Fodor's 15th Edition

D0497429

The Carolinas and Georgia

The Guide for All Budgets

Completely Updated

Where to Stay, Eat, and Explore

On and Off the Beaten Path

When to Go, What to Pack

Maps, Travel Tips, and Web Sites

Parts of this book appear in *Fodor's The South*

Fodor's Travel Publications • New York, Toronto, London, Sydney, Auckland
www.fodors.com

Fodor's The Carolinas and Georgia

EDITOR: Diane Mehta

Editorial Contributors: Andrew Collins, Robert Fleming, Hollis Gillespie, Mary Sue Lawrence.

Editorial Production: Tom Holton

Maps: David Lindroth, *cartographer;* Rebecca Baer and Bob Blake, *map editors*

Design: Fabrizio La Rocca, *creative director;* Guido Caroti, *art director;* Melanie Marin, *photo editor;* Jolie Novak, *senior picture editor*

Cover Design: Pentagram

Production/Manufacturing: Angela L. McLean

Cover Photo (Blue Ridge Parkway, NC): Kelly Culpepper/Transparencies, Inc.

Copyright

Fifteenth Edition

ISBN 1–4000–1203–1

ISSN 1525–5832

Important Tip

Although all prices, opening times, and other details in this book are based on information supplied to us at press time, changes occur all the time in the travel world, and Fodor's cannot accept responsibility for facts that become outdated or for inadvertent errors or omissions. So **always confirm information when it matters,** especially if you're making a detour to visit a specific place.

Special Sales

Fodor's Travel Publications are available at special discounts for bulk purchases for sales promotions or premiums. Special editions, including personalized covers, excerpts of existing guides, and corporate imprints, can be created in large quantities for special needs. For more information, contact your local bookseller or write to Special Markets, Fodor's Travel Publications, 1745 Broadway, New York, NY 10019. Inquiries from Canada should be directed to your local Canadian bookseller or sent to Random House of Canada, Ltd., Marketing Department, 2775 Matheson Boulevard East, Mississauga, Ontario L4W 4P7. Inquiries from the United Kingdom should be sent to Fodor's Travel Publications, 20 Vauxhall Bridge Road, London SW1V 2SA, England.

CONTENTS

Maps

ON THE ROAD WITH FODOR'S

A trip takes you out of yourself. Concerns of life at home completely disappear, driven away by more immediate thoughts—about, say, what marvels will beguile the next day, or where you'll have dinner. That's where Fodor's comes in. We make sure that you know all your options, so that you don't miss something that's around the next bend just because you didn't know it was there. Mindful that the best memories of your trip might have nothing to do with what you came to the South to see, we guide you to sights large and small all over the region. You might set out to explore mansions and drink mint juleps in Savannah, but back at home you find yourself unable to forget the rivers and swampland of Georgia's Okefenokee wildlife refuge. You might set out to relax on the beaches of North Carolina's Outer Banks, but back at home you find yourself unable to forget lifting off the sane dunes on a hang-glider, or scuba diving offshore among the many shipwrecks that populate the coast. With Fodor's at your side, serendipitous discoveries are never far away.

About Our Writers

Our success in showing you every corner of the Carolinas and Georgia is a credit to our extraordinary writers. Although there's no substitute for travel advice from a good friend who knows your style, our contributors are the next best thing—the kind of people you would poll for travel advice if you knew them.

Hollis Gillespie was born in Southern California but moved to Atlanta in 1989 and almost immediately swapped her Valley Girl accent for a Southern drawl. A prolific travel writer and foreign-language interpreter, she writes a weekly humor column called "Mood Swings" for *Creative Loafing,* Atlanta's alternative newsweekly.

Robert Fleming is a Wilmington-based freelance writer and Internet entrepreneur. A transplanted New Jersey native, he quickly discovered the splendor of his adopted state, from the Smokies to the Outer Banks. In addition to updating the North Carolina chapter, Rob has been a regular contributor for Fodor's and has had travel-related articles published in other regional periodicals.

South Carolina's **Mary Sue Lawrence** is a freelance writer and editor whose features on travel, entertainment, health, and business have appeared in national and British magazines. She is a South Carolina native and a proud descendant of General William Moultrie. She lives in downtown Charleston, and is a frequent Fodor's contributor.

Andy Collins, a former resident of Atlanta, has authored more than a dozen guidebooks, including *Fodor's Gay Guide to the USA.* He updated the Destination and Smart Travel Tips chapters and has edited previous editions of this guide. He also writes a syndicated weekly newspaper column and has contributed to *Travel & Leisure* and *The Holland Herald.*

You can rest assured that you're in good hands—and that no property mentioned in the book has paid to be included. Each has been selected strictly on its merits, as the best of its type in its price range.

How to Use This Book

Up front is Smart Travel Tips A to Z, arranged alphabetically by topic and loaded with tips, Web sites, and contact information. Destination: The Carolinas and Georgia helps get you in the mood for your trip. Subsequent chapters in The Carolinas and Georgia are arranged regionally by state. These chapters are divided geographically; within each area, towns are covered in logical geographical order, and attractive stretches of road between them are indicated by the designation En Route. To help you decide what you'll have time to visit, all chapters begin with our writers' favorite itineraries. (Mix itineraries from several chapters, and you can put together a really exceptional trip.) The A to Z section that ends every chapter lists additional resources.

Icons and Symbols

★ Our special recommendations
✕ Restaurant
🏠 Lodging establishment

✕🏠 Lodging establishment whose restaurant warrants a special trip

⚠ Campgrounds

☺ Good for kids (rubber duck)

☞ Sends you to another section of the guide for more information

✉ Address

☎ Telephone number

☉ Opening and closing times

🎟 Admission prices (those we give apply to adults; substantially reduced fees are almost always available for children, students, and senior citizens)

Numbers in white and black circles ③ ❸ that appear on the maps, in the margins, and within the tours correspond to one another.

For hotels, you can assume that all rooms have private baths, phones, TVs, and air-conditioning unless otherwise noted and that all hotels operate on the European Plan (with no meals) if we don't specify another meal plan. We always list a property's facilities but not whether you'll be charged extra to use them, so when pricing accommodations, do ask what's included. For restaurants, it's always a good idea to book ahead; we mention reservations only when they're essential or are not accepted. All restaurants we list are open daily for lunch and dinner unless stated otherwise; dress is mentioned only when men are required to wear a jacket or a jacket and tie. Look for an overview of local dining-out habits in the Pleasures and Pastimes section that follows each chapter introduction.

Don't Forget to Write

Your experiences—positive and negative—matter to us. If we have missed or misstated something, we want to hear about it. We follow up on all suggestions. Contact the Carolinas and Georgia editor at editors@fodors.com or c/o Fodor's at 1745 Broadway, New York, New York 10019. And have a fabulous trip!

Karen Cure

Karen Cure
Editorial Director

The United States

The Carolinas and Georgia

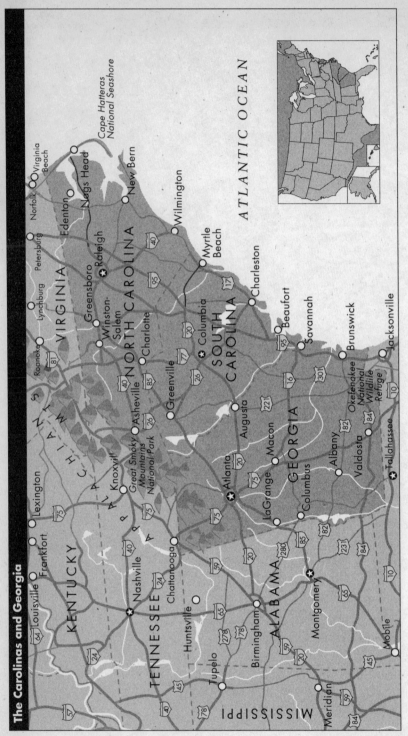

ESSENTIAL INFORMATION

AIR TRAVEL

BOOKING

Price is just one factor to consider when booking a flight: frequency of service and even a carrier's safety record are often just as important. Major airlines offer the greatest number of departures. Smaller airlines—including regional and no-frills airlines—usually have a limited number of flights daily. On the other hand, low-cost airlines usually are cheaper, and their fares impose fewer restrictions, such as advance-purchase requirements. Safetywise, low-cost carriers as a group have a good history—about equal to that of major carriers.

When you book **look for nonstop flights** and **remember that "direct" flights stop at least once.** Try to avoid connecting flights, which require a change of plane. For more booking tips and to check prices and make on-line flight reservations, log on to www.fodors.com.

CARRIERS

➤ MAJOR AIRLINES: American (☎ 800/433–7300). Continental (☎ 800/525–0280). Delta (☎ 800/221–1212). Northwest Airlines/KLM (☎ 800/225–2525). TWA (☎ 800/221–2000). United (☎ 800/241–6522). US Airways (☎ 800/428–4322).

➤ SMALLER AIRLINES: Air Canada (☎ 800/776–3000). AirTran (☎ 770/994–8258 or 800/247–8726). American Eagle (☎ 800/433–7300). Atlantic Southeast/Delta Connection (☎ 800/221–1212 or 800/282–3424). ComAir (☎ 800/221–1212). Continental Express (☎ 800/525–0280). Eastwind (☎ 888/327–8946). Kiwi (☎ 800/538–5494). Midway (☎ 800/446–4392). Midwest Express (☎ 800/452–2022). Northwest Airlink (☎ 800/225–2525). Southwest (☎ 800/435–9792). Spirit (☎ 800/772–

7117). TW Express (☎ 800/221–2000).

➤ FROM THE U.K.: American (☎ 0345/789–789). British Airways (☎ 0345/222–111). Delta (☎ 0800/414–767).

For further information on airports and airlines serving the Carolinas and Georgia, see individual state chapters.

CHECK-IN AND BOARDING

Assuming that not everyone with a ticket will show up, airlines routinely overbook planes. When everyone does, airlines ask for volunteers to give up their seats. In return, these volunteers usually get a certificate for a free flight and are rebooked on the next flight out. If there are not enough volunteers, the airline must choose who will be denied boarding. The first to get bumped are passengers who checked in late and those flying on discounted tickets, so **get to the gate and check in as early as possible,** especially during peak periods.

Always **bring a government-issued photo I.D. to the airport;** even when it's not required, a passport is best.

CUTTING COSTS

The least expensive airfares to the Carolinas and Georgia usually must be purchased in advance and are nonrefundable. It's smart to **call a number of airlines,** and when you are quoted a good price, **book it on the spot**—the same fare may not be available the next day. Always **check different routings** and look into using different airports. Travel agents, especially low-fare specialists (☞ Discounts & Deals), are helpful.

Consolidators are another good source. They buy tickets for scheduled international flights at reduced rates from the airlines, then sell them at prices that beat the best fare available directly from the airlines, usually without restrictions. Sometimes you can even get your money back if you need to return the ticket. Carefully read the fine print detailing penalties for changes and cancellations, and **confirm your consolidator reservation with the airline.**

➤ CONSOLIDATORS: **Cheap Tickets** (☎ 800/377–1000). **Discount Airline Ticket Service** (☎ 800/576–1600). **Unitravel** (☎ 800/325–2222). **Up & Away Travel** (☎ 212/889–2345, WEB www.upandaway.com). **World Travel Network** (☎ 800/409–6753).

ENJOYING THE FLIGHT

For more legroom, **request an emergency-aisle seat.** Don't sit in the row in front of the emergency aisle or in front of a bulkhead, where seats may not recline. If you have dietary concerns, **ask for special meals when booking.** These can be vegetarian, low-cholesterol, or kosher, for example. On long flights, try to maintain a normal routine, to help fight jet lag. At night, **get some sleep.** By day, **eat light meals, drink water** (not alcohol), and **move around the cabin** to stretch your legs. For additional jet-lag tips consult *Fodor's FYI: Travel Fit & Healthy* (available at bookstores everywhere).

FLYING TIMES

Flying time to Atlanta is 2½ hours from New York, two hours from Chicago, 4½ hours from Los Angeles, two hours from Dallas, and nine hours from London. By plane, Charlotte is an hour northeast of Atlanta, Raleigh 75 minutes northeast, Wilmington an hour and 45 minutes east, and Charleston, Hilton Head, and Savannah an hour east–southeast.

HOW TO COMPLAIN

If your baggage goes astray or your flight goes awry, complain right away. Most carriers require that you **file a claim immediately.**

➤ AIRLINE COMPLAINTS: U.S. Department of Transportation **Aviation Consumer Protection Division** (⊠ C-75, Room 4107, Washington, DC 20590, ☎ 202/366–2220, WEB www.dot.gov/airconsumer). **Federal Aviation Administration Consumer Hotline** (☎ 800/322–7873).

AIRPORTS

➤ AIRPORT INFORMATION: **Hartsfield Atlanta International Airport** (⊠ 6000 N. Terminal Pkwy., ☎ 404/530–6600, WEB www.atlanta-airport. com). **Raleigh-Durham International Airport** (⊠ 1600 Terminal Blvd., ☎ 919/840–2100, WEB www.rdu.com). **Charleston International Airport** (⊠ 5500 International Blvd., ☎ 843/767–7000). **Savannah International Airport** (⊠ 400 Airways Ave., ☎ 912/964–0514, WEB www. savannahairport.com).

For more information on airports serving the Carolinas and Georgia, see the A to Z section at the end of each regional section in individual state chapters.

BIKE TRAVEL

Throughout coastal Georgia, South Carolina, and North Carolina, hills are few and the scenery remarkable. You'll find a number of extensive, in many cases marked, bike routes throughout North Carolina's Outer Banks, around Savannah and Georgia's coastal islands, and throughout greater Charleston and coastal South Carolina's Lowcountry. Serious enthusiasts, especially those of mountain biking, might take to the more precipitous parts of North Carolina and Georgia, which are the Great Smoky Mountains and north Georgia mountains, respectively.

There are dozens of local bike clubs throughout the area. To reach one of these groups, which generally welcome people who are visiting the area, and which can provide detailed advice on local routes and rental shops, contact the local tourist board or visit the appropriate tourism Web site (☞ Web sites), many of which have information on or links to area cycling resources. Many tourist boards also distribute bike maps.

BIKES IN FLIGHT

Most airlines accommodate bikes as luggage, provided they are dismantled and boxed. Airlines sell bike boxes, which are often free at bike shops, for about $5 (it's at least $100 for bike bags). International travelers can sometimes substitute a bike for a piece of checked luggage at no charge;

otherwise, the cost is about $150. Domestic and Canadian airlines charge $50–$75.

BOOKS AND VIDEOS

Before your trip you may want to read some books or watch some movies about the region, which, like the rest of the South, has given rise to a substantial literary heritage: novels, drama, and poetry, as well as short stories and songs. Its authors have many a Pulitzer to their names, among them Georgia-born Caroline Miller for fiction (*Lamb in His Bosom,* 1934). You can choose from works by Thomas Wolfe, Reynolds Price, Pat Conroy, and Flannery O'Connor, to name just a few. Charles Frazier's 1997 novel *Cold Mountain,* about the journeys of a Confederate soldier in western North Carolina, won a National Book Award.

The area has produced writers of popular fiction as varied as Margaret Mitchell (*Gone With the Wind*), Kaye Gibbons, and Anne Rivers Siddons. The late journalist Charles Kuralt was a North Carolinian, whose books included *Charles Kuralt's America.* Tom Wolfe, not to be confused with North Carolina's Thomas Wolfe, weaves tales of success and failure in modern Atlanta in his novel *A Man in Full.* Although not authored by a Southerner, John Berendt's nonfiction *Midnight in the Garden of Good and Evil* is a tale of modern-day mayhem in sultry Savannah that reads like a novel.

One important element in Southern culture is the region's passion for history, defined as both personal, family history and regional history, which to those who live means both personal family and the history of the region. To understand the importance of the Civil War period, view Ken Burns's nine-episode PBS television documentary *The Civil War.* Shelby Foote's three-volume history, *The Civil War,* is excellent, as is James McPherson's one-volume *Battle Cry of Freedom,* another history of the war.

The classic treatise on the culture of the South is W. J. Cash's ground-breaking *The Mind of the South,* published more than 50 years ago. The *Oxford Book of the American South,* edited by Edward L. Ayers and Bradley C. Mittendorf, is an outstanding collection of Southern writing about the region from the 18th century to the present.

Alfred Uhry's *Driving Miss Daisy,* a Pulitzer Prize–winning play and award-winning film, portrays an aspect of relationships between the races in the South. Black Southern writers, of both fiction and nonfiction, are now, increasingly, getting the recognition they deserve. Although she currently lives in San Francisco, Alice Walker (from Eatonton, Georgia) made her mark with the book *The Color Purple,* later a film. Maya Angelou is one of the region's most celebrated poets.

For more recent examples of the region's rich literary tradition, look no farther than *New Stories from the South,* an annual compendium of the best fiction from Southern writers, edited by Shannon Ravenel. In the anthology *Rebel Yell: Stories by Contemporary Southern Gay Authors,* editor Jay Quinn chooses authors who explore themes of growing up, falling in love, and accepting themselves in a part of the world that has not always been especially tolerant of gays and lesbians.

In film, both Robert De Niro and Robert Mitchum have portrayed ex-convict Max Cady in the film-noir thriller *Cape Fear,* so named for an inlet on North Carolina's coastline. Some of the misconceptions about the South persisted as a result of the James Dickey novel-turned-movie *Deliverance,* about a group of friends on a canoeing trip in Georgia backcountry. Also originally a novel, the film *To Kill a Mockingbird* not only crystallizes the depths of prejudice and bigotry in the South, but also conveys a message of hope as a region struggles to come to terms with its past.

When it comes to music, you'll find that some of the biggest names across multiple genres were born and bred in the region. Artists such as James Taylor, Dizzy Gillespie, Otis Redding, Johnny Mercer, and Travis Tritt prove that musical tastes in these parts are as varied as the landscape.

Before they were touring the world and selling millions of albums, bands like R.E.M. and the B-52's cut their teeth in the college town of Athens, Georgia. In fact, Athens still plays a significant role in shaping pop music trends. For the hip-hop scene, however, Atlanta is the place to be: TLC, Toni Braxton, and OutKast all hail from these parts.

Still, rock and country reign as the average Southerner's first choice. Charlie Daniels's rowdy blend of the two makes him a favorite son, whereas the lesser-known Gram Parsons is a cult figure who never sold many records but influenced countless fellow musicians, from the Rolling Stones to the Byrds. Top-shelf rock journalist Stanley Booth touches on many other of the South's finest blues and rock-and-roll artists in *Rhythm Oil: A Journey Through the Music of the American South*.

BUS TRAVEL

Regional bus service, provided by Greyhound, is abundant throughout the Carolinas and Georgia. It's a handy and affordable means of getting around; if it's a simple matter of getting from one city to another, and you've got a bit of time on your hands, consider this option. Remember that buses sometimes make frequent stops, which may delay you but may also provide you the chance to see parts of the region you might not otherwise. For a comparison of different ways of getting around the region, *see* Transportation to and Around the Carolinas and Georgia.

CUTTING COSTS

Greyhound offers the **North America Discovery Pass,** which allows unlimited travel in the United States within any 7-, 10-, 15-, 21-, 30-, 45-, or 60-day period ($199–$549, depending on length of the pass), and the similar International Ameripass (for non–U.S. residents only), which offers 4- to 60-day passes for $135–$494. Greyhound also has senior citizen, children's, and student discounts.

➤ BUS INFORMATION: **Greyhound** (☎ 800/231–2222, WEB www.greyhound.

com) operates passenger buses connecting many towns and cities in the region.

BUSINESS HOURS

Banks are usually open weekdays from 9 to 4 and some Saturday mornings, the post office from 8 to 5 weekdays and often on Saturday morning. Shops in urban and suburban areas, particularly in indoor and strip malls, typically open at 9 or 10 daily and stay open until anywhere from 6 PM to 10 PM on weekdays and Saturday, and until 5 or 6 on Sunday. Hours vary greatly, so call ahead when in doubt.

CAMERAS AND PHOTOGRAPHY

The *Kodak Guide to Shooting Great Travel Pictures* (available at bookstores everywhere) is loaded with tips.

➤ PHOTO HELP: **Kodak Information Center** (☎ 800/242–2424).

EQUIPMENT PRECAUTIONS

Don't pack film and equipment in checked luggage, where it is much more susceptible to damage. X-ray machines used to view checked luggage are becoming much more powerful and therefore are much more likely to ruin your film. Always **keep film and tape out of the sun.** Carry an extra supply of batteries, and **be prepared to turn on your camera or camcorder** to prove to security personnel that the device is real. Always **ask for hand inspection of film,** which becomes clouded after repeated exposure to airport X-ray machines, and **keep videotapes away from metal detectors.**

CAR RENTAL

Rates vary from city to city, generally being lowest in destinations with busy airports, where there's the greatest competition. Below are sample rates, for both economy- and luxury-car rentals, quoted by the most popular agencies in two major cities (note that unlimited mileage is nearly always included).

In Atlanta daily rates range from about $37 to $52 for an economy car to $76–$100 for a luxury car; weekly rates range from $190 to $285 for an economy car to $390–$530 for a luxury car. Atlanta has an additional 7% sales tax, and at the airport location an 11% concession recoupment fee and a 3% airport excise tax are also added.

In Raleigh daily rates range from about $28 to $44 for an economy car to $66–$88 for a luxury car; weekly rates range from $140 to $205 for an economy car to $350–$440 for a luxury car. Raleigh has an additional 8% sales tax and a 5% local transportation tax, and at the airport a 10% concession recoupment fee also is added.

These rates are typical of those found in larger cities in the Carolinas and Georgia, but specials and deals may be available based on dates of travel and length of contract. It's important to **reserve a car well in advance of your expected arrival.**

➤ MAJOR AGENCIES: **Alamo** (☎ 800/327–9633, WEB www.alamo.com). **Avis** (☎ 800/331–1212; 800/879–2847 in Canada; 02/9353–9000 in Australia; 09/525–1982 in New Zealand; 0870/606–0100 in the U.K., WEB www.avis.com). **Budget** (☎ 800/527–0700; 0870/156–5656 in the U.K., WEB www.budget.com). **Dollar** (☎ 800/800–4000; 0800/085–4578 in the U.K.; 02/9223–1444 in Australia, WEB www.dollar.com). **Hertz** (☎ 800/654–3131; 800/263–0600 in Canada; 020/8897–2072 in the U.K.; 02/9669–2444 in Australia; 09/256–8690 in New Zealand, WEB www.hertz.com). **National Car Rental** (☎ 800/227–7368; 020/8680–4800 in the U.K., WEB www.nationalcar.com).

CUTTING COSTS

To get the best deal, **book through a travel agent who will shop around.** Also **price local car-rental companies,** although the service and maintenance may not be as good as those of a major player. Remember to ask about required deposits, cancellation penalties, and drop-off charges if you're planning to pick up the car in one city and leave it in another. If you're traveling during a holiday period, also make sure that a confirmed reservation guarantees you a car.

Some off-airport locations offer lower rates, and their lots are only minutes from the terminal via complimentary shuttle. Also ask whether certain frequent-flyer, American Automobile Association (AAA), corporate, or other such promotions are accepted and whether the rates might be lower the day before or after you had originally intended to travel. In some cases you'll find that the same agency offers a region's cheapest luxury car rates but priciest economy cars, or that the cheapest agency in one city may have high rates in another. It pays to check around.

Also, although an economy car is almost always your cheapest option, agencies sometimes offer upgrade specials that cost only a dollar or two more per day. Think carefully about how much and where you'll be using the car before choosing among economy, compact, standard, luxury, and premium; it may be worth the extra few dollars per day for a more substantial vehicle if you're traveling long distances, driving up into the mountains or over rugged terrain, traveling with more than a couple of passengers, or using the car extensively.

INSURANCE

When driving a rented car you are generally responsible for any damage to or loss of the vehicle as well as for any property damage or personal injury that you may cause. Before you rent, see what coverage your personal auto-insurance policy and credit cards provide.

For about $15 to $20 per day, rental companies sell protection, known as a collision- or loss-damage waiver (CDW or LDW), that eliminates your liability for damage to the car.

In most states you don't need a CDW if you have personal auto insurance or other liability insurance. However, **make sure you have enough coverage to pay for the car.** If you do not have auto insurance or an umbrella policy that covers damage to third parties, purchasing liability insurance and a CDW or LDW is highly recommended.

REQUIREMENTS AND RESTRICTIONS

In the Carolinas and Georgia you must be 21 to rent a car, and rates may be higher if you're under 25. You'll pay extra for child seats (about $3 a day), which are compulsory for children under five, and for additional drivers (about $2 per day). Non-U.S. residents need a reservation voucher (for prepaid reservations that were made in the traveler's home country), a passport, a driver's license, and a travel policy that covers each driver, when picking up a car.

SURCHARGES

Before you pick up a car in one city and leave it in another, **ask about drop-off charges or one-way service fees,** which can be substantial. Note, too, that some rental agencies charge extra if you return the car before the time specified in your contract. To avoid a hefty refueling fee, **fill the tank just before you turn in the car,** but be aware that gas stations near the rental outlet may overcharge.

CAR TRAVEL

A car is your most practical and economical means of traveling around the Carolinas and Georgia. Atlanta, Savannah, Charleston, Myrtle Beach, and Asheville can also be explored fairly easily on foot or by using public transit and cabs, but a car is helpful to reach many of the most intriguing nearby museums, parks, restaurants, and lodgings.

Although you'll make the best time traveling along the South's extensive network of interstate highways, keep in mind that U.S. and state highways offer some delightful scenery and the opportunity to stumble on funky roadside diners, leafy state parks, and historic town squares. Although the area is rural, it's still densely populated, so you'll rarely drive for more than 20 or 30 mi—even on local roads—without passing roadside services, such as gas stations, restaurants, and ATMs.

Among the most scenic highways in the Carolinas and Georgia, consider U.S. 78 across Georgia; U.S. 25, 19, 74, and 64 through the Great Smoky Mountains of western North Carolina; U.S. 17 from Brunswick, Georgia, along the coast through South Carolina and North Carolina; and the Blue Ridge Parkway from the eastern fringes of the Great Smoky Mountains through western North Carolina into Virginia.

For a comparison of different ways of getting around the region, *see* Transportation to and Around the Carolinas and Georgia.

RULES OF THE ROAD

State lawmakers now set speed limits, even for federal interstate highways. Limits vary from state to state and from rural to urban areas, so **check posted speeds frequently.**

Always **strap young children into approved child-safety seats.**

CHILDREN IN THE CAROLINAS AND GEORGIA

Most of the Carolinas and Georgia is ideal for travel with kids. This is an enjoyable part of the country for family road trips, and things are relatively affordable—you'll have no problem finding inexpensive kid-friendly hotels and family-style restaurants. Just keep in mind that a number of fine, antiques-filled B&Bs and inns punctuate the landscape, and these places are less suitable for kids—some of them flat-out refuse to accommodate children. Also, some of the quieter and more rural parts of the region—although exuding history—lack child-oriented attractions.

If you are renting a car, don't forget to **arrange for a car seat** when you reserve. For general advice about traveling with children consult *Fodor's FYI: Travel with Your Baby* (available in bookstores everywhere).

FLYING

If your children are two or older, **ask about children's airfares.** As a general rule, infants under two not occupying a seat fly at greatly reduced fares or even for free.

Experts agree that it's a good idea to use safety seats aloft for children weighing less than 40 pounds. Airlines set their own policies: U.S. carriers usually require that the child be ticketed, even if he or she is young enough to ride free, since the seats must be strapped into regular seats. Do **check your airline's policy about using safety seats during takeoff and**

landing. And since safety seats are not allowed everywhere in the plane, get your seat assignments early.

When reserving, **request children's meals or a freestanding bassinet** if you need them. But note that bulkhead seats, where you must sit to use the bassinet, may lack an overhead bin or storage space on the floor.

LODGING

Most hotels in the Carolinas and Georgia allow children under a certain age to stay in their parents' room at no extra charge, but others charge for them as extra adults; be sure to **find out the cutoff age for children's discounts.**

SIGHTS AND ATTRACTIONS

Places that are especially appealing to children are indicated by a rubber-duckie icon (🐤) in the margin.

CONSUMER PROTECTION

Whenever shopping or buying travel services in the Carolinas and Georgia, **pay with a major credit card,** if possible, so you can cancel payment or get reimbursed if there's a problem. If you're doing business with a particular company for the first time, **contact your local Better Business Bureau and the attorney general's offices** in your state and (for U.S. businesses) the company's home state as well. Have any complaints been filed? Finally, if you're buying a package or tour, always **consider travel insurance** that includes default coverage (☞ Insurance).

➤ BBBs: **Council of Better Business Bureaus** (✉ 4200 Wilson Blvd., Suite 800, Arlington, VA 22203, ☎ 703/276–0100, FAX 703/525–8277, WEB www.bbb.org).

CUSTOMS AND DUTIES

IN AUSTRALIA

Australian residents who are 18 or older may bring home $A400 worth of souvenirs and gifts (including jewelry), 250 cigarettes or 250 grams of tobacco, and 1,125 ml of alcohol (including wine, beer, and spirits). Residents under 18 may bring back $A200 worth of goods. Prohibited items include meat products. Seeds, plants, and fruits need to be declared upon arrival.

➤ INFORMATION: **Australian Customs Service** (Regional Director, ✉ Box 8, Sydney, NSW 2001; ☎ 02/9213–2000 or 1300/363263; 1800/020504 for quarantine-inquiry line; FAX 02/9213–4043; WEB www.customs.gov.au).

IN CANADA

Canadian residents who have been out of Canada for at least seven days may bring home C$750 worth of goods duty-free. If you've been away fewer than seven days but more than 48 hours, the duty-free allowance drops to C$200; if your trip lasts 24–48 hours, the allowance is C$50. You may not pool allowances with family members. Goods claimed under the C$750 exemption may follow you by mail; those claimed under the lesser exemptions must accompany you. Alcohol and tobacco products may be included in the seven-day and 48-hour exemptions but not in the 24-hour exemption. If you meet the age requirements of the province or territory through which you reenter Canada, you may bring in, duty-free, 1.14 liters (40 imperial ounces) of wine or liquor *or* 24 12-ounce cans or bottles of beer or ale. If you are 19 or older you may bring in, duty-free, 200 cigarettes and 50 cigars. Check ahead of time with the Canada Customs Revenue Agency or the Department of Agriculture for policies regarding meat products, seeds, plants, and fruits.

You may send an unlimited number of gifts worth up to C$60 each duty-free to Canada. Label the package UNSOLICITED GIFT—VALUE UNDER $60. Alcohol and tobacco are excluded.

➤ INFORMATION: **Canada Customs and Revenue Agency** (✉ 2265 St. Laurent Blvd. S, Ottawa, Ontario K1G 4K3, ☎ 204/983–3500, 506/636–5064, 800/461–9999, WEB www.ccra-adrc.gc.ca/).

IN NEW ZEALAND

Homeward-bound residents 17 or older may bring back $700 worth of souvenirs and gifts. Your duty-free allowance also includes 4.5 liters of wine or beer; one 1,125-ml bottle of spirits; and either 200 cigarettes, 250 grams of tobacco, 50 cigars, or a combination of the three up to 250 grams. Prohibited items include meat products, seeds, plants, and fruits.

➤ INFORMATION: **New Zealand Customs** (Head office: ✉ The Customhouse, 17–21 Whitmore St., Box 2218, Wellington, ☎ 09/300–5399 or 0800/428–786, WEB www.customs.govt.nz).

IN THE U.K.

From countries outside the European Union, including the United States, you may bring home, duty-free, 200 cigarettes or 50 cigars; 1 liter of spirits or 2 liters of fortified or sparkling wine or liqueurs; 2 liters of still table wine; 60 milliliters of perfume; 250 milliliters of toilet water; plus £145 worth of other goods, including gifts and souvenirs. If returning from outside the EU, prohibited items include meat products, seeds, plants, and fruits.

➤ INFORMATION: **HM Customs and Excise** (✉ Dorset House, Stamford St., Bromley, Kent BR1 1XX, U.K., ☎ 020/7202–4227, WEB www.hmce.gov.uk).

DINING

The restaurants listed are the cream of the crop in each price category. They are indicated in the text by a ✕ icon. Properties indicated by a ✕☐ icon are lodging establishments whose restaurant warrants a special trip.

RESERVATIONS AND DRESS

Reservations are always a good idea: they are mentioned only when they're essential or not accepted. Book as far ahead as you can, and reconfirm as soon as you arrive. Dress is only mentioned when men are required to wear a jacket or a jacket and tie.

DISABILITIES
AND ACCESSIBILITY

The Carolinas and Georgia rank on a par with the rest of America in their accessibility for persons with disabilities or special needs. A drawback is the abundance of historic accommodations, restaurants, and attractions with narrow staircases, doorways, and small rooms that fail to conform to the Americans with Disabilities Act

(ADA) guidelines. Increasingly, however, businesses throughout the region—especially those in densely populated areas—are changing to improve accessibility.

RESERVATIONS

When discussing accessibility with an operator or reservations agent, **ask hard questions.** Are there any stairs, inside *or* out? Are there grab bars next to the toilet *and* in the shower/ tub? How wide is the doorway to the room? To the bathroom? For the most extensive facilities meeting the latest legal specifications, **opt for newer accommodations.**

➤ COMPLAINTS: **Aviation Consumer Protection Division** (☞ Air Travel) for airline-related problems. **Departmental Office of Civil Rights** (for general inquiries, ✉ U.S. Department of Transportation, S-30, 400 7th St. SW, Room 10215, Washington, DC 20590, ☎ 202/366–4648, FAX 202/ 366–3571, WEB www.dot.gov/ost/docr/ index.htm). **Disability Rights Section** (✉ NYAV, U.S. Department of Justice, Civil Rights Division, 950 Pennsylvania Ave. NW, Washington, DC 20530, ☎ 202/514–0301 for ADA information line; 800/514–0301; 202/ 514–0383 for TTY; 800/514–0383 for TTY, WEB www.usdoj.gov/crt/ada/ adahom1.htm).

TRAVEL AGENCIES

In the United States, the Americans with Disabilities Act requires that travel firms serve the needs of all travelers. Some agencies specialize in working with people with disabilities.

➤ TRAVELERS WITH MOBILITY PROBLEMS: **Access Adventures** (✉ 206 Chestnut Ridge Rd., Scottsville, NY 14624, ☎ 716/889–9096, dltravel@ prodigy.net), run by a former physical-rehabilitation counselor. **Accessible Vans of America** (✉ 9 Spielman Rd., Fairfield, NJ 07004, ☎ 877/ 282–8267, FAX 973/808–9713, WEB www.accessiblevans.com). **CareVacations** (✉ No. 5, 5110–50 Ave., Leduc, Alberta T9E 6V4, Canada, ☎ 780/ 986–6404 or 877/478–7827, FAX 780/ 986–8332, WEB www.carevacations. com), for group tours and cruise vacations. **Flying Wheels Travel** (✉ 143 W. Bridge St., Box 382, Owatonna, MN 55060, ☎ 507/451–

5005, FAX 507/451–1685, WEB www.
flyingwheeltravel.com).

DISCOUNTS AND DEALS

Be a smart shopper and **compare all
your options** before making decisions.
A plane ticket bought with a promotional coupon from travel clubs,
coupon books, and direct-mail offers
or on the Internet may not be cheaper
than the least expensive fare from a
discount ticket agency. And always
keep in mind that what you get is just
as important as what you save.

DISCOUNT RESERVATIONS

To save money, **look into discount
reservations services** with toll-free
numbers, which use their buying
power to get a better price on hotels,
airline tickets, even car rentals. When
booking a room, always **call the
hotel's local toll-free number** (if one
is available) rather than the central
reservations number—you'll often get
a better price. Always ask about
special packages or corporate rates.

➤ AIRLINE TICKETS: ☎ 800/FLY–
ASAP.

➤ HOTEL ROOMS: **Accommodations
Express** (☎ 800/444–7666, WEB www.
accommodationsexpress.com). **Central Reservation Service (CRS)**
(☎ 800/548–3311, WEB www.
roomconnection.net). **Hotel Reservations Network** (☎ 800/964–6835,
WEB www.hoteldiscount.com). **Players
Express Vacations** (☎ 800/458–6161,
WEB www.playersexpress.com). **Quik-
book** (☎ 800/789–9887, WEB www.
quikbook.com). **RMC Travel**
(☎ 800/245–5738, WEB www.
rmcwebtravel.com). **Steigenberger
Reservation Service** (☎ 800/223–
5652, WEB www.srs-worldhotels.com).
Turbotrip.com (☎ 800/473–7829,
WEB www.turbotrip.com).

PACKAGE DEALS

Don't confuse packages and guided
tours. When you buy a package, you
travel on your own, just as though
you had planned the trip yourself.
Fly/drive packages, which combine
airfare and car rental, are often a
good deal.

GAY AND LESBIAN TRAVEL

Attitudes about gays and lesbians
tend toward the disapproving in some
parts of the South, especially outside
urban areas. On the whole, however,
despite a reputation for conservative-
minded residents, this part of the
country is not any more hostile or
dangerous for lesbians and gays—
traveling solo or together—than the
rest of America. It's prudent, however, to show an awareness of your
surroundings and exercise a degree of
discretion whenever you're venturing
into unfamiliar territory.

As for lesbian and gay resources,
there are several major newspapers
serving the community throughout
the Carolinas and Georgia, notably
Southern Voice, based in Atlanta, plus
a host of smaller local papers in the
Carolinas. The gay nightlife and
social scenes in Atlanta rival those of
virtually any comparably sized cities
in the North America, and you'll also
find thriving gay communities of
varying sizes in Savannah, Charlotte,
Charleston, Raleigh-Durham, and
Columbia. With a much lower profile
than most cities with large gay popu-
lations, Asheville is something of a
well-kept secret; it has sizable lesbian
and gay communities and a high
number of gay-friendly businesses and
accommodations.

For details about the gay and lesbian
scene, consult *Fodor's Gay Guide to
the USA* (available in bookstores
everywhere). The book provides
information on the gay scenes in
Asheville, Atlanta, Charleston, Charlotte, Raleigh–Durham, and Savannah.

➤ GAY- AND LESBIAN-FRIENDLY TRAVEL
AGENCIES: **Different Roads Travel** (✉
8383 Wilshire Blvd., Suite 902, Beverly Hills, CA 90211, ☎ 323/651–
5557 or 800/429–8747, FAX 323/651–
3678, lgernert@tzell.com). **Kennedy
Travel** (✉ 314 Jericho Turnpike,
Floral Park, NY 11001, ☎ 516/352–
4888 or 800/237–7433, FAX 516/354–
8849, WEB www.kennedytravel.com).
Now, Voyager (✉ 4406 18th St., San
Francisco, CA 94114, ☎ 415/626–
1169 or 800/255–6951, FAX 415/626–
8626, WEB www.nowvoyager.com).
Skylink Travel and Tour (✉ 1006
Mendocino Ave., Santa Rosa, CA
95401, ☎ 707/546–9888 or 800/
225–5759, FAX 707/546–9891), serving lesbian travelers.

GUIDEBOOKS

Plan well, and you won't be sorry. Guidebooks are excellent tools—and you can take them with you. *Fodor's Road Guide USA: Georgia, North Carolina, South Carolina* provides listings of thousands of sights, motels and hotels, and restaurants throughout the region. *Compass American Guides: Georgia, Compass American Guides: North Carolina*, and *Compass American Guides: South Carolina*, with their handsome photos and historical, cultural, and topical essays, are good companions to this guide. For additional perspectives on Atlanta check out *Fodor's CITYGUIDE Atlanta*.

HEALTH

PESTS AND OTHER HAZARDS

Mosquitoes, seasonal black flies, and other insects known to North America proliferate in the humid and often lush Southern states. **Exercise common precautions and wear lotions or sprays that keep away such pests.**

HOLIDAYS

Major national holidays include New Year's Day (Jan. 1); Martin Luther King, Jr., Day (3rd Mon. in Jan.); President's Day (3rd Mon. in Feb.); Memorial Day (last Mon. in May); Independence Day (July 4); Labor Day (1st Mon. in Sept.); Thanksgiving Day (4th Thurs. in Nov.); Christmas Eve and Christmas Day (Dec. 24 and 25); and New Year's Eve (Dec. 31).

INSURANCE

The most useful travel-insurance plan is a comprehensive policy that includes coverage for trip cancellation and interruption, default, trip delay, and medical expenses (with a waiver for preexisting conditions).

Without insurance you will lose all or most of your money if you cancel your trip, regardless of the reason. Default insurance covers you if your tour operator, airline, or cruise line goes out of business. Trip-delay covers expenses that arise because of bad weather or mechanical delays. Study the fine print when comparing policies.

Always **buy travel policies directly from the insurance company**; if you buy them from a cruise line, airline, or tour operator that goes out of business you probably will not be covered for the agency or operator's default, a major risk. Before making any purchase, **review your existing health and home-owner's policies** to find what they cover away from home.

If you are traveling from outside the United States or Canada, *see* Insurance *in* For International Travelers.

➤ TRAVEL INSURERS: **Access America** (✉ 6600 W. Broad St., Richmond, VA 23230, ☎ 800/284–8300, FAX 804/673–1491 or 800/346–9265, WEB www.accessamerica.com). **Travel Guard International** (✉ 1145 Clark St., Stevens Point, WI 54481, ☎ 715/345–0505 or 800/826–1300, FAX 800/955–8785, WEB www.travelguard.com).

FOR INTERNATIONAL TRAVELERS

For information on customs restrictions, *see* Customs and Duties.

CAR TRAVEL

In the Carolinas and Georgia gasoline costs $.90–$1.25 a gallon. Stations are plentiful. Most stay open late (24 hours along large highways and in big cities), except in rural areas, where Sunday hours are limited and where you may drive long stretches without a refueling opportunity. Highways are well paved. Interstate highways—limited-access multilane highways whose numbers are prefixed by "I–"—are the fastest routes. Interstates with three-digit numbers encircle or intersect urban areas, which may have other limited-access expressways, freeways, and parkways as well. Tolls may be levied on limited-access highways. So-called U.S. highways and state highways are not necessarily limited access, but many have several lanes.

Along larger highways roadside stops with rest rooms, fast-food restaurants, and sundries stores are well spaced. State police and tow trucks patrol major highways and lend assistance. If your car breaks down on an interstate, pull onto the shoulder and wait for help, or have your passengers wait while you walk to an emergency phone. If you carry a cell phone, dial *55, noting your location on the small green roadside mileage markers.

Driving in the United States is on the right. Do **obey speed limits** posted along roads and highways. Watch for lower limits in small towns and on back roads. Georgia and the Carolinas require front-seat passengers to wear seat belts. On weekdays between 6 AM and 10 AM and again between 4 PM and 7 PM **expect heavy traffic,** especially in big cities like Atlanta and Charlotte. To encourage carpooling, some freeways have special lanes for what are designated high-occupancy vehicles (HOV)—cars carrying more than one passenger.

Bookstores, gas stations, convenience stores, and rest stops sell maps ($3–$5) and multiregion road atlases ($10 and up).

CONSULATES AND EMBASSIES

➤ AUSTRALIA: **Australian Embassy** (✉ 1601 Massachusetts Ave. NW, Washington, DC 20036, ☎ 202/797–3000).

➤ CANADA: **Canadian Embassy** (✉ 501 Pennsylvania Ave. NW, Washington, DC 20001, ☎ 202/682–1740).

➤ NEW ZEALAND: **New Zealand Embassy** (✉ 37 Observatory Circle NW, Washington, DC 20008, ☎ 202/328–4800).

➤ UNITED KINGDOM: **British Embassy** (✉ 19 Observatory Circle NW, Washington, DC 20008, ☎ 202/588–7800).

CURRENCY

The dollar is the basic unit of U.S. currency. It has 100 cents. Coins include the copper penny (1¢); the silvery nickel (5¢), dime (10¢), quarter (25¢), and half-dollar (50¢); and the golden $1 coin, replacing a now-rare silver dollar. Bills are denominated $1, $5, $10, $20, $50, and $100, all green and identical in size; designs vary. The exchange rate at press time was US$1.58 per British pound, 64¢ per Canadian dollar, 54¢ per Australian dollar, and 46¢ per New Zealand dollar.

ELECTRICITY

The U.S. standard is AC, 110 volts/60 cycles. Plugs have two flat pins set parallel to each other.

EMERGENCIES

For police, fire, or ambulance, **dial 911** (0 in rural areas).

INSURANCE

Britons and Australians need extra medical coverage when traveling overseas.

➤ INSURANCE INFORMATION: In the U.K.: **Association of British Insurers** (✉ 51–55 Gresham St., London EC2V 7HQ, U.K., ☎ 020/7600–3333, FAX 020/7696–8999, WEB www.abi.org.uk). In Australia: **Insurance Council of Australia** (✉ Level 3, 56 Pitt St., Sydney NSW 2000, ☎ 02/9253–5100, FAX 02/9253–5111, WEB www.ica.com.au). In Canada: **RBC Insurance** (✉ 6880 Financial Dr., Mississauga, Ontario L5N 7Y5, Canada, ☎ 905/816–2400 or 800/668–4342 in Canada, FAX 905/816–2498, WEB www.royalbank.com). In New Zealand: **Insurance Council of New Zealand** (✉ Box 474, Wellington, New Zealand, ☎ 04/472–5230, FAX 04/473–3011, WEB www.icnz.org.nz).

MAIL AND SHIPPING

You can buy stamps and aerograms and send letters and parcels in post offices. Stamp-dispensing machines can occasionally be found in airports, bus and train stations, office buildings, drugstores, and the like. You can also deposit mail in the stout, dark blue, steel bins at strategic locations everywhere and in the mail chutes of large buildings; pickup schedules are posted.

For mail sent within the United States, you need a 37¢ stamp for first-class letters weighing up to 1 ounce (23¢ for each additional ounce) and 23¢ for postcards. You pay 80¢ for 1-ounce airmail letters and 70¢ for airmail postcards to most other countries; for mail to Canada and Mexico you need a 60¢ stamp for a 1-ounce letter and 50¢ for a postcard. An aerogram—a single sheet of lightweight blue paper that folds into its own envelope, stamped for overseas airmail—costs 70¢.

To receive mail on the road, have it sent c/o General Delivery at your destination's main post office (use the correct five-digit zip code). You must pick up mail in person within 30 days and show a driver's license or passport.

PASSPORTS AND VISAS

When traveling internationally, **carry your passport** even if you don't need one (it's always the best form of I.D.) and **make two photocopies of the data page** (one for someone at home and another for you, carried separately from your passport). If you lose your passport, promptly call the nearest embassy or consulate and the local police.

Visitor visas are not necessary for Canadian citizens, or for citizens of Australia and the United Kingdom who are staying fewer than 90 days.

➤ AUSTRALIAN CITIZENS: **Australian State Passport Office** (☎ 131–232, WEB www.passports.gov.au). **United States Consulate General** (✉ MLC Centre, 19–29 Martin Pl., 59th floor, Sydney, NSW 2000, ☎ 02/9373–9200; 1902/941–641 for fee-based visa-inquiry line, WEB www.usis-australia.gov/index.html).

➤ CANADIAN CITIZENS: **Passport Office** (to mail in applications: ✉ Department of Foreign Affairs and International Trade, Ottawa, Ontario K1A 0G3, ☎ 819/994–3500 or 800/567–6868, WEB www.dfait-maeci.gc.ca/passport).

➤ NEW ZEALAND CITIZENS: **New Zealand Passport Office** (☎ 04/474–8100 or 0800/22–5050, WEB www.passports.govt.nz). **Embassy of the United States** (✉ 29 Fitzherbert Terr., Thorndon, Wellington, ☎ 04/462–6000 WEB usembassy.org.nz). **U.S. Consulate General** (✉ Citibank Bldg., 3rd floor, 23 Customs St. E, Auckland, ☎ 09/303–2724, WEB usembassy.org.nz).

➤ U.K. CITIZENS: **London Passport Office** (☎ 0870/521–0410, WEB www.passport.gov.uk). **U.S. Consulate General** (✉ Queen's House, 14 Queen St., Belfast, Northern Ireland BT1 6EQ, ☎ 028/9032–8239, WEB www.usembassy.org.uk). **U.S. Embassy** (enclose a SASE to ✉ Consular Information Unit, 24 Grosvenor Sq., London W1 1AE, for general information; ✉ Visa Branch, 5 Upper Grosvenor St., London W1A 2JB, to submit an application via mail; ☎ 09068/200–290 for recorded visa information; 09055/444–546 for operator service, both with per-minute charges; WEB www.usembassy.org.uk).

TELEPHONES

All U.S. telephone numbers consist of a three-digit area code and a seven-digit local number. Within many local calling areas, dial only the seven-digit number; but in larger cities or regions with more than one area code (such as Atlanta and Charlotte), dial "1" then all 10 digits whether for local or long-distance calls. To call between area-code regions, dial "1" then all 10 digits; the same goes for calls to numbers prefixed by "800," "888," "877," and "866"—all toll-free. For calls to numbers preceded by "900" you must pay—usually dearly.

For international calls, dial "011" followed by the country code and the local number. For help, dial "0" and ask for an overseas operator. The country code is 61 for Australia, 64 for New Zealand, 44 for the United Kingdom. Calling Canada is the same as calling within the United States. Most local phone books list country codes and U.S. area codes. The country code for the United States is 1.

For operator assistance, dial "0." To obtain someone's phone number, call directory assistance, 555–1212 or occasionally 411 (free at some public phones). To have the person you're calling foot the bill, phone collect; dial "0" instead of "1" before the 10-digit number.

At pay phones, instructions are usually posted. Usually you insert coins in a slot (25¢–50¢ for local calls) and wait for a steady tone before dialing. When you call long-distance, the operator will tell you how much to insert; prepaid phone cards, widely available in various denominations, are easier. Call the number on the back, punch in the card's personal identification number when prompted, then dial your number.

For more information on area codes and making long-distance calls, *see* Telephones.

LODGING

With the exception of Atlanta, Savannah, and Charleston, most lodging rates in the region fall below the national average. They do vary a great deal seasonally, however—coastal areas as well as the Great Smoky Mountains tend to have significantly higher rates in summer. All major chains are well represented in this part of the country, both in cities and suburbs, and interstates are lined with inexpensive to moderate chains. It's not uncommon to find clean but extremely basic discount chains offering double rooms for as little as $25 to $40 nightly along the busiest highways.

In cities and some large towns you might want to forgo a modern hotel in favor of a historic property—there are dozens of fine old hotels, many of them fully restored and quite a few offering better rates than chain properties with comparable amenities and nowhere near the style.

The lodgings listed are the cream of the crop in each price category. They are denoted in the text by a 🏠 icon; lodging establishments whose restaurant warrants a special trip are denoted by a ✕🏠 icon. Facilities that are available are listed—but not any extra costs associated with those facilities. When pricing accommodations, **always ask what's included and what costs extra.**

Assume that hotels operate on the **European Plan** (EP, with no meals) unless it is specified that they use the **Continental Plan** (CP, with a Continental breakfast), **Breakfast Plan** (BP, with a full breakfast), **Modified American Plan** (MAP, with breakfast and dinner), or the **Full American Plan** (FAP, with all meals).

APARTMENT AND VILLA RENTALS

If you want a home base that's roomy enough for a family and comes with cooking facilities, **consider a furnished rental.** These can save you money, especially if you're traveling with a group. Home-exchange directories sometimes list rentals as well as exchanges.

➤ INTERNATIONAL AGENTS: **Hideaways International** (✉ 767 Islington St., Portsmouth, NH 03801, ☎ 603/430–4433 or 800/843–4433, FAX 603/430–4444, WEB www.hideaways.com; membership $129). **Vacation Home Rentals Worldwide** (✉ 235 Kensington Ave., Norwood, NJ 07648, ☎ 201/767–9393 or 800/633–3284, FAX 201/767–5510, WEB www.vhrww.com).

BED-AND-BREAKFASTS AND INNS

Historic B&Bs and inns are found in just about every region in the Carolinas and Georgia and include quite a few former plantation houses and lavish Southern estates. In many rural or less touristy areas, B&Bs offer an affordable and homey alternative to chain properties, but in tourism-dependent destinations you can expect to pay, for a historic inn, about the same as or more than for a full-service hotel. Many of the South's finest restaurants are also found in country inns.

CAMPING

The Carolinas and Georgia are popular for RV and tent camping, with facilities throughout the area, especially in state and national parks. For more information on parks and other campgrounds, contact the state tourism offices (☞ Visitor Information) or *see* Contacts and Resources *in* regional A to Z sections and *in* the A to Z section at the end of each state chapter.

HOME EXCHANGES

If you would like to exchange your home for someone else's, **join a home-exchange organization,** which will send you its updated listings of available exchanges for a year and will include your own listing in at least one of them. It's up to you to make specific arrangements.

➤ EXCHANGE CLUBS: **HomeLink International** (✉ Box 47747, Tampa, FL 33647, ☎ 813/975–9825 or 800/638–3841, FAX 813/910–8144, WEB www.homelink.org; $98 per year). **Intervac U.S.** (✉ 30 Corte San Fernando, Tiburon, CA 94920, ☎ 800/756–4663, FAX 415/435–7440, WEB www.intervacus.com; $90 yearly fee for a listing, on-line access, and a catalog; $50 without catalog).

HOSTELS

No matter what your age, you can **save on lodging costs by staying at hostels.** In some 4,500 locations in more than 70 countries around the world, Hostelling International (HI), the umbrella group for a number of national youth-hostel associations, offers single-sex, dorm-style beds and, at many hostels, rooms for couples and family accommodations. Membership in any HI national hostel association, open to travelers of all ages, allows you to stay in HI-affiliated hostels at member rates; one-year membership is about $25 for adults (C$26.75 in Canada, £13 in the U.K., A$52 in Australia, and NZ$40 in New Zealand); hostels run about $10 to $30 per night. Members have priority if the hostel is full; they're also eligible for discounts around the world, even on rail and bus travel in some countries.

➤ ORGANIZATIONS: Hostelling International—American Youth Hostels (✉ 733 15th St. NW, Suite 840, Washington, DC 20005, ☎ 202/783–6161, FAX 202/783–6171, WEB www. hiayh.org). Hostelling International—Canada (✉ 400–205 Catherine St., Ottawa, Ontario K2P 1C3, Canada, ☎ 613/237–7884 or 800/663–5777, FAX 613/237–7868, WEB www. hostellingintl.ca). Youth Hostel Association of England and Wales (✉ Trevelyan House, Dimple Rd., Matlock, Derbyshire DE4 3YH, ☎ 0870/870–8808, FAX 0169/592–702, WEB www.yha.org.uk). Australian Youth Hostel Association (✉ 10 Mallett St., Camperdown, NSW 2050, Australia, ☎ 02/9565–1699, FAX 02/9565–1325, WEB www.yha. com.au). Youth Hostels Association of New Zealand (✉ Level 3, 193 Cashel St., Box 436, Christchurch, ☎ 03/379–9970, FAX 03/365–4476, WEB www.yha.org.nz).

HOTELS

All hotels listed have private bath unless otherwise noted.

➤ TOLL-FREE NUMBERS: Adam's Mark (☎ 800/444–2326, WEB www. adamsmark.com). Baymont Inns (☎ 800/428–3438, WEB www. baymontinns.com). Best Western (☎ 800/528–1234, WEB www.bestwestern. com). Choice (☎ 800/424–6423, WEB www.choicehotels.com). Clarion (☎ 800/424–6423, WEB www.choicehotels. com). Colony (☎ 800/777–1700). Comfort Inn (☎ 800/424–6423, WEB www.choicehotels.com). Days Inn (☎ 800/325–2525, WEB www.daysinn. com). Doubletree and Red Lion Hotels (☎ 800/222–8733, WEB www. hilton.com). Embassy Suites (☎ 800/362–2779, WEB www.embassysuites. com). Fairfield Inn (☎ 800/228–2800, WEB www.marriott.com). Four Seasons (☎ 800/332–3442, WEB www. fourseasons.com). Hilton (☎ 800/445–8667, WEB www.hilton.com). Holiday Inn (☎ 800/465–4329, WEB www.sixcontinentshotels.com). Howard Johnson (☎ 800/654–4656, WEB www.hojo.com). Hyatt Hotels & Resorts (☎ 800/233–1234, WEB www. hyatt.com). La Quinta (☎ 800/531–5900, WEB www.laquinta.com). Marriott (☎ 800/228–9290, WEB www. marriott.com). Omni (☎ 800/843–6664, WEB www.omnihotels.com). Quality Inn (☎ 800/424–6423, WEB www.choicehotels.com). Radisson (☎ 800/333–3333, WEB www.radisson. com). Ramada (☎ 800/228–2828, WEB www.ramada.com). Renaissance Hotels & Resorts (☎ 800/468–3571, WEB www.renaissancehotels.com/). Ritz-Carlton (☎ 800/241–3333, WEB www.ritzcarlton.com). Sheraton (☎ 800/325–3535, WEB www.starwood. com). Westin Hotels & Resorts (☎ 800/228–3000, WEB www.westin. com). Wyndham Hotels & Resorts (☎ 800/822–4200, WEB www. wyndham.com).

MOTELS

➤ TOLL-FREE NUMBERS: Budget Hosts Inns (☎ 800/283–4678). Econo Lodge (☎ 800/553–2666, WEB www. econolodge.com). Friendship Inns (☎ 800/453–4511). Motel 6 (☎ 800/466–8356, WEB www.motel6.com). Rodeway (☎ 800/228–2000, WEB www. rodeway.com). Super 8 (☎ 800/848–8888, WEB www.super8.com).

MEDIA

NEWSPAPERS AND MAGAZINES

There's no major regional newspaper that serves the area, but the *Atlanta*

Journal-Constitution ranks among the most influential dailies in the Carolinas and Georgia (as well as nationwide); just about every city with a population of greater than 40,000 or 50,000 also publishes its own daily paper.

Most major cities have very good alternative newsweeklies with useful Web sites and information on area dining, arts, and sightseeing—these are usually free and found in restaurants, coffeehouses, bookstores, tourism offices, hotel lobbies, and some nightclubs. Of particular note is Atlanta's *Creative Loafing,* which has separate editions for a number of additional Southern cities and regions including Charlotte and Raleigh-Durham, where it's called *Spectator,* and Greenville, South Carolina. Visit its Web site (www.cln.com) to find links to each of these editions, as well as to other useful alternative newsweeklies in Athens (GA), Augusta (GA), Columbia (SC), Asheville, Charleston, Greensboro/Winston-Salem, Myrtle Beach, Savannah, and Wilmington (NC).

The monthly features magazine *Southern Living* gives a nice sense of travel, food, and lifestyle issues relevant to the region. Local lifestyles magazines serve Asheville, Atlanta, Charleston, Charlotte, Macon, Raleigh, Savannah, and several other cities. These publications have colorful stories and dining and entertainment coverage; they're worth picking up prior to your visit, especially if you're planning an extended stay; virtually all of these have useful Web sites, too.

RADIO AND TELEVISION

All the major television and radio networks have local affiliates and channels throughout the Carolinas and Georgia, and the CNN empire is based in Atlanta.

MONEY MATTERS

As with most of America, credit and debit cards are accepted at the vast majority of shops, sit-down restaurants, and accommodations in the Carolinas and Georgia. Common exceptions include small, independent stores and also B&Bs in more rural areas. Banks—as well as convenience stores, groceries, and even nightclubs—with ATMs are easy to find in just about every community.

Although the cost of living remains fairly low in most parts of the South, travel-related costs (such as dining, lodging, museums, and transportation) have become increasingly steep in Atlanta over the years and can also be dear in resort communities throughout the Carolinas and Georgia.

Prices throughout this guide are given for adults. Substantially reduced fees are almost always available for children, students, and senior citizens. For information on taxes, *see* Taxes.

CREDIT CARDS

Throughout this guide, the following abbreviations are used: **AE,** American Express; **D,** Discover; **DC,** Diners Club; **MC,** MasterCard; and **V,** Visa.

➤ REPORTING LOST CARDS: **American Express** (☎ 800/441–0519). **Diners Club** (☎ 800/234–6377). **Discover** (☎ 800/347–2683). **MasterCard** (☎ 800/622–7747). **Visa** (☎ 800/ 847–2911).

NATIONAL AND STATE PARKS

National and state parks abound in the Carolinas and Georgia and have lots of visitor facilities, including campgrounds, picnic grounds, hiking trails, boating, and ranger programs. State forests are usually somewhat less developed. For more information contact the state tourism offices (☞ Visitor Information) or parks departments (☞ Contacts and Resources, at the end of each state chapter).

NATIONAL PARK PASSES

Look into discount passes to save money on park entrance fees. For $50, the National Parks Pass admits you (and any passengers in your private vehicle) to all national parks, monuments, and recreation areas, as well as other sites run by the National Park Service, for a year. (In parks that charge per person, the pass admits you, your spouse and children, and your parents, when you arrive together.) Camping and parking are extra. The $15 Golden Eagle Pass, a hologram you affix to your National Parks Pass, functions as an upgrade, granting entry to all sites run by the NPS, the U.S. Fish and Wildlife Service, the U.S. Forest Service, and the Bureau of Land Management (BLM). The upgrade, which expires with the parks pass, is sold by most national-park, Fish-and-Wildlife, and BLM fee stations. A percentage of the proceeds from pass sales funds National Parks projects.

Both the Golden Age Passport ($10), for U.S. citizens or permanent residents who are 62 and older, and the Golden Access Passport (free), for those with disabilities, entitle holders (and any passengers in their private vehicles) to lifetime free entry to all national parks, plus 50% off fees for the use of many park facilities and services. (The discount doesn't always apply to companions.) To obtain them, you must show proof of age and of U.S. citizenship or permanent residency—such as a U.S. passport, driver's license, or birth certificate—and, if requesting Golden Access, proof of disability. The Golden Age and Golden Access passes, as well as the National Parks Pass, are available at any NPS-run site that charges an entrance fee. The National Parks Pass is also available by mail and via the Internet.

➤ PASSES BY MAIL AND ON-LINE: **National Park Foundation** (WEB www.nationalparks.org). **National Parks Pass** (✉ 27540 Ave. Mentry, Valencia, CA 91355, ☎ 888/GO–PARKS or 888/467–2757, WEB www.nationalparks.org); include a check or money order payable to the National Park Service for the pass, plus $3.95 for shipping and handling.

➤ PASSES BY MAIL: **National Parks Pass** (✉ 27540 Ave. Mentry, Valencia, CA 91355, ☎ 888/GO–PARKS, WEB www.nationalparks.org).

PACKING

Georgia is hot and humid in the summer and sunny and mild in the winter. Smart but casual attire works fine almost everywhere you'll go, with a few exceptions requiring more formal dress, most of them in Atlanta. For colder months pack a lightweight coat, slacks, and sweaters; you'll need heavier clothing in some mountainous areas, where cold, damp weather

prevails and snow is not unusual. Keeping summer's humidity in mind, **pack absorbent natural fabrics that breathe;** bring an umbrella, but leave the plastic raincoat at home. You'll want a jacket or sweater for summer evenings and for too-cool air-conditioning. And **don't forget insect repellent.**

In your carry-on luggage, **pack an extra pair of eyeglasses or contact lenses and enough of any medication** you take to last a few days longer than the entire trip. You may also ask your doctor to write a spare prescription using the drug's generic name, since brand names may vary from country to country. In luggage to be checked, **never pack prescription drugs or valuables.** To avoid customs delays, carry medications in their original packaging. And don't forget to carry with you the addresses of offices that handle refunds of lost traveler's checks. Check *Fodor's How to Pack* (available in bookstores everywhere) for more tips.

CHECKING LUGGAGE

How many carry-on bags you can bring with you is up to the airline. Most allow two, but not always, so make sure that everything you carry aboard will fit under your seat or in the overhead bin, and get to the gate early. Note that if you have a seat at the back of the plane, you'll probably board first, while the overhead bins are still empty.

If you are flying internationally, note that baggage allowances may be determined not by piece but by weight—generally 88 pounds (40 kilograms) in first class, 66 pounds (30 kilograms) in business class, and 44 pounds (20 kilograms) in economy.

Airline liability for baggage is limited to $1,250 per person on flights within the United States. On international flights it amounts to $9.07 per pound or $20 per kilogram for checked baggage (roughly $640 per 70-pound bag) and $400 per passenger for unchecked baggage. You can buy additional coverage at check-in for about $10 per $1,000 of coverage, but it excludes a rather extensive list of items, shown on your airline ticket.

Before departure, **itemize your bags' contents** and their worth, and label the bags with your name, address, and phone number. (If you use your home address, cover it so potential thieves can't see it readily.) Inside each bag, **pack a copy of your itinerary.** At check-in, **make sure that each bag is correctly tagged** with the destination airport's three-letter code. If your bags arrive damaged or fail to arrive at all, file a written report with the airline before leaving the airport.

SAFETY

Even in the more urban and tourism-dependent places, you have little cause of worry about theft or crime—just exercise common sense. Be wary of suspicious-looking figures and keep valuables hidden away or locked up, if possible. Especially in urban areas and along major highways, never leave valuables in your unattended car. Wherever you venture in this part of the world, folks are generally happy to offer directions and advice.

SENIOR-CITIZEN TRAVEL

To qualify for age-related discounts, **mention your senior-citizen status up front** when booking hotel reservations (not when checking out) and before you're seated in restaurants (not when paying the bill). When renting a car, ask about promotional car-rental discounts, which can be cheaper than senior-citizen rates.

➤ EDUCATIONAL PROGRAMS: **Elderhostel** (✉ 11 Ave. de Lafayette, Boston, MA 02111-1746, ☎ 877/426–8056, FAX 877/426–2166, WEB www.elderhostel.org).

STUDENTS IN THE CAROLINAS AND GEORGIA

➤ IDs AND SERVICES: **STA Travel** (☎ 212/627–3111 or 800/781–4040, FAX 212/627–3387, WEB www.sta.com). Travel Cuts (✉ 187 College St., Toronto, Ontario M5T 1P7, Canada, ☎ 416/979–2406 or 800/667–2887 in Canada, FAX 416/979–8167, WEB www.travelcuts.com).

TAXES

SALES TAX

Sales taxes are as follows: Georgia 4%; North Carolina 4.5%; and South Carolina 5%. Some counties or cities may impose an additional 1% to 3% tax. Most municipalities also levy a lodging tax (usually exempt at small inns with only a few rooms, but rules vary regionally) and, in some cases, a restaurant tax. The hotel taxes in the South can be rather steep, greater than 10% in Georgia and many counties in North Carolina.

TELEPHONES

AREA CODES

To place a long-distance call within the United States, you need to dial "1" followed by the three-digit area code, and then the seven-digit number. Over the past several years—with a steep increase in the number of cellular phones, fax machines, and second lines—dozens of new area codes have been added. Some cities are now served by multiple area codes; in these places it's often necessary to dial the full 10-digit number (including area code), sometimes preceded by "1," even when placing local calls. In Atlanta, for example, you must dial an area code before dialing the local number. If in doubt, dial "0" when you arrive to check with an operator, or ask your hotel's front desk.

Note that several area codes were added to the region in 2001–2002; 980 now overlays with the existing 803 code in Charlotte, North Carolina; 984 now overlays with the existing 919 code in the Raleigh-Durham area; and 470 has joined 678 and 770 in metro Atlanta. Also, 478 now replaces 912 in parts of 23 Georgia counties, including Macon and Milledgeville; and 229 replaces 912 in 38 counties in southwestern Georgia, including Albany, Valdosta, Tifton, and Thomasville.

LONG-DISTANCE CALLS

Competitive long-distance carriers make calling within the United States relatively convenient and let you avoid hotel surcharges. By dialing an "800" number, you can get connected to the long-distance company of your choice.

If you want to charge a long-distance call to the person you're calling, you can call collect by dialing "0" instead of "1" before the 10-digit number, and an operator will come on the line to assist you (the party you're calling, however, has the right to refuse the call). It's far less costly to purchase a long-distance phone card—these are available in different denominations from convenience stores, gas stations, and newsstands and offer rates that are competitive with those set by most major long-distance carriers.

➤ LONG-DISTANCE CARRIERS: **AT&T** (☎ 800/225–5288). **MCI** (☎ 800/888–8000). **Sprint** (☎ 800/366–2255).

For information on directory and operator assistance, international calls, and public phones, *see* Telephones *in* For International Travelers.

TIME

Georgia and the Carolinas fall in the eastern standard time (EST) zone, which is the same as New York and Florida, making it three hours ahead of California.

TIPPING

At restaurants a 15%–20% tip is standard for waiters, depending on the level of service provided. The same goes for taxi drivers, bartenders, and hairdressers. Coat-check operators usually expect $1; bellhops and porters should get 50¢–$1 per bag; hotel maids should get about $1 per day of your stay—$2 in upscale hotels. A concierge typically receives a tip of $5–$10, with an additional gratuity for special services or favors. On package tours conductors and drivers usually get around $2 per person per day; check whether this has already been figured into your cost. For local sightseeing tours you may individually tip the driver-guide $1 if he or she has been helpful or informative. Ushers in theaters do not expect tips.

TOURS AND PACKAGES

Because everything is prearranged on a prepackaged tour or independent vacation, you spend less time planning—and often get it all at a good price.

BOOKING WITH AN AGENT

Travel agents are excellent resources. But it's a good idea to collect brochures from several agencies as some agents' suggestions may be influenced by relationships with tour and package firms that reward them for volume sales. If you have a special interest, **find an agent with expertise in that area**; ASTA (☞ Travel Agencies) has a database of specialists worldwide.

Make sure your travel agent knows the accommodations and other services of the place being recommended. Ask about the hotel's location, room size, beds, and whether it has a pool, room service, or programs for children, if you care about these. Has your agent been there in person or sent others whom you can contact?

Do some homework on your own, too: local tourism boards can provide information about lesser-known and small-niche operators, some of which may sell only direct.

BUYER BEWARE

Each year consumers are stranded or lose their money when tour operators—even large ones with excellent reputations—go out of business. So **check out the operator.** Ask several travel agents about its reputation, and try to **book with a company that has a consumer-protection program.** (Look for information in the company's brochure.) In the United States, members of the National Tour Association and the United States Tour Operators Association are required to set aside funds to cover your payments and travel arrangements in the event that the company defaults. It's also a good idea to choose a company that participates in the American Society of Travel Agents' Tour Operator Program (TOP); ASTA will act as mediator in any disputes between you and your tour operator.

Remember that the more your package or tour includes the better you can predict the ultimate cost of your vacation. Make sure you know exactly what is covered, and **beware of hidden costs.** Are taxes, tips, and transfers included? Entertainment and excursions? These can add up.

➤ TOUR-OPERATOR RECOMMENDATIONS: **American Society of Travel**

Agents (☞ Travel Agencies). **National Tour Association** (NTA; ⊠ 546 E. Main St., Lexington, KY 40508, ☎ 859/226–4444 or 800/682–8886, WEB www.ntaonline.com). **United States Tour Operators Association** (USTOA; ⊠ 342 Madison Ave., Suite 1522, New York, NY 10173, ☎ 212/599–6599 or 800/468–7862, FAX 212/599–6744, WEB www.ustoa.com).

TRAIN TRAVEL

Amtrak has a number of routes that pass through the Carolinas and Georgia; however, many areas are not served by train, and those cities that do have service usually only have one or two arrivals and departures each day. Major cities served include Atlanta, GA; Charleston, SC; Charlotte, NC; Columbia, SC; Durham, NC; Greensboro, NC; Greenville, SC; Hilton Head, SC; Raleigh, NC; Savannah, GA; and Winston-Salem, NC. For a comparison of different ways of getting around the region, *see* Transportation to and Around the Carolinas and Georgia.

➤ TRAIN INFORMATION: **Amtrak** (☎ 800/872–7245).

CUTTING COSTS

Amtrak offers different kinds of rail passes that allow for travel within certain regions, including a set number of stops, at a significant savings over the standard posted fare. They also have a **North American rail pass** that offers you unlimited travel with the United States and Canada within any 30-day period ($674 peak, $475 off-peak). For non–U.S. residents only, they have several kinds of **USA rail passes,** offering unlimited travel for 15–30 days. Amtrak also has senior citizen, children's, disability, and student discounts, as well as occasional deals that allow a second or third accompanying passenger to travel for half price or even free. The **Amtrak Vacations** program customizes entire vacations, including hotels, car rentals, and tours.

TRANSPORTATION TO AND AROUND THE CAROLINAS AND GEORGIA

Although a car is your best bet for getting around the region, it's worth considering several strategies for getting about conveniently and economically.

If you're planning to spend more than several days and visit more than a couple of cities, you might consider driving your own car rather than flying in and renting one—especially if you live anywhere within 500 mi of the region (i.e., the mid-Atlantic states, the Midwest, or elsewhere in the South) and you're traveling with three or more in your group.

If coming by plane, plan to fly into one of the region's major airports, to which fares tend to be considerably lower than to smaller regional facilities. The sheer competition and wealth of connections at Atlanta's busy Hartsfield Airport make it an excellent choice—car-rental rates here are also highly competitive. Charlotte-Douglas International Airport, in North Carolina, is the second-best choice for a central location.

It's difficult to find direct flights to most of the other airports in the Carolinas and Georgia, especially if flying from outside the region. However, within the area check to see what airfares are between some smaller cities—very often airlines offer specials for popular shorter routes like Atlanta to Savannah or Charlotte to Hilton Head.

If you're trying to save money, you have a fair amount of time, and you're interested in taking in the landscape without having to drive, consider getting around via bus—Greyhound (☞ Bus Travel) has frequent and regular service to virtually every city in the region. Some routes, such as those near the coastal areas and over the mountainous interior section, can be quite breathtaking. And if you book at least a couple of days ahead, you'll find the rates quite reasonable. A bit less practical is relying on train travel (☞ Train Travel), as Amtrak's coverage within the region is a bit spotty, and round-trip fares are sometimes substantially higher than bus fares for comparable routes—occasionally even more than the corresponding air fares.

TRAVEL AGENCIES

A good travel agent puts your needs first. Look for an agency that has been in business at least five years, emphasizes customer service, and has someone on staff who specializes in your destination. In addition, **make sure the agency belongs to a professional trade organization.** The American Society of Travel Agents (ASTA), with more than 24,000 members in some 140 countries, is the largest and most influential in the field. Operating under the motto "Without a travel agent, you're on your own," it maintains and enforces a strict code of ethics and will step in to help mediate any agent-client disputes if necessary. ASTA also maintains a Web site that includes a directory of agents. (If a travel agency is also acting as your tour operator, *see* Buyer Beware *in* Tours and Packages.)

➤ LOCAL AGENT REFERRALS: **American Society of Travel Agents** (ASTA; ✉ 1101 King St., Suite 200, Alexandria, VA 22314, ☎ 800/965–2782 24-hr hot line, FAX 703/739–3268, WEB www.astanet.com). **Association of British Travel Agents** (✉ 68–71 Newman St., London W1T 3AH, U.K., ☎ 020/7637–2444, FAX 020/7637–0713, WEB www.abtanet.com). **Association of Canadian Travel Agents** (✉ 130 Albert St., Suite 1705, Ottawa, Ontario K1P 5G4, ☎ 613/237–3657, FAX 613/237–7052, WEB www.acta.ca). **Australian Federation of Travel Agents** (✉ Level 3, 309 Pitt St., Sydney NSW 2000, Australia, ☎ 02/9264–3299, FAX 02/9264–1085, WEB www.afta.com.au). **Travel Agents' Association of New Zealand** (✉ Level 5, Tourism and Travel House, 79 Boulcott St., Box 1888, Wellington 6001, ☎ 04/499–0104, FAX 04/499–0827, WEB www.taanz.org.nz).

VISITOR INFORMATION

For general information and brochures before you go, contact the state tourism bureaus below.

➤ TOURIST INFORMATION: **Georgia Department of Industry, Trade and Tourism** (✉ 285 Peachtree Center Ave., N.E. Marquis Tower II, Suite 1100, Atlanta, GA 30303, ☎ 404/656–3553 or 800/847–4842, FAX 404/651–9462, WEB www.georgia.org).

North Carolina Travel and Tourism Division (✉ 301 N. Wilmington St., Raleigh, NC 27601, ☎ 919/715–5900 or 800/847–4862, FAX 919/733–2616, WEB www.visitnc.com). **South Carolina Department of Parks, Recreation, and Tourism** (✉ 1205 Pendleton St., Suite 106, Columbia, SC 29201, ☎ 803/734–0122 or 888/SC–SMILE, FAX 803/734–0138, WEB www.travelsc.com).

WEB SITES

Do check out the World Wide Web when planning your trip. You'll find everything from weather forecasts to virtual tours of famous cities. Be sure to **visit Fodors.com** (www.fodors.com), a complete travel-planning site. You can research prices, check out bargains, and book plane tickets, hotel rooms, rental cars, vacation packages, and more. In addition, you can post your pressing questions in the Travel Talk section. Other planning tools include a currency converter and weather reports, and there are loads of links to travel resources.

For more information on events in the Carolinas and Georgia, try visiting the Web sites of major newspapers and alternative newsweeklies in the area (☞ Media). Also take a look at the Web sites listed for regional and local tourism offices in the A to Z sections throughout each chapter.

WHEN TO GO

Spring is probably the most attractive season in this part of the United States. Throughout the region the blooming of cherry blossoms is followed by those of azaleas, dogwoods, and camellias from April into May, with apple blossoms blooming in May. Summer can be hot and humid in many areas, but temperatures will be cooler along the coasts or in the mountains. Folk, crafts, art, and music festivals tend to take place in summer, as do sports events. State and local fairs are held mainly in August and September, although there are a few as early as the first part of July and as late as October. Fall can be a delight, with spectacular foliage, particularly in the mountains. The region is large, so conditions vary; *see* the individual state chapters for more information.

CLIMATE

In winter temperatures generally average in the low 40s inland, in the 60s by the shore. Summer temperatures, modified by mountains in some areas, by water in others, range from the high 70s to the mid-80s and now and then the low 90s.

➤ FORECASTS: **Weather Channel Connection** (☎ 900/932–8437), 95¢ per minute from a Touch-Tone phone.

The following are average daily maximum and minimum temperatures for key cities.

ATLANTA, GEORGIA

Jan.	52F	11C	May	79F	26C	Sept.	83F	28C
	36	2		61	16		65	18
Feb.	54F	12C	June	86F	30C	Oct.	72F	22C
	38	3		67	19		54	12
Mar.	63F	17C	July	88F	31C	Nov.	61F	16C
	43	6		70	21		43	6
Apr.	72F	22C	Aug.	86F	30C	Dec.	52F	11C
	52	11		70	21		38	3

RALEIGH, NORTH CAROLINA

Jan.	50F	10C	May	78F	26C	Sept.	81F	27C
	29	− 2		55	13		60	16
Feb.	52F	11C	June	85F	29C	Oct.	71F	22C
	30	− 1		62	17		47	8
Mar.	61F	16C	July	88F	31C	Nov.	61F	16C
	37	3		67	19		38	3
Apr.	72F	22C	Aug.	87F	31C	Dec.	52F	11C
	46	8		66	18		30	−1

CHARLESTON, SOUTH CAROLINA

Jan.	59F	15C	May	81F	27C	Sept.	84F	29C
	41	6		64	18		69	21
Feb.	60F	16C	June	86F	30C	Oct.	76F	24C
	43	7		71	22		59	15
Mar.	66F	19C	July	88F	31C	Nov.	67F	19C
	49	9		74	23		49	9
Apr.	73F	23C	Aug.	88F	31C	Dec.	59F	11C
	56	13		73	23		42	6

FESTIVALS AND SEASONAL EVENTS

The Carolinas and Georgia hold plenty of delightful festivals and special events throughout the year. Call local or state visitor information offices for further information.

➤ DECEMBER: **Christmas** is celebrated all over the South, with events in almost every city. Highlights include Old Salem Christmas, which re-creates a Moravian Christmas in Winston-Salem, North Carolina. The annual Festival of Trees in Atlanta highlights specially decorated trees, and Savannah glows with candlelight tours of the Historic District. **New Year's** events include the Peach Bowl, played in Atlanta, and First Night festivals held in the downtown areas of Asheville, Athens, Charleston, Charlotte, Greenville, Raleigh, and Savannah.

➤ JANUARY: In South Carolina, Orangeburg invites the country's finest coon dogs to compete in the **Grand American Coon Hunt. Martin Luther King Jr. Week** is celebrated in Atlanta with lectures, exhibits, and rallies.

➤ FEBRUARY: In North Carolina, Asheville has an annual **Arts and Crafts Show** at the Grove Park Inn. Chapel Hill stages the **Carolina Jazz Festival.** Regional runners race in the **Memorial Health Tybee Marathon and Half Marathon** in Savannah, Georgia.

➤ MARCH: The Old South comes alive: **antebellum mansion and garden tours** are given in Charleston and Beaufort, South Carolina. A **Revolu-**

tionary War battle is reenacted on the anniversary of the Battle of Guilford Courthouse in Greensboro, North Carolina. Spring is celebrated with a cherry blossom festival in Macon, Georgia, and SpringFest on Hilton Head Island, South Carolina. St. Patrick's Day in Savannah is one of the nation's largest celebrations of the day. Aiken, South Carolina, has its own horse-racing Triple Crown, including Thoroughbred trials, harness races, and steeplechases.

➤ APRIL: Spring festivals abound, including dogwood festivals in Atlanta, Georgia, and Fayetteville, North Carolina. The World Grits Festival is held near Charleston in St. George, South Carolina. In Wilkesboro, North Carolina, MerleFest is a celebration of Merle Watson; the highlight is Doc Watson's renowned bluegrass picking. The Biltmore Estate, in Asheville, North Carolina, hosts the Festival of Flowers, a breathtaking display with more than 50,000 tulips, hundreds of varieties of azaleas, and dogwood and cherry trees. The Masters Golf Tournament in Augusta, Georgia, attracts top pros and thousands of spectators. More than 25,000 participate in the Cooper River Bridge Run and Walk, in Charleston, South Carolina.

➤ MAY: Festivals take to the air this month with the annual Hang Gliding Spectacular in Nags Head, North Carolina. Over Memorial Day weekend, Anderson, South Carolina, hosts Pontiac GMC's Freedom Weekend Aloft, the second-largest hot-air balloon rally in the country. Spoleto Festival USA, in Charleston, South Carolina, is one of the world's biggest arts festivals; Piccolo Spoleto, running concurrently, showcases local and regional talent. In South Carolina, Beaufort's Gullah Festival highlights the fine arts, customs, language, and dress of Lowcountry African-Americans.

➤ JUNE: Popular arts festivals such as the juried Virginia-Highland Summerfest flourish throughout Atlanta. June is the time for Durham, North Carolina's, renowned American Dance Festival. Summer gets under way at the Sun Fun Festival on Myrtle

Beach's Grand Strand on the South Carolina coast. In Greenwood, South Carolina, the Festival of Flowers has been going strong since the 1967.

➤ JULY: Independence Day celebrations are annual traditions around the South. Clog and figure dancing are part of the Shindig on the Green, in Asheville, North Carolina. The annual Highland Games & Gathering of the Scottish Clans is held on Grandfather Mountain near Linville, North Carolina.

➤ AUGUST: The Georgia Mountain Fair, a mountain crafts and music extravaganza, is held in Hiawassee. August music festivals include a Beach Music Festival on Jekyll Island, Georgia, and the annual Mountain Dance and Folk Festival, in Asheville, North Carolina.

➤ SEPTEMBER: Truly a festival month, September welcomes local events throughout the South. In Georgia, Stone Mountain Park is the site of the Yellow Daisy Festival, celebrating this flower and also arts and crafts. North Carolina holds an Apple Festival in Hendersonville. The Candlelight Tour of Houses and Gardens is held in Charleston during this month and October.

➤ OCTOBER: Autumn brings more celebrations of food, including the Big Pig Jig in Vienna, Georgia, celebrating the glories of authentic Southern barbecue. The annual Highland Games, a celebration of Scottish heritage, is held at Stone Mountain Park in Georgia. A barbecue and parade of pigs guarantee fun at the Lexington Barbecue Festival, in North Carolina. The annual Woolly Worm Festival takes place in Banner Elk, North Carolina. The South Carolina State Fair is a Columbia highlight. Oktoberfest is celebrated in Helen, Georgia, and in Walhalla, South Carolina. The "ghost capital of the world"—Georgetown, South Carolina—stages a Ghost Tour.

➤ NOVEMBER: Christmas preparations include the Mistletoe Market in Albany, Georgia. Autumn food festivals include the Catfish Festival in Society Hill, South Carolina, and the Chitlin' Strut, in Salley, South Carolina.

1 DESTINATION: THE CAROLINAS AND GEORGIA

THE INCONGRUOUS SOUTH

NORTH CAROLINA, South Carolina, and Georgia—their many differences notwithstanding—share as strong a regional identity as any three states in the union. Each is marked at one end by a low Atlantic coastal plain and at the other by a jaunty tangle of Appalachian Mountain peaks. Connecting these two extremes are vast expanses of largely agrarian countryside, scruffy pine forest, and increasingly unchecked suburban sprawl. The endearing yet provincial Old South, characterized by down-home meat-and-three lunch joints and rambling country inns, still exists—in some cases within the shadows of Atlanta's and Charlotte's cloud-busting skyscrapers. But in the 21st century you have to crane your neck a little to see what sets the Carolinas and Georgia apart from the rest of the world.

Forever united by a common history and culture, these three states are becoming increasingly worldly and homogeneous, as opportunity seekers from other lands flock here in record numbers. Georgia, in particular, is growing at breakneck speed—according to the 2000 census, it has 18 of the nation's 100 fastest-growing counties. And several major headquarters—Bank of America, CNN, Coca-Cola—have earned Charlotte and Atlanta international business clout.

It all surpasses what Henry Grady envisioned when he popularized the term *New South*. In a speech delivered to the New England Club of New York in 1886, the longtime editor of the *Atlanta Constitution* made the case that the South was an ideal area for industrial investment. The growth and progress of Atlanta would serve, he said, as an example for the rest of the region. They did. And today the convergence of the Old South and the New South is nowhere more evident than in these three states.

Atlanta is a sprawling city in the heart of a spaghetti knot of interstate highways. Underground, however, beneath the viaducts that cover the original streets and railroad yards of old Atlanta, is an entertainment capital and Heritage Row, a historic district that recalls the city's different stages, from the wilderness years to the days of King Cotton, from the Civil War siege to the present day.

The South has a history of controversy—of slavery and civil strife—but it also has a history of beauty and warmth. In South Carolina the Gullah rhythms of African-Americans who have saved and made sacred the language, music, and traditions of ancestors who were brought to the Sea Islands as slaves are part of the cadence of life. Now German accents join the chorus. In upstate Spartanburg County, the automaker BMW operates Zentrum, a 28,000-square-ft visitor center, with a museum for its collection of vintage and current automobiles, motorcycles, racing cars, and aero engines.

Everything from Astroturf to Zantac has come from North Carolina's Research Triangle area (Raleigh–Durham–Chapel Hill), where gleaming research and medical centers set on lush campuses employ tens of thousands of people who believe in the power and promise of technology. Every year for nearly a century those who believe in another kind of promise have made their way to the Blue Ridge Mountains and the Southern gospel music festival at Grandfather Mountain's McRae Meadow. Here thousands of participants are reminded of a time when "the Word" was delivered outdoors in oratory and song.

To really experience the Carolinas and Georgia, you should really get around and explore a bit—this is not a one-dimensional place. In the classic South valued assets are stately old homes, rich recreational resources, and scenery that shifts effortlessly from tropical palms and sandy beaches to meandering roads and mountainsides. The states are the locations for many notable firsts: South Carolina's Beth Elohim Reform Temple was the birthplace of Reform Judaism in America, and the University of North Carolina at Chapel Hill was founded more than three centuries ago as the nation's first state institution of higher education.

The temperate weather draws people like moths to a flame. But if climate is king, then construction is queen in the New South, leaving her mark on even the sleepiest backwaters. Consider Brunswick, North Carolina's southernmost coastal county, whose reputation was built around its pristine beaches, golf courses, and historic sites. Now the number of building permits issued in Brunswick each year is rivaled only by that of Las Vegas.

Take what you want from these notions. The South, after all, writes Shannon Ravenel, cofounder of Algonquin Books in Chapel Hill, is a "state of mind." And should that state seem incongruous at times, well, that's all right. So what if a profusion of Atlanta road names include the word *Peachtree* (more than 60 at last count)? Don't mind that Georgia calls itself the Peach State although South Carolina is actually the nation's largest producer of fresh-market peaches. And when North Carolinians call their town of Beaufort "bow-furt," while South Carolinians pronounce their Beaufort "bew-fert," just say no problem, and chalk it up to the South.

Amid the changing landscape, growing population, and increasingly influential culture, the rock of the South is the Southerner. As T. S. Eliot (born in Missouri) explained, "Culture is not merely the sum of several activities, but a way of life." Carolinians and Georgians perpetuate the culture of the South, the way of life that still calls for civility. Here people know there's a proper way of doing things, and they believe in manners. So when you arrive, put your stereotypes aside and know that you're entering a slightly different sensibility and try to revel in it.

— Updated by Andy Collins

WHAT'S WHERE

Georgia

Georgia has contrasting landscapes and varied cities and towns, each reflecting its own version of Southern charm. The northern part of the state has the Appalachian Mountains and their waterfalls; Dahlonega, the site of an early gold rush; and Alpine Helen, a re-created Bavarian village in the Blue Ridge Mountains.

Also in the north are the region's urban hub, Atlanta, one of the nation's fastest-growing big cities and a vital banking center, and Macon, an antebellum town with thousands of cherry trees. To the southwest lies a network of bucolic all-American towns—including Americus, Tifton, and Thomasville—plus the river city of Columbus. East of Atlanta, historic Augusta and the college city of Athens have many fine old homes and an abundance of picturesque scenery.

If you drive some five hours southeast from Atlanta, you'll reach Savannah, which has the nation's largest historic district, filled with restored colonial and 19th-century buildings. From Savannah the state's 100-mi Atlantic coast runs south to the Florida border. Along this stretch is a string of lush, subtropical barrier islands including historic Sapelo Island and the Golden Isles, the elegant seaside communities of Jekyll, Sea, and St. Simons islands. Farther south is Cumberland Island National Seashore, a sanctuary of marshes, beaches, forests, lakes, and ponds. Much of southern Georgia consists of gator-infested swampland, including the mysterious rivers and lakes of the Okefenokee.

North Carolina

Historic sights and natural wonders abound in North Carolina, from Old Salem, where the 1700s spring to life in modern-day Winston-Salem, to the Great Smoky and Blue Ridge mountains, in the west, where waterfalls cascade over high cliffs into gorges thick with evergreens. On the Cape Hatteras and Cape Lookout national seashores, tides wash over the wooden skeletons of ancient shipwrecks, and lighthouses stand as they have for 200 years. The rugged beaches that fringe the Outer Banks are among the most beautiful in the country, and the many outdoors activities—hang gliding, windsurfing, kayaking, birdwatching, and nature hikes, not to mention intensely fresh seafood—attract peace- and adventure-seeking vacationers alike. Here, too, you'll find sophisticated cities such as Charlotte and Raleigh, world-class golf in the Pinehurst Sandhills, and the rich soil of the gently rolling Piedmont, which has supported generations of both farmers and potters.

South Carolina

South Carolina's scenic Lowcountry shoreline is punctuated by the lively port city of Charleston, decked out with fine museums (several in restored antebellum homes), and is anchored by the recreational resorts of Myrtle Beach and Hilton Head at either end of the coast. The state capital, Columbia, is set in the fertile interior, and the Blue Ridge Mountains form the western border of the state. Also to the west are the rolling fields of Thoroughbred Country, which is noted for top racehorses and sprawling mansions, and Upcountry, at the state's northwestern tip, with incredible mountain scenery and white-water rafting.

PLEASURES AND PASTIMES

Dining

Time was when "dinner" in the South meant the midday meal—the principal meal of the day—and the lighter evening meal was known as "supper." But no more. Now, dinner is the last meal of the day, and grits aren't just for breakfast anymore. In fact, dishes such as chili grits and shrimp with cheese grits are popping up as entrées on the states' most sophisticated menus. And it's not just in major cities that you'll find upscale cuisine. In Blowing Rock, a small resort town in the mountains of North Carolina, one chef regularly whips up wild creations such as grilled ostrich with vegetable tortilla lasagna and smoked apple ketchup. Purists can take heart, however, as there's still plenty of down-home cookin' to be had—country ham and fried chicken, biscuits and corn bread, collard and turnip greens—and South Carolina's Lowcountry kitchens continue to ooze with she-crab soup, stuffed oysters, and pecan pie. Barbecue, which in the South is only a noun, never a verb, is served in a stunning number of ways, the meat (usually pork) dressed in everything from vinegar and red pepper to sweet mustard.

History

Long before 16th-century explorers Giovanni de Verrazano and Hernando de Soto came calling on what is today the Carolinas and Georgia, the land was occupied by the indigenous peoples of many tribes. The history of one of the mightiest, the Cherokee, is chronicled in the state-of-the-art Museum of the Cherokee Indian, in Cherokee, North Carolina, beneath the shadow of the Great Smoky Mountains. Farther south, the Charleston Museum, founded in 1773 as the first public museum in the United States, still welcomes visitors. Across the region, colonial history comes alive at Revolutionary War sites—at Kings Mountain National Military Park, in Upcountry South Carolina, for example, and in Guilford Courthouse National Military Park, in Greensboro, North Carolina. In 1799 America's first gold rush got its start east of Charlotte; the Reed Gold Mine State Historic Site marks the spot. In Georgia, meanwhile, Savannah stands as testimony to the antebellum era, as do many of the towns lining U.S. 441, such as Madison and Milledgeville and, just to the south, Macon. The entire Confederate treasury, last seen at Chennault Plantation, in Lincolnton, Georgia, remains nowhere to be found, though rumor has it the gold is hidden somewhere on the grounds. A century after the Civil War, the South was the center of another wrenching conflict: the civil rights movement. Landmarks and memorials of the campaign, including Martin Luther King Jr.'s Ebenezer Baptist Church in Atlanta, can be found across the region.

Music

Travel along the coast of the Carolinas and Georgia during the summer months, and you'll hear the strains of beach music, sanctified oldies such as "Under the Boardwalk," by the Drifters. The focal point of this music is a dance ritual, the shag. South Carolina's Myrtle Beach, site of a huge annual festival celebrating beach music and the shag, also has a large number of country venues. Out of clubs and bars in the region's college towns have come scores of alternative rock bands and many national headliners, including R.E.M. and Hootie and the Blowfish. For bluegrass head to the mountains of North Carolina; for classical try Charleston's Spoleto Festival USA; and if you want a little of everything, sidle up to the listening stations in the Georgia Music Hall of Fame, in Macon. It honors the amazing number of music industry leaders and artists who hail from the state—from Toni Braxton, James Brown, and Ray Charles to Al Green, Isaac Hayes, and Lena Horne.

Outdoor Activities and Sports

Though the Carolinas and Georgia have professional baseball, basketball, football, and hockey teams, college sports—especially football and basketball—elicit the most fiery loyalty. School colors don't matter when it comes to fishing and boating, though, and Southerners do a lot of both. There are huge bays and sounds here, natural and man-made lakes, the Atlantic Ocean and Intracoastal Waterway, as well as rivers for white-water rafting and flat-water canoeing. If beaches are your passion, take your pick: the windswept shores of North Carolina's Outer Banks, the bustling resorts at South Carolina's Myrtle Beach, or Georgia's lush barrier islands. The myriad courses of Southern Pines and Pinehurst in North Carolina's Sandhills are a golfer's fantasy. The region's mountains, from the Blue Ridge to the Great Smokies, have well-marked hiking trails, including parts of the Appalachian Trail, to take you away from everyday bustle. But if it's sound and motion you crave, then that most Southern of sports, stock car racing (NASCAR), is just the ticket.

FODOR'S CHOICE

No two people will agree on what makes a perfect vacation, but it's fun and helpful to know what others think. There are so many special places in the Carolinas and Georgia, but a few that stand out. For detailed information about each entry, refer to the appropriate chapter.

Special Moments

Historic District, Savannah, Georgia. Architecture buffs will have a field day strolling by the hundreds of restored buildings within a 2½-square-mi area.

Okefenokee National Wildlife Refuge, southeastern Georgia. Savor nature at its most primeval as alligators and frogs bellow their respective mating calls in spring.

Martin Luther King Jr. Center, Atlanta, Georgia. The eternal flame burning at Martin Luther King Jr.'s tomb in front of the downtown center inspires reflection.

Cape Hatteras National Seashore, North Carolina. Stretching from Oregon Inlet to Ocracoke Island, this scenic coastline is dotted with beach communities, wildlife refuges, and beaches cluttered only by wild sea oats.

Kitty Hawk, Nag's Head, North Carolina. Hang-gliding on the sand dunes, in the place where, thanks to the Wright Brothers, aviation began, is an inimitable way to enjoy the Outer Banks.

Old Salem, Winston-Salem, North Carolina. A 1700s village of brick-and-wood structures peopled by tradesmen and gentlewomen in period costume provides a slice of living history.

Cypress Gardens, Moncks Corner, South Carolina. A boat tour among the spring blossoms reflecting in the black waters of the gardens is a visual dazzler.

Dining

Elizabeth on 37th, Savannah, Georgia. Crab cakes, cream cake, and country ham are among the fine regional specialties in this elegant early 20th-century mansion in the city's Victorian district. $$$–$$$$

Dillard House, Clayton, Georgia. On a plateau overlooking the Little Tennessee River Valley, this charming cluster of cottages and motel-style rooms is justly famous for its dining room serving heaping platters of all-you-can-eat Southern favorites. $–$$$

Mrs. Wilkes Dining Room, Savannah, Georgia. Expect long lines waiting to devour the reasonably priced, well-prepared Southern food, served family style at big tables. $$

Magnolia Grill, Durham, North Carolina. Innovative, eye-catching food with piquant flavors defines this bistro, which puts a fresh spin on traditional Southern cooking. $$$$

Second Empire, Raleigh, North Carolina. Art on a plate. Elegance and epicurean innovation are the bywords at this renovated Victorian-era mansion just blocks from the capitol. $$$$

Woodlands Inn, Summerville, South Carolina. Locals flock from Charleston for fantastic, sophisticated meals. Menu options are vast—from Kobe beef with seared foie gras to apple-wood-smoked salmon lasagna to Colorado lamb with goat cheese pierogi. $$$$

Charleston Grill, Charleston, South Carolina. Chef Bob Waggoner's place, with famously fabulous new South cuisine, is, according to locals, what all other area restaurants are measured on. $$$–$$$$

Collectors Cafe, Myrtle Beach, South Carolina. This pleasantly arty spot includes a gallery, so you can shop after you try the delicious black-bean or scallop cakes. $$$–$$$$

Magnolias, Charleston, South Carolina. Lots of Lowcountry dishes—uptown "down South" cuisine—and a magnolia theme infuse this popular restaurant in a refurbished warehouse. $$$–$$$$

McCrady's, Charleston, South Carolina. Join the fans who rave, justifiably, over the food at this elegant, if formal, restaurant in a 1778 tavern. $$$–$$$$

Peninsula Grill, Charleston, South Carolina. Superb, elegant dining makes the restaurant at Planters Inn a favorite with Charleston's jet set. $$$–$$$$

Alice's Fine Foods, Charleston, South Carolina. Locals love the casual cafeteria-style buffet, which is stocked with everything from fried chicken and ribs to collard greens and macaroni-and-cheese pie. $–$$

Lodging

Melhana Grand Plantation and Resort, Thomasville, Georgia. A sprawling 50-acre estate, this former plantation now comprises a 30-room resort surrounded by shaded glens and bridal paths. Note the exquisite dining—both the room and the meals. $$$$

Four Seasons Hotel, Atlanta, Georgia. Whether you come in torn jeans or a Prada suit, the famously graceful staff know how to treat you. Add to that the cascading marble staircases, elegant terraces, and immensely comfortable beds—this is as plush as it gets. Already one of the South's most luxurious hotels, it has also undergone a $1 million inner face-lift. $$$–$$$$

Henderson Village, Perry, Georgia. If you long for a rustic-style elegance—fine antiques, wraparound porches—this cluster of Southern houses on a green with a fine restaurant is a charming base if you're in Macon. $$$–$$$$

Jekyll Island Club Hotel, Jekyll Island, Georgia. This former private hunting retreat for the wealthy—with wraparound verandas and Queen Anne–style towers and turrets—now has luxurious guest rooms and cottages. There are two excellent restaurants; the Grand Dining Room emphasizes local ingredients, especially seafood, prepared with Southern flair. $$$–$$$$

Kehoe House, Savannah, Georgia. Elegance, refinement, and Victorian opulence make a stay at this inn a grand experience in every way. $$$–$$$$

Windsor Hotel, Americus, Georgia. This 1890s small-town monument to Victorian architecture is truly one of the South's best treasures of American heritage. The impressive restaurant serves both straightforward and innovative Southern fare—from surf and turf and baked ham to grilled chicken glazed with raspberries and Chipotle chilies. $$

The Carolina, Pinehurst, North Carolina. Thanks to its serene location and style, attentive service, round-the-calendar blooming flora, and recreational activities, including tennis and bicycling, the world's largest golf resort—with eight courses—attracts more than golfers. $$$$

Fearrington House, Chapel Hill, North Carolina. Once a working farm and now a community in the style of a country village, this unusual inn comes with mascots (cows) and has modern rooms overlooking a courtyard, garden, and pasture. You'll get top-notch service in genteel surroundings. $$$$

Grove Park Inn, Asheville, North Carolina. The city's premier resort, tucked away in the Blue Ridge Mountains and with countless sports and entertainment activities, Grove Park Inn has been the haunt of folks as varied as Thomas Edison and Michael Jordan since its opening in 1913. $$$$

First Colony Inn, Nags Head, North Carolina. Four-poster beds, English antiques, and whirlpool tubs lend an air of romance to this inn by the ocean, reminiscent of the beach hotels of years past. $$$–$$$$

Charleston Place, Charleston, South Carolina. Even the lobby—with a handblown Venetian-glass chandelier, an Italian marble floor, and antiques from Sotheby's—is world class. Rooms are furnished with period reproductions. Conveniently, the hotel is also in the historic district and is surrounded by boutiques. $$$$

John Rutledge House Inn, Charleston, South Carolina. The elegant John Rutledge House has ornate ironwork on its facade and is impeccably furnished and maintained. It's one of Charleston's most luxurious small inns. $$$$

Kingston Plantation, Myrtle Beach, South Carolina. If you want to remove yourself from the bustle but want the convenience of shops and restaurants, come to this self-contained resort among 145 acres of ocean-side woodlands. There are a spa and a marina, and its beach is broad. $$$–$$$$

Westin Resort, Hilton Head Island, South Carolina. On lushly landscaped oceanfront—the island's quietest stretch—the resort excels at making sure you really do get away from it all, and have plenty to do while you're doing it. $$$

Historic Houses and Gardens

Callaway Gardens, Pine Mountain, Georgia. This is one of the country's biggest—14,000 acres ensconced in the foothills of the Appalachian Mountains. There are thousands of azaleas and other blooms, 50 species of butterflies, birds of prey, and miles of nature trails. Also on the resort's grounds are golf courses, a lakefront beach, bicycling trails, and tennis courts.

Carter Presidential Center Library, Atlanta, Georgia. Built as a legacy to President Jimmy Carter's administration, the Carter Center is a splendid landscaped estate with meticulously tended Japanese gardens that provide a tranquil vantage point of Atlanta's cityscape.

Robert Toombs House, Washington, Georgia. The former home of U.S. senator Robert Toombs, who served as secretary of state during the Civil War, this Greek Revival mansion is furnished with 19th-century antiques and other personal items from Toombs's estate.

Biltmore Estate, Asheville, North Carolina. This castle is part of an 8,000-acre estate masterminded by premier landscape architect Frederick Law Olmsted and contains an Italian garden, a walled garden, a conservatory, the Biltmore Forest, and meandering woodland trails.

Orton Plantation Gardens, Winnabow, North Carolina. Aside the Cape Fear River, these gardens were established in 1725, and descendants of the original owners continue to maintain the 20 lush acres of trails, informal gardens, and sculpted formal gardens filled with azaleas, camellias, and other ornamentals.

Sarah P. Duke Gardens, Durham, North Carolina. The gardens occupy 55 acres of Duke University's West Campus. They include native plants, an Asiatic garden, a rock garden and fishpond, a circular rose garden, and an enormous wisteria-covered pergola offering a grand view of the core of the landscaped gardens, the Terraces.

Drayton Hall, Charleston, South Carolina. Unfurnished and unrestored, this mid-18th-century National Historic Landmark is considered the nation's finest example of unspoiled Georgian-Palladian architecture.

Magnolia Plantation and Gardens, Charleston, South Carolina. The 50-acre informal garden was begun in 1685. You can canoe through the Waterfowl Refuge, explore the Audubon Swamp Garden, or meander along 500 acres of wildlife trails. The Manor House offers a look at plantation life.

Middleton Place, Charleston, South Carolina. These are the nation's oldest landscaped gardens, dating to 1741, with terraced lawns and ornamental lakes (including the famous Butterfly Lakes). The place is ablaze with roses, azaleas, camellias, and magnolias in floral allées.

2 GEORGIA

Geographically speaking, Georgia is the largest state east of the Mississippi River. Its varied terrain ranges from the foothills of the Appalachian Mountains, in the north, to the great coastal plain that stretches from the state's center toward the shore to the beaches of the Golden Isles and the Okefenokee National Wildlife Refuge, in the southeast. From progressive Atlanta to antebellum Macon and colonial Savannah, each of Georgia's cities and towns has a unique charm.

Updated by
Hollis Gillespie

FROM THE AIR, and during spring, the sight of Georgia might mislead you into believing the entire state is hidden under trees, or at least under the ubiquitous kudzu vines, which blanket everything if not vigilantly kept at bay. This might give the landscape a deceptively monotonous appearance, but this is just superficial. Of course, anything worth exploring is worth delving beneath its surface. With Georgia you don't even have to delve that far because from the ground it's immediately apparent that the multiedged Peach State is anything but monotonous.

Its landscape encompasses the hazy blue foothills of the Appalachian Mountains, in the north, the coastal plain, which connects the heartland to the unspoiled beaches of the Atlantic, and the mysterious black-water swamps of the state's southern end. Most people travel its interstate highways (I–75, I–85, I–95, and I–16), but the adventurous traveler who decides to explore the state's byways will be rewarded with pristine vistas and detours through charming towns.

Within the landscape lies a rich diversity of unusual flora, including mountain laurels, rhododendrons, azaleas, and camellias. Spanish moss drapes live oak trees in the southern and coastal areas, and flat fields of white puffy cotton line the horizon through the middle of the state. Known for its peaches, Georgia is also proud of its apples, and the fruit trees' soft blooms create splendid sights in spring. Hiking in the north Georgia mountains could reveal their wealth of deer charging through the forest. Along the coast alligators, egrets, and herons take curiosity-seekers in stride.

As varied as its landscape, Georgia's citizens reflect the diversity of early settlers, Native American peoples, and, to this day, a constant stream of new arrivals from all parts of the globe. During the 18th century not only English and Scottish immigrants but also Jewish settlers, both Sephardic and Ashkenazic, and German religious refugees (the Salzburgers) arrived to take up positions of importance and prominence in the Georgia colony. Africans and Native peoples—chiefly Cherokee and Creek—added their cultural spice to the mix, creating a state that is richer in ethnic character than is often recognized. Irish immigrants arriving throughout the 19th century and Greeks, Middle Easterners, and Asians during the late 19th and early 20th centuries contributed to the state's diversity. Georgians speak with accents that vary from the classic, slightly nasal mountain "twang" to the distinctive, soft coastal lilt of upper-crust Savannahians.

Georgia's towns each define in their own way that famous Southern charm of fable and film. Bustling Atlanta, the state capital since the Civil War ended in 1865, has been compared with Margaret Mitchell's heroine, Scarlett O'Hara, the classic Steel Magnolia: gentle in form but brash and tough in substance. Colonial Savannah, with the nation's largest historic district, lures all sorts to its 21 cobblestone squares, giant parterre gardens, waterfront gift shops, jazz bars, and parks. Dahlonega, site of the nation's early gold rush in 1828, is a typical example of the small Georgia town, with its central square dominated by a county courthouse. Macon, full of flowering Japanese cherry trees and images of both the antebellum and Victorian South, celebrates its heritage as the home of poet and flutist Sidney Lanier. A few small towns are named for glittering foreign capitals that they resemble not in the slightest: Vienna (pronounced vy-*en*-ah), Madrid (may-*drid*), Rome, Athens, Cairo (*cay*-row), and so forth.

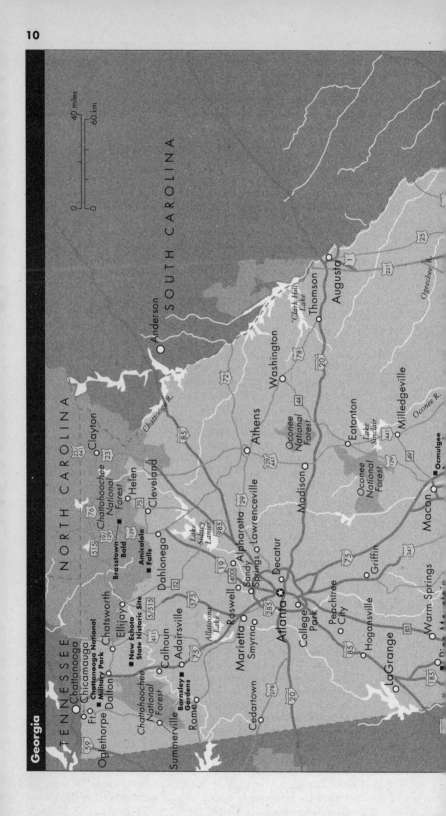

40 miles

60 km

TENNESSEE

NORTH CAROLINA

SOUTH CAROLINA

Chattanooga
Ft. Chicamauga
Chattanooga National
Military Park

Oglethorpe
Dalton

Chatsworth

Chattahoochee
National
Forest

Summerville

Barnsley
Gardens
Rome

Cedartown

278

20

Calhoun

New Echota
State Historic Site

Adairsville

75

Ellijay

411

5/515

515

197
129

Brasstown
Bald

Amicalola
Falls

Marietta

Smyrna

College
Park

Atlanta

285

Decatur

Sandy
Springs

400

Roswell

575

Allatoona
Lake

52

Dahlonega

19

Alpharetta

985

Lake
Sidney
Lanier

Lawrenceville

129

75

Helen

Cleveland

76

Chattahoochee
National
Forest

221
441

Clayton

23

85

129
441

Athens

72

Chattooga R.

Anderson

Washington

78

20

Clark Hill
Lake

Thomson

Augusta

11

25

221

Ogeechee R.

144

Oconee
National
Forest

Madison

Eatonton

Lake
Sinclair

441

Milledgeville

Oconee R.

Oconee
National
Forest

129

49

Ocmulgee

Macon

341

Griffin

75

Peachtree
City

Hogansville

85

LaGrange

85

Warm Springs

Pine Mountain

Peachtree

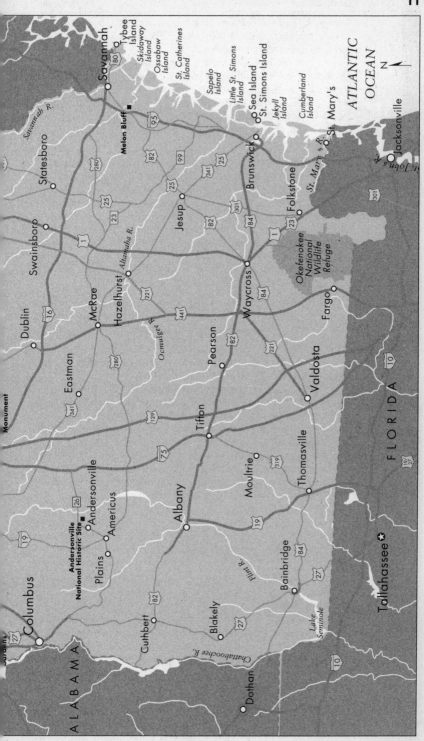

Georgia's 100-mi coast runs from the mouth of the Savannah River south to the mouth of the St. Marys River. The seaside resort communities blend Southern elegance with a casual sensibility. St. Simons Island, about 70 mi south of Savannah, attracts a laid-back crowd of anglers, beachgoers, golfers, and tennis players. On nearby Jekyll Island, the lavish lifestyle of America's early 19th-century rich and famous is still evident in their stately Victorian "cottages." Cumberland Island's protected forests and miles of sandy coastline, the rustically beautiful Sapelo Island, the isolated solitude of Little St. Simons Island, and the dark waters of the Okefenokee are favorite haunts of nature lovers.

Other historical riches include 1,000-year-old Native American homesites and burial mounds, antebellum mansions, war heroes' memorials, and intriguing monuments built by eccentric folk artists and obsessive gardeners. Georgia's many state parks have superb facilities for white-water rafting, canoeing, fishing, golf, and tennis, and nature trails wind through mountain forests delicately laced with wild rhododendrons, dogwoods, and azaleas.

Pleasures and Pastimes

Dining

Dining in Georgia has its ups and downs. Areas that have attracted substantial tourism have respectable to downright outstanding restaurants. Others lag far behind, with their best offerings chain restaurants or the local barbecue joint.

Atlanta sets the culinary pace, of course, with cutting-edge fare from outstanding chefs. Dress in Atlanta—and elsewhere in the state—is casual unless otherwise noted. Classic meat-and-threes—diners serving a meat entrée with three side dishes—abound throughout Georgia. On the byways of Georgia, barbecue stands and restaurants still cook the whole pig, serving customers its meat pulled off the bone for sandwiches or its tender ribs, both bathed in tangy sauce. Brunswick stew, a hunter's stew that traditionally contained the day's catch, is the standard accompaniment. Some of these places are full-fledged restaurants; others have no place to sit at all. If you're off the beaten path, these establishments offer your best chance for decent food.

CATEGORY	COST*
$$$$	over $30
$$$	$20–$30
$$	$10–$20
$	under $10

*per person for a main course at dinner

Historic Sites

You may want to plan your trip with Georgia's historic sites in mind. From the moment you enter the state along the interstate highways, brown markers with white lettering alert you to the locations of the state's principal historical sights along those routes. Georgia's towns constitute a special glimpse into the past. Savannah, founded in 1733, can be viewed from carriage or bus via specialty tours, by private car, or on foot; it's an excellent walking city. Augusta, founded in 1736, has a fine Riverwalk, a restored downtown, and the 19th- and 20th-century houses of Olde Town and Summerville. Macon, founded in 1823, is known for its wealth of fine antebellum and Victorian mansions that may be viewed by private car or on specialty tours. You'll find more than a fair share of battlefields to explore, including the dark woods and open fields of Chickamauga, and unusual historic sites such as New Echota, the lost capital of the Cherokee Nation.

Lodging

Most national and some international hotel and motel chains have establishments in Georgia. Bed-and-breakfast inns abound throughout the state, some providing exquisite lodging, others perfunctory but usually comfortable accommodations. Campsites are marked along the interstate highways, and the state has a fine network of parks, some of which offer campsites and overnight facilities. Always telephone ahead to B&Bs and campsites for reservations, as these are popular accommodations.

CATEGORY	ATLANTA AND SAVANNAH*	OTHER AREAS*
$$$$	over $240	over $175
$$$	$170–$240	$125–$175
$$	$100–$170	$75–$125
$	under $100	under $75

All prices are for a standard double room, excluding 13% tax and service.

Nightlife

No night in Georgia need ever be boring. Clubs, music venues, theater, film, symphony, and comedy revues all make nightlife hum. Blues and jazz, country and western, gospel, and rock and roll are all part of this region's—and Georgia's—homegrown musical tradition. Local composers and performers who made their marks on the national music scene include Savannah's Johnny Mercer; Macon's Otis Redding and the Allman Brothers; and Augusta's James Brown, the godfather of soul. Macon's Little Richard and Albany's Ray Charles still perform. Local groups that have gained national and international fame include R.E.M. and the B-52's, from Athens; Indigo Girls, from Decatur; and Black Crowes, from Marietta. In country-and-western music, Travis Tritt started out in Marietta and Trisha Yearwood in Monticello. To hear rising new stars, not to mention the cadre of reigning hip-hop royalty with roots in Georgia, call local radio stations for information about venues.

In the classical department, opera diva Jessye Norman is from Augusta, and violinist Robert McDuffie is from Macon. The state abounds in symphony orchestras, chamber groups, and classical and jazz ensembles, many of which perform on college campuses. For details contact a local college campus or consult the local newspaper.

Theater is vital not only in Atlanta but also throughout the state, which was the first home of thespians Joanne Woodward (Thomasville), Julia and Eric Roberts (Smyrna), Holly Hunter (Conyers), Melvin Douglas (Macon), Pernell Roberts (Waycross), and playwright Alfred Uhry (Atlanta). If you can catch a performance of *Swamp Gravy,* by residents of Colquitt, Georgia, or *Reach of Song,* based on the poetry of mountain poet Byron Herbert Reece, you'll enjoy traditional local subject matter and music.

Outdoor Activities and Sports

For the sports enthusiast Georgia has a full plate of activities—fishing, camping, golf and tennis, sailing and rowing. There's also a beloved baseball team, the Atlanta Braves. Hiking abounds: at the Chattahoochee Nature Center, outside Atlanta, you can see birds and other woodland animals in their natural habitat while hiking through 124 acres of lush forests and wetlands. Another outdoor favorite is Stone Mountain Park and its Walk Up Trail, an atmospheric jaunt up the west side of the mountain culminating in a rigorous 825-ft climb to the peak. It's well worth the challenge, as the ensuing panoramic view of Atlanta is stunning.

Exploring Georgia

Georgia has several distinct touring areas; the state is large, and you'd need more than a week to hit even some of the highlights. The foothills of the Appalachian Mountains run from west to east in north Georgia, making this a popular destination for tourists, especially in spring and fall. Atlanta alone warrants serious exploration. The coast offers plenty for the history aficionado; it's a good place to start if you have just a few days. From Savannah, Georgia's oldest city, to Augusta, its third oldest, colonial and Civil War history awaits at every turn. It's in east Georgia where you'll see most of the columned antebellum homes that people have come to expect. The coastal islands have fine beaches and nature-focused expeditions. The best spot for would-be naturalists, of course, is the Okefenokee Natural Wildlife Refuge. Southwest Georgia, with its pastoral agricultural towns, numerous options for antiquing, and the bustling river city of Columbus, makes an agreeable weekend adventure.

Great Itineraries

IF YOU HAVE 3 DAYS

Explore the coast to get a true taste of what early Georgia was all about. Spend a day and night in ▣ **Augusta,** being sure to visit Meadow Garden, home of George Walton, youngest signer (at age 26) of the Declaration of Independence. Exhibits at the Morris Museum of Southern Art range from luminous 19th-century landscapes to folk art and the challenging abstracts of Augusta native Jasper Johns. Give the remaining two days over to an exploration of ▣ **Savannah.** Stay at a B&B (be sure to make reservations, especially for weekends) and tour some of the city's fine restored homes. Spend some time along Riverfront Plaza, enjoying the waterfront, dining in restaurants, and just plain kicking back. Other must-see sights include the 1815 Isaiah Davenport House and the Colonial Park Cemetery, the final resting place for some of America's founders.

IF YOU HAVE 7 DAYS

Add a three-day trip to ▣ **Atlanta** to the above itinerary, using the final extra day to partake of the recreations and resorts of ▣ **Jekyll Island,** along the coast. In Atlanta history enthusiasts will want to visit the Atlanta History Center and its gardens, touring its two house museums. A fine small museum, the African-American Panoramic Experience, chronicles the history of blacks in America. In Grant Park, the Atlanta Cyclorama contains a truly huge painting of the 1864 Battle of Atlanta. The Chattahoochee National Recreational Area is a great spot for joggers, walkers, hikers, and nature lovers. At Stone Mountain Park you can see the Confederate Memorial (the world's largest sculpture), two Civil War museums, and the Road to Tara Museum.

IF YOU HAVE 10 DAYS

Follow the seven-day itinerary. Then take a run up to the north Georgia mountains, visiting **Clayton,** with its many art and antiques shops; ▣ **Dahlonega,** where you can pan for gold in "them thar hills"; and **Chickamauga,** site of one of the Civil War's most important conflicts. The north Georgia mountains are glorious from spring through fall. Then turn south back through Atlanta and visit the heart of the state, taking in ▣ **Macon,** with its antebellum and Victorian homes and museums.

When to Tour Georgia

Spring is the best time to visit, although autumn, especially beginning in early October, when the hardwoods change color, is another glorious season. Spring in middle Georgia is splendid, with azaleas and other flowers in full bloom. Many garden and historic home tours are scheduled at this time. And in Savannah you can tour some of the most spectacular of the city's private gardens.

ATLANTA

Though steeped in history, Atlanta nevertheless remains a comparatively new city by East Coast standards, having been founded only in 1837 as the end of the Western & Atlantic railroad line (it was first named Marthasville in honor of the then-governor's daughter, nicknamed Terminus for its rail location, and then changed soon after to Atlanta, the feminine of Atlantic—as in the railroad). Today the fast-growing city remains a transportation hub, not just for the country but for the world: Hartsfield Atlanta International Airport is one of the nation's busiest in daily passenger flights. Direct flights to Europe, South America, and Asia have made metro Atlanta easily accessible to the more than 1,000 international businesses that operate here and the more than 50 countries that have representation in the city through consulates, trade offices, and chambers of commerce. The city has emerged as a banking center and is the world headquarters for such Fortune 500 companies as CNN, Coca-Cola, Delta Airlines, Holiday Inn Worldwide, and United Parcel Service.

Atlanta's character has evolved from a mix of peoples: transplanted Northerners and those from elsewhere account for more than half the population and have undeniably affected the mood and character of the city. Irish immigrants had a major role in the city's early history, along with Germans and Austrians; the Hungarian-born Rich brothers founded Atlanta's principal department store. And the immigrants keep coming. In the past two decades Atlanta has seen spirited growth in its Asian and Latin-American communities. Related restaurants, shops, and institutions have become part of the city's texture.

For more than four decades Atlanta has been linked to the civil rights movement. Among the many accomplishments of which Atlanta's African-American community is proud is the Nobel Peace Prize that Martin Luther King Jr. won in 1964. Dr. King's widow, Coretta Scott King, continues to operate the King Center, which she founded after her husband's assassination in 1968. In 1972 Andrew Young was elected the first black congressman from the South since Reconstruction. After serving as ambassador to the United Nations during President Jimmy Carter's administration, Young was elected mayor of Atlanta. Since his term ended in the early '90s, Young has kept busy being co-chairman of the Atlanta Committee for the Olympic Games, chairman of the Metro Atlanta Chamber of Commerce, and president of the National Council of Churches.

The traditional South—which in romantic versions consists of lacy moss dangling from tree limbs; thick, sugary Southern drawls; a leisurely pace; and luxurious antebellum mansions—rarely reveals itself here. Even before the Civil War, the columned house was a rarity—and prior to the construction boom of the 1850s, houses of any kind were rare. The frenetic pace of rebuilding that characterized the period after the Civil War continues unabated. Still viewed by die-hard Southerners as the heart of the Old Confederacy, Atlanta has become the best example of the New South, a fast-paced modern city proud of its heritage.

In the past two decades Atlanta has experienced unprecedented growth—the official city population remains steady, at about 420,000, but the metro population has grown in the past decade by nearly 40%, from 2.9 million to 4.1 million people. A good measure of this growth is the ever-changing downtown skyline, along with skyscrapers constructed in the Midtown, Buckhead, and outer perimeter (fringing I–285) business districts. Since the late 1970s dozens of dazzling skyscrapers designed by such luminaries as Philip Johnson, I. M. Pei, and Marcel Breuer have reshaped the city's profile. Residents, however, are less likely to measure the city's growth by skyscrapers than by increasing traffic jams, crowds, higher prices, and the ever-burgeoning subdivisions that continue to push urban sprawl farther and farther into surrounding rural areas. The core of Atlanta revolves around five counties. The city of Atlanta is primarily in Fulton and DeKalb counties, with its southern end and the airport in Clayton County. Outside I–285, Cobb and Gwinnett counties, to the northwest and northeast, respectively, are experiencing much of Atlanta's population increase.

Atlanta's lack of a grid system confuses many drivers, even locals. Some streets change their names along the same stretch of road, including the city's most famous thoroughfare, Peachtree Street, which follows a mountain ridge from downtown to suburban Norcross, outside I–285N: it becomes Peachtree Road after crossing I–85 and then splits into Peachtree Industrial Boulevard beyond the Buckhead neighborhood and the original Peachtree Road, which heads into Chamblee. Adding to the confusion, more than 60 other streets in the metropolitan area use the word *Peachtree* in their names. Before setting out anywhere, get the complete street address of your destination, including landmarks, cross streets, or other guideposts, as street numbers and even street signs often are difficult to find.

Downtown Atlanta

Downtown Atlanta clusters around the hub known as Five Points. Here you'll find the MARTA station that intersects the north–south and east–west transit lines. On the surface Five Points is formed by the intersection of Peachtree Street with Marietta, Broad, and Forsyth streets.

Numbers in the text correspond to numbers in the margin and on the Downtown Atlanta and Sweet Auburn map.

A Good Walk

This walk branches in three directions, which are most efficiently managed by taking MARTA trains to get quickly from one spot to the next. The valiant will, of course, prefer to go it on foot. Begin at **Woodruff Park** ①, and then proceed north on Peachtree Street, noting Atlanta's **Flatiron Building** ② on the west side of Peachtree and the **Candler Building** ③ on the east side of the street. Nearby on Peachtree Street at John Wesley Dobbs Avenue is the modern **Georgia-Pacific Center** ④, and across from it are **Margaret Mitchell Park** ⑤ and the **Atlanta-Fulton Public Library** ⑥. Continuing north up Peachtree Street, note the sprawling **Peachtree Center** ⑦ complex, which includes the small but worthwhile **Atlanta International Museum of Art and Design** ⑧. Walk east on Baker Street one block to Courtland Street; head north on Courtland until you reach Ralph McGill Boulevard, and go one block east to the corner of Piedmont Road. Here you'll find an open-air folk art exhibition known as the **Folk Art Park** ⑨.

Return to Peachtree Center and take the subway one stop to the **Five Points MARTA station** ⑩, from which you can walk north on Peachtree Street to the **William-Oliver Building** ⑪. (From Folk Art Park you can also follow Ralph McGill Boulevard west to Peachtree and retrace your steps south to the William-Oliver Building.) From here go east on Edgewood Avenue, and just ahead you'll see the **Hurt Building** ⑫, a rare Atlanta example of Chicago-style architecture. Around the corner on

Marietta Street at Broad Street is the handsome **Bank of America Building** ⑬, and nearby is the **Statue of Henry Grady** ⑭, right across from the building now housing the newspaper he founded, the *Atlanta Journal-Constitution* ⑮. At Marietta Street and Techwood Drive, **Centennial Olympic Park** ⑯ hosts concerts and special events. Adjacent to the park is **CNN Center** ⑰, which you may tour (by reservation). At the rear of the center is the **Georgia Dome** ⑱.

At the CNN Center/Georgia Dome station, take MARTA one station to the Five Points station and exit at the sign for **Underground Atlanta** ⑲. After taking a rest and a restorative snack in its food court, wander the maze of subterranean streets here and leave through the Central Avenue exit of Underground Atlanta, bearing slightly south toward the **Georgia Railroad Freight Depot** ⑳. Across the plaza from the depot is the **World of Coca-Cola Pavilion** ㉑, with fun memorabilia on display. Across Martin Luther King Jr. Drive at Central Avenue is the historic **Shrine of the Immaculate Conception** ㉒, one of many historic churches still operating in downtown. Just south of the shrine are the neo-Gothic **City Hall** ㉓, with a modern addition housing a permanent art collection, which is on Mitchell Street, and the Renaissance-style **Georgia State Capitol** ㉔, on Washington Street.

TIMING

This walk requires at least a day, assuming you don't spend much time at any one location. If you plan to walk at a more leisurely pace, finish the first day at the Folk Art Park, and allow another half day for the rest of the walk. If you plan tours of CNN Center, the Georgia Dome, and World of Coca-Cola, you'll need an additional half day. If you tour these sights at length, it will probably take two full days to cover the territory. The terrain is fairly level and not too taxing.

Sights to See

OFF THE
BEATEN PATH
★

ATLANTA CYCLORAMA & CIVIL WAR MUSEUM – In Grant Park (named for a New England–born Confederate colonel, not the U.S. president), you'll find a huge circular painting, completed by a team of expert European panorama artists shortly after the Civil War, depicting the 1864 Battle of Atlanta. The museum has one of the best Civil War bookstores anywhere. To reach the Cyclorama by car, take I–20 east to Exit 59A, turn right onto Boulevard, and then take a right at the next traffic light into Grant Park; follow signs to the Cyclorama. ✉ *Grant Park, 800 Cherokee Ave., Grant Park,* ☎ *404/658–7625,* WEB *www.webguide. com/cyclorama.html.* 🎫 *$5.* ☉ *June–early Sept., daily 9:30–5:30; early Sept.–May, daily 9:30–4:30.*

⑥ **Atlanta-Fulton Public Library.** The Marcel Breuer–designed building houses, on its fourth floor, a large collection of *Gone With the Wind* memorabilia and newspapers from most major cities in the United States and elsewhere. ✉ *1 Margaret Mitchell Sq., Downtown,* ☎ *404/730–1700.* ☉ *Mon. and Fri.–Sat. 9–6, Tues.–Thurs. 9–8, Sun. 2–6.*

★ ⑧ **Atlanta International Museum of Art and Design.** In the Peachtree Center in the Marriott Marquis Two Tower, this museum mounts major international exhibitions covering such subjects as textiles, puzzles, boxes, masks, and baskets. Exhibits focus on arts and crafts, design, and culture from around the globe. ✉ *285 Peachtree Center Ave., Downtown,* ☎ *404/688–2467,* WEB *www.atlantainternationalmuseum. org.* 🎫 *Free.* ☉ *Weekdays 11–5.*

⑮ *Atlanta Journal-Constitution.* The building containing the business offices and printing plant for the city's—and the state's—dominant newspaper has a lobby that displays front-page news of historic events, an old printing press, and photographs of famous former employees. ⊠ *72 Marietta St., Downtown,* ☎ *404/614–2688.* ⊙ *Tours have been postponed indefinitely; call for information.*

⑬ Bank of America Building. Originally a Chicago-style edifice known as the Empire Building, this handsome 1901 classic was designed by Atlanta architect Phillip Trammel Shutze. In 1929 Shutze refashioned the first three floors, bestowing on them a decidedly Renaissance look. This is one of the city's first steel-frame structures, and at 14 stories one of its tallest, but during the renovation Shutze resheathed the base with masonry. ⊠ *35 Broad St., Downtown.*

❸ Candler Building. Asa G. Candler, founder of the Coca-Cola Company, engaged the local firm of Murphy and Stewart to design this splendid terra-cotta and marble building in 1906. The ornate bronze and marble lobby shouldn't be missed. ⊠ *84 Peachtree St., Downtown* ⊙ *Daily 9–5.*

⑯ Centennial Olympic Park. This 21-acre urban landscape, the largest urban park to be developed in this country in more than two decades, was the central venue for the 1996 Summer Olympics. The park's Fountain of Rings (the world's largest using the Olympic symbol) centers a court of 24 flags, each of them representing the Olympic Games as well as the host countries of the modern Games. The seating in the fountain amphitheater allows you to enjoy the water and music spectacle (five tunes are programmed and timed to coincide with water displays). The park has a 6-acre great lawn and pathways formed by commemorative brick paving stones. ⊠ *Marietta St. and Techwood Dr., Downtown,* ☎ *404/223–4412; 404/222–7275 for information,* WEB *www. centennialpark.com.* ⊙ *Daily 7 AM–11 PM.*

㉓ City Hall. When the 14-story neo-Gothic building, designed by Atlanta architect G. Lloyd Preacher, was erected in 1929, critics dubbed it the Painted Lady of Mitchell Street. The newer wing, with its five-story glass atrium and beautiful marble entryway, houses a splendid permanent collection of art. ⊠ *68 Mitchell St., Downtown,* ☎ *404/330–6000,* WEB *www.ci.atlanta.ga.us.* ⊙ *Weekdays 8:30–5.*

⑰ CNN Center. The home of Ted Turner's Cable News Network occupies all 14 floors of this dramatic structure on the edge of downtown. The 45-minute CNN studio tour begins with a ride up the world's longest escalator to an eighth-floor exhibit about Turner's global broadcasting empire. Tours are not open to children under age 6. ⊠ *1 CNN Center, Downtown,* ☎ *404/827–2300,* WEB *www.cnn.com/studiotour. Reservations required 48 hrs in advance held with credit card.* ☎ *50-min tour $8.* ⊙ *Daily 9–5.*

⑩ Five Points MARTA Station. Even if you're driving everywhere, it's worth visiting the busiest public-transit rail station in the city, bustling with people and pushcart vendors. It also has its own entrance to underground Atlanta, via a tunnel below Peachtree Street. On the practical side, this MARTA station serves Underground Atlanta and nearby Woodruff Park, Georgia State University, and numerous businesses; the station is at the crossroads of MARTA's east–west and north–south lines. Stand on the corner of Peachtree and Alabama streets, outside the station, and notice the old-fashioned gas streetlight, with its historic marker proclaiming it the **Eternal Flame of the Confederacy.** ⊠ *Peachtree and Alabama Sts., Downtown.*

❷ Flatiron Building. The English-American Building, as it was originally known, was designed by Bradford Gilbert. Similar to the famous New York City Flatiron Building, built in the early 1900s, this one dates from

1897 and is the city's oldest high-rise. ⊠ *74 Peachtree St., Downtown.*
⊙ *Weekdays 8:15–5:30.*

❾ Folk Art Park. Revitalizing an ignored part of the city, the park pays
homage to an important American art form by gathering works that
reflect the diverse styles of American (especially Southern) folk art. Works
by more than a dozen artists are on display, among them Harold Rit-
tenberry, Howard Finster, and Eddie Owens Martin. Martin's brightly
painted totems and snake-top walls replicate portions of *Pasaquan* (the
legendary visionary environment that Martin created at his farm near
Columbus, Georgia). ⊠ *Ralph McGill Blvd. at Courtland St., Baker
St., and Piedmont Ave., Midtown.*

❽ Georgia Dome. This arena accommodates 71,500 spectators with good
visibility from every seat; it's the site of Atlanta Falcons football games,
major rock concerts, conventions, and trade shows. The white, plum,
and turquoise 1 million-square-ft facility is crowned with the world's
largest cable-supported oval, giving the roof a circus-tent top. ⊠ *1 Georgia Dome Dr., Downtown,* ☎ *404/223–8687,* WEB *www.gadome.com.*
☒ *Tour $2 (groups of 15 or more only).* ⊙ *Tours daily every hr 10–4.*

❹ Georgia-Pacific Center. The towering, 52-story structure occupies the
site of the old Loew's Grand Theatre, where *Gone With the Wind* premiered in 1939. From certain angles the red-marble high-rise appears
to be flat against the sky. The **High Museum of Art Folk Art and Photography Galleries** is inside. ⊠ *133 Peachtree St., at John Wesley
Dobbs Ave., Downtown Museum:* ⊠ *Georgia-Pacific Center, 133
Peachtree St. NE, gallery entrance on 30 John Wesley Dobbs Ave., Sweet
Auburn,* ☎ *404/577–6940 for information line,* WEB *www.high.org.* ☒
Free. ⊙ *Mon.–Sat. 10–5, first Thurs. of every month 10–8.*

❷⓿ Georgia Railroad Freight Depot. After downtown's oldest extant building was constructed in 1869 to replace the one torched by Sherman's
troops in 1864, it burned again in 1935 and was rebuilt in its present
form. It is now used by several downtown companies as a banquet hall
and for special events. It may be viewed only by appointment. ⊠ *65
Martin Luther King Jr. Dr., Downtown,* ☎ *404/656–3850.*

★ **❷❹ Georgia State Capitol.** A Renaissance-style edifice, the capitol was
dedicated on July 4, 1889. The gold leaf on its dome was mined in nearby
Dahlonega. Inside, the **Georgia Capitol Museum** houses exhibits on
the history of the capitol building. On the grounds, state historical markers commemorate the 1864 Battle of Atlanta, which destroyed 90%
of the city. Statues memorialize a 19th-century Georgia governor and
his wife (Joseph and Elizabeth Brown), a Confederate general (John
B. Gordon), and a former senator (Richard B. Russell). Former governor and president Jimmy Carter is depicted with his sleeves rolled
up, a man at work. ⊠ *Capitol Sq., Downtown,* ☎ *404/656–2844,* WEB
www.sos.state.ga.us/museum. ⊙ *Guided tours weekdays at 10, 11, 1,
and 2 (during legislative session, Jan.–Mar., the first 2 tours operate
at 9:30 and 10:30).*

OFF THE
BEATEN PATH

HAMMONDS HOUSE GALLERIES AND RESOURCE CENTER – Dr. Otis Thrash
Hammonds donated his handsome Eastlake Victorian house and his fine
collection of Victorian furniture and paintings to the city of Atlanta as an
art gallery and resource center. The permanent and visiting exhibitions
are devoted chiefly to work by African-American artists, although art from
anywhere in the African-influenced world can be a focus. ⊠ *503 Peeples
St., West End,* ☎ *404/752–8730,* WEB *www.hammmondshouse.org.* ☒
$2. ⊙ *Tues.–Fri. 10–6, weekends 1–5.*

HERNDON HOME – Alonzo Herndon emerged from slavery and founded both a chain of successful barbershops and the **Atlanta Life Insurance Company.** He traveled extensively and influenced the cultural life around Atlanta's traditionally black colleges. Alonzo's son, Norris, created a foundation to preserve the handsome beaux arts home as a museum and heritage center. ✉ *587 University Pl., near Morris Brown College, West End,* ☎ *404/581–9813,* WEB *www.theherndonhome.org.* 🎟 *$5.* 🕐 *Tues.–Sat. 10–4; tours every hr.*

⑫ **Hurt Building.** Named for Atlanta developer Joel Hurt, this restored 1913 Chicago-style high-rise, with its intricate grillwork and sweeping marble staircase, has a lower level of shops and art galleries. The excellent City Grill restaurant is at the top of the sweeping staircase. ✉ *50 Hurt Plaza, Downtown.*

⑤ **Margaret Mitchell Park.** A cascading waterfall and columned sculpture are highlights of this park named for Atlanta's most famous author, whose masterpiece and only novel is *Gone With the Wind.* ✉ *Margaret Mitchell Sq., Midtown.*

⑦ **Peachtree Center.** John Portman designed this skyscraper complex, built between 1960 and 1992, which contains shops, offices, and restaurants. Across the street, connected to Peachtree Center by skywalks, is the massive **Atlanta Market Center.** Two additional Portman creations, the **Atlanta Marriott Marquis** and the **Hyatt Regency Hotel,** are also connected to the center by skywalks. A MARTA stop is available at Peachtree Center. ✉ *225 Peachtree St., Downtown,* ☎ *404/654–1255,* WEB *www.peachtreecenter.com.*

㉒ **Shrine of the Immaculate Conception.** During the Battle of Atlanta, Thomas O'Reilly, the church's pastor, persuaded Union forces to spare his church and several others around the city. That 1848 structure was then replaced by this much grander building, whose cornerstone was laid in 1869. O'Reilly, a native of Ireland, was interred in the basement of the church. The church was nearly lost to fire in 1982 but has been exquisitely restored. The vestibule is always open, allowing you to view the interior, or you may contact the rectory for an appointment. ✉ *48 Martin Luther King Jr. Dr., at Central Ave., Downtown,* ☎ *404/521–1866.* 🕐 *Weekdays 8:30–5, Sat. 9–7, Sun. 7–3.*

⑭ **Statue of Henry Grady.** New York artist Alexander Doyle's bronze sculpture honors the post–Civil War editor of the *Atlanta Constitution* and early advocate of the so-called New South. Much about Grady is reminiscent of Ted Turner, the contemporary Atlanta media mogul. The memorial was raised in 1891, after Grady's untimely death at age 39. ✉ *Marietta and Forsyth Sts., Downtown.*

⑲ **Underground Atlanta.** This six-block entertainment and shopping district, dotted with historic markers, was created from the web of underground brick streets, ornamental building facades, and tunnels that fell into disuse in 1929, when the city built viaducts over the train tracks. Merchants then moved their storefronts to the new viaduct level, leaving the original street level for storage. Today it houses restaurants, clubs, art galleries, shopping emporiums, and a food court, making it a good stop on a walking tour. ✉ *50 Upper Alabama St., Downtown,* ☎ *404/523–2311,* WEB *www.underatl.com.*

⑪ **William-Oliver Building.** Walk through the lobby of this art deco gem and admire the ceiling mural, brass grills, and elevator doors. Formerly an office building, it has been renovated for luxury downtown residences and won a prestigious award for historic preservation from the Atlanta Urban Design Commission. ✉ *32 Peachtree St., Downtown.*

❶ **Woodruff Park.** Named for the city's great philanthropist Robert W. Woodruff, the late Coca-Cola magnate, the triangular park fills during lunchtime on weekdays with executives, street preachers, politicians, Georgia State University students, and homeless people. ⊠ *Bordered by Pryor, Houston, and Peachtree Sts., Downtown.*

🕐 ㉑ **World of Coca-Cola Pavilion.** At this three-story, $15 million special-exhibit facility, you can sip samples of 38 Coca-Cola Company products from around the world and study memorabilia from more than a century's worth of corporate archives. Everything Coca-Cola, the gift shop, sells everything from refrigerator magnets to evening bags. ⊠ *55 Martin Luther King Jr. Dr., Downtown,* ☎ *404/676–5151,* WEB *www.woccatlanta.com.* ⌑ *$6.* ◷ *June–Aug., Mon.–Sat. 9–6, Sun. 11–6; Sept.–May, Mon.–Sat. 9–5, Sun. noon–6.*

OFF THE BEATEN PATH | **ZOO ATLANTA –** This zoo has nearly 1,000 animals living in naturalistic habitats, such as the Ford African Rain Forest, Flamingo Lagoon, Masai Mara (re-created plains of Kenya), and Sumatran Tiger exhibits. Sibling gorillas Kudzoo and Olympia are always hits. Don't miss the popular Chinese panda exhibit, consisting of two precocious bears named Yang Yang and Lun Lun. To reach the zoo by car, take I–20 east to Exit 59A, turn right on Boulevard, then right again at the next light into Grant Park. Follow signs to the zoo. ⊠ *Grant Park, 800 Cherokee Ave., Grant Park,* ☎ *404/624–5600,* WEB *www.zooatlanta.org.* ⌑ *$16.* ◷ *Daily 9:30–4:30.*

Sweet Auburn

Between 1890 and 1930 the historic Sweet Auburn district was Atlanta's most active and prosperous center of black business, entertainment, and political life. Following the Depression, the area went into an economic decline that lasted until the 1980s, when the residential area where civil rights leader Rev. Martin Luther King Jr. was born, raised, and later returned to live was declared a National Historic District.

Numbers in the text correspond to numbers in the margin and on the Downtown Atlanta and Sweet Auburn map.

A Good Walk

Start your walk in the Martin Luther King Jr. National Historic District, the heart of Sweet Auburn, where you can get a sense of what the civil rights movement and its principal leader were all about. First visit the **Martin Luther King Jr. Birth Home** ㉕, on Auburn Avenue, and on the next block west, the **Martin Luther King Jr. Center for Nonviolent Social Change** ㉖, where Dr. King is entombed. Next stop at the nearby **Ebenezer Baptist Church** ㉗, where Dr. King preached along with his grandfather, father, and brother. Proceed a few blocks west near the I–75/85 overpass to enjoy the **John Wesley Dobbs Plaza** ㉘, a good place to take a breather. The **Odd Fellows Building** ㉙, on the other side of Auburn Avenue just after you walk under the expressway, is a handsome structure not to be missed. At this point, go south on Bell Street and walk one block to Edgewood Avenue to visit the **Sweet Auburn Curb Market** ㉚. Walk three blocks west on Edgewood Avenue, and you'll reach the **Baptist Student Center** ㉛, a fine example of Victorian architecture. Returning north to Auburn Avenue, you'll see the **Atlanta Daily World Building** ㉜ and next to it the **African-American Panoramic Experience (APEX)** ㉝. Continue down Auburn Avenue just a few steps and enter the lobby of the **Atlanta Life Insurance Company** ㉞ to view its fabulous art collection. Now, proceed across the street and finish your walk with a stop at the **Auburn Avenue Research Library on African-American Culture and History** ㉟.

Downtown Atlanta and Sweet Auburn

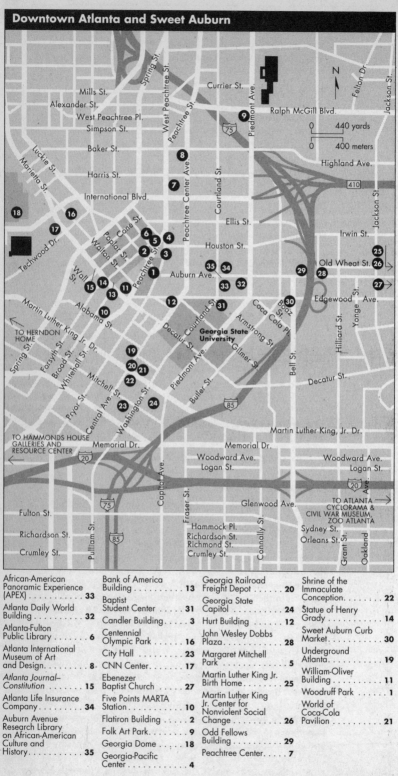

TIMING
This is a leisurely walk along level sidewalks, with shops and historic sites along the way. If you stop for tours, you'll fill an entire day. If you simply stroll and look, the walk should take an hour or two.

Sights to See

★ ③③ **African-American Panoramic Experience (APEX).** The museum's quarterly exhibits chronicle the history of black people in America. Videos illustrate the history of Sweet Auburn, the name bestowed on Auburn Avenue by businessman John Wesley Dobbs, who fostered business development for African-Americans on this street. ⊠ *135 Auburn Ave., Sweet Auburn,* ☎ *404/521–2739,* WEB *www.apexmuseum.org.* ⚏ *$3.* ☉ *June–Aug., Tues.–Sat. 10–5, Sun. 1–5; Sept.–May, Tues.–Sat. 10–5.*

③② **Atlanta Daily World Building.** This simple two-story brick building, banded with a white frieze of lion's heads, was constructed in the early 1900s; since 1945 it has housed one of the nation's oldest black newspapers (it's no longer a daily, however). Alexis Reeves, publisher and CEO, is the granddaughter of William A. Scott II, who founded the paper as a weekly in 1928. ⊠ *145 Auburn Ave., Sweet Auburn,* ☎ *404/659–1110,* WEB *www.atlantadailyworld.com.*

③④ **Atlanta Life Insurance Company.** The landmark enterprise founded by Alonzo Herndon, a former slave, was in modest quarters at 148 Auburn Avenue until the modern complex at No. 100 was opened in 1980. The lobby holds an exhibition of art by black artists from the United States and Africa. ⊠ *100 Auburn Ave., Sweet Auburn,* ☎ *404/659–2100.* ☉ *Weekdays 8–5.*

③⑤ **Auburn Avenue Research Library on African-American Culture and History.** This unit is an extension of the **Atlanta-Fulton Public Library** system, and houses a noncirculating library with about 35,000 volumes devoted to African-American subjects. Special exhibits, programs, and tours are free to the public. The archives division contains art and artifacts, ephemera, oral histories, pamphlets, prints, rare periodicals, rare books, manuscript collections, photographs, and memorabilia. ⊠ *101 Auburn Ave., Sweet Auburn,* ☎ *404/730–4001,* WEB *http://aarl.af. public.lib.ga.us.* ☉ *Mon.–Thurs. 10–8, Fri.–Sun. noon–6.*

③① **Baptist Student Center.** Adjacent to the Georgia State University campus, this restored Victorian building once contained the Coca-Cola Company's first bottling plant. ⊠ *125 Edgewood Ave., Sweet Auburn,* ☎ *404/659–8726,* WEB *www.gsu.edu/~wwwbsu.*

②⑦ **Ebenezer Baptist Church.** A Gothic Revival–style building completed in 1922, the church became known as the spiritual center of the civil rights movement after Martin Luther King Jr. won the Nobel Peace Prize in 1964. Members of the King family have preached at the church for three generations; Dr. King's funeral was held here. The grand building has just been restored extensively to its appearance during the '60s, when Dr. King preached inside it. A tour of the church includes an audiotape outlining the history of the building, though the congregation itself now occupies the building across the street. ⊠ *407 Auburn Ave., Sweet Auburn,* ☎ *404/688–7263.* ⚏ *Free.* ☉ *Tours weekdays 9–5.*

②⑧ **John Wesley Dobbs Plaza.** John Wesley Dobbs was an important civic leader whose legacy includes coining the name *Sweet Auburn* for Atlanta's black business and residential neighborhood. The plaza, which was built for the 1996 Olympic Games, has a life mask of Dobbs himself; children playing in the plaza may view the street through the mask's eyes. ⊠ *Auburn Ave. adjacent to I–75/85 overpass, Sweet Auburn.*

★ ㉕ **Martin Luther King Jr. Birth Home.** This modest Queen Anne–style historic home is managed by the National Park Service, which also has a visitor center across the street from the Martin Luther King Jr. Center for Nonviolent Social Change. The visitor center contains a multimedia exhibit focused on the civil rights movement and Dr. King's role in it. To sign up for tours, go to the fire station (⊠ 39 Boulevard, Sweet Auburn). ⊠ *501 Auburn Ave., Sweet Auburn,* ☎ *404/331–6922,* WEB *www. thekingcenter.org.* ⊠ *Free.* ☉ *Daily guided ½-hr tours every hr 10–5.*

㉖ **Martin Luther King Jr. Center for Nonviolent Social Change.** The Martin Luther King Jr. National Historic District occupies several blocks on Auburn Avenue, a few blocks east of Peachtree Street in the black business and residential community of Sweet Auburn. The neighborhood is the birthplace of Martin Luther King Jr., who was born here in 1929. After Dr. King's assassination in 1968, his widow, Coretta Scott King, established the center, which exhibits personal items, such as King's Nobel Peace Prize, Bible, and tape recorder, along with memorabilia and photos chronicling the civil rights movement. In the courtyard in front of Freedom Hall, on a circular brick pad in the middle of the rectangular Meditation Pool, is Dr. King's white-marble tomb; the inscription reads: FREE AT LAST! Nearby, an eternal flame burns. A chapel of all faiths sits at one end of the reflecting pool. ⊠ *449 Auburn Ave., Sweet Auburn,* ☎ *404/524–1956,* WEB *www.thekingcenter.org.* ☉ *Daily 9–5.*

㉙ **Odd Fellows Building.** The Georgia Chapter of the Grand United Order of Odd Fellows was a trade and social organization for African-Americans. In 1912 the membership erected this handsome Romanesque Revival–style building housing meeting rooms, a theater, commercial spaces, and a community center. African-featured terra-cotta figures adorn the splendid entrance. Now handsomely restored, the building houses offices. ⊠ *250 Auburn Ave., Sweet Auburn.*

㉚ **Sweet Auburn Curb Market.** The market, an institution on Edgewood Avenue since 1923, sells vegetables, fish, flowers, prepared foods, and meat. Individual stalls are operated by separate owners, making this a true public market. Don't miss the splendid totemic sculptures by young Atlanta artist Carl Joe Williams. The pieces were placed as part of Atlanta's Olympic art program. ⊠ *209 Edgewood Ave., Sweet Auburn,* ☎ *404/659–1665.* ☉ *Mon.–Thurs. 8–6, Fri.–Sat. 8–7.*

Midtown

Just north of downtown lies this thriving area, a hippie hangout in the late '60s and '70s and now housing a large segment of the city's gay population, along with young families, young professionals, artists, and musicians. Formerly in decline, Midtown has evolved into one of the city's most interesting and sought-after neighborhoods. Confirming its other facet as one of the city's most burgeoning business centers, its gleaming office towers now define a skyline that nearly rivals that of downtown, and the renovated mansions and bungalows in its residential section have made it a city showcase.

Numbers in the text correspond to numbers in the margin and on the Atlanta Neighborhoods map.

A Good Drive

From downtown take Piedmont Avenue about a half mile to **SciTrek** ㊱, a science museum all ages will enjoy. Turn left from Piedmont Avenue onto Ponce de Leon Avenue and drive two blocks to Peachtree Street; then turn right and find the 1929 **Fox Theatre** ㊲ and, across the street, the **Georgian Terrace** ㊳, a luxury suites hotel. From Peachtree Street circle around the block, turning right onto 3rd Street to Juniper Street; then turn right on Juniper Street, continue two blocks, and turn right onto North Avenue. Turn right again onto Peachtree Street to view the **Bank of America Plaza Tower** ㊴. Continuing up Peachtree Street to Peachtree Place (one block south of 10th Street), you'll find the **Margaret Mitchell House** ㊵, the restored building where the Pulitzer Prize–winning author lived while completing *Gone With the Wind*. Across the street to the north is the new home of the **Federal Reserve Bank** ㊶. Walk west two blocks on 10th Street, then turn right onto West Peachtree Street, and continue north to its intersection with 14th Street, where you'll see Philip Johnson's distinctive One Atlantic Center. Turn left onto 18th Street to reach the **Center for Puppetry Arts** ㊷. Take 18th Street east back to Peachtree Street, turn left, and continue on to the **Woodruff Arts Center** ㊸, which includes the modern structure of the **High Museum of Art** ㊹. From this point travel two blocks north on Peachtree Street to **Rhodes Memorial Hall** ㊺. From here take Beverly Road east off Peachtree Street for about a quarter mile to Montgomery Ferry Drive; turn a quick dogleg left, then right, continuing on Beverly to Park Lane, and then turn right onto Park Lane and drive about a quarter mile to where it intersects the Prado. Here, these two streets dead-end onto Piedmont Avenue, where you'll enter the **Atlanta Botanical Garden** ㊻, which adjoins **Piedmont Park** ㊼, bounded by Piedmont Avenue, 10th Street, and Westminster Drive.

TIMING

This drive is best accomplished between midmorning (about 9:30) and midafternoon (3:30) to avoid rush-hour traffic. Give yourself between four and five hours to visit all the sights. Each place has parking no more than a few steps away, and often it's free.

Sights to See

㊻ **Atlanta Botanical Garden.** Occupying 30 acres inside Piedmont Park, the grounds contain 15 acres of display gardens, including a serene Japanese garden, a 15-acre hardwood forest with walking trails, and the Fuqua Conservatory, which has unusual and threatened flora from tropical and desert climates. A permanent Fuqua Conservatory exhibit of tiny, brightly colored poison-dart frogs is popular, especially with children. ⊠ *1345 Piedmont Ave., at the Prado, Midtown,* ☎ *404/876–5859.* WEB *www.atlantabotanicalgarden.org.* ⊡ *$10; free Thurs. after 3.* ☉ *Mar.–Sept., Tues.–Sun. 9–7; Oct.–Feb., Tues.–Sun. 9–6.*

㊴ **Bank of America Plaza Tower.** Built in 1992, the skyscraper has a graceful birdcage roof easily visible from the interstate; it's the South's tallest building, at 1,023 ft. The elegant marble central lobby is worth a glimpse. ⊠ *600 Peachtree St., Midtown.*

★ ㊷ **Center for Puppetry Arts.** At this interactive museum you can see puppets from around the world and attend puppet-making workshops. Elaborate performances, which include original dramatic works and classics adapted for the museum theater, are presented by professional puppeteers—youngsters and adults alike are spellbound. In particular, the popular Christmas performances of *The Velveteen Rabbit* and *The Shoemaker and the Elf* are truly magical experiences. ⊠ *1404 Spring St., at 18th St., Midtown,* ☎ *404/873–3391,* WEB *www.puppet.org.* ⊡ *$5; special exhibits and programs extra.* ☉ *Mon.–Sat. 9–5, Sun. 11–5.*

㊶ **Federal Reserve Bank.** Don't miss this grand, recently renovated monetary museum whose exhibits explain the story of money as a medium of exchange and the history of the U.S. banking system. Items displayed include rare coins, uncut sheets of money, and a gold bar. There are a tour and a video, *The Fed Today.* ⊠ *1000 Peachtree St., Midtown,*

Atlanta Neighborhoods

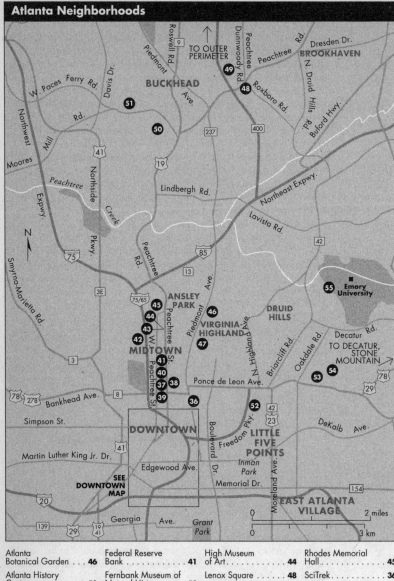

☎ *404/498–8764 or 800/498–8318,* WEB *www.frbatlanta.org.* ☉ *Weekdays 9–4.*

❸⓿ Fox Theatre. One of a dwindling number of vintage movie palaces in the nation, the Fox was built in 1929 in a fabulous Moorish-Egyptian style to be the headquarters of the Shriners Club. The interior's crowning glory is its skylike ceiling—complete with clouds and stars above Alhambra-like minarets. Threatened by demolition in the 1970s, the Fox was saved from the wrecker's ball by concerted civic action and is still a prime venue for musicals, rock concerts, dance performances, and film festivals. ⊠ *660 Peachtree St., Midtown,* ☎ *404/881–2100; 404/876–2041 for Atlanta Preservation Center,* WEB *www.foxtheatre. org.* 🎫 *Tour, conducted by Atlanta Preservation Center, $10.* ☉ *Tours Mon., Wed., and Thurs. at 10, Sat. at 10 and 11.*

❸❽ Georgian Terrace. Originally built in 1911 as a fine beaux arts–style hotel, the Georgian Terrace, designed by William L. Stoddart, housed the stars of the film *Gone With the Wind* when it premiered at the nearby Loew's Theater (now demolished) in 1939. President Calvin Coolidge also slept here. Stars of the Metropolitan Opera stayed at the hotel when the Met used to make its annual trek to Atlanta, and according to locals, Enrico Caruso routinely serenaded passersby from its balconies. Renovated with style and historic sensitivity, the building is now a luxury hotel. ⊠ *459 Peachtree St., Midtown,* ☎ *404/897–1991,* WEB *www. thegeorgianterrace.com.*

❹❹ High Museum of Art. The permanent holdings of this high-tech museum built in 1983 focus on American decorative arts and African art. The Uhry Print Collection contains works by French impressionists and other European artists. In 1991 the American Institute of Architects listed the sleek structure, designed by Richard Meier, among the 10 best works of American architecture of the decade. ⊠ *Woodruff Arts Center, 1280 Peachtree St., MARTA Arts Center station, Midtown,* ☎ *404/ 733–4444 recorded information,* WEB *www.high.org.* 🎫 *$8 (varies for special events).* ☉ *Tues.–Sat. 10–5, Sun. noon–5 (hrs often extended for special exhibits).*

❹⓿ Margaret Mitchell House. Although the author of *Gone With the Wind* detested the turn-of-the-20th-century house (she called it "the dump") where she lived when she wrote her masterpiece, determined volunteers got backing to restore the house and open it to the public. To many Atlantans, the Margaret Mitchell House is a lightning rod, symbolizing the conflict between promoting the city's heritage and respecting its varied roots. The house has been gutted by arsonists twice, in 1995 and '96, the second time within days of a major restoration. Although Mitchell is the city's most famous author, her fame derived from writing a book that includes stereotypes of African-Americans that many find offensive. Yet others point out that before her tragically early death, Mitchell secretly helped to fund medical school scholarships to Morehouse College for scores of African-American college students. Both supporters and critics of the house hold their views passionately. The visitor center exhibits photographs, archival material, and personal possessions, including her original typewriter. ⊠ *990 Peachtree St., at Peachtree Pl., Midtown,* ☎ *404/249–7015,* WEB *www.gwtw.org.* 🎫 *$12.* ☉ *Daily 9:30–5.*

❹❼ Piedmont Park. The city's outdoor recreation center, this park is a major venue for special events. Tennis courts, a swimming pool, and paths for walking, jogging, and rollerblading are part of the attraction, but many retreat to the park's great lawn for picnics with a smashing view of the

Midtown skyline. Each April the park hosts the popular Dogwood Festival. ⊠ *Piedmont Ave. between 10th St. and the Prado, Midtown.*

㊺ Rhodes Memorial Hall. Headquarters of the **Georgia Trust for Historic Preservation,** this former residence is one of the finest works of Atlanta architect Willis F. Denny II. Built at the northern edge of the city in 1904 for Amos Giles Rhodes, the wealthy founder of a Southern furniture chain, the hall has stained-glass windows that depict the heroes of the Confederacy. ⊠ *1516 Peachtree St., Midtown,* ☎ *404/881–9980,* WEB *www.georgiatrust.org/rhodes.html.* ⊠ *$5.* ☉ *Weekdays 11–4, Sun. noon–3.*

★ ☾ ㊱ SciTrek. The Science and Technology Museum of Atlanta covers 96,000 square ft and has rotating exhibitions and daily science demonstrations at the Coca-Cola Science Show Theater. About 150 hands-on exhibits occupy four environments: *Simple Machines; Light, Color, and Perception; Electricity and Magnetism;* and *Kidspace,* for children ages 2–7. The Information Petting Zoo exhibits "cybercritters." ⊠ *395 Piedmont Ave., Midtown,* ☎ *404/522–5500,* WEB *www.scitrek.org.* ⊠ *$7.50.* ☉ *Mon.–Sat. 10–5, Sun. noon–5.*

㊸ Woodruff Arts Center. The center houses the world-renowned **Atlanta Symphony Orchestra,** the **High Museum of Art,** the **Alliance Theatre,** and the **14th Street Playhouse,** which includes several repertory companies. Both theaters present contemporary dramas, classics, and frequent world premieres. ⊠ *1280 Peachtree St., Midtown,* ☎ *404/733–4200,* WEB *www.woodruffcenter.org.*

Buckhead

Atlanta's sprawl doesn't lend itself to walking between major neighborhoods, so take a car or MARTA to reach Buckhead. Many of Atlanta's trendy restaurants, music clubs, chic shops, and hip art galleries are concentrated in this neighborhood. Finding a parking spot on the weekends and at night can be a real headache, and waits of two hours or more are common in the hottest restaurants.

Numbers in the text correspond to numbers in the margin and on the Atlanta Neighborhoods map.

A Good Drive

Begin this drive at the intersection of two splendid shopping malls. The older and larger of the two is **Lenox Square** ㊽. Across the street you'll find the elegant shops of **Phipps Plaza** ㊾. Leaving Phipps Plaza, exit onto Peachtree Road and turn right (south), traveling about ⅓ mi to West Paces Ferry Road. Turn right and proceed to the **Atlanta History Center** ㊿. Leaving the center, head back to West Paces Ferry Road and then turn left, driving about ½ mi to reach the **Georgia Governor's Mansion** ㉛.

From Buckhead a 4-mi drive north along Peachtree-Dunwoody Road takes you by some of the city's most impressive residential dwellings and leads you straight to the popular **Perimeter Mall,** a sprawling "shop-opolis" bolstered with nearby megastores and home-designer outlets. Its location is at the northern crest of I–285, the freeway circling the city in an approximate 10-mi radius, thus delineating the inner and outer perimeters of metro Atlanta. Loosely speaking, the Perimeter area, which is most heavily focused along this northern section of I–285, has become one of the nation's fastest-growing "edge cities," complete with hundreds of trendy restaurants, office towers, mostly business-oriented hotels, and condo and housing subdivisions galore.

Simply driving the distance around the five sights, looking briefly at each one, will consume, generally, no more than 30 minutes. Allot several hours if you want to shop or tour the Atlanta History Center and Georgia Governor's Mansion. And give yourself at least another two hours if you wish to explore the Perimeter area north of Buckhead—a section that's plagued by heavy traffic much of the time.

Sights to See

★ ⑤⓪ **Atlanta History Center.** The museum highlights materials native to Georgia, with a floor of heart pine and polished Stone Mountain granite. Displays are provocative, juxtaposing *Gone With the Wind* romanticism with the grim reality of Ku Klux Klan racism. Also on the 33-acre site are the elegant 1928 **Swan House;** the **Tullie Smith Farm,** with a two-story plantation plain house (1840s); and **McElreath Hall,** an exhibition space for artifacts from Atlanta's history. ⊠ *130 W. Paces Ferry Rd., Buckhead,* ☎ *404/814–4000,* WEB *www.atlantahistorycenter.com.* ☞ *$12.* ☉ *Mon.–Sat. 10–5:30, Sun. noon–5:30.*

⑤① **Georgia Governor's Mansion.** Built in 1967, this 24,000-square-ft Greek Revival mansion contains 30 rooms and sits on 18 acres originally belonging to the Robert Maddox family (no relation to Georgia governor Lester Maddox, who was its first occupant). Federal-period antiques fill the public rooms. ⊠ *391 W. Paces Ferry Rd., Buckhead,* ☎ *404/261–1858.* ☉ *Free guided tours Tues.–Thurs. 10–11:30.*

④⑧ **Lenox Square.** Local shoppers come for the more than 250 stores and several good restaurants at this mall. ⊠ *3393 Peachtree Rd., Buckhead,* ☎ *404/233–6767,* WEB *www.shopsimon.com.*

④⑨ **Phipps Plaza.** The mall is one of Atlanta's premier shopping areas, with upscale chain stores, specialty shops, and restaurants. It also includes a 14-screen movie theater. ⊠ *3500 Peachtree Rd., Buckhead,* ☎ *404/ 262–0992 or 800/810–7700,* WEB *www.shopsimon.com.*

Virginia-Highland and the Emory Area

Restaurants and art galleries are the backbone of Virginia-Highland/Morningside, northeast of Midtown. Like Midtown, this residential area was down-at-the-heels only 25 years ago. Reclaimed by writers, artists, and a few visionary developers, Virginia-Highland (and its bordering Morningside neighborhood, to the north) today offers intriguing shopping and delightful walking. Nightlife hums here as well. To the east, the Emory University area is studded with envious mansions and expansive landscaping.

Numbers in the text correspond to numbers in the margin and on the Atlanta Neighborhoods map.

A Good Drive

This tour meanders through some residential areas, such as Druid Hills, the location for the film *Driving Miss Daisy,* by local playwright Alfred Uhry. The neighborhood was designed by the firm of Frederick Law Olmsted, which also designed New York's Central Park. Begin at the **Carter Presidential Center** ⑤②, the central attraction in a sub-neighborhood called Poncey Highlands, because it lies south of Ponce de Leon Avenue and south of Virginia-Highland. The former president's center is bounded by Freedom Parkway, which splits and encircles the facility. To reach it from downtown, drive on Ralph McGill Boulevard about 1 mi east of I–75/85 (Exit 248C) to where the boulevard intersects with Freedom Parkway.

From the center take a left, drive only one short block on Highland Avenue to Ponce de Leon Avenue, and turn right (east), continuing for 1 mi to Clifton Road; next, take a left onto Clifton Road and almost immediately enter the driveway for the **Fernbank Museum of Natural History** (53). On the east end of this extensive forest and recreational-educational preserve lies **Fernbank Science Center** (54). Nearby on Emory University's campus visit the **Michael C. Carlos Museum** (55), an exquisite contemporary structure.

TIMING

You can drive this tour in about 15 minutes without stops. If you spend a few hours at each sight, it can easily take a full day.

Sights to See

★ (52) **Carter Presidential Center.** This complex occupies the site where Union general William T. Sherman orchestrated the Battle of Atlanta (1864). The museum and archives detail the political career of former president Jimmy Carter. The center itself, which is not open to the public, focuses on conflict resolution and human rights issues. It sponsors foreign-affairs conferences and projects on such matters as the world food supply. Outside, the Japanese-style garden is a serene spot to unwind. ✉ *1 Copenhill Ave., Virginia-Highland,* ☎ *404/331–3942,* WEB *www.cartercenter.org.* *$5.* ⏲ *Mon.–Sat. 9–4:45, Sun. noon–4:45.*

(53) **Fernbank Museum of Natural History.** The largest natural history museum south of the Smithsonian Institution in Washington, D.C., holds a permanent exhibit, *A Walk Through Time in Georgia.* You can meander through 15 galleries to explore the earth's natural history. The museum's IMAX theater shows films about the natural world. The café, with an exquisite view overlooking the forest, serves great food. ✉ *767 Clifton Rd., Emory,* ☎ *404/370–0960; 404/370–0019 IMAX; 404/370–0850 for directions hot line,* WEB *www.fernbank.edu/museum/.* *Museum $12, IMAX $10, combination ticket $17.* ⏲ *Museum Mon.–Sat. 10–5, Sun. noon–5; IMAX Mon.–Thurs. 10–5, Fri. 6:30 PM–10 PM, Sat. 10–5, Sun. noon–5.*

(54) **Fernbank Science Center.** The museum focuses on geology, space exploration, and ecology; it's best for younger children. Special seasonal programs for children under 5, priced at 50¢, are offered weekends at 1:30 from October through November, from early December through the first week of January, from the end of January to March 15, and during the summer. ✉ *156 Heaton Park Dr., Emory,* ☎ *404/378–4311,* WEB *http://fsc.fernbank.edu/.* *Museum free, planetarium shows $2.* ⏲ *Mon. 8:30–5, Tues.–Fri. 8:30 AM–10 PM, Sat. 10–5, Sun. 1–5; planetarium shows Tues.–Fri. at 3:30 and 8, weekends at 3:30.*

★ (55) **Michael C. Carlos Museum.** Housing a permanent collection of more than 16,000 objects, this excellent museum designed by renowned American architect Michael Graves exhibits artifacts from Egypt, Greece, Rome, the Near East, the Americas, and Africa. European and American prints and drawings cover the Middle Ages through the 20th century. The gift shop has rare art books, jewelry, and art-focused items for children. The museum's Caffé Antico is a good lunch spot. ✉ *Emory University, 571 S. Kilgo St., Emory,* ☎ *404/727–4282,* WEB *http://carlos.emory.edu/.* *Suggested donation $5.* ⏲ *Tues.–Wed. 10–5, Thurs. 10–9, Fri.–Sat. 10–5, Sun. noon–5.*

OFF THE BEATEN PATH

INMAN PARK AND LITTLE FIVE POINTS – Since this once grand neighborhood—about 4 mi east of downtown—was laid out by famous developer Joel Hurt in 1889, the area has faded and flourished a number of times, which explains the vast gaps in opulence evident by examining much of the architecture here. Huge, ornate Victorian mansions sit next to humble shotgun shacks. But no matter the exact address or style of home—be it modest or massive—all of Inman Park now commands considerable cachet among all types, from young families to empty nesters to gays and lesbians. Here you'll also find the delightfully countercultural Little Five Points section, ground zero for Atlanta funk. Though many of the storefronts here where Moreland, Euclid, and McLendon avenues intersect defy description, all are delightful. Check out the fascinating but almost scary **Urban Tribe Tattoo and Piercing Studio** (⊠ 1131 Euclid Ave., Inman Park, ☎ 404/659–6344). There's a plethora of colorful vintage-clothing stores here, including **Clothing Warehouse** (⊠ 420 Moreland Ave., Inman Park, ☎ 404/524–5074). In a former garage, **Groovy Girls Clothing Exchange** (⊠ 211 Moreland Ave., Inman Park, ☎ 404/659–3669) is a wonderland of edgy fashion pieces from the past.

Other Area Attractions

Atlanta's suburbs have excellent entertainment options. It is essential to drive to these venues, so plan your visits with Atlanta's notorious rush hours in mind.

★ **Château Élan.** A 16th-century-style French château has Georgia's best-known winery, ensconced in 2,400 rolling acres about an hour north of downtown Atlanta. Château Élan is also a complete resort: European luxury blends with Southern hospitality at the 274-room inn and spa with private villas, golf courses, and an equestrian center. ⊠ *100 Rue Charlemagne, Braselton I–85 to GA 211, Exit 126 (Chestnut Mountain/Winder)*, ☎ *770/932–0900 or 800/233–9463, FAX 770/271–6005, WEB www.chateauelan.com.* ☞ *Winery tours and tastings free.* ☉ *Wine market daily 10–9. Tours weekdays at 11, 12:30, 2, 3:30; Sat. hourly 11–5; Sun. noon–4.*

☾ **Chattahoochee Nature Center.** Birds and animals in their natural habitats may be seen from nature trails and a boardwalk winding through 124 acres of woodlands and wetlands. A gift shop, indoor exhibits, birds-of-prey aviaries, and a picnic area are on the property. Naturalist guides accompany evening canoe floats from May through August. ⊠ *9135 Willeo Rd., Roswell*, ☎ *770/992–2055, WEB www.chattnaturecenter.com.* ☞ *$3.* ☉ *Mon.–Sat. 9–5, Sun. noon–5.*

★ **Decatur Historical Courthouse.** Known as the Old Courthouse on the Square, this charming building was constructed in 1823 and now houses the DeKalb Welcome Center. One reason to visit this historical site is its location—it's right in the center of delightful Decatur Square, a quaint town quad with a sophisticated artistic feel, teeming with interesting specialty shops and delectable coffeehouses and cafés. Lively downtown Decatur is one of metro Atlanta's favorite spots for sidewalk-strolling and window-shopping. ⊠ *101 E. Court Sq., Decatur, Ponce de Leon Ave. east 8 mi to Decatur Sq. at Clairmont Ave.*, ☎ *404/373–1088, FAX 404/373–8287, WEB www.dekalbhistory.org.* ☉ *Weekdays 9–4.*

Kennesaw Mountain National Battlefield. A must for Civil War buffs, this 2,884-acre park with 16 mi of hiking trails was the site of several crucial battles in June 1864. The visitor center contains a small museum with exhibits of Civil War weapons, uniforms, and other items recovered from the battlefield. A 10-minute slide presentation explains the battles. ⊠ *Old U.S. 41 and Stilesboro Rd. (look for signs on I–75N), Kennesaw*, ☎ *770/427–4686, WEB www.nps.gov/kemo.* ☞ *Free.* ☉ *Daily 7:30–dusk.*

☺ **Six Flags over Georgia.** Atlanta's major theme park, with eight sections, heart-stopping roller coasters, and water rides (best saved for last to prevent being damp all day), is a child's ideal playground. The Georgia Scorcher, a roller coaster that you ride standing up, moves at 54 mph. The park also has well-staged musical revues, concerts by top-name artists, and other performances. Take MARTA's west line to the Hightower station and then the Six Flags bus. ✉ *I–20W at 7561 Six Flags Pkwy., Austell,* ☎ *770/739–3400,* WEB *www.sixflags.com.* ✆ *All-inclusive 1-day pass $39.99, parking $9 or $12 (depending on the lot).* ⊙ *June–Aug., daily 10 AM–11 PM; Mar.–May and Sept.–Oct., weekends from 10, closing times vary.*

☺ **Stone Mountain Park.** This 3,200-acre state park 15 mi east of Atlanta has the largest exposed granite outcropping on earth. The Confederate Memorial on the north face of the 825-ft-high domed mountain is the world's largest sculpture, measuring 90 ft by 190 ft. The park has a skylift to the mountaintop, a steam locomotive ride around the mountain's base, an antebellum plantation, a swimming beach, a campground, a hotel, a resort, a wildlife preserve, restaurants, and two Civil War museums. Summer nights are capped with a laser light show, and annual events such as the Yellow Daisy Festival and the Scottish Highland Games are popular in the fall. ✉ *U.S. 78E (Stone Mountain Pkwy.), Stone Mountain,* ☎ *770/498–5600,* WEB *www.stonemountainpark.com.* ✆ *Per car $7; annual pass $30; day pass to all attractions $13.91 for GA residents, $17.12 for out-of-state visitors; additional fees for special events.* ⊙ *Daily 6 AM–midnight.*

OFF THE BEATEN PATH	**EAST ATLANTA VILLAGE –** This earthy outpost of edgy-cool shops and restaurants evolved when a cadre of proprietors with dreams much bigger than their bank accounts spurned the high rents of fancier parts of town and set up businesses in this then-blighted but beautiful ruin of a neighborhood 4 mi southeast of downtown. Soon artists and trendoids began soaking up the ensuing creative atmosphere, and like attracted like. Years later East Atlanta, which is centered at Flat Shoals and Glenwood avenues, just southeast of Moreland Avenue at I–20, now ranks among the hippest neighborhoods in metro Atlanta. The majestic homes have almost all been renovated, and what remains unrestored seems simply to romanticize the area's hint of "fashionable" danger. The coffeehouse **Sacred Grounds** (✉ 508 Flat Shoals Ave., East Atlanta, ☎ 404/524–4779) is the credited cornerstone for the new wave of jazzy businesses here. Check out the delightfully funky gift shop **Traders** (✉ 485 Flat Shoals Ave., East Atlanta, ☎ 404/522–3006). And stop by **Space Tribe** (✉ 490 Flat Shoals Ave., East Atlanta, ☎ 404/688–0780), where the funkadelic inventory is out of this world.

Dining

Atlanta has sophisticated kitchens run by world-class chefs, myriad ethnic restaurants, and classic Southern establishments serving such regional favorites as fried chicken, Brunswick stew, fried catfish, and hush puppies. There's no shortage of urban chic in the dining scene, but traditional Southern fare—including Cajun and creole, country-style and plantation cuisine, coastal and mountain dishes—continues to thrive.

The local taste for things sweet and fried holds true for restaurants serving traditional Southern food. Tea in the South comes iced and sweet; if you want hot tea, specify hot. Desserts in the region are legendary. Catch the flavor of the South at breakfast and lunch in modest establishments that serve only these meals. Reserve evenings for culinary exploration, including some of the new restaurants that present traditional ingredients and dishes in fresh ways. The influx of Asian immigrants makes Atlanta the perfect city to sample Thai, Vietnamese, Japanese, and authentic Chinese cuisines.

Downtown

$$$$ ✕ **City Grill.** It's the poshest power-lunch spot in Atlanta and has made
★ the most of its grand location in the elegantly renovated historic Hurt Building. Dinners are prix fixe, and an impressive wine list accompanies the equally impressive menu. ⊠ *50 Hurt Plaza, Downtown,* ☎ *404/524–2489. AE, D, DC, MC, V. Closed Sun. No lunch Sat.*

$$–$$$$ ✕ **Atlanta Grill.** With an outdoor veranda overlooking Peachtree Street, this restaurant in the Ritz-Carlton, Atlanta, has taken dining in the hotel from formal to casual. Chef Peter Zampaglione focuses on regional Southern ingredients and specializes in grilled seafood and game. Savor such Southern culinary artworks as molasses-grilled pork tenderloin and dry-rubbed Carolina chicken. ⊠ *181 Peachtree St., Downtown,* ☎ *404/221–6550. AE, D, DC, MC, V.*

$$–$$$$ ✕ **Food Studio.** No less stylish for being a piece of a former plow fac-
★ tory, the restaurant gleams with high-tech and industrial touches. From the same group that made South City Kitchen a success, the Studio is known for innovative American food—but has added a few more traditional dishes, such as the braised beef short ribs with maple-soy glazed carrots. Desserts range from the parfaitlike frozen lemon-basil bombe to mango mousse. ⊠ *887 W. Marietta St., Studio K-102, King Plow Arts Center, Downtown,* ☎ *404/815–6677. Reservations essential. AE, DC, MC, V. No lunch weekends.*

$$–$$$ ✕ **Mumbo Jumbo.** After you pass both the long bar that skirts the left
★ side of the establishment and the posh clientele, you'll approach sleek young staffers who will conduct you to your table. The menu emphasizes game in cool weather, fish and shellfish in summer, and regional ingredients and locally grown produce year-round. Tempting dishes include braised hen-of-the-woods mushrooms with roasted tomatoes and caramelized garlic; braised rabbit legs with goat-cheese macaroni; and sautéed halibut with fennel salad and smoked-eel butter. ⊠ *89 Park Pl., Downtown,* ☎ *404/523–0330. Reservations essential. AE, D, DC, MC, V. No lunch weekends.*

$–$$ ✕ **ACE Barbecue Barn.** Delicious ribs and chopped rib tips, baked chicken and dressing, and sweet-potato pie are the draws at this slightly worn down-home restaurant. It's near the Martin Luther King Jr. Center. ⊠ *30 Bell St. NE, Sweet Auburn,* ☎ *404/659–6630. No credit cards. Closed Tues.*

$–$$ ✕ **Max Lager's American Grill & Brewery.** Line up a tasting of the house brews—the pale ale and brown ale are tops—and then order the Gulf Coast gumbo, the "Maximum" T-bone (an 18-ounce steak), or one of the popular specialty pizzas. This lively brewpub near the city's major high-rise buildings is hopping after business hours. The pub has its own root and ginger beers, which are brewed here. ⊠ *320 Peachtree St., Downtown,* ☎ *404/525–4400. AE, D, DC, MC, V.*

$ ✕ **Thelma's Kitchen.** After losing her original location to the Centennial Olympic Park, Thelma Grundy moved her operation down the road to the street level of the somewhat renovated Roxy Hotel. Brighter, spiffier, and more cheerful than the earlier spot, it has okra pancakes, fried catfish, "cold" slaw, and macaroni and cheese, all of which are among the best in town. Thelma's desserts are stellar. ⊠ *768 Marietta St. NW, Downtown,* ☎ *404/688–5855. Reservations not accepted. No credit cards. Closed weekends. No dinner.*

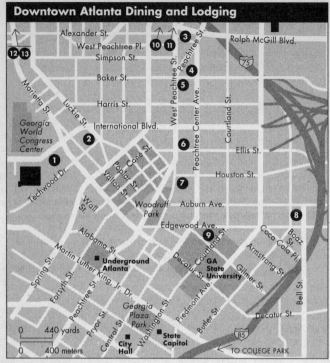

Downtown Atlanta Dining and Lodging

Midtown

$$$–$$$$ ★ ✕ **The Abbey.** Established in 1968, the restaurant is housed in a former church. Stained-glass windows and celestial music played by a harpist in the former choir loft reinforce the headiness. Dishes range from the dramatic Pommery mustard–crusted veal chop to the tandoori-seared tuna. Finish your meal with sweet abandon: the white chocolate–and–roasted banana napoleon is worth losing control over. ⊠ *163 Ponce de Leon Ave., Midtown,* ☎ *404/876–8532. Reservations essential. AE, D, DC, MC, V. No lunch.*

$$$–$$$$ ★ ✕ **Park 75.** It's a swank place and is considered a prominent jewel in Atlanta's culinary crown. Chef Kevin Hickey has created a sumptuous menu, with offerings that include smoked Copper River salmon and baby-chicken stew. Delightfully, it's possible to reserve a table in the middle of the kitchen and observe the master at work while sampling a constant steam of delicacies. ⊠ *75 14th St., Four Seasons Hotel, Midtown,* ☎ *404/253–3840. AE, D, MC, V. No dinner Sun.*

$$$ ✕ **Terra di Siena.** Siena native Ricardo Campinoti imported his love of Tuscany when he opened this fine, upscale Italian bistro, in the same building as the breathtaking Fox Theatre. Entrées include a creative collection of traditional Tuscan dishes, often accented with Southern-style cooking techniques (turning out such dishes as sautéed shrimp with puree of local peas). ⊠ *654 Peachtree St., Midtown,* ☎ *404/885–7505. Reservations essential. AE, MC, V. Closed Mon. No lunch Sat.*

$$–$$$ ✕ **Sotto Sotto.** Atlanta's hot spot close to downtown is an adventurous take on Italian cuisine. The former commercial space hops with young, hip patrons dining on grilled scallops with white beans and truffle oil, tortelli with roasted eggplant and walnuts, spaghetti with sun-dried mullet roe, and utterly perfect *panna cotta* (a custard of cooked cream). ⊠ *313 N. Highland Ave., Inman Park,* ☎ *404/523–6678. Reservations essential. AE, MC, V. No lunch.*

SOUTHERN FLAVORS

GEORGIA IS AN EXCELLENT **PLACE** to sample Southern food. In Atlanta and Savannah you'll find restaurants that serve the finest traditional cuisine, as well as more innovative cooking. Remember that Southern food varies widely across the region and even within states. Nothing reflects this more than barbecue, and few culinary differences produce as many passionate opinions. Taste as you travel, and add to the debate.

Locals in Georgia and Mississippi generally prefer tomato-based sauces on ribs or chopped meat—but variations abound. In North Carolina barbecue is chopped pork piled on a bun with hand-cut coleslaw on top. Sauces range from vinegar and pepper (and little else) to Lexington style, with some tomato in the mix. And North Carolinians serve hush puppies (deep-fried ball-shape cornmeal fritters) with barbecue, which, for them, does not generally include ribs. For the rest of the South, the hush puppy is reserved for fried fish, whether fin or shell.

In South Carolina mustard-based barbecue sauces are widely savored, whether on chopped meat or on ribs. In eastern Alabama (and the Florida Panhandle), you'll find a unique white sauce for barbecue. Memphis-style 'cue is famous for its dry rub, although there is also a "wet" style, in which the same spices, moistened, are rubbed on the ribs. In parts of Tennessee, barbecued mutton is traditional.

Prior to the Depression, there were two sorts of cooking in the South—country food and the elegant plantation fare drawn from French and English models. More recent country cooking blends European, African, and Native American styles and has come to be the defining Southern cuisine in most people's minds. But in the past many an elegant table was set with European-based dishes, especially along the coasts.

Gumbo, the spicy soup that is so clearly from this region, is a more apt metaphor for the South's demographics than the term *melting pot* because the word *gumbo* reflects all that comes to the Southern table (and to Southern culture) from its people. The term is African, from *ngombo*, which meant "okra" in that part of the world. And what would gumbo be without okra? But gumbo is also French: a proper gumbo is based on a *roux*, a sauté of fat and flour cooked to the color of peanut butter. The cook might sauté vegetables for a gumbo, making a kind of *sofrito*, a legacy from the Spanish settlers in the lower part of Louisiana. Using sassafras or filé powder to thicken gumbo is a legacy of Southern Native Americans.

One defining ingredient in Southern cooking is corn—another Native American legacy. Parch the corn with lye, which swells the grains, and you get hominy. Grind the corn, white or yellow, and you have grits. Sift the grits, and you have cornmeal for making corn bread, fluffy spoon bread, corn pone, hoecakes, hush puppies, johnnycake (or Native American "journey" cake). Ferment the grain, and you get corn whiskey, also known as white lightning or moonshine (and arguably like Southern grappa).

When traveling in Georgia and the rest of the South, you'll find the area's diversity on its tables. Many of the region's chefs use the traditional ingredients to craft "new" Southern dishes as a way of restoring that sense of elegant dining to the region's cuisine. Others wouldn't get near that sort of style, preferring to do the original dishes proud. Take your pick: either way you'll dine divinely.

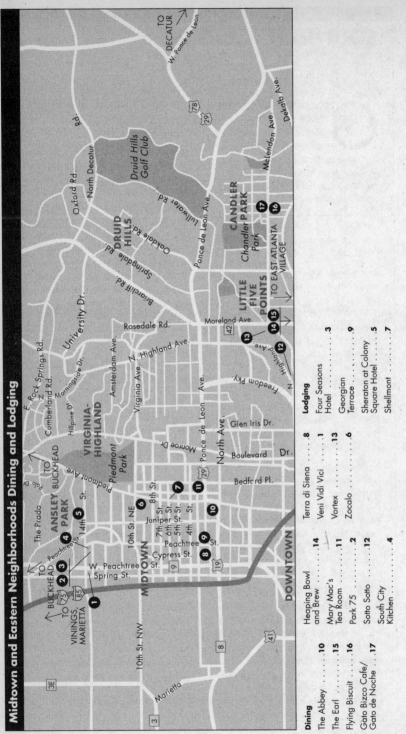

Midtown and Eastern Neighborhoods Dining and Lodging

36

Dining

The Abbey **10**
The Earl **15**
Flying Biscuit **16**
Gato Bizco Cafe/
Gato de Noche **17**
Heaping Bowl
and Brew **14**
Mary Mac's
Tea Room **11**
Park 75 . . . . **2**
Sotto Sotto **12**
South City
Kitchen **4**
Terra di Siena **8**
Veni Vidi Vici **1**
Vortex **13**
Zocalo **6**

Lodging

Four Seasons
Hotel **3**
Georgian
Terrace **9**
Sheraton at Colony
Square Hotel . . . **5**
Shellmont **7**

$$–$$$ ✕ **South City Kitchen.** The culinary traditions of South Carolina's Low-country inspire the cooking at this cheerful restaurant. The spare, art-filled interior attracts a hip crowd. This is the place to get fried green tomatoes with goat cheese, she-crab soup, or buttermilk fried chicken. The chef prepares catfish in many intriguing ways. Crab hash, served with poached eggs and chive hollandaise, is a classic. Do not skip the chocolate pecan pie. ⊠ *1144 Crescent Ave., Midtown,* ☎ *404/873–7358. AE, MC, V.*

$$–$$$ ✕ **Veni Vidi Vici.** Gleaming woods, contemporary styling, and an out-
★ door boccie court and dining patio create the perfect place for an in-dulgent Italian meal. Start with *piatti piccoli* (savory appetizers), then try one of the following: beef tenderloin, rack of lamb, or the excel-lent osso buco. Gnocchi with Gorgonzola is another favorite, or order one of the fragrant rotisserie meats. ⊠ *41 14th St., Midtown,* ☎ *404/875–8424. AE, D, DC, MC, V. No lunch weekends.*

$$ ✕ **Zocalo.** Come to this inviting open-air patio restaurant—warmed
★ in the frigid winter months by giant heaters—if you want some of the best Mexican food in town. Spicy *chipotle*-pepper shrimp and creamy *poblano*-pepper soup are delicious proof of the chef's culinary prowess. The bar has an excellent selection of epicurean tequilas. ⊠ *187 10th St., Midtown,* ☎ *404/249–7576. Reservations not accepted. AE, D, MC, V.*

$–$$ ✕ **Mary Mac's Tea Room.** Local celebrities and ordinary folk line up for the country-fried steak, fried chicken, and fresh vegetables. Here, in the Southern tradition, lunch is called "dinner," and the evening meal is referred to as "supper." Waitresses will call you "honey" and pat your arm to assure you that everything's all right. It's a great way to experience Southern food and hospitality all at once. ⊠ *224 Ponce de Leon Ave., Midtown,* ☎ *404/876–1800. No credit cards. No dinner Sun.*

Buckhead

$$$$ ✕ **Dining Room, The Ritz-Carlton, Buckhead.** If you like the style of an old gentlemen's club, you'll appreciate this elegant, restrained room, with formal hunt scenes on the walls, romantic lighting, and generously spaced tables. Chef Bruno Menarch ensures a delectable daily assort-ment of creative options on the prix-fixe menu. Specialties have included veal loin with lemongrass, tomato confit, and chanterelle mushrooms. ⊠ *3434 Peachtree Rd., Buckhead,* ☎ *404/237–2700. Reservations es-sential. Jacket and tie. AE, D, DC, MC, V. Closed Sun. No lunch.*

$$$$ ✕ **Seeger's.** Celebrated chef Guenter Seeger, formerly at the Dining
★ Room in the Ritz-Carlton, presides over this sophisticated, sleek place. Some find it a bit noisy, but after the first fragrant, flavorful bite you'll forget about the volume. The smoked salmon with horseradish cream and the grilled squab are outstanding. Local inspirations include sweet-onion tarts with pecan sauce. Your prix-fixe options are a vegetable menu and, in season, an entire menu based on truffles. ⊠ *111 W. Paces Ferry Rd., Buckhead,* ☎ *404/846–9779. Reservations essential. Jacket required. AE, D, DC, MC, V. Closed Sun. No lunch.*

$$$–$$$$ ✕ **Morton's.** This Chicago transplant sticks to quintessential steakhouse
★ classics: filet Oskar, a filet mignon topped with lump crab meat, fresh asparagus, and béarnaise sauce; and fillet Diane, which is topped with sautéed mushrooms and a demiglace sauce. Morton's is in the Peachtree Lenox building. ⊠ *3379 Peachtree Rd., Buckhead,* ☎ *404/816–6535. AE, D, MC, V. No dinner Sun.*

$$–$$$ ✕ **Aria.** Here, chef Gerry Klaskala is known for making masterful en-
★ trées of rustic heartiness that also appeal to the epicurean palate. His signature talent is best captured by his love of "slow foods"—braises, stews, steaks, and chops cooked over a roll-top French grill. This

38

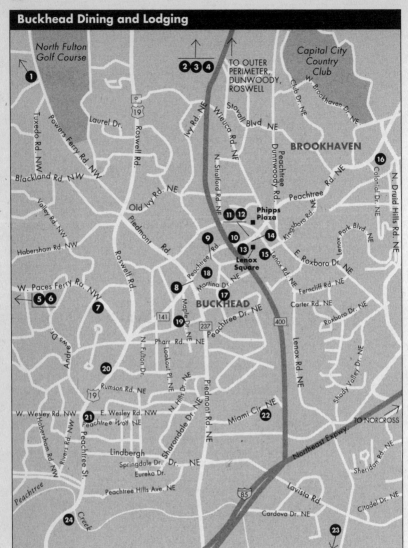

Dining

Aria	19
Brasserie Le Coze	14
Canoe	5
Colonnade Restaurant	23
Dining Room, The Ritz-Carlton, Buckhead	12
Eclipse di Luna	22
Horseradish Grill	1
Joël	6
La Grotta Ristorante Italiano	21
Meritage	17
Morton's	9
Oh...Maria!	8
Seeger's	7
Toulouse	24
Vino!	20

Lodging

Crowne Plaza Atlanta Ravinia	2
Doubletree Hotel	10
Embassy Suites Hotel	18
Holiday Inn Select Atlanta Perimeter	4
Ritz-Carlton, Buckhead	11
Sheraton Buckhead	15
Sierra Suites Atlanta Brookhaven	16
Swissôtel	13
W Atlanta	3

makes for very weighty plates, but still Klaskala lovingly flavors every ounce. For example, pork shoulder is presented with a delicious balsamic reduction and Gorgonzola polenta. Don't miss renowned pastry chef Kathryn King's mouthwatering dessert menu, including Valrhona chocolate cream pie with Drambuie sauce. ✉ *490 E. Paces Ferry Rd., Buckhead,* ☎ *404/233–7673. Reservations essential. Jacket and tie. AE, D, DC, MC, V. Closed Sun. No lunch.*

$$–$$$ ✕ **Brasserie Le Coze.** This bistro draws raves from critics and foodies
★ alike. Shoppers stream into this glowing, wood-paneled space with comfortable banquettes, and once they try the comforting bistro-style fare, they forget they're in a mall. Traditional dishes include coq au vin, and seared codfish in a white-bean stew. *Vacherin* (meringue rings placed on a pastry base) filled with ice cream is one of many extravagant desserts. ✉ *3393 Peachtree Rd., Lenox Sq., near Neiman Marcus, Buckhead,* ☎ *404/266–1440. AE, DC, MC, V. Closed Sun.*

$$–$$$ ✕ **Canoe.** This popular spot on the banks of the Chattahoochee River
★ brims with appreciative patrons nearly all day. In nice weather the outdoor dining spaces allow the best view of the river. The restaurant has built a national reputation based on such dishes as herb-crusted grouper with roasted sweet-corn succotash, oak-roasted duck breast, and slow-roasted Carolina rabbit. Sunday brunch is superb. ✉ *4199 Paces Ferry Rd. NW, Buckhead,* ☎ *770/432–2663. AE, D, DC, MC, V.*

$$–$$$ ✕ **Horseradish Grill.** Once a red horse barn, this establishment is now
★ painted gray with white trim and has arched windows across the front that brighten the space. It may be a little noisy, but it's a must for authentic, if upscale, Southern dishes. The menu changes seasonally, with entrées ranging from autumn venison stew to "crispy-spit" roasted duck. ✉ *4320 Powers Ferry Rd., Buckhead,* ☎ *404/255–7277. AE, D, DC, MC, V.*

$$–$$$ ✕ **Joël.** Chef Joël Antunes, former executive chef at the heralded Dining Room in the Ritz Carlton Buckhead, spices up this chic French
★ brasserie with Mediterranean and Asian influences. Signature entrées include roast lobster with fried vermicelli, snow peas, and Thai sauce; braised beef ribs with tamarind and rutabaga; and sea bass with tomato lasagna and tapenade. ✉ *3290 Northside Pkwy., Berkeley Park,* ☎ *404/233–3500. Reservations essential. AE, DC, MC, V. Closed Sun.– Mon.*

$$–$$$ ✕ **La Grotta Ristorante Italiano.** Overlook the location in the ground level of a posh condominium—though the burgundy-and-cream interior is elegant—and know that this is an expertly managed dining room. Old northern Italian favorites are the core of the menu. Savor prosciutto with grilled pears and mascarpone cheese, then try the potato-and-herb gnocchi tossed in a crayfish cream sauce. ✉ *2637 Peachtree Rd., Buckhead,* ☎ *404/231–1368. Reservations essential. AE, D, DC, MC, V. Closed Sun. No lunch.*

$$–$$$ ✕ **Meritage.** In this snazzy space you'll find a serious menu of contemporary American food, prepared with tremendous care. Of note is pumpkin seed–encrusted sea scallops, crab-stuffed salmon wrapped in rice paper, and roasted quail stuffed with white truffles. A lengthy dessert list includes similarly elaborate creations. ✉ *3125 Piedmont Rd., Buckhead,* ☎ *404/231–6700. AE, D, DC, MC, V. Closed Sun. No lunch.*

$$–$$$ ✕ **Vino!** The Mediterranean colors here impart warmth and intimacy, which is perfect for enjoying tapas and the good selection of wines by the glass (and you also can eat a full meal). Tapas ($5–$6) are traditional; among the best are shaved fennel with citrus and olive oil, and Spanish serrano ham (similar to prosciutto). ✉ *2900 Peachtree Rd., Buckhead,* ☎ *404/816–0511. AE, DC, MC, V. Closed Sun.*

$–$$$ ✕ **Oh . . . Maria!** It's touted as Atlanta's premiere upscale Mexican eatery,
★ so don't expect to find plastic baskets of chips on your table. This gor-

geously decorated restaurant makes good on its mission to introduce the South to sumptuous Mexican haute cuisine, with such offerings as lobster sautéed in regional herbs topped with chipotle-pecan salsa and red mole poblano. ⊠ *3167 Peachtree Rd., Buckhead,* ☎ *404/261–2032. AE, D, DC, MC, V.*

$$ ✕ **Toulouse.** Open spaces enclosed by warm, rough-brick walls characterize this attractive room. The food is inspired—in theory—by the cooking of southwestern France, but in execution it clearly draws on some American influences. The country potato soup is a perfect cold-weather meal. Especially wonderful are the roast chicken, duck confit with blueberry vinaigrette, and crème brûlée. ⊠ *2293B Peachtree Rd., Peachtree Walk, Buckhead,* ☎ *404/351–9533. AE, DC, MC, V. No lunch.*

$-$$ ✕ **Colonnade Restaurant.** For traditional Southern food—oyster stew, ham steak, and turkey and dressing—insiders head here, an Atlanta institution since 1927. The interior, with patterned carpeting, is a classic version of a 1950s restaurant. ⊠ *1879 Cheshire Bridge Rd., Buckhead,* ☎ *404/874–5642. Reservations not accepted. No credit cards.*

$ ✕ **Eclipse di Luna.** This hot spot has captured the fancy of twen-
★   tysomethings, who flock here on weekends. Lunch is sandwiches and salads, and evening fare is tapas ($3) and wine by the glass. *Patatas bravas* (potatoes with olive oil and spicy sauce), tender braised chicken with saffron and garlic, and flan will take you to Castile. The restaurant is tucked at the very end of Miami Circle, a to-the-trade-only design center. ⊠ *764 Miami Circle, Buckhead,* ☎ *404/846–0449. AE, DC, MC, V. Closed Mon.*

Inman Park, Candler Park, and East Atlanta Village

$-$$ ✕ **The Earl.** A scrappy yet delightful addition to the East Atlanta bar scene, the Earl offers a hearty menu of classic pub food, as well as a few entrées that are more innovative. Don't let the comically eclectic interior fool you: the food is surprisingly substantial and well prepared, considering the no-nonsense digs. There's a casual stage in the corner, too—this one of the city's favorite rock venues. ⊠ *488 Flat Shoals Ave., East Atlanta Village, East Atlanta,* ☎ *404/522–3950. AE, MC, V.*

$-$$ ✕ **Flying Biscuit.** There's an hour-long wait on weekends for the big,
★   fluffy biscuits. Other huge hits at this garage sale–decorated spot include egg dishes, turkey sausage, and bean cakes with tomatillo salsa, as well as a side item called Pudge, a dense mound of mashed potatoes and rosemary. Note that the formerly all-day breakfast café now serves dinner, too. ⊠ *1655 McLendon Ave., Candler Park,* ☎ *404/687–8888. Reservations not accepted. AE, D, MC, V.*

$-$$ ✕ **Gato Bizco Cafe/Gato de Noche.** It's weird but it works. This pocket of a café is actually two restaurants in one. By day it's the popular breakfast-and-lunch joint Gato Bizco, where people line up for fabulous omelets or hearty midday fare. Then Wednesday–Saturday evenings the place transforms into Gato de Noche, a culinary incubator for chef Mike Geier's whimsical creations. Try fresh salmon cakes with papaya salsa or a coconut red-curry rice bowl with fresh garden vegetables. At either time you're in for a treat. ⊠ *1660 McClendon Ave., Candler Park,* ☎ *404/371–0889. AE, MC, V. Closed Mon.–Tues. No dinner Sun.*

$-$$ ✕ **Heaping Bowl and Brew.** Trendoids and scenesters from all over town are devoted to this eatery in ultrahip East Atlanta Village. Meals come in big bowls, be it noodles, seared salmon, mashed potatoes, or southwestern-style chicken. Specials often depend on what's growing fresh in the garden that day. ⊠ *469 Flat Shoals Ave., East Atlanta Village, East Atlanta,* ☎ *404/523–8030. AE, D, MC, V.*

$-$$ ✕ **Vortex.** Talk about a funky design: you enter this restaurant through
★   the mouth of a massive, spiral-eyed skull. The restaurant's motto,

printed on waitstaff T-shirts, is IT'S NEVER TOO LATE TO START WASTING YOUR LIFE. But beyond the shenanigans are tasty delights, particularly the hefty burgers. A little-known perk is the bar's amazingly extensive selection of top-shelf liquor, consistently voted "Best in Atlanta" by the city's namesake magazine. ⊠ *438 Moreland Ave., Little Five Points,* ☏ *404/688–1828. AE, MC, V.*

Metro Atlanta

$$$$ ✕ **Asher.** This swank spot serves up a creative prix fixe menu from which diners may opt for such delicacies as grilled rack of venison with African squash purée and lobster wrapped in Savoy cabbage with white truffle oil. The dining room, an inviting alcove filled with unique antiques, is one reason why those in the know consider it one of the most romantic restaurants in the metro area. ⊠ *1085 Canton St., Roswell (21 mi north of Atlanta),* ☏ *770/650–9398. AE, D, MC, V. No lunch.*

$–$$$$ ✕ **Hi Life Kitchen & Cocktails.** This hip restaurant 20 mi northeast of downtown Atlanta presents an eclectic menu of American favorites, but devotees swear by the Lobster Menu, a heaping plate of lobster prepared three ways—chilled, steamed, and roasted. The meal ends with the dessert of the day. The design is trendy upscale, with light-wood and wrought-iron accents. ⊠ *3380 Holcomb Bridge Rd., Norcross,* ☏ *770/409–0101. AE, MC, V. No lunch weekends.*

$$–$$$ ✕ **The Crab House.** Get your seafood fix here. The menu lists a dizzying variety of fish, along with lobster, crab, and other shell-dressed creatures prepared any number of inventive ways. The seafood-and-salad bar is popular, thanks to its selection of fresh crab, shelled shrimp, Louisiana crawfish, and freshly shucked oysters. For all this, you'll have to drive to Marietta, a suburb 21 mi northwest of Atlanta. ⊠ *2175 Cobb Pkwy., Marietta (20 mi northwest of Atlanta),* ☏ *770/955–2722. AE, D, DC, MC, V.*

$$–$$$ ✕ **Lickskillet Farm.** Although the name of this elegantly rustic farmhouse, which General Sherman once used as a hospital, has a name that suggests greasy-spoon down-home cooking, the chefs at Lickskillet run a serious—and commendable—kitchen. Sample such exquisite entrées as pan-flashed salmon, apple-wood-smoked pork chops, and smoked sea scallops. For starters, don't miss the roasted, stuffed Vidalia onion, made from a classic family recipe. ⊠ *1380 Old Roswell Rd., Roswell (20 mi north of Atlanta),* ☏ *770/475–6484. AE, D, DC, MC, V. No lunch Sat. and Mon.*

$$–$$$ ✕ **Oscar's.** This friendly, upscale bistro continues to wow both locals and big-city types who don't mind venturing 10 mi south of downtown. Behind the prosaic facade of a former pawn shop, you'll discover a dazzling interior of peppermint-stripe lights, mod tableware, and light-wood furnishings. The inventive menu includes intriguing appetizers—lobster-and-cabbage pockets with shiitake mushrooms and crab-and-avocado *tian* (a Provençal-style gratin). For a main course try the Georgia stuffed trout with Swiss cardoons and melted tomatoes. ⊠ *3725 Main St., College Park,* ☏ *404/766–9688. AE, MC, V.*

$$ ✕ **Cafe Alsace.** This tiny culinary enclave in historic downtown Decatur serves estimable (and affordable) French food accented with German touches. Take the tasty spaetzle dishes, created around homemade Alsatian noodles: in the *au saumon* version, the noodles are baked with salmon chunks, garlic, basil, and cheese—and that alone is worth a visit. ⊠ *121 E. Ponce de Leon Ave., Decatur (6 mi east of Atlanta),* ☏ *404/373–5622. AE, D, MC, V. Closed Mon. No lunch Sat.*

$$ ✕ **Food 101.** It was a smash hit as soon as it opened, and no wonder, given the gut-filling comfort food—stuffed pork chop with mashed potatoes, gravy, and string beans; and turkey with stuffing, giblet gravy, and cranberry sauce. Wine drinkers especially love this place for its selection of 50 American wines by the glass. ⊠ *4969 Roswell Rd., #200, Sandy Springs (6 mi north of Atlanta),* ☎ *404/497–9700. AE, MC, V. No lunch weekends.*

$$ ✕ **Villa Christina.** Look no farther for elegant Italian food with a twist. You enter down a lighted path resplendent with gardens, a waterfall, and a stone bridge. Once inside, you'll see that the dining room doubles as an art gallery, with two murals depicting a glorious Tuscan landscape. From the kitchen comes seared wild striped sea bass on a bed of spinach, and grilled Tuscan veal chops with a sweet-onion brûlée of Parma ham; and the house specialty, Christina's seafood cioppino, a medley of succulent shellfish swimming in a saffron-tomato stew. ⊠ *4000 Perimeter Summit Blvd., Dunwoody (14 mi north of Atlanta),* ☎ *404/303–0133. AE, D, DC, MC, V. Closed Sun. No lunch Sat.*

$–$$ ✕ **El Mexica Gourmet.** The owners of El Mexica insist that by sampling the authentic fare from their kitchen you'll learn quickly that Mexican cuisine is not all tacos and enchiladas—though if that's what you're up for, you'll find plenty of that here, too. Alongside those Mexican staples dig into specialties like *carne tampiquena* (charbroiled steak smothered with sautéed onions and peppers) and red snapper Veracruz (panfried with a fresh tomato sauce). ⊠ *11060 Alpharetta Hwy., Suite 172 (behind Applebee's), Roswell (20 mi north of Atlanta),* ☎ *770/594–8674. AE, MC, V.*

$–$$ ✕ **Watershed.** Indigo Girl Emily Saliers and three of her friends launched
★   this casual restaurant–cum–gift shop. Chef Scott Peacock makes the planet's best shrimp salad, homemade flat bread, chicken salad with white truffles, homemade pimento cheese with sharp cheddar and egg, and lusty desserts—any and all are worth the trip. Consider the Georgia pecan tart with a scrumptious shortbread crust. Also an *enoteca* (wine bar), Watershed sells wine both retail in bottles and by the glass at the comfy bar. When she's not in the recording studio, Saliers makes a fine sommelier and loves to talk about wine. ⊠ *406 W. Ponce de Leon Ave., Decatur (6 mi north of Atlanta),* ☎ *404/378–4900. AE, MC, V.*

Lodging

One of America's most popular convention destinations, Atlanta offers plenty of variety in terms of lodgings. More than 76,000 rooms are in metro Atlanta, with about 12,000 downtown, close to the Georgia World Congress Center, Atlanta Civic Center, Atlanta Merchandise Mart, and Omni Coliseum. Other clusters are in Buckhead, in the north I–285 perimeter, and around Hartsfield Atlanta International Airport.

Downtown

$$$–$$$$ 🏨 **Omni Hotel at CNN Center.** The hotel is adjacent to the home of Ted Turner's Cable News Network. The lobby combines traditional and modern accents, with marble floors, Oriental rugs, and exotic floral and plant arrangements. Rooms have large windows and contemporary-style furniture, including a sofa. Guests have access to the Downtown Athletic Club and two small meeting rooms. ⊠ *100 CNN Center (by Omni MARTA), Downtown, 30305,* ☎ *404/659–0000 or 800/843–6664,* FAX *404/525–5050,* WEB *www.omnihotels.com. 470 rooms, 15 suites. 2 restaurants, lobby lounge, business services, parking (fee). AE, D, DC, MC, V.*

$$$–$$$$ 🏨 **Ritz-Carlton, Atlanta.** Traditional afternoon tea—served in the inti-
★   mate, sunken lobby beneath an 18th-century chandelier—sets the mood. Notice the 17th-century Flemish tapestry when you enter from Peachtree Street. Some of the most luxurious guest rooms are decorated with marble writing tables, plump sofas, four-poster beds, and white-marble bathrooms. The Atlanta Grill is one of downtown's few

outdoor dining spots. ✉ *181 Peachtree St. (opposite Peachtree Center MARTA), Downtown, 30303,* ☎ *404/659–0400 or 800/241–3333,* FAX *404/688–0400,* WEB *www.ritzcarlton.com. 441 rooms, 13 suites. Restaurant, bar, laundry service, business services, parking (fee). AE, D, DC, MC, V.*

$$–$$$$ 🛏 **Atlanta Marriott Marquis.** Immense and coolly contemporary, the building seems to go up forever as you stand under the lobby's huge fabric sculpture that hangs from the skylighted roof 47 stories above. Guest rooms, which open onto this atrium, are decorated in dark greens and neutral shades. Major suites have live plants and fresh flowers; two suites have grand pianos and ornamental fireplaces. ✉ *265 Peachtree Center Ave., Downtown, 30303,* ☎ *404/521–0000 or 800/932–2198,* FAX *404/586–6299,* WEB *www.marriott.com. 1,675 rooms, 69 suites. 4 restaurants, indoor-outdoor pool, health club, 2 bars, business services, meeting rooms, parking (fee). AE, D, DC, MC, V.*

$$–$$$ 🛏 **Hyatt Regency Atlanta.** This was John Portman's first atrium-centered building, and it became the model for his other hotels, including the San Francisco Embarcadero and the Atlanta Marriott Marquis. The blue-bubble top stands out against the Atlanta skyline. Expect the careful service and quality facilities typical of Hyatt hotels. Constructed in 1967, it was the first major hotel to be built downtown since the 1920s. From the exterior the most notable feature is the space-age blue dome crowning the structure, which houses a revolving cocktail lounge. Inside is a spectacular 22-story skylighted atrium, a John Portman trademark, which encompasses a massive aviary and another cocktail lounge beneath a stunning suspended canopy. The exposed glass elevators zipping up and down the length of the atrium are also a Portman trademark. ✉ *265 Peachtree St. (connected by skywalk to Peachtree Center), Downtown, 30303,* ☎ *404/577–1234 or 800/233–1234,* FAX *404/588–4137,* WEB *www.hyatt.com. 1,206 rooms, 58 suites. 4 restaurants, pool, health club, bar, business services, parking (fee). AE, D, DC, MC, V.*

$–$$ 🛏 **Quality Hotel Downtown.** This quiet, older downtown hotel, two blocks off Peachtree Street, has a marble lobby with sofas and a grand piano, with paid entertainment. Modest-size rooms are decorated in teal and navy. It's priced reasonably for its location and thus has become popular during conventions due to its proximity to the World Congress Center and the show marts; prices go up when conventions are in town. ✉ *89 Luckie St., Downtown, 30303,* ☎ *404/524–7991 or 888/729–7705,* FAX *404/524–0672,* WEB *www.qualityinn.com. 75 rooms. Pool, parking (fee). AE, D, DC, MC, V.*

Midtown

$$$–$$$$ 🛏 **Four Seasons Hotel.** From the lobby a sweeping staircase leads up to a refined but welcoming bar and to Park 75, the hotel's American-chic dining establishment. Rose-hue marble creates a warm feeling in the public spaces and lounges. Amenities abound throughout—marble bathrooms with extra-large soaking tubs, pale lemon or celadon color schemes, and polished brass chandeliers—and let's not forget their famously comfortable mattresses (Julia Roberts declared on Oprah that her favorite place to relax is in a Four Seasons bed). The hotel prides itself on its immensely courteous staff—a phone call to reception is considered scandalous if it exceeds two rings before it's answered. Stewards and other staff members are on hand—sightlessly—till the moment you need their help. ✉ *75 14th St., Midtown, 30309,* ☎ *404/881–9898 or 800/819–5053,* FAX *404/873–4692,* WEB *www.fourseasons.com. 226 rooms, 18 suites. Restaurant, pool, health club, spa, bar, high-speed Internet, business services, meeting rooms, parking (fee). AE, D, DC, MC, V.*

$$–$$$$ 🛏 **Georgian Terrace.** Spend a night where Enrico Caruso and the Metropolitan Opera stars once lodged. This fine 1911 hotel, across the street from the Fox Theatre, is on the National Register of Historic Places. From its beginning it has housed the rich and famous, but it fell into disrepair for a few decades—and now has undergone a restoration, with an added matching tower. The lobby is sleek and plush, and breathtaking terraces traverse the exterior, making it one of the most popular wedding-reception venues in the city. All units are suites with balconies (and washer-dryers); they are pastel and plush, providing competent if not luxurious comfort. ✉ *659 Peachtree St., Midtown, 30308,* ☎ *404/897–1991 or 800/651–2316,* ℻ *404/724–0642,* WEB *www.thegeorgianterrace.com. 326 suites. Restaurant, kitchens, kitchenettes, pool, health club, convention center, meeting rooms, parking (fee). AE, D, DC, MC, V.*

$$$　🏨 **Sheraton at Colony Square Hotel.** Theatricality and opulence are epitomized by the moodily lighted lobby with overhanging balconies, live piano music, and fresh flowers. Rooms are modern, with muted tones; those on higher floors have city views. The hotel is two blocks from MARTA's Arts Center station and two blocks from the Woodruff Arts Center and the High Museum of Art; it anchors the Colony Square complex of office, residential, and retail buildings. ✉ *188 14th St., Midtown, 30361,* ☎ *404/892–6000 or 800/422–7895,* ℻ *404/872–9192,* WEB *www.starwood.com. 467 rooms, 32 suites. Restaurant, pool, lobby lounge, meeting rooms, parking (fee). AE, D, DC, MC, V.*

INNS AND GUEST HOUSES

$$–$$$$　🏨 **Shellmont.** The house, on the National Register of Historic Places, was named for the shell motif that adorns it. It was designed in 1891 by Massachusetts-born, Atlanta-reared architect Walter T. Downing and has antique stained, leaded, and beveled glass, enhanced by artfully carved woodwork and charming hand-painted stencils. Guest rooms have American-made Victorian-style antiques and CD players. ✉ *821 Piedmont Ave., Midtown, 30306,* ☎ *404/872–9290 or 404/872–5379,* WEB *www.shellmont.com. 5 rooms, 2 suites, 1 carriage house. AE, D, DC, MC, V. BP.*

Buckhead and Outer Perimeter

$$$–$$$$　🏨 **Crowne Plaza Atlanta Ravinia.** You can't beat the convenience—it anchors Atlanta's Perimeter Center and is near several Fortune 500 companies, so it's perfect for convention-center attendees. It's a 10- to 20-minute trip north of Buckhead and downtown, but you don't need to travel far for shopping and other excitement because there is plenty of upscale shopping and dining nearby. All rooms are furnished opulently and have hair dryers and upscale bath amenities. ✉ *4435 Ashford-Dunwoody Rd., Dunwoody 30346,* ☎ *770/395–7700 or 800/227–6963,* ℻ *770/392–9503,* WEB *www.crowneplazaravinia.com. 459 rooms, 36 suites. 3 restaurants, tennis court, indoor pool, gym, hot tub, lounge, Internet, laundry service, free parking. AE, D, DC, MC, V.*

$$$–$$$$　🏨 **Ritz-Carlton, Buckhead.** Decorated with 18th- and 19th-century
★　　antiques and art, this is an elegant gem of a hotel. The richly paneled Lobby Lounge is a respite for shoppers from nearby Lenox Square mall and Phipps Plaza; afternoon tea or cocktails is popular here. The Dining Room is one of the city's finest restaurants; don't pass up the Wine Bar, either—the lounge hosts informative wine tastings, which both novices and aficionados attend. The spacious rooms are furnished with traditional reproductions and have luxurious white-marble baths. ✉ *3434 Peachtree Rd., Buckhead, 30326,* ☎ *404/237–2700 or 800/ 241–3333,* ℻ *404/239–0078,* WEB *www.ritzcarlton.com. 524 rooms, 29 suites. 3 restaurants, pool, health club, hot tub, bar, parking (fee). AE, D, DC, MC, V.*

$$$–$$$$　🏨 **Swissôtel.** Sleek and efficient, this stunner has a chic, modern glass and white-tile exterior with curved walls and Biedermeier-style interi-

ors. Convenient to Lenox Square mall, a prime shopping and dining destination, the hotel is popular with business travelers. The restaurant, the Palm, is noted for its steaks. ✉ *3391 Peachtree Rd., Buckhead, 30326,* ☎ *404/365–0065 or 800/253–1397,* FAX *404/365–8787,* WEB *www. swissotel.com. 349 rooms, 16 suites. Restaurant, pool, spa, gym, health club, bar, business services, parking (fee). AE, D, DC, MC, V.*

$$–$$$ 🏨 **Sheraton Buckhead.** This modern, eight-floor hotel has the advantage of being right across from the Lenox Square mall (Shangri-la to Georgians). Rooms have contemporary furnishings; some have a desk and chair, others sofas. All are equipped with amenities, such as hair dryers, coffeemakers, and irons with ironing boards. ✉ *3405 Lenox Rd., Buckhead, 30326,* ☎ *404/261–9250 or 888/625–5144,* FAX *404/ 848–7391,* WEB *www.starwood.com. 355 rooms, 7 suites. Restaurant, pool, bar, parking (fee). AE, D, DC, MC, V.*

$$–$$$ 🏨 **W Atlanta.** An ultrachic member of the W hotel chain, this Perimeter property makes good on its promise to pamper business travelers. Guest rooms are sweepingly large, with oversize wet bars and all the comforts of home (assuming your home is a dazzling showcase of impeccable taste). In your room you'll find a lush terry robe and a coffeemaker complete with the hotel's own brand of specialty coffee. Baths are outfitted with high-end-salon shampoos, conditioners, and soaps. ✉ *111 Perimeter Center W, Dunwoody 30346,* ☎ *770/396– 6800 or 888/625–5144,* FAX *770/394–4805,* WEB *www.starwood.com/ whotels. 252 rooms, 23 suites. Restaurant, pool, gym, hot tub, sauna, lounge, Internet, free parking. AE, D, DC, MC, V.*

$–$$$ 🏨 **Embassy Suites Hotel.** Just blocks from the Phipps Plaza and Lenox Square malls, this modern high-rise offers different kinds of suites— from deluxe presidential (with wet bars) to more basic sleeping- and sitting-room combinations. All rooms open to a 16-story sunlighted atrium towering above the lobby. Rates include afternoon cocktails. ✉ *3285 Peachtree Rd., Buckhead, 30305,* ☎ *404/261–7733 or 800/ 362–2779,* FAX *404/261–6857,* WEB *www.embassysuites.com. 317 suites. Restaurant, indoor pool, gym, parking (fee). AE, D, DC, MC, V. BP.*

$$ 🏨 **Doubletree Hotel.** If the complimentary fresh-baked chocolate-chip cookies that welcome you don't convince you to stay here, maybe the spacious rooms and reasonable rates—given the excellent location— will. The hotel offers complimentary transportation within 2 mi of the hotel and is adjacent to the Buckhead MARTA station. ✉ *3342 Peachtree Rd., Buckhead, 30326,* ☎ *404/231–1234 or 800/222–8733,* FAX *404/231–5236,* WEB *www.doubletree.com. 222 rooms, 8 suites. Restaurant, health club, free parking. AE, D, DC, MC, V.*

$–$$ 🏨 **Holiday Inn Select Atlanta Perimeter.** If frills come second to comfort and familiarity, consider this hotel—which generally caters to the briefcase set—with a superb location in the Perimeter business district. Rooms are reliably appointed with coffeemakers, hair dryers, and work desks. ✉ *4386 Chamblee-Dunwoody Rd., Dunwoody 30341,* ☎ *770/ 457–6363 or 800/465–4329,* FAX *770/936–9592,* WEB *www.hiselect. com/atl-perimeter. 250 rooms, 2 suites. Restaurant, pool, gym, lounge, laundry service, free parking. AE, D, DC, MC, V.*

$–$$ 🏨 **Sierra Suites Atlanta Brookhaven.** The feel is modern southwestern—rife with pastel Indian prints—at this comfortable hotel, just 1 mi north of Lenox Square. Cream-and-green color schemes decorate the one-bedroom studio suites with kitchenettes (no ovens). ✉ *3967 Peachtree Rd., Brookhaven 30319,* ☎ *404/237–9100 or 800/474–3772,* FAX *404/237–0055,* WEB *www.sierrasuites.com. 92 suites. Pool, gym, laundry service. AE, D, DC, MC, V.*

Nightlife and the Arts

The Arts

For the most complete schedule of cultural events, check the *Atlanta Journal-Constitution*'s Friday "Weekend Preview" and Saturday "Leisure" sections. Also available for cultural and entertainment listings is the city's lively and free alternative newsweekly, *Creative Loafing*.

Tickets for the Fox Theatre, Atlanta Civic Center, and other locations are handled by **TicketMaster** (☎ 404/249–6400 or 800/326–4000). **Ticket-X-Press, Inc.** (☎ 404/231–5888) is a good ticket outlet.

CONCERTS

The **Atlanta Symphony Orchestra (ASO),** now under the musical direction of Robert Spano, is now more than a half century old, with 14 Grammy awards to its credit. It performs the fall–spring subscription series in the 1,800-seat Symphony Hall at **Woodruff Arts Center** (✉ 1280 Peachtree St., Midtown, ☎ 404/733–5000). In summer the orchestra regularly plays with big-name popular and country artists in Chastain Park's **outdoor amphitheater** (✉ 4469 Stella Dr., Chastain Park, ☎ 404/733–4800).

Emory University (✉ N. Decatur Rd. at Clifton Rd., Emory, ☎ 404/727–6187, FAX 404/727–6421), an idyllic suburban campus, has four venues where both internationally renowned guest artists and faculty and student groups perform. Expect quality music from various ensembles, including woodwind, brass, jazz, and vocal.

Georgia State University (✉ Art and Music Bldg., Peachtree Center Ave. and Gilmer St., Downtown, ☎ 404/651–4636 or 404/651–3676), with the entrance on Gilmer Street and free parking at the corner of Edgewood and Peachtree Center avenues, sponsors many concerts (about 80%) that are free and open to the public. Performances by faculty, student, and local groups and guest artists focus on jazz and classical. There are also performances at the **Rialto Center for the Performing Arts** (✉ 80 Forsyth St., ☎ 404/651–4727, WEB www.rialtocenter.org), an old movie theater the university turned into a performance venue.

DANCE

The **Atlanta Ballet** (✉ 1400 W. Peachtree St., Midtown, ☎ 404/873–5811), founded in 1929, is the country's oldest continuously operating ballet company. Thanks to artistic director John McFall—who has choreographed such dance greats as Mikhail Baryshnikov and Cynthia Gregory—it has been internationally recognized for its productions of classical and contemporary works. Performances are usually at the Fox Theatre but sometimes take place elsewhere. Artistic director John McFall, only the third in the company's history, brings a constant stream of innovative ideas and vision to the group.

FESTIVALS

The **Atlanta Jazz Festival,** held Memorial Day weekend, gathers the best local, national, and international musicians to give mostly free concerts at Atlanta's Piedmont Park. For information contact the **Atlanta Bureau of Cultural Affairs** (☎ 404/817–6815, FAX 404/817–6827).

The **Montreux/Atlanta International Music Festival** began in 1988, when Atlanta joined with Montreux, Switzerland, to cohost a music festival featuring jazz, blues, gospel, reggae, and classical. The festival typically starts during Labor Day weekend, with performances in Piedmont Park (free) and Chastain Park (expensive). For information contact the **Atlanta Bureau of Cultural Affairs** (☎ 404/817–6815, FAX 404/817–6827).

OPERA

The **Atlanta Opera** (✉ 728 W. Peachtree St., Midtown, ☎ 404/881–8801 or 800/356–7372) usually mounts four main-stage productions each year from spring through fall at the Fox Theatre. Major roles are performed by national and international guest artists, while the chorus and orchestra come from the local community. Call **TicketMaster** (☎ 404/817–8700) for information.

PERFORMANCE VENUES

Atlanta Civic Center (✉ 395 Piedmont Ave., Midtown, ☎ 404/523–6275) presents touring Broadway musicals, pop music, and dance concerts.

Fox Theatre (✉ 660 Peachtree St., Midtown, ☎ 404/881–2100), a dramatic faux-Moorish theater, is the principal venue for touring Broadway shows and national productions, as well as the home of the Atlanta Opera and the Atlanta Ballet.

Georgia Tech Center for the Performing Arts (✉ 349 FerstDr., Georgia Tech, ☎ 404/894–9600), at the Georgia Institute of Technology, offers performances that run the gamut, from classical to jazz, from dance to theater. The highly regarded student-operated theater, DramaTech, is in the James E. Dull Theatre. There's ample free parking.

Rialto Center for the Performing Arts (✉ 80 Forsyth St., Downtown, ☎ 404/651–4727), developed by Georgia State University in a beautifully renovated and restructured former movie theater, shows film, theater, and dance, as well as musical performances by local and international performers.

Spivey Hall (campus: ✉ 5900 N. Lee St., Morrow, ☎ 770/961–3683) is a gleaming, modern, acoustically magnificent performance center at Clayton College and State University, 15 mi south of Atlanta in Morrow. The hall is considered one of the country's finest concert venues. Internationally renowned musicians perform everything from chamber music to jazz.

Variety Playhouse (✉ 1099 Euclid Ave., Inman Park, ☎ 404/524–7354), a former movie theater, is one of the cultural anchors of the hip Little Five Pointsneighborhood. Its denizens don't don fancy frocks to listen to rock, bluegrass and country, blues, reggae, folk, jazz, and pop.

Woodruff Arts Center (✉ 1280 Peachtree St., Midtown, ☎ 404/733–4200) houses the Alliance Theatre and the Atlanta Symphony Orchestra.

THEATER

Check local newspaper listings for information on the outstanding companies in Atlanta and its suburbs.

Actor's Express (✉ 887 W. Marietta St., Downtown, ☎ 404/607–7469), an acclaimed theater group, presents an eclectic selection of classic and cutting-edge productions in the 150-seat theater of the **King Plow Arts Center** (✉ 887 W. Marietta St., ☎ 404/885–9933, WEB www.kingplow.com), a stylish artists' complex hailed by local critics as a showplace of industrial chic. For an evening of dining and theater, plan dinner at the Food Studio, at the King Plow Arts Center.

Alliance Theatre (✉ 1280 Peachtree St., Midtown, ☎ 404/733–4200), Atlanta's premier professional theater, presents everything, from Shakespeare to the latest Broadway and off-Broadway shows from New York, in the Woodruff Arts Center.

↻ **Atlanta Shakespeare Tavern** (✉ 499 Peachtree St., Midtown, ☎ 404/ 874–5299) produces plays by the Bard and his peers, as well as by contemporary dramatists. Performances vary in quality but are always fun. The Elizabethan-style playhouse is a tavern, so alcohol and pub-style food are available. It also houses the Kaleidoscope Children's Theater (same phone), which presents classics, such as *The New Adventures of the Three Musketeers,* on most weekends during the day.

14th Street Playhouse (✉ 175 14th St., Midtown, ☎ 404/733–4750 or 404/733–4754) is part of the Woodruff Arts Center. The house has three theaters, a 400-seat main stage, a 200-seat second stage, and an 90-seat third stage, which are rented for special productions. There is no resident company. Musicals, plays, and sometimes opera are presented.

Horizon Theatre Co. (✉ 1083 Austin Ave., Little Five Points, Inman Park, ☎ 404/584–7450) is a professional troupe that was established in 1983; it produces premieres of provocative and entertaining contemporary plays in its 185-seat theater.

Nightlife

The pursuit of entertainment—from Midtown to Buckhead—is known as the "Peachtree shuffle." Atlanta's vibrant nightlife includes everything from coffeehouses to sports bars, from country line dancing to high-energy dance clubs. Atlanta has long been known for having more bars than churches, and in the South that's an oddity.

Most bars and clubs are open seven nights, until 2 AM–4 AM. Those with live entertainment usually charge a cover.

ACOUSTIC

Eddie's Attic (✉ 515B N. McDonough St., Decatur, ☎ 404/377–4976) is a good spot for catching local and some national acoustic, folk, pop, and country-music acts. It has a full bar and restaurant and is right near the Decatur MARTA station. Covers range from $6 to $12.

BARS

The **Beluga Martini Bar** (✉ 3115 Piedmont Rd., Buckhead, ☎ 404/ 869–1090) has caviar, smoked salmon, champagne by the glass, and other light fare in an intimate, comfortable space with live music.

For Irish fun, food, beer, and music (both live and on CD), head to **Irish Bred Pub & Grill** (✉ 94 Upper Pryor St., Downtown, ☎ 404/524– 5722). The food ranges from *boxty* (potato pancakes with savory fillings) to Irish stew made with lamb, cottage pie, and whiskey trifle.

Limerick Junction (✉ 822 N. Highland Ave., Virginia-Highland, ☎ 404/ 874–7147), a lively Irish pub, showcases singers from the large Atlanta community that ably render traditional Irish music, as well as performers from the Old Sod itself. It has a rollicking, good-time feeling about it. Parking is dreadful, so consider a cab. A small cover may be charged.

Manuel's Tavern (✉ 602 N. Highland Ave., Virginia-Highland, ☎ 404/ 525–3447) is a neighborhood saloon where families, politicians, writers, students, and professionals gather to brainstorm and partake of the tavern's menu of pleasantly upscale pub food. When the Atlanta Braves play, the crowd gathers around the wide-screen TVs.

Vortex (✉ 898 Peachtree St., Midtown, ☎ 404/875–1667) has a friendly style, knowledgeable bartenders, live bands, and hearty pub fare, making it a local favorite.

To make it through the door at **Tongue & Groove** (✉ 3055 Peachtree Rd., Buckhead, ☎ 404/261–2325), you must dress up—long dresses for ladies and jackets for men. Live music—sometimes rock, sometimes salsa—alternates with recorded tunes. The light-fare menu is as chic as the sense of style here. Covers range from $5 to $10, depending on the program.

COMEDY

The **Punchline** (✉ 280 Hilderbrand Dr., Balconies Shopping Center, Sandy Springs, ☎ 404/252–5233), Atlanta's oldest comedy club, books major national acts. The small club is popular, so you need a reservation. Cover charges vary and can be upward of $20 for some acts, but it's usually worth it.

COUNTRY

Buckboard Country Music Showcase (✉ 2080 Cobb Pkwy., Windy Hill, ☎ 770/955–7340), a 425-seat house, has a large dance floor, pool tables, and two full bars; it serves food of the hamburgers, nachos, and chicken fingers variety. The house band is the Buckboard Bandits, and Nashville-based bands play on Thursday night. The cover charge is $5–$10.

The 44,000-square-ft **Cowboys Concert Hall** (✉ 1750 N. Roberts Rd., Kennesaw, ☎ 770/426–5006) attracts national talent twice monthly on Friday. On Wednesday, Thursday, Friday, and Sunday, line-dancing classes and couple-dancing lessons are taught. The cover is $5, unless an unusually high-profile act is slated.

GAY AND LESBIAN

Backstreet (✉ 845 Peachtree St., Midtown, ☎ 404/873–1986), though it draws men and women of all affinities, has been Midtown's mainstay gay club for nearly two decades. Downstairs is the dance floor with recorded music, and upstairs is Charlie Brown's Cabaret, with female impersonators. As the club is open 24 hours, membership is required; quarterly memberships cost $10, entitling cardholders to free admission Sunday through Thursday and $5 covers Friday and Saturday.

JAZZ AND BLUES

Blind Willie's (✉ 828 N. Highland Ave., Virginia-Highland, ☎ 404/873–2583) showcases New Orleans– and Chicago-style blues that sends crowds into a frenzy. The name honors Blind Willie McTell, a native of Thomson, Georgia, whose original compositions include "Statesboro Blues," made popular by the Macon, Georgia–based Allman Brothers. Cajun and zydeco are also on the agenda from time to time. Cover charges run in the $10 range.

Dante's Down the Hatch (✉ 3380 Peachtree Rd., Buckhead, ☎ 404/266–1600) is popular for its music and sultry sensibility. Regular entertainers include the Paul Mitchell Trio, which conjures silky-smooth jazz in the "hold" of a make-believe sailing ship.

Fuzzy's Place (✉ 2015 N. Druid Hills Rd., Druid Hills, ☎ 404/321–6166), a crowded and smoke-filled neighborhood bar, begins the day by serving lunch to the denizens of nearby office buildings. By night it's a restaurant with a surprisingly sophisticated menu, sports bar, and blues room. The finest local talent holds forth on the stage, including the venerable Francine Reed, one of Atlanta's favorite entertainers. There's usually no cover.

Sambuca Jazz Cafe (✉ 3102 Piedmont Rd., Buckhead, ☎ 404/237–5299), with decent dining, a lively bar, and good live jazz, attracts a trendy young set.

Whiskers (⊠ 8371 Roswell Rd., in a shopping center at Northridge Rd., Sandy Springs, ☎ 770/992–7445) hosts blues and rock groups, with some of the best local talent. There's no cover.

ROCK

Masquerade (⊠ 695 North Ave., Poncey-Highland; ☎ 404/577–8178) is a grunge hangout with music, from disco to techno, from industrial rock to swing. Basic bar food is available. The mix of people reflects the club's three separate spaces, dubbed Heaven, Hell, and Purgatory. The cover is $2–$10.

Smith's Olde Bar (⊠ 1578 Piedmont Ave., Ansley Park, ☎ 404/875–1522) schedules different kinds of talent, both local and regional, in its acoustically fine performance space. Food is available in the downstairs restaurant. Covers vary depending on the act but are usually $5–$10.

Star Community Bar (⊠ 437 Moreland Ave., Inman Park, ☎ 404/681–9018) is highly recommended for those who enjoy garage bands and rockabilly. Bands are featured almost nightly, with covers varying depending on the act. The bar is fully equipped, with an all-Elvis jukebox and an Elvis shrine that must be seen to be believed.

Outdoor Activities and Sports

Participant Sports

At almost any time of the year, in parks, private clubs, and neighborhoods throughout the city, you'll find Atlantans pursuing everything from tennis to soccer to rollerblading. **Atlanta Sports & Fitness** magazine (☎ 404/843–2257), available free at many health clubs and sports and outdoors stores, is a good link to Atlanta's athletic community. Pick up **Georgia Athlete** at gyms and sports stores if you need a guide to individual sporting events.

BIKING AND ROLLERBLADING

Piedmont Park (⊠ Piedmont Ave. between 10th St. and the Prado, Piedmont Park) is closed to traffic and is popular for rollerblading and other recreational activities. **Skate Escape** (⊠ 1086 Piedmont Ave., across from the park, Midtown, ☎ 404/892–1292) rents bikes and skates.

GOLF

Golf is enormously popular here, as the large number of courses attest. The only public course within sight of downtown Atlanta is the **Bobby Jones Golf Course** (⊠ 384 Woodward Way, Buckhead, ☎ 404/355–1009), named after the famed golfer and Atlanta native and occupying a portion of the site of the Battle of Peachtree Creek. Despite having some of the city's worst fairways and greens, the immensely popular 18-hole, par-71 course is always crowded. At Chastain Park, the 18-hole, par-71 **North Fulton Golf Course** (⊠ 216 W. Wieuca Rd., Sandy Springs, ☎ 404/255–0723) has one of the best layouts and lies within the I–285 perimeter.

Stone Mountain Park (⊠ U.S. 78, Stone Mountain, ☎ 770/498–5715) has two courses. Stonemont, an 18-hole, par-72 course with several challenging and scenic holes, is the better of the two. The other course, Lakemont, is also 18-hole, par 72.

JOGGING AND RUNNING

Chattahoochee National Recreation Area contains different parcels of land that lie in 16 separate units spread along the banks of the Chattahoochee River, much of which has been protected from development. The area is crisscrossed by 70 mi of trails. ⊠ 1978 Island Ford Pkwy., Roswell, ☎ 770/399–8070. ☉ Daily 7–7.

Bitsy Grant Tennis Center (✉ 2125 Northside Dr., Buckhead, ☎ 404/609–7193), named for one of Atlanta's best-known players, is the area's best public facility, with 13 clay courts (6 of which are lighted) and 10 lighted hard courts. Charges are $2 per person per hour for the hard courts during the day and $2.50 at night (courts close around 10 PM), $3–$3.50 for the clay courts, which close around 7 PM. The clubhouse closes at 8 PM.

Piedmont Park, Atlanta's most popular park, has 12 lighted hard courts. Access the tennis center from Park Drive off Monroe Drive; even though the sign says DO NOT ENTER, the security guard will show you the parking lot. Courts are always open, but personnel keep specific hours. Costs are $1.50 per person per hour before 6 PM and $1.75 after 6. ✉ *Piedmont Ave. between 10th St. and the Prado, Midtown.* ☎ FAX *404/853–3461.* ⊙ *Weekdays 9–9, weekends 9:30–6.*

Spectator Sports

BASEBALL

Major League Baseball's best overall team the past decade, the **Atlanta Braves** (✉ Turner Field, I–75/85, Exit 246 [Fulton St.]; I–20, westbound Exit 58A [Capitol Ave.], eastbound Exit 56B [Windsor St./Spring St.], Downtown, ☎ 404/522–7630) play in Turner Field, formerly the Olympic Stadium.

BASKETBALL

The **Atlanta Hawks** (✉ Philips Arena, 1 CNN Center, Downtown, ☎ 404/827–3800) had a proud Olympics moment in '96 when then-coach Lenny Wilkens was selected to head the U.S. Olympic men's basketball team in Atlanta.

FOOTBALL

The **Atlanta Falcons** (✉ Georgia Dome, 1 Georgia Dome Dr., Downtown, ☎ 404/223–9200, WEB www.atlantafalcons.com), currently under coach Dan Reeves, have made the playoffs seven times in their history.

HOCKEY

The National Hockey League's young **Atlanta Thrashers** (✉ Philips Arena, 1 CNN Center, Downtown, ☎ 404/827–5300, WEB www.atlantathrashers.com) debuted during the 1999–2000 season. Named for the state bird, the brown thrasher, the team is backed by Atlanta's sports and media mogul Ted Turner.

Shopping

Atlanta's department stores, specialty shops, large enclosed malls, and antiques markets draw shoppers from across the Southeast. Most stores are open Monday–Saturday 10–9, Sunday noon–6. Many downtown stores close Sunday. Sales tax is 7% in the city of Atlanta and Fulton County and 6%–7% in the suburbs.

Shopping Centers

Brookwood Square (✉ 2140 Peachtree Rd., Buckhead) is an arrangement of unusual shops, including the Vespermann Gallery and the Piano Gallery, Atlanta's Steinway dealership.

Buckhead, a village with many specialty shops and strip malls, is no minor shopping destination. At Peachtree Plaza, at the intersection of Peachtree Road and Mathieson Drive, you'll find Beverly Bremer's Silver Shop, devoted to fine antique silver, and Irish Crystal Co., offering fine cut glass and linens. Down Maple Drive off Peachtree Road you'll find Yesteryear, dealing in antique books, next to the Atlanta Guitar Center. Boutiques and gift shops, and some fine restaurants, line

Grandview Avenue (off Peachtree Road), and another similar collection runs down East Shadowlawn Avenue. East Village Square (Buckhead Avenue and Bolling Way) has art galleries and restaurants. Across from Lenox Square, the Around Lenox Shopping Center includes Tower Records–Video–Books. Andrews Square, on East Andrews Drive, is a good conglomeration of shops, eateries, nightspots, and galleries. Next to it, Cates Center has similar stores.

Lenox Square mall (✉ 3393 Peachtree Rd., Buckhead, ☎ 404/233–6767, WEB www.shopsimon.com), one of Atlanta's oldest and most popular shopping centers, has branches of Neiman Marcus, Rich's (the regional department store), Crate & Barrel, and Macy's looming next to specialty shops such as Geode (fine art jewelry) and Mori (luggage and travel gifts). You'll do better at one of the several good restaurants here—even for a quick meal—than at the food court.

Peachtree Center Mall (✉ 231 Peachtree St., Downtown, ☎ 404/524–3787), downtown, does steady business. Stores here are chiefly specialty shops, such as International Records and Tapes, the Architectural Book Center, and the Atlanta International Museum gift shop.

Perimeter Mall (✉ 4400 Ashford-Dunwoody Rd., Dunwoody), known for upscale family shopping, has Nordstrom, the High Museum of Art Gift Shop, Gap Kids, and the Nature Company, as well as branches of Rich's, Sears Roebuck, and JCPenney, and a good food court.

Phipps Plaza (✉ 3500 Peachtree Rd., Buckhead, ☎ 404/262–0992 or 800/810–7700, WEB www.shopsimon.com) has branches of Tiffany & Co., Saks Fifth Avenue, Birmingham-based Parisian, Lord & Taylor, and Abercrombie & Fitch alongside such shops as Skippy Musket (unique jewelry, collectibles, and decorative items for the home).

Underground (✉ 50 Upper Alabama St., Downtown, ☎ 404/523–2311) has galleries, such as African Pride, with objets d'art from Africa; specialty shops, including Hats Under Atlanta; and Habersham Vineyard & Winery, a tasting room for Georgia wines. The classic chicory-laced New Orleans coffee and beignets at Café du Monde are the perfect way to refuel.

Outlets

The interstate highways leading to Atlanta have discount malls similar to those found throughout the country. Worth noting is the huge cluster around both sides of Exit 149 off I–85, 60 mi north of the city. Also, the **North Georgia Premium Outlets** mall (✉ 800 Rte. 400, at Dawson Forest Rd., Dawsonville, ☎ 706/216–3609) is worth the 45 minutes it takes to get there from Atlanta's northern perimeter. This shopping center has more than 140 stores, including Williams-Sonoma for cookware; OshKosh B'gosh, a clothing store for children; Music for a Song, dealing in discount CDs and tapes; Stone Mountain Handbags, specializing in quality leather goods; and numerous designer outlet shops not found in most malls.

Specialty Shops

ANTIQUES

Buckhead has several antiques shops, most of them along or near Peachtree Road; expect rare goods and high prices here. Venture into Virginia-Highland and the city's suburban towns to find all sorts of treasures.

Bennett Street (✉ 116 Bennett St., Buckhead, ☎ 404/352–4430, WEB www.buckhead.org/bennettstreet) has art galleries, including Out of the Woods; antiques shops, such as Kelim; and a good restaurant, **Fratelli**

di Napoli (✉ 2101B Tula St., Buckhead, ☎ 404/351–1533), making it easy to spend an entire day here. The Stalls on Bennett Street is a good antiques market.

Chamblee Antique Row, at Peachtree Road and Broad Street in the suburban town of Chamblee just north of Buckhead and about 10 mi north of downtown, is a browser's delight. For information contact the Chamblee Antique Dealers Association (☎ 770/458–1614, WEB www.antiquerow.com).

Little Five Points (✉ Moreland and Euclid Aves., Inman Park) attracts "junking" addicts, who find happiness in Atlanta's version of Greenwich Village, characterized by vintage clothing stores, art galleries, used-record and -book shops, and some stores that defy description.

Miami Circle, off Piedmont Road, is an upscale enclave for antiques and decorative arts lovers. Drop in for a snack at Eclipse di Luna (✉ Miami Circle, Buckhead, ☎ 404/846–0449).

Stone Mountain Village (✉ Main St., Stone Mountain, ☎ 770/879–4971 for visitor center) is a 19th-century village beside a railroad track at the foot of Stone Mountain. Storefronts are exquisitely decorated at holiday time. Shops of note include **Stone Mountain Handbags Factory Store** (☎ 770/498–1316), which sells designer bags, such as Coach and Dooney & Bourke, at discount prices. **Stone Mountain General Store** (☎ 770/469–9331) is a quaint outpost offering bulk items, handmade crafts, and nickel candy. The village is 17 mi from downtown. For a quick snack have a coffee milkshake at **Continental Park Café** (✉ 941 Main St., Stone Mountain, ☎ 770/413–6448).

2300 Peachtree Road is one of Buckhead's most stylish complexes—it has more than 25 antiques shops, art galleries, and enough home furnishing stores to fill multiple mansions (✉ just north of Midtown, near Peachtree Memorial Dr. intersection, Buckhead).

Virginia-Highland is one of the city's gentrified areas, full of art galleries, restaurants, fashionable boutiques, antiques shops, and bookstores. Atlanta designer **Bill Hallman** (✉ 792 N. Highland Ave., Virginia-Highland, ☎ 404/876–6055) showcases his own designs at his eponymous boutique. There's lots of memorabilia from **20th Century Antiques** (✉ 1044 N. Highland Ave., Virginia-Highland, ☎ 404/892–2065).

ART GALLERIES

The city bursts with art galleries—some well established, others new, some conservative, others cutting edge. For more information on the Atlanta art gallery scene, including openings and location maps, consult *Museums & Galleries* (☎ 770/992–7808), a magazine distributed free at welcome centers and select area galleries.

Fay Gold Gallery (✉ 247 Buckhead Ave., East Village Sq., Buckhead, ☎ 404/233–3843) displays works by nationally renowned contemporary artists. **Jackson Fine Art Gallery** (✉ 3115 E. Shadowlawn Ave., Buckhead, ☎ 404/233–3739) exhibits fine art photography. **Modern Primitive** (✉ 1393 N. Highland Ave., Virginia-Highland, ☎ 404/892–0556) has a fascinating assembly of folk and visionary art from around the state and the region. **Marcia Wood Gallery** (✉ 1831 Peachtree St., Buckhead, ☎ 404/351–5709) shows exquisite original paintings by such notable artists as Daniel Troppy and Ruth Laxson. **Vespermann Gallery** (✉ 2140 Peachtree Rd., Brookwood Sq., Buckhead, ☎ 404/350–9698) has lovely handblown glass objects.

Chapter 11 (✉ 6237 Roswell Rd., Sandy Springs, ☎ 404/256–5518) is a great place to find recently published titles at good prices. **Yesteryear** (✉ 3201 Maple Dr., Buckhead, ☎ 404/237–0163) is the destination of choice for antiquarians. Its strengths include military history, Georgiana, and old cookbooks.

DeKalb Farmers Market (✉ 3000 E. Ponce de Leon Ave., Decatur, ☎ 404/377–6400) has 175,000 square ft of exotic fruits, cheeses, seafood, sausages, breads, and delicacies from around the world. The cafeteria-style buffet, with a selection of earthy and delicious hot foods and salads, alone is worth the trip. **East 48th St. Market** (✉ 2462 Jett Ferry Rd., at Mt. Vernon Rd., Williams at Dunwoody Shopping Center, Dunwoody, ☎ 770/392–1499) sells Italian deli meats, fabulous breads, cheeses, and Italian prepared foods. Shop at **Eatzi's Market & Bakery** (✉ 3221 Peachtree Rd., Buckhead, ☎ 404/237–2266) for prepared foods, imported cheeses, great breads, and fine wines. The healthwise can take comfort at **Whole Foods Market** (✉ 2111 Briarcliff Rd., Druid Hills, ☎ 404/634–7800), with a dizzying amount of additive- and pesticide-free foods and baked goods.

Atlanta A to Z

To research prices, get advice from other travelers, and book travel arrangements, visit www.fodors.com

AIR TRAVEL TO AND FROM ATLANTA

Atlanta is served by AirTran, America West, American, Atlantic Southeast Airlines, Continental, Delta, GP Express, Markair, Midwest Express, National, Northwest, TWA, United, and US Airways, as well as many international carriers.

AIRPORTS AND TRANSFERS

Hartsfield Atlanta International Airport is 13 mi south of downtown.
➤ AIRPORT INFORMATION: **Hartsfield Atlanta International Airport** (✉ 6000 N. Terminal Pkwy., Hapeville, ☎ 404/530–6600, WEB www.atlanta-airport.com).

Atlanta Airport Shuttle operates vans every quarter hour between 7 AM and 11 PM daily. The downtown trip, $14 one-way, $22 round-trip, takes about 20 minutes and stops at major hotels. Vans also go to the Buckhead/Lenox area: $20 one-way, $30 round-trip.

If your luggage is light, take MARTA (Metropolitan Atlanta Rapid Transit Authority) high-speed trains between the airport and downtown and other locations. Trains operate 5 AM–1 AM weekdays and 6 AM–12:30 AM weekends. The trip downtown takes about 15 minutes to the Five Points station, and the fare is $1.75.

From the airport to downtown the taxi fare is $22 for one person, $26 for two, and $30 for three or more, including tax. From the airport to Buckhead, the fare is $35 for one, $36 for two, and $39 for three or more. With a reasonable advance reservation, Carey-Executive Limousine will provide 24-hour service. Buckhead Safety Cab and Checker Cab offer 24-hour service.
➤ TAXIS AND SHUTTLES: **Airport Shuttle Bus** (☎ 770/932–9127). **Atlanta Airport Shuttle** (☎ 404/766–5312). **Buckhead Safety Cab** (☎ 404/233–1152). **Carey-Executive Limousine** (☎ 404/223–2000). **Checker Cab** (☎ 404/351–1111). **MARTA** (☎ 404/848–4711).

BUS TRAVEL TO AND FROM ATLANTA

Greyhound Bus Lines provides transportation to downtown Atlanta. Amtrak operates its Thru-Way bus service daily from Birmingham and Mobile, Alabama, to Atlanta's Brookwood station. Another bus goes daily from the station to Macon.

➤ BUS INFORMATION: **Amtrak** (✉ 1688 Peachtree St., Buckhead, ☎ 404/881–3060 or 800/872–7245, WEB www.amtrak.com). **Greyhound Bus Lines** (✉ 232 Forsyth St., Downtown, ☎ 404/584–1731 or 800/231–2222, WEB www.greyhound.com).

BUS TRAVEL WITHIN ATLANTA

The Metropolitan Atlanta Rapid Transit Authority (MARTA), with a fleet of about 700 buses, operates 150 routes covering 1,500 mi. The fare is $1.75, and exact change is required. Weekly and monthly Trans-Cards give you a slight discount. Service is very limited outside the perimeter set by I–285, except for a few areas in Clayton, DeKalb, and Fulton counties.

➤ BUS INFORMATION: **Metropolitan Atlanta Rapid Transit Authority** (☎ 404/848–4711).

CAR TRAVEL

The city is encircled by I–285. Three interstates—I–85, running northeast–southwest from Virginia to Alabama; I–75, north–south from Michigan to Florida; and I–20, east–west from South Carolina to Texas—also crisscross Atlanta.

TRAFFIC

Some refer to Atlanta as the Los Angeles of the South, because driving is virtually the only way to get to most parts of the city. Although the congestion hasn't quite caught up to L.A.'s, Atlantans have grown accustomed to frequent delays at rush hour—the morning and late-afternoon commuting periods seem to get longer every year. Beware: the South as a whole may be laid-back, but Atlanta drivers are not; they tend to drive faster than drivers in other Southern cities.

EMERGENCIES

For 24-hour emergency rooms contact Georgia Baptist Medical Center, Grady Memorial Hospital, Northside Hospital, and Piedmont Hospital.

➤ EMERGENCY SERVICES: **Ambulance, police** (☎ 911).

➤ HOSPITALS: **Georgia Baptist Medical Center** (✉ 303 Parkway Dr., Downtown, ☎ 404/265–4000). **Grady Memorial Hospital** (✉ 80 Butler St., Downtown, ☎ 404/616–4307). **Northside Hospital** (✉ 1000 Johnson Ferry Rd., Dunwoody, ☎ 404/851–8000). **Piedmont Hospital** (✉ 1968 Peachtree Rd., Buckhead, ☎ 404/605–5000).

➤ 24-HOUR PHARMACIES: **CVS** (✉ 1943 Peachtree Rd., Buckhead, ☎ 404/351–7629; ✉ 1554 N. Decatur Rd., Emory, ☎ 404/373–4192; ✉ 2350 Cheshire Bridge Rd., Buckhead, ☎ 404/486–7289).

LODGING

BED-AND-BREAKFASTS

Bed & Breakfast Online can provide detailed cyber-brochures on inns in Atlanta and the surrounding Georgia territory.

➤ RESERVATION INFORMATION: **Bed & Breakfast Online** (✉ Box 829, Madison, TN 37116, WEB www.bbonline.com/ga, ☎ 615/868–1946).

SUBWAY TRAVEL

MARTA has clean and safe rapid-rail subway trains with somewhat limited routes that link downtown with many major landmarks. The system's two main lines cross at the Five Points station downtown. Trans-Cards and information on public transportation are available at Rides

Stores, open weekdays 7–7 and Saturday 8:30–5; Rides Stores are at the airport, Five Points station, the headquarters building by Lindbergh station, and Lenox station. You can also buy TransCards at Kroger and Publix groceries. Obtain free transfers, needed for some bus routes, by pressing a button on the subway turnstile or requesting one from the driver.

FARES AND SCHEDULES
Trains run 5 AM–1 AM, and large parking lots (free) are at most stations beyond downtown. Tokens ($1.75 each) can be bought from machines outside each station.
➤ SUBWAY INFORMATION: **MARTA** (☎ 404/848–4711, WEB www. itsmarta.com).

TAXIS
Taxi service in Atlanta can be uneven. Drivers often lack correct change, so be prepared either to charge your fare (many accept credit cards) or insist that the driver obtain change. Drivers can also appear as befuddled as you may be by Atlanta's notoriously winding and hilly streets, so if your destination is something other than a major hotel or popular sight, come with directions.

Taxi fares start at $2 on entry, $1.75 for the first mile, with 25¢ for each additional ¼ mi, $1 per extra passenger, and $18 per hour of waiting time. Within the Downtown Convention Zone a flat rate of $6 for one person plus $1 per additional passenger will be charged for any destination. Buckhead Safety Cab and Checker Cab offer 24-hour service.
➤ TAXI COMPANIES: **Buckhead Safety Cab** (☎ 404/233–1152). **Checker Cab** (☎ 404/351–1111).

TOURS
BUS TOURS
Gray Line of Atlanta has tours of downtown, Midtown, Buckhead, the King Center, and sometimes Stone Mountain.
➤ FEES AND SCHEDULES: **Gray Line of Atlanta** (☎ 770/449–1806 or 800/ 593–1818, FAX 770/249–9397, WEB www.americancoachlines.com/ Grayline.htm).

WALKING TOURS
The Atlanta Preservation Center offers several walking tours of historic areas and neighborhoods for $10 each; tours usually last from one to two hours. Especially noteworthy are tours of Sweet Auburn, the neighborhood associated with Martin Luther King Jr. and other leaders of Atlanta's African-American community; Druid Hills, the verdant, genteel neighborhood where *Driving Miss Daisy* was filmed; and the Fox Theatre, the elaborate 1920s picture palace.
➤ FEES AND SCHEDULES: **Atlanta Preservation Center** (☎ 404/876– 2041; 404/876–2040 for tour hot line, WEB www.preserveatlanta.com).

TRAIN TRAVEL
Amtrak operates the *Crescent* train, with daily service to Atlanta's Brookwood station from New York; Philadelphia; Washington, D.C.; Baltimore; Charlotte, North Carolina; and Greenville, South Carolina. It also goes daily from New Orleans to New York through Atlanta.
➤ TRAIN INFORMATION: **Amtrak** (✉ 1688 Peachtree St., Buckhead, ☎ 404/881–3060 or 800/872–7245, WEB www.amtrak.com).

VISITOR INFORMATION
The Atlanta Convention & Visitors Bureau (ACVB) has information on Atlanta and the outlying area. The ACVB has several visitor in-

formation centers in Atlanta: Hartsfield Atlanta International Airport, in the atrium of the main ticketing terminal; Underground Atlanta; Georgia World Congress Center; and Lenox Square mall.

➤ TOURIST INFORMATION: **Atlanta Convention & Visitors Bureau** (✉ 233 Peachtree St., Suite 2000, Downtown, 30303, ☎ 404/222–6688 or 800/285–2682, www.atlanta.net; ✉ Underground Atlanta, 65 Upper Alabama St., Downtown; Georgia World Congress Center, 285 International Blvd., Downtown, ☎ 404/223–4000, WEB www.gwcc.com; ✉ Lenox Mall, 3393 Peachtree Rd., Buckhead; WEB www.shopsimon.com).

SAVANNAH

The very sound of the name *Savannah* conjures up misty images of mint juleps, handsome mansions, and a somewhat decadent city moving at a lazy Southern pace. It's hard even to say "Savannah" without drawling. Well, brace yourself. The mint juleps are there all right, along with the moss and the mansions and the easygoing pace, but this Southern belle rings with surprises. Take, for example, St. Patrick's Day: Savannah has a St. Patrick's Day celebration second only to New York's. The greening of Savannah began in 1812, and everybody in town talks a blue (green) streak about St. Patrick's Day. Everything turns green on March 17, including scrambled eggs and grits.

Savannah's modern history began on February 12, 1733, when English general James Edward Oglethorpe and 120 colonists arrived at Yamacraw Bluff on the Savannah River to found the 13th and last colony in the New World. As the port city grew, people from England and Ireland, Scottish Highlanders, French Huguenots, Germans, Austrian Salzburgers, Sephardic and Ashkenazic Jews, Moravians, Italians, Swiss, Welsh, and Greeks all arrived to create what could be called a rich gumbo.

In 1793 Eli Whitney of Connecticut, who was tutoring on a plantation near Savannah, invented a mechanized means of "ginning" seeds from cotton bolls. Cotton soon became king, and Savannah, already a busy seaport, flourished under its reign. Waterfront warehouses were filled with "white gold," and brokers trading in the Savannah Cotton Exchange set world prices. The white gold brought in solid gold, and fine mansions were built in the prospering city.

In 1864 Savannahians surrendered their city to Union general Sherman rather than see it torched. Later, following World War I and the decline of the cotton market, the city's economy virtually collapsed, and its historic buildings languished for more than 30 years. Elegant mansions were razed or allowed to decay, and cobwebs replaced cotton in the dilapidated riverfront warehouses.

In 1955 Savannah's spirits rose again. News that the exquisite Isaiah Davenport House (✉ 324 E. State St.) was to be destroyed prompted seven outraged ladies to raise money to buy the house. They saved it the day before the wrecking ball was to swing. Thus was born the Historic Savannah Foundation, the organization responsible for the restoration of downtown Savannah, where more than 1,000 restored buildings form the 2½-square-mi Historic District, the nation's largest. Many of these buildings are open to the public during the annual tour of homes, and today Savannah is one of the country's top 10 cities for walking tours.

John Berendt's wildly popular *Midnight in the Garden of Good and Evil* has lured many people to Savannah since the book's publication in 1994. A nonfiction account of a notorious 1980s shooting, the book brings to life such Savannah sites as Monterey Square, Mercer House, and Bonaventure Cemetery. Clint Eastwood's film adaptation, only loosely based on the book, was neither a box-office nor a critical success, but the public's interest in Savannah has remained intense—to the consternation of old-timers who find the story's characters less than savory and the nosy Northerners a nuisance. Other Savannahians have rolled out the welcome mat, while still others have hiked prices, profiting from the tourist dollars.

Georgia's founder, General James Oglethorpe, laid out the city on a perfect grid. The Historic District is neatly hemmed in by the Savannah River, Gaston Street, East Street, and Martin Luther King Jr. Boulevard. Streets are arrow-straight, public squares of varying sizes are tucked into the grid at precise intervals, and each block is sliced in half by narrow, often unpaved streets. Bull Street, anchored on the north by City Hall and the south by Forsyth Park, charges down the center of the grid and lunges around the five public squares that stand in its way.

Numbers in the text correspond to numbers in the margin and on the Savannah Historic District map.

The Historic District

A Good Walk and Drive

You can cover historic Savannah on foot, but to save time and energy, you might want to drive part of this tour. Start at the **Savannah Visitors Center** ⑯, on Martin Luther King Jr. Boulevard. In the same building, the **Savannah History Museum** ⑰ is an ideal introduction to the city's history. There is public parking next to the center and museum.

Exit the parking lot and turn left (north), walking or driving two short and one very long blocks on Martin Luther King Jr. Boulevard to the **Scarborough House** ⑱, which contains the Ships of the Sea Museum. Cross Martin Luther King Jr. Boulevard and continue two blocks east on West Congress Street, past Franklin Square to **City Market** ⑲. Skirting around Franklin Square north on Montgomery Street, go two blocks to West Bay Street and turn right.

From this point continue east on West Bay Street four blocks to Bull Street. On your left you'll see **City Hall** ⑳. Continue east along West Bay Street (which now becomes East Bay Street) to **Factors Walk** ㉑, which lies south of River Street and the Savannah River. If you're driving, leave your car here to continue on foot (be sure to choose long-term parking, as the short-term meters are monitored vigilantly). Step down from Factors Walk toward the river and visit **Riverfront Plaza** ㉒, which is best seen on foot.

At this point, if you're driving, you'll probably want to get back in your car to continue the tour. Return to East Bay Street and head west two long blocks back to Bull Street. Walk four blocks south on Bull Street to **Wright Square** ㉓; then turn right (west) and go two blocks to Telfair Square, where you can stop at the **Telfair Mansion and Art Museum** ㉔. Stroll around Telfair Square and then continue east on West York Street back toward Wright Square, and turn right on Bull Street, heading two blocks south to the **Juliette Gordon Low Birthplace/Girl Scout National Center** ㉕. Two more short blocks south from the Low House on Bull Street, and you'll reach **Chippewa Square** ㉖. Continue south on Bull Street to the Gothic Revival **Green-Meldrim House** ㉗. Next, walk four blocks south on Bull Street to **Monterey Square** ㉘. Proceed two blocks farther south from Monterey Square to **Forsyth Park** ㉙, the divide between East and West Gaston streets.

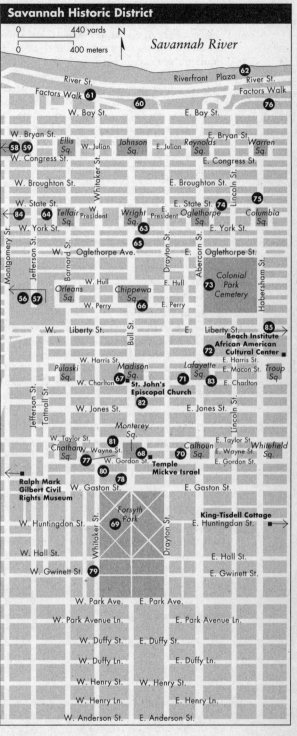

Savannah Historic District

From the park walk east on East Gaston Street and go one block to Abercorn Street; then turn left (north) on Abercorn Street to Calhoun Square and note the **Wesley Monumental Church** ⑦⓪. Continue north on Abercorn four blocks to Lafayette Square and view the **Andrew Low House** ⑦①. Northeast of Lafayette Square looms the **Cathedral of St. John the Baptist** ⑦②, on East Harris Street. Two blocks north, at the intersection of Abercorn and East Oglethorpe streets, is the huge **Colonial Park Cemetery** ⑦③. Proceeding two blocks north on Abercorn Street from the cemetery takes you to Oglethorpe Square; across from the square is the **Owens-Thomas House and Museum** ⑦④. From the house walk east on East President Street two blocks to Columbia Square. Northwest of the square on East State Street stands the **Isaiah Davenport House** ⑦⑤. From here continue north up Habersham Street to **Emmet Park** ⑦⑥, a splendid park to relax in at the end of your tour.

TIMING

This is a long but comfortable walk, as Savannah has no taxing hills. Allow a full day to see everything along this route, especially if you plan to read all the historic markers and explore the sights thoroughly, stopping for tours. Driving around the squares can be slow—but you can drive the entire route in two hours, a pace that allows for some stopping along the way. Allow extra time if you want to linger in Riverfront Plaza for a half hour or so.

Sights to See

⑦① **Andrew Low House.** This residence was built in 1848 for Andrew Low, a native of Scotland and one of Savannah's merchant princes. The home later belonged to his son William, who married Juliette Gordon. After her husband's death, she founded the Girl Scouts in this house on March 12, 1912. The house has 19th-century antiques, stunning silver, and some of the finest ornamental ironwork in Savannah. ✉ *329 Abercorn St., Historic District,* ☎ *912/233–6854,* *www.andrewlow. com.* 💲 *$7.* ☉ *Mon.–Wed. and Fri.–Sat. 10:30–3:30, Sun. noon–3:30.*

Beach Institute African-American Cultural Center. It's in the building that housed the first school for African-American children in Savannah, established after emancipation (1867). The center exhibits works by African-American artists from the Savannah area and around the country. ✉ *502 E. Harris St., Historic District,* ☎ *912/234–8000,* WEB *www.kingtisdell.org/beach.* 💲 *$3.50.* ☉ *Tues.–Sat. noon–5.*

⑦② **Cathedral of St. John the Baptist.** Soaring over the city, the French Gothic-style cathedral, with pointed arches and free-flowing traceries, is the seat of the diocese of Savannah. It was founded in 1799 by the first French colonists to arrive in Savannah. Fire destroyed the early structures; the present cathedral dates from 1874. ✉ *222 E. Harris St., Historic District,* ☎ *912/233–4709.* ☉ *Weekdays 9–5.*

⑥⑥ **Chippewa Square.** Daniel Chester French's imposing bronze statue of General James Edward Oglethorpe, founder of Savannah and Georgia, anchors the square. Also note the **Savannah Theatre,** on Bull Street, which claims to be the oldest continuously operated theater site in North America. ✉ *Bull St. between Hull and Perry Sts., Historic District.*

⑥⓪ **City Hall.** Built in 1905 on the site of the Old City Exchange (1799–1904), this imposing structure anchors Bay Street. Notice the bench commemorating Oglethorpe's landing on February 12, 1733. ✉ *1 Bay St., Historic District,* ☎ *912/651–6410.* ☉ *Weekdays 8–5.*

⑤⑨ **City Market.** Alas, the original 1870s City Market was razed years ago to make way for a dreary-looking parking garage. Next to the garage you'll find this popular pedestrians-only area that encompasses galleries, nightclubs, restaurants, and shops. ☒ *Between Franklin Sq. and Johnson Sq. on W. St. Julian St., Historic District.*

★ ⑦ **Colonial Park Cemetery.** The park is the final resting place for Savannahians who died between 1750 and 1853. You may want to stroll the shaded pathways and read some of the old tombstone inscriptions. There are several historical plaques, one of which marks the grave of Button Gwinnett, a signer of the Declaration of Independence. ☒ *Oglethorpe and Abercorn Sts., Historic District.*

Columbia Square. When Savannah was a walled city (1757–90), Bethesda Gate (one of six) was here. The square was laid out in 1799. ☒ *Habersham St. between E. State and E. York Sts., Historic District.*

⑦ **Emmet Park.** The lovely tree-shaded park is named for Robert Emmet, a late-18th-century Irish patriot and orator. ☒ *Borders E. Bay St., Historic District.*

⑥ **Factors Walk.** A network of iron walkways connects Bay Street with the multistory buildings that rise up from the river level, and iron stairways descend from Bay Street to Factors Walk. Cobblestone ramps lead pedestrians down to River Street (these are serious cobblestones, so wear comfortable shoes) ☒ *Bay St. to Factors Walk, Historic District.*

⑥ **Forsyth Park.** The park forms the southern border of Bull Street. On its 20 acres it has a glorious white fountain dating to 1858, Confederate and Spanish-American War memorials, and the Fragrant Garden for the Blind, a project of Savannah garden clubs. There are tennis courts and a tree-shaded jogging path. Outdoor plays and concerts often take place here. At the northwest corner of the park, in **Hodgson Hall**, a 19th-century Italianate–Greek Revival building, you'll find the **Georgia Historical Society**, which shows selections from its collection of artifacts and manuscripts. ☒ *501 Whitaker St., Historic District,* ☎ *912/651–2128,* WEB *www.georgiahistory.com.* ☾ *Tues.–Sat. 10–5.*

★ ⑥ **Green-Meldrim House.** Designed by New York architect John Norris and built in 1850 for cotton merchant Charles Green, this Gothic Revival mansion cost $90,000 to build—a princely sum back then. The house was bought in 1892 by Judge Peter Meldrim, whose heirs sold it to **St. John's Episcopal Church** to use as a parish house. General Sherman lived here after taking the city in 1864. Sitting on **Madison Square**, the house has such Gothic features as a crenellated roof, oriels, and an external gallery with filigree ironwork. Inside are mantels of Carrara marble, carved black-walnut woodwork, and doorknobs and hinges of either silver plate or porcelain. ☒ *1 W. Macon St., Historic District,* ☎ *912/233–3845.* ☒ *$5.* ☾ *Tues., Thurs., and Fri. 10–4, Sat. 10–1. Closed last 2 wks of Jan. and 2 wks before Easter.*

★ ⑦ **Isaiah Davenport House.** The proposed demolition of this historic Savannah structure galvanized the city's residents into action to save their treasured buildings. Semicircular stairs with wrought-iron trim lead to the recessed doorway of the redbrick federal mansion that master builder Isaiah Davenport built for himself between 1815 and 1820. Three dormered windows poke through the sloping roof of the stately house, and the interior has polished hardwood floors, fine woodwork and plasterwork, and a soaring elliptical staircase. Furnishings, from the 1820s, are Hepplewhite, Chippendale, and Sheraton. ☒ *324 E. State St., Historic District,* ☎ *912/236–8097,* WEB *www.davenportsavga.com.* ☒ *$7.* ☾ *Mon.–Sat. 10–4, Sun. 1–4.*

Johnson Square. The oldest of James Oglethorpe's original 24 squares was laid out in 1733 and named for South Carolina governor Robert

Johnson. A monument marks the grave of Nathanael Greene, a hero of the Revolutionary War. The square was once a popular gathering place: Savannahians came here to welcome President Monroe in 1819, to greet the Marquis de Lafayette in 1825, and to cheer for Georgia's secession in 1861. ⊠ *Bull St. between Bryan and Congress Sts., Historic District.*

⑥⑤ Juliette Gordon Low Birthplace/Girl Scout National Center. This majestic Regency town house, attributed to William Jay (built 1818–21), was designated in 1965 as Savannah's first National Historic Landmark. "Daisy" Low, founder of the Girl Scouts, was born here in 1860, and the house is now owned and operated by the Girl Scouts of America. Mrs. Low's paintings and other artwork are on display in the house, restored to the style of 1886, the year of Mrs. Low's marriage. ⊠ *142 Bull St., Historic District,* ☎ *912/233–4501,* ⓦⓔⓑ *www. girlscouts.org/birthplace.* ☞ *$8.* ⊙ *Mon.–Tues. and Thurs.–Sat. 10–4, Sun. 12:30–4:30.*

OFF THE
BEATEN PATH
    KING-TISDELL COTTAGE – Tucked behind a picket fence is this museum dedicated to the preservation of African-American history and culture. The Negro Heritage Trail Tour visits this little Victorian house. Broad steps lead to a porch, and dormer windows pop up through a steep roof. The interior is furnished to resemble a middle-class African-American coastal home of the 1890s. To reach the cottage by car, go east on East Bay Street to Price Street and turn south (right) on this street; continue for about 30 blocks to East Huntington Street and take a left (east). The building is in the middle of the block. ⊠ *514 E. Huntington St., Historic District,* ☎ *912/234–8000,* ⓦⓔⓑ *www.kingtisdell.org.* ☞ *$3.50.* ⊙ *By appointment.*

Lafayette Square. Named for the Marquis de Lafayette, the square contains a graceful three-tier fountain donated by the Georgia chapter of the Colonial Dames of America. ⊠ *Abercorn St. between E. Harris and E. Charlton Sts., Historic District.*

Madison Square. A statue on the square, laid out in 1839 and named for President James Madison, depicts Sergeant William Jasper hoisting a flag and is a tribute to his bravery during the Siege of Savannah. Though mortally wounded, Jasper rescued the colors of his regiment in the assault on the British lines. ⊠ *Bull St. between W. Harris and W. Charlton Sts., Historic District.*

⑥⑧ Monterey Square. Commemorating the victory of General Zachary Taylor's forces in Monterrey, Mexico, in 1846, this is the fifth and southernmost of Bull Street's squares. A monument honors General Casimir Pulaski, the Polish nobleman who lost his life in the Siege of Savannah during the Revolutionary War. Also on the square is Temple Mickve Israel. ⊠ *Bull St. between Taylor and Gordon Sts., Historic District.*

★ **⑦④ Owens-Thomas House and Museum.** English architect William Jay's first Regency mansion in Savannah is the city's finest example of that architectural style. Built in 1816–19, the English house was constructed mostly with local materials. Of particular note are the curving walls of the house, Greek-inspired ornamental molding, half-moon arches, stained-glass panels, and Duncan Phyfe furniture. In 1825 the Marquis de Lafayette bade a two-hour au revoir from a wrought-iron balcony to a crowd below. ⊠ *124 Abercorn St., Historic District,* ☎ *912/ 233–9743,* ⓦⓔⓑ *www.telfair.org.* ☞ *$8.* ⊙ *Mon. noon–5, Tues.–Sat. 10–5, Sun. 1–5.*

RALPH MARK GILBERT CIVIL RIGHTS MUSEUM – In Savannah's Historic District, this history museum has a series of 15 exhibits on segregation, from emancipation through the civil rights movement. The role of black and white Savannahians in ending segregation in their city is detailed in these exhibits, largely derived from archival photographs. The museum also has touring exhibits. ⊠ *460 Martin Luther King Jr. Blvd., Historic District,* ☎ *912/231–8900,* FAX *912/234–2577.* 🖃 *$4.* ☉ *Mon.–Sat. 9–5.*

Reynolds Square. John Wesley, who preached in Savannah and wrote the first English hymnal in the city in 1736, is remembered here. A monument to the founder of the Methodist Church is shaded by greenery and surrounded by park benches. The **Olde Pink House** (⊠ 23 Abercorn St., Historic District), built in 1771, is one of the oldest buildings in town. Now a restaurant, the porticoed pink-stucco Georgian mansion has been a private home, a bank, and headquarters for a Yankee general during the Civil War. ⊠ *Abercorn St. between E. Bryant and E. Congress Sts., Historic District.*

62 **Riverfront Plaza.** Here you can watch a parade of freighters and pugnose tugs; youngsters can play in the tugboat-shape sandboxes. River Street is the main venue for many of the city's celebrations, including the First Saturday festivals, when flea marketers, artists, and artisans display their wares and musicians entertain the crowds. ⊠ *River St. between Abercorn and Barnard St., Historic District.*

57 **Savannah History Museum.** This museum in a restored railway station is an excellent introduction to the city. Exhibits range from old locomotives to a tribute to Savannah-born songwriter Johnny Mercer. On top of the **site of the Siege of Savannah,** it marks the spot where in 1779 the colonial forces, led by Polish count Casimir Pulaski, laid siege to Savannah in an attempt to retake the city from the redcoats. They were beaten back, and Pulaski was killed while leading a cavalry charge against the British. The dead lie underneath the building. ⊠ *303 Martin Luther King Jr. Blvd., Historic District,* ☎ *912/238–1779,* WEB *www.chsgeorgia.org/historymuseum.cfm.* 🖃 *$4.* ☉ *Daily 9–5.*

56 **Savannah Visitors Center.** Come here for free maps and brochures, friendly advice, and an audiovisual overview of the city. The starting point for a number of guided tours, the center is in a big 1860 redbrick building with high ceilings and sweeping arches. It was the old Central of Georgia railway station. The parking lot is a good spot to leave your car while you explore the nearby Historic District. ⊠ *301 Martin Luther King Jr. Blvd., Historic District,* ☎ *912/944–0455,* WEB *www.savannahvisit.com.* ☉ *Weekdays 8:30–5, weekends 9–5.*

58 **Scarborough House.** This exuberant Greek Revival mansion, built during the 1819 cotton boom for Savannah merchant prince William Scarborough, was designed by English architect William Jay. Scarborough was a major investor in the steamship *Savannah.* The house has a Doric portico capped by one of Jay's characteristic half-moon windows. Four massive Doric columns form a peristyle in the atrium entrance hall. Inside is the **Ships of the Sea Museum,** with displays of ship models, including steamships, a nuclear-powered ship (the *Savannah*), China clippers with their sails unfurled, and Columbus's vessels. ⊠ *41 Martin Luther King Jr. Blvd., Historic District,* ☎ *912/232–1511,* WEB *www.shipsofthesea.org.* 🖃 *$5.* ☉ *Tues.–Sun. 10–5.*

64 **Telfair Mansion and Art Museum.** The oldest public art museum in the Southeast was designed by William Jay in 1819 for Alexander Telfair and sits across the street from **Telfair Square.** Within its marble rooms are American, French, and Dutch impressionist paintings; German tonalist paintings; a large collection of works by Kahlil Gibran; plaster casts of the Elgin Marbles, the Venus de Milo, and the Laocoön, among other classical sculptures; and some of the Telfair family furnishings, including a Duncan Phyfe sideboard and Savannah-made silver. ⊠ *121 Barnard St., Historic District,* ☎ *912/232–1177,* WEB *www.telfair.org.* ⌑ *$8, free Sun.* ☼ *Mon. noon–5, Tues.–Sat. 10–5, Sun. 1–5.*

Temple Mickve Israel. A Gothic Revival synagogue on Monterey Square houses the third-oldest Jewish congregation in the United States; its founding members settled in town five months after the establishment of Savannah in 1733. The synagogue's collection includes documents and letters (some from George Washington, James Madison, and Thomas Jefferson) pertaining to early Jewish life in Savannah and Georgia. ⊠ *20 E. Gordon St., Historic District,* ☎ *912/233–1547,* WEB *www.mickveisrael.org.* ☼ *Weekdays 10–noon and 2–4.*

⓱ **Wesley Monumental Church.** This Gothic Revival–style church memorializing the founders of Methodism is patterned after Queen's Kerk in Amsterdam. Noted for its magnificent stained-glass windows, the church celebrated a century of service in 1968. ⊠ *429 Abercorn St., Historic District,* ☎ *912/232–0191.* ☼ *By appointment only.*

⓺ **Wright Square.** Named for James Wright, Georgia's last colonial governor, the square has an elaborate monument in its center that honors William Washington Gordon, founder of the Central of Georgia Railroad. A slab of granite from Stone Mountain adorns the grave of Tomo-Chi-Chi, the Yamacraw chief who befriended General Oglethorpe and the colonists. ⊠ *Bull St. between W. State and W. York Sts., Historic District.*

Midnight in the Garden of Good and Evil

Town gossips can give you the best introduction to a city, and as author John Berendt discovered, Savannah's not short on them. In his 1994 best-seller, *Midnight in the Garden of Good and Evil,* Berendt shares the juiciest of tales imparted to him during the eight years he spent here wining and dining with Savannah's high society and dancing with her Grand Empress, drag queen the Lady Chablis, among others. By the time he left, there had been a scandalous homicide and several trials: the wealthy Jim Williams was accused of killing his assistant and sometime lover, Danny Hansford.

Before you set out, find a copy of the book, pour yourself a cool drink, and enter an eccentric world of cutthroat killers and society backstabbers, voodoo witches, and garden-club ladies. Then head over to the Historic District to follow the characters' steps. By the end of this walking tour, you'll be hard-pressed to find the line between Berendt's creative nonfiction and Savannah's reality. Note: unless otherwise indicated, the sights on this tour are not open to the public.

A Good Walk

Begin at the southwest corner of Monterey Square, site of the **Mercer House** ⑦, whose construction was begun by songwriter Johnny Mercer's great-grandfather just before the Civil War. Two blocks south on Bull Street is the **Armstrong House** ⑱, an earlier residence of Jim Williams, the main character in the book. Walk south through Forsyth Park to the corner of Park Avenue and Whitaker Street. The **Forsyth Park Apartments** ⑲, where author John Berendt lived, are on the southwest corner of Forsyth Park. Then turn back north through the park. At the midpoint of the park's northern edge, turn north up Bull Street in the direction of Monterey Square. Turn left on West Gordon

Street off Bull Street and walk toward the corner of West Gordon Street and Whitaker Street, where you'll reach **Serena Dawes's House** ⑳. Next, cross West Gordon Street, walk north on Bull Street in front of Mercer House, cross Wayne Street, and you'll find that the first house on the left facing Bull Street at Wayne Street is **Lee Adler's Home** ㉛, which sits across from Monterey Square's northwest corner. Continue walking north on Bull Street and take a right (east) on East Jones Street. **Joe Odom's first house** ㉜ is the third house on the left before Drayton Street.

Continue on East Jones Street to Abercorn Street and turn left (north), walking two blocks on Abercorn Street to East Charlton Street and the **Hamilton-Turner House** ㉝, now a B&B inn. Then swing around Lafayette Square to East Harris Street, and take it about six blocks west to Pulaski Square at Barnard Street; turn right (north) on Barnard Street through Orleans Square and continue north to Telfair Square. On foot, you may elect to head west down West York Street to find the **Chatham County Courthouse** ㉞, scene of all those trials, two blocks away. Finally, take either Whitaker Street or Abercorn Street south to Victory Drive and turn left. Go through Thunderbolt to Whatley Avenue, and turn left again. Whatley Avenue leads directly to Bonaventure Road, which curves in both directions; bear left, and on your right about a quarter mile up the road is **Bonaventure Cemetery** ㉟.

TIMING

Allow a leisurely two hours to walk the main points of the tour, plus another hour to visit the cemetery.

Sights to See

⑦⑧ **Armstrong House.** Antiques dealer Jim Williams lived and worked in this residence before purchasing the Mercer House. On a late-afternoon walk past the mansion, Berendt met Mr. Simon Glover, an 86-year-old singer and porter for the law firm of Bouhan, Williams, and Levy, occupants of the building. Glover confided that he earned a weekly $10 for walking the deceased dogs of a former partner of the firm up and down Bull Street. Baffled? So was the author. Behind the house's cast-iron gates are the offices of Frank Siler, Jim Williams's attorney, who doubles as keeper of Uga, the Georgia Bulldog mascot. ✉ *447 Bull St., Historic District.*

㉟ **Bonaventure Cemetery.** A cemetery east of downtown is the final resting place for Danny Hansford. The haunting female tombstone figure from the book's cover has been removed to protect surrounding graves from sightseers. Now you can view the figure at the Telfair Mansion. ✉ *330 Bonaventure Rd., Eastside,* ☎ *912/651–6843.*

㉞ **Chatham County Courthouse.** The courthouse was the scene of three of Williams's murder trials, which took place over the course of about eight years. An underground tunnel leads from the courthouse to the jail where Williams was held in a cell that was modified to allow him to conduct his antiques business. ✉ *133 Montgomery St., Historic District.*

⑦⑨ **Forsyth Park Apartments.** Here was Berendt's second home in Savannah; from his fourth-floor rooms he pieced together the majority of the book. While parking his newly acquired 1973 Pontiac Grand Prix outside these apartments, Berendt met the Lady Chablis coming out of her nearby doctor's office, freshly feminine from a new round of hormone shots. ✉ *Whitaker and Gwinnett Sts., Historic District.*

㉝ **Hamilton-Turner House.** After one too many of Joe Odom's deals went sour, Mandy Nichols, his fourth fiancée-in-waiting, left him and took over his third residence, a Second Empire–style mansion dating from

1873. Mandy filled it with 17th- and 18th-century antiques and transformed it into a successful museum through which she led tour groups. The elegant towering hulk is at the southeast corner of Lafayette Square. The house was sold in the late '90s and has since become the elegant Hamilton-Turner Inn. ⊠ *330 Abercorn St., Historic District.*

㉘ Joe Odom's first house. At this stucco town house, Odom, a combination tax lawyer, real-estate broker, and piano player, hosted a 24-hour stream of visitors. The author met Odom through Mandy Nichols, a former Miss Big Beautiful Woman, who stopped by to borrow ice one time after the power had been cut off, a frequent occurrence. ⊠ *16 E. Jones St., Historic District.*

㉑ Lee Adler's Home. Just north of the Mercer House, in half of the double town house facing West Wayne Street, Lee Adler, the adversary of Jim Williams, runs his business of restoring historic Savannah properties. Adler's howling dogs drove Williams to his pipe organ, where he churned out a deafening version of César Franck's *Pièce Heroïque.* Later, Adler stuck reelection signs in his front lawn, showing his support for the district attorney who prosecuted Williams three times before he was finally found not guilty. ⊠ *425 Bull St., Historic District.*

㊆ Mercer House. This redbrick Italianate mansion on the southwest corner of Monterey Square became Jim Williams's Taj Mahal; here he ran a world-class antiques dealership and held *the* Christmas party of the season; here also Danny Hansford, his sometime house partner, succumbed to gunshot wounds. Williams himself died here of a heart attack in 1990, near the very spot where Hansford fell. Today his sister lives quietly among the remnants of his Fabergé collection and his Joshua Reynolds paintings, in rooms lighted by Waterford crystal chandeliers. ⊠ *429 Bull St., Historic District.*

㊾ Serena Dawes's House. Near the intersection of West Gordon and Bull streets, this house was owned by Helen Driscoll, also known as Serena Dawes. A high-profile beauty in the 1930s and '40s, she married into a Pennsylvania steel family. After her husband accidentally and fatally shot himself in the head, she retired here, in her hometown. Dawes, Berendt writes, "spent most of her day in bed, holding court, drinking martinis and pink ladies, playing with her white toy poodle, Lulu." Chief among Serena's gentlemen callers was Luther Driggers, rumored to possess a poison strong enough to wipe out the entire city. ⊠ *17 W. Gordon St., Historic District.*

Other Area Attractions

Ebenezer. When the Salzburgers arrived in Savannah in 1734, Oglethorpe sent them up the Savannah River to establish a settlement. The first effort was assailed by disease, and they sought his permission to move to better ground. Denied, they moved anyway and established Ebenezer. Here, they engaged in silkworm production and, in 1769, built the Jerusalem Church, which still stands. After the revolution, the silkworm operation never resumed, and the town faded into history. Descendants of these Protestant religious refugees have preserved the church and assembled a few of the remaining buildings, moving them to this site from other locations. Be sure to follow Route 275 to its end and see Ebenezer Landing, where the Salzburgers came ashore. ⊠ *Ebenezer Rd., Rte. 21–Rte. 275, Rincon (25 mi north of Savannah).*

Old Fort Jackson. About 2 mi east of Broad Street via President Street, you'll see a sign for the fort, which is 3 mi from the city. Purchased in 1808 by the federal government, this is the oldest standing fort in Georgia. It was garrisoned in 1812 and was the Confederate headquarters of the river batteries. The brick edifice is surrounded by a tidal moat, and there are 13 exhibit areas. Battle reenactments, blacksmithing demonstrations, and programs of 19th-century music are among the fort's activities for tour groups. ☒ *1 Ft. Jackson Rd., Fort Jackson,* ☎ *912/232–3945,* WEB *www.chsgeorgia.org/fortjackson.cfm.* ☒ *$3.50.* ☻ *Daily 9–5.*

★ ☻ **Fort Pulaski National Monument.** Named for Casimir Pulaski, a Polish count and Revolutionary War hero, this must-see sight for Civil War buffs was built on Cockspur Island between 1829 and 1847. Robert E. Lee's first assignment after graduating from West Point was as an engineer here. During the Civil War the fort fell, on April 11, 1862, after a mere 30 hours of bombardment by newfangled rifled cannons. The restored fortification, operated by the National Park Service, has moats, drawbridges, massive ramparts, and towering walls. The park has trails and picnic areas. It's 14 mi east of downtown Savannah; you'll see the entrance on your left just before U.S. 80 reaches Tybee Island. ☒ *U.S. 80, Fort Pulaski,* ☎ *912/786–5787,* WEB *www.nps.gov/fopu.* ☒ *$3.* ☻ *Daily 9–5.*

Melon Bluff. On a centuries-old 3,000-acre plantation that has been in one family since 1735, Melon Bluff includes a nature center and facilities for canoeing, kayaking, bird-watching, hiking, and other outdoor activities. You can camp here or stay at one of the three B&B inns ($$–$$$): Palmyra Plantation, an 1850s cottage; the Ripley Farmhouse, a classic rural house with a tin-covered roof; and an old barn, renovated to contain nine guest rooms. From Melon Bluff you can visit nearby **Seabrook Village,** a small but growing cluster of rural buildings from an African-American historic community; **Old Sunbury,** whose port made it a viable competitor to Savannah until the Revolutionary War ended its heyday; **Fort Morris,** which protected Savannah during the revolution; and **Midway,** an 18th-century village with a house museum and period cemetery. To reach Melon Bluff, take I–95 south from Savannah (about 30 mi) to Exit 76 (Midway/Sunbury), turn left, and go east for 3 mi. The other sites mentioned here are all within a short drive. ☒ *2999 Islands Hwy., Midway,* ☎ *912/884–5779 or 888/246–8188,* FAX *912/884–3046,* WEB *www.melonbluff.com.*

Mighty Eighth Air Force Heritage Museum. The famous World War II squadron the Mighty Eighth Air Force was formed in Savannah in January 1942 and shipped out to the United Kingdom. Flying Royal Air Force aircraft, the Mighty Eighth became the largest air force of the period, with some 200,000 combat crew personnel. Many lost their lives during raids on enemy factories or were interned as prisoners of war. Exhibits begin with the prelude to World War II and the rise of Adolf Hitler and continue through Desert Storm. ☒ *175 Bourne Ave. (I–95, Exit 102, to U.S. 80), Pooler (14 mi west of Savannah),* ☎ *912/748–8888,* WEB *www.mightyeighth.org.* ☒ *$8.* ☻ *Daily 9–5.*

☻ **Skidaway Marine Science Complex.** On the grounds of the former Modena Plantation, Skidaway has a 14-panel, 12,000-gallon aquarium with marine and plant life of the continental shelf. Other exhibits highlight coastal archaeology and fossils of the Georgia coast. Nature trails overlook marsh and water. ☒ *30 Ocean Science Circle, Skidaway Island (8 mi south of Savannah),* ☎ *912/598–2496.* ☒ *$2.* ☻ *Weekdays 9–4, Sat. noon–5.*

Tybee Island. *Tybee* is an Indian word meaning "salt." The Yamacraw Indians came to this island in the Atlantic Ocean to hunt and fish, and legend has it that pirates buried their treasure here. The island is about 5 mi long and 2 mi wide, with seafood restaurants, chain motels, condos, and shops—most of which sprang up during the 1950s and haven't changed much since. The entire expanse of white sand is divided into a number of public beaches, where you can shell and crab, charter fishing boats, and swim. It's 18 mi east of Savannah; take Victory Drive (U.S. 80), sometimes called Tybee Road, onto the island. On your way here stop by Fort Jackson and Fort Pulaski National Monument. Nearby, the misnamed Little Tybee Island, actually larger than Tybee Island, is entirely undeveloped. Contact **Tybee Island Convention and Visitors Bureau** (⊠ Box 491, Tybee Island 31328, ☎ 800/868–2322, WEB www.tybeevisit.com).

Dining

Savannah has excellent seafood restaurants, though locals also have a passion for spicy barbecued meats. The Historic District yields culinary treasures, especially along River Street. Several of the city's restaurants—such as Elizabeth on 37th, 45 South, the Olde Pink House, and Sapphire Grill—have been beacons that have drawn members of the culinary upper crust to the region for decades. From there they explored and discovered that such divine dining isn't isolated to Savannah's Historic District, as nearby Thunderbolt, Skidaway, Tybee, and Wilmington islands also have a collection of remarkable restaurants.

$$$–$$$$ ✕ **Elizabeth on 37th.** Regional specialties are the hallmark at this ac-
★   claimed restaurant that goes so far as to credit local produce suppliers on its menu. Chef Elizabeth Terry manages to make dishes such as Maryland crab cakes and a plate of roasted shiitake and oyster mushrooms sit comfortably beside Southern-fried grits and country ham. The extravagant Savannah cream cake is the way to finish your meal in this elegant turn-of-the-20th-century mansion with hardwood floors and spacious rooms. ⊠ *105 E. 37th St., Victorian District,* ☎ *912/236–5547. Reservations essential. AE, D, DC, MC, V. No lunch.*

$$$–$$$$ ✕ **45 South.** This popular Southside eatery is small and stylish, with
★   a contemporary mauve-and-green interior. The game-heavy menu often includes a confit of tender rabbit with morels and mashed potatoes. ⊠ *20 E. Broad St., Victorian District,* ☎ *912/233–1881. Reservations essential. AE, D, DC, MC, V. Closed Sun. No lunch.*

$$–$$$ ✕ **Belford's Steak and Seafood.** In the heart of City Market, Belford's is great for Sunday brunch, when so many of the downtown venues are closed. A complimentary glass of sparkling wine arrives at your table when you place your order. Brunch entrées include egg dishes, such as smoked salmon Florentine and crab frittatas. The lunch and dinner menus focus on seafood, including Georgia pecan grouper and Lowcountry shrimp and grits. ⊠ *315 W. St. Julian St., Historic District,* ☎ *912/233–2626. AE, D, DC, MC, V.*

$$–$$$ ✕ **Bistro Savannah.** High ceilings, burnished heart-pine floors, and gray-
★   brick walls lined with local art contribute to the bistro-ish qualities of this spot by City Market. The menu has such specialties as seared beef tenderloin with shiitakes, scallions, corn pancakes and horseradish sauce, and shrimp and *tasso* (seasoned cured pork) on stone-ground grits. Another treat is the crispy roasted duck. ⊠ *309 W. Congress St., Historic District,* ☎ *912/233–6266. AE, MC, V. No lunch.*

$$–$$$ ✕ **Cafe@Main.** This upscale but easygoing restaurant offers a compendium of Continental and regional American dishes, such as pork tenderloin with mashed potatoes and fresh green beans, and potato-onion-crusted grouper. Also of note is the wine list, with an unusually extensive selection of by-the-glass offerings. ⊠ *1 W. Broughton St., Historic District,* ☎ *912/447–5979. AE, MC, V.*

$$–$$$ ✕ **Georges' of Tybee.** From the proprietors of the North Beach Grill came Tybee's first fine restaurant. The warmly lighted interior, with

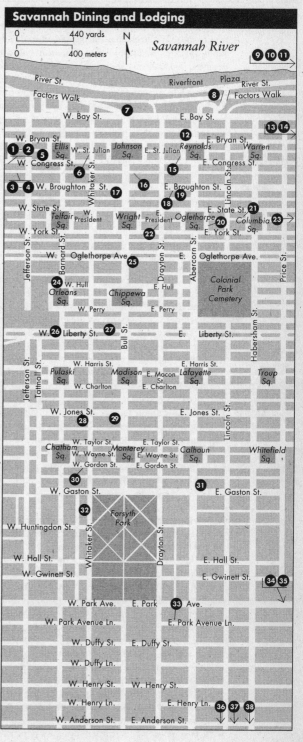

Savannah Dining and Lodging

its inviting dining room, with a lovely stone fireplace and dark rose-painted walls, is a fine place to spend a romantic evening. Duck liver and frisée salad, and Thai-barbecued Muscovy duck breast are popular. Lobster, crab, and four-cheese ravioli with carrots, snow peas, and arugula, in a saffron-cream sauce, is also outstanding. ⊠ *1105 E. U.S. 80, Tybee Island,* ☎ *912/786–9730. AE, MC, V. Closed Mon. No lunch.*

$$–$$$ ✕ **Il Pasticcio.** Sicilian Pino Venetico turned this former department store
★ into his dream restaurant—a bistro-style place gleaming with steel, glass, and tile, and a lively, hip, young crowd to populate it. The menu changes frequently, but fresh pastas and sauces are a constant. Don't miss the second-floor art gallery. Excellent desserts, including a superior tiramisu, make this one worth seeking out. ⊠ *2 E. Broughton St., Historic District,* ☎ *912/231–8888. AE, D, DC, MC, V. No lunch.*

$$–$$$ ✕ **Olde Pink House.** The brick Georgian mansion was built in 1771 for James Habersham, one of the wealthiest Americans of his time. One of Savannah's oldest buildings, the tavern has original Georgia pine floors, Venetian chandeliers, and 18th-century English antiques. The she-crab soup is a light but flavorful version of this Lowcountry specialty. Regional ingredients find their way into many of the dishes, including the black grouper stuffed with blue crab and served with a Vidalia onion sauce. ⊠ *23 Abercorn St., Historic District,* ☎ *912/232–4286. AE, MC, V. No lunch.*

$$–$$$ ✕ **Sapphire Grill.** Savannah's young and restless pack this trendy haunt
★ nightly. Chef Chris Nason focuses his seasonal menus on local ingredients, such as Georgia white shrimp, crab, and fish. Vegetarians will delight in his elegant vegetable presentations—perhaps including roasted sweet onions, spicy peppers, wild mushrooms, or roasted shallots. Chocoholics: get the remarkably delicious, intensely potent chocolate flan. ⊠ *110 W. Congress St., Historic District,* ☎ *912/443–9962. Reservations essential. AE, D, DC, MC, V. No lunch.*

$$–$$$ ✕ **Savannah Steak House.** This art-filled, dashing restaurant with a striking collage on its ceiling has made an impressive splash in Savannah dining circles. The menu offers a tremendously varied number of inventive delicacies. Traditionalists might stick with the hefty rib-eye steak, but if you're game for something more exotic, consider "wild" entrées like ostrich fillet, wild-boar chili, and antelope medallions. ⊠ *423 W. Congress St., Historic District,* ☎ *912/232–0092. AE, MC, V. Closed Sun.*

$$–$$$ ✕ **17 Hundred and 90.** Chef Deborah Noelk keeps a creative kitchen
★ in this restaurant—in a rustic structure dating to the 13th colony and tucked in among ancient oaks dripping with Spanish moss. The restaurant is in Savannah's oldest inn of the same name. Entrées include pan-seared veal medallions with artichoke hearts and capers in a lemon butter; roasted half duckling with a port wine lingonberry sauce; and local shrimp stuffed with scallops and crabmeat and served with a lemon beurre blanc sauce. There is a ghost story to go with dinner, so make sure the waiter fills you in. ⊠ *307 E. Presidents St., Historic District,* ☎ *912/231–8888. AE, D, DC, MC, V. No lunch weekends.*

$$–$$$ ✕ **The Lady & Sons.** Expect to take your place in line, along with locals, here. Everyone patiently waits to attack the buffet, which is stocked for both lunch and dinner with such specials as moist, crispy fried chicken; the best baked spaghetti in the South; green beans cooked with ham and potatoes; tender, sweet creamed corn; and homemade lemonade. The interior of this 1870s-era building, painted pale pink with faux ivy tendrils draped along its perimeter, is bright, cheerful, and busy. Owner Paula H. Deen's book, *The Lady & Sons: Savannah Country Cookbook,* includes recipes for the most popular dishes. ⊠ *311 W. Congress St., Historic District,* ☎ *912/233–2600. AE, D, MC, V. No dinner Sun.*

$$ ✕ **Johnny Harris.** What started as a small roadside stand in 1924 has grown into one of the city's mainstays, with a menu that includes steaks, fried chicken, seafood, and meats spiced with the restaurant's famous tomato-and-mustard sauce. The lamb barbecue is a treat, and their sauces are now so famous that they bottle them for take-home and shipping. There's live music Friday and Saturday night, except on the first Saturday night of the month, when there's dancing. ⊠ *1651 E. Victory Dr., Eastside,* ☎ *912/354–7810. AE, D, DC, MC, V. Closed Sun.*

$$ ✕ **Mrs. Wilkes Dining Room.** Folks line up for a culinary orgy of fine
★ Southern food, served family style at big tables. For breakfast there are eggs, sausage, piping hot biscuits, and grits. At lunch try fried or roast chicken, collard greens, okra, mashed potatoes, and corn bread. ⊠ *107 W. Jones St., Historic District,* ☎ *912/232–5997. Reservations not accepted. No credit cards. Closed Jan. and weekends. No dinner.*

$$ ✕ **North Beach Grill.** The tiny kitchen of this casual beachfront locale serves up a taste of the Caribbean. The jerk-rubbed fish tacos with fruit salsa—which you'll be hard-pressed to find prepared right in the South— are wonderful. Also expect to be tempted by the grilled okra and by the sea bass topped with caramelized onions with cilantro-lime beurre blanc. You can come in a swimsuit for lunch, but throw on something casual for dinner. ⊠ *41A Meddin Dr., Tybee Island,* ☎ *912/786–9003. Reservations not accepted. D, MC, V. Closed weekdays Dec.–Jan.*

$–$$ ✕ **Nita's Place.** Juanita Dixon has a reputation for perfectly prepar-
★ ing down-home Southern cooking at this renowned steam-table operation, which remains authentic (despite now being housed in a more polished-looking space than its original location). People flock here for salmon patties, baked chicken, perfectly cooked okra, outstanding squash casserole, and homemade desserts. The fresh vegetables and other side dishes alone are worth the trip, if only for the sheer number (11) from which to choose: rutabagas, fried corn, string beans, potato salad, collard greens, sautéed spinach, black-eyed peas, macaroni and cheese, fried sweet potatoes, baked sweet potatoes, and Nita's famous squash casserole. ⊠ *129 E. Broughton St., Historic District,* ☎ *912/ 238–8233. Reservations not accepted. MC, V. Closed Sun. No dinner Mon.–Thurs.*

$–$$ ✕ **Red Hot & Blue.** Their motto is: "Best Barbecue You'll Ever Have in
★ a Building that Hasn't Already Been Condemned!" With such specialties as pulled-pig spare ribs, pork spare ribs, beef brisket, smoked chicken, and smoked sausage, all meticulously smoked over hickory wood for a long time, this place may be worth the drive to the Southside for barbecue aficionados, even if it is a chain location. ⊠ *11108 Abercorn St., Southside,* ☎ *912/961–7422. Reservations not accepted. MC, V.*

$–$$ ✕ **SoHo South Cafe.** This is not your normal soup-and-salad pit stop— it's a soup-and-salad pit stop for epicureans. The tuna salad in your tuna-salad sandwich will be made to order—from the café's own recipe, no less—and the smoked ham and Brie on a baguette is enough to make your taste buds swoon. The soups are also fittingly fabulous. ⊠ *12 W. Liberty St., Historic District,* ☎ *912/233–1633. MC, V. Closed Sun. Dinner served 6–9:30 Fri.–Sat. only.*

$–$$ ✕ **Toucan Cafe.** This colorful café has food to satisfy every kind of eater— the menu is sympathetic to vegetarian tastes but doesn't leave meat eaters out in the cold. Offerings include Indian veggie *samosas* with curried broccoli, Jamaican jerk chicken, and rib-eye steaks. ⊠ *531 Stephenson Ave., Southside,* ☎ *912/352–2233. AE, D, MC, V. Closed Sun.*

$–$$ ✕ **Yanni's Greek Cuisine.** A gregarious waitstaff serves a wonderful,
★ authentic Greek cuisine in this Southside eatery with walls emblazoned by murals of Mediterranean seaside panoramas. Menu items include Grecian shrimp kebabs with feta, garlic, onions and tomatoes, as well as salmon sautéed in a creamy white-wine and dill sauce. There

is plenty of pork, beef, and chicken to choose from as well, all prepared with finesse. ✉ *11211 Abercorn Expressway, Southside,* ☎
912/925–6814. AE, D, MC, V. Closed Sun.

$ ╳ **Creole Red.** This jaunty little no-frills storefront café is patronized
with great enthusiasm by locals. Everybody seems to love the delicious
and inexpensive Louisiana specialties, from fresh crawfish étouffée to
deviled crabs, served with warmth and aplomb by the friendly proprietor
and staff. ✉ *409 W. Congress St., Historic District,* ☎ *912/234–6690.
MC, V.*

Lodging

Although Savannah has its share of chain hotels and motels, the city's
most distinctive lodgings are the more than two dozen historic inns,
guest houses, and B&Bs gracing the Historic District.

If the term *historic inn* brings to mind images of roughing it in shabby-
genteel mansions with antiquated plumbing, you're in for a surprise.
Most of these inns are in mansions with the requisite high ceilings, spacious rooms, and ornate carved millwork. And most do have canopy,
four-poster, or Victorian brass beds. But amid all the antique surroundings, there is modern luxury: enormous baths, many with
whirlpools or hot tubs; film libraries for in-room VCRs; and turndown
service with a chocolate, a praline, even a discreet brandy on your night-
stand. Continental breakfast and afternoon refreshments are often included in the rate. Prices have risen since the filming of *Midnight in
the Garden of Good and Evil.* Special seasons and holidays, such as
St. Patrick's Day, push prices up a bit as well. On the other hand, weekdays and the off-season can yield excellent bargains.

Inns and Guest Houses

$$$$ ▥ **Gastonian.** Guest rooms at this inn, built in 1868, have working
  ★   fireplaces and antiques from the Georgian and Regency periods; most
also have whirlpool tubs or Japanese soak tubs. The Caracalla Suite
is named for the oversize whirlpool tub built in front of the fireplace.
At breakfast you'll find such specialty items as ginger pancakes. Afternoon tea, evening cordials, and complimentary wine are other treats.
✉ *220 E. Gaston St., Historic District, 31401,* ☎ *912/232–2869 or
800/322–6603,* FAX *912/232–0710,* WEB *www.gastonian.com. 14 rooms,
3 suites. Internet. AE, D, MC, V. BP.*

$$$–$$$$ ▥ **Ballastone Inn.** This sumptuous inn occupies an 1838 mansion that
   ★   once served as a bordello. Rooms are handsomely furnished, with lux-
urious linens on canopy beds, antiques and fine reproductions, and a col-
lection of original framed prints from *Harper's* scattered throughout. On
the garden level rooms are small and cozy, with exposed brick walls, beam
ceilings, and, in some cases, windows at eye level with the lush court-
yard. Most rooms have working gas fireplaces, and three have whirl-
pool tubs. Afternoon tea and free passes to a nearby health club are
included. ✉ *14 E. Oglethorpe Ave., Historic District, 31401,* ☎ *912/
236–1484 or 800/822–4553,* FAX *912/236–4626,* WEB *www.ballastone.
com. 14 rooms, 3 suites. In-room VCRs, bicycles. AE, MC, V. BP.*

$$$–$$$$ ▥ **Eliza Thompson House.** Eliza Thompson was a socially prominent
widow when she built her fine town house around 1847; today the lovely
Victorian edifice remains one of the oldest B&Bs in Savannah. The lov-
ingly weathered exterior still retains the majestic beauty of its stately hey-
day, when regal homes were all the rage. A peaceful garden courtyard
provides a quiet respite where you can read or simply breathe in the flo-
ral scents. The rooms are lavishly decorated, with marble baths and rare
antiques, boasting walls painted in deep primaries, such as forest green
or pencil yellow—which provide stunning backdrops for the plush bed-

ding and other designer accents. Continental breakfast and complimentary afternoon wine and cheese are served in the parlor or on the patio, with its fine patio, the latter of which has a fine Ivan Bailey sculpture. ✉ *5 W. Jones St., Historic District, 31401,* ☎ *912/236–3620 or 800/348–9378,* FAX *912/238–1920,* WEB *www.elizathompsonhouse.com. 25 rooms. MC, V. BP.*

$$$–$$$$ 🏠 **Foley House Inn.** Two town houses, built 50 years apart, form this
★ elegant inn. Proprietor Phillip Jenkins often entertains during the evening wine-and-dessert service—he plays lively numbers on the baby grand piano in the parlor. Most rooms have antiques and reproductions; five rooms have whirlpool tubs. A carriage house to the rear of the property has less expensive rooms. ✉ *14 W. Hull St., Historic District, 31401,* ☎ *912/232–6622 or 800/647–3708,* FAX *912/231–1218,* WEB *www.foleyinn.com. 17 rooms, 2 suites. In-room VCRs. AE, MC, V. BP.*

$$$–$$$$ 🏠 **Kehoe House.** A fabulously appointed 1890s B&B, the Victorian Kehoe House has brass-and-marble chandeliers, a courtyard garden, and a music room. On the main floor a double parlor holds two fireplaces and sweeps the eye upward with its 14-ft ceilings. Turndown service is included. Rates include access to the Downtown Athletic Club. ✉ *123 Habersham St., Historic District, 31401,* ☎ *912/232–1020 or 800/820–1020,* FAX *912/231–0208,* WEB *www.kehoehouse.com. 13 rooms, 2 suites. Meeting room. AE, D, DC, MC, V. BP.*

$$–$$$$ 🏠 **Magnolia Place Inn.** Looking out directly across breathtaking Forsyth
★ Park, this opulent 1878 inn dazzles. There are regal antiques, prints, and porcelain from around the world—you'd expect one of Savannah's wealthy old cotton merchants to occupy such a mansion. Many rooms have Jacuzzis and fireplaces. With expansive verandas, lush terraces, and soaring ceilings, the Magnolia Place Inn typifies Savannah's golden era. ✉ *503 Whitaker St., Historic District, 31401,* ☎ *912/236–7674 or 800/ 238–7674,* FAX *912/231–1218,* WEB *www.magnoliaplaceinn.com. 13 rooms, 3 suites, 2 town houses. In-room VCRs, Internet. AE, MC, V. BP.*

$$–$$$ 🏠 **Claudia's Manor.** Proprietors Claudia and Larry Collins create a warm and inviting feeling in this sweeping Spanish Mediterranean home in the southern reaches of the city's Historic District, just a half mile south of Forsyth Park. Some of the accommodations in this turn-of-the-20th-century house have themed decors—one has African furnishings, and another is a homage to the East. Each of the large suites has a pair of queen-size beds. ✉ *101 E. 35th St., Historic District, 31401,* ☎ *912/ 233–2379 or 800/773–8177,* FAX *912/238–5919,* WEB *www.claudiasmanor. com. 4 rooms, 3 suites. AE, DC, MC, V. Internet, business services, meeting room. BP.*

$$–$$$ 🏠 **The Manor House.** Built for the Lewis Byrd family in the 1830s, this
★ majestic historic structure (it's the city's oldest building south of Liberty Street) once housed Union officers during General Sherman's Civil War march to the sea. All rooms are suites with a master bedroom and a separate cozy sitting area, and each has been decorated with a delightful individuality. Some even come complete with fireplace and kitchen. The Manor House also oversees three additional properties off-site from the main inn: a gorgeous, antiques-filled loft suite on Factors Walk overlooking the historic Savannah waterfront; a large historic town house complete with formal dining room on Broughton Street; and a magnificent, two-bedroom oceanfront town house with two sprawling private decks on Tybee Island. ✉ *201 W. Liberty St., Historic District, 31401,* ☎ *912/ 233–9597 or 800/462–3595,* WEB *www.manorhouse-savannah.com. 8 suites. In-room VCRs, some whirlpool baths. AE, D, DC, MC, V. BP.*

$$–$$$ 🏠 **The President's Quarters.** You'll be impressed even before you enter
★ this lovely inn, which has an exterior courtyard so beautiful and inviting it has become a popular wedding-reception spot. Each room in this classic Savannah inn, fashioned out of a pair of meticulously restored

1860s town houses, is named for an American president. Some rooms have four-poster beds, working fireplaces, and private balconies. Expect to be greeted with wine and fruit, and a complimentary afternoon tea will tempt you with sweet cakes. Turndown service includes a glass of port or sherry. There are also rooms in an adjacent town house. ✉ *225 E. President St., Historic District, 31401,* ☎ *912/233–1600 or 800/ 233–1776,* FAX *912/238–0849,* WEB *www.presidentsquarters.com. 11 rooms, 8 suites. Some hot tubs. D, DC, MC, V. BP.*

$–$$ 🛏 **Bed & Breakfast Inn.** So called, the owner claims, because it was the first such property to open in Savannah more than 20 years ago, the inn is a restored 1853 federal-style row house on historic Gordon Row near Chatham Square. The courtyard garden is a lovely cluster of potted tropical flowers surrounding an inviting koi pond. A sweeping renovation has added private baths to all the rooms but managed to keep many elements of the original charm, such as beamed ceilings and exposed-brick walls; only the Garden Suite has a full kitchen. Afternoon pastries, lemonade, coffee, and tea are served. ✉ *117 W. Gordon St., Historic District, 31401,* ☎ *912/238–0518,* FAX *912/233– 2537,* WEB *www.savannahbnb.com. 15 rooms. AE, D, MC, V. BP.*

$–$$ 🛏 **Green Palm Inn.** This inn is quite a pleasing little discovery. Origi-
★ nally built in 1897 but renovated top to bottom by owners Jack Moore and Rick Ellison, it's now a B&B. The elegant furnishings, meant to reflect a minimized subtropical aesthetic, were inspired by Savannah's British colonial heritage; some rooms have fireplaces. A separate cottage has two bedrooms, a fireplace, and a lush garden with a marble wading pool. ✉ *548 E. President St., Historic District, 31401,* ☎ *912/447–8901 or 888/606–9510,* FAX *912/236–4626,* WEB *www.greenpalminn.com. 5 suites, 1 cottage. Fans, cable TV. AE, MC, V. BP.*

$–$$ 🛏 **17th Street Inn.** The deck of this 1920 inn, which is adorned with plants, palms, and swings, is a gathering place where you can chat, sip wine, and enjoy breakfast both with other guests and your hosts: Susie Morris and her spouse, Stuart Liles. Steps from the beach, the inn has two-story porches and brightly colored rooms, each with a double iron bed. ✉ *12 17th St., Box 114, Tybee Island 31328,* ☎ *912/786–0607 or 888/909–0607,* FAX *912/786–0601,* WEB *www.tybeeinn.com. 8 rooms, 1 condo. Kitchenettes. D, MC, V. CP.*

Hotels and Motels

$$$–$$$$ 🛏 **Hyatt Regency Savannah.** When this riverfront hotel was built in 1981, preservationists opposed the construction of the seven-story modern structure in the Historic District. The main architectural features are the towering atrium and glass elevators. Rooms have modern furnishings, marble baths, and balconies overlooking either the atrium or the Savannah River. MD's Lounge is the ideal spot to have a drink and watch the river traffic drift by. Windows, the hotel's restaurant, serves a great Sunday buffet. ✉ *2 W. Bay St., Historic District, 31401,* ☎ *912/238–1234 or 800/233–1234,* FAX *912/944–3673,* WEB *www.savannah-online.com/hyatt. 325 rooms, 22 suites. Restaurant, bar, indoor pool, health club, lounge, business services, meeting rooms. AE, D, MC, V.*

$$$ 🛏 **Mulberry Inn.** This Holiday Inn–managed property is ensconced in
★ an 1860s livery stable that later became a cotton warehouse and then a Coca-Cola bottling plant. Gleaming heart-pine floors and antiques, including a handsome English grandfather clock and an exquisitely carved Victorian mantel, make it unique. Deluxe-grade rooms, as expected, have extras; the 24 suites have living rooms and wet bars. The café is a notch nicer than most other Holiday Inn restaurants. An executive wing, at the back of the hotel, is geared to business travelers. ✉ *601 E. Bay St., Historic District, 31401,* ☎ *912/238–1200 or 800/ 465–4329,* FAX *912/236–2184,* WEB *www.savannahhotel.com. 145 rooms,*

24 suites. Restaurant, bar, café, some in-room VCRs, some microwaves, some refrigerators, outdoor pool, outdoor hot tub, Internet, meeting room. AE, D, DC, MC, V.

$$$ ★ ⊡ **Planters Inn.** Formerly the John Wesley Hotel, this inn is housed in a structure built in 1812, and though it retains the regal tone of that golden age, it still offers all the intimate comforts you would expect from an upscale inn. The inn's 60 guest rooms are all decorated in the finest fabrics and Baker furnishings (a '20s design style named for the Dutch immigrant cabinetmaker). According to lore, a (good) ghost inhabits the hotel, floating through the hallways and rearranging skewed paintings hanging in the hallway. ⊠ *29 Abercorn St., Historic District, 31401,* ☎ *912/232–5678,* FAX *912/236–2184,* WEB *www.plantersinnsavannah.com. 60 rooms. Cable TV, hot tubs. AE, D, DC, MC, V.*

$$–$$$ ⊡ **Marshall House.** This restored hotel, with original pine floors, woodwork, and bricks, caters to business travelers while providing the intimacy of a B&B. Different spaces reflect different parts of Savannah's history, from its founding to the Civil War. Artwork is mostly by local artists. You can listen to live jazz on weekends in the hotel lounge. Café M specializes in local cuisine, such as Southern pot-au-feu, a seafood-rich Lowcountry dish with okra and greens, and Georgia smoked quail. Guests get free passes to a downtown health club. ⊠ *123 E. Broughton St., Historic District, 31401,* ☎ *912/644–7896 or 800/589–6304,* FAX *912/234–3334,* WEB *www.marshallhouse.com. 65 rooms, 3 suites. Restaurant, lounge, meeting room. AE, D, MC, V.*

$$–$$$ ⊡ **River Street Inn.** The interior of this 1817 converted warehouse is so lavish that it's hard to believe the five-story building once stood vacant in a state of disrepair. Today the 86 guest rooms are filled with antiques and reproductions from the era of King Cotton. One floor has charming souvenir and gift shops and a New Orleans–style restaurant. ⊠ *115 E. River St., Historic District, 31401,* ☎ *912/234–6400 or 800/678–8946,* FAX *912/234–1478,* WEB *www.riverstreetinn.com. 86 rooms. 2 restaurants, 3 bars, shops, billiards, business services, meeting rooms. AE, D, DC, MC, V. BP.*

Nightlife and the Arts

Savannah's nightlife reflects the city's laid-back personality. Some clubs have live reggae, hard rock, and other contemporary music, but most stick to traditional blues, jazz, and piano-bar vocalists. After-dark merrymakers usually head for watering holes on Riverfront Plaza or the south side.

Bars and Nightclubs

The **Bar Bar** (⊠ 219 W. St. Julian St., Historic District, ☎ 912/231–1910), a neighborhood hangout, has pool tables, games, and a varied beer selection. Once a month at **Club One Jefferson** (⊠ 1 Jefferson St., Historic District, ☎ 912/232–0200), a gay bar, the Lady Chablis bumps and grinds her way down the catwalk, lip-synching disco tunes in a shimmer of sequin and satin gowns; the cover is $5. **Kevin Barry's Irish Pub** (⊠ 114 W. River St., Historic District, ☎ 912/233–9626) has a friendly vibe, a full menu until 1 AM, and traditional Irish music from Wednesday to Sunday; it's *the* place to be on St. Patrick's Day. The rest of the year there's a mix of tourists and locals of all ages. Go to **M.D.'s Lounge** (⊠ 2 W. Bay St., Historic District, ☎ 912/238–1234) if you have a classy nightcap in mind. The bar is literally perched above the Savannah River and surrounded by windows big enough to be glass walls. **Stogies** (⊠ 112 W. Congress St., Historic District, ☎ 912/233–4277) has its own humidor where patrons buy expensive cigars. It's a fun spot if you can take the smoke.

Coffeehouses

Thanks to a substantial student population, the city has sprouted coffeehouses as if they were spring flowers. **Christy's Espresso Delights** (⊠ 7400 Abercorn St., Highland Park, ☎ 912/356–3566) is a full-service espresso café with a wonderful selection of fine desserts and a light-lunch menu. The **Express** (⊠ 39 Barnard St., Historic District, ☎ 912/233–4683) is a warm, unassuming bakery and café that serves specialty coffees along with decadent desserts and tasty snacks. **Gallery Espresso** (⊠ 6 E. Liberty St., Historic District, ☎ 912/233–5348) is a combined coffee haunt and art enclave, with gallery shows; it stays open late.

Jazz and Blues Clubs

Bayou Café and Blues Bar (⊠ 14 N. Abercorn St., at River St., Historic District, ☎ 912/233–6414) has acoustic music during the week and the Bayou Blues Band on the weekend. The food is Cajun. **Cafe Loco** (⊠ 1 Old Hwy. 80, Tybee Island, ☎ 912/786–7810), a few miles outside Savannah, showcases local blues and acoustics acts. You can rollick with Emma Kelly, the undisputed "Lady of 6,000 Songs," at **Hard Hearted Hannah's East** (⊠ 20 E. Broad St., Historic District, ☎ 912/233–2225) Tuesday through Saturday.

Outdoor Activities and Sports

Boating

At the **Bull River Yacht Club Marina** (⊠ 8005 Old Tybee Rd., Tybee Island, ☎ 912/897–7300), you can arrange a dolphin tour, a deep-sea fishing expedition, or a jaunt through the coastal islands. **Lake Mayer Park** (⊠ Montgomery Crossroads Rd. and Sallie Mood Dr., Cresthill, ☎ 912/652–6780) has paddleboats, sailing, canoeing, and an in-line skating and hockey facility. **Saltwater Charters** (⊠ 111 Wickersham Dr., Skidaway Island, ☎ 912/598–1814) provides packages ranging from two-hour sightseeing tours to 13-hour deep-sea fishing expeditions. Water taxis to the coastal islands are also available. Public boat ramps are found at **Bell's on the River** (⊠ 12500 Apache Ave., off Abercorn St., Windward, ☎ 912/920–1113), on the Forest River. **Savannah Islands Expressway** (⊠ adjacent to Frank W. Spencer Park, Skidaway Island, ☎ 912/231–8222) offers boat ramps on the Wilmington River. **Savannah Marina** (⊠ Thunderbolt) provides ramps on the Wilmington River.

Golf

Bacon Park (⊠ 1 Shorty Cooper Dr., Southside, ☎ 912/354–2625), a public course with 27 holes, is par 72 for 18 holes and has a lighted driving range. **Henderson Golf Club** (⊠ 1 Al Henderson Dr., at I–95, Exit 94 to Rte. 204, Southside, ☎ 912/920–4653) is an 18-hole, par-71 course about 15 mi from downtown Savannah. The **Mary Calder Golf Course** (⊠ W. Lathrop Ave., West Chatham, ☎ 912/238–7100) is par 35 for its 9 holes.

Jogging and Running

Savannah's low-lying coastal terrain makes it an ideal place for joggers. **Forsyth Park** (⊠ Bull St. between Whitaker and Drayton Sts., Historic District) is a flat, pleasant place to walk, jog, or run. **Tybee Island** has a white-sand beach that is hard packed and relatively debris free, making it a favorite with runners. For suburban jogging trails head for **Daffin Park** (⊠ 1500 E. Victory Dr., Edgemere), with level sidewalks available during daylight hours. **Lake Mayer Park** (⊠ Montgomery Crossroads Rd. and Sallie Mood Dr., Southside) has 1½ mi of level asphalt available 24 hours a day.

Tennis

Bacon Park (⊠ 6262 Skidaway Rd., Southside, ☎ 912/351–3850) has 16 lighted asphalt courts. Fees are $2.50 an hour per person. **Forsyth Park** (⊠ Drayton St. and Park Ave., Historic District, ☎ 912/652–6780) contains four lighted courts available until about 10 PM; there is no charge to use them. **Lake Mayer Park** (⊠ Montgomery Crossroads Rd. and Sallie Mood Dr., Southside, ☎ 912/652–6780) has eight asphalt lighted courts available at no charge and open 8 AM–10 PM (until 11 PM May–September).

Shopping

Find your own Lowcountry treasures among a bevy of handcrafted wares—handmade quilts and baskets; wreaths made from Chinese tallow trees and Spanish moss; preserves, jams, and jellies. The favorite Savannah snack, and a popular gift item, is the benne wafer. It's about the size of a quarter and comes in different flavors. Savannah has a wide collection of colorful businesses—revitalization is no longer a goal but an accomplishment. Antiques malls and junk emporiums beckon you with their colorful storefronts and eclectic offerings, as do the many specialty shops and bookstores clustered along the moss-embossed streets.

Shopping Districts

City Market (⊠ W. St. Julian St. between Ellis and Franklin Sqs., Historic District) has sidewalk cafés, jazz haunts, shops, and art galleries. **Riverfront Plaza/River Street** (⊠ Historic District) is nine blocks of shops in renovated waterfront warehouses where you can find everything from popcorn to pottery.

Specialty Shops

ANTIQUES

Alexandra's Antique Gallery (⊠ 320 W. Broughton St., Historic District, ☎ 912/233–3999) is a four-level extravaganza of items from kitsch to fine antiques. **Arthur Smith Antiques** (⊠ 402 Bull St., Historic District, ☎ 912/236–9701) has four floors showcasing 18th- and 19th-century European furniture, porcelain, rugs, and paintings.

ART GALLERIES

Compass Prints, Inc./Ray Ellis Gallery (⊠ 205 W. Congress St., Historic District, ☎ 912/234–3537) sells original artwork, prints, and books by internationally acclaimed artist Ray Ellis. **Gallery Espresso** (⊠ 6 E. Liberty St., Historic District, ☎ 912/233–5348) has a new show every two weeks focusing on work by local artists. A true coffeehouse, it stays open until the wee hours. **Gallery 209** (⊠ 209 E. River St., Historic District, ☎ 912/236–4583) is a co-op gallery, with paintings, watercolors, pottery, jewelry, batik, stained glass, weavings, and sculptures by local artists. **Off the Wall** (⊠ 206 W. Broughton St., Historic District, ☎ 912/233–8840) exhibits artists from everywhere, including Savannah. **Jack Leigh Gallery** (⊠ 132 E. Oglethorpe Ave., Historic District, ☎ 912/234–6449) displays the work of Jack Leigh, whose photograph of Bonaventure Cemetery graces the cover of *Midnight in the Garden of Good and Evil.*

Savannah College of Art and Design (⊠ 516 Abercorn St., Historic District, ☎ 912/525–5200), a private art college, has restored at least 40 historic buildings in the city, including 12 galleries. Work by faculty and students is often for sale, and touring exhibitions are frequently in the on-campus galleries. Stop by Exhibit A, Pinnacle Gallery, and the West Bank Gallery, and ask about other student galleries. Garden for the Arts has an amphitheater and shows performance art.

BENNE WAFERS

Byrd Cookie Company & Gourmet Marketplace (⌧ 6700 Waters Ave., Highland Park, ☎ 912/355–1716), founded in 1924, is the best place to get the popular cookies that are also sold in numerous gift shops around town.

BOOKS

For regional to general Southern subjects and Americana, visit the **Book Lady** (⌧ 17 W. York St., Historic District, ☎ 912/233–3628), in a 200-year-old house for more than two decades. The shop also has an on-line search service. **E. Shaver Booksellers** (⌧ 326 Bull St., Historic District, ☎ 912/234–7257) is the source for 17th- and 18th-century maps and new books on regional subjects; the shop occupies 12 rooms. **V. & J. Duncan** (⌧ 12 E. Taylor St., Historic District, ☎ 912/232–0338) specializes in antique maps, prints, and books.

COUNTRY CRAFTS

Charlotte's Corner (⌧ 1 W. Liberty St., Historic District, ☎ 912/233–8061) carries expensive and moderately priced Savannah souvenirs, children's clothes and toys, and beachwear.

Savannah A to Z

To research prices, get advice from other travelers, and book travel arrangements, visit www.fodors.com

AIR TRAVEL TO AND FROM SAVANNAH

CARRIERS

Savannah is served by AirTran Airways, ASA, Comair, Continental Express, Delta, United Express, and US Airways/Express for domestic flights.

AIRPORTS AND TRANSFERS

Savannah International Airport is 18 mi west of downtown. Despite the name, international flights are nonexistent. The foreign trade zone, a locus for importing, constitutes the "international" aspect.

➤ AIRPORT INFORMATION: **Savannah International Airport** (⌧ 400 Airways Ave., West Chatham, ☎ 912/964–0514, WEB www.savannahairport.com).

AIRPORT TRANSFER

Vans operated by McCall's Limousine Service leave the airport daily for downtown locations. The trip takes 15 minutes, and the one-way fare is $16 for one-way, $30 round-trip for one person; the two-person rate is $11 per person one-way, $22 per person round-trip. Routes can include other destinations in addition to downtown. Advance reservation is required.

Taxi service is an easy way to get from the airport to downtown; try AAA Adam Cab Incorporated and Yellow Cab Company; the one-way fare is about $20, plus $5 for each addition person. By car take I–95 south to I–16 east into downtown Savannah.

➤ TAXIS AND SHUTTLES: **AAA Adam Cab Incorporated** (☎ 912/927–7466). **McCall's Limousine Service** (☎ 912/966–5364). **Yellow Cab Company** (☎ 912/236–1133).

BUS TRAVEL TO AND FROM SAVANNAH

➤ BUS INFORMATION: **Greyhound/Trailways** (⌧ 610 W. Oglethorpe Ave., Downtown, ☎ 912/233–8186 or 800/231–2222).

BUS TRAVEL WITHIN SAVANNAH

Chatham Area Transit (CAT) operates buses in Savannah and Chatham County Monday through Saturday from 6 AM to 11 PM, Sunday from

9 to 7. Some lines may stop running earlier or may not run on Sunday. The CAT Shuttle operates throughout the Historic District; the cost is 75¢ one-way. Buses require 75¢ in exact change.

➤ Bus Information: **Chatham Area Transit** (☎ 912/233–5767, WEB www.catchacat.org).

CAR TRAVEL

I–95 slices north–south along the eastern seaboard, intersecting 10 mi west of town with east–west I–16, which dead-ends in downtown Savannah. U.S. 17, the Coastal Highway, also runs north–south through town. U.S. 80, which connects the Atlantic to the Pacific, is another east–west route through Savannah.

EMERGENCIES

Candler Hospital and Memorial Health University Medical Center are the area hospitals with 24-hour emergency rooms.

➤ Emergency Services: **Ambulance, police** (☎ 911).

➤ Hospitals: **Candler Hospital** (⊠ 5353 Reynolds St., Kensington Park, ☎ 912/692–6000). **Memorial Health University Medical Center** (⊠ 4700 Waters Ave., Fairfield, ☎ 912/350–8000).

➤ 24-Hour Pharmacies: **CVS Pharmacy** (⊠ Medical Arts Shopping Center, 4725 Waters Ave., Fairfield, ☎ 912/355–7111).

LODGING

BED-AND-BREAKFASTS

Bed & Breakfast Online can provide detailed cyber-brochures on inns in Atlanta as well as the surrounding area.

➤ Reservation Information: **Bed & Breakfast Online** (⊠ Box 829, Madison, TN 37116, WEB www.bbonline.com/ga, ☎ 615/868–1946).

TAXIS

AAA Adam Cab Co. is a reliable 24-hour taxi service. Calling ahead for reservations could yield a flat rate. Taxis start at 60¢ and cost $1.20 for each mile. Yellow Cab Company is a another dependable taxi service; it has comparable rates.

➤ Taxi Companies: **AAA Adam Cab Co.** (☎ 912/927–7466). **Yellow Cab Company** (☎ 912/236–1133).

TOURS

HISTORIC DISTRICT TOURS

Beach Institute African-American Cultural Center is headquarters for the Negro Heritage Trail Tour. A knowledgeable guide traces the city's more than 250 years of black history. Tours, which begin at the Savannah Visitors Center, are at 1 and 3 and cost $15.

Carriage Tours of Savannah takes you through the Historic District by day or by night at a 19th-century clip-clop pace, with coachmen spinning tales and telling ghost stories along the way. A romantic evening tour in a private carriage costs $65 ($85 on Friday and Saturday evenings), and although champagne can no longer be included, you may bring whatever refreshments you wish; regular tours are a more modest $17 per person.

Garden Club of Savannah runs spring tours of private gardens tucked behind old brick walls and wrought-iron gates. It costs $20 and finishes with tea at the Green-Meldrim House.

Old Town Trolley Tours has narrated 90-minute tours traversing the Historic District. Trolleys stop at 13 designated stops every half hour daily 9–4:30; you can hop on and off as you please. The cost is $18–$22.

➤ Fees and Schedules: **Beach Institute African-American Cultural Center** (☎ 912/234–8000). **Carriage Tours of Savannah** (☎ 912/236–

6756). **Garden Club of Savannah** (☎ 912/238–0248). **Old Town Trolley Tours** (☎ 912/233–0083).

Gray Line conducts a four-hour tour to Isle of Hope and the Lowcountry, including Thunderbolt (a shrimping community) and Wormsloe Plantation Site. Options include walking tours, minibus tours, and trolley tours. The cost is $17–$22.

Historic Savannah Foundation, a preservation organization, leads tours of the Historic District and the Lowcountry. Preservation, *Midnight in the Garden of Good and Evil,* the Golden Isles, group, and private tours also are available. In addition, the foundation leads specialty excursions to the fishing village of Thunderbolt; the Isle of Hope, with its stately mansions lining Bluff Drive; the much-photographed Bonaventure Cemetery, on the banks of the Wilmington River; and Wormsloe Plantation Site, with its mile-long avenue of arching oaks. Fees for the specialty tours start at $75 per hour, with a two-hour minimum for a private group of up to five people.

Square Routes provides customized strolls and private driving tours that wend through the Historic District and other parts of the Lowcountry. In-town tours focus on the city's architecture and gardens, and specialized tours include the *Midnight in the Garden of Good and Evil* walk. Tours usually last two hours and start at $35 per person, with a minimum of two people per tour.

➤ FEES AND SCHEDULES: **Gray Line** (☎ 912/234–8687 or 800/426–2318). **Historic Savannah Foundation** (☎ 912/234–4088 or 800/627–5030). **Square Routes** (☎ 912/232–6866 or 800/868–6867).

Much of the downtown Historic District can easily be explored on foot. Its grid shape makes getting around a breeze, and you'll find any number of places to stop and rest.

A Ghost Talk Ghost Walk tour should send chills down your spine during an easy 1-mi jaunt through the old colonial city. Tours, lasting an hour and a half, leave from the middle of Reynolds Square, at the John Wesley Memorial. Call for dates, times, and reservations; the cost is $10.

Savannah-by-Foot's Creepy Crawl Haunted Pub Tour is a favorite. It seems there are so many ghosts in Savannah they're actually divided into subcategories. On this tour, charismatic guide and storyteller Greg Proffit specializes in those ghosts that haunt taverns only, regaling you with tales from secret subbasements discovered to house skeletal remains, possessed gum-ball machines, and animated water faucets. Tours traditionally depart from the Six Pence Pub, where a ghost named Larry likes to fling open the bathroom doors, but routes are open to customizing, so call for departure times and locations; the cost is $15.

➤ FEES AND SCHEDULES: **A Ghost Talk Ghost Walk Tour** (✉ Reynolds Sq., Congress and Abercorn Sts., Historic District, ☎ 912/233–3896). **Savannah-By-Foot's Creepy Crawl Haunted Pub Tour** (☎ 912/398–3833). **Six Pence Pub** (✉ 245 Bull St., Historic District).

TRAIN TRAVEL

Amtrak has regular service along the eastern seaboard, with daily stops in Savannah. The Amtrak station is 4 mi southwest of downtown. Cab fare into the city is $7–$10, depending on the number of passengers.

➤ TRAIN INFORMATION: **Amtrak** (✉ 2611 Seaboard Coastline Dr., Telfair Junction, ☎ 912/234–2611 or 800/872–7245, WEB www.amtrak.com).

VISITOR INFORMATION

➤ TOURIST INFORMATION: **Savannah Area Convention & Visitors Bureau** (✉ 101 E. Bay St., Historic District, 31401, ☎ 912/644–6401 or 877/728–2662, 🄵🄰🄷 912/944–0468, 🅆🄴🄱 www.savcvb.com).

THE COASTAL ISLES AND THE OKEFENOKEE

Jekyll, St. Simons, and Sea Islands

The coastal isles are a string of lush, subtropical barrier islands meandering lazily down Georgia's Atlantic coast from Savannah to the Florida border. The islands have a long history of human habitation; Native American relics have been found here that date from about 2500 BC. The four designated Golden Isles—Little St. Simons Island, Sea Island, St. Simons Island, and Jekyll Island—are great vacation spots. The best way to appreciate the barrier islands' rare ecology is to visit Sapelo and Cumberland islands—part of Georgia's coastal isles—or to take a guided tour.

Each coastal isle has a distinct personality, shaped by its history and ecology. All the Golden Isles but Little St. Simons are connected to the mainland by bridges in the vicinity of Brunswick; these are the only coastal isles accessible by automobile. Little St. Simons Island, a privately owned retreat with guest accommodations, is reached by a launch from St. Simons. Sapelo Island is accessible by ferry from the visitor center just north of Darien (on the mainland). The Cumberland Island National Seashore is reached by ferry from St. Marys. About 60 mi inland is the Okefenokee National Wildlife Refuge, which has a character all its own.

Lodging prices quoted here may be much lower during nonpeak seasons, and specials are often available during the week in high season. All Georgia beaches are in the public domain.

Numbers in the margin correspond to points of interest on the Coastal Isles map.

Sapelo Island

⑧⑥ *8 mi east of Darien.*

In Sapelo's fields you might find chips of Guale Indian pottery dating as far back as 2000 BC and shards of Spanish ceramics from the 16th century. On the northern end, remains of the Chocolate Plantation recall the island's French heritage and role during the plantation days of the 19th century. Today researchers occupy the southern sector of the island, studying ecology at the Sapelo Island National Estuarine Research Reserve and evaluating the marshland at the Marine Institute. The organizations' studies are instrumental in preserving Sapelo's delicate ecosystem and others like it throughout the world.

You can explore many historical periods and natural environments here, but facilities on the island are limited for the most part to drinking fountains and rest rooms. Bring insect repellent, especially in summer, and leave your pets at home.

Start your visit at the **Sapelo Island Visitors Center** (✉ Rte. 1, Box 1500, Darien 31305, ☎ 912/437–3224; 912/485–2300 for group tours; 912/485–2299 for camping reservations, 🅆🄴🄱 www.gacoast.com/navigator/sapelo.html). To get here from downtown Darien, go north on Route 99 for 8 mi, following signs for the Sapelo Island National Estuarine

The Coastal Isles

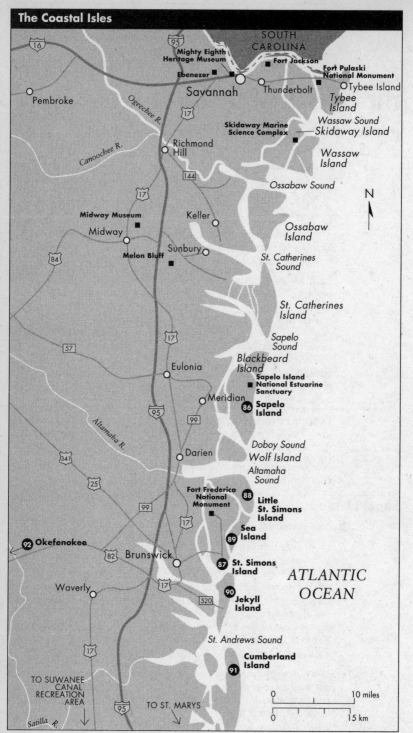

SOUTH CAROLINA

Mighty Eighth
Heritage Museum

Fort Jackson

Fort Pulaski
National Monument

Ebenezer

Savannah

Thunderbolt

Tybee Island

Pembroke

Tybee
Island

Wassaw Sound

Skidaway Marine
Science Complex

Skidaway Island

Ogeechee R.

Richmond
Hill

Wassaw
Island

Canoochee R.

Ossabaw Sound

Midway Museum

Keller

Ossabaw
Island

Midway

Sunbury

St. Catherines
Sound

Melon Bluff

St. Catherines
Island

Sapelo
Sound

Blackbeard
Island

Eulonia

Sapelo Island
National Estuarine
Sanctuary

Meridian

86 Sapelo
Island

Doboy Sound

Wolf Island

Darien

Altamaha
Sound

Altamaha R.

Fort Frederica
National
Monument

88 Little
St. Simons
Island

89 Sea
Island

92 Okefenokee

Brunswick

87 St. Simons
Island

ATLANTIC
OCEAN

Waverly

90 Jekyll
Island

St. Andrews Sound

Cumberland
Island

91

TO SUWANEE
CANAL
RECREATION
AREA

TO ST. MARYS

Satilla R.

N

0   10 miles

0   15 km

Research Reserve. At the visitors center you'll see an exhibition on the island's history, culture, and ecology. Here you can purchase a ticket good for a round-trip ferry ride and bus tour of the island. The sights that make up the bus tour vary depending on the day of the week but always included are the marsh, the sand dune ecosystem, and the wildlife management area. On Saturday the tour includes the 80-ft **Sapelo Lighthouse,** built in 1820, a symbol of the cotton and lumber industry once based out of Darien's port. To see the island's **Reynolds Mansion,** schedule your tour for Wednesday. Reservations are required for tours. If you wish to stay overnight on Sapelo, you can either camp or choose from several B&B inns. If you stay overnight (and only if you do), you may visit the beach and, on a tour, the **Hog Hammock Community,** the few remaining sites on the south Atlantic coast where ethnic African-American culture has been preserved. Hog Hammock's 65 residents are descendants of slaves who worked the island's plantations during the 19th century. You can rent a bicycle at your hotel if you want to tour the area, but you cannot bring a bicycle on the ferry.

Dining and Lodging

$-$$ ✕ **Mudcat Charlie's.** It's plastic forks and plates all the way at this casual eatery. Local seafood—crab stew, fried oysters, and shrimp—is the specialty. The steaks, burgers, and pork chops are good, too. Peach and apple pies are made on the premises. It's between Brunswick and Darien on U.S. 17, 8 mi from Sapelo Island. ⊠ *250 Ricefield Way,* ☎ *912/261–0055. AE, D, DC, MC, V.*

$$ 🏠 **Open Gates.** Fine antiques fill the public spaces and guest rooms of this comfortable white-frame Victorian house, which dates from 1876. Breakfast specialties include fresh fig preserves, plantation (puffed) pancakes, and hunter's casserole (a baked egg strata). Innkeeper Carolyn Hodges offers guided tours of the Altamaha River. ⊠ *Vernon Sq., Box 1526, Darien 31305,* ☎ *912/437–6985,* 𝙵𝙰𝚇 *912/882–9427,* 𝚆𝙴𝙱 *www. opengatesbnb.com. 4 rooms, 2 with bath. Pool, library. No credit cards. BP.*

St. Simons Island

87   *22 mi south of Darien, 6 mi south of Brunswick.*

As large as Manhattan, with more than 14,000 year-round residents, St. Simons is the Golden Isles' most complete resort destination. Fortunately, all this development has not spoiled the natural beauty of the island's regal live oaks, beaches, and salt marshes. Here you can swim and sun, golf, bike, hike, go fishing, horseback ride, tour historic sites, and feast on fresh local seafood at more than 50 restaurants.

Many sights and activities are in the **village** area along Mallory Street at the more developed south end of the island, where you'll find shops, several restaurants, pubs, and a popular public pier. For $10 a quaint "trolley" takes you on a 1½-hour guided tour of the island, leaving from near the pier several times a day in high season; tours run less frequently in winter.

🛝   **Neptune Park** (⊠ 550 Beachview Dr., ☎ 912/638–2393), on the island's south end, has picnic tables, a children's play park, miniature golf, and beach access. A swimming pool ($3 per person), with showers and rest rooms, is open each summer in the **Neptune Park Casino.**

St. Simons Lighthouse, a beacon since 1872, is virtually the symbol of St. Simons. The **Museum of Coastal History,** in the lightkeeper's cottage, has a permanent exhibit of coastal history. ⊠ *101 12th St.,* ☎ *912/638–4666,* 𝚆𝙴𝙱 *www.saintsimonslighthouse.org.* 🎟 *$4, including lighthouse.* ⊙ *Mon.–Sat. 10–5, Sun. 1:30–5.*

At the burgeoning north end of the island there's a marina, a golf club, and a housing development, as well as **Fort Frederica National Monument,** the ruins of a fort built by English troops in the mid-1730s as a bulwark against a Spanish invasion from Florida. Around the fort are the foundations of homes and shops. Start at the **National Park Service Visitors Center,** which has a film and displays. ⊠ *Off Frederica Rd. just past Christ Episcopal Church,* ☎ *912/638–3639,* WEB *www.nps.gov/fofr.* ☞ *$4 per car.* ☉ *Daily 8–5.*

Consecrated in 1886 following an earlier structure's desecration by Union troops, the white-frame Gothic-style **Christ Episcopal Church** is surrounded by live oaks, dogwoods, and azaleas. The interior has beautiful stained-glass windows. ⊠ *6329 Frederica Rd.,* ☎ *912/638–8683.* ☞ *Donations suggested.*

Dining and Lodging

$$–$$$$ ✕ **Georgia Sea Grill.** This tiny and very popular place presents eclectic dishes, with fresh local seafood the house specialty. Standouts include tender shrimp au gratin, as well as fresh seafood prepared five different ways. Nightly specials are prepared personally by the chef–owners. ⊠ *310B Mallory St.,* ☎ *912/638–1197. D, MC, V. Closed Mon. May–Sept.; Sun.–Mon. Oct.–Apr. No lunch.*

$$–$$$ ✕ **CARGO Portside Grill.** Don't miss this superb seaside pub, a short drive across the bridge in the small city of Brunswick. The menu reads like a foodie's wish list, with succulent coastal and cross-coastal fare from many ports. All of it is creatively presented by owner–chef Alix Kanegy, formerly of Atlanta's Indigo Coastal Grill. Specials have included pasta Veracruz with grilled chicken, smoked tomatoes, poblano peppers, and caramelized onions in a chipotle cream sauce; in season, soft-shell crab is often on the menu. ⊠ *1423 Newcastle St., Brunswick,* ☎ *912/267–7330. MC, V. Closed Sun.–Mon.*

$$–$$$ ✕ **Redfern Café.** A popular spot with locals, the Redfern has up to six specials nightly in addition to the regular menu. Fried oysters in a light cornmeal coating, shrimp and crab bisque with corn fritters, and the crab cakes are specialties. ⊠ *200 Redfern Village,* ☎ *912/634–1344. Reservations essential. MC, V. Closed Sun.*

$–$$$ ✕ **P. G. Archibald's.** In the village this lively restaurant and nightclub has a "bayou Victorian" style, with lots of antiques and memorabilia. The menu highlights seafood as well as basic steak and chicken dishes, plus oysters prepared 15 ways. Blue-crab soup is a local favorite, and the huge seafood platter could easily feed two. Open late, the restaurant also presents live entertainment Thursday through Saturday. ⊠ *440 King's Way,* ☎ *912/638–3030. AE, DC, MC, V.*

$ ✕ **Rafters Blues Club, Restaurant and Raw Bar.** If you're looking for cheap, great food and a raucous good time, this place serves it up by the boatload. Revelers sit at long wooden-plank picnic tables and heartily partake in the offerings of both the prodigious bar and the equally generous kitchen. The restaurant serves ocean fare prepared in interesting ways—a seafood burrito, for example. Rafters is open late and presents live entertainment Wednesday through Saturday. ⊠ *315½ Mallory St.,* ☎ *912/634–9755. AE, D, MC, V. Closed Sun.*

$$$$ ☷ **The Lodge at Sea Island Golf Club.** This small but opulent lodge has assumed its place among the coast's most exclusive accommodations. Dashingly decorated rooms and suites all have water or golf-course views, and you can expect to be pampered by 24-hour butler service. You can also choose from among four stellar restaurants for dining. The lodge serves as the clubhouse for the Sea Island Golf Club (although this whole complex lies on St. Simons Island, so don't let the title disorient you) and encompasses a trophy room, locker rooms, and the Sea Island Golf Learning Center. ⊠ *St. Simons Island 31522,* ☎ *912/638–3611 or 866/*

465–3563, WEB *www.golflodge.com. 40 rooms, 2 suites. 4 restaurants, bar, in-room VCRs, 2 18-hole golf courses, tennis court, pool, health club, hot tub, lounge, Internet, meeting room. AE, D, DC, MC, V.*

$$$ 🏨 **King and Prince Beach and Golf Resort.** Most people who visit feel it's worth the expense to get a room with easy beach access at this cushy retreat. Guest rooms are spacious, and villas have two or three bedrooms. The villas are owned by private individuals, so the total number available for rent varies from time to time. ✉ *201 Arnold Rd., Box 20798, 31522,* ☎ *912/638–3631 or 800/342–0212,* FAX *912/634–1720,* WEB *www.kingandprince.com. 148 rooms, 10 suites, 43 villas. 2 restaurants, bar, golf privileges, 2 tennis courts, 1 indoor and 4 outdoor pools, 3 hot tubs, bicycles, lounge, Internet. AE, D, MC, V.*

$$ 🏨 **Holiday Inn Express.** With brightly decorated rooms at great prices, this nonsmoking facility is an excellent midprice option. The six King Executive rooms have sofas and desks. ✉ *Plantation Village, 299 Main St., 31522,* ☎ *912/634–2175 or 800/787–4666,* FAX *912/634–2174. 60 rooms. Cable TV, pool, bicycles, laundry service, meeting room. AE, D, MC, V.*

$–$$ 🏨 **Sea Palms Golf and Tennis Resort.** Given this resort's emphasis on golf and tennis, it's an ideal milieu if you're the sports-minded type. Rooms have balconies overlooking the golf course, and they are large—so large they're touted as the biggest standard guest rooms in the Golden Isles. The furnishings are somewhat unimaginative, however. This is a contemporary complex with fully furnished villas (suites), most with kitchens, nestled on an 800-acre site. Guests also enjoy beach club privileges. ✉ *5445 Frederica Rd., 31522,* ☎ *912/638–3351 or 800/ 841–6268,* FAX *912/634–8029,* WEB *www.seapalms.com. 149 rooms, 26 suites. 2 restaurants, bar, 27-hole golf course, 3 tennis courts, 2 pools, health club, bicycles, volleyball, children's programs, convention center. AE, DC, MC, V.*

RENTALS

For St. Simons condo and cottage rentals, contact **Golden Isles Realty** (✉ 330 Mallory St., 31522, ☎ 912/638–8623 or 800/337–3106, FAX 912/638–6925). **Trupp-Hodnett Enterprises** (✉ 520 Ocean Blvd., 31522, ☎ 912/638–5450 or 800/627–6850, FAX 912/638–2983) provides boat rentals.

Little St. Simons Island

🟤 *10–15 mins by ferry from the Hampton River Club Marina on St. Simons Island.*

Six miles long, 2–3 mi wide, and skirted by Atlantic beaches and salt marshes teeming with birds and wildlife, this privately owned resort is custom-made for *Robinson Crusoe*–style getaways. The island's only development is a rustic but comfortable guest compound. Guided tours, horseback rides, canoe trips, fly-fishing lessons, and other extras can be arranged, some for no additional charge. Inquire about the advisability of bringing children, as there are some limitations. In summer day tours can be arranged.

The island's forests and marshes are inhabited by deer, armadillos, horses, raccoons, gators, otters, and more than 200 species of birds. As a guest you're free to walk the 6 mi of undisturbed beaches, swim in the mild surf, fish from the dock, and seine (you and others take a net, walk into the ocean, and drag the net back to shore) for shrimp and crabs in the marshes. There are also horses to ride, nature walks with experts, and other island explorations via boat or the back of the hotel's pickup truck. From June through September up to 10 nonguests per day may visit the island by reservation; the $75 cost includes the ferry to the island, an island tour by truck, lunch at the lodge, and a beach walk. Contact the Lodge on Little St. Simons Island for more information.

Dining and Lodging

$$$$ ✕🏨 **Lodge on Little St. Simons Island.** A recent winner of *Condé Nast Traveler*'s "Best Small Hotel in North America" title, this gorgeous resort cites full capacity at a mere 30 guests. Meals are included—platters are heaped with fresh fish, homemade breads, and pies. You also get complimentary drinks during cocktail hour. Transportation from St. Simons Island, transportation on the island, and interpretive guides are also provided. ⊠ *Box 21078, 31522,* ☎ *912/638–7472 or 888/733–5774,* ⅢA *912/634–1811,* ⅢE *www.littlestsimonsisland.com. 14 rooms, 1 suite. Restaurant, pool, beach, boating, fishing, bicycles, horseback riding. AE, D, MC, V. FAP.*

Sea Island

89 *5 mi northeast of St. Simons Island.*

Separated from St. Simons Island by a narrow waterway and a good many steps on the social ladder, Sea Island has been the domain of the well-heeled and the Cloister Hotel since 1928. There is no entrance gate, and nonguests are free to admire the beautifully planted grounds and to drive past the mansions lining Sea Island Drive. The owners of the 180 or so private cottages and villas treat the hotel like a country club, and their tenants may use the hotel's facilities. For rentals contact **Sea Island Cottage Rentals** (⊠ Box 30351, 31561, ☎ 912/638–5112 or 800/732–4752, ⅢA 912/638–5824).

Lodging

$$$$ 🏨 **The Cloister.** The Cloister undeniably lives up to its celebrity status as a grand coastal resort. You can get a spacious, comfortably appointed room or suite in the Spanish Mediterranean–style hotel—designed by Florida architect Addison Mizner—or in the property's later-built Ocean Houses, which offer 56 dramatic suites connected by lavish house parlors with fireplaces and staffed bars. The state-of-the-art spa at the Cloister is in a beautiful building all its own. You also get access to the nearby Sea Island Golf Course. ⊠ *Sea Island 31561,* ☎ *912/638–3611 or 800/732–4752,* ⅢA *912/638–5823,* ⅢE *www.cloister.com. 274 rooms, 32 suites. 4 restaurants, bar, cable TV, 3 18-hole golf courses, 18 tennis courts, 2 pools, health club, spa, bicycles, 2 lounges, children's programs, business services, airport shuttle. AE, D, DC, MC, V. FAP.*

Jekyll Island

90 *18 mi south of St. Simons Island, 90 mi south of Savannah.*

For 56 winters, between 1886 and 1942, America's rich and famous faithfully came south to Jekyll Island. Through the Gilded Age, the Great War, as World War I was originally known, the Roaring '20s, and the Great Depression, Vanderbilts and Rockefellers, Morgans and Astors, Macys, Pulitzers, and Goodyears shuttered their 5th Avenue castles and retreated to the serenity of their wild Georgia island. Here they built elegant "cottages," played golf and tennis, and socialized. Early in World War II the millionaires departed for the last time. In 1947 the state of Georgia purchased the entire island for the bargain price of $675,000.

Jekyll Island is still a 7½-mi playground but is no longer restricted to the rich and famous. The golf, tennis, fishing, biking, and jogging, the water park, and the picnic grounds are open to all. One side of the island is lined by nearly 10 mi of hard-packed Atlantic beaches; the other, by the Intracoastal Waterway and picturesque salt marshes. Deer and wild turkeys inhabit interior forests of pine, magnolia, and moss-veiled live oaks. Egrets, pelicans, herons, and sandpipers skim the gentle surf. Jekyll's clean, mostly uncommercialized public beaches are free and open year-round. Bathhouses with rest rooms, changing areas, and showers are open at regular intervals along the beach. Beachwear, suntan lotion, rafts, snacks, and drinks are available at the **Jekyll Shopping Center,** facing the beach at Beachview Drive.

The **Jekyll Island Museum Visitor Center** gives tram tours of the Jekyll Island National Historic Landmark District. Tours originate at the museum's visitor center on Stable Road and include several millionaires' residences in the 240-acre historic district. Faith Chapel, illuminated by Tiffany stained-glass windows, is open for meditation daily 2–4. ⊠ *381 Riverview Dr., I–95, Exit 29,* ☎ *912/635–2762 or 800/841–6586,* FAX *912/635–4004.* 🎫 *$10.* ◷ *Daily 9–5, tours daily 10–3.*

Dining and Lodging

$$$ ✕ **Grand Dining Room.** In the Jekyll Island Club Hotel, the dining room
★ sparkles with silver and crystal. The cuisine reflects the elegance of the private hunting club that flourished from the late 19th century to the World War II era and which brought a fine chef and staff in from New York's Delmonico's. Enjoy the blue-crab cakes, grilled pork with Vidalia onion, and local seafood. The restaurant has its own label pinot noir and chardonnay, made by Mountain View Vineyards. ⊠ *371 Riverview Dr.,* ☎ *912/635–2600. Reservations essential. AE, D, DC, MC, V.*

$$ ✕ **Courtyard at Crane.** This notable addition to the island's restaurant scene offers alfresco dining in the courtyard of Crane Cottage, part of the Jekyll Island Club Hotel. The menu focuses on creative salads and entrées inspired by the world-famous kitchens of the Napa/Sonoma Valley wine country. You might sample the Mediterranean platter of grilled vegetables, imported olives, and fresh mozzarella with *crostini*; or a lobster-salad croissant with avocado, red onion, apple-wood-smoked bacon, tomato, and alfalfa sprouts. ⊠ *371 Riverview Dr., Jekyll Island Club Hotel,* ☎ *912/635–2600. AE, D, DC, MC, V. Closed Sun.*

$$ ✕ **SeaJay's Waterfront Cafe & Pub.** Convivial and festive, with a swamp-shack style, this tavern serves delicious—and inexpensive—seafood, including a crab chowder that locals love. This is also the home of a wildly popular shrimp-boil buffet: a Lowcountry all-you-can-eat feast of local shrimp, corn on the cob, smoked sausage, and new potatoes served in a pot. ⊠ *Jekyll Harbor Marina,* ☎ *912/635–3200. AE, MC, V.*

$$$–$$$$ 🏨 **Jekyll Island Club Hotel.** This sprawling 1886 resort, the focal point
★ of which is a four-story clubhouse—with couches and a fireplace—has wraparound verandas and Queen Anne–style towers and turrets. Guest rooms, suites, apartments, and cottages are custom-decorated with mahogany beds, armoires, and plush sofas and chairs. Two beautifully restored former "millionaires' cottages"—the Crane Cottage and the Cherokee Cottage—add 23 elegant guest rooms to this gracefully groomed compound. Note the B&B packages—they're a great deal. ⊠ *371 Riverview Dr., 31527,* ☎ *912/635–2600 or 800/535–9547,* FAX *912/635–2818,* WEB *www.jekyllclub.com. 139 rooms, 15 suites. 3 restaurants, bar, cable TV, 13 tennis courts, pool, beach, bicycles, croquet, lounge, Internet, meeting room. AE, D, DC, MC, V.*

$$–$$$$ 🏨 **Beachview Club.** They literally raised the roof on an old motel to
★ build this luxury all-suites lodging. Stucco walls are painted light yellow, and big old oak trees shade the grounds. Efficiencies have either one king- or two queen-size beds, a desk, and a kitchenette. All rooms either are on the oceanfront or have at least a partial ocean view from the balcony, and some rooms are equipped with a hot tub and gas fireplace. The interior design reflects an understated island theme. An attempt to target the corporate crowd has proven effective, and the

unique meeting room in the Bell Tower accommodates up to 35 people for business events. Higher-end suites have full kitchens. ⊠ *721 N. Beachview Dr., 31527,* ☎ *912/635–2256 or 800/299–2228,* FAX *912/ 635–3770,* WEB *www.beachviewclub.com. 21 efficiencies, 7 suites. Restaurant, bar, some kitchenettes, microwaves, pool, hot tub, Internet, meeting room. AE, D, DC, MC, V.*

$$–$$$ 🏨 **Holiday Inn Beach Resort.** Amid natural dunes and oaks in a secluded oceanfront location, this hotel has a private beach. Each room has a balcony, but none has an ocean view (though it's a short walk away). The boardwalk out to the beach meanders through a lovely regional landscape, thick with palm trees and other native flora. ⊠ *200 S. Beachview Dr., 31527,* ☎ *912/635–3311 or 800/753–5955,* FAX *912/ 635–2901,* WEB *www.sixcontinentshotels.com. 198 rooms. Restaurant, bar, 2 tennis courts, pool, health club, bicycles, lobby lounge, playground. AE, D, DC, MC, V.*

$–$$ 🏨 **Jekyll Inn.** This popular oceanfront spread's 15 verdant acres space the buildings generously apart. Popular with families, the inn accommodates children under 17 free when they stay with parents or grandparents. Packages include summer family-focused arrangements and romantic getaways. The Italian restaurant offers basic, hearty fare. ⊠ *975 N. Beachview Dr., 31527,* ☎ *912/635–2531 or 800/431–5190,* FAX *912/635–2332,* WEB *www.jekyllinn.com. 188 rooms, 66 villas. Restaurant, 2 bars, refrigerators, pool, volleyball, lobby lounge, playground, children's programs, laundry service, meeting room. AE, D, DC, MC, V.*

RENTALS

Jekyll's more than 200 rental cottages and condos are handled by **Jekyll Realty** (⊠ Box 13096, 31527, ☎ 912/635–3301 or 888/333–5055, FAX 912/635–3303). **Parker-Kaufman Realty** (⊠ Box 13126, 31527, ☎ 912/635–2512 or 888/453–5955, FAX 912/635–2190) is a small outfit that provides cottage and condo rental information.

Outdoor Activities and Sports

GOLF

The **Jekyll Island Golf Club** (⊠ 322 Capt. Wylly Rd., ☎ 912/635–2368) has 63 holes, including three 18-hole, par-72 courses, and a clubhouse. Greens fees are $35, good all day, and carts are $14.50 per person per course. There's also a 9-hole, par-36 course, the **Historic Oceanside Nine** (⊠ N. Beachview Dr., ☎ 912/635–2170), where the millionaires used to play. Greens fees are $21, and carts are $7.25 for every 9 holes.

NATURE CENTER

ℭ The **Coastal Encounters Nature Center** runs summer programs for children and families on the ecology of the coastal islands. Programs and excursions are individually priced. At the center are exhibits about the fauna of the region. ⊠ *100 S. Riverview Dr.,* ☎ *912/635–9102,* WEB *http://coastalgeorgia.com/coastalencounters.* ▣ *Donation.* ☉ *Mon.–Sat. 9–5.*

TENNIS

The **Jekyll Island Tennis Center** (⊠ 400 Capt. Wylly Rd., ☎ 912/635–3154) has 13 clay courts, with seven lighted for nighttime play; it hosts eight USTA-sanctioned tournaments throughout the year. Costs are $14 per hour daily 9–6 and $16 per hour for lighted courts (available until 10 PM); reservations for lighted courts are required and must be made prior to 6 PM the day of play.

☉ **Summer Waves,** an 11-acre water park, has an 18,000-square-ft wave pool, water slides, a children's activity pool with two slides, and a circular river for tubing and rafting. You are not permitted to bring your own equipment. ⊠ *210 S. Riverview Dr.,* ☎ *912/635–2074,* WEB *www. summerwaves.com.* ⊡ *$14.95.* ☉ *Late May–early Sept. (and some additional weekends in early May and late Sept.), Sun.–Fri. 10–6, Sat. 10–8 (hrs vary at beginning and end of season).*

Cumberland Island

91 *47 mi south of Jekyll Island, 115 mi south of Savannah to St. Marys via I–95, 45 mins by ferry from St. Marys.*

The largest, most southerly, and most accessible of Georgia's primitive coastal islands is Cumberland Island, a 16- by 3-mi sanctuary of marshes, dunes, beaches, forests, lakes and ponds, estuaries, and inlets. Waterways are homes for gators, sea turtles, otters, snowy egrets, great blue herons, ibises, wood storks, and more than 300 other species of birds. In the forests are armadillos, wild horses, deer, raccoons, and an assortment of reptiles.

After the ancient Guale Indians came 16th-century Spanish missionaries, 18th-century English soldiers, and 19th-century planters. During the 1880s the Thomas Carnegie family (he was the brother of industrialist Andrew) of Pittsburgh built several lavish homes here, but the island remained largely as nature created it. In the early 1970s the federal government established the **Cumberland Island National Seashore** and opened this natural treasure to the public. There is no transportation on the island itself, and the only public access to the island is via the *Cumberland Queen,* a reservations-only, 146-passenger ferry based near the National Park Service Information Center at St. Marys. Ferry bookings are heavy in summer, but cancellations and no-shows often make last-minute space available. Reservations may be made up to 11 months in advance.

From the park-service docks at the island's south end, you can follow wooded nature trails, swim and sun on 18 mi of undeveloped beaches, go fishing and bird-watching, and view the ruins of Thomas Carnegie's great estate, **Dungeness.** You can also join history and nature walks led by park-service rangers. Bear in mind that summers are hot and humid and that you must bring everything you need, including your own food, soft drinks, sunscreen, and a reliable insect repellent. ⊠ *Cumberland Island National Seashore, Box 806, 31558,* ☎ *912/882–4335,* FAX *912/673–7747,* WEB *www.nps.gov/cuis.* ⊡ *Round-trip ferry $12, day pass $4, annual pass $20.* ☉ *Mid-May–Sept., ferry departure from St. Marys daily at 9 and 11:45, from Cumberland Mar.–Nov., Wed.–Sat. at 10:15, 2:45, and 4:45, Sun.–Tues. at 10:15 and 4:45. No ferry service Dec.–Feb. Tues.–Wed.*

Dining and Lodging

$$$$ ✕🏠 **Greyfield Inn.** Cumberland Island's only accommodations are in a turn-of-the-20th-century Carnegie family home. Greyfield's public areas are filled with family mementos, furnishings, and portraits (you may feel as though you've stepped into one of Agatha Christie's mysterious Cornwall manors). Prices include all meals, transportation, tours led by a naturalist, and bike rentals. ⊠ *8 N. 2nd St., Box 900, Fernandina Beach, FL 32035,* ☎ *904/261–6408,* FAX *904/321–0666,* WEB *www.greyfieldinn.com. 13 rooms, 4 suites. Restaurant, bar, bicycle rentals. AE, D, MC, V. FAP.*

$ ⚠ **Camping.** The island has three primitive camping sites in a National Wilderness Area. Reservations are required for all camping at these sites, and the rate is $2 per person per day. To reach the sites (Hickory Hill, Yankee Paradise, and Brickhill Bluff), start north of Sea Camp dock and then hike (with all equipment) from 4 to 10 mi. Equipment must include rope to suspend provisions from trees for critter control. Non-wilderness Stafford Beach is good for novice backpackers. A half mile from the dock, with rest rooms and showers adjacent to campsites, Sea Camp is the ideal spot for first-time campers ($4 per person per day). Also available are 16 campsites that can accommodate a maximum of 60 persons. Reservations are required (recommended at least two months in advance), no pets or fires are allowed, and a seven-day stay is the limit. Bring all required equipment. The beach is just beyond the dunes. To make a reservation, contact the Cumberland Island National Seashore.

MAINLAND

$$ ✕ **Greek Mediterranean Grill.** It's a block from the St. Marys River, but the sky-blue murals and Greek proprietors make it seem more like the Mediterranean than the South. Traditional Greek dishes, such as *pastitsio* (pasta and ground beef baked with cinnamon and white cream sauce) and moussaka, are the mainstay. ✉ *122 Osborne St., St. Marys,* ☎ *912/576–2000. No credit cards.*

$$–$$$ 🏠 **Spencer House Inn.** This comfortable Victorian inn dates from 1872 and is named for the sea captain who built it as a hotel. Some rooms have expansive balconies that overlook the neatly tended grounds; others have antique claw-foot bathtubs. Innkeepers Mike and Mary Neff reside here and will prepare picnic lunches if you ask. The inn makes a perfect base for a tour of historic St. Marys and the waterfront and is convenient to the *Cumberland Queen* ferry. ✉ *200 Osborne St., St. Marys 31558,* ☎ *912/882–1872,* FAX *912/882–9427,* WEB *www.spencerhouseinn.com. 13 rooms, 1 suite. No room phones, no room TVs. AE, D, MC, V. BP.*

Okefenokee National Wildlife Refuge

65 mi southwest of Brunswick, 42 mi west of St. Marys.

★ ❾❷ Covering 730 square mi of southeastern Georgia and spilling over into northeastern Florida, the **Okefenokee,** with its mysterious rivers and lakes, bristles with seen and unseen life. Scientists agree that the Okefenokee, the largest intact freshwater wetlands in the contiguous United States, is not duplicated anywhere else on earth. The impenetrable Pinhook Swamp, to the south, part of the same ecosystem, adds another 100 square mi. If the term *swamp* denotes a dark, dank place, the Okefenokee is never that. Instead, it is a vast peat bog with numerous and varied landscapes, including aquatic prairies, towering virgin cypress, sandy pine islands, and lush subtropical hammocks. During the last Ice Age 10,000 years ago, it was part of the ocean flow. Peat began building up 7,000 years ago atop a mound of clay, now 120 ft above sea level. Two rivers, the St. Marys and the Suwanee, flow out of the refuge, and it provides at least a part-time habitat for myriad species of birds, mammals, reptiles, amphibians, and fish.

As you travel by canoe or speedboat among the water lilies and the great stands of live oaks and cypress, be on the lookout for, among many others, alligators, otters, bobcats, raccoons, opossums, white-tailed deer, turtles, bald eagles, red-tailed hawks, egrets, muskrats, herons, cranes, and red-cockaded woodpeckers. The black bears tend to be more reclusive.

The Seminole people, in their migrations south toward Florida's Everglades, once took refuge in the Okefenokee. The last Native Americans to occupy the area, they were evicted by the army and Georgia's militia in the 1830s. When the Okefenokee acquired its present status of federal preserve (1937), the white homesteaders living on its fringe were forced out.

Noting the many floating islands, the Seminole named this unique combination of land and water "Land of the Quivering Earth." If you have the rare fortune to walk one of these bogs, you will find the earth does indeed quiver, rather like fruit gelatin in a bowl.

The Okefenokee Swamp Park, 8 mi south of Waycross, is a nonprofit development. The northern entrance to the refuge is here. There are two other gateways to the swamp: an eastern entrance at the U.S. Fish and Wildlife Service headquarters in the Suwanee Canal Recreation Area, near Folkston; and a western entrance at Stephen C. Foster State Park, outside the town of Fargo. You may take an overnight canoeing-camping trip into the interior, but the Okefenokee is a wildlife refuge and designated national wilderness, not a park. Access is restricted by permit. The best way to see the Okefenokee up close is to take a day trip at one of the three gateways. Plan your visit between September and April to avoid the biting insects that emerge in May, especially in the dense interior.

South of Waycross, via U.S. 1, **Okefenokee Swamp Park** has orientation programs, exhibits, a 1⅓-mi nature trail, observation areas, wilderness walkways, an outdoor museum of pioneer life, and boat tours into the swamp that reveal its unique ecology. A boardwalk and 90-ft tower are excellent places to glimpse cruising gators and birds. You may arrange for guided boat tours at an additional cost. A 1½-mi train tour passes by a Seminole village and stops at Pioneer Island, a re-created pioneer homestead, for a 30-minute walking tour. ⊠ *5700 Swamp Park Rd., Waycross 31501*, ☎ *912/283–0583*, FAX *912/283–0023*, WEB *www.okefenokee.com.* ⊑ *$10, plus $4–$8 extra for boat-tour packages.* ☉ *Daily 8–5.*

Stephen C. Foster State Park, 18 mi northeast of Fargo via Route 177, is an 80-acre island park within the Okefenokee National Wildlife Refuge. The park encompasses a large cypress-and-black-gum forest, a majestic backdrop for one of the thickest growths of vegetation in the southeastern United States. Park naturalists leading boat tours will spill out a wealth of Okefenokee lore while you observe alligators, birds, and native trees and plants. You may also take a self-guided excursion in rental canoes and a motorized flat-bottom boat. Campsites and cabins are available. ⊠ *Rte. 1, Box 131, Fargo 31631*, ☎ *912/637–5274.* ⊑ *$5 per vehicle to National Wildlife Refuge.*

Suwanee Canal Recreation Area, 8 mi southwest of Folkston via Route 121, is administered by the U.S. Fish and Wildlife Service. Stop first at the visitor center, with exhibits on the Okefenokee's flora and fauna. A boardwalk takes you over the water to a 50-ft observation tower. The concession has equipment rentals and daily food service; you may sign up here for one- or two-hour guided boat tours. Hikers, bicyclists, and private motor vehicles are welcome on the Swamp Island Drive; several interpretive walking trails may be taken along the way. Picnicking is allowed. Wilderness canoeing and camping in the Okefenokee's interior are by reserved permit only (for which a fee is charged). Permits are hard to get, especially in cool weather. Call **refuge headquarters** (☎ 912/496–3331) when it opens at 7 AM *exactly* two months in advance of your desired starting date. Guided overnight canoe trips can be arranged by refuge concessionaire Carl E. Glenn Jr. ✉ *Rte. 2, Box 3325, Folkston 31537,* ☎ *912/496–7156;* ✉ *Refuge headquarters: Rte. 2, Box 3330, Folkston 31537,* ☎ *912/496–7836.* ☜ *$5 per car; 1-hr tours $11; 2-hr tours $19.* ☉ *Refuge Mar.–Sept. 10, daily 6:30 AM–7:30 PM; Sept. 11–Feb., daily 8–6.*

Lodging

$$–$$$ 🏠 **The Inn at Folkston.** This craftsman-style inn, just 7 mi from the refuge, has a huge front veranda and four working gas-log fireplaces. Guest rooms are individually decorated. The romantic Lighthouse Room, for example, has a king-size bed and screened-in porch with a fireplace. The Garden Room woos romantics with a whirlpool tub, and the Oriental Room has an Asian theme. ✉ *509 W. Main St., Folkston 31537,* ☎ *912/496–6256 or 888/509–6246,* 〖WEB〗 *www.innatfolkston.com. 4 rooms. Hot tub, library. AE, MC, V. BP.*

$ ⚠ **Laura S. Walker State Park.** Named for a Waycross teacher who championed conservation, the park, 9 mi northeast of Okefenokee Swamp Park, has campsites with electrical and water hookups. Be sure to pick up food and supplies on the way to the park. Boating and skiing are permitted on the 120-acre lake, and there's an 18-hole championship golf course. Rustic cabins cost $21.40 per night, plus $2 parking. ✉ *5500 Laura Walker Rd., Waycross 31503,* ☎ *912/287–4900 or 800/864–7275. 44 campsites. Picnic area, pool, fishing, playground.*

$ ⚠ **Stephen C. Foster State Park.** The park has two-room furnished cottages, each capable of sleeping eight, and campsites with water, electricity, rest rooms, and showers. Because of roaming wildlife and poachers and because of the park's location inside the refuge, the gates close between sunset and sunrise. If you're staying overnight, stop for groceries before you get here. Cottages cost $66–$86 per night, depending on the season. ✉ *Fargo 31631,* ☎ *912/637–5274 or 800/864–7275. 66 campsites.*

The Coastal Isles and the Okefenokee A to Z

To research prices, get advice from other travelers, and book travel arrangements, visit www.fodors.com

AIR TRAVEL
CARRIERS

Glynco Jetport is served by Delta affiliate Atlantic Southeast Airlines (ASA), with flights from Atlanta.
➤ AIRLINES AND CONTACTS: **Atlantic Southeast Airlines** (☎ 800/282–3424).

AIRPORTS
The coastal isles are served by Glynco Jetport, 6 mi north of Brunswick near the coastal isles.
➤ AIRPORT INFORMATION: **Glynco Jetport** (✉ 500 Connole St., ☎ 912/265–2070, 800/235–0859, 〖WEB〗 www.glynncountyairports.com).

BOAT AND FERRY TRAVEL
Cumberland Island and Little St. Simons are accessible only by ferry or private launch. You also can get to Sapelo Island by ferry.

BUS TRAVEL
Greyhound Bus Lines serves Savannah, Brunswick, and Waycross.
➤ BUS INFORMATION: **Greyhound Bus Lines** (☎ 800/231–2222, 〖WEB〗 www.greyhound.com).

CAR TRAVEL

From Brunswick take the Jekyll Island Causeway ($2 per car) to Jekyll Island and the Torras Causeway to St. Simons and Sea Island. You can get by without a car on Jekyll Island and Sea Island, but you'll need one on St. Simons. You cannot bring a car to Cumberland Island or Little St. Simons.

VISITOR INFORMATION

The Brunswick and the Golden Isles Visitors Center provides helpful information on all of the Golden Isles. Reservations are centralized through the Georgia State Parks department (Reservation Resource). ➤ TOURIST INFORMATION: **Brunswick and the Golden Isles Visitors Center** (✉ 2000 Glynn Ave., Brunswick 31520, ☎ 912/264–5337 or 800/933–2627, WEB www.bgivb.com). **Georgia State Parks** (☎ 800/864–7275 for reservations; 770/398–7275 within metro Atlanta; 404/656–3530 for general park information; WEB www.gastateparks.org).

ATHENS TO MACON TO AUGUSTA

If it's traces of the old South you crave, you'll want to take in Georgia's Antebellum Trail, a former stagecoach route that is now a highway, U.S. 441. It is dotted with small towns, like Madison, Eatonton, and Milledgeville, saturated in historic architecture: you'll find an abundance of white-columned mansions, shaded verandas, and magnolia gardens reminiscent of pre–Civil War days. Try to plan a visit in April or October, when these towns host community tours of their homes and gardens.

Begin in Athens—with its historic homes, thriving music, and entertainment scene, and the University of Georgia—following the Antebellum Trail south to Macon. A visit to Washington and Augusta necessitates a side trip east along U.S. 78 and I–20, but both are well worth the detour, as they are steeped in history and tradition.

Athens

70 mi east of Atlanta via I–85 north to Rte. 316.

Athens, an artistic jewel of the American South, is known as a breeding ground for such famed rock groups as the B-52's and R.E.M. Because of this distinction, creative types from all over the country flock to its trendy streets in hopes of becoming, or catching a glimpse of, the next big act to take the world by storm. At the center of this artistic melee is the University of Georgia (UGA). With more than 28,000 students, UGA is an influential ingredient in the Athens mix, giving the quaint but compact city a distinct flavor that falls somewhere between a misty Southern enclave, a rollicking college town, and a smoky, jazz club–studded alleyway. It truly is a fascinating blend of Mayberry R.F.D. and MTV. The effect is as irresistible as it is authentic.

Although the streets bustle at night with students taking in the coffeehouse and concert life, Athens's quieter side also flourishes. The streets are lined with many gorgeous old homes, some of which are open to the public. Most prominent among them is the **Athens Welcome Center** (✉ 280 E. Dougherty St., ☎ 706/353–1820, WEB www.visitathensga.com), in the town's oldest surviving residence, the 1820 Church-Waddel-Brumby House. Athens has several splendid Greek Revival buildings, including the **university chapel,** on campus, built in 1832. The **university president's house** (✉ 570 Prince Ave.), on campus, was built in the late 1850s. The **Taylor-Grady House** (✉ 634 Prince Ave.) was constructed in 1844. The 1844 **Franklin House** (⊠ 480 E. Broad St.) has been restored and reopened as an office building.

Just outside the Athens city limits is the **State Botanical Gardens of Georgia,** a tranquil, 313-acre wonderland of aromatic gardens and woodland paths. It has a massive conservatory overlooking the International Garden that functions as a welcome foyer and houses an art gallery, gift shop, and café. ⊠ *2450 S. Milledge Ave., off U.S. 129/441,* ☎ *706/542–1244,* ⊞ *www.uga.edu/botgarden.* ⊠ *Free.* ☉ *Grounds Apr.–Sept., weekdays 8–8; Oct.–Mar., weekdays 8–6. Visitor center Tues.–Sat. 9–4:30, Sun. 11:30–4:30.*

Dining and Lodging

$–$$$ ✕ East–West Bistro. This popular bistro—one of the busiest spots downtown—has a bar, formal dining upstairs, and casual dining downstairs. The most interesting selections downstairs are the small plates that allow you to sample cuisines from around the world—from wasabi-crusted tilapia to salmon in rice paper. Specials include sautéed corvina (sea bass) topped with macadamia-nut kimchi, and spinach-and Swiss cheese–stuffed flank steak. The quieter upstairs room serves a more expensive classic Italian menu. ⊠ *351 E. Broad St.,* ☎ *706/546–9378. AE, D, MC, V.*

$–$$$ ✕ Last Resort Grill. This is a pleasant place to unwind—especially with the restaurant's cheery sidewalk café section. The cuisine is a cross between Tex-Mex and California, with items such as salmon and blackbean quesadillas, and grilled shiitake mushrooms and feta cheese tossed with pasta. ⊠ *174 W. Clayton St.,* ☎ *706/549–0810. AE, D, MC, V.*

$$ ✕ Harry Bissett's. Get primed to taste the offerings at one of the best restaurants in Athens, where you can expect sumptuous Cajun recipes straight from the streets of New Orleans. Nosh on oysters on the half shell at the raw bar while waiting for a table (if it's the weekend, expect to wait a while). Popular main dishes include amberjack Thibodaux (broiled fresh fillet smothered in crawfish étouffée) and chicken Rochambeau (a terrine of chicken breast, béarnaise sauce, shaved ham, and wine sauce). ⊠ *279 E. Broad St.,* ☎ *706/353–7065. AE, D, MC, V. No lunch Mon.*

$ ✕ Weaver D's Fine Foods. Besides serving some of the best soul food in Athens-Clarke County, this place represents a piece of musical history: R.E.M. was so inspired by Weaver D's service motto, "Automatic for the People," that the band named its 1992 album after it. The cooks specialize in hearty home-style meals—fish and chicken, barbecued pork, meat loaf, and steak with gravy. All entrées come with vegetables picked fresh from the garden. ⊠ *1016 E. Broad St.,* ☎ *706/353–7797. No credit cards.*

$$–$$$ ▥ Magnolia Terrace. This B&B is housed in a 1912 mansion right in the middle of the historic district. Each room is decorated with a mishmash of antiques. The rooms are warmly appointed with individual care, favoring rich, stately hues, such as burnt orange and velvet red. Some are carpeted with intricate Persian rugs, and others have large claw-foot tubs. Many have working fireplaces. ⊠ *288 Hill St., 30601,* ☎ *706/548–3860,* ⅀ *706/369–3439,* ⊞ *www.magnoliaterrace.com. 8 rooms, 1 suite. AE, D, MC, V. BP.*

$$ ▥ Nicholson House. This 19th-century house, on 6 acres of an 18th-century land grant originally deeded to William Few, one of Georgia's two signers of the U.S. Constitution, literally is a two-over-two log house. Later additions and changes hide this original structure beneath a 1947 colonial revival exterior. The inn has a wide front veranda with rocking chairs. Rooms are decorated in rich colors, and furnishings are a mix of antiques and good reproductions. ⊠ *6295 Jefferson Rd., 30607,* ☎ *706/*

353–2200, FAX *706/353–7799,* WEB *www.bbonline.com/ga/nicholson. 7 rooms, 2 suites. AE, D, MC, V. BP.*

$ ⊡ **Best Western Colonial Inn.** Just a half mile from the UGA campus, it's a favorite among relatives who come to attend graduation. Don't expect to be blown away by the architectural design, as the hotel building itself, like the rooms it offers, is basic. Rooms, however, are still quite comfortable, with thick flowery bedspreads; each room comes equipped with a coffeemaker. Excellent freshly baked cookies are offered every afternoon. Directly across the street is the Varsity Drive-In, where hungry students feast on smothered hot dogs and heaps of fries. ⊠ *170 N. Milledge Ave., 30607,* ☎ *706/546–7311 or 800/528–1234,* FAX *706/546–7959,* WEB *www.bestwestern.com. 69 rooms. Some microwaves, some refrigerators, pool. AE, D, DC, MC, V.*

Nightlife and the Arts

THE ARTS

The **Classic Center** (⊠ 300 N. Thomas St., ☎ 706/357–4444) puts on a splendid variety of plays and other theatrical performances. The ul-tramod **Georgia Theater** (⊠ 215 N. Lumpkin St., ☎ 706/549–9918) doubles as a movie house and concert hall, showcasing edgy cinema and booking local bands. **UGA's Performing Arts Center** (⊠ South Campus on River Rd., ☎ 706/542–4400) routinely has world-class music recitals—by the Atlanta Symphony Orchestra, for example—and modern dance shows.

NIGHTLIFE

For boisterous rockabilly tunes check out **Bumpers** (⊠ 1720 Commerce Dr., ☎ 706/369–7625). The **40 Watt Club** (⊠ 285 W. Washington St., ☎ 706/549–7871) has been the launching pad of numerous well-known rock groups, such as R.E.M. In the '30s and '40s famed jazz greats such as Bessie Smith and Cab Calloway regularly performed at the **Morton Theatre** (⊠ 195 W. Washington St., ☎ 706/613–3770), listed on the National Register of Historic Places; it is now a performing arts center, presenting musicals, concerts, and modern dance.

Madison

30 mi south of Athens via U.S. 129/441, 60 mi east of Atlanta via I–20.

Directly south of Athens you'll find this small treasure of a town—filled with plenty of restaurants and irresistible antiques shops and gift boutiques. Here you'll also get to see some well-preserved examples of antebellum and Victorian architecture, a treat because so few buildings in Atlanta escaped the torches of the Union troops. Madison's homes are well preserved largely because of a curious stroke of luck: when General Sherman burned a path through Georgia during the Civil War, he left Madison intact because of his friendship with U.S. senator Joshua Hill, a Madison resident and Union sympathizer. That's how Madison earned the moniker "the town that Sherman refused to burn." Hill's former home (not open to the public) is now one of Madison's most cherished mansions.

The **Madison-Morgan Cultural Center,** housed in an early 20th-century schoolhouse built in Romanesque Revival style, has tools and furniture from the late 19th century and a restored classroom of the period, plus information and printed guides on the Joshua Hill house and other historic sites in town. ⊠ *434 S. Main St.,* ☎ *706/342–4743,* WEB *www.morgan.public.lib.ga.us/madmorg.* ⊡ *$3.* ☉ *Tues.–Sat. 10–5, Sun. 2–5.*

At **Heritage Hall** (⊠ 277 S. Main St., ☎ 706/342–9627) you can take a guided tour of a preserved 1833 Greek Revival home and learn about aspects of antebellum highbrow society life.

Dining and Lodging

$–$$ ✕ **Yesterday Cafe.** The brick walls of this former pharmacy are lined with archival black-and-white photographs. Patrons come from counties far away to delight in the traditional but updated Southern fare: country-fried steak with mashed red-skin potatoes, fresh vegetables, and buttermilk pie from an old recipe. The full Southern breakfast, served Tuesday through Sunday, is outstanding. ⊠ *120 Fairplay St., Rutledge (10 mi west of Madison),* ☎ *706/557–9337. AE, MC, V. No dinner Sun.–Wed.*

$ ✕ **Ye Olde Colonial Restaurant.** Housed in a renovated bank building (complete with seating accommodations in the former vault), this cafeteria-style restaurant is a must for hungry patrons passing through Madison. The buffet is a complete cornucopia of Southern faves: butter beans, country-fried steak, sweet-potato casserole, fried chicken, corn bread, cobbler, and, of course, iced tea. ⊠ *108 W. Washington St.,* ☎ *706/342–2211. AE, D, MC, V. Closed Sun.*

$$–$$$ ⊡ **The Farmhouse Inn.** This inn is on a farm that has been in Melinda Hartney's family for generations. Rooms have private entrances (from the outside); the rooms are off a common area where everyone enjoys breakfast and late-afternoon gatherings. Over the barn is an apartment suite. The inn is 6 mi east of Madison. ⊠ *1051 Meadow La., 30650,* ☎ *706/342–7933,* WEB *www.thefarmhouseinn.com. 5 rooms, 1 suite. AE, MC, V. BP.*

$$ ⊡ **Burnett Place.** This charming B&B right in the heart of town is housed in a gorgeous federal-style home built in the early 1800s. The guest rooms are spacious and inviting, and the proprietors are friendly and knowledgeable about the history of the region. ⊠ *317 Old Post Rd., 30650,* ☎ *706/342–4034,* WEB *www.burnettplace.com. 3 rooms. MC, V. BP.*

Eatonton

22 mi south of Madison on U.S. 129/441.

Right in the middle of the Antebellum Trail, Eatonton is a historical trove of houses that still retain the rare Southern antebellum architecture that survived Sherman's torches. But this is not the only thing for which this idyllic town is so proud. Take a look at the courthouse lawn, it's not your imagination—that really is a giant statue of a rabbit. This small town is the birthplace of celebrated novelist Joel Chandler Harris of Br'er Rabbit and Uncle Remus fame. The **Uncle Remus Museum,** built from authentic slave cabins, houses countless carvings, paintings, and other artwork depicting the characters made famous by the imaginative author. It's on the grounds of a park. ⊠ *Turner Park, U.S. 441,* ☎ *706/485–6856.* ▣ *50¢.* ☉ *Wed.–Mon. 10–5. Closed Tues.*

The **Eatonton-Putnam Chamber of Commerce** (⊠ 105 Sumter St., ☎ 706/485–7701) provides printed maps detailing landmarks from the upbringing of Eatonton native Alice Walker, who won the Pulitzer Prize for her novel *The Color Purple.* It also has information on the many fine examples of antebellum architecture in Eatonton, including descriptions and photographs of the town's prize antebellum mansions, and a walking tour of Victorian antebellum homes.

Lodging

$$ ⊡ **Crockett House.** With its aromatic gardens, majestic wraparound porch, and in-room fireplaces, this B&B nestled in a restored 1895 Victorian home is perfect for a romantic getaway. Make sure to get a room with an old-fashioned claw-foot bathtub. All rooms have working fireplaces. ✉ *671 Madison Rd., 31024,* ☎ *706/485–2248,* WEB *www. bbonline/ga/crocketthouse. 5 rooms. AE, MC, V. BP.*

Milledgeville

20 mi south of Eatonton on U.S. 441.

Locals believe ghosts haunt what remains of the antebellum homes in Milledgeville. Laid out as the state capital of Georgia in 1803 (a title it held until Atlanta assumed the role in 1868), the town was not as fortunate as Madison in escaping being torched during the Civil War. Sherman's troops stormed through with a vengeance after the general heard hardship stories from Union soldiers who had escaped from a prisoner-of-war camp in nearby Andersonville. The 1838 Greek Revival **Old Governor's Mansion** became Sherman's headquarters during the war. His soldiers are said to have tossed government documents out of the windows and fueled their fires with Confederate money. Guided tours of the building, now a museum home, are given daily. ✉ *120 S. Clark St.,* ☎ *478/453–4545.* ✆ *$5.* ☼ *Mon.–Sat. 10–4, Sun. 2–4.*

On West Hancock Street is the Georgia College and State University campus. One of its most famous students was prolific Southern novelist and short-story writer Flannery O'Connor, author of such acclaimed novels as *Wise Blood* and *The Violent Bear It Away.* O'Connor did most of her writing at the family farm, Andalusia, just north of Milledgeville on U.S. 441. The **Flannery O'Connor Room,** inside the **Ina Russell Library,** has many of the author's handwritten manuscripts on display. It also contains O'Connor's typewriter and some of her furniture. ✉ *231 W. Hancock St.,* ☎ *478/445–4047.* ✆ *Free.* ☼ *Weekdays 9–4.*

Dining and Lodging

$–$$ ✕ **Brewers Downtown Café.** Pocketed nicely in a historic building, this warmly decorated restaurant specializes in Californian/Mediterranean fare with such entrées as braised mussels and steak prepared Tuscan-style. ✉ *138 W. Hancock St.,* ☎ *478/452–5966. AE, D, MC, V. Closed Sun.*

$–$$ ✕ **The Brick.** This bar-restaurant has a comfortable, worn-at-the-elbows appeal—which is all important when you're about to consume massive pizzas with tasty toppings like feta cheese and spinach. The menu also has salads and calzones. ✉ *136 W. Hancock St.,* ☎ *478/452–0089. AE, D, MC, V. Closed Sun.*

$–$$ 🏠 **Antebellum Inn.** Each room in this pre–Civil War mansion has beautiful period antiques. The Southern breakfasts are fabulous. Proprietress Dianne Johnson is a bird lover, and you'll get a kick out of all the birds and woodland creatures that flock to her gardens in the morning, attracted to the many decorative feeders. ✉ *200 N. Columbia St., 31061,* ☎ *478/453–3993,* WEB *www.bbonline/ga/antebelluminn. 5 rooms. Pool. AE, MC, V. BP.*

Macon

32 mi southwest of Milledgeville via U.S. 441 to Rte. 49, 85 mi southeast of Atlanta via I–75.

At the state's geographic center, Macon, founded in 1823, has more than 100,000 flowering cherry trees, which it celebrates each March with a knockout festival. Its antebellum and Victorian homes are among the state's best preserved.

★ Among the city's many sites is the **Georgia Music Hall of Fame,** appropriately located in Macon as a tribute to the city's extensive contribution to American music. The museum pays tribute to the Georgians who have helped to define America's musical culture. Among the honorees are Ray Charles, James Brown, the Allman Brothers Band, Chet Atkins, R.E.M., and the B-52's. Exhibits also celebrate classical musicians including Robert Shaw, the late director emeritus of the Atlanta Symphony Orchestra; opera singers Jessye Norman and James Melton; and violinist Robert McDuffie. ⊠ *200 Martin Luther King Jr. Blvd.,* ☎ *478/750–8555,* WEB *www.gamusichall.com.* ✄ *$8.* ☉ *Mon.–Sat. 9–5, Sun. 1–5.*

☾ The **Georgia Sports Hall of Fame,** with its old-style ticket booths, has the look and feel of an old ballpark. Exhibits honor sports at all levels, from prep and college teams to professional. ⊠ *301 Cherry St.,* ☎ *478/752–1585,* WEB *www.gshf.org.* ✄ *$6.* ☉ *Mon.–Sat. 9–5, Sun. 1–5.*

★ The unique **Hay House,** designed by the New York firm T. Thomas & Son, is a virtual study in fine Italianate architecture prior to the Civil War. The marvelous stained-glass windows and many technological advances, including indoor plumbing, make a tour worthwhile. ⊠ *934 Georgia Ave.,* ☎ *478/742–8155,* WEB *www.georgiatrust.org/hay.html.* ✄ *$6.* ☉ *Mon.–Sat. 10–5, Sun. 1–5.*

African-American entrepreneur Charles H. Douglass built the **Douglass Theatre** in 1921. Great American musicians have performed here, among them Bessie Smith, Ma Rainey, Cab Calloway, Duke Ellington, and locals Little Richard and Otis Redding. It is currently a venue for movies, plays, and other performances. You can take a guided tour of the building. ⊠ *355 Martin Luther King Jr. Blvd.,* ☎ *478/742–2000,* WEB *www.douglasstheatre.org.* ✄ *$2.* ☉ *Tues.–Sat. 9–5.*

☾ The **Macon Museum of Arts and Sciences and Mark Smith Planetarium** displays everything from a whale skeleton to fine art. Discovery House, an interactive exhibit for children, is modeled after an artist's garret. ⊠ *4182 Forsyth Rd.,* ☎ *478/477–3232,* WEB *www.masmacon.com.* ✄ *$7.* ☉ *Mon.–Thurs. and Sat. 9–5, Fri. 9–9, Sun. 1–5.*

Just 3 mi east of downtown, the **Ocmulgee National Monument,** a significant archaeological site, was occupied for more than 10,000 years and was at its peak under the Mississippian peoples who lived here between AD 900 and AD 1100. There are a reconstructed earth lodge and displays of pottery, effigies, and jewelry of copper and shells discovered in the burial mound. ⊠ *1207 Emery Hwy. (take U.S. 80 east),* ☎ *478/752–8257,* WEB *www.nps.gov/ocmu.* ✄ *Free.* ☉ *Daily 9–5.*

The **Tubman African American Museum** honors the former slave who led more than 300 people to freedom as one of the conductors of the Underground Railroad. A mural depicts several centuries of black culture. The museum also has an African artifacts gallery. ⊠ *340 Walnut St.,* ☎ *478/743–8544,* WEB *www.tubmanmuseum.com.* ✄ *$3.* ☉ *Mon.–Sat. 9–5, Sun. 2–5.*

OFF THE BEATEN PATH   **MUSEUM OF AVIATION –** This museum at Robins Air Force Base has an extraordinary collection of 90 vintage aircraft including a MiG, an SR-71 (Blackbird), a U-2, and assorted other flying machines from past campaigns. From Macon take I–75 south to Exit 146 (Centerville/Warner Robins), and turn left onto Watson Boulevard, 7 mi to Route 247/U.S. 129, then right for 2 mi. ⊠ *Rte. 247/U.S. 129 at Russell Pkwy., Warner Robins, 20 mi south of Macon,* ☎ *478/926–6870,* WEB *www.museumofaviation.org.* ✄ *Free; film $2.* ☉ *Daily 9–5.*

Dining and Lodging

$$ ✕ **Naple's on Forsyth.** This romantic enclave serves Italian food inspired by the Southern region of the country. Specials include homemade pastas, pungent pestos, and spaghetti *al scoglio,* which is a virtual seafood stew over linguine. The restaurant is quite romantic, and conversation is kept to a pleasant murmur. ✉ *4524 Forsyth Rd.,* ☎ *478/471–7017. AE, DC, MC, V. Closed Sun. No lunch Sat.*

$$$–$$$$ ✕🏠 **Henderson Village.** At this resort, 38 mi south of Macon, you'll
★ find stunning 19th- and early 20th-century Southern homes clustered around a green. Guest rooms have a rustic-style elegance, with fine antiques and access to inviting wraparound porches; suites are even nicer, with fireplaces and whirlpool tubs. Buttermilk-yellow walls add warmth to the fine 1838 Langston House restaurant, which is perfect for a meal of Southern-style turbot and pan-seared beef fillet. ✉ *125 S. Langston Circle, Perry 31069,* ☎ *478/988–8696 or 888/615–9722,* 🗚 *912/ 988–9009,* WEB *www.hendersonvillage.com. 19 rooms, 5 suites. Restaurant, bar, in-room VCRs, pool, hot tub, hiking, horseback riding, fishing, library, meeting rooms. AE, MC, V. BP.*

$$$–$$$$ 🏠 **1842 Inn.** With its grand white-pillared front porch and period antiques, this inn offers a true taste of antebellum grandeur, and it's easy to see why this place is considered to be one of America's top inns. The rooms have an aristocratic flair, with plush coverlets and embroidered pillows. There are also loveseats, ornate window stoops, and tile fireplaces, as well as period antiques and heirloom-quality accessories. In the morning you can eat breakfast in your room, in one of the parlors, or in the gorgeous courtyard. It's an easy walk to downtown and the historic district. ✉ *353 College St. 31201,* ☎ *800/336– 1842,* ☎ 🗚 *478/741–1842,* WEB *www.the1842inn.com. 21 rooms, 1 guest house. Cable TV, laundry services, hot tub, Internet. AE, DC, MC, V. BP.*

Washington

38 mi east of Athens via U.S. 78, 100 mi east of Atlanta via I–20 to Exit 154, 100 mi northeast of Macon via U.S. 129 to I–20 to Rte. 47.

Washington, the first city chartered in honor of the country's first president, is a living museum of Southern culture. Brick buildings, some of which date to the American Revolution, line the lively downtown area, which bustles with people visiting shops, cafés, and antiques shops. Residents live and work downtown, giving Washington a little-city appeal that distinguishes it from most other small Southern towns. The Confederate treasury was moved here from Richmond in 1865, and soon afterward the half-million dollars in gold vanished. This mysterious event has been the inspiration for many a treasure hunt, as many like to believe the gold is still buried somewhere in Wilkes County.

The **Washington Historical Museum** (✉ 308 E. Robert Toombs Ave., ☎ 706/678–2105, WEB www.ohwy.com/ga/w/washismu.htm) houses a collection of Civil War relics, including the camp chest of Jefferson Davis. The **Robert Toombs House** (✉ 216 E. Robert Toombs Ave., ☎ 706/ 678–2226) is furnished with 19th-century antiques, some of which are the personal items of the former U.S. senator for which it is named, who served as secretary of state for the Confederacy during part of the Civil War.

Be sure to stop by historic **Callaway Plantation,** 4 mi west of downtown. Here, at a site dating to 1785, you can experience the closest thing to an operating plantation. Among a cluster of buildings on the estate you'll find a blacksmith's house, schoolhouse, and weaving house. An ancient family cemetery is also fun to explore. During the second week of both April and October the estate comes alive with Civil War reenactments and activities such as butter-churning and quilting demonstrations. ✉ *U.S. 78,* ☎ *706/678–7060,* WEB *www.ohwy.com/ga/ c/calplant.htm.* ☒ *$4.* ☉ *Tues.–Sat. 10–5, Sun. 2–5.*

Dining and Lodging

$–$$ ✕ **Another Thyme Café.** This eating establishment has at least three things going for it: homemade breads and desserts (including pecan pie), location (right on the square in downtown Washington), and excellent salads and sandwiches (try the grilled vegetables on focaccia). Dinner runs slightly more upscale but stays regional with fried green tomatoes, sweet-potato chips, and fried seafood. ✉ *5 E. Public Sq.,* ☎ *706/ 678–1672. AE, D, MC, V. Closed Sun. No dinner Sun.–Thurs.*

$$ ▨ **Maynard's Manor.** Expect to be greeted with a pleasant wine-and-cheese service. Fireplaces in the main house warm the public spaces of this 1820 classic revival structure. You might find it fun to join the others who gather in the library and parlor for conversation and light refreshments. The day begins with coffee, tea, and juice in the main hall at 7 AM, followed by a full breakfast in the morning rooms. In the evening there's a dessert service conducted in the parlor, where a buffet of homemade sweets beckons. The proprietors make sure you return to turned-down bedding once you retire to your room for the evening, one of the little touches of luxury in which this inn takes pride. ✉ *219 E. Robert Toombs Ave., 30673,* ☎ *706/678–4303,* WEB *www.kudcom.com/ maynard. 6 rooms, 1 suite. Library, lounge. MC, V. BP.*

Augusta

55 mi east of Washington via U.S. 78 and I–20, 150 mi east of Atlanta via I–20, 70 mi southwest of Columbia, SC, via I–20.

Although Augusta escaped the ravages of Union troops during the Civil War, nature itself was not so kind. On a crossing of the Savannah River, the town was flooded many times before modern-day city planning redirected the water into a collection of small lakes and creeks. Now the current is so mild that citizens gather to send bathtub toys downstream every year in the annual Rubber Duck Race.

Augusta is Georgia's third-oldest city, founded in 1736 by James Edward Oglethorpe, who founded Savannah in 1733. The city was named for Augusta, Princess of Wales, wife of Frederick Louis, Prince of Wales. Augusta served as Georgia's capital from 1785 to 1795. The well-maintained paths of **Riverwalk** (between 5th and 10th streets) curve along the Savannah River and are the perfect place for a leisurely stroll. **Olde Town,** lying along Telfair and Greene streets, is a restored neighborhood of Victorian homes. The 1845 tree-lined **Augusta Canal** is another pleasant place for a walk. Many antebellum and Victorian homes of interest are spread throughout the city.

Meadow Garden was the home of George Walton, one of Georgia's three signers of the Declaration of Independence and, at age 26, its youngest signer. It has been documented as Augusta's oldest extant residence. ✉ *1320 Independence Dr.,* ☎ *706/724–4174,* WEB *www. downtownaugusta.com/meadowgarden.* ☒ *$3.* ☉ *Weekdays 10–4, weekends by appointment.*

The **Morris Museum of Southern Art** has a splendid collection of Southern art, from early landscapes, antebellum portraits, and Civil War art, through neo-impressionism and modern contemporary art. ✉ *Riverfront Center, 1 10th St., 2nd floor,* ☎ *706/724–7501,* WEB *www.themorris. org.* ☒ *$3, free on Sun.* ☉ *Tues.–Sat. 10–5, Sun. noon–5.*

🕙 Children love the National Science Center's **Fort Discovery,** an inter-active museum with a moonwalk simulator, a bike on square wheels, a hot-air balloon, and a little car propelled by magnets. ⊠ 1 7th St., ☎ 706/821–0200 or 800/325–5445, WEB www.nationalsciencecenter. org/fortdiscovery. 🎫 $8. ⊙ Mon.–Sat. 10–5, Sun. noon–5.

Dining and Lodging

$$–$$$$ ✕ **La Maison on Telfair.** Augusta's finest restaurant, operated by chef–owner Heinz Sowinski, presents a classic menu of game, sweetbreads, and, with a nod to the chef's heritage, Wiener schnitzel. The experi-ence is enhanced by the quiet and elegant style here. ⊠ 404 Telfair St., ☎ 706/722–4805. AE, D, DC, MC, V. Closed Sun. No lunch.

$$–$$$ 🏨 **Partridge Inn.** A National Trust Historic hotel, this restored inn sits at the gateway to Summerville, a hilltop neighborhood of summer homes dating to 1800. There's a splendid view of downtown Augusta from the roof. Rooms are elegant, and have double-line cordless phones and high-speed Internet lines. The hotel's exterior has 12 common balconies and a breathtaking upper veranda accented with shaded architectural porticos over wood-plank flooring, creating a truly lustrous reprieve for a quick coffee and newspaper read. There's also videoconferenc-ing for those who can't bear to be out of sight of their business part-ners. ⊠ 2110 Walton Way, 30904, ☎ 706/737–8888 or 800/476–6888, FAX 706/731–0826, WEB www.partridgeinn.com. 133 rooms, 26 suites. Restaurant, bar, some kitchens, pool, gym, lounge, rooftop concierge floor, Internet, meeting room. AE, D, DC, MC, V. BP.

Spectator Sports

GOLF

In early April Augusta hosts the much-celebrated annual **Masters Tour-nament** (WEB www.masters.org), one of pro golf's most distinguished events. Tickets for actual tournament play are not available to the gen-eral public, but you can try to get tickets for one of the practice rounds earlier in the week—which, for golf addicts, is still hugely entertain-ing. Tickets are awarded on a lottery basis; write to the Masters Tour-nament Practice Rounds office (⊠ Box 2047, Augusta, GA 30903) by July 15 of the year preceding the tournament.

Athens to Macon to Augusta A to Z

To research prices, get advice from other travelers, and book travel ar-rangements, visit www.fodors.com

AIR TRAVEL

CARRIERS

Atlantic Southeast Airlines (ASA), Delta, and US Airways all serve the Athens, Macon, and Augusta area.

AIRPORTS

Athens Ben Epps Airport is served by US Airways. Augusta Regional Airport is served by Delta, ASA, and US Airways Express. Middle Geor-gia Regional Airport is served by Atlantic Southeast Airlines.

➤ AIRPORT INFORMATION: **Athens Ben Epps Airport** (⊠ 1010 Ben Epps Dr., ☎ 706/613–3420, WEB www.athensairport.net). **Augusta Regional Airport** (⊠ 1501 Aviation Way, ☎ 706/798–3236). **Middle Georgia Regional Airport** (⊠ 1000 Terminal Dr., Rte. 247 at I–75, ☎ 478/788–3760).

BUS TRAVEL

Greyhound Bus Lines serves Athens, Augusta, Macon, Madison, Milledgeville, and Washington.

FARES AND SCHEDULES

➤ Bus Information: **Greyhound Bus Lines** (☎ 800/231–2222, WEB www.greyhound.com).

CAR TRAVEL

U.S. 441, known as the Antebellum Trail, runs north–south, merging with U.S. 129 for a stretch and connecting Athens, Madison, Eatonton, and Milledgeville. Macon is on Route 49, which splits from U.S. 441 at Milledgeville. Washington lies at the intersection of U.S. 78, running east from Athens to Thomson, and Route 44, running south to Eatonton. I–20 runs east from Atlanta to Augusta, which is about 93 mi east of U.S. 441.

EMERGENCIES

➤ Emergency Services: **Ambulance, police** (☎ 911).

➤ Hospitals: **Doctors Hospital** (✉ 3651 Wheeler Rd., Augusta, ☎ 706/651–3232). **Medical Center** (✉ 1199 Prince Ave., Athens, ☎ 706/549–9977). **Macon Northside Hospital** (✉ 400 Charter Blvd., Macon, ☎ 478/757–8200).

➤ 24-Hour Pharmacies: **CVS** (✉ 1271 Gray Hwy., Macon, ☎ 478/743–6979 or 912/743–8936).

LODGING

BED-AND-BREAKFASTS

Bed & Breakfast Online has detailed cyber-brochures on inns in Atlanta and surrounding areas.

➤ Reservation Information: **Bed & Breakfast Online** (✉ Box 829, Madison, TN 37116, WEB www.bbonline.com/ga, ☎ 615/868–1946).

TAXIS

Augusta Cab Company provides transportation throughout Augusta-Richmond County. There is a $1.75 initial charge, plus $1.50 per mile.

Your Cab Company is a reliable, 24-hour taxi service in Athens. Rates, based on a grid of designated area zones, start at $3. The fare to downtown from the airport costs $6.

➤ Taxi Companies: **Augusta Cab Company** (☎ 706/724–3543). **Your Cab Company** (☎ 706/546–5844).

TOURS

The Augusta Cotton Exchange conducts free tours of its historic brick building, with exhibits from its past as an arbiter of cotton prices. It also has Saturday van tours throughout the historic district of Augusta; the fee is $10 per person.

Classic City Tours conducts daily walking tours starting from the steps of the Athens Welcome Center at 2 PM. The 1½-hour tour takes participants through the city's antebellum neighborhoods. The fee is $10 per person ($8 per person for groups of 10 or more).

➤ Tour Operators: **Augusta Cotton Exchange** (☎ 706/724–4067). **Classic City Tours** (☎ 706/208–8687).

VISITOR INFORMATION

Georgia Welcome Center provides maps and brochures about prominent historical and recreational sites around the state.

➤ Tourist Information: **Athens Convention and Visitors Bureau** (✉ 300 N. Thomas St., 30601, ☎ 706/357–4430 or 800/653–0603, FAX 706/549–5636, WEB www.visitathensga.com). **Eatonton-Putnam Chamber of Commerce** (✉ 105 Sumter St., Eatonton 31024, ☎ 706/485–7701, WEB www.eatonton.com). **Georgia Welcome Center** (✉ Box 211090, Martinez 30917, ☎ 706/737–1446). **Macon-Bibb County Con-**

vention and Visitors Bureau (⊠ 200 Cherry St., 31201, ☎ 478/743–3401 or 800/768–3401, WEB www.maconga.org). **Madison/Morgan County Chamber of Commerce** (⊠ 115 E. Jefferson St., Madison 30605, ☎ 706/342–4454, WEB www.madisonga.org). **Milledgeville Convention and Visitors Bureau** (⊠ 200 W. Hancock St., 31061, ☎ 478/452–4687, WEB www.milledgevillecvb.com). **Washington-Wilkes Chamber of Commerce** (⊠ 104 E. Liberty St., Box 661, Washington 30673, ☎ 706/678–2013, WEB www.washingtonga.org).

NORTH GEORGIA

As an antidote to the congestion of city life, nothing beats the clear skies, cascading waterfalls, and tranquil town squares of north Georgia. Within a half-day's drive from Atlanta, you'll find yourself in the middle of a refreshing cluster of old Southern towns and nature sites that pepper the northern region of the state—the heart of Appalachia.

In Dahlonega, Cleveland, Helen, Clayton, and Ellijay, north and northeast of Atlanta, you'll find shops selling handmade quilts, folk-art pottery, antiques, and loads of Grandma's chowchow in gingham-capped mason jars. These towns also offer plenty of activities—you can descend into a gold mine, explore a re-created Alpine village, or go apple picking. To the northwest are two of Georgia's most important historic sites: New Echota State Historic Site and Chickamauga and Chattanooga National Military Park. And whether your preference is rustic or romantic, there are plenty of B&Bs and campgrounds to accommodate you.

Dahlonega

65 mi north of Atlanta via Rte. 400/U.S. 19.

Hoards of fortune seekers stormed the town of Dahlonega (named after the Cherokee word for "precious yellow metal") in the early 1800s after the discovery of gold in the hills nearby, but by 1849 miners were starting to seek riches elsewhere. In fact, the famous call "There's gold in them thar hills!" originated as an enticement to miners in the Georgia mountains to keep their minds away from the lure of the gold rush out West. It worked for a while, but government price fixing eventually made gold mining unprofitable, and by the early 1920s Dahlonega's mining operations had halted completely.

Many former mining settlements became ghost towns but not Dahlonega. Today it thrives as a rustic country outpost with an irresistible town square rife with country stores, art galleries, coffeehouses, gem shops, old small-town businesses, and even a sophisticated restaurant or two. The gold mines are still here but are open mainly for show. **Consolidated Gold Mine** gives guided tours. You enter the mine, which has been reconstructed for safety, pass through a breathtaking stone passage, and then begin a descent down 120 ft into the mine's depths to gaze at the geological wonders. Guides expound on historical mining techniques and tools, such as the "widowmaker," a drill that kicks up mining dust and that caused disease in many miners. You'll also be invited to pan for gold prospector style, from a long wooden sluice. ⊠ *185 Consolidated Rd.,* ☎ *706/864–8473,* WEB *www.consolidatedgoldmine.com.* ☜ *$10.* ☉ *Daily 10–5.*

The **Gold Museum,** in the present-day courthouse on the square, has coins, tools, and a 5½-ounce nugget. The building is the oldest in north Georgia, and if you look closely at the bricks that form the building's foundation, you'll notice a sprinkling of gold dust in their formation. (A U.S. Mint operated in this modest boomtown from 1838 to 1861—

it closed and was later destroyed by fire, but the foundation remained intact.) Along with the exhibits, the museum shows a short film celebrating the region's history through interviews with Appalachian old-timers. ⊠ *Public Sq.,* ☎ *706/864–2257,* WEB *www.dahlonega.org/museum/goldmuseum.html.* ☒ *$2.50.* ⊘ *Mon.–Sat. 9–5, Sun. 10–5.*

OFF THE
BEATEN PATH
AMICALOLA FALLS – Rushing waters will tumble your troubles away in no time. This is the highest waterfall east of the Mississippi, with waters plunging an eye-popping 729 ft through a cluster of seven cascades. The surrounding state park is dotted with scenic campsites and cottages strategically situated near a network of nature trails, picnic sites, and fishing streams. ⊠ *Off Rte. 52, 18 mi west of Dahlonega,* ☎ *706/265–8888,* WEB *www.ngeorgia.com/parks/amicalola.html.* ☒ Parking $2. ⊘ *Daily 7 AM–10 PM.*

Dining and Lodging

$$–$$$ ✕ **Renée's Café & Wine Bar.** This fine yet casual restaurant in a 19th-century restored residence lies within walking distance of the village square. The contemporary cuisine has regional and Mediterranean accents, such as crawfish tails with spinach tortellini and Gorgonzola Alfredo sauce. Upstairs, patient patrons wait for their tables in a warmly lighted bar or attend one of the monthly wine tastings. ⊠ *135 N. Chestatee St.,* ☎ *706/864–6829. AE, MC, V. No lunch.*

$–$$ ✕ **Smith House.** One of the most popular dining destinations in the north Georgia mountains, Smith House has all-you-can-eat family-style meals that'll have the tables groaning under the weight of the heaping plates. Potatoes, fried chicken, peas, cobbler—you name a Southern dish, and it's probably offered here. ⊠ *84 S. Chestatee St.,* ☎ *706/864–2348,* WEB *www.smithhouse.com. AE, D, MC, V. Closed Mon.*

$$ ▥ **Blueberry Inn & Gardens.** The inn, which crowns the crest of a low hill, takes its name from the wild blueberries growing on its 55 acres. Porch rocking chairs welcome you at the end of a busy day of touring. Gracious hosts Phyllis and Harry Charnley have built a structure reminiscent of a 1920s farmhouse. Rooms are decorated with antiques and family pieces. On the grounds are mountain laurel, oaks, and dogwoods, along with flowering plants of all kinds. ⊠ *400 Blueberry Hill, 30533,* ☎ *706/219–4024 or 877/219–4024,* FAX *706/219–4793,* WEB *www.blueberryinnandgardens.com. 12 rooms. MC, V. BP.*

$$ ▥ **Worley Homestead.** This pristine B&B occupies an 1845 mansion with two garden courtyards. Everyone sits family style at the large, formally set dining room table; breakfast includes caramelized French toast, casseroles, ham, sausage, and cheese grits. Often on weekend evenings the proprietors arrange a wine table with cheese and crackers in the entry foyer. Rooms are beautifully furnished. The B&B is right at the southern tip of the Appalachian Trail, and near the entrance to Chattanooga National Forest. ⊠ *410 W. Main St., 30533,* ☎ *706/864–7002,* WEB *www.bbonline.com/ga/worley. 7 rooms. MC, V. BP.*

Outdoor Activities and Sports

Appalachian Outfitters (⊠ 1236 Golden Ave. [Box 793], Dahlonega 30533, ☎ 800/426–7177, 800/426–7117, WEB www.appoutga.com) provides equipment and maps for self-guided canoeing and kayaking expeditions on the Chestatee River. River trails begin at its outpost in town and extend to Route 400.

Shopping

Golden Memories Antiques (⊠ 121 S. Public Sq., ☎ 706/864–7222) has an impressive number of local rocks and minerals and Coca-Cola collectibles for sale. **Amber Rose Quilts** (⊠ 10 S. Chestatee St., ☎ 706/864–5326) carries a splendid selection of hand-stitched quilts. **Quigley's**

Antiques and Books (⊠ 170-B N. Public Sq., ☎ 706/864–0161) sells used and rare books, Blue Ridge china, vintage trunks, and old toys.

Cleveland

25 mi northeast of Dahlonega via U.S. 19 to U.S. 129, 75 mi northeast of Atlanta via I–985 and U.S. 129.

In Cleveland's tiny town square you'll find a number of antiques shops where you might just uncover some dusty bargains. Note the **Old White County Courthouse,** which was constructed by slaves in the mid-1800s and resembles Philadelphia's Independence Hall. ⊠ *1 Cleveland Sq.,* ☎ *706/865–3225,* WEB *www.georgiamagazine.com/counties/white.* ⊡ *Free.* ⊙ *Thurs.–Sat. 10–6.*

Ⓒ By far Cleveland's biggest claim to fame is **Babyland General Hospital,** best known for starting the pandemonium-causing craze for Cabbage Patch Kids in the late 1970s; it was here that the dolls were first produced. The makeshift "hospital" is housed in what actually was a medical clinic, and the dolls are displayed in a fake cabbage field. ⊠ *73 W. Underwood St.,* ☎ *706/865–2171,* WEB *www.cabbagepatchkids. com.* ⊡ *Free.* ⊙ *Mon.–Sat. 9–5, Sun. 10–5.*

Shopping

Mary T's Auction and Antique (⊠ 233 Friendship Rd., ☎ 706/865–0575) sells antique furniture, china, and crystal, as well as Waverly fabrics and Sedgefield lamps. At **Mount Yonah Gifts** (⊠ 3745 Helen Hwy., ☎ 706/865–5003) you'll find plenty of colorful curios: pottery, birdhouses, ornamental concrete statuaries, and fountains. **Rocks Relics and Beads** (⊠ 5419 U.S. 129, ☎ 706/865–6932) carries minerals and rocks from local mines and others from all over the world. It also has one of the best selections of antique and ornamental beads in the state.

Helen

13 mi north of Cleveland via Rte. 75.

When Helen was founded at the turn of the 20th century, it was a simple little lumber outpost. By the 1960s it was in danger of turning into a ghost town because of a logging bust. Local business leaders came up with a plan to save the town: they transformed the tiny village of 300 into a virtual theme town, and "Alpine Helen" was born. Today businesses along Helen's central streets sport a distinctive German facade, giving you the impression that you've stumbled on a Bavarian vista in the middle of Appalachia. (There's also a scattering of Swiss, Belgian, Danish, Dutch, and Scandinavian facades.) Everywhere you look are beer halls, steepled roofs, flowering window boxes, and billboards written in Renaissance script. As phony as it all is, the effect is contagious and makes you feel as if you've walked into a fairy tale.

The entrance to the village is particularly picturesque, with a narrow bridge traversing a pretty section of the Chattahoochee River. Along Main Street are a multitude of patio cafés lushly shaded by trees. A network of cobblestone walkways and plazas spans a thicket of bakeries and little shops selling Bavarian-theme souvenirs. Costumed shop workers add to the charade. A faux castle that can't be missed is the **Castle Inn,** long considered a gateway of sorts to this manufactured Bavarian oasis in the middle of the Georgia mountains. ⊠ *8590 Main St.,* ☎ *706/878–3140, 877/878–3140,* WEB *www.castleinn-helen.com.*

OFF THE
BEATEN PATH

BRASSTOWN BALD – The highest mountain in Georgia, at 4,784 ft, rises in the heart of the Chattahoochee National Forest. Expect a dramatic vantage from which you can view four states—Tennessee, North Carolina, South Carolina, and Georgia. And sight is not the only sense that gets an aesthetic pick-me-up at Brasstown Bald: bushels of wildflowers in the spring and autumn give a boost to the nose. ⊠ *Off Rte. 180, 18 mi northwest of Helen via Rte. 17,* ☎ *706/896–2556, 706/745–6928.* ⌂ *Parking $3, shuttle to mountain from lot $2.* ☉ *Daily 10–6.*

Dining and Lodging

$$–$$$$ ✕ **Hofbrauhaus Inn.** This beer hall, which shares its name with a famous counterpart in Munich, welcomes a convivial and lively bunch. The menu is saturated with hearty German food, including schnitzel and *bratkartoffeln* (fried potatoes); there are also plenty of options for other international fare, including Hungarian goulash, broiled African lobster tails, and *bistecca alla lupe* (char-grilled beef tenderloin with a creamy Parmesan sauce). ⊠ *Main St.,* ☎ *706/878–2248. AE, D, DC, MC, V.*

$–$$ ✕ **Farmer's Market Café.** This cheerfully decorated eatery has hearty, reasonably priced American fare—seafood, sandwiches, salads, and vegetable plates. You won't go hungry soon after a visit here. ⊠ *63 Chattahoochee St.,* ☎ *706/878–3705. AE, D, DC, MC, V.*

$$$$ ▥ **Brasstown Valley Resort.** It's contemporary, upscale, and has lodge-style accommodations, plus a full line of sports activities: tennis, golf, hiking trails, and a fitness center. The rooms are comfortable and spacious, in an elegant but rustic style. Some have fireplaces and balconies overlooking the breathtaking valley. It's 28 mi northwest of Helen, just off U.S. 76 but surrounded by verdant woods and mountain vistas. ⊠ *6321 U.S. 76, Young Harris 30582,* ☎ *706/379–9900 or 800/201–3205,* FAX *706/379–4615,* WEB *www.brasstownvalley.com. 102 rooms, 32 cottages, 5 suites. Restaurant, bar, cable TV, 18-hole golf course, 4 tennis courts, pool, health club, hot tub, sauna, hiking, convention center. AE, D, DC, MC, V. BP.*

$–$$ ▥ **Fieldstone Inn.** Many of the beautifully appointed rooms in this massive lodge in the mountains are decorated with cherry-wood furniture and have a gorgeous view of Lake Chatuge. You can relax in the lobby before a towering fieldstone fireplace and admire the landscape from the floor-to-ceiling window that faces out across the lake. A nearby marina has boat rentals, including pontoons, paddleboats, sailboats, and kayaks. Sizable discounts are available in winter. It's 25 mi north of Helen. ⊠ *3499 U.S. 76, Hiawassi 30546,* ☎ *706/896–2262 or 800/ 545–3408,* FAX *706/896–4128,* WEB *www.fieldstoneinn.com. 66 rooms. Restaurant, cable TV, tennis court, pool, convention center. AE, D, DC, MC, V. BP.*

Shopping

Gift World of Helen (⊠ 8614 Main St., ☎ 706/878–2504) sells candles, ceramics, knives, and T-shirts, among other items. Check out **Festival of Arts and Crafts** (⊠ 8600 Main St., ☎ 706/878–1283) for its wood carvings and handcrafted dolls. **Jolly's Toys** (⊠ 8800 Main St., ☎ 706/878–2262) has wooden American and European toys. At **Kaiser Bill's II** (⊠ 8635 Main St., ☎ 706/878–1408) you'll find collectible beer steins and figurines.

Clayton

35 mi northeast of Helen via Rte. 356, Rte. 197, and U.S. 76; 106 mi northeast of Atlanta via I–85, I–985, and U.S. 23; 95 mi southwest of Asheville, NC, via I–40 and U.S. 23.

Clayton bills itself as the place "where spring spends the summer"— because of the characteristically mild temperatures during Georgia's otherwise sweltering summer months. An unassuming mountain town, Clayton is near spectacular **Tallulah Gorge State Park,** which at nearly 1,000 ft is the deepest canyon in the United States after the Grand Canyon and was a popular early 20th-century destination for Atlantans. The state of Georgia has designated more than 20 mi of the state park as walking and mountain-biking trails. There are also a 63-acre lake with a beach, a picnic shelter, and about 50 tent and RV sites. ⊠ *U.S. 441, Tallulah Falls,* ☎ *706/754–7970; 706/754–7979 for camping reservations,* WEB *www.ngeorgia.com/parks/tallulah.html.* ⌨ *Parking $2.* ⊙ *Daily 8–dusk.*

Clayton is rich in art galleries, flea markets, and antiques shops. The **Main Street Gallery** (⊠ 641 Main St., ☎ 706/782–2440), one of the state's best sources for folk art, carries works by regional artists, including Sarah Rakes, O. L. Samuels, Jay Schuette, and Rudy Bostick.

Dining and Lodging

$$$–$$$$ ✕🏠 **Glen-Ella Springs Country Inn.** This restored old hotel draws from
★ far and wide with its rustic charm, restful location, and fine food emphasizing regional specialties, such as trout pecan, pickled shrimp, and Lowcountry shrimp on grits. Rooms have no TVs but plenty of reading material, and they open onto common porches with rocking chairs. The splendid grounds invite hiking and exploring. The restaurant's cuisine has been showcased in many books, including *Great Cooking with Country Inn Chefs,* by Gail Greco. You have to BYOB. ⊠ *1789 Bear Gap Rd., Rte. 3, Box 3304, Clarkesville 30523 (15 mi south of Clayton),* ☎ *706/754–7295 or 877/456–7527,* FAX *706/754–1560,* WEB *www. glenella.com. 12 rooms, 4 suites. Restaurant, pool, hiking, meeting room. AE, MC, V. BP.*

$–$$$ ✕🏠 **Dillard House.** An inviting cluster of cottages and motel-style
★ rooms, this establishment sits on a plateau in the Little Tennessee River valley. Some rooms and the glass-walled Dillard House Restaurant ($$) have vistas of the Blue Ridge Mountains. The restaurant serves all-you-can-eat platters of Southern favorites such as country ham, fried chicken, barbecue, corn on the cob, acorn squash, and cabbage casserole. Breakfast is a gut buster. The rooms are uniquely furnished; even floor plans differ. Some have stone fireplaces and interior French doors, others have window-seat alcoves and butler hutches, and many open onto a large rocking-chair front porch. ⊠ *768 Franklin St., Box 10, Dillard 30537 (7 mi north of Clayton),* ☎ *706/746–5348 or 800/541–0671,* FAX *706/ 746–3680,* WEB *www.dillardhouse.com. 75 rooms, 25 chalets, 4 cottages, 6 suites. Restaurant, cable TV, hot tub, some kitchens, some refrigerators, tennis courts, stables. AE, D, DC, MC, V.*

Ellijay

84 mi west of Clayton via U.S. 76, 37 mi northwest of Dahlonega via Rte. 52, 80 mi north of Atlanta via I–75, I–575, and Rte. 5/515.

Although billed as "Georgia's apple capital," Ellijay is also popular among antiques aficionados. The town, on the site of what had been a Cherokee village called Elatseyi (meaning "place of green things"), has a colorful cluster of crafts shops, antiques markets, and art galleries.

The most popular time to visit Ellijay is in the fall, when roadside stands brimming with delicious ripe apples dot the landscape. The annual **Georgia Apple Festival** takes place here in mid-October. In addition to showcasing the many manifestations of the crisp fruit—apple butter, apple pie, apple cider, and so on—the festival offers a host of arts and crafts shows.

During the apple festival you can tour rows upon rows of ripening apple trees at **Hillcrest Orchards** (⊠ 9696 Rte. 52, ☏ 706/273–3838, WEB www.georgiamagazine.com/hillcrest, ⊠ $3). Pick your own apples and then feast on homemade jellies, jams, breads, and doughnuts. Also on the orchard's premises are a petting zoo and a picnic area.

Lodging

$$–$$$ 🏨 **Whitepath Lodge.** From every room here you get panoramic vistas of the tranquil north Georgia mountains. The main lodge has eight suites, each with two bedrooms, three baths, and a fully equipped kitchen. The Shenandoah Lodge has six two-floor suites with fireplaces and multi-level decks overlooking the woods. If you're a sports enthusiast, you'll be happy with all the recreational activities nearby—18-hole golf courses, mountain biking, horseback riding, tubing, seasonal white-water rafting, boating, canoeing, kayaking, and fishing. ⊠ *987 Shenandoah Dr., 30540,* ☏ *706/276–7199 or 888/271–7199,* WEB *www.whitepathlodge. com. 14 suites. AE, D, DC, MC, V. Restaurant, some kitchens, pool, basketball, tennis, hiking, meeting rooms.*

Outdoor Activities and Sports

There are plenty of options for fishing, canoeing, and kayaking on the Cartecay River, which runs through town. **Mountaintown Outdoor Expeditions** (⊠ Rte. 52, ☏ 706/635–2524) arranges outdoor adventures for people of all skill levels.

Shopping

Mountain Treasures (⊠ 511 Rte. 52, ☏ 706/635–5590) sells mountain home furnishings with a comfortable lodge motif. **Ellijay Antiques Mall** (⊠ 66 N. Main St., ☏ 706/276–7622) is a fun collective that spans 7,000 square ft, with everything from clocks to ceramic curios.

New Echota State Historic Site

71 mi northwest of Atlanta via I–75 north to Rte. 225, 43 mi southwest of Ellijay via U.S. 76 to Rte. 136.

From 1825 to 1838 New Echota was the capital of the Cherokee Nation, whose constitution was patterned after that of the United States. There was a council house, a printing office, a Supreme Court building, and the *Cherokee Phoenix,* a newspaper that utilized the Cherokee alphabet developed by Sequoyah. Some buildings have been entirely reconstructed, and some originals have simply been restored. A museum details the site's history. ⊠ *Rte. 225, 1 mi east of I–75, near Calhoun,* ☏ *706/624–1321,* WEB *www.georgiastateparks.org.* ⊠ *$3.50.* ⊙ *Tues.–Sat. 9–5, Sun. 2–5:30.*

About 15 mi north of New Echota, the beautifully restored two-story brick **Chief Vann House,** with an intricately carved interior, was commissioned in 1805 by a leader of the Cherokee Nation, who hired Moravian artisans to construct it. Of mixed Scottish and Cherokee parentage, Chief James Vann owned numerous slaves who worked on the construction of the house. Before he died, he became known as a rogue— he killed his brother-in-law in a duel and shot his mother. ⊠ *Rte. 225 at Rte. 52, Chatsworth,* ☏ *706/695–2598,* WEB *www.alltel.net/~vannhouse.* ⊠ *$2.50.* ⊙ *Tues.–Sat. 9–5, Sun. 2–5:30.*

Dining and Lodging

$$ ✕ **La Scala.** Piero Barba from Capri, Italy, established this outpost of Italian cooking in 1996. The menu is dominated by classic dishes: osso buco, braciola, seafood, and pasta. The wine list, which Barba claims is the largest in north Georgia, includes French, American, and Italian

wines. ⊠ *413 Broad St., Rome (30 mi southwest of Calhoun),* ☎ *706/238–9000. AE, D, DC, MC, V. Closed Sun. No lunch.*

$–$$ 🏨 **Claremont House.** Jeff and Linda Williams's beautifully restored 1890s Victorian inn has huge rooms furnished with period antiques. Breakfast is sumptuous, with stuffed French toast and the like. ⊠ *906 E. 2nd Ave., Rome 30161 (30 mi southwest of Calhoun),* ☎ *706/291–0900 or 800/254–4797,* FAX *706/802–0551,* WEB *www.theclaremonthouse.com. 4 rooms, 1 cottage. AE, D, MC, V. BP.*

Chickamauga and Chattanooga National Military Park

110 mi northwest of Atlanta via I–75 and Rte. 2, 42 mi north of New Echota State Historic Site via I–75, 8 mi south of Chattanooga, TN, via U.S. 27.

This site, established in 1890 as the nation's first military park, was the scene of one of the Civil War's bloodiest battles (30,000 casualties), which ended in the Union capture of Chattanooga. The normally thick cedar groves and foliage covering Chickamauga were supposedly so trampled that the area resembled an open field, and so shot up were the trees that a sweet cedar smell mingled with the blood of fallen soldiers. Monuments, battlements, and weapons adorn the road that traverses the 8,000-acre park, with markers explaining the action. An excellent visitor center has reproduction memorabilia, books, and a film on the battle. ⊠ *U.S. 27, Fort Oglethorpe, 12 mi south of Chattanooga,* ☎ *706/866–9241,* WEB *www.nps.gov/chch.* 🎫 *Free.* ☉ *Mid-Aug.–mid-June, daily 8–4:45; mid-June–mid-Aug., daily 8–5:45.*

Lodging

$$–$$$ 🏨 **Gordon-Lee Mansion.** To capture the feeling of the Civil War era, stay overnight at this antebellum mansion, which served as a field hospital during the battle. You stay in the log house, formerly Congressman Gordon Lee's office, and have the run of two bedrooms, a living room with fireplace, and a full kitchen, where you prepare your own breakfast. ⊠ *217 Cove Rd., Chickamauga 30707,* ☎ *706/375–4728 or 800/487–4728, 800/487–4728,* FAX *706/375–9499,* WEB *www.fhc.org/gordon-lee. 4 rooms, 1 cottage. MC, V. BP.*

North Georgia A to Z

To research prices, get advice from other travelers, and book travel arrangements, visit www.fodors.com

BUS TRAVEL

Greyhound Bus Lines serves Calhoun, Dalton, and Rome.

FARES AND SCHEDULES

➤ BUS INFORMATION: **Greyhound Bus Lines** (☎ 800/231–2222, WEB www.greyhound.com).

CAR TRAVEL

U.S. 19 runs north–south, passing through Dahlonega and up into the north Georgia mountains. U.S. 129 runs northwest from Athens, passing through Cleveland and subsequently merging with U.S. 19. Route 75 stems off U.S. 129 and goes through Helen and up into the mountains. U.S. 23/441 runs north through Clayton; U.S. 76 runs west from Clayton to Dalton, merging for a stretch with Route 5/515. Route 52 runs along the edge of the Blue Ridge Mountains, passing through Ellijay. I–75 is the major artery in the northwesternmost part of the state and passes near the New Echota State Historic Site and the Chickamauga and Chattanooga National Military Park.

EMERGENCIES

➤ EMERGENCY SERVICES: **Ambulance, police** (☎ 911).

➤ HOSPITALS: **Laurelwood/Blairsville Hospital** (⊠ 214 Hospital Circle, Blairsville, ☎ 706/745–8641).

➤ PHARMACIES: **CVS** (⊠ 220 Old Orchard Sq., Ellijay, ☎ 706/635–2538; ⊠ 43 Hwy. 515, Blairsville, ☎ 706/745–9601; ⊠ Hwy. 441, ☎ 706/782–2722).

LODGING

BED-AND-BREAKFASTS

Bed & Breakfast Online has detailed cyber-brochures on inns in Atlanta and surrounding areas.

➤ RESERVATION INFORMATION: **Bed & Breakfast Online** (⊠ Box 829, Madison, TN 37116, WEB www.bbonline.com/ga, ☎ 615/868–1946).

OUTDOORS AND SPORTS

FISHING

Upper Hi Fly Fishing and Outfitters offers personalized guided trout and fly-fishing trips in the southern Appalachian Mountains. It also operates a full-service fly-fishing shop with state-of-the-art equipment.

➤ CONTACTS: **Upper Hi Fly Fishing and Outfitters** (☎ 706/896–9075, WEB www.upper-hi-fly.com).

HIKING

Fort Mountain State Park has campgrounds amid prehistoric rock formations, plus hiking, mountain biking, horseback riding, miniature golf, fishing, boating, and swimming. It's 8 mi east of Chatsworth via Route 52.

A network of hiking trails—filled with ancient Indian carvings and historical markers—is dotted with cabins and camping accommodations run by Trackrock Campground and Cabins. It also has fishing and horseback riding. It's 9 mi east of Blairsville via Route 180.

➤ CONTACTS: **Fort Mountain State Park** (⊠ 181 Fort Mountain Park Rd., Chatsworth 30705, ☎ 706/695–2621, WEB www.ngeorgia.com/parks/fort.html). **Trackrock Campground and Cabins** (⊠ 4887 Trackrock Campground Rd., Blairsville 30512, ☎ 706/745–2420, WEB www.trackrock.com).

➤ TOURIST INFORMATION: **Alpine Helen–White County Convention and Visitors Bureau** (⊠ Box 730, Helen 30545, ☎ 706/878–2181 or 800/858–8027, WEB www.helenga.org). **Blairsville/Union County Chamber of Commerce** (⊠ 385 Blue Ridge Hwy., Blairsville 30512, ☎ 706/745–5789, WEB www.blairsvillechamber.com). **Clayton Chamber of Commerce** (⊠ Box 702, 30525-0702, ☎ 706/782–4512, FAX 706/782–4596, WEB www.claytoncham.org). **Dahlonega-Lumpkin Chamber of Commerce** (⊠ 13 Park St. S, Dahlonega 30533, ☎ 706/864–3513 or 800/231–5543, FAX 706/864–7917, WEB www.dahlonega.org). **Gilmer County Chamber of Commerce** (⊠ 5 Westside Sq., Ellijay 30540, ☎ 706/635–7400, WEB www.gilmerchamber.com). **Helen Welcome Center** (⊠ 726 Bruckenstrasse, Box 730, 30545, ☎ 706/878–2181 or 800/858–8027, FAX 706/878–4032, WEB www.helenga.com). **White County Chamber of Commerce** (⊠ 122 N. Main St., Cleveland 30528, ☎ 706/865–5356, WEB www.whitecountychamber.org).

SOUTHWEST GEORGIA

It's best to meander through southwest Georgia slowly—as deliberately as the drawl that drips sweetly off the lips of the locals who inhabit the many speck-on-the-map towns that pepper this region. Here travelers come to escape the rigors and daily grind of the state's more densely settled communities. You'll encounter few high-tech diversions, few cell phone–addled commuters, and few gripes about traffic jams and suburban sprawl. Many locals here are content to spend the afternoon fanning themselves on the front porches, rarely—if ever—locking the screen door behind them.

Within a day's drive of Atlanta you'll encounter the rolling agricultural landscapes of southwest Georgia—farming enterprises that have kept generations literally rooted to their hometowns. Peanuts, cotton, corn, tobacco, and other crops flourish throughout the countryside, usually punctuated by large groves of pecan trees.

Petite country hamlets beckon with their charming town squares and elegant B&Bs. Hogansville, for example, attracts antiques and flea-market aficionados on their way south to LaGrange and Columbus. Jog in a southeasterly direction to the Andersonville National Historic Site, the nation's only museum dedicated to American prisoners of war. A short distance afield you can explore Americus and Plains, two more towns seemingly cut from the pages of the past. Farther south await Tifton and Thomasville, often cited as among the nation's most appealing small towns, thanks to inviting town squares, shaded glens, and an easygoing air; you'll also find some fine country inns here. In southwest Georgia the inclination simply to relax is contagious—it can saturate you slowly but completely, like syrup on a stack of pancakes.

Hogansville

56 mi southwest of Atlanta via I–85.

Just an hour southwest of Atlanta, tiny yet surprisingly urbane Hogansville, which began as a textile-mill and cotton-trading center in the mid-19th century, has now increased its cachet by becoming a haven of artsy, creative-minded types. Spirited entrepreneurs and restaurateurs have snapped up—and then spruced up—crumbled storefronts, converting them into an eclectic mix of antiques stores and eateries.

Dining and Lodging

$$–$$$ ★ ✕ **Hogan's Heroes.** Set inside a restored and converted gas station, this trendy eatery serves authentically rendered Italian food prepared with a sophistication that belies the restaurant's jokey name—consider the *zuppa di pesce* (fish soup) of clams, green-lip mussels, scallops, shrimp, squid, octopus, and Maine lobster. Devotees credit this café, which opened in the late '80s, with spurring Hogansville's revitalization. ✉ *218 U.S. Hwy. 29, Hogansville,* ☎ *706/637–4953. AE, D, MC, V. Closed Sun.–Mon.*

$$$ **Serenbe Farm.** Just 36 mi southwest of Atlanta, you'll find the quintessence of serene rural Georgia in this 360-acre farm. Most accommodations are in a converted 1930s horse barn or a lakeside cottage; each room radiates with individual personality, reflected in handmade patchwork quilts and heirlooms from the owners' folk-art collection. There's also a two-bedroom cottage with a full kitchen that's perfect for families. You can also count on a supreme breakfast made from ingredients fresh from the farm gardens. ✉ *10950 Hutcheson Ferry Rd., Palmetto 30268 (about 35 mi northeast of LaGrange via I–85),* ☎ *770/463–2610,* FAX *770/463–4472,* WEB *www.serenbe.com. 7 rooms, 1 cottage. Some cable TV, pool, Internet, meeting rooms. No credit cards. BP.*

$$ **Fair Oaks Inn at the Plantation.** This pretty six-room home in downtown Hogansville is on the former estate of William Hogan, the plantation owner after whom the town is named (he received this honor for having donated land for the town's railroad depot). Sweeping verandas and antiques-appointed rooms create a relaxing, old-world style. ⊠ *703 E. Main St., Hogansville 30230,* ☎ *706/637–8289, 4 rooms, 2 suites. MC, V. BP.*

$$ 🏨 **Grand Hotel.** This striking 1890s hotel in picture-perfect Hogansville is fronted by a two-story veranda. Period antiques fill these rooms, all with rustic hardwood floors and gas-log fireplaces. Included is a full breakfast in the hotel's Sweets Shoppe, where you can buy various treats—shortbreads, cheese straws, petit fours, cream puffs—to snack on later. Also complimentary are evening cocktails and hors d'oeuvres. There's great shopping and dining within walking distance. ⊠ *303 E. Main St., Hogansville 30230,* ☎ *706/637–8828 or 800/324–7625,* FAX *706/637–4522,* WEB *www.thegrandhotel.net. 5 rooms, 5 suites. Cable TV, some hot tubs, in-room data ports. MC, V. BP.*

LaGrange

15 mi southwest of Hogansville via U.S. 29, 70 mi southwest of Atlanta via I–85.

The city of LaGrange got its name from the Marquis de Lafayette, who—while traveling through the west Georgia countryside in the early 1800s—commented that the scenery reminded him of his own verdant estate in La Grange, France. Troup County officials were so touched by the compliment that they christened their new county seat in honor of the French town to which the area had been so favorably compared. By the turn of the 20th century textile mills employed many of the town's residents, and as this industry tapered off in the '60s, LaGrange waned economically. Things have improved since then, though, with the development of a major industrial park at the southwest edge of town, which has attracted a number of major companies, including Georgia Pacific, Duracell, and Mobil.

Today this community of about 30,000 has a burgeoning arts scene that would do the refined origins of its name proud. The **Chattahoochee Valley Art Museum** anchors beautiful downtown LaFayette Square and shows exhibits by regional contemporary artists. The museum occupies a restored 19th-century county jail. ⊠ *112 Hines St.,* ☎ *706/882–3267.* 🎟 *Free.* ☉ *Tues.–Fri. 9–5, Sat. 11–5.*

You'll find a smattering of galleries and boutiques in downtown La-Grange, among them **Gallery on the Square** (⊠ 9 E. LaFayette Sq., ☎ 706/883–6680), which specializes in Southern regional paintings, stained glass, and pottery.

Dining and Lodging

$$ ✕ **Cleve's Place.** This friendly, family-popular tavern lighted with Tiffany-style lamps is chock-full of memorabilia, from vintage cola and ice cream signs to antique toys. The kitchen turns out hefty portions of traditional favorites—hickory burgers and cornmeal-battered catfish—and fajitas. ⊠ *Sawmill Plaza, 1841 Roanoke Rd.,* ☎ *706/884–2222. AE, D, DC, MC, V. Closed Sun.*

$ 🏨 **Best Western LaGrange Inn.** Ordinary but perfectly comfortable, this downtown chain property has rooms outfitted with standard furnishings, including coffeemakers. ⊠ *1601 LaFayette Pkwy., 30241,* ☎ *706/882–9540 or 800/528–1234,* FAX *706/882–3929,* WEB *www.bestwestern.com. 100 rooms. Pool, meeting room. AE, D, DC, MC, V. CP.*

Pine Mountain

18 mi southeast of LaGrange via U.S. 27.

Although Pine Mountain attracts a healthy pack of tourists every year, most are lured by the surrounding area's large-scale attractions and then are pleasantly surprised that the small-town burg has a folksy, inviting downtown square. Spend a bit of time here, shop browsing and chatting with the friendly locals.

⟳ Just south of the village lies the main draw of this area: **Callaway Gardens** is a 14,000-acre family-style golf and tennis resort with elaborate gardens. This botanical wonderland was developed in the 1930s by a couple determined to breathe new life into the area's dormant cotton fields. The **Day Butterfly Center** has more than 1,000 varieties flying free. **Creek Lake** is well stocked with largemouth bass and bream. ⊠ *U.S. 27, Pine Mountain,* ☎ *706/663–2281 or 800/282–8181,* WEB *www.callawaygardens.com.* ☞ *$12; free to overnight guests.* ☉ *Mar.–Aug., daily 7–7; Sept.–Feb., daily 8–5.*

A few miles northwest of town, you can further commune with nature
⟳ at the **Pine Mountain Wild Animal Safari.** Either drive yourself or ride a bus through a 500-acre animal preserve in which you won't believe you're still in Georgia. Camels, llamas, antelopes, and hundreds of other exotic animals traipse around freely, often coming close to vehicles. An added plus is the **Old McDonald's Farm,** a petting zoo with jovial monkeys and writhing-reptile pits. ⊠ *1300 Oak Grove Rd.,* ☎ *706/663–8744 or 800/367–2751,* WEB *www.animalsafari.com.* ☞ *$12.95 summer, $11.95 spring and fall, $10.95 winter.* ☉ *Oct.–May, daily 10–5:30, June–Sept., 10–7:30.*

Dining and Lodging

$–$$ ✕ **McGuire's Family Restaurant.** This friendly, reasonably priced country kitchen serves breakfast anytime but doesn't stop there: the menu ranges broadly, with burgers, salads, chicken, and even an occasional quail entrée. And what would a quintessential Georgia dinner be without fried green tomatoes? Get yours here, hot and inexpensive. ⊠ *324 Main St.,* ☎ *706/663–2640. MC, V.*

$$–$$$ ⬚ **Callaway Gardens.** This sprawling resort dwarfs many nearby towns,
★ with lots of places to eat and shop and endless landscaped and wild grounds. Accommodations range from fairly basic motel-style guest rooms to fully furnished cottages and villas, all of them with lovely panoramic vistas and verdant garden settings. A 10-mi paved bike trail meanders through the property. There's great fishing in 13 stocked ponds, and the golf courses are famously impressive. Various meal and recreation packages are available. ⊠ *U.S. 27, Pine Mountain 31822,* ☎ *706/663–2281 or 800/282–8181,* FAX *706/663–5068,* WEB *www.callawaygardens. com. 775 units. 5 restaurants, 2 bars, 2 seasonal cafés, 4 18-hole golf courses, 10 tennis courts, lake, health club, beach, fishing, bicycles, Ping-Pong, racquetball, volleyball, lounge, shops. AE, D, DC, MC, V.*

$$–$$$ ⬚ **Chipley Murrah House B&B.** Just 1 mi from Callaway Gardens and on the fringe of downtown Pine Mountain, this lavish inn occupies a high-style Queen Anne Victorian dating to 1895. A favorite perch in this period-decorated house is the wraparound porch, decked out with rockers, swings, and wicker chairs. Hardwood flooring, 12-ft ceilings, and decorative molding are among the beautifully preserved original details. There's also a fully furnished country cottage with three bedrooms. ⊠ *207 W. Harris St., 31822,* ☎ *706/663–9801 or 888/782–0797,* WEB *www.bbonline.com/ga/chipley. 4 rooms, 1 cottage. MC, V. BP.*

Shopping

In downtown Pine Mountain, check out the **Anne Tutt Gallery** (⊠ 709 Garden View Dr., ☎ 706/663–8032) for its selection of paintings, etchings, and designer jewelry. Don't miss **Now and Then Antiques** (⊠ 116 Main St., ☎ 706/663–2000), a former gas station–turned–curio shop of old local crafts, including antique pottery, finger puppets, and weavings. **Country Gardens** (⌧ 155 Main St., ☎ 706/663–7779) offers an enchanting collection of eclectic plants, gifts, and antiques.

Warm Springs

14 mi east of Pine Mountain via Rte. 18 and Rte. 194, 75 mi south of Atlanta via I–85 and Rte. 41.

The village of Warm Springs was the summer White House during the presidency of Franklin D. Roosevelt. After Roosevelt died here in 1945, Warm Springs became blighted, but in the '80s an influx of crafts and antiques shops revitalized it. At the south end of town, you can tour the **Little White House Historic Site,** the restored vacation home of President Roosevelt, who first visited Warm Springs in 1924 to take the therapeutic hot waters after he contracted polio. In 1932 he built what became known as the Little White House, a simple three-bedroom cottage. It contains his personal effects and looks much as it did the day he died here. The pools where Roosevelt once took his therapy are now open for tours. ⌧ *401 Little White House Rd.,* ☎ *706/ 655–5870.* ⌦ *$5.* ☉ *Daily 9–4:45.*

Lodging

$$ 🏠 **Magnolia Hall.** Painted green with taupe shutters, this handsome Victorian cottage about 15 mi south of both Pine Mountain and Warm Springs has gingerbread trim and a wraparound porch. Rooms are soundproof, and each has a thermostat. A terrific breakfast, with such dishes as stuffed French toast, bacon pie, and lemon biscuits, is served in the formal dining room. ⌧ *127 Barnes Mill Rd., Hamilton 31811,* ☎ *706/628– 4566,* 🌐 *www.magnoliahallbb.com. 3 rooms, 2 suites. AE, MC, V. BP.*

Columbus

45 mi south of Warm Springs via U.S. 27 and Rte. 85, 45 mi south of LaGrange via I–185, 105 mi south of Atlanta via I–85 and I–185, 90 mi east of Montgomery, AL, via I–85 and U.S. 280.

Touted as "Georgia's West Coast" because of its 12-mi Riverwalk along the Chattahoochee, Columbus—the state's third-largest city (population 185,000) sprouted from what was originally a prosperous mill town in 1827. Gracious antebellum and Victorian homes line the streets of downtown, along with character-rich shotgun shacks that once belonged to the mill's laborers.

This is the hometown of John Pemberton, the pharmacist who created Coca-Cola. The 1840 four-room **Pemberton House** is one of several buildings that constitute **Heritage Corner,** which you can visit via a guided walking tour given by the Historic Columbus Foundation, headquartered in an 1870 building. Other structures here include the one-room **log cabin** that's said to be the oldest extant structure in Muscogee County; the 1828 federal-style **Walker-Peters-Langdon House;** and the 1840s **Woodruff Farm House.** ⌧ *700 Broadway,* ☎ *706/322–3181.* ⌦ *$5 per person tour (2-person minimum).* ☉ *Tours weekdays at 11 and 2, weekends at 2.*

Military buffs and anybody else with an interest in the nation's Civil War past should make it a point to visit the **Port Columbus National Civil War Naval Museum,** which has been lauded for its interactive approach and high-tech exhibits. This is one of the nation's most innovative Civil War museums. You can walk the decks of partially reconstructed Civil War ships. The museum is heavily focused on the Confederate navy and its ultimate influence on the U.S. navy's subsequent development. ⊠ *1002 Victory Dr.,* ☎ *706/327–9798,* WEB *www.portcolumbus.org.* ⊡ *$4.50.* ☾ *Daily 9–5.*

The Riverwalk, a linear park that's ideal for jogging, strolling, biking, and rollerblading, is also the site of Columbus State University's **Coca-Cola Space Science Center,** which houses a planetarium, an observatory, a replica of an Apollo space capsule, a space shuttle, and other space-related exhibits. ⊠ *701 Front Ave.,* ☎ *706/649–1470,* WEB *www.ccssc.org.* ⊡ *Free; planetarium show $4.* ☾ *Tues.–Thurs. 10–4, Fri. 10–7, Sat. 1:30–7, Sun. 1:30–4.*

★ One of the city's most notable attractions, the current **Columbus Museum,** which opened in its current 86,000-square-ft location in 1989, is the state's second-largest art museum. Collections focus heavily on American art ranging from colonial portraiture to the Ashcan School to provocative contemporary works. Other exhibits concentrate on science and the history of the Chattahoochee Valley. ⊠ *1251 Wynnton Rd.,* ☎ *706/649–0713,* WEB *www.columbusmuseum.com.* ⊡ *Free.* ☾ *Tues.–Wed. and Fri.–Sat. 10–5, Thurs. 10–9, Sun. 1–5. Closed Mon.*

Dining and Lodging

$–$$ ✕ **Country's Barbecue.** In a city of great barbecue restaurants, it's no small matter that this place has been a favorite since it opened in 1975. The original location on Mercury has plenty of fans, but you should also consider a second outpost downtown close to the Riverwalk. Expect massive portions of fried chicken, hickory- and oak-smoked barbecued smoked ham, ribs, pulled pork, and a surfeit of extras. ⊠ *3137 Mercury Dr.,* ☎ *706/563–7604;* ⊠ *1329 Broadway,* ☎ *706/ 596–8910. MC, V.*

$–$$ ✕ **Olive Branch Cafe.** This dapper downtown eatery presents a menu heavily influenced by the islands of the Mediterranean. The lamb loin is a feast, and the fried–goat cheese Greek salad puts a distinctive spin on a traditional favorite. ⊠ *1032 Broadway,* ☎ *706/322–7410. AE, MC, V. Closed Sun.*

$ ✕ **Gabby's Diner.** If you're feeling nostalgic, take a dive back in time at this '50s diner with Formica counters and a hopping jukebox. Plates are piled high with good-time comfort food. Portions are enormous, from the breakfasts to the burgers to the concrete-thick malteds. Kids eat free on Wednesday. ⊠ *4641 Warm Springs Rd.,* ☎ *706/221–9031. No credit cards.*

$$–$$$ ▥ **Columbus Hilton.** On the site of a vast 1860s complex of warehouses, ★ factories, mills, and a Confederate arsenal, this hotel is a key component of the Iron Works Convention Center, and it uses many of the original industrial materials. Millstones and conveyor belts decorate the lobby. Rooms are done in shades of eggplant and hunter green, and many overlook the Riverwalk park. With a terrific location and a reliable restaurant (Pemberton's) with a great Sunday brunch, the Hilton is a focal point of the city's downtown revival. ⊠ *800 Front Ave., 31901,* ☎ *706/324–1800 or 800/774–1500,* FAX *706/576–4413,* WEB *www.hilton.com. 175 rooms. 2 restaurants, bar, lounge, in-room data ports, cable TV, pool, laundry service, meeting rooms, free parking. AE, D, DC, MC, V.*

$$–$$$ ▥ **Gates House Inn.** This exquisitely restored inn with lush gardens looks straight from the pages of a Victorian-period novel. The owners spent years restoring and decorating this 1880 twin-chimney colonial revival, taking great care to preserve the original features. Rooms have Oriental rugs and family antiques. In warm weather you can take breakfast on the front porch and relax on the antique wicker furniture; selections change often but might include homemade sourdough and brown sugar, cinnamon, and pecan French toast. ⊠ *737 Broadway, 31901,* ☎ *706/*

324–6464 or 800/891–3187, FAX 706/324–2070, WEB *www.gateshouse. com. 3 rooms, 1 suite. Free parking. AE, MC, V. BP.*

$–$$ 🏠 **Country Inn and Suites.** It's a reliable chain property that's ideal if you're staying more than a few days. The rooms and suites—decorated in a country style, with gingham-printed fabrics and grapevine wreaths on the walls—are spacious, and all have coffeemakers and other helpful amenities. ✉ *1720 Fountain Ct., 31904,* ☎ *706/660–1880 or 800/ 456–4000,* FAX *706/243–3473,* WEB *www.countryinns.com. 49 rooms, 13 suites. Microwaves, refrigerators, pool, gym, free parking. AE, D, MC, V. CP.*

Plains

55 mi southeast of Columbus via U.S. 27 and U.S. 280.

The small farming town of Plains proudly bills itself as "the town that cultivated a president" because it is the home of former U.S. president Jimmy Carter, who was born here in 1924. Carter and his wife, Rosalynn (who was also born here), still live in a sprawling ranch house in Plains, and he still teaches Sunday school twice a month at the local **Maranatha Baptist Church** (✉ 148 Rte. 45, ☎ 229/824–7896).

At the **Jimmy Carter National Historic Site** you can still see the late 1880s railroad depot that housed his 1976 presidential campaign headquarters, the 360-acre **Jimmy Carter Boyhood Farm** (currently being restored to its 1930s appearance), and the former **Plains High School,** in which Jimmy and Rosalynn were educated—it now contains a museum and visitor center. You can visit these places and tour the town either by picking up a self-guided tour book at the visitor center or renting an audio cassette. ✉ *300 N. Bond St.,* ☎ *229/824–4104,* WEB *www.nps. gov/jica.* 🎫 *Free.* ☉ *Daily 9–5.*

For a guided tour of this amiable and appealing community, contact **Plain Peanuts** (✉ 616 Main St., ☎ 229/824–3462; 🎫 $5; ☉ daily 9– 5), which will squire you around in a van driven by a guide well versed in the art of country-spun gossip and tall tales. Sites range from the prominent to the mundane (such as the late, ex-first brother Billy Carter's dilapidated gas station).

Lodging

$ 🏠 **Plains Bed & Breakfast Inn.** Smack in the center of town, this graciously renovated B&B captures the dignity of the old South—while charging quite reasonable rates. Each of the four large rooms is decorated with turn-of-the-20th-century antiques. A grand veranda wraps around the facade of this Victorian mansion, which is crowned by a circular turret. Expect breakfast in the morning to be a traditional Southern gutbuster. ✉ *100 Church St., 31780,* ☎ *229/824–7252. 4 rooms. V. BP.*

Americus

11 mi east of Plains via U.S. 280, 133 mi south of Atlanta via U.S. 19.

In this charming small-town hamlet, the past and present coincide pleasantly along the bustling streets of the downtown square, around which you'll find numerous shops. You'll also see the magnificent Windsor Hotel, a Victorian castle built in 1892 that—with its dazzling assemblage of turrets, towers, and verandas (not to mention its grand dining room)—is an important draw for tourists.

About 10 mi northeast of Americus via Route 49, you can visit a solemn reminder of the Civil War's tragic toll, the **Andersonville National Historic Site.** This infamous prisoner-of-war penitentiary is the nation's only POW museum. Inside you'll find photographs, artifacts, and high-tech exhibits detailing not just the plight of Civil War POWs, but also prison life and conditions affecting all of America's 800,000 prisoners of war since the Revolutionary War. Some 13,000 Union prisoners died—mostly from disease, neglect, and malnutrition—at Andersonville during its 14-month tenure at the tail of the war. At the conclusion of the Civil War, the Swiss-born commandant of Andersonville was tried, convicted, and hanged. Appropriately, the exterior of this 10,000-square-ft memorial of sorts looms forbiddingly over the rural countryside, with barred windows and jutting towers. ⊠ *496 Cemetery Rd., Andersonville,* ☎ *229/924–0343,* WEB *http://andersonville. areaparks.com/.* ⊡ *Free.* ◔ *Daily 8:30–5.*

Dining and Lodging

$$ ✕▥ **Windsor Hotel.** This jewel of a hotel garnered awards from the
★ National Trust for Historic Preservation. Built in 1892, it's a monument to Victorian architecture and remains one of the South's best showcases of American heritage. All rooms have 12-ft ceilings, and the circular Carter Presidential Suite is the entire floor of the hotel's tallest tower. On site is the Grand Dining Room ($$–$$$, no dinner Sunday), an elegant restaurant that serves a varied menu with a focus on Southern food, such as corn chowder, crab cakes, and pecan-crusted salmon. ⊠ *125 W. Lamar St., 31709,* ☎ *229/924–1555 or 888/297–9567,* FAX *229/928–0533,* WEB *www.windsor-americus.com. 41 rooms, 12 suites. Restaurant, bar, fans. AE, D, MC, V.*

Shopping

Americus is known for its antiques and gift shops, a highlight being the **Americus Antique Mall** (⊠ 201 W. Forsyth St., ☎ 229/924–6999), a collective of 23 different dealers. **Country Comforts** (⊠ 701 S. Martin Luther King Jr. Blvd., ☎ 229/928–0077) sells handcrafted furniture, gift baskets, and Southern food products.

Tifton

72 mi southeast of Americus via U.S. 280 and I–75, 183 mi south of Atlanta via I–75.

There's something extremely genial about the tiny towns of rural Georgia, especially as you get closer to the Florida border. Tifton exemplifies this friendliness, and takes great pride in having ranked 54th in Norman Crampton's noted book, *Top 100 Best Small Towns in America.* What else would you expect of a town with a main street called "Love Avenue"? On a typical warm day you'll find neighbors walking to each others' porches for mint juleps or covered-dish dinners. Historically one of the more prosperous small towns in the state (it's wealth drawn chiefly from tobacco farming), Tifton is an antiquing favorite among Georgians in the know.

Drop by the **Tifton Museum of Arts & Heritage** (⊠ 285 Love Ave., ☎ 229/382–3600; ⊡ free; ◔ Tues.–Fri. 1–5), which is housed in a 1900 Romanesque brick church sparkling with stained glass. Exhibits of varied media are held year-round.

Dining and Lodging

$ ✕ **Sonny's Bar-B-Q.** There's nothin' fancy here—just smoky-good pork ribs, sliced beef, and turkey served with heaping mounds of cole slaw and beans. ⊠ *1616 U.S. 82, Tifton,* ☎ *229/386–0606. MC, V.*

$–$$ ▥ **Hummingbird's Perch Bed and Breakfast.** Innkeeper Francis Wilson has created a diverting retreat with this Cape Cod–style inn just 5 mi north of downtown Tifton. Peaceful grounds surround the house. ⊠ *1802 Lee Ave., 31794,* ☎ *229/382–5431,* WEB *www.stay-in-ga. com/inns/hummingbird.htm. 3 rooms. No credit cards. BP.*

$ 🏨 **Econo Lodge.** The inexpensive but reliable chain property by the Tifton Mall is also a short distance from tennis facilities and a golf course. ✉ *1025 W. 2nd St., 31794,* ☎ *229/382–0280,* FAX *229/386–0316,* WEB *www.econolodge.com. 76 rooms. Playground. AE, D, DC, MC, V. CP.*

Thomasville

55 mi south of Tifton via U.S. 319, 236 mi south of Atlanta via I–75 and U.S. 319, 38 mi north of Tallahassee, FL, via U.S. 319.

Like some of the other inviting small towns in this part of the state, Thomasville—which is just a short drive from the Florida border—prides itself on its carefully cultivated downtown square, which draws thousands of people each spring to an Annual Rose Bud Parade (the short winters in this part of the state encourage bountiful flower and vegetable gardens). The town has been a major commercial and manufacturing hub since it was incorporated in 1826, producing everything from cotton gins to tobacco to crates and baskets. Thomasville became a desirable winter retreat among wealthy Northerners in the late 1800s. Many fine old plantations and homes remain from this gilded era.

On the downtown square, converted turn-of-the-century shop fronts range from snazzy to shabby-chic, and a quaint coffeehouse and kitchen-specialty store, **Buon Appetito** (✉ 107 S. Broad St., ☎ 229/228–7175), provides shoppers a respite with jazzy java drinks.

Outdoors enthusiasts regularly take to the miles of walking trails at the **Birdsong Nature Center** (✉ 2106 Meridian Rd., ☎ 229/377–4408, WEB www.tfn.net/birdsong; ✉ $5; ☉ Wed. and Fri.–Sat. 9–5, Sun. 1–5), which encompasses 565 acres of lush fields, forests, swamps, and butterfly gardens. It's a wondrous haven for birds and scores of other native wildlife. Nature programs are offered year-round.

Dining and Lodging

$$ ✕ **Mom and Dad's Italian Restaurant.** That's definitely oregano in the air you'll smell on entering Mom and Dad's—but also expect to hear a Southern drawl wafting overhead. These go together perfectly here, a great place for rich, cheesy, thick-red-tomato-sauce Italian food. The garlic bread is served warm and strong enough to turn your breath into a blowtorch. ✉ *1800 Smith Ave.,* ☎ *229/226–6265. MC, V. Closed Sun.–Mon.*

$$$$ ✕🏨 **Melhana Grand Plantation Resort.** On this sprawling 50-acre plantation—listed on the National Register of Historic Places—there are 30 buildings on grounds dotted with shade trees, gardens, bridal paths, and hunting trails. Most rooms are massive, with gorgeous four-poster beds and antique writing desks. A highlight here is Melhana's Chapin Dining Room ($$$–$$$$, jacket and reservations required, no lunch). The meals here are every bit as exquisite as the surroundings in which they are served. ✉ *301 Showboat La., 31792,* ☎ *229/226–2290 or 888/920–3030,* FAX *229/226–4585,* WEB *www.melhana.com. 18 rooms, 11 suites, 2 cottages. Restaurant, bar, cable TV, indoor pool, tennis court, health club, spa, horseback riding, library, concierge. AE, D, MC, V. CP.*

$$–$$$ 🏨 **Serendipity Cottage Bed and Breakfast.** In a quiet residential neighborhood a short walk from the downtown square, this immaculate 4,600-square-ft house has four rooms, each decorated to reflect a distinctive style. Accents may include a hand-crocheted bed canopy, thick brass bedposts, hand-painted fireplace screens, or lace linens dripping with intricate needlework. ✉ *339 E. Jefferson St., 31792,* ☎ *229/226–8111 or 800/383–7377,* FAX *912/226–2656,* WEB *www.serenbe.com. 4 rooms. AE, D, MC, V. BP.*

Country Oaks Municipal Golf Course (⊠ Rte. 122 [Pavo Rd.], ☎ 229/ 225–433) has a par-71, 18-hole golf course with 6,200 yards of tight fairways and Bermuda greens in peaceful woods.

Shopping

Adding character to the square is the **Bookshelf** (⊠ 108 E. Jackson St., ☎ 229/228–7767), a respected bookstore of antique and vintage books that serves as a community-binding gathering spot for local literati. **Holly-brook, Inc.** (⊠ 110 South Broad St., ☎ 229/225–1771) is an odyssey of imported and domestic home furnishings.

Southwest Georgia A to Z

To research prices, get advice from other travelers, and book travel arrangements, visit www.fodors.com

BUS TRAVEL

Greyhound Bus Lines serves Americus, Columbus, LaGrange, Thomasville, and Tifton.
➤ Bus Information: **Greyhound Bus Lines** (☎ 800/231–2222, WEB www.greyhound.com).

CAR TRAVEL

A car is your best way to tour this part of Georgia; I–75 runs north–south through the eastern edge of the region and connects to several U.S. and state highways that traverse the region, and I–85 runs southwest through LaGrange and Columbus.

EMERGENCIES

➤ Emergency Services: **Ambulance, police** (☎ 911).
➤ Hospitals: **Columbus Doctors Hospital** (⊠ 616 19th St., Columbus, ☎ 706/322–0753). **John D. Archibold Memorial Hospital** (⊠ 915 Gordon St., Thomasville, ☎ 229/336–5646).

TAXIS

Yellow Cab in Columbus and Thomasville provides 24-hour taxi service.
➤ Taxi Companies: **Yellow Cab** (☎ 706/322–1616 in Columbus; 229/ 226–1717 in Thomasville).

VISITOR INFORMATION

➤ Tourist Information: **Americus-Sumter Tourism Council** (⊠ Windsor Hotel, 125 W. Lamar St., Box 275, Americus 31709, ☎ 229/928–6059 or 888/278–6837). **Columbus Convention and Visitors Bureau** (⊠ 1000 Bay Ave., The Riverwalk, Box 2768, 31902, ☎ 706/322–3181 or 800/999–1613, WEB www.columbusga.com). **LaGrange-Troup County Chamber of Commerce** (⊠ 111 Bull St., Box 636, LaGrange 30241, ☎ 706/884–8671, WEB www.lagrangechamber.com). **Thomasville Welcome Center** (⊠ Broad St., Thomasville 31792, ☎ 229/227–7099 or 800/704–2350, WEB www.thomasvillega.com). **Tifton-Tift County Tourism Association** (⊠ 115 W. 2nd St., Box 273, Tifton 31793, ☎ 229/382–6200, WEB www.tiftontourism.com). **Warm Springs Welcome Center** (⊠ 69 Broad St., Warm Springs 31830, ☎ 706/655–3322 or 800/327–1927, WEB www.warmspringsga.com).

GEORGIA A TO Z

To research prices, get advice from other travelers, and book travel arrangements, visit www.fodors.com.

AIRPORTS

Hartsfield Atlanta International Airport is 13 mi south of downtown. Numerous regional airports serve the state. For information on the state's local airports, *see* the A to Z coverage at the end of each regional section in this chapter.

➤ AIRPORT INFORMATION: **Hartsfield Atlanta International Airport** (✉ 6000 N. Terminal Pkwy., ☎ 404/530–6600, WEB www.atlanta-airport.com).

BIKE TRAVEL

With a membership of about 3,000, the Southern Bicycle League has promoted bicycling across Georgia and the South for more than 20 years. The Bicycle Ride Across Georgia (BRAG) is an annual event, and the same organization holds numerous shorter bicycling events throughout the year. Advance application is required.

➤ CONTACTS: **Bicycle Ride Across Georgia** (☎ 770/921–6166, WEB www.brag.org). **Southern Bicycle League** (✉ Box 870387, Stone Mountain 30087, ☎ 770/594–8350, WEB www.bikesbl.org).

BUS TRAVEL

Greyhound Bus Lines serves several dozen towns statewide.

➤ BUS INFORMATION: **Greyhound Bus Lines** (☎ 800/231–2222, WEB www.greyhound.com).

CAR TRAVEL

Although Savannah and several of the state's most visited communities have highly walkable downtowns, a car is your most convenient and practical way to tour the state. This is even true in most of Atlanta, a city where distances between attractions, restaurants, and hotels can be vast.

Georgia is traversed east and west by several interstate highways. North and south are covered by I–75, running from northwest through the center of the state to the Florida line; I–85 runs from the northeastern part of the state through the west to Alabama; I–95 runs along the Georgia coast from South Carolina to Florida. I–85 and I–75 converge in Atlanta near its downtown; this nexus is called the Connector. Running east and west, I–20 stretches from Birmingham, Alabama, to Augusta, Georgia, running through the center of downtown Atlanta on its way. From Macon I–16 leads directly east to Savannah, where it ends. Scenic routes include U.S. 76, a good highway running east–west through the north Georgia mountains, and U.S. 441, running north–south from the mountains to the Florida line. Along the way U.S. 441 links numerous charming small towns and is lined with barbecue joints of worth. On the west side of the state, various pleasant small towns are connected by U.S. 19, the north–south route of choice prior to development of the interstate and still a good option if I–75 comes to a standstill, as it routinely does.

ROAD CONDITIONS

For road information call the Georgia Department of Transportation.

➤ CONTACTS: **Georgia Department of Transportation** (☎ 404/656–1267, WEB www.dot.state.ga.us).

RULES OF THE ROAD

The speed limit on interstates is 55 mph in metropolitan areas and up to 70 mph elsewhere. Right turns on red lights are permitted unless indicated.

EMERGENCIES
➤ EMERGENCY SERVICES: **Ambulance, police** (☎ 911).

LODGING
BED-AND-BREAKFASTS
For home stays Bed & Breakfast Atlanta represents 80–100 homes and can find lodging in carriage houses, apartments, and B&B inns.
➤ RESERVATION SERVICES: **Bed & Breakfast Atlanta** (✉ 1608 Briarcliff Rd., Suite 5, Atlanta 30306, ☎ 404/875–0525 or 800/967–3224, FAX 404/875–8198).

OUTDOORS AND SPORTS
FISHING
The Georgia Department of Natural Resources, Game and Fish Division has free pamphlets covering Georgia's regulations, and has maps detailing good fishing spots.
➤ CONTACTS: **Georgia Department of Natural Resources, Game and Fish Division** (✉ 2070 U.S. 278, Social Circle 30025, ☎ 770/918–6400, WEB www.state.ga.us).

TRAIN TRAVEL
Amtrak serves Atlanta and Savannah from major cities along the eastern seaboard, as well as New Orleans. Amtrak's Thru-Way bus service connects daily from Birmingham and Mobile, Alabama, to Atlanta's Brookwood Amtrak station. Another bus runs from Brookwood to Macon.

FARES AND SCHEDULES
➤ TRAIN INFORMATION: **Amtrak** (☎ 800/872–7245, WEB www.amtrak.com).

VISITOR INFORMATION
The Georgia Department of Industry, Trade, and Tourism operates visitor centers (most of them just off major interstate highways) in Augusta, Columbus, Kingsland, Lavonia, Plains, Ringgold, Savannah, Sylvania, Tallapoosa, Valdosta, and West Point. Housed under the Georgia Department of Natural Resources, Parks, Recreation & Historic Sites division has information on Georgia's parks.
➤ TOURIST INFORMATION: **Georgia Department of Industry, Trade, and Tourism** (✉ Box 1776, Atlanta 30301, ☎ 404/656–3590 or 800/847–4842, FAX 404/651–9063, WEB www.georgia.org). **Georgia Department of Natural Resources, Parks, Recreation & Historic Sites** (✉ 205 Butler St. SE, Suite 1352, Atlanta 30334, ☎ 404/656–3530; 800/864–7275 for reservations; 770/389–7275 for local reservations, WEB www.state.ga.us).

3 NORTH CAROLINA

Indulge yourself in the historical sites and natural wonders of North Carolina, from Old Salem in Winston-Salem, where the 1700s spring to life today, to the Great Smoky and Blue Ridge mountains. On the Cape Hatteras and Cape Lookout national seashores, lighthouses stand as they have for 200 years, and unspoiled beaches stretch for miles. You'll find sophisticated shopping and dining in Charlotte; first-class golf in the Sandhills; and high technology, health care, and culture within the Triangle, a shape traced by Raleigh, Durham, and Chapel Hill.

By Lisa H.
Towle

Updated by
Rob Fleming

THE FIRST STANZA OF NORTH CAROLINA'S OFFICIAL toast reads: "Here's to the land of the longleaf pine/ The summer land where the sun doth shine/ Where the weak grow strong and the strong grow great/ Here's to 'Down Home,' the Old North State!" Sure, it's hyperbolic, but it's catchy and rhythmic. It also speaks to a deeper truth: as much as geography, people have shaped the state's landscape over the years. In a moving tribute that was both videotaped and printed, the late Charles Kuralt, television journalist, author, and inveterate traveler, noted that North Carolina—his "state of grace"—has been the home of Whistler's mother, Billy Graham, Michael Jordan, Chief Manteo, and three U.S. presidents.

In 1524 the explorer Giovanni da Verrazano landed on what is now North Carolina's shore and wrote in his log that it was ". . . as pleasant and delectable [a land] to behold as is possible to imagine." Sixty years later the New World's first English-speaking settlers found their way to the state's eastern edge, which is bordered by 300 mi of beaches, islands, and inlets. Hernando de Soto searched for gold in the western part of the state, an area bounded by two ranges of the southern Appalachians, the Blue Ridge Mountains and the Great Smoky Mountains. In 1540 he and his band of Spanish explorers met the centuries-long residents of the area, the Cherokee, at the ancient village of Guasili, close by what is today the town of Murphy. Several centuries later, in 1799, the first gold rush in the United States got its start in the heartland, the Piedmont—near Concord, to be exact—when young Conrad Reed discovered a 17-pound nugget that would eventually be identified as gold. And although North Carolina was the last state to secede during the Civil War, the state provided more troops and supplies to the Confederacy than any other Southern state and suffered the most casualties.

Thanks to efforts of the state and many determined citizens, this history and more has been carefully preserved. A lot of it can be found along 1,500 mi of roads designated by the state's Department of Transportation as Scenic Byways. Thirty-one such byways (all marked with signs) crisscross the state. The soul of North Carolina can be glimpsed on these meandering routes. Here the views can quickly shift from panoramic to intimate, and the jasmine and galax, azaleas and rhododendrons, magnolias and dogwoods, and soft Spanish moss grow undisturbed.

Unlike many other states, North Carolina does not have one city that stands head and shoulders above all others. Rather, because of a confluence of circumstance, custom, and capitalistic acuity, a number of centers of business, art, and education have grown up throughout the state. Citizens, from African-American to Quaker, are proud of their contributions to North Carolina's development and protective of the areas and unique cultures from which they sprang. Indeed, some have described the Old North State as a collection of fiercely independent city-states reminiscent of those in ancient Greece or 19th-century Italy. Taken as a whole, North Carolina is now more urban and suburban than rural. You won't find gritty, noisy, oversize cities here, though. Instead, the pace is a bit slower. Manners and smiles still count, and canopies of hardwoods and pine trees characterize cities and countryside alike.

Thanks to its temperate climate, world-class schools, and one of the most dynamic economies in the nation, North Carolina attracts residents in record numbers. These new inhabitants have come from around the world and around the country, and their myriad artistic, cul-

North Carolina

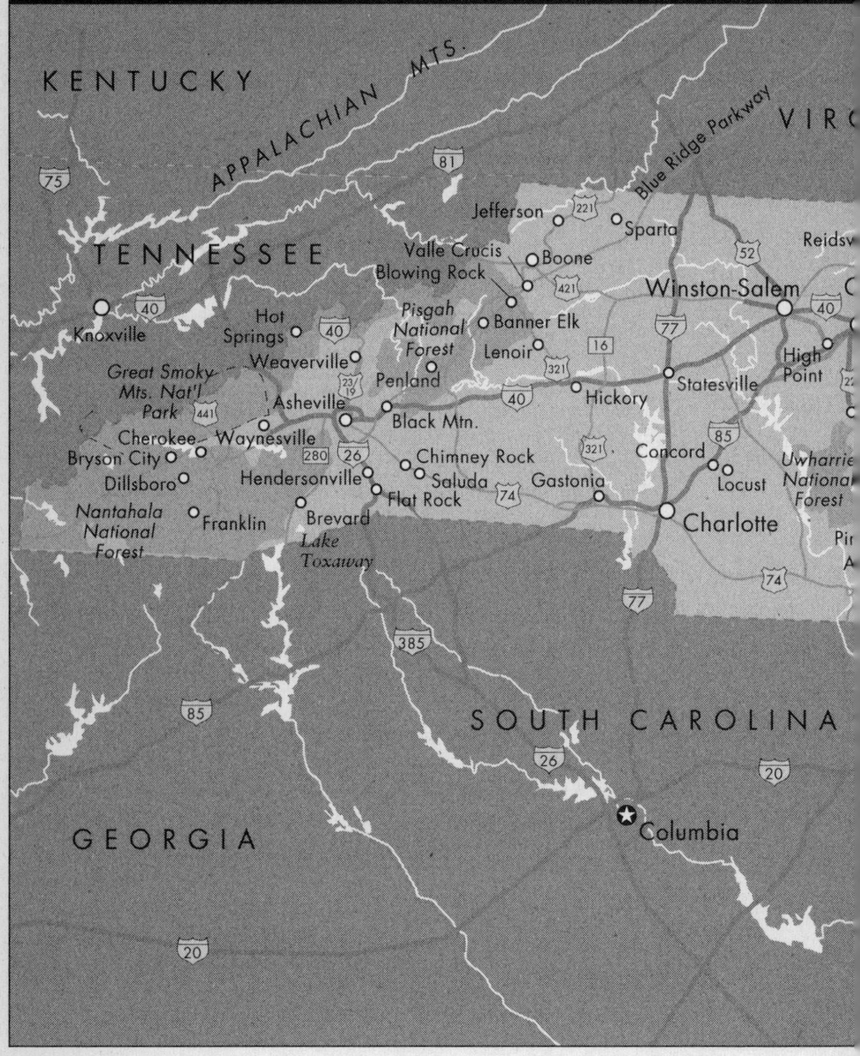

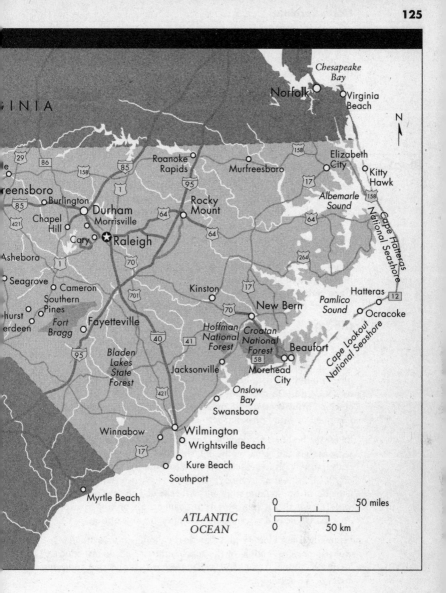

tural, culinary, spiritual, and academic influences have been unmistakable. Ultimately, however, what newcomers find to be one of North Carolina's great appeals is its timelessness. In 1749 Peter Jefferson, the father of Thomas Jefferson, and his group of surveyors discovered a river in western North Carolina. Because they believed it to be a large, undiscovered branch of the Mississippi River, the surveyors dubbed it the New River. Later, archaeologists determined that it is actually the oldest river in the United States and the second oldest in the world, after the Nile. Today, amid majestic scenery, its two forks continue to flow.

Pleasures and Pastimes

Beaches

From the thin band of barrier islands known as the Outer Banks, along the northern coastline, to the area around Wilmington and the Cape Fear Coast to the South Brunswick Islands, near the South Carolina border, North Carolina's beaches are a year-round destination. You can visit national seashores or wildlife refuges, go surfing, diving, fishing, hiking, bird-watching, hang gliding—or just watch the waves. North Carolinians are proud that the nation's first national seashore, Cape Hatteras, is in their state, as is Roanoke Island, where the country's first European settlers landed more than 400 years ago.

Dining

In North Carolina's cities, risotto and dim sum have become as common as grits and corn bread. Ethnic specialties of all kinds are available, as well as contemporary American cuisine. The Sandhills, too, have a number of sophisticated restaurants. But you can find plenty of good old-fashioned Southern cooking, including Southern-fried chicken, Brunswick stew, ham, vegetables, biscuits, and fruit cobblers. Chopped or sliced pork barbecue is still a big item.

By far the best fare around the Outer Banks is fresh seafood. Raw bars serve oysters and clams on the half shell, and seafood houses offer fresh crabs (soft-shells in season, which is early in the summer) and whatever local fish—tuna, wahoo, mahimahi—have been hauled in that day. Cuisine in the Wilmington and Morehead City areas is strong on seafood, whether it's shrimp, Atlantic blue crab, or king mackerel, but pork barbecue and international cuisines are also options.

From Cherokee County to Asheville the dining choices are many: upscale restaurants, middle-of-the-road country fare, and fast-food eateries. Fresh mountain trout and such game meats as pheasant and venison are regional specialties.

Unless otherwise noted, neat, casual wear (including golf wear in the Sandhills) is acceptable throughout North Carolina.

CATEGORY	COST*
$$$$	over $25
$$$	$17–$25
$$	$10–$17
$	under $10

*per person for a main course at dinner

Historic Places

You'll find plenty of ways to get out of the fast lane and onto the back roads that lead to places where history is kept alive. Whether it's the site of a key battle in the Revolutionary War or the largest troop surrender of the Civil War, a Quaker settlement, or studios where artisans carry on a 200-year-old tradition in pottery, North Carolina cherishes its past. Places to visit are as varied as the site of man's first flight and the architectural legacies of America's industrial barons.

Lodging

In North Carolina's cities you'll find everything from economy motels to convention hotels to bed-and-breakfasts in lovely historic districts. Most major chains are represented, and some hotels offer great weekend packages. A few warnings, though: during the twice-a-year furniture market in High Point, when 75,000 people descend on the city, empty hotel rooms and rental cars are almost impossible to find. May is graduation time for all of the Triangle's colleges and universities. Hotels and restaurants are booked, in some cases, years in advance.

Most lodging options in the Sandhills are in the luxury resort category, with full amenities and services. Many of the prices quoted are for golf packages. However, there are some chain motels in Southern Pines and Aberdeen, as well as B&Bs in the area.

Motels and hotels are clustered up and down the Outer Banks, with rental properties in all the towns that dot the Cape Hatteras National Seashore. If you're going to Wilmington and the Cape Fear Coast, and New Bern and the Central (or Crystal) Coast, you can choose from chains, condos, and resorts overlooking water, whether it's a river or the ocean. There are also in-town guest houses. Lodging options in the western mountains range from posh resorts to mountain cabins, country inns, and economy chain motels. When you're planning your trip, always ask about special packages and possible off-season rates.

CATEGORY	COST*
$$$$	over $175
$$$	$125–$175
$$	$75–$125
$	under $75

All prices are for a standard double room, excluding 6%–12% tax (depending on county).

Outdoor Activities

North Carolina's unique geological and biological resources give outdoor enthusiasts lots of options. There are hundreds of choices if you want to rough it, from primitive camping to family camping. Hikers and backpackers come here for the trails—from one-day hikes to week-long trips. Quite a few stables offer rental horses, and some have llama treks. Hard-core mountain bikers can ride a 27-mi loop through the Great Smoky Mountains National Park. Local outfitters regularly conduct white-water rafting trips. The state has eight ski resorts, and if you like height but not snow, there's hang gliding across the dunes at Nags Head.

Exploring North Carolina

Charlotte, the state's largest city, is known as a center of high finance in the South, and prides itself on its cosmopolitan flair. The cities of the Triad (Greensboro, Winston-Salem, and High Point), in the upper Piedmont, showcase the legacies of some of the state's founding families. The Triangle (Raleigh, Durham, and Chapel Hill), in the central Piedmont, is the hub of higher education, scientific research, and state-sponsored cultural resources. The Sandhills, on the Coastal Plain, is a favorite among antiques lovers and is recognized worldwide as a major golfing destination. On the Outer Banks comes solitude in the form of miles of pristine shore. Boating, scuba diving, and fishing are the main pastimes in Morehead City and the Central Coast, whereas history is alive in genteel New Bern. Wilmington and the Cape Fear Coast aren't just resort vacation spots—they're a thriving business and cultural center for the southeastern portion of North Carolina. In the western mountains, which are anchored by the city of Asheville, you'll find everything from hiking trails and Southern crafts to boot-scoot music and Brahms.

Great Itineraries

North Carolina is a large state, and touring it comfortably from end to end could easily take two weeks, although you could whiz through in a week. Many people focus each trip on one region: mountains, Piedmont, or Coastal Plain. A week could be spent in each of these, but there are many worthwhile trips of shorter duration.

IF YOU HAVE 3 DAYS

Start your tour of the Outer Banks from its north end, coming in on U.S. 158. Drive north on Route 12 your first morning there to spend time in **Corolla,** visiting the Currituck Beach Lighthouse. After lunch head south through **Kitty Hawk, Kill Devil Hills,** and **Nags Head,** with a stop at the Wright Brothers National Memorial. Spend the first night (and the next) on ☷ **Roanoke Island,** where you'll take the second day to visit historical locations and the North Carolina Aquarium. On Day 3 leave Roanoke and spend the day along the **Cape Hatteras National Seashore,** visiting sights on **Hatteras Island** in the morning and ☷ **Ocracoke Island** in the afternoon.

IF YOU HAVE 5 DAYS

☷ **Asheville** is the logical starting point for a tour of the North Carolina mountains. It will take the full first day to cover the Biltmore Estate and neighboring village. Day 2 should be devoted to the attractions south of Asheville, including **Chimney Rock** and the Carl Sandburg Home National Historical Site, in **Flat Rock.** Another day back in Asheville will allow you to visit the remaining area attractions, including Pack Place. On the fourth morning begin your journey up the **Blue Ridge Parkway,** lingering at the many scenic stopping points along the way, and arrive in the ☷ **Boone** area for the night. Day 5 will be occupied with High Country activities, including a visit to the Tweetsie Railroad, in **Blowing Rock.**

IF YOU HAVE 7 DAYS

With a full week at your disposal you can do a whirlwind tour from one end of North Carolina to the other. Start your journey by touring the Biltmore Estate in ☷ **Asheville.** Next head for ☷ **Charlotte;** be sure to visit Discovery Place and the Mint Museum of Craft & Design during your day here. The Triad and the historical attractions of Old Salem are the focus of the third day; overnight in ☷ **Winston-Salem.** The next two days will allow time for a taste of the Triangle, including the Duke University campus and Sarah Duke Gardens, in **Durham;** the Morehead Planetarium and Franklin Street shopping, in **Chapel Hill;** and the museums and capital area of ☷ **Raleigh.** Your sixth day should be spent in the Sandhills area enjoying antiques shops and the world-class golf in ☷ **Pinehurst.** Wind up your visit in ☷ **Wilmington,** where you can visit the historic downtown and USS *North Carolina* Battleship Memorial, or just head for the nearby beaches.

When to Tour North Carolina

North Carolina particularly shines in the spring (April and May) and fall (September and October), when the weather is temperate and the trees and flowers burst with color. At these times you'll avoid the peak tourist season. Summer trips are best spent in the mountains or at the coastal beaches, where temperatures are significantly cooler. In winter many mountain attractions close just as the ski resorts open for the season.

CHARLOTTE

Although Charlotte dates from Revolutionary War times (it is named for King George III's wife, Queen Charlotte), its Uptown is distinctively New South, with gleaming skyscrapers and broad streets. Uptown encompasses all of downtown Charlotte, a center of government, commerce, and culture. It also has some fashionable historic neighborhoods that are noted for their architecture and their winding, tree-shaded streets. Public art—such as the sculptures at the four corners of Trade and Tryon streets—is increasingly displayed in the city. Erected at Independence Square, the sculptures symbolize Charlotte's beginnings: a gold miner (commerce), a mill worker (the city's textile heritage), an African-American railroad builder (transportation), and a mother holding her baby aloft (the future). Residents of the Queen City take enormous pride in their city being not only the largest city in the Carolinas but also the second-largest banking center in the nation.

Heavy development has created some typical urban problems. Outdated road systems in this metropolis make traffic a nightmare during rush hour, and virtually all the city's restaurants are packed on weekends. But the locals' Southern courtesy is contagious, and people still love the laid-back pleasures of jogging, picnicking, and sunning in Freedom Park.

You'll be able to walk around Uptown and the Fourth Ward, and buses are adequate for getting around within the city limits. Cars, however, remain the best bet for touring.

Numbers in the text correspond to numbers in the margin and on the Charlotte map.

Uptown Charlotte

Uptown Charlotte is ideal for walking. The city was laid out in four wards around Independence Square, at Trade and Tryon streets. The Square, as it is known, is the center of the Uptown area.

A Good Walk

Stop first at **INFO! Charlotte** (✉ 330 S. Tryon St., Uptown, ☎ 704/331–2700) for information on a self-guided walking tour of the Fourth Ward and a historic tour of Uptown, as well as maps and brochures. Take a stroll north on Tryon Street and enjoy this revitalized area, noting the outdoor sculptures on the plazas and the creative architecture of some of the newer buildings, including the **Bank of America Corporate Center** ①.

Walk two blocks west on Trade Street to the **First Presbyterian Church** and begin exploring the **Fourth Ward** ②, Charlotte's "old" city. Next head south to North Tryon Street just above 6th Street, where you will find the science and technology museum **Discovery Place** ③, a leading attraction. Finish your walk at the **Mint Museum of Craft & Design** ④, which showcases North Carolina's rich crafts tradition.

TIMING

You can spend a pleasant half day to a day touring these areas. Allow an hour to browse through the Bank of America Corporate Center and Founders Hall. You can tour the Fourth Ward in an hour or so. The bulk of your time will be spent in Discovery Place, which can occupy as much of the day as you wish. You can avoid the workday bustle by visiting on the weekend, but note Discovery Place's Sunday hours.

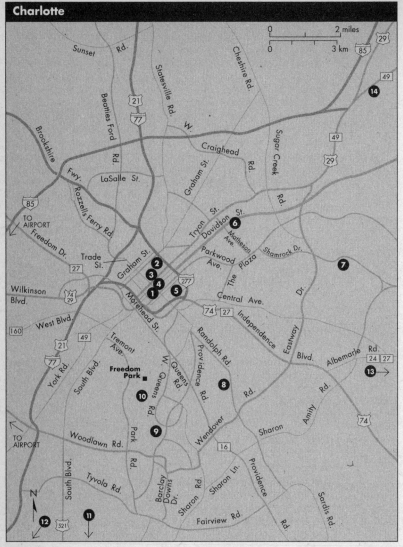

Charlotte

Afro-American Cultural
Center. **5**

Bank of America
Corporate Center **1**

Charlotte Museum of
History and Hezekiah
Alexander Homesite . . **7**

Charlotte Nature
Museum **10**

Discovery Place **3**

Fourth Ward **2**

James K. Polk
Memorial. **11**

Lowe's Motor
Speedway **14**

Mint Museum of Art . . : **8**

Mint Museum of
Craft & Design **4**

North Davidson
Arts District (NoDA) . . **6**

Paramount's
Carowinds. **12**

Reed Gold Mine State
Historic Site **13**

Wing Haven Gardens
and Bird Sanctuary. . . **9**

Sights to See

1 Bank of America Corporate Center. This 60-story structure with a crownlike top designed by Cesar Pelli is one of the city's most striking buildings. Its main attractions are three monumental frescoes by Ben Long, whose themes are making/building, chaos/creativity, and planning/knowledge. Also in the tower are the **North Carolina Blumenthal Performing Arts Center** and the restaurants, shops, and exhibition space of **Founders Hall**. ⊠ *100 N. Tryon St., Uptown.*

★ ☺ **3 Discovery Place.** At Charlotte's premier attraction, the wonderful hands-on **Science Museum** is a priority; also allow at least two hours for the **aquariums**, the three-story **rain forest**, the **Omnimax theater**, and **Kelly Space Voyager Planetarium**, the largest in the United States. A ham radio room, a puppet theater, and a 10-ft model of an eyeball that you can walk through are other highlights. Check the schedule for special exhibits. ⊠ *301 N. Tryon St., Uptown,* ☎ *704/372–6261 or 800/935–0553,* WEB *www.discoveryplace.org.* ☜ *$7.50 for 1 area, plus $3 for any additional area visited.* ☉ *Sept.–May, weekdays 9–5, Sat. 9–6, Sun. 1–6; June–Aug., Mon.–Sat. 9–6, Sun. 1–6.*

2 Fourth Ward. Charlotte's popular old neighborhood began as a political subsection created for electoral purposes in the mid-1800s. The architecture and sensibility of this quiet, homespun neighborhood provide a feeling for life in a less hectic time. A brochure available at INFO! Charlotte includes 18 historic places of interest. Be sure to stop by **Old Settlers Cemetery**, behind the **First Presbyterian Church** (⊠ 200 W. Trade St., Uptown, ☎ 704/332–5123), which contains tombstones that date from the 1700s. The Gothic Revival church, which takes up a city block and faces West Trade Street, reflects the prosperity of the early settlers and their descendants. **Fourth Ward Park** is an oasis in the middle of the city. **Alexander Michael's** (⊠ 401 W. 9th St., Uptown/Fourth Ward, ☎ 704/332–6789) is a warm and worn neighborhood bar. **Poplar Street Books** is housed in the Victorian Young-Morrison House (⊠ 226 W. 10th St., Uptown). U.S. president William Taft spent the night in the **McNinch House** (⊠ 511 N. Church St., Uptown), now a restaurant, when he visited Charlotte in 1909. **Spirit Square** (⊠ 345 N. College St., Uptown), in a former church, includes galleries, a performing arts center, and classrooms that used to be the sanctuary for the First Baptist Church. The **public library** (⊠ 310 N. Tryon St., Uptown), which contains a mural reproducing a Romare Bearden painting, is open weekdays 9–9, Saturday 9–6, and Sunday 2–6.

4 Mint Museum of Craft & Design. A sister to the Mint Museum of Art, the museum is in what used to be an upscale women's clothing store. The gallery alone is 16,000 square ft. Add on the permanent collections of ceramics, glass, fiber, metal, and wood, and you have one of the country's major crafts museums. You can use your receipt from the crafts museum to enter the Mint Museum of Art free on the same day. ⊠ *220 N. Tryon St., Uptown,* ☎ *704/337–2000,* WEB *www.mintmuseum.org.* ☜ *$6.* ☉ *Tues.–Sat. 10–5, Sun. noon–5.*

Greater Charlotte

Beyond Uptown and farther afield lie many of Charlotte's most interesting sights, from gardens to museums. You can reach the ones listed below by car or by city bus; for visits elsewhere a car is essential.

A Good Tour

From Uptown follow 7th Street east and turn north on North Myers Street to visit the galleries of the **Afro-American Cultural Center** ⑤. Backtrack to North Davidson Street, turn right, and continue for just over

2 mi to Matheson Avenue, the start of the **North Davidson Arts District (NoDa)** ⑥. This revived main street of a former mill village—now with a collection of singular galleries, bars, coffeehouses, shops, and artist's residences—extends north to 36th Street. Travel east on 36th Street less than a mile to the Plaza, turn right, and go south to Shamrock Drive and turn left toward the **Charlotte Museum of History and Hezekiah Alexander Homesite** ⑦, where you can see the county's oldest building. Return west on Eastway Drive and follow it south until it becomes Wendover Road. Continue 1⅔ mi to Randolph Road and then turn right to reach the **Mint Museum of Art** ⑧, a wide-ranging collection in a former mint. The next stop, **Wing Haven Gardens and Bird Sanctuary** ⑨, is in Myers Park, a handsome neighborhood. More experience with nature can be found at the **Charlotte Nature Museum** ⑩, next to Freedom Park.

TIMING

Within a few miles of each other, these sites can easily be covered on foot over two days.

Sights to See

❺ **Afro-American Cultural Center.** In a historic former church, this center, with its galleries and theater, is a showcase for art, music, drama, and dance. ⊠ *401 N. Myers St., Uptown,* ☎ *704/374–1565,* WEB *www.aacc-charlotte.org.* ☞ *Free.* ☉ *Tues.–Sat. 10–6, Sun. 1–5.*

❼ **Charlotte Museum of History and Hezekiah Alexander Homesite.** The stone house, built in 1774, is the oldest dwelling in the county. Alexander and his wife, Mary, reared 10 children in this house and farmed the land. Seasonal events commemorate the early days. Permanent and rotating exhibits in the museum span 300 years of southern Piedmont history. ⊠ *3500 Shamrock Dr., East Charlotte/Merchandise Mart,* ☎ *704/568–1774,* WEB *www.charlottemuseum.org.* ☞ *Museum and homesite $6; free Sun.* ☉ *Tues.–Sat. 10–5, Sun. 1–5; tours by costumed docents weekdays 1:15 and 3:15.*

☝ ⑩ **Charlotte Nature Museum.** Although affiliated with Discovery Place, the museum is in the southeast section of the city. You'll find a butterfly pavilion, live animals, nature trails, Indian relics, a puppet theater, and hands-on exhibits just for children. ⊠ *1658 Sterling Ave. (next to Freedom Park), Uptown,* ☎ *704/372–0471,* WEB *www.discoveryplace.org.* ☞ *$4.* ☉ *Weekdays 9–5, Sat. 10–5, Sun. 1–5.*

★ ⑧ **Mint Museum of Art.** Built in 1836 as a U.S. Mint, this building has served as a home for art since 1936. Among the holdings in its impressive permanent collections are American and European paintings, furniture, and decorative arts; African, pre-Columbian, and Spanish colonial art; porcelain and pottery; and regional crafts and historic costumes. On the day you visit this museum your receipt will entitle you to free admission to downtown's Mint Museum of Craft & Design. ⊠ *2730 Randolph Rd., East Charlotte/Merchandise Mart,* ☎ *704/337–2000,* WEB *www.mintmuseum.org.* ☞ *$6.* ☉ *Tues. 10–10, Wed.–Sat. 10–5, Sun. noon–5.*

❻ **North Davidson Arts District (NoDa).** Historic NoDa is as funky as Uptown is elegant. Creative energy flows through the reclaimed textile mill and mill houses, cottages, and commercial spaces of this north Charlotte neighborhood where you'll find both the kooky and the conformist—artists, musicians, and dancers; street vendors; and restaurateurs—sharing space. The heart of this architecturally significant district is the **Neighborhood Theatre** (⊠ *511 E. 36th St., North Davidson Arts District,* ☎ *704/358–9298*), a converted movie house that seats 300 and presents all manner of performance art. **Center of the Earth** (✉ 3204 N. Davidson St., North Davidson Arts District, ☎ 704/375–5756) and **Blue Pony Gallery and Press** (✉ 3202-A N. Davidson St., North Davidson Arts District, ☎ 704/334–9390) are representative of the contemporary art galleries that have made a home here. Adding to the spice of this compact enclave are several notable restaurants and working-class bars. **Fat City** (✉ 3127 N. Davidson St., North Davidson Arts District, ☎ 704/343–0242) serves deli food and mixed drinks, and attracts an eclectic clientele. **Pat's/23 Studio** (✉ 3203 N. Davidson St., North Davidson Arts District, ☎ 704/358–0539) offers food, beverage, poetry, and comedy. To truly experience NoDa, attend a nighttime Gallery Crawl, held the first and third Fridays of every month. The crawls, which run officially from 6 to 9:30, have gained a regional reputation for their informal and entertaining nature.

❾ Wing Haven Gardens and Bird Sanctuary. In Myers Park, one of Charlotte's loveliest neighborhoods, 4 acres of formal gardens and wild woodlands developed by the Clarkson family house more than 135 species of birds. ✉ *248 Ridgewood Ave., South Park,* ☎ *704/331–0664,* 🌐 *www.winghavengardens.com.* ⛁ *Free.* ☉ *Sun. 2–5, Tues. 3–5, Wed. 10–noon, or by appointment.*

Other Area Attractions

Historic sites, a speedway, and a theme park provide plenty to explore beyond the city.

⓫ James K. Polk Memorial. A state historic site south of Charlotte marks the humble 1795 birthplace and childhood home of the 11th president. Guided tours of the log cabins (replicas of the originals) are available. ✉ *308 S. Polk St., Pineville,* ☎ *704/889–7145.* ⛁ *Free.* ☉ *Apr.–Oct., Mon.–Sat. 9–5, Sun. 1–5; Nov.–Mar., Tues.–Sat. 10–4, Sun. 1–4.*

⓮ Lowe's Motor Speedway. Learn all about NASCAR racing, one of the nation's fastest-growing sports, at this state-of-the-art, 167,000-seat facility; browse through the gift shop; or even take a "hot laps" (160 mph) lesson at the track through the **Richard Petty Driving Experience** (☎ 704/455–9443) or **Fast Track Driving School** (☎ 704/455–1700). Classes are given year-round, though intermittently. ✉ *5555 Concord Pkwy. S, University/Speedway Concord, northeast of Charlotte,* ☎ *704/455–3200 or 800/455–3267,* 🌐 *www.lowesmotorspeedway.com.* ⛁ *$10–$60; prices vary.* ☉ *Racing season runs Apr.–Nov.*

☝ ⓬ Paramount's Carowinds. A 100-acre amusement park on the South Carolina state line has rides and attractions based on films. Costumed movie characters and actors greet visitors, and the Palladium offers musical concerts with star entertainers. Rides include the heart-stopping Drop Zone. ✉ *14523 Carowinds Blvd., South Charlotte/Pineville,* ☎ *704/588–2600 or 800/888–4386,* 🌐 *www.carowinds.com.* ⛁ *$40.* ☉ *Late Mar.–May and mid-Aug.–early Oct., weekends; June–mid-Aug., daily. Park usually opens around 10; closing hrs vary.*

☝ ⓭ Reed Gold Mine State Historic Site. This area, east of Charlotte in Cabarrus County, is where America's first documented gold rush began, following Conrad Reed's discovery of a 17-pound nugget in 1799. Forty-minute guided underground tours of the gold mine are available, as well as seasonal gold panning, walking trails, and a stamp mill. ✉ *9621 Reed Mine Rd., north of Rte. 24/27, Locust, follow signs beyond town,* ☎ *704/721–4653.* ⛁ *Free; gold panning $2 per pan.* ☉ *Apr.–Oct., Mon.–Sat. 9–5, Sun. 1–5; Nov.–Mar., Tues.–Sat. 10–4, Sun. 1–4; call for tour schedules.*

Dining

$$$$ ✕ **Étienne's Townhouse.** Chef-owner Étienne Jaulin and his wife, Amanda, serve exquisitely prepared American cuisine with a French twist. The restaurant has a country-club-elegant style—with crown molding and white linen. The menu shifts frequently as Jaulin encourages sous chefs to go to the market and "come back with something fun." The end result may be thousand-layer salmon terrine or roasted Dover sole with a sweet pea vanilla sauce. ⊠ *1011 Providence Rd., South Park,* ☎ *704/335–1546. AE, D, DC, MC, V. No dinner Sun.*

$$–$$$ ✕ **Campania.** Warmth is the byword for this restaurant in a country-club community. The walls are golden and textured, there is richly toned wood and lots of candlelight, and the music is genuine Italian, from opera to contemporary. The food, too, is about as authentic as it gets outside southern Italy. The *gamberoni mergellina,* shrimp sautéed in garlic butter and herbs, is sublime. Another option is linguine *posillipo,* which pairs clams with red or white sauce; the veal chops are also popular. ⊠ *6414 Rea Rd., South Park,* ☎ *704/541–8505. AE, D, MC, V. No dinner Sun.*

$$–$$$ ✕ **Latorre's.** The emphasis at this downtown retreat is on the heat, color, and tastes of Latin America. Art splashed with vibrant shades of mango, lemon, and salmon complement exposed-brick walls and hardwood floors. Live salsa and merengue music is sometimes offered. It's the perfect backdrop for the likes of orange-and-cumin-encrusted salmon over black-bean rice cakes and tender grilled *chimichurri* (a piquant Argentinian herb sauce) flank steak served with tortillas and three salsas. ⊠ *118 W. 5th St., Uptown,* ☎ *704/377–4448,* WEB *www.lattores.net. AE, MC, V. Closed Sun.*

$$–$$$ ✕ **Providence Café.** The signature purple awnings and trendy furnishings lend atmosphere to the original of this lively spot. The menu may be comfortably predictable—with chicken, beef, seafood, and pasta options—but the focaccia baked daily on the premises stands out. It's a great place for Sunday brunch, and on Wednesday evening there's live jazz. ⊠ *110 Perrin Pl., South Park,* ☎ *704/376–2008;* ⊠ *15205 John Jay Delaney Dr., South Park,* ☎ *704/540–2244;* ⊠ *8708 J. W. Clay Blvd., University/Speedway,* ☎ *704/549–0050. AE, D, DC, MC, V.*

$–$$ ✕ **Landmark Diner.** This spacious and informal place in the Eastland Mall neighborhood is a cut above most other inexpensive restaurants, and it's open until 3 AM on weeknights and 24 hours on weekends. The chocolate cream pie and chef's salad with grilled chicken are must-tries. ⊠ *4429 Central Ave., East Charlotte/Merchandise Mart,* ☎ *704/532–1153. Reservations not accepted. AE, DC, MC, V.*

$–$$ ✕ **Thai House.** Fiery pleasures await you here if you're an adventurous diner. Sample from a selection of vegetarian, seafood, and classic Thai dishes—the food has proved so popular here that the owners opened two more branches. The *satays* (skewers of meat, fish, or poultry with peanut sauce) are mild enough for any taste buds, and you can order many dishes as spicy or mild as you wish. ⊠ *3210 N. Sharon Amity Rd., East Charlotte/Merchandise Mart,* ☎ *704/532–6868;* ⊠ *Tower Plaza Shopping Center, 8652 Pineville-Matthews Rd., No. 1000, South Charlotte/Pineville,* ☎ *704/542–6300;* ⊠ *4918 Central Ave., East Charlotte/Merchandise Mart,* ☎ *704/535–6716. AE, D, DC, MC, V.*

$–$$ ✕ **300 East.** The gentrified, leafy Dilworth neighborhood in which this
★ casual spot resides doesn't lack for older, refurbished houses. Even so, 300 East makes its mark, and not just because of its brightly hued signage, private dining nooks and crannies, and open-air patio. The bold menu—Thai pork tenderloin with banana-mango salsa and saffron rice, for instance, or penne with duck and lobster—attracts a hip and eclec-

tic bunch. Here, people-watching is as much fun as eating. ⊠ *300 East Blvd., South Park,* ☎ *704/332–6507. AE, D, DC, MC, V. Closed Wed.*

$ ✕ **College Place Restaurant.** Expect simple down-home cooking—and plenty of it. Come for breakfast or lunch (7–3), and know that you'll have to work hard to spend more than $5. Breakfasts in particular are big and include any combination of eggs, pancakes, grits, bacon, and sausage, among other items. Lunch has lots of vegetable choices (12), meats, homemade corn bread, and cobblers. This cafeteria and grill is close to the convention center. ⊠ *300 S. College St., Uptown,* ☎ *704/343–9268. No credit cards. Closed weekends. No dinner.*

Lodging

Hotels and Motels

$$$ ⊞ **Adam's Mark.** This is the city's largest convention hotel, within walking distance of the convention center. The expansive main lobby, with its woodwork and shades of green and gray, feels a bit clubby. Guest rooms are done in blues and plums. Bravo!—its popular signature restaurant, which serves northern Italian cuisine—is known for its singing waiters. ⊠ *555 S. McDowell St., Uptown, 28204,* ☎ *704/372–4100 or 800/444–2326,* ⅋ *704/348–4646,* ⟦WEB⟧ *www.adamsmark.com. 631 rooms, 21 suites. Restaurant, indoor-outdoor pool, health club, sauna, racquetball, bar, dry cleaning, laundry service, concierge, business services, meeting room, airport shuttle, free parking. AE, D, DC, MC, V.*

$$$ ⊞ **The Park.** Executives, entertainers, sports stars, and heads of state
★ appreciate the privacy and pampering as well as the parklike setting of this hotel on a former estate in the southeast corner of the city. Antique furnishings, polished marble, and art grace the public areas, and the hotel owns more than 20 paintings by French artist Yolanda Ardisonne. Guest rooms, with lush fabrics, seem more like a home than a hotel. ⊠ *2200 Rexford Rd., South Park, 28211,* ☎ *704/364–8220 or 800/334–0331,* ⅋ *704/365–4712,* ⟦WEB⟧ *www.theparkhotel.com. 187 rooms, 7 suites. Restaurant, minibars, 18-hole golf course, 9-hole putting green, pool, health club, massage, spa, piano bar, business services, meeting room, airport shuttle, free parking. AE, D, DC, MC, V.*

$$ ⊞ **Hyatt Charlotte at SouthPark.** The focal point of the four-story atrium is a Mexican water fountain surrounded by 25-ft olive trees. Scalini, the restaurant, serves northern Italian cuisine; the Club piano bar is a favorite. The hotel, with contemporary rooms, lies within walking distance of the upscale South Park Mall. ⊠ *5501 Carnegie Blvd., South Park, 28209-3462,* ☎ *704/554–1234 or 800/233–1234,* ⅋ *704/554–8319,* ⟦WEB⟧ *www.hyatt.com. 258 rooms, 4 suites. Restaurant, indoor pool, health club, hot tub, sauna, piano bar, business services, airport shuttle. AE, D, DC, MC, V.*

$ ⊞ **Bradley Motel.** Clean and functional is what you get with this motel, which has been family-owned and -operated since 1959. Popular with families and NASCAR fans, the Bradley, near the airport and the coliseum, fills up on race weekends. The rooms are large, with full ceramic baths. There's a Mexican restaurant adjacent. ⊠ *4200 S. I–85 Service Rd., Airport/Coliseum, 28214,* ☎ *704/392–3206,* ⅋ *704/392–5040. 21 rooms. AE, D, MC, V.*

$ ⊞ **Comfort Inn–Lake Norman.** This economy motel, north of Charlotte on I–77 near Lake Norman and Davidson College, offers basic guest rooms with coffeemakers; some come with whirlpool baths. Jogging trails are nearby. ⊠ *20740 Torrence Chapel Rd., North Charlotte/Lake Norman, Cornelius 28031,* ☎ *704/892–3500 or 800/848–9751,* ⅋ *704/892–6473,* ⟦WEB⟧ *www.choicehotels.com. 84 rooms, 6 suites. Some in-room VCRs, some microwaves, pool, business services, meeting room. AE, D, DC, MC, V. CP.*

$ 🖬 **Sterling Inn.** This economy option has an upscale sensibility. Rooms are large and tastefully decorated. The inn is near several restaurants. Every room of this motel, which is close by Queens College as well as I–77 and I–85, has oversize beds and coffeemakers. ⊠ *242 E. Woodlawn Rd., Airport/Coliseum, 28217,* ☎ *704/525–5454,* FAX *704/525–5637. 100 rooms. Refrigerators, health club, laundry service, airport shuttle, meeting room, free parking. AE, D, DC, MC, V. CP.*

Bed-and-Breakfasts

$$$–$$$$ 🖬 **Morehead Inn.** Although it's now a commercial venture catering to corporate clients, this grand colonial revival B&B in the Dilworth neighborhood was once a private estate and still has all the comforts of a beautiful home. ⊠ *1122 E. Morehead St., South Park, 28204,* ☎ *704/376–3357 or 888/667–3432,* FAX *704/335–1110,* WEB *www.moreheadinn.com. 8 rooms, 2 suites, 1 2-bedroom apartment. In-room VCRs, meeting room. AE, DC, MC, V. CP.*

$$$ 🖬 **Inn Uptown.** This 1891 brick château on the edge of the historic Fourth Ward neighborhood is popular because of its proximity to Uptown businesses and attractions. Many rooms have fireplaces. Most fun is the Tower Room, with its spiral staircase leading to a tower with a whirlpool bath and skyline view. ⊠ *129 N. Poplar St., Uptown, 28202,* ☎ *704/342–2800 or 800/959–1990,* FAX *704/342–2222,* WEB *www.innuptown.com. 6 rooms. Business services. AE, D, DC, MC, V. BP.*

$$–$$$ 🖬 **Homeplace.** This spotless early 20th-century Victorian gem in a res-
★   idential neighborhood has a wraparound porch, fireplaces, and 10-ft ceilings and is full of antiques and memorabilia. Rooms, with four-poster beds, are country Victorian in style. The no-smoking inn is best for adults and older children. ⊠ *5901 Sardis Rd., South Park, 28270,* ☎ *704/365–1936,* FAX *704/366–2729,* WEB *www.bbonline.com/nc/homeplace/. 2 rooms, 1 suite. AE, MC, V. BP.*

Nightlife and the Arts

The Arts

The key venue for performing arts is the **North Carolina Blumenthal Performing Arts Center,** or PAC (⊠ 130 N. Tryon St., Uptown, ☎ 704/372–1000). It houses several resident companies, including the Charlotte Symphony Orchestra, North Carolina Dance Theatre, Charlotte Repertory Theatre, and Opera Carolina. PAC also presents national tours of Broadway musicals. The **Spirit Square Center for the Arts & Education** (⊠ 345 N. College St., Uptown, ☎ 704/372–7469) is an interdisciplinary arts center with classes, exhibits, and national acts, such as Wynton Marsalis and Jerry Jeff Walker.

Verizon Wireless Amphitheater (⊠ 707 Pavilion Blvd., University/Speedway, ☎ 704/549–1292) spotlights big-name concerts (Tom Petty, Reba McEntire, *NSYNC) from spring through fall. The **Paladium Amphitheater,** at Paramount's Carowinds (⊠ 14523 Carowinds Blvd., South Charlotte/Pineville, ☎ 704/588–2600 or 800/888–4386), presents stars in concert from midspring through midfall.

Nightlife

Comedy Zone (⊠ 516 N. College St., Uptown, ☎ 704/348–4242) showcases live comedy nightly Tuesday through Saturday. The **Double Door Inn** (⊠ 218 E. Independence Blvd., Uptown, ☎ 704/376–1446; no credit cards) is a staple of the national blues circuit and offers live music nightly. Eric Clapton, Junior Walker, and Stevie Ray Vaughn are among the legends who've played this laid-back venue. **Ri Ra** (⊠ 208 N. Tryon St., Uptown, ☎ 704/333–5554), Gaelic for "uproar" or "a lot of fun," is filled with Irish food, ale, and, on Sunday night, live traditional

Irish music. Other musical styles are presented Thursday through Saturday. Snazzy **Swing 1000** (✉ 1000 Central Ave., Uptown, ☎ 704/334–4443) jumps with 1940s supper club atmosphere and a seven-piece house orchestra, which plays nightly.

Outdoor Activities and Sports

Participant Sports

CAMPING

Near Charlotte, campsites, fishing, and live animal exhibits can be found at **McDowell Park and Nature Reserve** (✉ 15222 York Rd., South Charlotte/Pineville, ☎ 704/588–5224). Next to the theme park, **Paramount's Carowinds** (✉ 14523 Carowinds Blvd., off I–77, South Charlotte/Pineville, ☎ 704/588–2600 or 800/888–4386), you can pitch a tent or park a mobile home right next to roller coasters. **Lake Norman State Park** (✉ Rte. 2, North Charlotte/Lake Norman Troutman, ☎ 704/528–6350) is ideal for hiking and water sports.

CANOEING

Inlets on Lake Norman and Lake Wylie are ideal for canoeing, as are some spots of the Catawba River. The Pee Dee River east of Charlotte and the New River in the mountains offer other options.

FISHING

You'll find good fishing in Charlotte's neighboring lakes and streams. A mandatory state license can be bought at local bait-and-tackle shops or over the phone (with a credit card) from the **North Carolina Wildlife Commission** (☎ 919/662–4370).

GOLF

There are more than 50 golf courses within a 40-mi drive of Uptown Charlotte. **Highland Creek Golf Club** (✉ 7001 Highland Creek Pkwy., University/Speedway, ☎ 704/875–9000), an 18-hole, par-72 course with a driving range, is considered by some to be the best public course in Charlotte. **Larkhaven Golf Club** (✉ 4801 Camp Stewart Rd., East Charlotte/Merchandise Mart, ☎ 704/545–4653) is a championship 18-hole, par-72 course with clubhouse and pro shop. **Paradise Valley Golf Center** (✉ 9309 N. Tryon St., University/Speedway, ☎ 704/548–1808) has an 18-hole, all-par-3 course. The driving range is a half mile down the street (✉ 9615 N. Tryon St., University/Speedway, ☎ 704/548–8114). **Woodbridge Golf Links** (✉ 922 New Camp Creek Church Rd., Kings Mountain, ☎ 704/482–0353), an attractive par-72 course, has 18 holes and a driving range.

TENNIS

Tennis courts are available in several Charlotte city parks, including Freedom, Hornet's Nest, Park Road, and Veterans. For details call the **Charlotte Park and Recreation Department** (☎ 704/336–3854).

Spectator Sports

AUTO RACING

NASCAR races, such as the Coca-Cola 600 and UAW/GM 500, draw huge crowds at the **Lowe's Motor Speedway** (✉ 5555 Concord Pkwy. S, Concord, northeast of Charlotte, ☎ 704/455–3200).

BASEBALL

The AAA minor league **Charlotte Knights,** an affiliate of the Chicago White Sox, play from April through August at Knights Castle (✉ 2280 Deerfield Dr., at I–77 and Gold Hill Rd., Exit 88, South Charlotte/Pineville, ☎ 704/357–8071 or 803/548–8050).

FOOTBALL

The National Football League's **Carolina Panthers** play from August through December in the 73,000-seat Ericsson Stadium (⊠ 800 S. Mint St., Airport/Coliseum, ☎ 704/358–7800).

Shopping

Charlotte is the largest retail center in the Carolinas. The majority of stores are in suburban malls, and villages and towns in outlying areas have regional specialties.

Shopping Malls

Carolina Place Mall (⊠ 11025 Carolina Place Pkwy., off I–277 at Pineville, South Charlotte/Pineville, ☎ 704/543–9300) is the only Charlotte shopping center with five anchors and interstate access. Ask for a visitor discount card at the customer service center. **SouthPark Mall** (⊠ 4400 Sharon Rd., South Park, ☎ 704/364–4411 or 888/364–4411), in the most affluent section of the city, offers high-end stores, including Tiffany & Co., Montblanc, Coach, Eddie Bauer, and Godiva Chocolatier. A concierge provides executive services, gift wrap, and delivery.

The **Outlet Marketplace** (⊠ off I–77, Fort Mill, SC, 18 mi south of Charlotte, ☎ 704/377–8630) carries well-known brands at a discount.

Specialty Stores

ANTIQUES

Waxhaw, Pineville, and Matthews are the best places to find antiques. Waxhaw sponsors an annual antiques fair each February. You can find a good selection of antiques and collectibles at the sprawling **Metrolina Expo** (⊠ off I–77 at 7100 N. Statesville Rd., North Charlotte/Lake Norman, ☎ 704/596–4643 or 800/824–3770) on the first and third weekends of the month.

BOOKS

You'll find a good selection of contemporary fiction, classics, and children's books at **Little Professor Book Center** (⊠ Park Road Shopping Center, 4139 Park Rd., South Park, ☎ 704/525–9239; ⊠ Jetton Village, 19910 N. Cove Rd., North Charlotte/Lake Norman, Cornelius, ☎ 704/896–7323).

FOOD AND PLANTS

The **Charlotte Regional Farmers Market** (⊠ 1801 Yorkmount Rd., Airport/Coliseum, ☎ 704/357–1269) sells produce, fish, plants, and crafts.

Charlotte A to Z

To research prices, get advice from other travelers, and book travel arrangements, visit www.fodors.com.

AIRPORTS AND TRANSFERS

Charlotte-Douglas International Airport is west of the city off I–85. Most major airlines serve the facility.

➤ AIRPORT INFORMATION: **Charlotte-Douglas International Airport** (⊠ 5501 Josh Birmingham Blvd., Airport/Coliseum, ☎ 704/359–4013, WEB www.charlotteairport.com).

AIRPORT TRANSFER

Taxis charge a set fee to designated zones. ₫From the airport to most destinations the cost is $15–$20 ($2 each additional person). Airport vans are approximately $8 per person to Uptown. By car take the Billy Graham Parkway, then Wilkinson Boulevard (U.S. 74) east to I–277, which leads to the heart of Uptown.

BUS TRAVEL TO AND FROM CHARLOTTE

Greyhound/Carolina Trailways serves the Charlotte area.

➤ BUS INFORMATION: **Greyhound/Carolina Trailways** (✉ 601 W. Trade St., Uptown, ☎ 704/372–0456 or 800/231–2222, WEB www. greyhound.com).

BUS TRAVEL WITHIN CHARLOTTE

Center City Circuit operates free shuttle service on four routes throughout Uptown beginning at 7 and 7:30. Look for the UPTOWN CIRCUIT street signs. Charlotte Transit provides public transportation throughout the city. Fares are $1 for local rides and $1.40 for express service within Charlotte.

FARES AND SCHEDULES

➤ BUS INFORMATION: **Center City Circuit** (☎ 704/332–2227). **Charlotte Transit** (☎ 704/336–3366).

CAR TRAVEL

Charlotte is a transportation hub; I–77 comes in from Columbia, South Carolina, to the south, and then continues north to Virginia, intersecting I–40 on the way. I–85 arrives from Greenville, South Carolina, to the southwest, and then goes northeast to meet I–40 between Winston-Salem and the Triangle. From the Triangle I–85 continues northeast and merges with I–95 in Petersburg, Virginia.

EMERGENCIES

➤ EMERGENCY SERVICES: **Ambulance, police** (☎ 911).
➤ HOSPITALS: **Carolinas Medical Center** (✉ 1001 Blythe Blvd., South Park, ☎ 704/355–2000). **Presbyterian Hospital** (✉ 200 Hawthorne La., East Charlotte/Merchandise Mart, ☎ 704/384–2273). **University Hospital** (✉ 8800 N. Tryon St., University/Speedway, ☎ 704/548–6000).
➤ LATE-NIGHT PHARMACIES: **Eckerd Drugs** (✉ Park Road Shopping Center, South Park, ☎ 704/523–3031; ✉ 3740 E. Independence Blvd., East Charlotte/Merchandise Mart, ☎ 704/536–3600).

TAXIS

Crown Cab and Yellow Cab have taxis and airport vans. University Towncar caters to business travelers. You won't pay more for the company's flat rate than you would for a cab ride.
➤ TAXI COMPANIES: **Crown Cab** (☎ 704/334–6666). **Yellow Cab** (☎ 704/332–6161). **University Towncar** (☎ 704/553–2424 or 888/553–2424).

TOURS

BOAT TOURS

The *Catawba Queen* paddle wheeler gives dinner cruises and tours on Lake Norman. Reservations are essential.
➤ FEES AND SCHEDULES: *Catawba Queen* (✉ Rte. 150, Exit 36, North Charlotte/Lake Norman, Mooresville, ☎ 704/663–2628).

TRAIN TRAVEL

Amtrak offers daily service from Charlotte to Washington, D.C., Atlanta, and points beyond, and there's daily service to cities in the Triangle.
➤ TRAIN INFORMATION: **Amtrak** (✉ 1914 N. Tryon St., Uptown, ☎ 704/376–4416 or 800/872–7245, WEB www.amtrak.com).

VISITOR INFORMATION

➤ TOURIST INFORMATION: **INFO! Charlotte** (✉ 330 S. Tryon St., Uptown, ☎ 704/331–2700 or 800/231–4636, WEB www.charlottecvb.org).

THE TRIAD

Greensboro, Winston-Salem, High Point

North Carolinians group six urban centers in the Piedmont into two threesomes: the Triad and the Triangle. Although this shorthand is a verbal convenience, it's also testament that the whole can be greater than the sum of the parts. Make no mistake, however. Although they share geography and the major arteries of the region and claim rich histories as well as institutions of higher learning, the Triad's leading cities have very distinct personalities. Greensboro, to the east, bustles as a center of commerce. Smaller Winston-Salem, to the west, will catch you by surprise with its eclectic arts scene. High Point, to the south, has managed to fuse the simplicity of Quaker forebears with its role as a world-class furniture market.

Greensboro

96 mi northeast of Charlotte, 26 mi east of Winston-Salem, 58 mi west of Durham.

With 200,000 citizens, Greensboro is the largest population center in the Triad, and thanks to spacious convention facilities, it's an increasingly popular destination for business travelers. Yet this city, named in honor of General Nathanael Greene, a Revolutionary War hero, takes pride in its role in American history and has taken great pains to preserve and showcase the sights of past eras.

With the exception of Old Greensborough and the downtown historic district, however, walking is not a comfortable sightseeing option. To tour the grand historic homes, glimpse monuments to famous native sons and daughters—Dolley Madison, Edward R. Murrow, O. Henry—or visit one of the many recreation areas, you'll need a car.

Guilford Courthouse National Military Park, the nation's first Revolutionary War park, has monuments, military memorabilia, and more than 200 acres with wooded hiking trails. It memorializes one of the earliest events in the city's history and a pivotal moment in the life of the colonies. On March 15, 1781, the Battle of Guilford Courthouse so weakened British troops that they surrendered seven months later at Yorktown. Today many families use the 3 mi of foot trails. ⊠ *2332 New Garden Rd., Northwest Metro,* ☎ *336/288–1776.* ⚑ *Free.* ☉ *Daily 8:30–5.*

Tannenbaum Park, a hands-on history experience near Guilford Courthouse National Military Park, draws you into the life of early settlers. With advance notice costumed reenactors will escort you through exhibits at the **Colonial Heritage Center,** in the visitor center. The restored **1778 Hoskins House** (tours by appointment) and a blacksmith shop and barn are on the property. The park has one of the most outstanding collections of original colonial settlement maps in the country. ⊠ *2200 New Garden Rd., Northwest Metro,* ☎ *336/545–5315.* ⚑ *Free.* ☉ *Tues.–Sat. 9–5, Sun. 1–5.*

Roam through a dinosaur gallery, learn about gems and minerals, and see the lemurs, snakes, and amphibians at the **Natural Science Center of Greensboro.** There are also a planetarium and a petting zoo. ⊠ *4301 Lawndale Dr., adjacent to Country Park, Northwest Metro,* ☎ *336/288–3769.* ⚑ *Science Center $6, planetarium $1; prices subject to change for special exhibits and events.* ☉ *Science Center Mon.–Sat. 9–5, Sun. 12:30–5; zoo Mon.–Sat. 10–4:30, Sun. 12:30–4:30.*

The **Greensboro Historical Museum,** in a Romanesque 1892 church, has exhibits about native son O. Henry and native daughter Dolley Madison, as well as one about the Woolworth sit-in, which launched the civil rights movement struggle to desegregate Southern eating establishments. Behind the museum are the graves of several Revolutionary War soldiers. ✉ *130 Summit Ave., Downtown,* ☎ *336/373–2043,* WEB *www.greensborohistory.org.* 🎫 *Free.* ☾ *Tues.–Sat. 10–5, Sun. 2–5.*

♨ **Greensboro Cultural Center at Festival Park,** an architectural showplace, houses 25 visual and performing arts organizations, five art galleries, rehearsal halls, a sculpture garden, a restaurant with outdoor café-style seating, and an outdoor amphitheater. **ArtQuest,** developed by educators and artists, is North Carolina's only permanent interactive children's art gallery. ✉ *200 N. Davie St., Downtown,* ☎ *336/373–2712.* 🎫 *Free; ArtQuest $3.* ☾ *Weekdays 8 AM–10 PM, Sat. 9–5, Sun. 2–5.*

♨ Exhibits and activities at the **Greensboro Children's Museum** are designed for children under 12. They can tour an airplane cockpit with an interactive screen, dig for buried treasure, or wrap themselves in a gigantic bubble. ✉ *220 N. Church St., Downtown,* ☎ *336/574–2898,* WEB *www.gcmuseum.com.* 🎫 *$5.* ☾ *Early Sept.–late May, Tues.–Sat. 9–5, Sun. 1–5; late May–early Sept., Mon.–Sat. 9–5, Sun. 1–5.*

Elm Street, with its turn-of-the-20th-century architecture, is the heart of **Old Greensborough** (✉ 100 block of N. Elm St. to 600 block of S. Elm St., with portions of several other streets, Downtown), which is listed on the National Register of Historic Places. Stop by the offices of **Downtown Greensboro, Inc.** (✉ 122 N. Elm St., Downtown, ☎ 336/ 379–0060) to collect your shopping guide and self-guided tour map.

In Old Greensborough, the elegant **Blandwood Mansion,** home of former governor John Motley Morehead, is considered the prototype of the Italian villa architecture that swept the country during the mid-19th century. Designed by noted architect Alexander Jackson Davis, the house still contains many of its original furnishings. ✉ *447 W. Washington St., Downtown,* ☎ *336/272–5003,* WEB *www.blandwood.org.* 🎫 *$5.* ☾ *Tues.–Sat. 11–2, Sun. 2–5.*

The **Weatherspoon Art Museum,** on the campus of the University of North Carolina–Greensboro, consists of six galleries and a sculpture courtyard. It is nationally recognized both for its permanent collection, which includes lithographs and bronzes by Henri Matisse, and for its changing exhibitions of 20th-century American art. ✉ *Tate and Spring Garden Sts., University,* ☎ *336/334–5770,* WEB *www.uncg.edu/wag/.* 🎫 *Free.* ☾ *Tues. and Thurs.–Fri. 10–5, Wed. 10–8, weekends 1–5.*

Dining and Lodging

$$$$ ✕ **Paisley Pineapple.** The dining is formal in this romantic Old Greensborough restaurant in a restored 1920s building. The fare on the extensive menu—rack of lamb, grilled veal tenderloin, and Black Angus beef—tends toward the hearty. On the lighter side are the soups (try the berry bisque if it's available) and fish such as Atlantic salmon poached in court bouillon. Upstairs, there's a bar with sofas and background music. ✉ *345 S. Elm St., Downtown,* ☎ *336/279–8488. AE, MC, V. Closed Sun. and Mon.*

$$$–$$$$ ✕ **Gate City Chop House.** This place has a lock on the upscale, everything-is-bigger-here steak house concept in the Triad. The look is masculine and clubby, and portions are geared for large appetites. Beef is the star, but there's plenty of good to say about other menu items, such as seafood (try the shrimp bisque) and salads. The wine list is respectable. ✉ *106 S. Holden Rd., West Metro,* ☎ *336/294–9977. AE, D, DC, MC, V. Closed Sun.*

$$-$$$ ✕ **Noble's Restaurant.** Murals of the Italian countryside adorn some walls, and from the upstairs seating area you can see the wood-burning tile oven and the slowly turning spit that turns out Tuscan-inspired cuisine. The menu changes regularly, but a typical entrée is grilled rack of lamb with polenta cake, sautéed spinach, oyster mushroom, and artichoke with a lamb jus. The piano bar on the lower level is a nice place to end the evening—a jazz trio plays Wednesday through Saturday. ✉ *172 Battleground Ave., Northwest Metro,* ☏ *336/333–9833. AE, D, MC, V.*

$$ ✕ **Casaldi's Cafe.** Light gray-green is the predominant color in this sleek little trattoria—the motif appears in the tile floors and the marble countertops, providing a powerful lure to sample the myriad pasta dishes. Especially popular are the spinach-and-walnut ravioli and the bow-tie pasta with chicken and mushrooms. ✉ *1310 Westover Terr., Northwest Metro,* ☏ *336/379–8191. Reservations not accepted. D, MC, V. Closed Sun.*

$$$$ ▥ **O. Henry Hotel.** Named for the renowned author, this is one of the newest and grandest establishments in the city. The furnishings evoke the arts and crafts style, with lots of wood, tapestries, and upholstery in warm tones. Particularly nice touches are the oversize rooms, tile bathrooms with standing shower stalls and separate tubs, and bed coverlets that are laundered daily. A complimentary breakfast buffet is served in a sunny pavilion overlooking a small garden. ✉ *624 Green Valley Rd., Northwest Metro, 27408,* ☏ *336/854–2000 or 800/965–8259,* FAX *336/854–2223,* WEB *www.o.henryhotel.com. 121 rooms, 10 suites. Restaurant, room service, in-room safes, refrigerator, pool, exercise room, laundry service, business services, meeting room, airport shuttle. AE, D, DC, MC, V. BP.*

$$$ ▥ **Greenwood Bed and Breakfast.** Eclectic antiques, art, and various other collections fill this 1905 craftsman-style home in historic Fisher Park. Owners Bob (a former New Orleans chef) and Dolly (a decorator) Guertin serve a full breakfast at the time of your choosing. Café au lait, French bread, eggs Benedict, and crêpes suzette come with freshly squeezed orange juice and fruit. Desserts are set out in the evening. This no-smoking B&B is best for older children. ✉ *205 N. Park Dr., Downtown, 27401,* ☏ *336/274–6350 or 877/374–7067,* WEB *www. greenwoodbb.com,* FAX *336/274–9943. 5 rooms. Pool, meeting room. AE, D, DC, MC, V. BP.*

$$-$$$ ▥ **Sheraton Greensboro Hotel at Four Seasons/Joseph S. Koury Convention Center.** Business travelers are the mainstay here, at the state's largest hotel, which is adjacent to the convention center. Accommodations are a notch above standard, and the hotel and its nearby sister property, the Park Lane Hotel (☏ *336/294–4565*), are convenient to major thoroughfares and the Four Seasons Town Centre, a three-story regional mall. ✉ *3121 High Point Rd., West Metro, 27407,* ☏ *336/292–9161 or 800/ 242–6556,* FAX *336/292–1407,* WEB *www.sheratongreensboro.com. 1,016 rooms, 78 suites. 5 restaurants, room service, pool, wading pool, health club, sauna, racquetball, 4 bars, nightclub, business services, convention center, meeting rooms, airport shuttle, kennel. AE, D, DC, MC, V.*

$-$$ ▥ **Biltmore Greensboro Hotel.** In the heart of the central business district, the Biltmore has an old-world but slightly faded feel, with 16-ft ceilings, a cage elevator, and a lobby area with walnut-paneled walls and a fireplace. Some guest rooms have Victorian or Victorian-style furniture and electric candle sconces. ✉ *111 W. Washington St., Downtown, 27401,* ☏ *336/272–3474 or 800/332–0303,* FAX *336/275–2523,* WEB *www.biltmorehotelgreensboro.com. 25 rooms, 4 suites. Minibars, refrigerator, business services, meeting room, airport shuttle. AE, D, DC, MC, V. CP.*

Nightlife and the Arts

The **Broach Theatre** (✉ 520 S. Elm St., Downtown, ☎ 336/378–9300) has professional adult (February–December) and children's (September–May) theater in the Old Greensborough historic district. The **Carolina Theatre** (✉ 310 S. Greene St., Downtown, ☎ 336/333–2605), a restored vaudeville venue, serves as one of the city's principal performing arts centers, showcasing dance, concerts, films, and plays.

The vast **Greensboro Coliseum Complex** (✉ 1921 W. Lee St., West Metro, ☎ 336/373–7474) hosts arts and entertainment events throughout the year, as well as professional, college, and amateur sports. The Greensboro Symphony (☎ 336/333–7490) and the Greensboro Opera Company (☎ 336/273–9472) perform at the Greensboro Coliseum Complex.

The **Eastern Music Festival** (✉ 200 N. Davie St., Downtown, ☎ 336/333–7450 or 877/833–6753), whose alumni include Wynton Marsalis, brings six weeks of classical music concerts to Greensboro in summer.

Outdoor Activities and Sports

CAMPING

You can rent a cabin or bring a tent to the **Greensboro KOA** (✉ 2300 Montreal Ave., Southeast Metro, ☎ 336/274–4143 or 800/562–4143). **Hagan-Stone Park** (✉ 5920 Hagan-Stone Rd., Southeast Metro, ☎ 336/674–0472) is a wildlife reserve with hiking, water sports, and other activities available.

GOLF

Golfers can choose from among 27 public courses and four driving ranges. **Bryan Park and Golf Club** (✉ 6275 Bryan Park Rd., Browns Summit, ☎ 336/375–2200) is a highly regarded 18-hole, par-72 course 6 mi north of Greensboro. The **Grandover Resort/Grandover Golf Club** (✉ One Thousand Club Rd., South Metro, ☎ 336/294–1800 or 800/472–6301) has two 18-hole, par-72 courses. The **Greensboro National Golf Club** (✉ 330 Niblick Dr., Summerfield, ☎ 336/342–1113), 15 minutes north of Greensboro, is an 18-hole, par-72 course.

The PGA's (Professional Golfers' Association) **Greater Greensboro Chrysler Classic** is held each April at the Forest Oaks Country Club (✉ U.S. 421S, Southeast Metro, ☎ 336/379–1570).

HIKING

The **Bog Garden** (✉ on Hobbs Rd. and Starmount Farms Dr., Northwest Metro, ☎ 336/373–2199) has an elevated wooden walkway through a swampy area with more than 8,000 individually labeled trees, shrubs, ferns, and wildflowers. There are walking trails and an exercise course at the 120-acre **Oka T. Hester Park** (✉ 910 Ailanthus St., South Metro, ☎ 336/373–2937).

TENNIS

Greensboro Jaycee Park (✉ Forest Lawn Dr. off Pisgah Church Rd., adjacent to Country Park, North Metro, ☎ 336/545–5342) has sports facilities, including a tennis center with 13 championship soft courts.

Shopping

OUTLET CENTERS

More than 75 stores and services constitute the **Burlington Manufacturers Outlet Center** (✉ off I–85, Exit 145, Burlington, ☎ 336/227–2872), which makes the area off I–85 near here—about 25 mi east of Greensboro—a trove for bargain hunters.

SPECIALTY STORES

Replacements, Ltd. (⊠ I–85/I–40 at Mt. Hope Church Rd., Exit 132, Metro East, ☎ 800/737–5223), the world's largest retailer of discontinued and active china, crystal, flatware, and collectibles, stocks nearly 6 million pieces of inventory and 125,000 patterns. The cavernous showroom is open 8 AM–9 PM daily, and free tours are given.

Side Trips from Greensboro

CHARLOTTE HAWKINS BROWN MEMORIAL STATE HISTORIC SITE
10 mi east of Greensboro.

On the site of the Palmer Institute, the memorial honors the African-American woman who founded the school in 1902. Before closing in 1971, this accredited preparatory school for African-Americans was recognized as one of the country's best and had expanded to more than 350 acres of land. There are a visitor center and a gift shop. ⊠ *6136 Burlington Rd., Sedalia, off I–85, Exit 135,* ☎ *336/449–4846,* WEB *www. chbfoundation.org.* 🎟 *Free.* ☉ *Oct.–Apr., Tues.–Fri. 10–4, Sun. 1–4; May–Sept., Mon.–Sat. 9–5, Sun. 1–5.*

CHINQUA-PENN PLANTATION
★ *25 mi north of Greensboro.*

The **Chinqua-Penn Plantation,** a National Register of Historic Places English-country mansion, was built by tobacco and utility magnate Jeff Penn and his wife, Betsy, in 1925. The Penns, world travelers, filled the 27-room house with an eclectic collection of artifacts representing 30 countries. The 22-acre estate also has a 1-mi walking trail, Chinese pagoda, a three-story clock tower, greenhouses, and formal gardens—even a cemetery for all the Penns' beloved dogs. ⊠ *2138 Wentworth St., Reidsville,* ☎ *336/349–4576 or 800/948–0947,* WEB *www.chinquapenn.com.* 🎟 *$13.* ☉ *Mar.–Dec., Tues.–Sat. 9–5, Sun. noon–5.*

Winston-Salem

81 mi north of Charlotte, 26 mi west of Greensboro.

Winston-Salem residents' donations to the arts are among the highest per capita in the nation: the city bills itself as the City of the Arts, and its museums show the benefits of this support. The North Carolina School of the Arts commands international attention. Salem College, the oldest women's college in the country, is here, as is Wake Forest University, where writer Maya Angelou teaches. Old Salem, a restored 18th-century Moravian town within the city, has been a popular attraction since the early 1950s.

Staff at the **Winston-Salem Visitor Center** (⊠ 601 N. Cherry St., Downtown, ☎ 336/777–3796 or 800/331–7018) will assist with directions and help you make dining and lodging reservations.

Founded in 1766 as a Moravian congregation town and backcountry
★ trading center, **Old Salem** has become one of the nation's most authentic and well-documented colonial sites. At this living history museum with more than 80 restored and original buildings, costumed interpreters recreate household activities and trades common in Salem in the late 18th and early 19th centuries. You can participate in African-American programs that include a stop by St. Philip's Church, the state's oldest-standing African-American church. Old Salem has many museum shops, the Old Salem Furniture & Accessories Shop, the 1816 Salem Tavern restaurant, and the Winkler Bakery (don't pass up the Moravian sugar cake). The village is a few blocks from downtown Winston-Salem and near Business I–40 (take the Old Salem/Salem College exit). ⊠ *600 S. Main St., Old Salem,* ☎ *336/721–7300 or 888/653–7253,* WEB *www.old-*

salem.org. ✉ *$15; combination ticket with Museum of Early Southern Decorative Arts $20.* ☉ *Mon.–Sat. 9–5, Sun. 12:30–5.*

★ The **Museum of Early Southern Decorative Arts (MESDA),** on the southern edge of Old Salem, is the only museum dedicated to exhibiting and researching the regional decorative arts of the early South. Twenty-four intricately detailed period rooms and seven galleries showcase the furniture, painting, ceramics, and metalware made and used regionally through 1820. The bookstore carries current and hard-to-find books on Southern decorative arts, culture, and history. ✉ *924 S. Main St., Old Salem,* ☎ *336/721–7360 or 888/653–7253,* WEB *www.mesda.org.* ✉ *$10; combination ticket with Old Salem $20.* ☉ *Mon.–Sat. 9:30– 5, Sun. 1:30–5.*

☺ The **SciWorks** complex includes a 120-seat planetarium, a 15-acre Environmental Park, and 45,000 square ft of interactive or hands-on exhibits, including the *Coastal Encounters* wet lab. ✉ *400 W. Hanes Mill Rd., North Metro,* ☎ *336/767–6730.* ✉ *Museum $7, the Works (planetarium, park, and museum) $8.* ☉ *Mon.–Sat. 10–5.*

You can take a guided tour through the exhibits on tobacco growing and auctioning at **R. J. Reynolds Whitaker Park,** view historical memorabilia related to the tobacco industry, and visit the gift shop. Tours of the factory floor are no longer offered, however. ✉ *1100 Reynolds Blvd., East Metro,* ☎ *336/741–5718.* ✉ *Free.* ☉ *Weekdays 8–6.*

☺ **Historic Bethabara Park,** set in a wooded 175-acre wildlife preserve, is the site of the first Moravian settlement (1753) in North Carolina. Bethabara—meaning "house of passage"—was to be temporary until the town of Salem was established. You can tour restored buildings such as the 1788 congregation house, explore the foundations of the town, or browse the colonial and medicinal gardens. Children love the reconstructed fort from the French and Indian War. Brochures for self-guided walking tour available year-round at the visitor center. ✉ *2147 Bethabara Rd., University,* ☎ *336/924–8191,* WEB *www.bethabarapark. org.* ✉ *$1.* ☉ *Exhibit buildings Apr.–Nov., weekdays 9:30–4:30, weekends 1:30–4:30; guided tours Apr.–Nov. or by appointment.*

The **Museum of Anthropology** has exhibits of peoples and cultures of the Americas, Asia, Africa, and Oceania. The museum shop holds special sales in May and December. ✉ *1834 Wake Forest Rd., Wake Forest Reynolda Campus University,* ☎ *336/758–5282.* ✉ *Free.* ☉ *Tues.– Sat. 10–4:30.*

Reynolda House Museum of American Art, formerly the home of tobacco magnate Richard Joshua Reynolds and his wife, Katherine, is filled with American paintings, prints, and sculptures by such artists as Thomas Eakins, Frederic Church, and Georgia O'Keeffe. There's also a costume collection, as well as vintage clothing and toys used by the Reynolds children. The museum is next to **Reynolda Village,** a collection of shops, restaurants, and gardens that fill the estate's original outer buildings. ✉ *2250 Reynolda Rd., University,* ☎ *336/725–5325,* WEB *www.reynoldahouse.org.* ✉ *$6.* ☉ *Tues.–Sat. 9:30–4:30, Sun. 1:30–4:30.*

Exhibits at the **Southeastern Center for Contemporary Art (SECCA),** near Reynolda House, showcase regional arts and crafts and works by nationally known artists. The Centershop sells many one-of-a-kind pieces. ✉ *750 Marguerite Dr., University,* ☎ *336/725–1904,* WEB *www.secca.org.* ✉ *$3.* ☉ *Tues.–Sat. 10–5, Sun. 2–5.*

Just 10 minutes south of the city, on land once claimed for Queen Elizabeth by Sir Walter Raleigh, is **Tanglewood Park.** The home of the late

William and Kate Reynolds is now open to the public; in addition to golfing, boating, hiking, fishing, horseback riding, and swimming, it puts on a holiday lights festival, the largest such display in the Southeast. The **Tanglewood Festival of Lights** runs from mid-November to January every year. ⊠ *U.S. 158 off I–40, South Metro, Clemmons,* ☎ *336/778–6300,* WEB *www.tanglewoodpark.org.* 🖾 *$2 per car; separate fees for each activity.* ☺ *Daily dawn–dusk.*

Dining and Lodging

$$$–$$$$ ✕ **Noble's Grille.** French and Mediterranean flavors are key to the menu, which changes nightly. Typical entrées, grilled or roasted over the omnipresent oak-and-hickory fire, might include Roquefort risotto–stuffed Portobello mushroom with roasted polenta and veal sweetbreads with garlic-mashed potatoes. The dining room, with tall windows and track lighting, has a view of the grill. ⊠ *380 Knollwood St., Metro West,* ☎ *336/777–8477,* WEB *www.noblesrestaurants.com. AE, DC, MC, V.*

$$$ ✕ **Opie's Southbound Grille.** Although housed in a building erected in 1913 as the headquarters for Southbound Railway, this place is anything but old-fashioned. A new menu each week brings surprises, from grilled steak with fried sweet potatoes to grilled ostrich topped with honeyed onions and spicy cantaloupe chutney. ⊠ *300 S. Liberty St., Downtown,* ☎ *336/723–0322. AE, MC, V. Closed Sun.–Mon. No lunch Sat.*

$$–$$$ ✕ **Leon's Café.** This quiet, well-kept eatery in a renovated building near Old Salem serves some of the tastiest food in town—fresh seafood, grilled duck with a berry cognac sauce, and other specialties. Stained-glass windows, artwork, and an open-air patio create an eye-pleasing experience. ⊠ *924 S. Marshall St., Old Salem,* ☎ *336/725–9593. AE, D, MC, V. No lunch.*

$$–$$$ ✕ **Old Salem Tavern Dining Room.** The costumed staff happily details the varied lunch and dinner menus, from which you might order traditional Moravian chicken pie or the bratwurst platter. You can also opt for something more innovative, such as fillet of beef with brandied green peppercorns. In the warm months drinks are served under the arbor, and outdoor seating draws diners to the covered back porch. ⊠ *736 S. Main St., Old Salem,* ☎ *336/748–8585. AE, D, MC, V.*

$$–$$$ ✕ **The Vineyards.** The innovative seasonal menu, with such dishes as grilled swordfish on a bed of black-eyed-pea salsa, and stuffed eggplant, keeps people coming back to this Reynolda Village restaurant, a participant in the Heart Healthy Dining Program (sponsored by Wake Forest University's Baptist Medical Center). The homemade bread pudding is considered the best in town. There's live music Thursday through Saturday. ⊠ *120 Reynolda Village Rd., University,* ☎ *336/748–0269. AE, MC, V. Closed Sun. No lunch.*

$$$–$$$$ 🏨 **Adam's Mark Winston Plaza Hotel.** Centrally located off I–40, the hotel occupies two towers connected by a climate-controlled skywalk. The East Tower has a traditional look, although the West Tower is a bit sleeker and more contemporary. The Cherry Street Bar, with its smoothly tailored living-room, is a great place to relax. ⊠ *425 N. Cherry St., Downtown, 27101,* ☎ *336/725–3500 or 800/444–2326,* FAX *336/721–2240,* WEB *www.adamsmark.com/winstonsalem. 603 rooms, 26 suites. Restaurant, room service, indoor pool, health club, sauna, steam room, 2 bars, dry cleaning, laundry service, business services, meeting room, parking (fee). AE, D, DC, MC, V.*

$$$ 🏨 **Brookstown Inn.** Handmade quilts, two-person tubs, and wine and cheese and freshly baked cookies in the lobby are just a few of the amenities at this inn. The rooms, with their rafters, high ceilings, and brick walls, retain the character of the 1837 textile mill this building once housed. ⊠ *200 Brookstown Ave., Old Salem, 27101,* ☎ *336/725–1120 or 800/845–4262,* FAX *336/773–0147,* WEB *www.brookstowninn.com.*

40 rooms, 31 suites. Exercise room, business services, meeting room. AE, DC, MC, V. CP.

$$–$$$ 🏨 **Henry F. Shaffner House.** Accessible to downtown and Old Salem, this B&B is a favorite with business travelers and honeymooning couples. The rooms in the restored English Tudor house are meticulously furnished in 19th-century Victorian elegance. Rates include afternoon tea and evening wine and cheese. ⊠ *150 S. Marshall St., Old Salem, 27101,* ☎ *336/777–0052 or 800/952–2256,* FAX *336/777–1188. 6 rooms, 3 suites. Restaurant, business services, meeting room. AE, MC, V. BP, CP.*

$$ 🏨 **Tanglewood Manor House Bed & Breakfast.** The former home of a branch of the Reynolds family includes 10 rooms in the antiques-filled manor house, 18 rooms in a more contemporary motel behind the house, and four cottages on Mallard Lake in Tanglewood Park. Those staying in the motel can purchase the Continental breakfast served in the manor house. Admissions to the park and swimming pool are included; a fishing license is extra. Greens fees at park courses are discounted. ⊠ *U.S. 158 off I–40, South Metro, Clemmons 27012,* ☎ *336/778–6300,* FAX *336/778–6379,* WEB *www.tanglewoodpark.org. 28 rooms, 4 cottages, guest house. Picnic area, driving range, 2 18-hole golf courses, pool, wading pool, fishing, horseback riding, playground, meeting room. AE, DC, MC, V. CP.*

$–$$ 🏨 **Comfort Inn–Cloverdale.** Off I–40 Business near downtown and Old Salem, this hotel is near the business and nightlife nexus of Winston-Salem. ⊠ *110 Miller St., Downtown, 27103,* ☎ *336/721–0220 or 800/228–5150,* FAX *336/723–2117,* WEB *www.choicehotels.com. 122 rooms. Microwaves, refrigerators, pool, exercise room, sauna, laundry service, meeting room. AE, D, DC, MC, V. CP.*

Nightlife and the Arts

THE ARTS

Many North Carolina School of the Arts musical and dramatic performances are held at the **Stevens Center** (⊠ 405 W. 4th St., Downtown, ☎ 336/721–1945), a restored 1929 movie palace downtown and part of the NCSA campus. The Broadway Preview Series stages first-run productions, featuring big-name actors, before they move on to Broadway engagements. Every two years the North Carolina Black Repertory Company hosts the **National Black Theatre Festival** (⊠ 610 Coliseum Dr., University, ☎ 336/723–2266). This weeklong showcase of African-American talent attracts tens of thousands of people, including a who's who of celebrities. The *New York Times* has hailed this event as "one of the most historic and culturally significant in the history of black theatre and American theatre in general." The festival usually held during the summer.

NIGHTLIFE

Burke Street Pub (⊠ 1110 Burke St., West Metro, ☎ 336/750–0097) is an Irish-style pub with music, dancing, games, and sports TV. In the Adam's Mark Winston Plaza, the **Cherry Street Bar** (⊠ 425 N. Cherry St., Downtown, ☎ 336/725–3500) has cozy chairs and a smart style. **Lucky 32** (⊠ 109 S. Stratford Rd., University, ☎ 336/777–0032), a fine bar adjoining a restaurant, caters to a professional crowd.

Outdoor Activities and Sports

BASKETBALL

Winston-Salem's Atlantic Coast Conference entry is the Wake Forest University **Demon Deacons** (☎ 336/758–3322 or 888/758–3322).

GOLF

Tanglewood Park Golf Club (⊠ Rte. 158, Clemmons, ☎ 336/778–6320) has two fine 18-hole, par-72 courses, the Reynolds Course and the Championship Course, where the Vantage Championship is played each year. The **Reynolds Park Golf Course** (⊠ 2931 Reynolds Park Rd., East Metro, ☎ 336/650–7660) has 18 holes with a view of the city skyline and a par 71.

Shopping

SHOPPING DISTRICTS AND MALLS

The **Art District,** at 6th and Trade streets (just behind the Winston-Salem Visitor Center), has several galleries and arts-and-crafts shops. **Reynolda Village** is near the Reynolda House Museum of American Art. **Stratford Place,** a collection of upscale shops, restaurants, and cafés, is off I–40 Business in the Five Points area, where Country Club, Miller Road, and 1st Street converge.

CRAFTS

All items at the **Piedmont Craftsmen's Shop and Gallery** (⊠ 1204 Reynolda Rd., University, ☎ 336/725–1516) are juried. An annual fair is held in November. **erl Originals** (⊠ 3069 Trenwest Dr., West Metro, ☎ 336/760–4373), near I–40 and Hanes Mall, has 8,000 square ft of gallery space and represents more than 300 artists.

High Point

76 mi northeast of Charlotte, 20 mi southwest of Greensboro.

Originally settled by Quakers in the 1700s, High Point was incorporated in 1859. Its name is derived from its former position as the highest point on the railroad between Goldsboro and Charlotte. It's also the childhood home of legendary jazz saxophonist John Coltrane. But today when people think of High Point, they think of furniture, for it is where the twice-a-year (April and October) International Home Furnishings Market, the largest wholesale furniture market in the world (not open to the public), takes place. Tens of thousands of buyers and others associated with the trade "go to market" and in the process lend a sophistication to this warm and hospitable city. More than 70 retail outlets here offer furniture and home accessories at bargain prices.

The **High Point Museum/Historical Park,** focusing on Piedmont history and Quaker heritage, includes the 1786 Haley House and a mid-1700s blacksmith shop and weaving house. Exhibits highlight furniture, pottery, communication, transportation, and military artifacts. Tours of the buildings are available weekends and are conducted by costumed staff. The park also serves as base camp for the Guilford Militia Living Historians. ⊠ *1859 E. Lexington Ave.,* ☎ *336/885–6859.* ☞ *Free.* ۞ *Museum Tues.–Sat. 10–4:30, Sun. 1–4:30; park buildings Sat. 10–4, Sun. 1–4.*

The **Furniture Discovery Center,** in a renovated fabric warehouse downtown, simulates the furniture design and manufacturing process. It has a Furniture Hall of Fame and an extensive miniature collection exhibited in room displays. ⊠ *101 W. Green Dr.,* ☎ *336/887–3876,* WEB *www.furniturediscovery.org.* ☞ *$5; combination ticket with Angela Peterson Doll and Miniature Museum $8.50.* ۞ *Apr.–Oct., weekdays 10–5, Sat. 9–5, Sun. 1–5; Nov.–Mar., Tues.–Fri. 10–5, Sat. 9–5, Sun. 1–5.*

The **Angela Peterson Doll and Miniature Museum** houses the collection begun by one woman and now including more than 2,000 dolls, costumes, miniatures, and dollhouses. ⊠ *101 W. Green Dr.,* ☎ *336/885–3655.* ☞ *$4; combination ticket with Furniture Discovery Center $8.50.* ۞ *Apr.–Oct., weekdays 10–4:30, Sat. 9–4:30, Sun. 1–4:30; Nov.–Mar., Tues.–Sat. 10–4:30, Sun. 1–4:30.*

OFF THE
BEATEN PATH

MENDENHALL PLANTATION – A few miles northwest of High Point is this well-preserved example of 19th-century Quaker domestic architecture. The Mendenhalls opposed slavery, and here you'll find one of the few surviving false-bottom wagons, used to help slaves escape to freedom on the Underground Railroad. ⊠ *603 W. Main St., Jamestown,* ☎ *336/454–3819.* ⊠ *$2.* ☉ *Mid-Apr.–Nov., Tue.–Fri. 11–2, Sat. 1–4, Sun. 2–4.*

Dining and Lodging

$$$ ✕ **Act I.** This easygoing respite from the fast-paced world is tucked in a commercial area of town, its three dining areas—atrium, lounge, and gallery—hung attractively with local art. Appealing, too, are the daily specials, which have included roasted duck in peach sauce and honey-mango shrimp. ⊠ *130 E. Parris Ave.,* ☎ *336/869–5614,* WEB *www. act1highpoint.com. AE, MC, V. No lunch Sat.*

$$–$$$ ✕ **J. Basul Noble's.** Locals hold this place in high esteem, and it's easy to see why. It's architecturally dramatic, with 10-ft pillars, a pyramid-shape glass ceiling, and a river-rock wall. The menu covers all the bases—fish, veal, pork, game, beef, and lamb. You could make a meal out of the fine breads (baked daily on the premises) and desserts. There's live jazz Thursday through Saturday. ⊠ *101 S. Main St.,* ☎ *336/889–3354,* WEB *www.noblesrestaurants.com. AE, DC, MC, V.*

$$–$$$ 🏨 **Radisson Hotel High Point.** The central location makes the Radisson a favorite with people coming to town for weekend shopping trips. Guest rooms are standard, but each suite is outfitted with furniture from the different manufacturers represented in the area. ⊠ *135 S. Main St., 27260,* ☎ *336/889–8888,* FAX *336/885–2737,* WEB *www.radisson.com/ highpoint. 239 rooms, 13 suites. Restaurant, indoor pool, gym, bar, business services, meeting room, airport shuttle, parking (fee). AE, D, DC, MC, V.*

$$ 🏨 **Toad Alley Bed & Bagel.** This three-story 1924 house, in a quiet neighborhood 1 mi north of downtown, is fronted by a wide wraparound porch. Rooms are distinguished by 9-ft ceilings and individual decorating schemes—in one there's a dramatic custom-designed four-poster bed. You can relax while sipping wine by the fireplace or on the front porch swing. ⊠ *1001 Johnson St., 27262,* ☎ *336/889–8349,* FAX *336/886–6646,* WEB *www.toadalley.com. 6 rooms. In-room VCRs. MC, V. BP.*

Nightlife and the Arts

Headquartered in High Point is the **North Carolina Shakespeare Festival.** The professional troupe performs from August through October and in December at the **High Point Theatre** (⊠ 1014 Mill St., ☎ 336/ 841–2273, WEB www.ncshakes.org).

Outdoor Activities and Sports

GOLF

There are six public golf courses in High Point: three have 18 holes, and three have 9. Pete Dye designed the notable par-72 course at **Oak Hollow** (⊠ 3400 N. Centennial St., ☎ 336/883–3260).

HIKING

The 376-acre **Piedmont Environmental Center** (⊠ 1220 Penny Rd., ☎ 336/883–8531, WEB www.piedmontenvironmental.com) has 11 mi of hiking trails adjacent to City Lake Park, with recreational activities and a nature preserve. There's also access to a 6-mi greenway trail.

TENNIS

In Oak Hollow Lake Park, the **Reitzel Tennis Center** (⊠ 3401 N. Centennial St., ☎ 336/883–3493) has 12 outdoor and 4 indoor courts. Reservations are a must.

Shopping

There are more than 70 retail furniture stores in and around High Point. The 36 stores in the **Atrium Furniture Mall** (⊠ 430 S. Main St., ☎ 336/882–5599) carry items by more than 700 manufacturers of furniture and home accessories.

Art shows rotate through the three exhibition spaces of **Theatre Art Galleries** (⊠ 220 E. Commerce Ave., ☎ 336/887–3415), open weekdays noon–5 and weekends by appointment but closed during market weeks in April and October.

The Triad A to Z

To research prices, get advice from other travelers, and book travel arrangements, visit www.fodors.com.

AIRPORTS

Just west of Greensboro, the Piedmont Triad International Airport is off Route 68 north from I–40; it's served by American, ATA, Continental, Delta, Eastwind, Northwest, United, and US Airways.

Taxi service to and from the airport is provided by Airport Express and other tour, charter, limousine, and cab services, including the Golden Eagle Cab Company and Piedmont Executive Transportation. ➤ AIRPORT INFORMATION: **Airport Express** (☎ 800/934–8779). **Golden Eagle Cab Company** (☎ 336/724–6481). **Piedmont Executive Transportation** (☎ 336/723–2179). **Piedmont Triad International Airport** (⊠ 6451 Bryan Blvd., Greensboro, ☎ 336/665–5666, WEB www.ptia.org).

BUS TRAVEL

Greyhound/Carolina Trailways serves Burlington, Greensboro, High Point, Lexington, and Winston-Salem.
➤ BUS INFORMATION: **Greyhound/Carolina Trailways** (☎ 800/231–2222, WEB www.greyhound.com).

CAR TRAVEL

Greensboro and Winston-Salem are on I–40, which runs east–west through North Carolina. From the east I–40 and I–85 combine coming into the Triad, but in Greensboro, I–85 splits off to go southwest to Charlotte. High Point is off a business bypass of I–85 southwest of Greensboro.

TOURS

Carolina Treasures and Tours offers a look at historic Winston-Salem.
➤ CONTACTS: **Carolina Treasures and Tours** (⊠ 1031 Burke St., ☎ 336/631–9144).

TRAIN TRAVEL

Amtrak serves Greensboro and High Point.
➤ TRAIN INFORMATION: **Amtrak** (☎ 800/872–7245, WEB www.amtrak.com).

VISITOR INFORMATION

➤ TOURIST INFORMATION: **Greensboro Area Convention and Visitors Bureau** (⊠ 317 S. Greene St., 27401, ☎ 336/274–2282 or 800/344–2282, WEB www.greensboro.org). **High Point Convention and Visitors Bureau** (⊠ 300 S. Main St., 27260, ☎ 336/884–5255 or 800/720–5255, WEB www.highpoint.org). **Winston-Salem Convention and Visitors Bureau** (⊠ Box 1409, 27102, ☎ 336/728–4200 or 800/331–7018; visitor center, ⊠ 601 N. Cherry St., ☎ 336/777–3796, WEB www.wscvb.com).

THE TRIANGLE
Raleigh, Durham, Chapel Hill

The cities of Raleigh, Durham, and Chapel Hill make up the Triangle, with Raleigh to the east, Durham to the north, Chapel Hill to the west, and, in the center, Research Triangle Park—a renowned complex of corporations and public and private research facilities set in 6,800 acres of lake-dotted pineland that attracts scientists, academicians, and businesspeople from all over the world. Throughout the Triangle, an area that's been characterized as "trees, tees, and PhDs," politics and basketball are always hot topics. The NCAA basketball championship has traded hands among the area's three major universities.

Raleigh

143 mi northeast of Charlotte, 104 mi east of Winston-Salem.

Raleigh is Old South and New South, down-home and upscale, all in one. Named for Sir Walter Raleigh (who established the first English colony on the coast in 1585), it's the state capital and the biggest of the three cities. Many of the state's largest and best museums are here, as are North Carolina State University and six other universities and colleges.

Numbers in the text correspond to numbers in the margin and on the Downtown Raleigh map.

A Good Walk

Downtown the streets are laid out in an orderly grid with the state capitol as the hub. Most downtown Raleigh attractions are state government buildings, historic buildings, and museums and are free to the public. Begin with a walk through **Oakwood Historic District** ⑮. Next, stroll by the **executive mansion** ⑯, the home of governors since 1891.

Follow Jones Street west past Wilmington Street to visit the **State Legislative Building** ⑰. Cross Jones Street to Bicentennial Plaza, flanked by the **North Carolina Museum of Natural Sciences** ⑱, to the west, and the **North Carolina Museum of History** ⑲, to the east. Continue south across Edenton Street to Capitol Square and the **state capitol** ⑳.

Starting just south of the capitol across Morgan Street and continuing for four blocks is the **Fayetteville Street Mall** ㉑, a pedestrians-only walkway. From the mall walk two blocks east on Hargett Street to **Exploris** ㉒, a children's museum. One block south is the **City Market** ㉓, a revitalized area between Blount and Person streets. Just south of the market are the studios and galleries of **Artspace** ㉔, at the corner of Blount and Davie streets.

TIMING

You'll need several hours just to hit the sights of this walk and even more time if you're the kind of person who tends to get hooked on museums.

Sights to See

㉔ **Artspace.** Adjacent to the Moore Square art district, Artspace is a private, nonprofit visual arts center offering open studios, exhibits, and galleries. The gift shop showcases the work of the resident artists, who are happy to talk to you about their work. ✉ *201 E. Davie St., Downtown,* ☎ *919/821–2787,* WEB *www.artspace.citysearch.com.* ✆ *Free.* ◷ *Tues.–Sat. 10–6.*

152

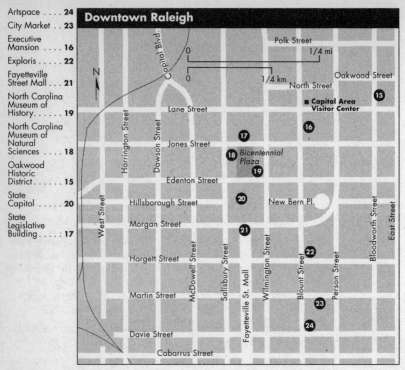

Downtown Raleigh

🅔 **City Market.** This revitalized area with cobblestone streets has specialty shops, art galleries, restaurants, a comedy club, and a small farmers' market. The free Entertainment Trolley shuttles between the market and other downtown restaurant and nightlife locations from 6:40 PM to 12:40 AM Thursday through Saturday. ⊠ *Martin St. and Moore Sq., Downtown,* ☎ *919/828–4555,* WEB *www.citymarket.citysearch.com.* ⊙ *Stores Mon.–Sat. 10–5:30, restaurants Mon.–Sat. 7 AM–1 AM, Sun. 11:30–10.*

🅖 **Executive Mansion.** The mansion is a brick early 20th-century Queen Anne cottage–style structure with gingerbread trim and manicured lawns. Tour hours vary; check with the Capital Area Visitor Center. ⊠ *200 N. Blount St., Downtown,* ☎ *919/733–3456.* ☞ *Free.*

🅒 🅤 **Exploris.** This 84,000-square-ft architectural showplace (the marble wall is a dazzler) is a learning center that stands apart from most other children's museums. It emphasizes a global perspective, as opposed to specific health and natural science topics. Exhibits explore language, culture, geography, trade, and communications. ⊠ *201 E. Hargett St., Downtown,* ☎ *919/834–4040,* WEB *www.exploris.org.* ☞ *$7.* ⊙ *Mon.–Sat. 9–5, Sun. noon–5.*

🅤 **Fayetteville Street Mall.** Extending from the state capitol to the Raleigh Civic and Convention Center, this pedestrian walkway provides entrance to a number of high-rise office buildings. The shops and restaurants in the area cater to the weekday business crowd.

🅞 **North Carolina Museum of History.** Founded in 1898, the museum is now in a state-of-the-art facility on Bicentennial Plaza. It uses artifacts, audiovisual programs, and interactive exhibits to bring the state's history to life. Exhibits include the *N.C. Sports Hall of Fame; N.C. Folklife;* and *Militaria, Politics, and Society.* ⊠ *5 E. Edenton St., Downtown,*

☎ *919/715–0200,* WEB *http://nchistory.dcr.state.nc.us/musuems.* 📧 *Free.* ⊙ *Tues.–Sat. 9–5, Sun. noon–5.*

★ ⓒ ⓲ **North Carolina Museum of Natural Sciences.** At 200,000 square ft, this museum is the largest of its kind in the Southeast. It has permanent exhibits and dioramas that celebrate the incredible diversity of species in the state's three regions—coast, piedmont, and mountains. There are enough animals and insects—including butterflies, hummingbirds, snakes, and a two-toed sloth—to qualify as a small zoo. One signature exhibit contains rare whale skeletons. The pièce de résistance, however, is the *Terror of the South* exhibit, featuring the dinosaur skeleton of "Acro," a giant carnivore that lived in the South 110 million years ago. ⊠ *11 W. Jones St., Downtown,* ☎ *919/733–7450 or 877/462–8724,* WEB *www.naturalsciences.org.* 📧 *Free.* ⊙ *Mon.–Sat. 9–5, Sun. noon–5.*

⓯ **Oakwood Historic District.** Many fine examples of Victorian architecture can be seen in this tree-shaded neighborhood. Self-guided walking tours of the area, which encompasses 20 blocks bordered by Person, Edenton, Franklin, and Watauga/Linden streets, are available at the **Capital Area Visitor Center.** Adjacent to historic Oakwood is **Oakwood Cemetery** (⊠ 701 Oakwood Ave., Downtown, ☎ 919/832–6077). Established in 1869, it is the resting place of 2,800 Confederate soldiers, Civil War generals, governors, and numerous U.S. senators. Free maps are available at the cemetery office.

⓴ **State Capitol.** A beautifully preserved example of Greek Revival architecture from 1840, the capitol once housed all the functions of state government. Today it's part museum, part executive offices. The capitol contains, under the domed rotunda, a copy of Antonio Canova's statue of George Washington depicted as a Roman general with tunic, tight-fitting body armor, and a short cape. ⊠ *Capitol Sq. (1 E. Edenton St.), Downtown,* ☎ *919/733–4994,* WEB *www.ah.dcr.state.nc.us/ sections/capitol.* 📧 *Free.* ⊙ *Weekdays 8–5, Sat. 10–4, Sun. 1–4.*

⓱ **State Legislative Building.** One block north of the state capitol, this complex hums with lawmakers and lobbyists when the legislature is in session. It's fun to watch from the gallery. A free guided tour is also available through the **Capital Area Visitor Center.** ⊠ *Salisbury and Jones Sts., Downtown,* ☎ *919/733–7928,* WEB *www.ncga.state.nc.us.* 📧 *Free.* ⊙ *Weekdays 8–5, Sat. 9–5, Sun. 1–5.*

Other Area Attractions

The city is spread out, so a car is almost a necessity for museums and parks beyond downtown.

OFF THE BEATEN PATH **AVA GARDNER MUSEUM –** This museum in the hometown of the legendary beauty and movie star has an extensive collection of memorabilia that trace her life from childhood on the farm to Hollywood glory days. It's about 30 mi east of Raleigh in downtown Smithfield. ⊠ *325 E. Market St., Smithfield,* ☎ *919/934–5830,* WEB *www.avagardner.org.* 📧 *$4.* ⊙ *Mon.–Sat. 9–5, Sun. 2–5.*

Joel Lane Museum House. The oldest dwelling in Raleigh was the home of the "father of Raleigh" and dates from the 1760s. Joel Lane sold the state the property on which the capital city grew. Costumed docents tell the story and show the restored house and beautiful period gardens. ⊠ *720 W. Hargett St., at St. Mary's St., Downtown,* ☎ *919/833–3431.* 📧 *$3.* ⊙ *Mar.–mid-Dec., Tues.–Fri. 10–2, Sat. 1–4.*

Mordecai Historic Park. You can see the Mordecai family's plantation home and other structures, including the house where President Andrew Johnson was born, in 1808. One-hour guided tours are given on the half hour. You can also board a trolley for a narrated 45-minute tour of historic Raleigh (March–December, Saturday noon–3; $5). ⊠ *1 Mimosa St., at Wake Forest Rd., University,* ☎ *919/834–4844.* ⊒ *$4.* ☉ *Weekdays 10–4.*

★ **North Carolina Museum of Art.** On the west side of Raleigh, the NCMA houses 5,000 years of artistic heritage, including one of the nation's largest collections of Jewish ceremonial art. Other exhibits range from ancient Egyptian times to the present, from the Old World to the New. The museum hosts touring exhibitions of works by such artists as Caravaggio and Rodin. The glass-wall **Museum Café** looks out on an outdoor performance center–cum–sculpture that when viewed from above spells the words PICTURE THIS. ⊠ *2110 Blue Ridge Rd., Northwest/Airport,* ☎ *919/839–6262; 919/833–3548 for restaurant,* WEB *www.ncartmuseum. org.* ⊒ *Free.* ☉ *Tues.–Thurs. and Sat. 9–5, Fri. 9–9, Sun. 11–6; tours Tues.–Sun. 1:30.*

○ **Pullen Park.** In summer crowds come to picnic and ride the 1911 Dentzel carousel, the train, and paddleboats. You can swim here in a large public indoor aquatic center or outdoor pool, play tennis, explore an arts-and-crafts center, or, if the timing is right, see a play at the Theater in the Park. ⊠ *520 Ashe Ave., near North Carolina State University, University,* ☎ *919/831–6468 or 919/831–6640,* WEB *www.raleigh-nc. org/parks&rec/pullenpark.htm.* ⊒ *Fees vary.* ☉ *Apr.–Oct., daily 10 AM–dusk; Mar. and Nov., Fri.–Sat. 10–5, Sun. 1–5; summer hrs vary.*

Dining and Lodging

$$$$ ★ ✕ **Second Empire.** Wood paneling, crown molding and high ceilings, floral arrangements, muted lighting, and well-spaced tables make for a calming and elegant dining experience. The menu, which changes monthly, has a regional flavor; the food is best described as art on a plate, intricately styled so that colors, textures, and tastes fuse. For an entrée you might get roasted mahimahi, paired with collard greens, butternut squash, and garlic cream. A wood-and-brass tavern on the lower level has a simpler and less expensive menu. ⊠ *300 Hillsborough St., Downtown,* ☎ *919/829–3663. AE, MC, V. Closed Sun. No lunch.*

$$$–$$$$ ✕ **Angus Barn.** A huge rustic barn houses a Raleigh tradition that is justifiably famous. The astonishing wine and beer list is 35 pages long. The restaurant is known for its steaks, baby-back ribs, prime rib, and fresh seafood and for its clubby Wild Turkey Lounge. Desserts are amazing. Reservations aren't accepted for Saturday dinner. ⊠ *U.S. 70W (Glenwood Ave.) near Aviation Pkwy., Northwest/Airport,* ☎ *919/781– 2444,* WEB *www.angusbarn.com. AE, D, DC, MC, V. No lunch.*

$$–$$$ ✕ **Greenshields Brewery & Pub.** You can sip beer and ale brewed on the premises with your soup, salad, sandwich, or such entrées as fish-and-chips, shepherd's pie, and steak in this English-style pub. Oak paneling and working fireplaces enhance the mood. There are also an open-air patio, and live music on Saturday night. ⊠ *214 E. Martin St., City Market, Downtown,* ☎ *919/829–0214,* WEB *www.greenshields.com. AE, D, MC, V.*

$$–$$$ ✕ **Irregardless Café.** The blond wood, brightly hued contemporary art, sunlighted dining areas, and well-spaced tables all underscore one theme: relaxation. The seasonal menu, although offering some meat-based dishes, emphasizes vegetarian items. Salads are amply portioned, and the breads, soups, and yogurts are homemade. There are live music every night, dancing on Saturday evening, and brunch on Sunday. The restaurant is midway between North Carolina State University and downtown. ⊠ *901 W. Morgan St., University,* ☎ *919/833– 8898. AE, D, DC, MC, V. No lunch Sat., no dinner Sun.*

$$–$$$ ✕ **Margaux's.** Eclectic is the key word for the cuisine at this intimate, dimly lighted north Raleigh fixture, where a massive stone fireplace warms the room. A blackboard lists the diverse specials, such as red-chili fettuccine with goat cheese, lamb with coconut curry sauce, or grilled shrimp and crawfish tostada with roasted corn, black beans, and salsa *verde.* ✉ *8111 Creedmoor Rd., Brennan Station Shopping Center, North Hills,* ☏ *919/846–9846. DC, MC, V.*

$$–$$$ ✕ **Tony's Bourbon Street Oyster Bar.** The mood here—already festive with red walls, feather masks, and street lamps from New Orleans—jumps up a notch with live music Friday and Saturday. Cajun and creole dishes, such as gumbo, jambalaya, and crawfish étouffée, are served in the large white-linen dining room or the large stainless-steel oyster bar. Cary, near the entrance to Research Triangle Park, is 25 minutes west of downtown Raleigh. ✉ *107 Edinburgh Dr., MacGregor Village Shopping Center, Cary,* ☏ *919/462–6226. AE, D, DC, MC, V. Closed Sun. No lunch.*

$ ✕ **Big Ed's City Market Restaurant.** A must for breakfast or lunch, Big Ed's is filled with antique farm implements and the owner's political memorabilia, including pictures of presidential candidates who have stopped at this landmark. Every Saturday morning a Dixieland band plays. Come here for down-home cookin' and make sure you indulge in the biscuits. ✉ *220 Wolfe St., City Market, Downtown,* ☏ *919/836–9909. Reservations not accepted. No credit cards. Closed Sun. No dinner.*

$$$–$$$$ ⊞ **Raleigh Marriott Crabtree Valley.** Fresh floral arrangements adorn the elegantly decorated public rooms of one of the city's most luxurious hotels. Standard rooms have soft colors, Asian floral prints, and dark cherry-wood furnishings. You can dine at the Crabtree Grill and at Quinn's, a lounge where light fare and drinks are served daily. ✉ *4500 Marriott Dr., U.S. 70 near Crabtree Valley Mall, University, 27612,* ☏ *919/781–7000 or 800/228–9290,* ℻ *919/781–3059,* 🖳 *www.marriotthotels.com/RDUNC. 375 rooms, 4 suites. Restaurant, lounge, indoor-outdoor pool, health club, hot tub, bar, laundry facilities, laundry service, concierge, business services, meeting room, airport shuttle. AE, D, DC, MC, V.*

$$–$$$ ⊞ **Hampton Inn & Suites.** In the southwest corner of Cary, right over the Raleigh line, this hotel is just minutes from Raleigh's Entertainment & Sports Arena, the State Fairgrounds, and North Carolina State University. Rooms are typical of the chain; you'll need a car to get to restaurants. ✉ *111 Hampton Woods La., Cary 27607,* ☏ *919/233–1798 or 800/426–7866,* ℻ *919/854–1166,* 🖳 *www.hampton-inn.com. 126 rooms. Kitchenettes, refrigerators, pool, exercise room, baby-sitting, laundry service, business services, meeting room. AE, D, DC, MC, V.*

$$–$$$ ⊞ **William Thomas House.** A stately but not stuffy Victorian home is a B&B on the edge of downtown Raleigh a few blocks from the governor's mansion. Rooms, named for family members, are traditionally and elegantly decorated and have oversize windows and 12-ft ceilings. The richly hued common rooms are filled with heirlooms, including a grand piano from 1863, and antique china. ✉ *530 N. Blount St., Downtown, 27604,* ☏ *919/755–9400 or 800/653–3466,* ℻ *919/755–3966,* 🖳 *www.williamthomashouse.com. 4 rooms. Fans, refrigerators, library. AE, D, DC, MC, V. BP.*

$$ ⊞ **North Raleigh Hilton.** This is a favorite spot for corporate meetings. The standard rooms are done in mauve and green, with traditional furniture and prints. You can dine in Lofton's restaurant and listen to the piano afterward in the lobby bar. Bowties is a popular nightspot for dancing. ✉ *3415 Wake Forest Rd., North Hills, 27609,* ☏ *919/872–2323 or 800/445–8667,* ℻ *919/876–0890,* 🖳 *www.hilton.com. 331 rooms, 7 suites. Restaurant, room service, indoor pool, exercise room,*

2 bars, nightclub, business services, meeting room, airport shuttle. AE, D, DC, MC, V.

$$ 🛏 **Ramada Inn Crabtree.** Pluses at this comfortable chain property are landscaped grounds large enough for a stroll and rooms done in muted autumnal colors. This may be the friendliest motel in town. It's also where football and basketball teams like to stay when they're here for a game, as evidenced by the sports memorabilia in the Brass Bell Lounge. ✉ *3920 Arrow Dr., U.S. 70 and Beltline/I–440, North Hills, 27612,* ☎ *919/782–7525 or 800/441–4712,* FAX *919/781–0435,* WEB *www. ramada.com. 157 rooms, 17 suites. Restaurant, room service, indoor pool, exercise room, bar, laundry service, business services, meeting room, airport shuttle. AE, D, DC, MC, V. CP.*

Nightlife and the Arts

THE ARTS

The **BTI Center for the Performing Arts** (✉ 1 E. South St., Downtown) is a multivenue complex that includes a 1,700-seat concert hall, 2,300-seat auditorium, 600-seat theater for opera, and 170-seat venue for live theater: **Memorial Auditorium** (☎ 919/831–6061) is home base for the North Carolina Theatre, which stages productions that have been on Broadway and off-Broadway. **Meymandi Concert Hall** (☎ 919/733–2750) hosts the North Carolina Symphony. **Fletcher Opera Theater** (☎ 919/831–6011) provides a showcase for the nationally acclaimed Carolina Ballet and productions of the Opera Company of North Carolina. And the **Kennedy Theater** (☎ 919/831–6011) stages shows of smaller, sometimes alternative theater groups.

The **North Carolina State University Arts Programs** (☎ 919/515–1100) include the Center Stage series, host to professional touring productions and world-class artists. All arts program performances are open to the public.

Alltel Pavilion at Walnut Creek (✉ 3801 Rock Quarry Rd., Southeast Metro, ☎ 919/831–6666), known as "the Creek," accommodates 20,000. Headliners appear spring through midfall and cover the musical spectrum. This is the most attended amphitheater on the East Coast.

NIGHTLIFE

The **Berkeley Café** (✉ 217 W. Martin St., Downtown, ☎ 919/821–0777) is one of the hottest gathering places in the Triangle for live music: rock and roll, R&B, and blues. **Bowties** (✉ North Raleigh Hilton, 3415 Wake Forest Rd., University, ☎ 919/878–4917) is a popular after-hours spot for dancing. **Cappers** (✉ 4216 Six Forks Rd., North Hills, ☎ 919/787–8963), a restaurant and tavern, is also *the* spot for jazz and blues. **Charlie Goodnight's Comedy Club** (✉ 861 W. Morgan St., University, ☎ 919/828–5233) combines dinner with a night of laughs. Alumni include Jay Leno, Jerry Seinfeld, and Elaine Boosler. **Tir na nog** (✉ 218 S. Blount St., Downtown, ☎ 919/833–7795) has Irish entertainers and Murphy's Irish Amber, Guinness, and even whiskey on tap. In the warehouse district is the **Warehouse Restaurant and Entertainment Center** (✉ 427 S. Dawson St., Downtown, ☎ 919/836–9966), with a huge dance floor and game room.

Outdoor Activities and Sports

BASKETBALL

Raleigh's Atlantic Coast Conference entry is the North Carolina State University **Wolfpack** (☎ 919/515–2106 or 800/310–7225).

BIKING

Raleigh has 40 mi of greenways for biking or walking, and maps are available through the **Raleigh Division of Transportation** (☎ 919/890–3285).

CAMPING

Try the **North Carolina State Fairgrounds** (⌧ 1025 Blue Ridge Rd., ☎ 919/821–7400) if you have an RV, as it's RVs only. The 5,439-acre **William B. Umstead State Park** (⌧ 8801 Glenwood Ave., ☎ 919/571–4170) is between Raleigh and Durham. **Clemmons State Forest** (⌧ 2411 Old Garner Rd., ☎ 919/553–5651) is near Clayton. **Jordan Lake** (⌧ 280 State Park Rd., ☎ 919/362–0586) is between Apex and Pittsboro.

FISHING

Jordan Lake, a 13,900-acre reservoir in Apex, is a favorite fishing spot. Others are Lake Wheeler, in Raleigh, and the Falls Lake State Recreation Area, in Wake Forest.

GOLF

There are 20 golf courses, either public or semiprivate, within a half-hour drive of downtown Raleigh. **Cheviot Hills Golf Course** (⌧ 7301 Capital Blvd., North Hills, ☎ 919/850–9983) is a par-71, 18-hole championship course. **Devil's Ridge Golf Club** (⌧ 5107 Links Land Dr., Holly Springs, ☎ 919/557–6100), about 15 mi from Raleigh, is a challenging par-72, 18-hole course with large, rolling greens. **Lochmere Golf Club** (⌧ 2511 Kildaire Farm Rd., Cary, ☎ 919/851–0611) provides a friendly environment, good value, and a challenge with 18 holes at par 71. A 30-minute drive from Raleigh is the **Neuse Golf Club** (⌧ 918 Birkdale Dr., Clayton, ☎ 919/550–0550), an attractive par-72, 18-hole course on the banks of the Neuse River.

HOCKEY

The NHL's **Carolina Hurricanes** play in the 21,000-seat **Raleigh Entertainment & Sports Arena** (⌧ 1400 Edwards Mill Rd., Northwest/Airport, ☎ 919/467–7825 or 888/645–8491).

JOGGING

Runners frequent Shelley Lake, the track at North Carolina State University, and the **Capital Area Greenway** system (☎ 919/831–6833 for a map).

Shopping

SHOPPING MALLS AND OUTLET CENTERS

Cameron Village Shopping Center (⌧ 1900 Cameron St., Downtown), Raleigh's first shopping center contains specialty shops and boutiques and restaurants. **Prime Outlets** (⌧ Exit 284 off I–40, Airport Blvd., Northwest/Airport, Morrisville, between Raleigh and Durham, ☎ 919/380–8700) is decidedly un-mall-like with its wooden floors and greenery. The area's only factory outlet center has more than 40 stores, including Off Fifth (Saks Fifth Avenue) and Geoffrey Beene.

ART AND ANTIQUES

City Market is a revitalized downtown shopping area with shops and art galleries. At **Artspace** (⌧ 201 E. Davie St., Downtown, ☎ 919/821–2787, WEB www.artspace.citysearch.com) you can visit artists' studios and purchase their works. The merchandise changes daily at **Carolina Antique Mall** (⌧ 1900 Cameron St., ☎ 919/833–8227), in Cameron Village, where 75 dealers stock the floor.

FOOD

Open year-round, the 60-acre **State Farmers' Market** (⌧ 1201 Agriculture St., Lake Wheeler Rd. and I–40, Southwest Metro, ☎ 919/733–7417 for market; 919/833–7973 for restaurants) includes a garden center, a seafood restaurant, and a down-home restaurant. **Wellspring Grocery** (⌧ 3540 Wade Ave., University, ☎ 919/828–5805) has outstanding produce, fresh-baked breads, health foods, and specialty items, as well as a place to sit and eat your purchases.

Durham

23 mi northwest of Raleigh on I–40 and Rte. 147 (Durham Fwy.).

Durham has three of North Carolina's 22 National Historic Landmarks and long ago shed its tobacco-town image. It is now known as the City of Medicine for the medical and research centers at Duke University, one of the top schools in the nation. With more than 20,000 employees, Duke is not only the largest employer in Durham but also one of the largest in the state. Warehouses and mills around the city have been converted to chic shops, offices, and condos.

Numbers in the text correspond to numbers in the margin and on the Durham map.

A Good Drive

Durham has some areas appropriate for a good walk, such as Duke University's campus. However, it's best to drive. Start your tour 1½ mi south of downtown, exiting the Durham Freeway (Route 147) at Fayetteville Street, along which you will find the **North Carolina Central University Art Museum** ㉕ and the **Hayti Heritage Center** ㉖.

The next stop is about 3 mi away. Return to the Durham Freeway and continue northwest to the exit at Chapel Hill Street. Follow Chapel Hill west into the West Campus of **Duke University**, which includes the **Duke Chapel** ㉗ and the **Sarah P. Duke Gardens** ㉘. Return to Chapel Hill Street and take it past the Durham Freeway to Duke Street and turn left. Head north toward downtown, stopping at **Brightleaf Square** ㉙. dFrom here it's a short drive to the **North Carolina Museum of Life and Science** ㉚. Continue north to reach the **Duke Homestead** ㉛. And conclude your tour at **West Point on the Eno** ㉜.

TIMING

You should allow 1–1½ days to explore these Durham highlights; select a number of sights that interest you if you have only a day.

Sights to See

㉙ **Brightleaf Square.** Named for the kind of tobacco once manufactured here, Brightleaf Square, with its flowering courtyard, striking turn-of-the-century architecture, upscale shops, and funky restaurants, is the shining star of a downtown revitalization effort. It anchors a larger arts and entertainment district, which includes the Carolina Theatre and Durham Bulls Athletic Park. ⊠ *905 W. Main St., Duke University,* ☎ *919/682–9229,* WEB *www.brightleaf.citysearch.com.*

★ ㉗ **Duke Chapel.** A Gothic-style gem built in the early 1930s, the chapel is the centerpiece of the campus. Modeled after Canterbury Cathedral, it has 77 stained-glass windows and a 210-ft bell tower. ⊠ *Chapel Dr., West Campus, Duke University,* ☎ *919/684–2572,* WEB *www.chapel. duke.edu.* ☉ *Daily 8 AM–9 PM.*

㉛ **Duke Homestead.** The Duke family empire began here in the 1860s with tobacco, and it is now a National Historic Landmark. You can tour the small wood-frame factories, pack house, and curing barn; guides demonstrate early manufacturing processes. The visitor center exhibits early tobacco advertising. ⊠ *2828 Duke Homestead Rd., Downtown,* ☎ *919/477–5498.* ▢ *Free.* ☉ *Apr.–Oct., Mon.–Sat. 9–5, Sun. 1–5; Nov.–Mar., Tues.–Sat. 10–4, Sun. 1–4.*

Duke University. A stroll along the wide tree-lined streets of this campus is a lovely way to spend a few hours. In all, the university encompasses 525 acres in the heart of Durham. The East Campus, off Broad Street, has Georgian architecture and the **Duke University Museum of Art** (⊠ Buchanan Blvd. at Trinity Ave., Duke University, ☎ 919/684–

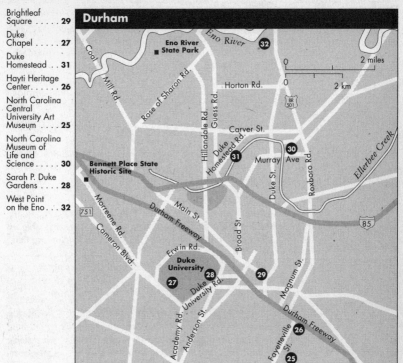

Durham

5135, WEB www.duke.edu), a showcase for pre-Columbian, African, Russian, European medieval, and Renaissance art. A mile or so away is the West Campus, dominated by the **Duke Chapel,** on Chapel Drive, and late-Gothic-style buildings. The sprawling medical school is on Erwin Road. A bus system and bike paths connect the campuses.

🔵**26** **Hayti Heritage Center.** One of Durham's oldest ecclesiastical structures, St. Joseph's A.M.E. Church, houses this center for African-American art and culture. In addition to exhibitions of traditional and contemporary art by local, regional, and national artists, the center hosts special events such as the Black Diaspora Film Festival. ⊠ *804 Old Fayetteville St., Downtown,* ☎ *919/683–1709 or 800/845–9835,* WEB *www.hayti.org.* 🎫 *Free; fees for special events vary.* ☉ *Weekdays 9–7:30, Sat. 9–3, Sun. hrs vary.*

🔵**25** **North Carolina Central University Art Museum.** African-American art is showcased at the nation's first publicly supported liberal arts college for African-Americans. Besides the permanent collection, known for its 19th-century masterpieces, you can see works by students and local artists. ⊠ *1801 Fayetteville St., South/NCCU University,* ☎ *919/560–6211,* WEB *www.nccu.edu/artmuseum.* 🎫 *Free.* ☉ *Tues.–Fri. 9–5, Sun. 2–5.*

☝ 🔵**30** **North Carolina Museum of Life and Science.** Here you can create a tornado, encounter dinosaurs on the prehistoric trail, view NASA artifacts, and ride a train through a wildlife sanctuary. The nature center has such native North Carolina animals as flying squirrels. The three-story **Magic Wings Butterfly House** has a tropical butterfly conservatory and includes the Insectarium, where you can see and hear live insects under high magnification and amplification. ⊠ *433 Murray Ave., off I–85, Downtown,* ☎ *919/220–5429,* WEB *www.ncmls.citysearch.com.* 🎫 *Museum $8, train ride $1.50.* ☉ *Mon.–Sat. 10–5, Sun. noon–5.*

★ ㉘ **Sarah P. Duke Gardens.** These 55 acres, complete with a wisteria-draped gazebo and a Japanese garden with a lily pond teeming with fat gold-fish, have more than 5 mi of pathways through formal plantings and woodlands. ⊠ *Main entrance on Anderson St., West Campus, Duke University,* ☎ *919/684–8861,* WEB *www.hr.duke.edu/dukegardens.* 🖃 *Free.* ⊙ *Daily 8–dusk.*

㉜ **West Point on the Eno.** Included in a city park on the banks of the Eno River are a 19th-century blacksmith shop, an 1880s home, and a re-stored mill dating from 1778. It's the site of an annual three-day folk-life festival surrounding the Fourth of July; musicians, artists, and craftspeople come from around the region. ⊠ *5101 N. Roxboro Rd. (U.S. 501N), North Metro,* ☎ *919/471–1623.* 🖃 *Free.* ⊙ *Mar.–Dec., daily 8–sunset; historic bldgs. weekends only 1–5.*

Other Area Attractions

Bennett Place State Historic Site. In this farmhouse, in April 1865, Con-federate general Joseph E. Johnston surrendered to U.S. general William T. Sherman, 17 days after Lee's surrender to Grant at Appomattox. The two generals then set forth the terms for a "permanent peace" be-tween the South and the North. Historical reenactments are held an-nually. ⊠ *4409 Bennett Memorial Rd., 10 mi from downtown, Downtown,* ☎ *919/383–4345.* 🖃 *Free.* ⊙ *Apr.–Oct., Mon.–Sat. 9–5, Sun. 1–5; Nov.–Mar., Tues.–Sat. 9–5, Sun. 1–5.*

Eno River State Park. The park's 2,733 acres include hiking trails, a picnic area, rough camping, and Class II rapids (after a heavy rain). ⊠ *6101 Cole Mill Rd., North Metro,* ☎ *919/383–1686.* 🖃 *Free.* ⊙ *Daily 8–sunset.*

Dining and Lodging

$$$$ ✕ **Magnolia Grill.** This bistro is consistently one of the area's finest,
★ most innovative places to dine. The food is as eye-catching as the art on the walls. On the daily menu you may find grilled jumbo sea scal-lops on spicy black beans with blood-orange-and-onion marmalade or grilled hickory-smoked pork tenderloin in a sun-dried cherry sauce. ⊠ *1002 9th St., Downtown,* ☎ *919/286–3609. MC, V. Closed Sun.–Mon. No lunch.*

$$–$$$ ✕ **Café Parizäde.** Soft lighting, white tablecloths, and an enclosed courtyard are among the inviting aspects of this Erwin Square bistro. One particularly fine appetizer is fried calamari with jalapeño-tomato salsa; popular entrées include fettuccine with fresh salmon and black-pepper dill cream, sesame pasta with scallops, and roast duck with fresh vegetables. ⊠ *2200 W. Main St., Downtown,* ☎ *919/286–9712. AE, D, DC, MC, V. No lunch weekends.*

$$–$$$ ✕ **George's Garage.** In the heart of happening 9th Street, George's is the latest success for well-known Triangle restaurateur Giorgios Bakat-sias, and it defies pigeonholing. It's part nouvelle restaurant, part mar-ket, part bar (sushi and drinks), and part bakery—all in a cavernous, pumped-up room. Fresh fish and Mediterranean fare are specialties, but there are also grilled chicken, pork, lamb, and beef. Live enter-tainment and dancing make this a popular after-hours hangout. ⊠ *737 9th St., Downtown,* ☎ *919/286–1431. AE, D, DC, MC, V.*

$$–$$$ ✕ **Pop's.** The roof is rough tin and the sculptures wrought-iron and steel industrial, and one latticework wall is covered in silk flowers and vines. Like the New South–Old South style, the menu mixes contem-porary Italian and down-home cuisine. You can get a grilled pork chop with polenta or *fritto misto* calamari (batter-fried squid) and other seafood. Arrive early; it fills up quickly. ⊠ *810 W. Peabody St., Down-town,* ☎ *919/956–7677. MC, V. No lunch weekends.*

$$$$ ✕⊞ **Washington Duke Inn & Golf Club.** On the campus of Duke Uni-
★ versity, this luxurious hotel overlooks a Robert Trent Jones golf course.
Rooms evoke the feeling of an English country inn, with floral bedspreads
and creamy striped wall coverings. On display in the public rooms are
memorabilia belonging to the Duke family, for whom the hotel and university are named. At the quietly sophisticated Fairview restaurant
($$$–$$$$), you can start with Moroccan–spiced lamb sausage or
chestnut soup with rosemary cream and then move on to entrées such
as breast of Muscovy duck with mashed white beans, roasted garlic,
and sweet-and-sour cranberry sauce. ⊠ *3001 Cameron Blvd., Duke Uni-
versity, 27706,* ☎ *919/490–0999 or 800/443–3853,* ℻ *919/688–0105,*
WEB *www.washingtondukeinn.com. 164 rooms, 7 suites. Restaurant, room
service, driving range, 18-hole golf course, putting green, 12 tennis courts,
pool, health club, bar, business services, laundry service, concierge,
meeting room, airport shuttle. AE, D, DC, MC, V.*

$$–$$$$ ⊞ **Arrowhead Inn.** Brick chimneys and tall Doric columns distinguish
this B&B inn in an 18th-century white-clapboard farmhouse. It's a few
miles outside Durham and has a cozy style, with antiques, heritage plants,
fireplaces, and a log cabin in the garden. ⊠ *106 Mason Rd., North
Metro, 27712,* ☎ *919/477–8430 or 800/528–2207,* ℻ *919/471–9538,*
WEB *www.arrowheadinn.com. 9 rooms, 2 suites. Picnic area, business
services. AE, D, DC, MC, V. BP.*

$$–$$$ ⊞ **Blooming Garden Inn.** Truly a bright spot in the Holloway Historic
District, this B&B is painted yellow outside. Inside, the inn explodes with
color and warmth, thanks to exuberant hosts Dolly and Frank Pokrass.
Breakfast might be walnut crepes with ricotta cheese and warm rasp-
berry sauce. A sister B&B, the Victorian Holly House, across the street,
accommodates extended stays. ⊠ *513 Holloway St., Downtown, 27701,*
☎ *919/687–0801 or 888/687–0801,* ℻ *919/688–1401,* WEB *www.
bloominggardeninn.com. 4 rooms, 2 suites. AE, D, DC, MC, V. BP.*

$$–$$$ ⊞ **Durham Marriott at the Civic Center.** Several fountains run through
the lobby entrance of this nine-floor hotel, which has reasonable rates
given the excellent location in the downtown art-and-entertainment district, atop the Durham Civic Center. Rooms are spacious and well ap-
pointed. Guests can use a health club one block away. ⊠ *201 Foster
St., Downtown, 27701,* ☎ *919/768–6000,* ℻ *919/768–6037,* WEB *www.
marriotthotels.com. 185 rooms, 2 suites. Restaurant, room service, in-
room safes, bar, exercise room, dry cleaning, laundry service, concierge
floor, business services, free parking. AE, D, DC, MC, V.*

Nightlife and the Arts

THE ARTS

The 1926 beaux arts **Carolina Theatre** (⊠ 309 W. Morgan St., Downtown, ☎ 919/560–3030) hosts film festivals, orchestras, and operas,
as well as the International Jazz Festival (March) and the Doubletake
Documentary Film Festival (May). Most of the performances at the
internationally known **American Dance Festival,** held annually in June
and July, take place at the **Page Auditorium** and **Reynolds Theater** (⊠
West Campus, Duke University, ☎ 919/684–4444). The old **Durham
Athletic Park** (⊠ 428 Morris St., Downtown) and **St. Joseph's Church**
(⊠ 804 Old Fayetteville St., Downtown), at the Hayti Heritage Center, are the venues for the two-day Bull Durham Blues Festival (☎ 800/
845–9835), presented early each September.

NIGHTLIFE

The **Edge** (⊠ 108 Morris St., Downtown, ☎ 919/667–1012) is a mul-
tilevel dance club with the feel of a slick renovated warehouse. There's
something for every taste: live music, a DJ, game rooms, even karaoke.

Outdoor Activities and Sports

BASEBALL

The **Durham Bulls,** a tradition since 1902, were immortalized in the hit movie *Bull Durham.* The AAA team, an affiliate of the Tampa Bay Devil Rays, plays at a 10,000-seat stadium near Downtown (⊠ 409 Blackwell St., North Metro, ☎ 919/687–6500).

BASKETBALL

Durham's Atlantic Coast Conference team is Duke's **Blue Devils,** which plays its home games at Cameron Indoor Stadium (⊠ Duke University, ☎ 919/681–2583 or 800/672–2583).

GOLF

Durham has four 18-hole public golf courses. **Duke University** (⊠ Cameron Blvd. and Science Dr., ☎ 919/681–2288) has a Robert Trent Jones course that is par 72. **Hillandale Golf Course** (⊠ Hillandale Rd., Duke University, ☎ 919/286–4211) has a par-71 George Cobb course.

TENNIS

The city's **Parks and Recreation Department** (☎ 919/560–4355) has information on the city's 72 public tennis courts.

Shopping

SHOPPING DISTRICTS AND MALLS

Durham's **9th Street** has funky shops and restaurants. **Brightleaf Square** (⊠ 905 W. Main St., Downtown, ☎ 919/682–9229) is an upscale shopping-entertainment complex housed in old tobacco warehouses downtown.

CRAFTS

One World Market (⊠ 1918 Perry St., Duke University, ☎ 919/286–2457) carries unique, affordable gifts. One goal of the store is to provide increased self-employment for low-income crafters from around the world.

FOOD

Fowler's Gourmet (⊠ 112 S. Duke St., Downtown, ☎ 919/683–2555) stocks everything from exotic spices to wines, fresh seafood, and European chocolates. Customized gift baskets are shipped all over the country. **Wellspring Grocery** (⊠ 621 Broad St., Downtown, ☎ 919/286–0765) has outstanding fresh produce, soups, salads, and sandwiches prepared daily.

Chapel Hill

12 mi southwest of Durham on U.S. 15/501, 28 mi northwest of Raleigh.

Chapel Hill may be the smallest city in the Triangle, but its reputation as a seat of learning—and of liberalism—looms large. The home of the nation's first state university, the 208-year-old University of North Carolina (UNC), Chapel Hill retains the feel of a quiet, tree-shaded village while crowded with students and retirees.

Morehead Planetarium, where the original Apollo astronauts and many since have trained, is one of the largest in the country. You can learn about the constellations and take in laser-light shows. ⊠ *250 E. Franklin St., University,* ☎ *919/962–1236; 919/549–6863 show information,* WEB *www.morehead.unc.edu.* ⊡ *$4.50.* ☉ *Mon. 12:30–5, Tues.–Fri. and Sun. 12:30–5 and 7–9:45, Sat. 10–5 and 7–9:45; call ahead for show times.*

★ **Franklin Street,** in the heart of downtown Chapel Hill, is lined with bicycle shops, bookstores, clothing stores, restaurants and coffee shops, and a movie theater.

Franklin Street runs along the northern edge of the **University of North Carolina** campus, which is filled with oak-shaded courtyards and stately old buildings. The **Louis Round Wilson Library** (⊠ South St., University, ☎ 919/962–0114) houses the largest single collection of state literature in the nation. Its **North Carolina Collection Gallery** (☎ 919/ 962–1172) has exhibits of rare books, photos, and oil portraits.Several historic rooms highlight topics in the state's history, such as the Walter Raleigh Room. The university's **Ackland Art Museum** (⊠ Columbia and Franklin Sts., University, ☎ 919/406–9837) showcases some of the Southeast's strongest collections of art from India and of Western art, as well as old-master paintings and sculptures. Of special interest is North Carolina folk art.

☾ The **ArtsCenter** (⊠ 300G E. Main St., Carrboro, ☎ 919/929–2787, WEB www.carrboro.com/artscenter.html) has exhibits, offers classes of all kinds for children, and hosts dance, theater, and music events.

The **North Carolina Botanical Garden,** south of downtown via U.S. 15/ 501 Bypass, has the largest collection of native plants in the Southeast. Nature trails wind through a 300-acre Piedmont forest; the herb garden and carnivorous plant collection are impressive. ⊠ *Old Mason Farm Rd., South Metro,* ☎ *919/962–0522,* WEB *www.unc.edu/depts/ncbg.* ☐ *Free.* ☉ *Apr.–Oct., weekdays 8–5, Sat. 10–6, Sun. 1–6; Nov.–Mar., weekdays 8–5, Sat. 9–5, Sun. 1–5.*

Dining and Lodging

$$–$$$ ✕ **Aurora.** Vaulted ceilings, skylights, and vivid hues of blue, lavender, mauve, and yellow help create a stylish and lively dining experience. The menu of northern Italian cuisine may include succulent sea scallops and shiitake mushrooms in rosemary and white wine, fresh chive pasta stuffed with four cheeses and tossed with walnut sauce, or veal with apples. ⊠ *1350 Raleigh Rd. (Rte. 54 Bypass), Metro East,* ☎ *919/ 942–2400,* WEB *www.aurorarestaurant.com. AE, MC, V. No lunch.*

$$–$$$ ✕ **Crook's Corner.** This small, often noisy restaurant is an exemplar of Southern chic. The menu changes often, and highlights such regional specialties as snapper with mint, pecans, and oranges, as well as hot-pepper jelly, crab gumbo, and buttermilk pie. A wall of bamboo and a waterfall fountain make the patio a delightful alfresco experience. Look for the pink pig atop the building. ⊠ *610 W. Franklin St., Downtown,* ☎ *919/929–7643. AE, D, DC, MC, V. No lunch.*

$$–$$$ ✕ **Pyewacket Restaurant.** What began as a hole-in-the-wall vegetarian restaurant in 1977 has become one of Chapel Hill's most popular eateries. Now with sleeker, larger digs and courtyard dining, Pyewacket has expanded its repertoire. Entrées range from Indonesian curried shrimp to spinach lasagna. ⊠ *431 W. Franklin St., Downtown,* ☎ *919/ 929–0297,* WEB *www.pyewacketrestaurant.com. AE, D, DC, MC, V. Closed Sun. No lunch.*

$–$$ ✕ **Mama Dip's Country Kitchen.** Mildred Edna Cotton Council (a.k.a. Mama Dip) is just about as well known in this town as another tall, gregarious Chapel Hillian, Michael Jordan. That's because she and her restaurant, which serves authentic home-style Southern meals in a roomy but simple setting, have been on the scene since the early '60s. Everything from chicken and dumplings, ribs, and country ham to fish, beef, salads, a mess of fresh vegetables, and melt-in-your-mouth buttermilk biscuits appear on the lengthy menu. ⊠ *408 W. Rosemary St., Downtown,* ☎ *919/942–5837. MC, V.*

$$$$ ✕⊞ **Fearrington House.** A member of the prestigious Relais & Châteaux
★ group, this country inn is on a 200-year-old farm that has been remade
into a residential community resembling a country village. The village
mascots, the "Oreo cows" (black on the ends, snow white in the middle), roam the pasture at the entrance. The inn's modern guest rooms,
overlooking a courtyard, gardens, and pasture, are furnished with antiques, English pine, and oversize tubs. The restaurant serves dressed-
up regional food, such as collard-pecan-pesto-stuffed chicken breast
with Hoop cheddar grits. Dinner is prix fixe. ✉ *2000 Fearrington Village Center, 8 mi south of Chapel Hill on U.S. 15/501, Pittsboro
27312,* ☎ *919/542–2121,* FAX *919/542–4202,* WEB *www.fearringtonhouse.
com. 29 rooms, 2 suites. 2 restaurants, 2 tennis courts, pool, croquet,
business services, meeting room. AE, MC, V. BP.*

$$$$ ✕⊞ **Siena Hotel.** Sam and Susan Longiotti's love for Siena, Italy, has
carried over to their posh European-style hotel. The lobby and rooms
have imported carved-wood furniture, along with fabrics and artwork
that conjure the Italian Renaissance. The public areas are filled with plush
furniture grouped for conversation. Tuscan cuisine is the hallmark of
Il Palio Ristorante ($$$). You won't be hurried here, which is a good
thing because it takes a while just to get through the antipasto while
you anticipate entrées such as *filetto di branzino*—black grouper filled
with greens and wrapped with prosciutto, in a saffron broth. ✉ *1505
E. Franklin St., North Metro, 27514,* ☎ *919/929–4000 or 800/223–
7379,* FAX *919/968–8527,* WEB *www.sienahotel.com. 68 rooms, 12 suites.
Restaurant, picnic area, room service, bar, laundry service, concierge,
business services, meeting room, airport shuttle. AE, DC, MC, V. BP.*

$$$–$$$$ ⊞ **Sheraton Chapel Hill.** The look of the guest rooms here differs a bit
from other area hotels, as they're done in a modern, Scandinavian style,
with fitted bedding and sleek furniture, including work desks. The mar-
ble lobby has a clean, spare look as well. Almost all the rooms offer a
view of pine-dotted grounds. This property, with its outdoor garden,
is conveniently located on U.S. 15/501 at the far edge of the Univer-
sity of North Carolina campus; it's easy access to Durham and Raleigh.
✉ *1 Europa Dr., University 27514,* ☎ *919/968–4900 or 800/325–3535,*
FAX *919/929–8170,* WEB *www.sheratonchapelhill.com. 168 rooms, 4
suites. Restaurant, room service, outdoor pool, exercise room, 2 bars,
business services, meeting rooms, airport shuttle. AE, D, DC, MC, V.*

Nightlife and the Arts

THE ARTS

The **Dean E. Smith Center** (✉ Skipper Bowles Dr., on the UNC cam-
pus, University, ☎ 919/962–7777) is the place not only for UNC
men's basketball games but for special events and concerts. **Playmak-
ers Repertory Company** (✉ Country Club Dr., on the UNC campus,
University, ☎ 919/962–7529), a nonprofit professional theater, per-
forms six plays annually (September–May) at the Paul Green Theatre.

NIGHTLIFE

The Chapel Hill area is the place to hear live rock and alternative bands.
Cat's Cradle (✉ 300 E. Main St., Carrboro, ☎ 919/967–9053) is
smoky and dark and presents entertainment nightly. The **West End Wine
Bar** (✉ 450 W. Franklin St., Downtown, ☎ 919/967–7599) attracts
professionals and postgraduates with its comprehensive wine list (more
than 80 vintages by the glass) and urbane sensibility.

Outdoor Activities and Sports

BASKETBALL

The University of North Carolina's **Tarheels** (☎ 919/962–2296 or
800/722–4335) are Chapel Hill's Atlantic Coast Conference team.

GOLF

There are three public golf courses in Orange County; Chapel Hill has one of them: **Finley Golf Course** (⊠ Finley Golf Course Rd., off Rte. 54 on the UNC campus, University, ☎ 919/962–2349) is a championship par-72, 18-hole course with a driving range and putting green.

TENNIS

There are 21 public courts in Chapel Hill. For information call the **Chapel Hill Parks and Recreation Department** (☎ 919/968–2784).

Shopping

SHOPPING DISTRICTS AND MALLS

Minutes from downtown, the lively **Eastgate Shopping Center** (⊠ between E. Franklin St. and U.S. 15/501, North Metro) sells everything from antiques to wine. **Fearrington Village,** a planned community 8 mi south of Chapel Hill on U.S. 15/501 in Pittsboro, has upscale shops selling art, garden items, handmade jewelry, and more. **Franklin Street** in Chapel Hill has a wonderful collection of shops, including bookstores, art galleries, crafts shops, and clothing stores.

BOOKS

At **McIntyre's Fine Books and Bookends** (⊠ Fearrington Village, U.S. 15/501, Pittsboro, ☎ 919/542–3030), an independent operation, you can read by the fire in one of the cozy rooms. It has extensive collections of travel and gardening books.

FOOD

A Southern Season (⊠ Eastgate Shopping Center, North Metro, ☎ 919/929–9466 or 800/253–3663) stocks a dazzling variety of cookware, books, wine, and treats, including barbecue sauces, peanuts, and hams. The adjoining Weathervane Café has indoor and alfresco dining.

The Triangle A to Z

To research prices, get advice from other travelers, and book travel arrangements, visit www.fodors.com.

AIRPORTS

The Raleigh-Durham International Airport, off I–40 between the two cities, is served by most major airlines. It takes about 20 minutes to get to any of the three cities from the airport.

➤ AIRPORT INFORMATION: **Raleigh-Durham International Airport** (⊠ 1600 Terminal Blvd., Morrisville, ☎ 919/840–2123, WEB www.rdu.com).

BUS TRAVEL

Greyhound/Carolina Trailways serves Raleigh, Durham, and Chapel Hill.

➤ BUS INFORMATION: **Greyhound/Carolina Trailways** (☎ 800/231–2222, WEB www.greyhound.com).

CAR TRAVEL

U.S. 1, which runs north–south through the Triangle and the Sandhills, also links to I–85 going northeast. U.S. 64, which makes an east–west traverse across the Triangle, continues eastward all the way to the Outer Banks. I–95 runs northeast–southwest to the east of the Triangle and the Sandhills, crossing U.S. 64 and I–40 from Virginia to South Carolina.

EMERGENCIES

For minor emergencies go to one of the many urgent-care centers in Raleigh, Cary, Durham, and Chapel Hill. Eckerd Drug Store and the Wal-Mart pharmacy are open 24 hours. Eckerd Drugs is open 8 AM–midnight weekdays and 9 AM–11 PM weekends.

➤ EMERGENCY SERVICES: **Ambulance, police** (☎ 911).
➤ 24-HOUR AND LATE-NIGHT PHARMACIES: **Eckerd Drug Store** (✉ Lake Boone Shopping Center, Wycliff Rd., Raleigh, ☎ 919/781–4070). **Eckerd Drugs** (✉ 3527 Hillsborough Rd., Durham, ☎ 919/383–5591). **Wal-Mart pharmacy** (✉ 6600 Glenwood Ave., Raleigh, ☎ 919/783–9693).

TAXIS

More than 25 taxi companies serve the Triangle; fares are calculated by the mile.
➤ TAXI COMPANIES: **City Taxi** (✉ Raleigh, ☎ 919/832–1489). **National Cab** (✉ Raleigh-Durham Airport, ☎ 919/469–1333). **Orange Cab** (✉ Durham, ☎ 919/682–6111).

TOURS

The Capital Area Visitor Center in Raleigh offers maps, brochures, and free guided and self-guided tours of government buildings; it's open weekdays 8–5, Saturday 10–4, and Sunday 1–4.

The Historic Chapel Hill/UNC Trolley Tour is given Wednesday 2–3, mid-April to mid-November. Departure is from the Horace Williams House, and the fare is $5; call for reservations.
➤ FEES AND SCHEDULES: **Capital Area Visitor Center** (✉ 301 N. Blount St., 27611, ☎ 919/733–3456). **Historic Chapel Hill/UNC Trolley Tour** (✉ Horace Williams House, 610 E. Rosemary St., ☎ 919/942–7818).

TRAIN TRAVEL

Amtrak serves Raleigh, Durham, and Cary; the *Carolinian* has one daily train northbound and one southbound; and the in-state *Piedmont* connects nine cities between Raleigh and Charlotte each day.
➤ TRAIN INFORMATION: **Amtrak** (☎ 800/872–7245, WEB www.amtrak.com).

TRANSPORTATION AROUND THE TRIANGLE

Capital Area Transit is Raleigh's public transport system. Fares are 75¢. Chapel Hill Transit, at 75¢ a ride, takes you around the city. Durham Area Transit Authority is Durham's intracity bus system. Fares are 75¢. The Triangle Transit Authority, which links downtown Raleigh with Cary, Research Triangle Park, Durham, and Chapel Hill, runs weekdays except major holidays. Rates start at $1.
➤ CONTACTS: **Capital Area Transit** (☎ 919/833–5701, WEB www.raleigh-nc.org/transit). **Chapel Hill Transit** (☎ 919/968–2769). **Durham Area Transit Authority** (☎ 919/683–3282). **Triangle Transit Authority** (☎ 919/549–9999).

VISITOR INFORMATION

The Durham Bullhorn provides 24-hour recorded information on events and activities.
➤ TOURIST INFORMATION: **Chapel Hill/Orange County Visitors Bureau** (✉ 501 W. Franklin St., Suite 104, Chapel Hill 27516, ☎ 919/968–2060 or 888/968–2060, WEB www.chocvb.org). **Downtown Chapel Hill Welcome Center** (✉ Old Post Office Building, 179 E. Franklin St., ☎ 919/929–9700). **Durham Convention and Visitors Bureau** (✉ 101 E. Morgan St., 27701, ☎ 919/687–0288 or 800/446–8604, WEB www.dcvb.durham.nc.us). **Durham Bullhorn** (☎ 919/688–2855 or 800/772–2855). **Greater Raleigh Convention and Visitors Bureau** (✉ Bank of America Bldg., 421 Fayetteville Street Mall, Suite 1505, 27601, ☎ 919/834–5900 or 800/849–8499, WEB www.raleighcvb.org).

THE SANDHILLS
Southern Pines, Pinehurst

Because of their sandy soil—they were once Atlantic beaches—the Sandhills weren't of much use to early farmers, most of whom switched to lumbering and making turpentine for a livelihood. Since the turn of the 20th century, however, this area with its gently undulating hills has proved ideal for golf and tennis. Promoters call it "the golf capital of the world"; the Tufts Archives honors the sport and the founding of Pinehurst. First-class resorts are centered on the 40 championship golf courses, including the famed Pinehurst Number 2, which have hosted PGA tournaments. Public tennis courts can be found in many communities, and the area has also long been popular with horse owners.

The Highland Scots who settled the area left a rich heritage perpetuated through festivals and gatherings. In colonial times English potters were attracted to the rich clay deposits in the soil, and today their descendants and others turn out beautiful wares sold in more than 40 local shops.

Southern Pines

104 mi east of Charlotte, 71 mi southwest of Raleigh.

Southern Pines, the center of the Sandhills, is a good place to start your visit to the area.

Sandhills Horticultural Gardens has a wetland area that can be observed from elevated boardwalks. It's part of a 32-acre series of gardens showcasing roses, fruits and vegetables, herbs, conifers, hollies, a formal English garden, pools, and a waterfall. ⊠ *2200 Airport Rd., Sandhills Community College campus,* ☏ *910/695–3882 or 800/338–3944,* WEB *www.sandhills.cc.nc.us/lsg/hort.html.* ✉ *Free.* ☉ *Daily sunrise–sunset.*

The **Shaw House,** the oldest structure in town (circa 1820), serves as headquarters for the Moore County Historical Association. It and two other restored historic houses on the property, all of which date to 1700, depict the lives of early settlers. ⊠ *S.W. Broad St. and Morganton Rd.,* ☏ *910/692–2051.* ✉ *$2, suggested donation.* ☉ *Apr.– Dec., Wed.–Sun. 1–4.*

Weymouth Center, former home of author and publisher James Boyd, hosts numerous concerts and lectures. Boyd, who died in 1944, was visited by many well-known writers; his home served as a cultural center for the area. The North Carolina Literary Hall of Fame is on the 24-acre property, as is a writer-in-residence program, which has hosted more than 600 writers. ⊠ *555 E. Connecticut Ave.,* ☏ *910/692– 6261,* WEB *www.weymouthcenter.org.* ✉ *Free.* ☉ *Weekdays 10–2; call ahead to arrange tours.*

Weymouth Woods Sandhills Nature Preserve, on the eastern outskirts of town, is a 571-acre wildlife preserve with 4 mi of hiking trails, a beaver pond, and a naturalist on staff. ⊠ *1024 N. Fort Bragg Rd., off U.S. 1,* ☏ *910/692–2167,* WEB *ils.unc.edu/parkproject/wewo.html.* ✉ *Free.* ☉ *Apr.–Oct., daily 9–7; Nov.–Mar., daily 9–6.*

OFF THE BEATEN PATH **CAMERON –** Cameron, which hasn't changed much since the 19th century, is the place to shop for antiques. Approximately 60 antiques dealers operate out of several stores. The town itself, off U.S. 1, has been declared a historic district. Most shops are open Tuesday through Saturday 10–5, Sunday 1–5; call the historic district office (☏ 910/245– 7001) for information. The town is 12 mi north of Southern Pines.

Dining and Lodging

$$$–$$$$ ✕ **Lob Steer Inn.** Salad and dessert bars complement generous broiled seafood and prime rib dinners at this casual, dimly lighted steak house. ⊠ *U.S. 1,* ☎ *910/692–3503. Reservations essential. AE, DC, MC, V. No lunch.*

$ ✕ **Sweet Basil.** This cozy corner café is run by a family whose considerable restaurant expertise shows in the service and the cooking: lots of homemade breads, hefty loaded sandwiches, and lush salads are offered. Special treats are the soups—especially the ginger-carrot and flavorful red-pepper varieties—and decadent desserts. Arrive early to avoid the lunch rush. ⊠ *134 Broad St.,* ☎ *910/693–1487. MC, V. Closed Sun. No dinner.*

$$$$ ▦ **Pine Needles Lodge and Golf Club.** One of the bonuses of staying at this informal lodge is the chance to meet Peggy Kirk Bell, a champion golfer and golf instructor. She built the resort with her late husband and continues to help run it. The club has even hosted the U.S. Women's Open. The rooms are done in a rustic chalet style; many have exposed beams. ⊠ *1005 Midland Rd., Box 88, 28387,* ☎ *910/692–7111 or 800/747–7272,* FAX *910/692–5349,* WEB *www.pineneedles-midpines.com. 71 rooms. Dining room, snack bar, driving range, 18-hole golf course, putting green, 2 tennis courts, pool, bicycles, bar, business services, meeting room, airport shuttle. AE, MC, V. FAP.*

$$$ ▦ **Mid Pines Inn and Golf Club.** This resort community includes a Georgian-style clubhouse and a golf course designed by Donald Ross that has been the site of numerous tournaments. The spacious rooms in the 1921 inn are Wedgwood blue, with American antiques or good copies. Jackets are required in the dining room. ⊠ *1010 Midland Rd., 28387,* ☎ *910/692–2114 or 800/323–2114,* FAX *910/692–4615,* WEB *www. pineneedles-midpines.com. 112 rooms, 5 houses, 7 villas. Dining room, snack bar, 18-hole golf course, putting green, 4 tennis courts, pool, gym, bar, recreation room, business services, meeting room, airport shuttle. AE, D, DC, MC, V. FAP.*

Outdoor Activities and Sports

There are many excellent 18-hole golf courses here. **Club at Longleaf** (⊠ 2001 Midland Rd., ☎ 910/692–6100 or 800/889–5323) was built on a former horse farm. The front nine of the par-71 course plays through posts, rails, and turns of the old racetrack. **Mid Pines Golf Club** (⊠ 1010 Midland Rd., ☎ 910/692–2114 or 800/323–2114) is a golf getaway with a Donald Ross–designed par-72 course. **Pine Needles Resort** (⊠ 1005 Midland Rd., ☎ 910/692–7111 or 800/747–7272) has a Donald Ross–designed par-71 course complemented by practice facilities, grass tennis courts, and an outdoor swimming pool. **Talamore at Pinehurst** (⊠ 1595 Midland Rd., ☎ 910/692–5884 or 800/552–6292), with its unusual llama caddies, is a par-71 course designed by Rees Jones.

Shopping

Country Bookshop (⊠ 140 N.W. Broad St., ☎ 910/692–3211), in the historic downtown district, often has regional authors do readings and signings. The store stocks a lot of everything, including children's books and classical and jazz CDs.

Pinehurst

6 mi west of Southern Pines.

Pinehurst, a New England–style village with quiet, shaded streets and immaculately kept cottages, was laid out in the late 1800s in a wagon-wheel design by landscape genius Frederick Law Olmsted. Annie Oakley lived here for a number of years and headed the gun club. Today it attracts sports enthusiasts, retirees, and tourists.

Tufts Archives recounts the founding of Pinehurst in the letters, pictures, and news clippings, dating from 1895, of James Walker Tufts, who served as president of the United States Golf Association. Golf memorabilia are on display. ✉ *Given Memorial Library, 150 Cherokee Rd.,* ☎ *910/ 295–6022 or 910/295–3642.* 🖾 *Free.* ☉ *Weekdays 9:30–5, Sat. 9:30– 12:30.*

Dining and Lodging

$ ✗ **Pinehurst Playhouse Restaurant.** This casual eatery in the shop-filled Theater Building is in the heart of the village. It's *the* place to meet for soups and sandwiches. ✉ *W. Village Green,* ☎ *910/295–8873. Reservations not accepted. No credit cards. Closed Sun. No dinner.*

$$$$ ✗🖾 **The Carolina.** The Carolina is the centerpiece of the Pinehurst Com-
★   pany Resorts, which includes the Holly Inn, the Manor Inn, and villas and condos. This stately hotel, in operation since 1901, has never lost the charm that founder James Tufts intended it to have. Civilized decorum rules in the spacious public rooms, on the rocker-lined wide verandas, and amid the gardens. Guest rooms are elegantly traditional. You can tee off on one of eight signature golf courses. Two blocks away, the 45-room Manor Inn, with its bar and grill, has the feel of a B&B. Manor Inn guests have access to all the resort facilities, including the very formal Carolina Dining Room. The esoteric menu changes daily. ✉ *1 Carolina Vista Dr., Box 4000, 28374,* ☎ *910/295–6811 or 800/ 487–4653,* ℻ *910/295–8503,* 🕸 *www.pinehurst.com. 338 rooms, 130 condos. 2 restaurants, room service, 8 18-hole golf courses, 24 tennis courts, 5 pools, health club, massage, windsurfing, boating, fishing, bicycles, croquet, bar, children's programs, concierge, business services, meeting room. AE, D, DC, MC, V.*

$$$$ ✗🖾 **Holly Inn.** This historic hotel, affiliated with the Pinehurst Resort, was the first in the village. Molding, lighting, and plumbing fixtures, based on research from local archives, recall the 1890s, the decade of its opening. Luxuries include silk hangers; embroidered robes; and afternoon sandwiches, cookies, and iced tea. A two-night stay is required. The menu at 1895, the bistro-style restaurant, changes seasonally. Inventive dinner entrées may include pinecone-smoked free-range chicken with truffles, tarragon-scented roast tenderloin of veal, and Carolina blue-crab hash. Jackets are requested at the restaurant. ✉ *Cherokee Rd., 28374,* ☎ *910/295–6811 or 800/487–4653,* ℻ *910/295–8503,* 🕸 *www.pinehurst.com. 78 rooms, 7 suites. Restaurant, room service, golf privileges, pool, croquet, bar, library, concierge, business services, meeting room. AE, DC, MC, V. MAP.*

$$$ ✗🖾 **Magnolia Inn.** This turn-of-the-20th-century inn, once just a hangout for golfing buddies, is tastefully decorated with unusual antiques. Most guest rooms are in the Victorian style with wicker and brass beds; bathrooms have original fixtures such as claw-foot tubs. The inn's dining rooms ($$$–$$$$), with their dusty-rose wallpaper and fireplaces, are cozy. The regional menu includes Magnolia duck–breast and leg of duck with a pear, sweet potato, and wild cherry glaze. There's also an English-style pub. ✉ *Magnolia and Chinquapin Rds., Box 818, 28370,* ☎ *910/295–6900 or 800/526–5562,* ℻ *910/215–0858,* 🕸 *www.themagnoliainn.com. 11 rooms. Dining room, golf privileges, pool, business services. AE, MC, V. BP.*

$$$–$$$$ 🖾 **Pine Crest Inn.** Chintz and mahogany fill the rooms of this slightly faded gem once owned by golfing great Donald Ross. The chefs whip up meals reminiscent of Sunday supper: homemade soups, fresh fish dishes, and the house special, stuffed pork chops. Mr. B's Bar is the liveliest nightspot in town. Guests have golf and tennis privileges at local clubs. ✉ *Dogwood Rd., Box 879, 28370,* ☎ *910/295–6121 or*

800/371–2545, FAX 910/295–4880, WEB *www.pinecrestinnpinehurst.com.* *40 rooms. Dining room, bar. AE, D, DC, MC, V. MAP.*

Outdoor Activities and Sports

GOLF

Pinehurst Resort and Country Club (✉ 1 Carolina Vista Dr., ☎ 910/ 295–6811 or 800/487–4653) has eight courses designed by such masters as Donald Ross, including the famed par-72 Number 2.

The par-71 **Pit Golf Links** (✉ Rte. 5, ☎ 910/944–1600 or 800/574– 4653) was designed by Dan Maples and sculpted from a 230-acre sand quarry.

HORSEBACK AND CARRIAGE RIDING

Riding instruction and carriage rides are available by appointment at **Pinehurst Stables** (✉ Rte. 5, ☎ 910/295–8456).

TENNIS

The **Lawn and Tennis Club of North Carolina** (✉ 1 Merrywood, ☎ 910/ 692–7270) has seven courts and a swimming pool. **Pinehurst Resort and Country Club** (✉ Carolina Vista Dr., ☎ 910/295–8556) is considered one of the best facilities in the country and has clay courts.

Aberdeen

5 mi southeast of Pinehurst, 5 mi southwest of Southern Pines.

Aberdeen, a small town of Scottish ancestry, has a beautifully restored early 20th-century train station and plenty of shops with antiques and collectibles. The **Bethesda Presbyterian Church,** on Bethesda Road east of town, was founded in 1790. The present wooden structure, which is used for weddings, funerals, and reunions, was built in the 1860s and still has preserved its slave gallery as well as exterior bullet holes from a Civil War battle. The cemetery, where many early settlers are buried, is always open.

Malcolm Blue Farm, one of the few remaining examples of the 19th-century Scottish homes that dotted the area, has farm buildings and an old gristmill. A September festival recalls life here in the 1800s. The farm and museum are part of the North Carolina Civil War Theme Trail. ✉ *Bethesda Rd.,* ☎ *910/944–7558; 910/944–9483 for museum.* 🎟 *Free.* ⊙ *Wed.–Sat. 1–4.*

OFF THE
BEATEN PATH

FORT BRAGG/POPE AIR FORCE BASE – This army–air force duo outside Fayetteville, 45 mi east of Aberdeen via Route 211 and U.S. 401, is one of the world's largest military complexes. Pope hosts an open house and air show annually (☎ 910/394–4183). Bragg, the biggest army post east of the Mississippi, is open year-round, and self-guided tours are available. The welcome center (☎ 910/907–2026, WEB www. bragg.army.mil), at the corner of Randolph and Knox streets on Fort Bragg, has maps indicating public access areas. Free sites include the 82nd Airborne Division War Memorial Museum (☎ 910/432–3443), which tells the story of this unit, famous from World War I through Desert Storm. ✉ *Off Rte. 24 or the All American Freeway. Some sites closed Mon.*

AIRBORNE AND SPECIAL OPERATIONS MUSEUM – The Army's newest museum tells the story of the fabled airborne and special-ops units through film and video, interactive displays, walk-through dioramas, and rare artifacts. The $22.5 million facility is in downtown Fayetteville. ✉ *100 Bragg Blvd.,* ☎ *910/483–3003,* WEB *www.asomf.org.* 🎟 *Museum free; Vistascope Theater $3; motion simulator $3. Tues.–Sat. 10–5, Sun. noon–5.*

Lodging

$–$$ ⊞ **Inn at Bryant House.** One block east of U.S. 1, this charming downtown B&B, built in 1913, is a home away from home. All rooms are individually decorated; some have canopy beds. The inn has golf packages and arranges tennis and horseback riding. ⊠ *214 N. Poplar St., 28315,* ☎ *910/944–3300 or 800/453–4019,* FAX *910/944–8898,* WEB *www.innatbryanthouse.com. 9 rooms, 7 with bath. Picnic area, business services. AE, D, MC, V. CP.*

Outdoor Activities and Sports

Legacy Golf Links (⊠ U.S. 15/501, ☎ 910/944–8825 or 800/344–8825) has the first American course designed by Jack Nicklaus II (par 72).

Seagrove

35 mi northwest of Pinehurst via Rte. 211 and U.S. 220.

Potters, some of whom are carrying on traditions that have been in their families for generations and others who are newer to the art, handcraft mugs, bowls, pitchers, platters, vases, and clay "face jugs" in the
★ **Seagrove** area. More than 90 potteries are scattered along and off Route 705 and U.S. 220. Some of the work of local artisans is exhibited in national museums, including the Smithsonian. Most shops are open Tuesday through Saturday 10–5.

★ The **North Carolina Pottery Center,** a museum and educational facility, has exhibitions of pottery from around the state and maps locating the various studios around the area. ⊠ *250 East Ave.,* ☎ *336/873–8430,* WEB *www.ncpotterycenter.com.* ☉ *Tues.–Sat. 10–4.*

Asheboro

13 mi north of Seagrove, 23 mi south of Greensboro on U.S. 64.

Asheboro, the seat of Randolph County, sits in the Uwharrie National Forest, a haven for hikers, bikers, horseback riders, and fisherfolk. This part of the southern Piedmont is a lovely place to view scenery and visit crafts shops.

★ ☾ The **North Carolina Zoological Park,** a 1,500-acre home for more than 1,100 animals and 60,000 exotic and tropical plants, was the first zoo in the country designed from the get-go as a natural habitat facility. The park includes the 300-acre African Pavilion, an aviary, a gorilla habitat, a Sonoran Desert habitat, and a 200-acre North American habitat with polar bears and sea lions. You can take a tram between areas. ⊠ *4401 Zoo Pkwy.,* ☎ *336/879–7000 or 800/488–0444,* WEB *www. nczoo.org.* ☞ *$10, including tram ride.* ☉ *Apr.–Oct., daily 9–5; Nov.–Mar., daily 9–4.*

The Sandhills A to Z

To research prices, get advice from other travelers, and book travel arrangements, visit www.fodors.com.

AIR TRAVEL

CARRIERS

US Airways Express serves the Moore County Airport with connections from the Charlotte, Raleigh, and Piedmont Triad airports.
➤ AIRLINES AND CONTACTS: **Moore County Airport** (⊠ Rte. 22, Southern Pines, ☎ 910/692–3212). **US Airways Express** (☎ 800/428–4322).

CAR TRAVEL

U.S. 1 runs north–south through the Sandhills and is the recommended route from the Raleigh-Durham area, a distance of about 70 mi.

EMERGENCIES

Moore Regional Hospital is an acute-care facility with an emergency room.

➤ EMERGENCY SERVICES: **Ambulance, fire, police** (☎ 911).

➤ HOSPITALS: **Moore Regional Hospital** (✉ 155 Memorial Dr., Pinehurst, ☎ 910/215–1000).

TRAIN TRAVEL

Both southbound and northbound Amtrak trains, one daily in each direction, stop in Southern Pines.

➤ TRAIN INFORMATION: **Amtrak** (☎ 800/872–7245, WEB www.amtrak.com).

VISITOR INFORMATION

Pinehurst Area Convention and Visitors Bureau serves the Pinehurst, Southern Pines, and Aberdeen areas. For details on local events call the events hot line. Moore County Parks and Recreation Department can provide recreation information.

➤ TOURIST INFORMATION: **Events Hot Line** (☎ 910/692–1600). **Moore County Parks and Recreation Department** (☎ 910/947–2504, WEB www.co.moore.nc.us). **Pinehurst Area Convention and Visitors Bureau** (✉ 1480 U.S. 15/501, Box 2270, Southern Pines 28388, ☎ 910/692–3330 or 800/346–5362, WEB www.homeofgolf.com).

THE OUTER BANKS

Cape Hatteras, Cape Lookout

North Carolina's Outer Banks, a series of barrier islands in the Atlantic Ocean, stretch from the Virginia state line south to Cape Lookout. Throughout history these waters have been the nemesis of shipping, gaining them the nickname the Graveyard of the Atlantic; the network of lighthouses and lifesaving stations draws lots of curious travelers, and the many submerged wrecks attract scuba divers. The islands' coves and inlets offered privacy to pirates—the notorious Blackbeard lived and died here.

For many years the Outer Banks remained isolated, with only a few families, which made their living by fishing. Times may have changed, but fishing still prevails as the industry of note here: about 40 million pounds of fish are caught here annually—a $27 million industry. Flounder and crab alone account for half the industry; other fish and seafood include bluefish, dolphin, mussels, clams, mackerel, marlin, shark, tuna, and shrimp. Many locals still use crab pots and process their catches in their backyards, and it's not unusual to see a fisherman arrive at a restaurant with a fresh catch and ask the chef to cook it up.

Today the islands, linked by bridges and ferries, have become popular destinations for vacationers. Much of the area is included in the Cape Hatteras and Cape Lookout national seashores. The largest towns are Kitty Hawk, Kill Devil Hills, Nags Head, and Manteo. Vacation rentals are popular—there are about 12,000 weekly rental cottages available on the Outer Banks. Rates run about $800–$1000 a week in summer.

On the inland side of the Outer Banks is the historic Albemarle region, a remote area of small villages and towns surrounding Albemarle

FIRST IN FLIGHT

DECEMBER 17, 1903, was a cold and windy day on the Outer Banks, but Wilbur and Orville Wright took little notice. The slightly built brothers from Ohio were undertaking an excellent adventure. With Orville at the controls, Wilbur running alongside, and the men of the nearby Lifesaving Service stations acting as ground crew, the fragile *Wright Flyer* lifted off from the dunes of Kill Devil Hills and flew 120 ft in 12 seconds.

John Daniels, an Outer Banker, photographed the instant the world forever changed: a heavier-than-air machine was used to achieve controlled, sustained flight with a pilot aboard. To prove that they were not accidental aviators, the Wrights made three more powered flights that day. Wilbur took his turn, flying 195 ft in a little over 15 seconds. Finally, it was Wilbur's chance again. In a 59-second period he took the first airplane 852 ft.

In fact, everything about the start of modern aeronautical science was very intentional. Wilbur and Orville began experimenting in 1899 with their first kite and achieved their goals in 1905, when they built a truly practical airplane. What happened in between, with their work in Kill Devil Hills, helped them solve the problems of mechanical flight, lift, propulsion, and control that had vexed scientists for hundreds of years.

It was the ideal combination of wind and sand and privacy that brought Wilbur and Orville to the then-remote corner of North Carolina: There they were welcomed and provided food and assistance. In 2003 the state will celebrate the Year of the Centennial of Flight, which will culminate in a special series of events at the Outer Banks and the Wright Brothers National Memorial. April 6, 2003, is the grand opening of the Aviation World's Fair, at Kill Devil Hills (☎ 252/441–4434). Activities during the year will include aerial tours of the memorial, parades, rallies, a kite festival, an antique airplane exhibit, and history programs and exhibits. From December 13 to 17, 2003, a celebration with aviation flyovers and aircraft-related events is planned. See the official Web site for information on all events (www.celebrate100.org).

— By Lisa H. Towle

Sound. Edenton was the colonial capital for a while, and many of its early structures are preserved.

You can tour the Outer Banks from the south end by taking a car ferry to Ocracoke Island or, as in the following route, from the north end. Driving the 120-mi stretch of Route 12 from Corolla to Ocracoke can be managed in a day, but be sure to allow plenty of time in summer to wait for the ferry connecting the islands and for exploring the undeveloped beaches, historic lifesaving stations, and charming beach communities stretched along the national seashores. Rentals are available throughout the area, with the highest concentration of accommodations between Kill Devil Hills and Nags Head. Mile markers (MM) indicate addresses for sites where there aren't many buildings. Be aware that during major storms and hurricanes the roads and bridges become clogged with traffic following the blue-and-white evacuation signs.

Numbers in the margin correspond to points of interest on the Outer Banks map.

Corolla, Duck, and Kitty Hawk

Kitty Hawk: 87 mi south of Norfolk, VA, via U.S. 17 and U.S. 158; 215 mi east of Raleigh via U.S. 64 and Rte. 12. Duck: 7 mi north of Kitty Hawk. Corolla: 19 mi north of Duck.

The small settlements of Corolla and Duck are largely seasonal residential enclaves full of summer rental condominiums. Upscale **Duck** has lots of restaurants and shopping outlets. The **Currituck Beach Lighthouse** (☉ Easter to Thanksgiving, daily 10–5), in **Corolla,** is the northernmost lighthouse on the Outer Banks. Weather permitting, you can climb to the top. Drive slowly in Corolla; wild ponies wander free here and always have the right of way. **Kitty Hawk,** with a few thousand permanent residents, is among the quieter of the beach communities, with fewer rental accommodations.

OFF THE BEATEN PATH

ELIZABETH CITY – This city's historic district has the largest number of pre–Civil War commercial buildings in the state. The **Museum of the Albemarle** (⊠ 1116 U.S. 17, ☎ 252/335–1453, WEB www.albemarle-nc. com/moa; ⊠ free; ☉ Tues.–Sat. 9–5, Sun. 2–5), an affiliate of the North Carolina Museum of History, has displays on local history. Elizabeth City is 50 mi northwest of Kitty Hawk on the Albemarle Sound.

MERCHANTS MILLPOND STATE PARK – A 200-year-old man-made millpond and an ancient swamp form one of the state's rarest ecosystems. Cypress and gum trees hung with Spanish moss reach out of the still, dark waters, which are ideal for canoeing. Fishing, hiking, and camping are also available. The park is 80 mi northwest of Kitty Hawk, on the mainland. ⊠ 71 U.S. 158, Gatesville, ☎ 252/357–1191. ⊠ Free. ☉ June–Aug., daily 8 AM–9 PM; Sept. and Apr.–May, daily 8–8; Oct. and Mar., daily 8–7; Nov.–Feb., daily 8–6.

Dining and Lodging

$$$ ✕ **Blue Point Bar & Grill.** The upscale spot with an enclosed porch overlooking Currituck Sound is as busy as a diner and as boldly colored—with a red, black, and chrome interior—but you won't find burgers, fries, or blue-plate specials here. Both the service and the menu, which stresses "Southern coastal cuisine," such as a seasonal seafood stew with saffron, citrus, tomatoes, and grilled roasted-garlic crostini, is decidedly uptown. Sunday brunch is served. ⊠ 1240 Duck Rd., Duck, ☎ 252/261–8090. Reservations essential. AE, D, MC, V. No lunch.

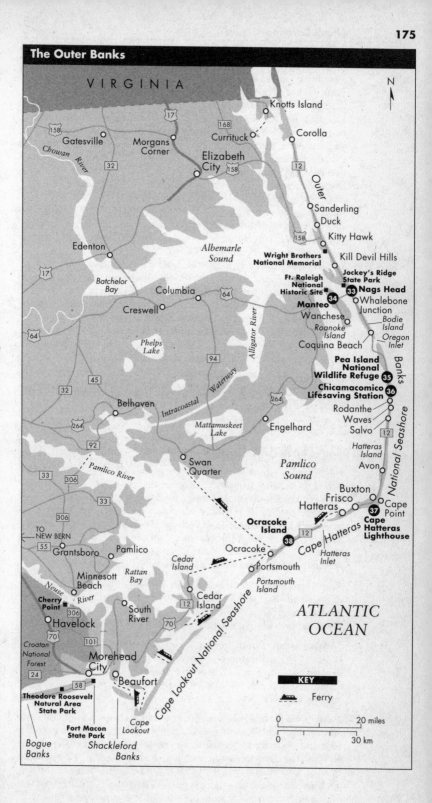

The Outer Banks

VIRGINIA

N

Knotts Island

158 Gatesville

Morgans Corner

168 Currituck

Corolla

Chowan River

32

17

Elizabeth City

158

12

Outer

Sanderling

Duck

158 Kitty Hawk

Edenton

Albemarle Sound

Wright Brothers National Memorial

Kill Devil Hills

Jockey's Ridge State Park

17

Batchelor Bay

Columbia

64

Ft. Raleigh National Historic Site

Manteo

(34)

(33) Nags Head

Whalebone Junction

Creswell

Wanchese

Roanoke Island

Bodie Island

64

Phelps Lake

94

Coquina Beach

Oregon Inlet

45

Alligator River

Pea Island National Wildlife Refuge

(35) Banks

32

Intracoastal Waterway

Chicamacomico Lifesaving Station

(36)

Belhaven

Mattamuskeet Lake

Engelhard

Rodanthe

Waves

Salvo

264

92

264

12

Pamlico River

Hatteras Island

33 306

Swan Quarter

Pamlico Sound

Avon

National Seashore

33

Buxton

Frisco

306

Hatteras

Cape Point

Ocracoke Island

(37)

Cape Hatteras Lighthouse

TO NEW BERN

55 Grantsboro

Pamlico

(38) 12

Ocracoke

Cape Hatteras

Minnesott Beach

Rattan Bay

Cedar Island

Hatteras Inlet

Cherry Point

Neuse River

Portsmouth

South River

Cedar Island

Portsmouth Island

306

12

ATLANTIC OCEAN

Havelock

70

101

70

Croatan National Forest

Morehead City

24

58

Beaufort

Cape Lookout National Seashore

Theodore Roosevelt Natural Area State Park

Fort Macon State Park

Cape Lookout

KEY

Ferry

Bogue Banks

Shackleford Banks

0   20 miles

0   30 km

$$$$ ✕🖼 **The Sanderling Inn.** This inn on a remote beach 5 mi north of Duck is a fine place to be pampered. Recreation choices include tennis, swimming, and nature walks through the Pine Island Sanctuary. Although it has all the contemporary conveniences, the resort has the wonderfully stately, mellow look of old Nags Head. With ceiling fans, wicker, and neutral tones, the rooms feel casual and summery. The Sanderling restaurant ($$$–$$$$; dinner reservations essential) occupies a renovated lifesaving station. On the seasonal menu you may find crab cakes, roast duckling, or fricassee of shrimp. The newer restaurant, the Left Bank ($$$; dinner only; reservations essential; jacket required) serves fine American food with a French influence. ⊠ *1461 Duck Rd., Sanderling 27949,* ☎ *252/261–4111 or 800/701–4111,* FAX *252/261–1638,* WEB *www.sanderlinginn.com. 88 rooms, 29 efficiencies. 2 restaurants, room service, minibars, golf privileges, 2 tennis courts, pool, health club, hot tub, spa, fishing, bicycles, hiking, racquetball, squash, bar, library, shop, meeting room. AE, D, MC, V. CP.*

$$$–$$$$ 🖼 **Advice 5¢.** The name may be quirky, but this contemporary B&B in Duck's North Beach area is very serious about guest care. Just a short walk from downtown shops and restaurants, Advice 5¢ also offers the use of the tennis courts and swimming pool at Sea Pines, a nearby property. Beds in each room are dressed with crisp, colorful linens. All rooms have private decks, ceiling fans, and baths stocked with thick cotton towels. ⊠ *111 Scarborough La., 27949,* ☎ *252/255–1050 or 800/238–4235,* WEB *www.advice5.com. 4 rooms, 1 suite. MC, V. Closed Dec.–Feb. CP.*

Outdoor Activities and Sports

Sea Scape Golf Course (⊠ 300 Eckner St., MM 2.5, Kitty Hawk, ☎ 252/261–2158) is a par-72 links course set amid the dunes.

Nags Head

③③   *4 mi south of Kill Devil Hills.*

Nags Head got its name because Outer Bankers hoping for shipwrecks would tie lanterns around the heads of their horses to lure merchant ships onto the shoals, thus profiting from the cargo that washed ashore (or which they brought ashore when they pirateered the boats). This is a somewhat commercialized and congested area, but, on the upside, you are convenient to plenty of restaurants, motels, hotels, and shops. Vacation rentals are a big industry here; older homes have wraparound porches, and most can house an entire family (or two).

Nags Head has 11 mi of **beach** with 33 public access areas, all with parking and some with rest rooms and showers. One point of interest is mile marker 11.5, the first North Carolina Historic Shipwreck Site. The USS *Huron* lies in 20 ft of water off the Nags Head Pier.

Coquina Beach (⊠ off Rte. 12, 8 mi south of U.S. 158), in the **Cape Hatteras National Seashore,** is considered the loveliest beach in the Outer Banks according to locals. The wide-beamed ribs of the shipwreck *Laura Barnes* rest in the dunes here. Free parking, showers, and picnic shelters are available.

🝙   **Jockey's Ridge State Park** has 400 acres that encompass the tallest sand dune in the East (about 88 ft), although it has lost some 22 ft since the 1930s thanks to the million visitors a year who carry sand away on their persons. The climb to the top is a challenge; nevertheless, it's a popular spot for hang gliding, kite flying, and sand boarding. You can also explore an estuary and several trails through the park. In summer join the free Sunset on the Ridge program: watch the sun disappear while you sit on the dunes and learn about their local legends and history. ⊠ *U.S. 158 Bypass, MM 12,* ☎ *252/441–7132.* 🝙 *Free.* ☉ *Daily 8–sunset.*

The **Tanger Outlet Center,** an outlet mall, includes 2-dozen stores, from designer clothes and shoes to casual attire, books, and sun glasses. ⊠ *U.S. 158 Bypass, MM 16,* ☎ *252/441–5634.* ⊙ *Mar.–Dec., Mon.–Sat. 9–9, Sun. 11–6; Jan.–Feb., call for hrs.*

Dining and Lodging

$$$–$$$$ ✕ **Windmill Point.** The menu changes here, but you can always count on the signature seafood trio: diners may choose any combination of three fish. The preparation is at the whim of the chef: lightly poached or grilled, and topped with roasted red pepper and capers, or shredded cucumber and dill, or a pineapple salsa. The restaurant has stunning views of the sound at sunset, eye-catching memorabilia from the luxury liner SS *United States,* and, yes, a real windmill. It's a reproduction of the German-style windmills used in the area a century ago. ⊠ *U.S. 158 Bypass, MM 16.5,* ☎ *252/441–1535. AE, D, DC, MC, V.*

$$–$$$$ ✕ **Owens' Restaurant.** In an old Nags Head–style clapboard cottage, this old-fashioned dining spot has been in the same family since 1946. Stick with the seafood or chops, at which they excel. Pecan-encrusted sea scallops are plump, tender, and intensely delicious. Also popular are Margarita sea scallops, coconut shrimp with an orange creole sauce, and filet mignon topped with lump crabmeat and asparagus béarnaise sauce. Seafood gumbo is studded with crawfish, Andouille sausage, and Tasso ham. Service is attentive and the wine list hefty. The 16-layer lemon and chocolate cakes are delicious. The brass-and-glass Station Keeper's Lounge has entertainment. ⊠ *U.S. 158, MM 17,* ☎ *252/441–7309. Reservations not accepted. AE, D, DC, MC, V. Closed Jan.–Feb. No lunch.*

$$–$$$ ✕ **Pier House Restaurant.** A sign above the entrance reads THE HAPPIEST PEOPLE IN THE WORLD PASS THROUGH THIS DOOR—no kidding, especially if you count the decidedly spectacular view over the ocean, the friendly service, and the tremendous selection of fresh seafood. This seasonal restaurant is literally *on* the crooked, rickety Nags Head Fishing Pier, which juts into the ocean, and while you're waiting for your food, you can stroll down and watch ruddy fishermen haul up their catch. It's open from 7 AM until 9 PM. At breakfast and lunch ($) you can get anything from seafood omelets to crab cakes to burgers and grilled-cheese sandwiches. ⊠ *U.S. 158, MM 12,* ☎ *252/441–4200. Reservations not accepted. AE, D, MC, V. Closed Thanksgiving–Easter. No dinner Oct.–Easter.*

$$–$$$ ✕ **RV's.** If fiery red sunsets, spicy marinated tuna, sweet scallops, or peanut butter pie mean anything to you, head immediately to this busy place on the Causeway between Nags Head and Roanoke Island. It's where locals come to eat, drink, and take in serene views of Roanoke Sound. Both lunch and dinner are served. Seafood choices range from clam chowder to barbecued shrimp to piquant crab cakes and tuna. You can also get steak, ribs, and chicken. Portions are huge. There are a little pier outside and an attached indoor-outdoor gazebo where you can get a drink. The marvelous turtle cake is a dieter's nightmare, with chocolate, pecans, and caramel. ⊠ *Nags Head Manteo Causeway, MM 16.5,* ☎ *252/441–4963. Reservations not accepted. MC, V. Closed Dec.–Jan.*

$ ✕ **Sam & Omie's.** This charming, no nonsense little niche, named after two fishermen who were father and son, is the oldest restaurant in the Outer Banks. Fishing illustrations hang on the walls, and Merle Haggard plays in the background. It's open daily 7–7 and serves every imaginable kind of seafood, plus other items. The chef has been serving she-crab soup for 22 years, and it's easy to see why locals love it. Also, try the fine marinated tuna steak, Cajun tuna bites, or frothy crab–asparagus soup. Diehard fans claim that Sam & Omie's serves the best oysters on the beach. Dress is beach-casual. ⊠ *U.S. 158, MM 16.5,* ☎ *252/441–7366. Reservations not accepted. D, MC, V.*

$$$–$$$$ **First Colony Inn.** You'll get great ocean views from the verandas that
★ encircle this historic three-story B&B. Two rooms have wet bars, kitch-
enettes, and whirlpool baths; others have four-poster or canopy beds,
handcrafted armoires, and English antiques. All rooms offer extras, such
as heated towel bars. The entire property is no-smoking. ⊠ *6720 S.
Virginia Dare Trail, 27959,* ☎ *252/441–2343 or 800/368–9390,* FAX
252/441–9234, WEB *www.firstcolonyinn.com. 26 rooms. Picnic area,
microwaves, refrigerators, pool, beach, croquet, library, business ser-
vices. AE, D, MC, V. CP.*

Outdoor Activities and Sports

GOLF

Nags Head Golf Links (⊠ 5615 S. Seachase Dr., MM 15, ☎ 252/441–
8074 or 800/851–9404) has a par-71, 18-hole course with ocean views.

HANG GLIDING

Kitty Hawk Kites (⊠ U.S. 158, MM 13, ☎ 800/334–4777, WEB www.
kittyhawk.com) offers lessons and gear. It's the oldest (and biggest) hang-
gliding school on the East Coast.

Roanoke Island

10 mi southwest of Nags Head.

On a hot July day in 1587, 117 men, women, and children left their
boat and set foot on Roanoke Island to make the first permanent En-
glish settlement in the New World. Three years later they disappeared
without a trace, leaving a mystery that continues to intrigue histori-
ans. Today Roanoke Island is a sleepy, well-kept place; much of the
12-mi-long island remains wild. In summer Roanoke and its two vil-
lages—picturesque Manteo and Wanchese—come alive. You get to the
❸❹ island by taking U.S. 64/264 from the U.S. 158 Bypass. **Manteo** has
some sights related to the island's history, as well as an aquarium.

A history, educational, and cultural arts complex opposite the waterfront
🔆 in Manteo, **Roanoke Island Festival Park** includes the *Elizabeth II* State
Historic Site. Costumed interpreters conduct tours of the 69-ft ship, a
re-creation of a 16th-century vessel, except when it is on educational voy-
ages in the off-season (call ahead). The complex also has an interactive
museum, a fossil pit, plays, concerts, arts-and-crafts exhibitions, and spe-
cial programs. ⊠ *Downtown Manteo,* ☎ *252/475–1500; 252/475–
1506 for 24-hr event hot line,* WEB *www.roanokeisland.com.* 🎟 *$8.* ☉
Mar. and Nov.–Dec., daily 10–5; Apr.–Oct., daily 9–7.

Clustered together on the outskirts of Manteo are the lush **Elizabethan
Gardens,** a re-creation of a 16th-century English garden, established
as a memorial to the first English colonists. They contain antique stat-
uary, wildflowers, rose gardens, and a sunken garden and are impec-
cably maintained by the Garden Club of North Carolina. ⊠ *1411 U.S.
64/264, 3 mi north of downtown Manteo,* ☎ *252/473–3234,* WEB
www.outerbanks.com/elizabethangardens. 🎟 *$5.* ☉ *Mid-Sept.–May,
daily 9–5; June–early Sept., daily 9–8.*

Fort Raleigh National Historic Site is a restoration of the original 1585
earthworks that mark the beginning of English colonial history in
America. Be sure to see the orientation film and then take a guided tour
of the fort. A nature trail leads to an outlook over Roanoke Sound.
Native American and Civil War history is also preserved here. ⊠ *Off
U.S. 64/264, 3 mi north of Manteo,* ☎ *252/473–5772,* WEB *www.nps.
gov/fora.* 🎟 *Free.* ☉ *Daily 9–5; extended hrs in summer.*

GO FLY A GLIDER

FOR THRILL-SEEKING VACATIONERS there's little that compares with a morning flight over the dunes at Jockey's Ridge State Park. The premier hang-gliding outfitter in the country, **Kitty Hawk Kites** (☎ 800/334–4777, WEB www.kittyhawk.com), in Nags Head—in business since 1974—offers beginner dune lessons at the place where, almost exactly 100 years ago, flying began. If sheer volume has anything to do with it, you're in good hands: with about 10,000 students lifting off every year, Kitty Hawk Kites is the largest hang-gliding school in the world.

The only requirement (besides having a little gumption) is that you weigh between 85 and 225 lbs. It's not difficult to run your 50-pound glider—about the weight of a five-year-old—down a hill. Fortunately, your instructor hauls it back *up* the hill.

You can go hang-gliding year-round, though the warmer it is, the less likely you are to catch a breeze—which means spring and fall are excellent times to fly. Summer, when the dunes are golden, and with the ocean in the east and the islands of the Outer Banks stretching out before you as you take off to the south, is a stunning time of year.

Beginner dune lessons at Jockey's Ridge State Park, including an hour of ground school and a three-hour lesson (five flights), cost $85. The Taste of Flight package—one beginner dune lesson and a tandem Aero-tow to 2,000 ft—is $175. Tandem Aero-tow lessons over the Currituck Sound run March–November and cost $110–$260 per flight, depending on altitude (from 1,500 ft to a mile high). Ask about other combination packages and group rates.

— By Diane Mehta

☺ The **Lost Colony,** begun in 1937, is the country's first and longest-running outdoor drama. Staged at the Waterside Amphitheatre, it reenacts the story of the first colonists, who settled here in 1587 and then disappeared. ⊠ *1409 U.S. 64/264,* ☎ *252/473–3414 or 800/488–5012,* WEB *www.thelostcolony.org.* ⊠ *$16 (reservations essential).* ☺ *Performances June–Aug., Sun.–Fri. at 8:30 PM.*

☺ **Manteo Booksellers** stocks an admirable collection of books oriented to local attractions, cuisine, history, nature, and fiction. Local authors are featured, and author readings are frequent. It's easy to get captivated and browse here for a long time. The children's section is quite large, and the staff is helpful and friendly. ⊠ *105 Sir Walter Raleigh St., Downtown Manteo,* ☎ *252/473–1221,* WEB *www.manteobooksellers.com.* ☺ *Summer, weekdays 10–8, weekends 10–6; fall–spring, daily 10–6.*

☺ The **North Carolina Aquarium at Roanoke Island,** overlooking Croatan Sound, occupies 68,000 square ft. There are touch tanks and a shoreline boardwalk with observation decks. *The Graveyard of the Atlantic* is the centerpiece exhibit. It is a 285,000-gallon ocean tank containing the re-created remains of the USS *Monitor,* sunken off Hatteras Island. The aquarium hosts a slew of workshops and field trips, from feeding fishes to learning about medicinal aquatic plants to kids' workshops. ⊠ *374 Airport Rd., off U.S. 64,* ☎ *252/473–3493 for aquarium; 252/473–3494 for educational programs,* WEB *www.aquariums.state.nc.us.* ⊠ *$4.* ☺ *Daily 9–5.*

OFF THE
BEATEN PATH

EDENTON – Rich with history, North Carolina's first permanent settlement and the colony's first capital is a placid, immensely scenic place on the north side of the Albemarle Sound (65 mi west of Manteo). Originally incorporated in 1715 with the name the Towne on Queen Anne's Creek, the spot was renamed Edenton seven years later in honor of Governor Charles Eden. A fine collection of 18th-century buildings has been well maintained. Stop by the **visitor center** (⊠ 108 N. Broad St., ☎ 252/482–2637) to hear tales about the colonists, such as the women of the Edenton Tea Party, who fought for liberty. An inexpensive pamphlet serves as a guide on a 1½-mi walking tour. Guided tours of the historic district are available—and are recommended.

Dining and Lodging

$$-$$$
✕ **Weeping Radish Brewery and Restaurant.** This Bavarian-style restaurant and microbrewery is known for its German cuisine and the annual Oktoberfest weekend held after Labor Day, which showcases German and blues bands. Brewery tours are offered free of charge on request. The beer is superb. There's also a gift shop. ⊠ U.S. 64, Manteo, ☎ 252/473–1157, WEB www.weepingradish.com. D, MC, V.

$–$$
✕ **Full Moon Café.** Come at lunch or dinner to this wonderfully cheerful bistro near the waterfront, with high ceilings, bright blue walls, and red-and-green-flowered tablecloths. The herbed hummus with roasted pita is fantastic, as are the crab cakes. Light eaters beware: even the Waldorf salad comes with a million pecans and apples. Expect lots of cheese on any dish that includes it. Choices include salads, veggie wraps, quesadillas, Cuban-style enchiladas, Lowcountry shrimp and grits, burgers of all kinds, and a dozen innovative and hearty sandwiches. The café also serves specialty cocktails and maintains a thoughtful wine list. ⊠ 306 Queen Elizabeth Ave., Manteo, ☎ 252/473–6666. AE, D, DC, MC, V. No dinner Sun.

$
✕ **Magnolia Grille.** Freddy and Pam Ortega, cheerful New York transplants, run this new and immensely popular lunch and dinner spot on Manteo's downtown waterfront. Choose anything from lean, char-grilled chili cheeseburgers to deli sandwiches, quesadillas, salads, and hearty chicken dishes. Quirkier options include spicy shrimp jammers (battered, filled with jalapeño cheese, and fried) or the specials, such as fried oyster sandwiches or burgers topped with crabmeat. The place is hopping, even at breakfast; lunch gets the overflow from nearby Festival Park. Do like the locals do: get takeout and savor your sandwich by the waterfront. Or come for a stack of pancakes at breakfast; the restaurant opens daily at 7 AM. ⊠ 408 Queen Elizabeth St., Manteo, ☎ 252/475–9877. AE, D, MC, V. No dinner Sun.–Mon.

$$$-$$$$
✕🏠 **Tranquil House Inn.** This charming 19th-century-style waterfront inn is only a few steps from shops, restaurants, and the Roanoke Island Festival Park. The mood of the individually decorated rooms is cozy: handmade comforters, Oriental rugs, and hardwood floors. Complimentary wine and cheese are served in the evening. The popular restaurant, 1587 ($$$), is known for its chop-house-style cuts and other inventive entrées: char-grilled duck breast with black mission fig and dried cherry spiked Bordelaise and the cornmeal-crusted Rockfish fillet. ⊠ 405 Queen Elizabeth Ave., Box 2045, Manteo 27954, ☎ 252/473–1404 or 800/458–7069, FAX 252/473–1526, WEB www.1587.com. 25 rooms. Restaurant, bicycles, business services, meeting room. AE, D, MC, V. Closed Dec.–Jan. CP.

$–$$
🏠 **Scarborough Inn.** Off Manteo's main road, within walking distance of popular shops and restaurants and about 3 mi from the beach, the two-story Scarborough is modeled after a turn-of-the-20th-century inn. Each spacious room is decorated differently and includes family heirlooms as well as modern conveniences such as coffeemakers. Out-

side on the wraparound porch of each room are benches and rocking chairs. ✉ *524 U.S. 64/264, Manteo 27954,* ☎ *252/473–3979,* WEB *www. scarborough-inn.com. 12 rooms. Microwaves, room service, refrigerators, bicycles. AE, D, DC, MC, V. CP.*

Cape Hatteras National Seashore

Extends 70 mi south of Nags Head.

★ **Cape Hatteras National Seashore** has more than 70 mi of unspoiled beaches stretching from south Nags Head to Ocracoke Inlet across three narrow islands: Bodie, Hatteras, and Ocracoke. The islands are linked by Route 12 and the Hatteras Inlet ferry. This coastal area is ideal for swimming, surfing, windsurfing, diving, boating, and other water activities. It's easy to find your own slice of beach as you drive south down Route 12, but park only in designated areas. If you want to swim, beware of strong tides and currents—there are no lifeguard stations. Fishing piers are in Rodanthe, Avon, and Frisco.

Hatteras Island

15 mi south of Nags Head.

The Herbert C. Bonner Bridge arches for 3 mi over Oregon Inlet and carries traffic to Hatteras Island, known as the "blue marlin capital of the world." The island, a 33-mi-long ribbon of sand, juts out into the Atlantic Ocean; at its most distant point (Cape Hatteras), Hatteras is 25 mi from the mainland. About 85% of the island belongs to Cape Hatteras National Seashore, and the remainder is privately owned in seven small, quaint villages strung along Route 12, the island's fragile lifeline to points north.

③⑤ **Pea Island National Wildlife Refuge** is made up of more than 5,000 acres of marsh. This birder's delight, with observation platforms and spotting scopes, is on the Atlantic flyway: more than 265 species are sighted regularly, including endangered peregrine falcons and piping plovers. Route 12 travels through marsh areas, and you can hike or drive, depending on the terrain. A visitor center, 5 mi south of Oregon Inlet on Route 12, has an informational display. Remember to douse yourself in bug spray, especially in the spring. ✉ *Pea Island Refuge Headquarters, Rte. 12,* ☎ *252/473–1131.* ✆ *Free.* ☉ *May–Sept., daily 9–4; Oct.–Apr., Thurs.–Sun. 9–4.*

③⑥ In the village of Rodanthe, the restored 1911 **Chicamacomico Lifesaving Station** has a museum that tells the story of the 24 stations that once lined the Outer Banks. These were the precursors to today's Coast Guard. Living-history reenactments are performed June through August. ✉ *Off Rte. 12,* ☎ *252/987–1552,* WEB *www.chicamacomico.org.* ✆ *Free.* ☉ *Apr.–Oct., Tues.–Sat. 9–5.*

③⑦ **Cape Hatteras Lighthouse,** about 30 mi south of Rodanthe, is a beacon to ships offshore. It was the first lighthouse built in the region, after being authorized by Congress in 1794 to help prevent shipwrecks. At 208 ft it is the tallest brick lighthouse in the world, and it's painted with distinctive black-and-white spirals. Endangered by the sea, in 1999 the lighthouse was actually picked up and moved slightly inland to its present location. In summer the principal keeper's quarters are open for viewing. Offshore lie the remains of the USS *Monitor,* a Confederate ironclad ship that sank in 1862. ✉ *Hatteras Island Visitor Center, off Rte. 12 near Buxton,* ☎ *252/995–4474,* WEB *www.nps.gov/caha.* ✆ *Free.* ☉ *Visitor center daily 9–5; climbing Apr.–mid-Oct., daily 10–2; summer, daily 10–6.*

Dining

$$–$$$ ✕ **Tides.** Just south of the entrance for the Cape Hatteras Lighthouse, this place is popular for its good service, well-prepared food, and homey manner. In addition to offering the usual seafood, the menu has chicken and ham. It's also a popular breakfast spot. ⊠ *Rte. 12, Buxton,* ☎ *252/995–5988. MC, V. Closed Dec.–early Apr. No lunch.*

Ocracoke Island

38 *Southwest of Hatteras Island.*

Much of Ocracoke Island is part of Cape Hatteras National Seashore. A free ferry that leaves every hour during the day will take you from Hatteras to the island in 40 minutes; other ferries leave from the mainland. Ocracoke was cut off from the world for a long time, but now the island is somewhat of a refuge for people seeking peace and quiet. A village of shops, motels, and restaurants is around Silver Lake Harbor, where the pirate Blackbeard met his death in 1718. The **Ocracoke Lighthouse,** the oldest operating lighthouse in North Carolina—it can be seen from 14 mi out at sea—is unfortunately not open for climbing but is a photographer's dream. The **Ocracoke Island Visitor Center** (⊠ Ocracoke Village, south end of Rte. 12 on Silver Lake, ☎ 252/ 928–4531), run by the National Park Service, provides plenty of useful information.

Ocracoke Island **beaches** are among the least populated and most beautiful on the Cape Hatteras National Seashore. Four public access areas have parking as well as off-road vehicle access. At the **Ocracoke Pony Pen** (⊠ Rte. 12, 6 mi southwest of the Hatteras-Ocracoke ferry landing), you can observe from a platform what some believe are the direct descendants of Spanish mustangs that once roamed wild on the island.

Dining and Lodging

$$ ✕▭ **Island Inn and Dining Room.** The inn, built as a private lodge back in 1901, shows its age a bit but is full of Outer Banks character. The rooms in the modern wing are good for families. The large rooms in the Crow's Nest, on the third floor, have the most architectural interest—they have cathedral ceilings and look out over the island. The restaurant ($–$$) is known for its oyster omelet, crab cakes, and hush puppies. This is a no-smoking property. ⊠ *Lighthouse Rd. and Rte. 12, Box 9, 27960,* ☎ *252/928–4351; 877/456–3466 for inn; 252/928–7821 for dining room;* ℻ *252/928–4352,* ⧉ *www.ocracokeislandinn. com. 35 rooms, 4 villas. Restaurant, cable TV, pool, lobby lounge, airport shuttle. AE, MC, V.*

Cape Lookout National Seashore

Southwest of Ocracoke Island via Cedar Island.

★   **Cape Lookout National Seashore** extends for 55 mi from Portsmouth Island to Shackleford Banks and includes 28,400 acres of uninhabited land and marsh. The remote, sandy islands are linked to the mainland by private ferries. Ferry service is available from Harkers Island to the Cape Lookout Light area, from Davis to Shingle Point, from the Atlantic to an area north of Drum Inlet, and from Ocracoke to Portsmouth Village. Portsmouth, a deserted village that was inhabited from 1753 until the early 1970s, is being restored and is open to the public from April to early November. To the south, wild ponies roam Shackleford Banks. Four-wheel-drive vehicles are allowed on the beach, and primitive camping is available.

The Outer Banks A to Z

To research prices, get advice from other travelers, and book travel arrangements, visit www.fodors.com.

AIR TRAVEL

CARRIERS

Outer Banks Airways provides charter service between the Dare County Regional Airport and major cities along the East Coast, as does Flightline Aviation, which flies into the First Flight depot, at the Wright Memorial in Kill Devil Hill.

➤ AIRLINES AND CONTACTS: **Outer Banks Airways** (☎ 252/441–7677). **Flightline Aviation** (☎ 800/916–3226).

AIRPORTS

The closest commercial airports are Raleigh-Durham, a five-hour drive, and, in Virginia, Norfolk International, a 1½-hour drive.

➤ AIRPORT INFORMATION: **Dare County Regional Airport** (✉ 410 Airport Rd., Manteo, ☎ 252/473–2600, WEB www.fly2mqi.com). **Norfolk International** (✉ 2200 Norview Ave., ☎ 757/857–3351, WEB www.norfolkairport.com).

BOAT AND FERRY TRAVEL

Seagoing folks travel the Intracoastal Waterway through the Outer Banks and the Albemarle region. Boats may dock at nearly 150 marinas, including Elizabeth City, Manteo Waterfront Docks, and National Park Service Silver Lake Marina, in Ocracoke.

For information about the state-run ferry system and its schedules and costs, call the North Carolina Department of Transportation's ferry information line. From Ocracoke there are car ferries to Cedar Island and Swan Quarter on the mainland. You need a reservation for the ferry.

FARES AND SCHEDULES

➤ BOAT AND FERRY INFORMATION: **Elizabeth City** (☎ 252/338–2886). **Manteo Waterfront Docks** (☎ 252/473–3320). **National Park Service Silver Lake Marina** (☎ 252/928–5111). **North Carolina Department of Transportation Ferry Information** (☎ 800/293–3779).

CAR TRAVEL

U.S. 158 links the Outer Banks with U.S. 17 leading to Norfolk, Virginia, and other places north. Route 12 goes north toward Corolla and south toward Ocracoke.

EMERGENCIES

Dial 911 for emergencies on Oregon Inlet, Roanoke Island, Hatteras Island, and Ocracoke Island. The Healtheast/Outer Banks Medical Center is open 24 hours a day. Beach Medical Care provides help around the clock. The Outer Banks Hospital, which opened in spring 2002 in Nags Head, is open daily and has 24-hour emergency care. For Coast Guard assistance call the number listed below. A CVS Pharmacy is open weekdays 8:30 AM–9 PM, Sat. 8:30–6, and Sun. 10–6.

➤ DOCTORS AND DENTISTS: **Beach Medical Care** (✉ 5200 N. Croatan Hwy., MM 1.5, Kitty Hawk, ☎ 252/261–4187). **Healtheast/Outer Banks Medical Center** (✉ 2808 S. Croatan Hwy., Nags Head, ☎ 252/441–7111). **Outer Banks Hospital** (✉ 4800 S. Croatan Hwy., Nags Head, ☎ 252/449–4500).

➤ EMERGENCY SERVICES: **Ambulance, police** (☎ 911). **Coast Guard** (☎ 252/995–6411).

➤ PHARMACIES: **CVS** (✉ 1101 S. Croatan Hwy., Kill Devil Hill, ☎ 252/441–3633).

LODGING
CAMPING

Camping is permitted in four designated areas along the Cape Hatteras National Seashore. These campgrounds can serve tents, trailers, and motor homes. All camping at Cape Lookout National Seashore is in the primitive style and is allowed from mid-April through mid-October. Be sure to take extralong tent stakes for sand, and don't forget insect repellent. All sites are available on a first-come, first-served basis, except Ocracoke, where reservations are accepted. For information about private campgrounds contact the Dare County Tourist Bureau.

➤ CONTACTS: **Cape Hatteras National Seashore** (✉ 1401 National Park Dr., Manteo 27954, ☎ 252/473–2111, WEB www.nps.gov/caha). **Cape Lookout National Seashore** (✉ 131 Charles St., Harkers Island 28531, ☎ 252/728–2250). **Dare County Tourist Bureau** (☎ 252/473–2138 or 800/446–6262).

OUTDOORS AND SPORTS
FISHING

Fishing, whether surf casting or deep-sea, is wonderful here. You don't need a license for saltwater fishing. You can board a charter boat or head your own craft out of Oregon Inlet Fishing Center or Pirates Cove Yacht Club and Marina in Manteo. For fishing regulations, call the North Carolina Division of Marine Fisheries.

➤ CONTACTS: **North Carolina Division of Marine Fisheries** (☎ 252/726–7021). **Oregon Inlet Fishing Center** (☎ 252/441–6301 or 800/272–5199). **Pirates Cove Yacht Club and Marina** (☎ 252/473–3906 or 800/367–4728).

SCUBA DIVING

About 2,000 shipwrecks have occurred off the coast of the Outer Banks—which means scuba-diving options are virtually unlimited. The USS *Monitor* is off-limits, however. The USS *Huron* Historic Shipwreck Preserve, which lies offshore between mile markers 11 and 12, is a popular diving site. Full-service dive shops include the Outer Banks Dive Center.

➤ CONTACTS: **Outer Banks Dive Center** (✉ 3917 S. Croatan Hwy., Nags Head, ☎ 252/449–8349, WEB www.obxdive.com).

KAYAKING

Carolina Outdoors, part of Kitty Hawk Kites, operates sea-kayaking Ecotours along the banks of the villages Duck and Manteo (in the latter's downtown area) and through wildlife refuges, islands, and even a maritime forest. It also rents kayaks. Kitty Hawk Sports (a different company altogether, opposite Jockeys Ridge) rents kayaks to the public and offers surf-kayaking lessons and ecotours.

➤ CONTACTS: **Carolina Outdoors** (☎ 252/334–4777; 252/441–4124 for reservations, WEB www.kittyhawk.com). **Kitty Hawk Sports** (✉ U.S. 158, MM 13, Nags Head, ☎ 252/441–6800, WEB www.khsports.com).

WATER SPORTS

Surfing and windsurfing are excellent on the Outer Banks, and parasailing and kite surfing have become increasingly popular. For lessons and rentals contact Kitty Hawk Watersports, the oldest water-sports outfitter in the area, offering sailing, windsurfing, parasailing, jet skiing, kite boarding, and kayaking. (It also has a retail store, Kitty Hawk Sports, at mile marker 12 on U.S. 158.) Bert's Surf Shop rents surfboards, offers private lessons, and runs 3- and 5-day surf school programs; it also has a retail shop.

➤ CONTACTS: **Kitty Hawk Water Sports** (✉ U.S. 158, MM 16.5, Nags Head, ☎ 252/441–2756, WEB www.khsports.com). **Bert's Surf Shop** (✉ U.S. 158, MM 11, Nags Head, ☎ 252/441–1939).

TAXIS

Beach Cabs, based in Nags Head, offers 24-hour service from Norfolk to Ocracoke and towns in between; a ride to the Norfolk airport will run you about $140. Coastal Cab serves the Outer Banks—from the southern shores down to Nags Head—and charges you $135 to get to the airport. Coastal Limo, which serves the entire 100 mi stretch of the Outer Banks, is quite a bargain: $68 for one or two people from Nags Head, Kill Devil Hills, or Kitty Hawk to the Norfolk airport. If you're farther south or are going to the airport at odd hours, the price increases, depending on what you need. The Outer Banks Limousine Service, headquartered in Kill Devil Hills, serves the entire area and Norfolk International Airport and runs around the clock; getting to the airport costs about $125 from Nags Head, though fees vary depending on where you are and when you're going.

➤ TAXI COMPANIES: **Beach Cabs** (☎ 252/441–2500 or 800/441–2503). **Coastal Cab** (☎ 252/449–8787). **Coastal Limo** (☎ 252/441–2262). **Outer Banks Limousine Service** (☎ 252/261–3133 or 800/828–5466).

TOURS

Historic Albemarle Tour, Inc., runs guided tours of Edenton and publishes a brochure on self-guided tour of the Albemarle region.

Kitty Hawk AeroTours leaves from the First Flight Airstrip or from Manteo for Kitty Hawk, Corolla, Cape Hatteras, Ocracoke, Portsmouth Island, and other areas along the Outer Banks. Tours take place March through Labor Day.

➤ FEES AND SCHEDULES: **Historic Albemarle Tour, Inc.** (✉ 1 Harding Sq., Washington, ☎ 252/974–2950 or 800/734–1117, WEB www. historicalbemarletour.com). **Kitty Hawk AeroTours** (✉ behind Wright Brothers Monument, U.S. 158, MM 8, Kill Devil Hills, ☎ 252/441–4460).

TRAIN TRAVEL

Amtrak is available to Norfolk, Virginia, about 75 mi to the north, but it does not serve the Outer Banks.

➤ TRAIN INFORMATION: **Amtrak** (☎ 800/872–7245, WEB www.amtrak.com).

VISITOR INFORMATION

Dare County Tourist Bureau operates three information centers. The Aycock Brown Welcome Center is open daily 9–5:30 and offers extensive resources, including photos, maps, and ferry schedules. The smaller Hatteras Island Welcome Center is right before Bodie Island. This center is open from Memorial Day to October 1, daily 9–5, and on weekends in April, May, and November. The Outer Banks Welcome Center on Roanoke Island, in Manteo, opened in 2002 and is open daily 9–5. It's a state-of-the-art center with touch screens—you can pick up a phone, push a number, and be connected to an accommodation instantly.

The National Park Service's group headquarters, at the Fort Raleigh National Historic Site in Manteo, has a 24-hour general information line about Cape Hatteras National Seashore, or you can write the superintendent at the address listed below.

The National Park Service, Cape Lookout National Seashore, has information about visiting Cape Lookout.

➤ VISITOR INFORMATION: **Aycock Brown Welcome Center** (✉ U.S. 158, MM 1.25, Kitty Hawk 27949, ☎ 252/261–4644). **Dare County Tourist Bureau** (✉ 704 S. U.S. 64/264, Box 399, Manteo 27954, ☎ 252/473–2138 or 800/446–6262, WEB www.outerbanks.org). **Hatteras Island Welcome Center** (☎ no phone). **National Park Service, Cape Lookout National Seashore** (✉ 131 Charles St., Harkers Island 28531, ☎ 252/728–2250, WEB www.nps.gov/calo). **National Park Service's**

Group Headquarters (✉ 1401 National Park Dr., Manteo, ☎ 252/473–2111 for 24-hr general information, 〖WEB〗 www.nps.gov/fora). **National Park Service's superintendent** (✉ Rte. 1, Box 675, Manteo 27954). **Outer Banks Welcome Center on Roanoke Island** (✉ 1 Visitors Center Circle, Manteo 27954, ☎ 877/298–4373).

NEW BERN AND THE CENTRAL COAST

Craven County—where you'll find New Bern, a good chunk of the 157,000-acre Croatan National Forest, and Cherry Point, the world's largest Marine Corps air station—is by turns genteel and historic, modern and commercialized, rural and wild. Golfers, boaters, and a growing number of retirees find the area a haven.

Neighboring Carteret County, with nearly 80 mi of ocean coastline, is known as the Central, or Crystal, Coast. It is composed of the south-facing beaches along the barrier island Bogue Banks (Atlantic Beach, Pine Knoll Shores, Indian Beach, Salter Path, and Emerald Isle), three mainland townships (Morehead City, Beaufort, and Newport), and a series of small, unincorporated "down-east" communities traversed by a portion of U.S. 70 that's been designated a Scenic Byway.

New Bern

112 mi southeast of Raleigh.

The pace is quiet and slow in New Bern, the second-oldest town in North Carolina. Settled in 1710 by Swiss and German colonists and named for Bern, Switzerland, the city has a heraldic Swiss black bear symbol that is everywhere. New Bern, the state capital from the period of English rule until immediately after the revolution, is where North Carolina's first newspaper was printed and Pepsi-Cola was invented. History is taken seriously here; it has more than 150 sites included in the National Register of Historic Places.

Sailors and sun seekers will enjoy the area, as the Neuse and Trent rivers are perfect for such activities as waterskiing and crabbing. The historic downtown area is filled with shops, many of them selling antiques. As in much of North Carolina, golf is a favorite New Bern pastime.

The reconstructed **Tryon Palace,** an elegant Georgian building, was the colonial capital and the home of Royal Governor William Tryon during the 1770s. It was rebuilt according to architectural drawings of the original palace and furnished with English and American antiques according to Governor Tryon's inventory. An audiovisual orientation will prepare you for a tour of the house led by costumed guides. In summer actors deliver monologues detailing a day in the life of everyday citizens and the governor. Tours of the 18th-century formal gardens are self-guided. The stately **John Wright Stanly House** (circa 1783), the **Dixon-Stevenson House** (circa 1826), and the **New Bern Academy** (circa 1809) are within or near the 13-acre Tryon Palace complex. ✉ 610 Pollock St., ☎ 252/514–4900. 🎟 *Self-guided tours $8; tours of garden, kitchen office, and stables $7; tour of all bldgs. and gardens $15.* ⊙ *Late May–early Sept., Mon.–Sat. 9–7, Sun. 1–7; early Sept.–late May, Mon.–Sat. 9–5, Sun. 1–5.*

Dining and Lodging

$$–$$$ ✕ **The Chelsea.** This two-story restored 1912 structure, originally the second drugstore of the pharmacist who invented Pepsi-Cola, retains some fine architectural details, such as its tin ceiling. It's a magnet for weekenders, who look forward to selecting from sandwiches (wrapped, pita, and burgers), large salads, and entrées such as shrimp and grits. The bar

is well stocked, and Pepsi, of course, is the nonalcoholic drink of choice. ⊠ *335 Middle St.,* ☎ *252/637–5469,* WEB *www.thechelsea.com. AE, D, DC, MC, V.*

$$–$$$ ✕ **The Flame.** The considerate staff at this dark, woodsy steak house, with furnishings vaguely reminiscent of the Victorian era, helps make dinners special. Steak, lobster, grilled shrimp, and teriyaki chicken are all good bets. Sunday brunch is popular. ⊠ *2303 Neuse Blvd.,* ☎ *252/ 633–0262. AE, D, DC, MC, V. No dinner Sun. No lunch Mon.–Sat.*

$ ✕ **Pollock Street Deli.** Good-size crowds gather in the tiny rooms of an authentic colonial house in the historic district and its sidewalk tables for classic deli treats or Sunday brunch. Service can be leisurely. ⊠ *208 Pollock St.,* ☎ *252/637–2480. AE, MC, V. No dinner Sun.*

$$$ ⌂ **Sheraton New Bern Hotel and Marina.** At the confluence of the Neuse and Trent rivers, this Sheraton—with marina facilities—is actually two properties in one. A hotel has guest rooms overlooking the Trent River, and rooms at the inn have either waterfront or city views. ⊠ *100 Middle St., 28560,* ☎ *252/638–3585 or 888/625–5144,* FAX *252/638– 8112,* WEB *www.newbernsheraton.com. 150 rooms, 22 suites. Restaurant, room service, pool, marina, exercise room, 2 bars, concierge, business services, meeting room, airport shuttle. AE, D, DC, MC, V.*

$$ ⌂ **Bridge Pointe Hotel & Marina.** On the Trent River, just across the bridge from the historic section of New Bern, this property has standard rooms with above-average views of the rivers that circle the eastern side of the city. The grounds also include a small lake, on which a few ducks reside. Next door is a steak house. ⊠ *101 Howell Rd., 28562,* ☎ *252/636–3637 or 877/283–7713,* FAX *252/637–5028,* WEB *www.bridgepointehotel.com. 116 rooms. Restaurant, pool, marina, lounge, laundry service, meeting rooms. AE, D, DC, MC, V.*

$$ ⌂ **Harmony House Inn.** This historic B&B has a fascinating past. At
★ one point, two brothers sawed the house in half, creating double hallways and stairs and a dividing wall. Today the only external hint of the dual identity is the double front doors. You sleep in spacious rooms that lodged Yankee soldiers during the Civil War. Rooms are furnished with a mix of antiques and reproductions. Complimentary white and dessert wines are served in the evening. ⊠ *215 Pollock St., 28560,* ☎ *252/636–3810 or 800/636–3113,* FAX *252/636–3810,* WEB *www. harmonyhouseinn.com. 10 rooms. Dining room, business services, airport shuttle. AE, D, MC, V. BP.*

Morehead City

35 mi southeast of New Bern.

Morehead City is a fishing and boating center across Bogue Sound from the barrier island Bogue Banks. Popular family beaches on the island are **Atlantic Beach** and **Emerald Isle.** Among the more developed areas are these beach towns, as well as Pine Knoll Shores.

☾ The **North Carolina Aquarium at Pine Knoll Shores,** in a maritime forest on Bogue Banks, has a 2,000-gallon salt-marsh tank with live alligators, a loggerhead turtle nursery, and a shipwreck exhibit. ⊠ *Salter Path Rd., MM 7, Atlantic Beach,* ☎ *252/247–4004,* WEB *www. aquariums.state.nc.us.* ▨ *$3.* ☉ *Daily 9–5.*

Dining and Lodging

$$–$$$ ✕ **Bistro by the Sea.** Although the stonework and stucco exterior hint at the Mediterranean style within, the cuisine defies any particular theme. Beef, chicken, and seafood all share space on the menu—favorites include stir-fry chicken with rice and wontons; and *capellini* tossed with pesto, fresh scallops, and vegetables. Vegetables are always garden fresh, and the service is consistently friendly. There are also a piano bar and cigar lounge. ✉ *4301 Arendell St.,* ☎ *252/247–2777. MC, V. Closed Sun.–Mon. in Jan. No lunch.*

\$\$–\$\$\$ ✕ **Sanitary Fish Market & Restaurant.** In 1938, when the Sanitary was founded, many fish houses were ill kept. The owners wanted to signal that theirs was different. Clean, simple, and generous are by-words at this waterfront place where diners sit on wooden benches. It can get noisy (the restaurant seats 600), but people from around the world gush about the food. ✉ *501 Evans St.,* ☎ *252/247–3111,* WEB *www.sanitaryfishmarket.com. D, MC, V. Closed Dec.–Jan.*

\$\$ 🏨 **Best Western Buccaneer.** The inn sits beside the Morehead Plaza shopping center, a 10-minute drive from Atlantic Beach. Rooms are attractive and comfortable. ✉ *2806 Arendell St., 28557,* ☎ *252/726–3115 or 800/682–4982,* FAX *252/726–3864,* WEB *www.bestwestern.com. 91 rooms. Restaurant, refrigerators, pool, bar, exercise room, business services, meeting room. AE, D, DC, MC, V. BP.*

\$\$ 🏨 **Windjammer Inn.** If you're focused on one thing—easy access to the ocean—this is the place for you. What you get here is straightforward—a comfortable oversize room with a private balcony and ocean view. The five-story, glass-enclosed elevator sets the inn apart from typical beach lodging. There's a two-night minimum stay on summer weekends. ✉ *Salter Path Rd. in Pine Knoll Shores, Atlantic Beach 28512,* ☎ *252/247–7123 or 800/233–6466,* FAX *252/247–0133,* WEB *www.windjammerinn. com. 46 rooms. Refrigerators, pool. AE, D, MC, V.*

Beaufort

3 mi east of Morehead City.

Beaufort, a small seaport with a bustling boardwalk, brims with charm. The third-oldest town in North Carolina, it was named for Henry Somerset, duke of Beaufort. Boat rides of all types are available for a fee at the town docks on Taylor's Creek.

The **Beaufort Historic Site,** in the center of town, consists of restored buildings dating from 1767 to 1859, including the **Carteret County Courthouse** and the **Apothecary Shop and Doctor's Office.** Don't miss the **Old Burying Grounds** (1731). Here Otway Burns, a privateer in the War of 1812, is buried under his ship's cannon; a nine-year-old girl who died at sea is buried in a rum keg; and an English soldier saluting the king is buried upright in his grave. Tours on an English-style double-decker bus and guided walking tours depart from the visitor center. ✉ *130 Turner St.,* ☎ *252/728–5225,* WEB *www.historicbeaufort.com.* 🎫 *Bus tour \$6, bus and walking tour \$10.* ☉ *Visitor center Easter–Oct., Mon.–Sat. 9:30–5, Sun. 1:30–4; Nov.–Easter, Mon.–Sat. 10–4, Sun. 1:30–4.*

Beaufort's **North Carolina Maritime Museum** documents the state's seafaring history and includes an exhibit about the infamous pirate Blackbeard and the discovery of his flagship near Beaufort Inlet. The museum includes the **Watercrafts Center,** across the street, which gives boatbuilding classes. Its education staff also provides year-round programs, including trips to the marsh and barrier islands. ✉ *315 Front St.,* ☎ *252/728–7317.* 🎫 *Free.* ☉ *Museum weekdays 9–5, Sat. 10–5, Sun. 1–5; watercrafts center Tues.–Fri. 9–5, Sat. 10–5, Sun. 1–5.*

Dining and Lodging

\$\$–\$\$\$ ✕ **Clawson's 1905 Restaurant and Pub.** Housed in what was a general store in the early 1900s and stuffed with memorabilia, Clawson's serves hearty food such as ribs, steaks, pasta, and local seafood. It gets very crowded in summer, so arrive early for both lunch and dinner. The coffee bar, Fishtowne Java, opens at 7 AM. ✉ *425 Front St.,* ☎ *252/*

Close-Up

NORTH CAROLINA'S PIRATES

NORTH CAROLINA'S COAST was a magnet for marauding sea dogs during the golden age of piracy, a period that spanned the 17th and 18th centuries. Among those who visited was Stede Bonnet, captured in the Cape Fear region in 1718 but able to escape; Anne Bonny, daughter of a plantation owner, wife of one pirate and lover of another; Charles Vane, whose crew mutinied; and Paul Williams, who accepted King George I's pardon, only to return to piracy.

The most notorious buccaneer of them all was Blackbeard, whose two-year reign of terror began in 1716: cultivating fear by strapping on six pistols and six knives, tying his luxuriant beard into pigtails and, legend has it, lighting matches under his hat to give the illusion that his head was smoking, Blackbeard attacked ships in the Caribbean and settlements along the coasts of Virginia and the Carolinas.

At least three of his ships sank in North Carolina's waters; archaeologists are retrieving artifacts from what is likely the flagship, *Queen Anne's Revenge,* which ran aground on a sandbar near Beaufort Inlet in May 1718. The following November a seafaring posse caught Blackbeard in one his favorite playgrounds, Ocracoke Inlet. The pirate was decapitated and his head hung from a conquering ship. Still sought are the hulks of Blackbeard's lost ships and his treasure.

— By Lisa H. Towle

728–2133, WEB *www.clawsonsrestaurant.com.* D, MC, V. Closed Sun., Sept.–Apr.

$$–$$$ 🏠 **The Cedars by the Sea.** Two side-by-side homes (circa 1768 and 1851) and a private cottage make up this romantic B&B in the historic district. All rooms are individually and elegantly decorated and reflect an eye for detail. They combine contemporary and antique furnishings from world travels, and many have fireplaces, four-poster beds, and original art. There's a small wine bar. The gardens are a favorite spot for wedding receptions. ✉ *305 Front St., 28516,* ☎ *252/728–7036 or 800/732–7036,* FAX *252/728–1685,* WEB *www.cedarsinn.com. 10 rooms. Dining room. AE, D, MC, V. BP.*

New Bern and the Central Coast A to Z

To research prices, get advice from other travelers, and book travel arrangements, visit www.fodors.com.

AIR TRAVEL

CARRIERS

➤ AIRLINES AND CONTACTS: **Midway** (☎ 800/446–1392, WEB www.midwayair.com). **US Airways Express** (☎ 800/428–4322, WEB www.usair.com).

AIRPORTS

US Airways Express and Midway fly into Craven County Regional Airport, where charter service and car rentals are available.
➤ AIRPORT INFORMATION: **Craven County Regional Airport** (✉ U.S. 70, New Bern, ☎ 252/638–8591).

BOAT AND FERRY TRAVEL

The Intracoastal Waterway provides access to many Central Coast destinations, including Beaufort, Morehead City, and Emerald Isle. Beaufort has plentiful anchorage and more than 35 marinas, including the Beaufort Town Docks and the Morehead City Yacht Basin.

New Bern can be reached via the Neuse River from Pamlico Sound. Several marinas are available here, including the Sheraton Grand Marina. You can dock for the day (but not overnight) at the public docks of Union Point Park.

For information about the state-run ferry system, call the North Carolina Department of Transportation's ferry information line.

FARES AND SCHEDULES
➤ BOAT AND FERRY INFORMATION: **Beaufort Town Docks** (☎ 252/728–2053). **Ferry information line** (☎ 800/293–3779). **Morehead City Yacht Basin** (☎ 252/726–6862). **Sheraton Grand Marina** (☎ 252/638–3585). **Union Point Park** (☎ 252/636–4060).

BUS TRAVEL

Greyhound/Carolina Trailways serves Morehead City and New Bern.
➤ BUS INFORMATION: **Greyhound/Carolina Trailways** (☎ 800/231–2222, WEB www.greyhound.com).

CAR TRAVEL

U.S. 70 connects New Bern, Morehead City, and Beaufort with points to the west, including Raleigh and I–95. East of Beaufort, U.S. 70 connects to Route 12, which continues on the Outer Banks via ferry. U.S. 17 leads north from New Bern toward the Albemarle region and south to Wilmington.

EMERGENCIES

For emergencies contact Carteret General Hospital, in Morehead City, or Craven Regional Medical Center, in New Bern.
➤ EMERGENCY SERVICES: **Ambulance, police** (☎ 911). **Coast Guard assistance** (☎ 252/247–4598).
➤ HOSPITALS: **Carteret General Hospital** (✉ 3500 Arendell St., ☎ 252/247–1616). **Craven Regional Medical Center** (✉ 2300 Neuse Blvd., ☎ 252/633–8111).

OUTDOORS AND SPORTS

BEACHES
Route 58 passes through all of the beach communities on the Bogue Banks, and locations are noted by mile markers (MM). Points of public access along the shoreline are marked by orange-and-blue signs. Lifeguards monitor some of the beaches. You can fish, swim, picnic, and hike at Fort Macon State Park, outside Morehead City.
➤ CONTACTS: **Fort Macon State Park** (☎ 252/726–3775).

FISHING
The Atlantic Beach King Mackerel Tournament (☎ 252/247–2334) is held on the Crystal Coast in September, and one of the largest and oldest sportfishing contests, the Big Rock Blue Marlin Tournament, is held in various locations each June. Fishing piers are found mostly on Bogue Banks and are closed during the winter. Dozens of charter boats operate year-round. In New Bern bass-fishing tournaments are popular.

GOLF
Golf courses are abundant, and locals prefer to play in the spring and fall months, when it's cooler. For a list of courses and help with reservations, contact the Crystal Coast Regional Golf Association. Two no-

table courses are the par-72, 18-hole course at Carolina Pines Golf and Country Club, off Route 70, between New Bern and Havelock, and the par-72, 18-hole course designed by Rees Jones at the semiprivate Emerald Golf Club, on the Route 70 Bypass.

➤ CONTACTS: **Carolina Pines Golf and Country Club** (✉ 390 Carolina Pines Blvd., ☎ 252/444–1000). **Crystal Coast Regional Golf Association** (✉ 801 Arendell St., Box 1193, Morehead City 28557, ☎ 888/991–7529). **Emerald Golf Club** (✉ 5000 Clubhouse Dr., ☎ 252/633–4440).

SCUBA DIVING

Morehead City is considered one of North America's top scuba-diving destinations by many. Two popular wreck sites are the *Schurz*, sunk in World War I, and the *Papoose*, a World War II tanker inhabited by docile sand sharks. The Olympus Dive Center has five dive boats and offers full- and half-day charters, equipment rental, and lessons.

➤ CONTACTS: **Olympus Dive Center** (✉ 713 Shephard St., Morehead City, ☎ 252/726–9432, WEB www.olympusdiving.com).

TAXI

A-1 Yellow Cab Co. serves Atlantic Beach, Beaufort, Morehead City, and the airport. Cherry Cab operates in the New Bern area.

➤ TAXI COMPANIES: **A-1 Yellow Cab Co.** (☎ 252/240–2700). **Cherry Cab** (☎ 252/447–3101).

VISITOR INFORMATION

The Carteret County Tourism Development Bureau operates two visitor centers, one in Morehead City and one on Route 58 just north of the Cameron Langston Bridge to Emerald Isle.

➤ TOURIST INFORMATION: **Carteret County Tourism Development Bureau** (✉ 3409 Arendell St., Morehead City 28557, ☎ 800/786–6962; ✉ 263 Rte. 58, Swansboro 28584, ☎ 252/393–3100, WEB www.sunnync.com). **Craven County Convention and Visitors Bureau** (✉ 314 S. Front St., New Bern 28560, ☎ 252/637–9400 or 800/437–5767, WEB www.visitnewbern.com).

WILMINGTON AND THE CAPE FEAR COAST

The Wilmington/Cape Fear Coast area, between the Cape Fear River and the Atlantic Ocean near the south end of the North Carolina coast, is simultaneously a beach resort and a shipping and trading center. Artists, golfers, history buffs, naturalists, and shoppers will all find something of interest here. The old seaport town of Wilmington has much to celebrate these days, including a once-decayed downtown that has been transformed with upscale places to shop and dine. On the surrounding Cape Fear Coast, you can tour old plantation houses and azalea gardens, study sea life at the state aquarium, or bask in the sun at nearby beaches.

Wilmington

130 mi south of Raleigh.

The city's long history, including its part in the American Revolution and its role as the main port of the Confederacy, is revealed in sights downtown and in the surrounding area. Chandler's Wharf, the Cotton Exchange, and Water Street Market are old buildings now used as shopping and entertainment centers. *Henrietta II*, a paddle wheeler similar to those that plied the waters of the Cape Fear River, has been put into service as a tourist vessel. Wilmington, also a college town, has special annual events such as the Azalea Festival, North Carolina Jazz Festival, Christmas candlelight tours, and fishing tournaments.

At the **USS *North Carolina* Battleship Memorial** you can tour a ship that participated in every major naval offensive in the Pacific during World War II. The self-guided tour takes about two hours, and a 10-minute film is shown throughout the day. Narrated tours on cassette can be rented. Warning: a climb down into the ship's interior is not for the claustrophobic. The ship can be reached by car or by taking the river taxi from Riverfront Park, Memorial Day through Labor Day, at a cost of $2 per person. ⊠ *Junction of U.S. 74/76 and U.S. 17 and 421, west bank of Cape Fear River, Downtown,* ☎ *910/251–5797,* WEB *www. battleshipnc.com.* ☎ *$8.* ☉ *Mid-May–mid-Sept., daily 8–8; mid-Sept.– mid-May, daily 8–5.*

The **Cotton Exchange,** a shopping-dining complex, is in a rambling restored cotton warehouse on the Cape Fear River in an area that has flourished as a trading center since pre–Civil War days. ⊠ *321 N. Front St., Downtown,* ☎ *910/343–9896,* WEB *www.shopcottonexchange.com.*

The **Cape Fear Museum** traces the natural, cultural, and social history of the lower Cape Fear region from its beginnings to the present. One exhibit follows the youth of one of Wilmington's most famous native sons, basketball superstar Michael Jordan. ⊠ *814 Market St., Downtown,* ☎ *910/341–7413.* ☎ *$5.* ☉ *Early Sept.–late May, Tues.–Sat. 9–5, Sun. 1–5; late May–early Sept., daily 9–5.*

Built in 1770 on the foundations of a jail, the **Burgwin-Wright Museum House** is a fine restoration of a colonial gentleman's town house and includes seven distinct period gardens. Open-hearth cooking demonstrations are presented one Saturday each month (call ahead). In April 1781 General Cornwallis used the house as his headquarters. ⊠ *224 Market St., Downtown,* ☎ *910/762–0570.* ☎ *$5.* ☉ *Tues.–Sat. 10–4.*

St. John's Museum of Art is known for its originals by Mary Cassatt, as well as for its works by North Carolina artists. Up to a dozen temporary exhibitions annually highlight art from many different parts of the world. The museum is housed in three buildings, including the 1804 Masonic Lodge Building, the oldest such lodge in the state. There is also a sculpture garden. ⊠ *114 Orange St., Downtown,* ☎ *910/763–0281,* WEB *www.stjohnsmuseum.com.* ☎ *$3.* ☉ *Tues.–Sat. 10–5, Sun. noon–4.*

The **Zebulon Latimer House,** built in 1852 in the Italianate style, is a reminder of opulent antebellum living. The Lower Cape Fear Historical Society is based here; it offers guided walking tours of the downtown historic district that depart from the house on Wednesday and Saturday mornings at 10. ⊠ *126 S. 3rd St., Downtown,* ☎ *910/762–0492,* WEB *latimer.wilmington.org.* ☎ *$6.* ☉ *Weekdays 10–4, weekends noon–5.*

Chandler's Wharf (⊠ 225 S. Water St., Downtown), on the Cape Fear River, contains shops and some seafood restaurants, such as Elijah's. It's a great place to conclude a tour of downtown Wilmington.

Greenfield Park offers picnic spots, bike paths, nature trails, and canoe and paddleboat rentals on a 150-acre lake bordered by cypress trees laden with Spanish moss. In April the park is ablaze with azaleas. ⊠ *S. 3rd St. (U.S. 421), 1 mi south of downtown, South Metro,* ☎ *910/ 341–7852.* ☎ *Free.* ☉ *Daily.*

At **Poplar Grove Historic Plantation,** an 1850 Greek Revival manor house 9 mi northeast of downtown, you can tour the manor house and outbuildings, see crafts demonstrations, shop in the country store, and pet the farm animals. ⊠ *10200 U.S. 17, North Metro,* ☎ *910/686–9989,* WEB *www.poplargrove.com.* ☜ *Guided tours $7.* ☉ *Feb.–Dec., Mon.– Sat. 9–5, Sun. noon–5.*

The **New Hanover County Arboretum** has 33 exhibits, including magnolia and patio gardens, 100 varieties of shade-loving camellias, a salt-spray garden, and a children's garden with a maze. ⊠ *6206 Oleander Dr., Midtown,* ☎ *910/452–6393.* ☜ *Free.* ☉ *Daily sunrise–sunset.*

OFF THE
BEATEN PATH

MOORE'S CREEK NATIONAL BATTLEFIELD – Military history buffs will appreciate this site, where American patriots defeated the Loyalists in 1776. The 85-acre park is also a wildlife habitat. ⊠ *200 Moores Creek Rd., Currie, 20 mi northwest of Wilmington on Rte. 210,* ☎ *910/283– 5591,* WEB *www.nps.gov/mocr.* ☜ *Free.* ☉ *Daily 8–5.*

Dining and Lodging

$$–$$$ ✕ **Pilot House.** This Chandler's Wharf restaurant is known for its seafood, pastas, fresh vegetables, and Carolina seafood bisque. You can dine indoors at tables with linen tablecloths secured by vases of fresh flowers or outdoors overlooking the Cape Fear River. Sunday brunch, which starts at 11:30, is popular. ⊠ *2 Ann St., Downtown,* ☎ *910/ 343–0200,* WEB *www.pilothouserest.com. AE, D, DC, MC, V.*

$$–$$$ ✕ **Water Street Restaurant and Sidewalk Café.** A restored two-story brick waterfront warehouse dating from 1835 holds an outdoor café and restaurant that serves up Greek, Mexican, and Middle Eastern dishes, as well as salads, pitas, burgers, and pasta. Seafood chowder is made daily on the premises. ⊠ *5 Water St., Downtown,* ☎ *910/343–0042. AE, MC, V.*

$–$$ ✕ **K-38 Baja Grill.** K-38 refers to the popular surfers' side road in Baja, Mexico, that leads to ideal waves—and the menu heavily references Baja culinary traditions. You won't find Americanized Mexican fare here; instead, sample tricolor corn tortillas with shrimp, scallops, and crab with cheese and roasted garlic cream, and chicken breast baked with artichokes, sun-dried tomatoes, green-chili pesto, and goat cheese cream. Rice, grilled vegetables, and fresh fruit accompany many dishes. ⊠ *5410 Oleander Dr., Midtown,* ☎ *910/395–6040,* WEB *www.k38baja. com. AE, D, MC, V.*

$$$–$$$$ ☷ **The Wilmingtonian.** Many clients at this historic garden-laced complex are businesspeople and members of the entertainment industry. Former commercial buildings, an antebellum home, and a convent have been meticulously transformed into luxurious suites, each in a different theme—classic movies, nautical heritage, country French, and so on. Many rooms have gas fireplaces and large whirlpool tubs. It's best for older children. ⊠ *101 S. 2nd St., Downtown, 28401,* ☎ *910/343– 1800 or 800/525–0909,* FAX *910/251–1149,* WEB *www.thewilmingtonian. com. 40 suites. Room service, in-room VCRs, library, laundry service, business services, meeting room. AE, D, DC, MC, V. CP.*

$$$ ☷ **Hilton-Riverside.** Overlooking the Cape Fear River on one side and the city on the other, the spacious Hilton is one of the most convenient places to stay in town. The lobby is plush; guest rooms are traditional, with dark woods and autumn colors. Rollicking parties are held poolside on summer weekends. ⊠ *301 N. Water St., Downtown, 28401,* ☎ *910/763–5900 or 800/445–8667,* FAX *910/763–0038,* WEB *www. wilmingtonhilton.com. 263 rooms, 11 suites. Restaurant, pool, exercise room, dock, bar, concierge floor, business services, meeting room, airport shuttle. AE, D, DC, MC, V.*

$$ ☷ **Catherine's Inn.** This two-story Italianate home, built in 1883 in what is now a historic district overlooking the Cape Fear River, is a B&B with

hardwood floors, a sunken garden, four-poster and canopy beds, and phones in each room. Many items were collected by the innkeepers over the years. Coffee is delivered to your door every morning. This is the only inn in the area with a direct river view. ⊠ *410 S. Front St., Downtown, 28401,* ☎ *910/251–0863 or 800/476–0723,* FAX *910/772–9550,* WEB *www.catherinesinn.com. 5 rooms. Dining room, library. MC, V. BP.*

$$ 🖫 **Hampton Inn.** This moderately priced chain motel is only 3 mi from downtown and 6 mi from Wrightsville Beach. Perks include in-room movies and free local calls. ⊠ *5107 Market St., Midtown, 28403,* ☎ *910/395–5045 or 800/426–7866,* FAX *910/799–1974,* WEB *www. hampton-inn.com. 118 rooms. Pool, exercise room, laundry service, business services, meeting room. AE, D, DC, MC, V. CP.*

Nightlife and the Arts

THE ARTS

The city has its own symphony orchestra, oratorio society, civic ballet, and concert association; and the North Carolina Symphony makes four appearances here each year. The annual **North Carolina Jazz Festival,** held in February, and the **Cape Fear Blues Festival,** in July, draw crowds. **Thalian Hall Center for the Performing Arts** (⊠ 310 Chestnut St., Downtown, ☎ 910/343–3664 or 800/523–2820), an opera house built between 1855 and 1858 and restored to its former grandeur, hosts more than 250 theater, dance, and musical performances each year. Theatrical productions are staged by the Thalian Association, Opera House Productions, and Tapestry Players.

NIGHTLIFE

Alleigh's (⊠ 4925 New Centre Dr., Midtown, ☎ 910/793–0999) suits many tastes, with a restaurant and five entertainment areas, including a game room, sports bar, and jazz/blues club. **Charley Brownz** (⊠ 21 S. Front St., Downtown, ☎ 910/245–9499) has nightly musical entertainment that ranges from reggae and rock to karaoke and DJ dance music.

Outdoor Activities and Sports

There are approximately 40 public-access golf courses in the Greater Wilmington area. **Beau Rivage Resort Golf Club** (⊠ 649 Rivage Promenade, South Metro, ☎ 910/392–9022 or 800/628–7080) is a par-72 course in a natural links setting. The **Cape Golf & Racquet Club** (⊠ 535 The Cape Blvd., Carolina Beach, ☎ 910/799–3110) is a par-72 resort course with 24 lakes and ponds and a driving range.

South Brunswick County, about 30–40 mi from Wilmington on the coast, has lots of wonderful golfing, especially the areas around Calabash, Sunset Beach, and Ocean Isle. **Lockwood Folly Golf Links** (⊠ 100 Club House Dr., Holden Beach, ☎ 910/842–5666 or 877/562–9663) is a semiprivate highly rated par-72 resort course. **Marsh Harbour Golf Links** (⊠ Rte. 179, Calabash, ☎ 910/579–3161 or 800/552–2660) has a highly rated par-71 course, offering views of marsh and marina activity. The par-70 **Oyster Bay Golf Links** (⊠ Rte. 179, Sunset Beach, ☎ 910/579–3528 or 800/552–2660) is known for its oyster-shell hazards and gator sightings. **Sea Trail Resort** (⊠ 211 Clubhouse Rd., Sunset Beach, ☎ 910/579–4350 or 800/624–6601) has three courses designed by Dan Maples, Rees Jones, and Willard Byrd, all of which are par 72.

Wrightsville Beach

12 mi east of Wilmington.

Wrightsville Beach is a small, quiet island community that's very family oriented. It has a number of fine restaurants, and beaches good for swimming, boating, and surfing.

Dining and Lodging

$$–$$$ ✕ **Oceanic Restaurant and Grill.** Thanks to three floors of seating, you'll have a panoramic view of the Atlantic for miles around—a great backdrop for the fresh seafood, steaks, and chicken. Dinner on the pier at sunset is a treat. ⊠ *703 S. Lumina St.,* ☏ *910/256–5551. AE, MC, V.*

$$$$ ✕⊟ **Blockade Runner Resort Hotel and Conference Center.** This oceanside complex is widely known for its Ocean Terrace Restaurant and supervised summer children's programs. Guest rooms, done in bright colors, overlook either the Intracoastal Waterway or, for a higher price, the ocean. Service can be uneven, especially at the height of the season, but the hotel's beachfront location and guaranteed parking keep them coming back. Spa privileges are another plus. The Ocean Terrace ($$–$$$, reservations essential) attracts crowds with its weekend buffets and jazz brunch on Sunday. Two-night minimum spring through fall weekends. ⊠ *275 Waynick Blvd., 28480,* ☏ *910/256–2251 or 800/541–1161,* FAX *910/256–5502,* WEB *www.blockade-runner.com. 147 rooms, 3 suites. Restaurant, refrigerators, indoor-outdoor pool, health club, beach, boating, parasailing, bicycles, volleyball, bar, children's programs, business services, meeting room, airport shuttle. AE, D, DC, MC, V.*

Kure Beach

17 mi south of Wilmington.

Kure Beach is a resort community that's a bit livelier than Wrightsville Beach as it's next to Carolina Beach, which has amusement parks and a boardwalk with bars. Historic site Fort Fisher and the North Carolina Aquarium (closed for renovations until at least mid-2002) provide further interest. In some places twisted live oaks still grow behind the dunes. The community has miles of beaches; public access points are marked by orange-and-blue signs.

Fort Fisher State Historic Site marks the largest and one of the most important earthworks fortifications in the South during the Civil War. A reconstructed battery and Civil War relics and artifacts from sunken blockade-runners are on site. The fort is part of the **Fort Fisher Recreation Area,** with 4 mi of undeveloped beach. ⊠ *U.S. 421,* ☏ *910/458–5538.* ▨ *Free.* ☉ *Apr.–Oct., Mon.–Sat. 9–5, Sun. 1–5; Nov.–Mar., Tues.–Sat. 10–4, Sun. 1–4.*

Dining and Lodging

$$–$$$ ✕ **Big Daddy's.** You can't miss this place—the huge sign outside sits next to the only stoplight in town. Inside the enormity continues: three dining areas seat nearly 500 people. And the menu is substantial, with more than 40 items. Although some chicken, steak, and prime rib are thrown in for good measure, seafood stars. It comes prepared almost any way you could want it, and portions are large. ⊠ *202 K Ave.,* ☏ *910/458–8622. AE, D, MC, V. Closed late Nov.–Feb.*

$$$ ⊟ **Docksider Inn.** The nautical theme is no surprise given that this hotel is just yards from the beach. The inn is furnished in light-color beach-type furniture. Owners Kip and Maureen Darling have another property a block away on Atlantic Avenue. The five contemporary luxury suites of Darlings by the Sea are for adults only. Each has an expansive ocean view, custom drapes, bed skirting, and cabinetry. There are whirlpools for two and wet bars. ⊠ *202 Fort Fisher Blvd. (U.S. 421), 28449,* ☏ *910/458–4200 or 800/383–8111,* FAX *910/458–6468,* WEB *www.docksiderinn.com. 34 rooms. Pool, beach. AE, D, MC, V.*

Southport

30 mi south of Wilmington.

This small town, which sits quietly at the mouth of the Cape Fear River, is listed on the National Register of Historic Places. An increasingly desirable retirement spot, Southport retains its village charm and character. Stately and distinctive homes, antiques stores, gift shops, and restaurants line streets that veer to accommodate ancient oak trees. The town, portrayed in Robert Ruark's novel *The Old Man and the Boy*, is ideal for walking; it's also popular with moviemakers—*Crimes of the Heart* was filmed here.

If you're approaching the town from Fort Fisher and Route 421, the **Southport–Fort Fisher Ferry,** a state-operated car ferry, provides a river ride between Old Federal Point at the tip of the spit and the mainland. The Old Baldy Lighthouse, on Bald Head Island, is seen en route. It's best to arrive 30 minutes prior to ferry departure, as it's first come, first served. ☎ 910/458–3329 or 800/293–3779. ⌨ *$3 per car.* ⊙ *Ferries run mid-Mar.–mid-Nov., daily every 45 mins 6:15 AM–9:15 PM; mid-Nov.–mid-Mar., daily every 1½ hrs 6:15 AM–4:45 PM.*

Lodging

$$–$$$ ⊡ **Bald Head Island Resort.** Reached by ferry from Southport, this private, self-contained, carless community complete with grocery store and restaurants has bleached-wood villas and shingle cottages. You can explore the semitropical island on foot, by bicycle, or in a golf cart. Pastimes are doing all manner of warm-weather outdoor activities, climbing to the top of the lighthouse, watching the loggerhead turtles, and taking a guided tour through the maritime forest. Accommodations include fully equipped rental condos, villas, cottages, and B&Bs; a two-night minimum stay is required. The ferry (☎ 910/457–5003) costs $15 per person round-trip and runs on the hour, 8–6 (except noon on weekdays), from Southport. Advance reservations are necessary for both the ferry and resort. ⊠ *Bald Head Island, 28461,* ☎ *910/457–5000 or 800/432–7368,* 𝐅𝐀𝐗 *910/457–9232,* 𝐖𝐄𝐁 *www.baldheadisland.com. 195 condos, villas, and cottages; 25 rooms in 2 B&Bs. 5 restaurants, 18-hole golf course, 4 tennis courts, pool, boating, fishing, croquet, baby-sitting, concierge, business services. AE, DC, MC, V.*

Outdoor Activities and Sports

For golf the par-72 **Gauntlet at St. James Plantation** (⊠ Rte. 211, ☎ 910/253–3008 or 800/247–4806) lives up to its reputation as a challenging course.

Winnabow

12 mi north of Southport, 18 mi south of Wilmington.

Winnabow is more of a crossroads than a town to visit; the draws here are gardens and a historic site, both off Route 133 near the Cape Fear

★   River. The house at **Orton Plantation Gardens** is not open to the public, but the 20 acres of beautiful, comprehensive gardens are great for strolling. The former rice plantation holds magnolias, ancient oaks, and all kinds of ornamental plants; the grounds are a refuge for waterfowl. Some or all of 35 movies have been made here. ⊠ *9149 Orton Rd. SE, off Rte. 133,* ☎ *910/371–6851,* 𝐖𝐄𝐁 *www.ortongardens.com.* ⌨ *$8.* ⊙ *Mar.–Aug., daily 8–6; Sept.–Nov., daily 10–5.*

At **Brunswick Town State Historic Site** you can explore the excavations of a colonial town; see Fort Anderson, a Civil War earthworks fort; and have a picnic. Special events include reenactments of Civil War en-

campments. ⊠ 8884 St. Phillips Rd., off Rte. 133, ☎ 910/371–6613.
🎟 Free. ⊙ Apr.–Oct., Mon.–Sat. 9–5, Sun. 1–5; Nov.–Mar., Tues.–Sat.
10–4, Sun. 1–4.

Wilmington and the Cape Fear Coast A to Z

To research prices, get advice from other travelers, and book travel arrangements, visit www.fodors.com.

AIR TRAVEL

AIRPORTS

US Airways, Atlantic Southeast Airlines, and Midway serve the Wilmington International Airport.
➤ AIRPORT INFORMATION: **Wilmington International Airport** (⊠ 1740 Airport Blvd., ☎ 910/341–4125, WEB www.flyilm.com).

BOAT AND FERRY TRAVEL

A state-run car ferry connects Fort Fisher with Southport on the coast.

FARES AND SCHEDULES

➤ BOAT AND FERRY INFORMATION: **Southport–Fort Fisher Ferry** (☎ 800/ 293–3779.)

BUS TRAVEL

Greyhound/Carolina Trailways serves the Union Bus terminal.
➤ BUS INFORMATION: **Greyhound/Carolina Trailways** (☎ 800/231–2222, WEB www.greyhound.com).

EMERGENCIES

For emergency medical attention contact the Cape Fear Memorial Hospital or the New Hanover Regional Medical Center, a trauma center.
➤ EMERGENCY SERVICES: **Ambulance, police** (☎ 911). **Coast Guard** (☎ 910/343–4881).
➤ HOSPITALS: **Cape Fear Memorial Hospital** (⊠ 5301 Wrightsville Ave., ☎ 910/452–8100). **New Hanover Regional Medical Center** (⊠ 2131 S. 17th St., ☎ 910/343–7000).

OUTDOORS AND SPORTS

BEACHES

Three beaches—Wrightsville, Carolina, and Kure—are within a short drive from Wilmington, and miles and miles of sand stretch northward to the Outer Banks and southward to South Carolina. The beaches offer activities from fishing to sunbathing to scuba diving, and the towns here have a choice of accommodations. Approximately 100 points of public access along the shoreline are marked by orange-and-blue signs. Some of the smaller beaches have lifeguards on duty, and many are accessible to people with disabilities. Some fishing piers are open to the public. Camping, fishing, swimming, and picnicking are permitted at Carolina Beach State Park.
➤ CONTACTS: **Carolina Beach State Park** (☎ 910/458–8206; 910/458–7770 for marina).

BOATING

A number of hotels provide docking facilities for guests. The Wilmington area has public marinas at Carolina Beach State Park and Wrightsville Beach. Public boat access is also offered at Atlantic Marina, Masonboro Boat Yard and Marina, Seapath Transient Dock, and Wrightsville Gulf Terminal.
➤ CONTACTS: **Carolina Beach State Park** (☎ 910/458–7770). **Wrightsville Beach** (☎ 910/256–6666).

FISHING

There's surf fishing on the piers that dot the coast, and charter boats are available for off-shore fishing. Four major tournaments, all offering substantial prize money, are held each year—the Cape Fear Marlin Tournament, the Wrightsville Beach King Mackerel Tournament, the East Coast Open King Mackerel Tournament, and the U.S. Open King Mackerel Tournament.

SCUBA DIVING

Wrecks such as the World War II tanker *John D. Gill* make for exciting scuba diving off the coast. Aquatic Safaris rents equipment and leads trips.
➤ CONTACTS: **Aquatic Safaris** (✉ 5751–4 Oleander Dr., Wilmington, ☎ 910/392–4386).

SURFING

Surfing and board sailing are popular at area beaches, and rentals are available at shops in Wilmington, Wrightsville Beach, and Carolina Beach.

TOURS

From April through December Cape Fear Riverboats, Inc., runs cruises aboard a stern-wheel riverboat, the *Henrietta III*, that departs from Riverfront Park. The cost is $18–$33. Cape Fear Tours gives walking and driving tours of the Wilmington Historic District, the mansions, and the beaches. Individual tours are $20 per hour.
➤ FEES AND SCHEDULES: **Cape Fear Tours** (✉ 8112 Sidbury Rd., Wilmington, ☎ 910/686–7744). **Cape Fear Riverboats, Inc.** (✉ docked at Hilton in downtown Wilmington, ☎ 910/343–1611 or 800/676–0162).

VISITOR INFORMATION

➤ TOURIST INFORMATION: **Cape Fear Coast Convention and Visitors Bureau** (✉ 24 N. 3rd St., Wilmington 28401, ☎ 910/341–4030 or 800/ 222–4757, WEB www.cape-fear.nc.us). **South Brunswick Islands Chamber of Commerce** (✉ 4948 Main St., Box 1380, Shalotte 28459, ☎ 910/754–6644 or 800/426–6644, WEB www.ncbrunswick.com).

THE MOUNTAINS

Cherokee, Asheville, and the High Country

The majestic peaks, meadows, and valleys of the Appalachian, Blue Ridge, and Smoky mountains characterize the western corner of the state, which is divided into three distinct regions: the southern mountains, with the Cherokee reservation; the northern mountains, known as the High Country (Blowing Rock, Boone, Banner Elk); and the central mountains, anchored by Asheville, for decades a retreat for the wealthy and famous. National parks, national forests, handmade-crafts centers, and the Blue Ridge Parkway are the area's main draws, providing prime shopping, skiing, hiking, bicycling, camping, fishing, canoeing, or just taking in the views.

At the southern terminus of the Blue Ridge Parkway and the North Carolina entrance to the Great Smoky Mountains lies the homeland of the Eastern Band of the Cherokee Indians. Through a combination of museums, dramas, assorted outdoor attractions, and the showing of everyday living, the Cherokee attempt to explain what's precious in their Land of the Blue Mist.

The biggest city in the mountains, Asheville has a lovely landscape, a choice of hotels and restaurants, and a thriving arts community. The city's revitalized downtown has good shopping, galleries, museums, restaurants, and nightlife.

Picture-book towns such as Boone, Blowing Rock, and Banner Elk have boomed in the 30 years since the introduction of snowmaking equipment. Luxury resorts now dot the valleys and mountaintops, and you can take advantage of the many crafts shops, music festivals, and theater offerings. The passing of each season is a visual event here, and autumn is the star.

Cherokee

165 mi west of Charlotte, 50 mi west of Asheville.

The 56,000-acre Cherokee reservation is known as the Qualla Boundary, and the town of Cherokee is its capital. Truth be told, there are two Cherokees. There's the Cherokee with the sometimes tacky pop culture, designed to appeal to the masses of tourists, many of whom are visiting the nearby Great Smoky Mountains National Park. But there's another Cherokee that explores the rich heritage of the tribe's Eastern Band. Although now relatively small in number—tribal enrollment is 12,500—these Cherokee and their ancestors have been responsible for keeping alive the Cherokee culture. They are the descendants of those who hid in the Great Smoky Mountains to avoid becoming part of the Trail of Tears, the forced removal of the Cherokee Nation to Oklahoma in the 19th century. They are survivors, extremely attached to the hiking, swimming, trout fishing, and natural beauty of their ancestral homeland.

The **Museum of the Cherokee Indian,** with displays and artifacts that cover 12,000 years, is one of the best Native American museums in the United States. Computer-generated images, lasers, specialty lighting, and sound effects help re-create events in the history of the Cherokee: for example, you'll see children stop to play a butter bean game while adults shiver along the snowy Trail of Tears. The museum has an art gallery, a gift shop, and an outdoor living exhibit of Cherokee life in the 15th century. ⊠ *U.S. 441 at Drama Rd.,* ☎ *828/497–3481,* WEB *www.cherokeemuseum.org.* ☒ *$8.* ☉ *June–Aug., Mon.–Sat. 9–8, Sun. 9–5; Sept.–May, daily 9–5.*

The **Qualla Arts and Crafts Mutual,** across the street from the Museum of the Cherokee Indian, is a cooperative that displays and sells items created by 300 Cherokee craftspeople. The store also has a large section of baskets, masks, and wood carvings. ⊠ *U.S. 441 at Drama Rd.,* ☎ *828/497–3103.* ☉ *June–Aug., daily 8–8; Sept.–Oct., daily 8–6; Nov.–May, daily 8–4:30.*

At the historically accurate, re-created **Oconaluftee Indian Village,** guides in native costumes will lead you through a village of 225 years ago while others demonstrate traditional skills such as weaving, pottery, canoe construction, and hunting techniques. ⊠ *U.S. 441 at Drama Rd.,* ☎ *828/497–2315,* WEB *www.dnet.net/~cheratt.* ☒ *$12.* ☉ *May 15–Oct. 25, daily 9:30–5.*

Every mountain county has significant deposits of gems and minerals, and at the **Smoky Mountain Gold and Ruby Mine,** on the Qualla Boundary, you can search for gems such as aquamarines. Children love panning precisely because it can be wet and messy. Here they're guaranteed a find. Gem ore can be purchased, too: gold ore costs $5 per bag. ⊠ *U.S. 441N,* ☎ *828/497–6574.* ☒ *$4–$10, depending on the gems.* ☉ *Mar.–Nov., daily 10–6.*

Dining and Lodging

$$–$$$ ✕ **Nantahala Village Restaurant.** This roomy rock-and-cedar restaurant with front-porch rocking chairs is about 10 mi southwest of Cherokee and is a local favorite. The food isn't fancy, but the choices—trout, chicken, country ham, and even some vegetarian options—are good and filling. Sunday brunch has some surprises, including *huevos rancheros* (tortilla with fried eggs and salsa) and eggs Benedict. ✉ *9400 U.S. 19W, Bryson City,* ☎ *828/488–9616 or 800/438–1507. MC, V. Closed late Nov.–early Mar.*

$$$ ✕⊞ **Hemlock Inn.** Even if you're not a guest at the inn, which is built on a small mountain that overlooks three valleys, you can make a reservation for dinner ($$) Monday through Saturday and for lunch on Sunday. The fixed-price all-you-can-eat meals are prepared with regional foods, including locally grown fruits and vegetables and mountain honey. Each cozy room is decorated with antiques and crafts. ✉ *Galbraith Creek Rd., 1 mi north of U.S. 19, Bryson City 28713,* ☎ *828/488–2885,* FAX *828/488–8985,* WEB *www.innbrook.com/hemlock/. 29 rooms. Restaurant, recreation room. D, MC, V. Closed Nov.–mid-Apr. MAP.*

$$ ⊞ **Holiday Inn Cherokee.** Guest rooms are standard chain fare, but the staff at this well-equipped, full-service facility is very friendly. The Chestnut Tree restaurant has dinner buffets that are veritable groaning boards, and the native crafts shop, the Hunting Ground, with works by local artists, is a nice touch. ✉ *U.S. 19, 28719,* ☎ *828/497–9181 or 800/465–4329,* FAX *828/497–5973,* WEB *www.hicherokee.com. 150 rooms, 4 suites. Restaurant, indoor pool, wading pool, sauna, recreation room, shop, playground, business services, meeting room. AE, D, DC, MC, V.*

Nightlife and the Arts

THE ARTS

Unto These Hills Outdoor Drama (✉ Mountainside Theater on Drama Rd., off U.S. 441N, ☎ 828/497–2111, WEB www.untothesehills.com) is a colorful and well-staged history of the Cherokee from the time of Spanish explorer Hernando de Soto's visit in 1540 to the infamous Trail of Tears. It runs from mid-June to mid-August and starts at $14.

NIGHTLIFE

The 175,000-square-ft **Harrah's Cherokee Casino** (✉ U.S. 19 off U.S. 441, ☎ 828/497–7777) has action 24 hours a day. Its 2,700 gaming machines, including video poker, video blackjack, and video craps, make it the largest casino within a 500-mi radius. The complex also has a 1,500-seat concert hall, three restaurants, and a child-care area. The casino is alcohol-free.

Outdoor Activities and Sports

FISHING

There are 30 mi of regularly stocked trout streams on the **Cherokee Indian Reservation.** To fish in tribal water, you need a tribal fishing permit, available at nearly two dozen reservation businesses. The $7 permit is valid for one day and has a creel limit of 100. For information call ☎ 828/497–5201 or 800/438–1601.

HIKING

In the downtown area you can cross the Oconaluftee River on a foot-bridge to **Oconaluftee Islands Park & Trail** (✉ across from Cherokee Elementary School on U.S. 441) and walk a trail around the perimeter of the Island Park, which also has picnic facilities. The flat 1½-mi **Oconaluftee River Trail** begins at the Great Smoky Mountains National Park entrance sign on U.S. 441 (near the entrance to the Blue Ridge Parkway) and ends at the Mountain Farm Museum–Park Visitor Center. A five-minute hike from the Mingo Falls Campground area (⊠ Big Cove Rd. about 4 mi north of Acquoni Rd.) will reward you with a view of the 200-ft-high **Mingo Falls.**

Great Smoky Mountains National Park

3 mi north of Cherokee.

★ Natural assets and proximity to several metro areas help make the **Great Smoky Mountains National Park** the most visited national park in the United States. No mountains in the world are older, and no place on Earth can claim such biological diversity: more than 1,600 types of wildflowers and more than 140 species of trees flourish in this wildlife sanctuary. The Appalachian Trail runs along the crest of the mountains through the park, the largest protected land area east of the Rocky Mountains. Within its 800 square mi (276,000 acres lie in North Carolina, 244,000 in Tennessee) are 800 mi of trails, more than 600 mi of trout streams, and some 200,000 acres of virgin forest.

The Smokies are so named because of the frequently occurring smoke-like blue mist that hovers in the air and can get so dense as to obscure mountaintops. In actuality, the "smoke" occurs when vegetation releases water vapor and natural oils produced by plants into the air. Along the twists and turns of the Blue Ridge Parkway are scores of scenic overlooks, and many byways lead to areas that grip the imagination.

U.S. 441 is the only road that passes all the way through the park. Fishing permits and visitor information are available at ranger stations at the north and south entrances. Depending on your location, the **Oconaluftee Visitors Center** (☎ 828/497–1900) is the terminus of the Blue Ridge Parkway or its starting point. Adjacent to the visitor center, at mile marker 469.1, is **Mountain Farm Museum,** a re-created pioneer homestead. ⊠ *107 Park Headquarters Rd., Gatlinburg, TN 37738,* ☎ *423/436–5615,* WEB *www.nps.gov/grsm.* ▨ *Free.*

Dillsboro

13 mi southeast of Cherokee on U.S. 441.

The tiny town of Dillsboro, in Jackson County, has a big reputation for good shopping, particularly if you favor folk art and crafts. The popular train rides of the **Great Smoky Mountains Railway** include six regular excursions and six special trips on diesel-electric or steam locomotives. Open-sided cars or cabooses are ideal for picture taking as the mountain scenery glides by. There's a train museum, too. ⊠ *119 Front St.,* ☎ *828/586–8811 or 800/872–4681,* WEB *www.gsmr.com.* ▨ *$28–$74; some rides include a meal.* ☉ *Mar.–Dec., call for schedule.*

Franklin

32 mi south of Cherokee on U.S. 441.

Franklin, the Macon County seat, lies at the convergence of U.S. 441, U.S. 64, and Route 28. In the 1500s Hernando de Soto came in search of gold and overlooked the wealth of gemstones for which this area is so famous. A dozen gem mines and nearly as many gem stores are nearby.

The **Scottish Tartans Museum** has the official registry of all publicly known tartans and is the only American extension of the Scottish Tartans Society. Scottish heritage can be traced in the research library. ⊠ *86 E. Main St.,* ☎ *828/524–7472,* WEB *www.scottishtartans.org.* ▨ *$1.* ☉ *Mon.–Sat. 10–5.*

Waynesville

17 mi east of Cherokee on U.S. 19.

This is where the Blue Ridge Parkway meets the Great Smokies. Pretty, arty Waynesville is the seat of Haywood County. About 40% of the county is occupied by the Great Smoky Mountains National Park, Pisgah National Forest, and the Harmon Den Wildlife Refuge.

The **Museum of North Carolina Handicrafts,** in the Shelton House (circa 1875), has a comprehensive exhibit of 19th-century heritage crafts as well as a working pioneer village and railroad memorabilia. ⊠ *307 Shelton St.,* ☎ *828/452–1551.* ☞ *$4.* ☉ *May–Oct., Tues.–Fri. 10–4.*

Cold Mountain, the vivid best-seller by Charles Frazier, has made a destination out of the real **Cold Mountain.** About 15 mi from Waynesville in the Shining Rock Wilderness Area of Pisgah National Forest, the 6,030-ft rise had stood in relative anonymity. But with the success of Frazier's book, people want to see the region that Inman and Ada, the book's Civil War–era protagonists, called home.

There are different ways to experience Cold Mountain. For a view of the splendid mass—or at least of the surrounding area—stop at any of a number of overlooks off the Blue Ridge Parkway. Try the Cold Mountain Parking Overlook, just past mile marker 411.9; the Wagon Road Gap parking area, at mile marker 412.2; or the Waterrock Knob Interpretative Station, at mile marker 451.2. You can climb the mountain, but beware, as the hike to the summit is rather strenuous. No campfires are allowed in Shining Rock, so you'll need a stove if you wish to cook. Inform the ranger station (☎ 828/877–3350) if you plan to hike or camp.

Lodging

$$$$ 🏠 **The Swag.** This exquisite, rustic inn sits high atop the Cataloochee Divide overlooking a swag—a deep depression in otherwise high ground. Its 250 wooded acres share a border with Great Smoky Mountains National Park and have access to hiking trails. Guest rooms and cabins were assembled from six authentic log structures transported here. All have rough wooden walls, exposed beams, and wooden floors and are furnished with early American crafts. A two-night minimum stay is required. ⊠ *2300 Swag Rd., 28786,* ☎ *828/926–0430 or 800/789–7672,* FAX *828/926–2036,* WEB *www.theswag.com. 16 rooms, 3 cabins. Dining room, pond, massage, sauna, badminton, croquet, racquetball, library, business services. AE, D, MC, V. Closed Nov.–Mar. FAP.*

Asheville

50 mi east of Cherokee, 115 mi west of Charlotte.

The largest and most cosmopolitan city in the mountains, Asheville has been rated America's favorite place to live among cities of its size. It has scenic beauty, a good airport and road system, a moderate four-season climate, and a thriving arts community. Banjo pickers are as revered as violinists, and mountain folks mix with city slickers. Experience the renaissance of the city's downtown, a pedestrian-friendly place with upscale shopping, art galleries, museums, restaurants, and nightlife.

Downtown Asheville is noted for its eclectic architecture. The **Battery Park Hotel** (1924) is neo-Georgian; the **Flatiron Building** (1924) is neoclassical; the **Basilica of St. Lawrence** (1912) is Spanish baroque; **Pack Place,** formerly known as Old Pack Library (1925), is in the Italian Renaissance style; the **S&W Cafeteria** (1929) is art deco. The city has the largest collection of art deco buildings in the Southeast after Miami.

The 92,000-square-ft **Pack Place Education, Arts & Science Center,** in downtown Asheville, houses the **Asheville Art Museum, Colburn Gem & Mineral Museum, Health Adventure,** and **Diana Wortham Theatre.** The **YMI Cultural Center,** also maintained by Pack Place, is across the street. ⊠ *2 S. Pack Sq., Downtown,* ☏ *828/257–4500,* WEB *www.packplace.org.* 🖃 *$6 for art museum, $4 each for other museums, $14 combination ticket.* ☉ *June–Oct., Tues.–Sat. 10–5, Sun. 1–5; Nov.–May, Tues.–Sat. 10–5.*

Asheville's most famous son, novelist Thomas Wolfe, grew up in a 29-room Queen Anne–style home that his mother ran as a boarding-house. The home, a state historic site, burned as a result of arson. It is closed while undergoing restoration. However, the visitor center at the **Thomas Wolfe Memorial** remains open, showing a video about Wolfe and displaying photographs and other memorabilia related to his career. Some items salvaged from the house are also here. Guided tours of the house's exterior and heirloom gardens are given. ⊠ *52 Market St., Downtown,* ☏ *828/253–8304.* 🖃 *$1.* ☉ *Apr.–Oct., Mon.–Sat. 9–5, Sun. 1–5; Nov.–Mar., Tues.–Sat. 10–4, Sun. 1–4.*

★ The astonishing **Biltmore Estate,** which faces Biltmore Village, was built in the 1890s as the private home of George Vanderbilt. This 250-room French Renaissance château is America's largest private residence (some of Vanderbilt's descendants still live on the grounds but open the bulk of the home and grounds to visitors). Richard Morris Hunt designed it, and Frederick Law Olmsted landscaped the original 125,000-acre estate (now 8,000 acres). It took 1,000 men five years to complete the gargantuan project. On view are the priceless antiques and art collected by the Vanderbilts, along with 75 acres of gardens and formally landscaped grounds. You can also see the state-of-the-art winery and take Christmas candlelight tours of the house. Allow a full day to tour the house and grounds. ⊠ *Exit 50 off I–40, South Metro,* ☏ *828/255–1700 or 800/624–1575,* WEB *www.biltmore.com.* 🖃 *$34; prices for special events vary.* ☉ *Jan.–Mar., daily 9–5; Apr.–Dec., daily 8:30–5.*

The **North Carolina Arboretum,** 426 acres that were part of the original Biltmore Estate, completes Frederick Law Olmsted's dream of creating a world-class arboretum in the western part of the state. Highlights include southern Appalachian flora in stunning settings, including the Blue Ridge Quilt Garden, with bedding plants arranged in patterns reminiscent of Appalachian quilts. There is also the formal Stream Garden, which capitalizes on the Bent Creek trout stream that runs through the grounds. An extensive network of trails is available for walking or mountain biking. ⊠ *100 Frederick Law Olmsted Way, 10 mi southwest of downtown Asheville, adjacent to Blue Ridge Pkwy. (near I–26 and I–40), South Metro,* ☏ *828/665–2492,* WEB *www.ncarboretum. org.* 🖃 *Free; call for group tour fees.* ☉ *Visitor education center Mon.–Sat. 9–5, Sun. noon–5; gardens and grounds daily 8 AM–7 PM.*

OFF THE BEATEN PATH

PENLAND SCHOOL OF CRAFTS – This world-famous institution about 45 mi northeast of Asheville on a remote mountaintop is the oldest and largest school for high-quality mixed-media arts and crafts in North America. It has classes in book and paper making, glassblowing, ceramics, textile arts, and other media. A gallery, open mid-April–early December, displays works (some are for sale; call to check hours and winter closing). Classes aren't open to the public, but you can call about a free campus tour. ⊠ *Penland Rd. off U.S. 19/23, Penland,* ☏ *828/765–2359 for school; 828/765–6211 for gallery and campus tours,* WEB *www.penland.org.*

Dining and Lodging

$$–$$$ ✕ **Café on the Square.** The local business crowd frequents this elegant and airy restaurant during lunch, but theatergoers favor it for dinner. All entrées are served with the Café salad and homemade bread. The menu's pasta dishes are particularly creative: for example, cracked-pepper fettuccine with scallops and shrimp in a white bean, tomato, and basil ragout. There's also patio dining. ⊠ *1 Biltmore Ave., Downtown,* ☎ *828/251–5565. AE, D, MC, V. Closed Sun. Nov.–May.*

$$–$$$ ✕ **The Market Place.** Clean lines, neutral colors, and brushed steel mobiles create a sophisticated style. The food offers refreshing twists on ingredients indigenous to the mountains (game and trout) and the South in general. Possible entrées are smoked trout and green-apple salad, or tenderloin of pork with a sweet-potato timbale. Iron gates open onto an exterior courtyard and dining patio. ⊠ *20 Wall St., Downtown,* ☎ *828/252–4162,* WEB *www.marketplace-restaurant.com. AE, MC, V. Closed Sun. No lunch.*

$$–$$$ ✕ **Vincenzo's.** There are two distinct halves of this pastel-hue *ristorante,* a casual trattoria downstairs and a more formal dining room upstairs. The trattoria serves an abbreviated version of the full northern Italian menu. Specialties include fillet of beef in a Gorgonzola cream sauce topped with pine nuts and caramelized shallots and chicken breast with prosciutto, sautéed spinach, and mushrooms in a sage-sherry cream sauce, served over fettuccine. The wine list is extensive. Smoking is allowed in the bistro, where you can find live music nightly. ⊠ *10 N. Market St., Downtown,* ☎ *828/254–4699. AE, D, DC, MC, V. No lunch.*

$$–$$$ ✕ **West Side Grill.** This '50s-style diner has a little bit of everything, including daily blue-plate specials, from "Mile-High" meat loaf to Southern-fried catfish. Vegetarians have a number of choices, including the focaccia veggie melt and the blackened garden burger. ⊠ *1190 Patton Ave., West Metro,* ☎ *828/252–9605. Reservations not accepted. AE, D, MC, V.*

$–$$ ✕ **Laughing Seed Café.** You'll get more than brown rice and beans at this vegetarian eatery. The extensive menu ranges from fruit drinks to sandwiches and pizzas to dinner specialties influenced by the flavors of India, China, and Morocco. Fruits and vegetables come from local organic farms during the growing season. Breads are baked daily on premises. There's outdoor dining. ⊠ *40 Wall St., Downtown,* ☎ *828/ 252–3445,* WEB *www.laughingseed.com. AE, D, MC, V. Closed Tues.*

$–$$ ✕ **Salsa.** In a diminutive space with a slightly retro-hippy look, you'll find spicy and highly creative Mexican and Caribbean fare in huge portions. Fire-roasted pepper tacos, black bean and goat cheese tacos, and plantains stuffed with herbs, meat, and vegetables are among the recommended entrées. Delicious desserts include caramelized mango. ⊠ *6 Patton Ave., Downtown,* ☎ *828/252–9805. AE, D, MC, V. Closed Sun.*

$$$$ ✕🏨 **Grove Park Inn Resort.** With its children's activities, special week-
★   end packages, and views of the Blue Ridge Mountains, this is Asheville's premier resort. Since the resort's opening in 1913, Henry Ford, Thomas Edison, and Michael Jordan have stayed here. The inn is furnished with oak antiques in the arts and crafts style. Although largely underground so as not to inhibit views, it has abundant light thanks to the inspired use of skylights and natural stone. Fireplace lounges, waterfalls, plunge pools, and a juice bar complete the experience. The restaurants offer plenty of choices: for example, Horizons specializes in game dishes from ostrich to boar; you can also order free-range chicken. ⊠ *290 Macon Ave., North Metro, 28804,* ☎ *828/252–2711 or 800/438–5800;* FAX *828/253–7053 for guests; 828/252–6102 reservations,* WEB *www. groveparkinn.com. 498 rooms, 12 suites. 4 restaurants, 18-hole golf*

course, putting green, 9 tennis courts, indoor pool, health club, hot tub, spa, shops, 3 bars, nightclub, playground, laundry service, concierge, business services, meeting room. AE, D, DC, MC, V.

$$$$ ★ ✕⚏ **Inn on Biltmore Estate.** Many people who have in the past come here to see this mansion have longed to lodge here overnight. In 2001 their wishes were granted when this posh ridge-top property opened. The hotel mimics the look of the Biltmore house with natural stone and copper. French manor houses inspired the interior, where windows offer mountain views. Nice touches include carriage rides around the estate and afternoon tea in the library. The dining room ($$$–$$$$) is bookended by large windows and a massive fireplace. Menus deftly blend local and international ingredients; dinner might begin with herbed goat cheese and then move on to pheasant with country ham. ⊠ Biltmore Estate, Exit 50 off I–40, South Metro, ☎ 800/922–0084, FAX 828/225–1629, WEB www.biltmore.com/inn. 131 rooms, 72 suites. Restaurant, room service, golf privileges, pool, health club, hot tub, mountain bikes, hiking, horseback riding, bar, library, shops, concierge, meeting rooms. AE, D, DC, MC, V.

$$$$ ★ ✕⚏ **Richmond Hill Inn.** Once a private residence, this elegant Victorian mansion is on the National Register of Historic Places. Many rooms in the mansion are furnished with canopy beds, Victorian sofas, and other antiques, whereas the more modern cottages have contemporary pine poster beds. Gabrielle's is known for its innovative cuisine, cherry-wood paneling, and three-tier chandelier. Reservations are necessary here but not at the Arbor Grille, in a glass-enclosed sun porch. Gabrielle's is only open to the public for dinner and Sunday brunch; jacket and tie are required. ⊠ 87 Richmond Hill Dr., North Metro, 28806, ☎ 828/252–7313 or 888/742–4536, FAX 828/252–8726, WEB www.richmondhillinn.com. 24 rooms, 3 suites, 9 cottages. 2 restaurants, croquet, library, business services, meeting room. AE, MC, V. BP.

$$$–$$$$ ✕⚏ **Haywood Park Hotel.** The lobby of this art deco downtown hotel, once a department store, has golden oak woodwork accented with gleaming brass. The suites are spacious, with baths done in Spanish marble. The hotel's elegant restaurant, 23 Page, has an oft-changing French-influenced menu. An entrée might be a grilled lamb chop with radicchio and artichoke mousse. There's live music every Friday evening during the summer. Adjoining the property is a shopping galleria. ⊠ 1 Battery Park Ave., Downtown, 28801, ☎ 828/252–2522 or 800/228–2522, FAX 828/253–0481, WEB www.haywoodpark.com. 33 suites. Restaurant, room service, exercise room, sauna, bar, shops, laundry service, concierge, business services, meeting room. AE, D, DC, MC, V. CP.

$$$–$$$$ ⚏ **Cedar Crest Victorian Inn.** Biltmore craftspeople constructed this beautiful cottage, with its lead-glass front door and corbeled brick fireplaces, as a private residence in 1891. The lovingly restored guest rooms are furnished with period antiques. You are treated to afternoon tea, evening coffee or chocolate and to a breakfast of fruit, pastry, and coffee. It's best for older children. ⊠ 674 Biltmore Ave., South Metro, 28803, ☎ 828/252–1389 or 800/252–0310, FAX 828/252–7667, WEB www.cedarcrestvictorianinn.com. 9 rooms, 2 cottage suites. Croquet, business services. AE, D, DC, MC, V.

$$–$$$ ⚏ **Comfort Inn.** This chain hotel, off I–240 near the River Ridge Outlet Mall, has a fireplace in a large sitting area. Most guest rooms are standard fare, but suites have private balconies and dinette areas. A walking trail surrounds the property. Pets are allowed. ⊠ 800 Fairview Rd., South Metro, 28803, ☎ 828/298–9141, FAX 828/298–6629, WEB www.choicehotels.com. 149 rooms, 28 suites. Pool, kitchenettes, exercise room, playground, business services, meeting room. AE, D, DC, MC, V. CP.

$$ 🏨 **Hampton Inn–Biltmore Square.** You can relax beside the fire in the lobby at this motel off I–26 that's 5 mi southwest of downtown. Some guest rooms have whirlpool baths. Cookies and coffee are served every evening. ⊠ *1 Rocky Ridge Rd., South Metro, 28806,* ☎ *828/667–2022 or 800/426–7866,* FAX *828/665–9680,* WEB *www.hampton-inn.com. 121 rooms. Indoor pool, exercise room, sauna, dry cleaning, laundry service, business services, meeting room, airport shuttle. AE, D, DC, MC, V. CP.*

$–$$ 🏨 **Mountaineer Inn.** A fixture along Tunnel Road, this family-owned inn is ever popular with families and others who care less about fanciness than they do about affordable, comfortable surroundings. A newer addition contains larger rooms. ⊠ *155 Tunnel Rd., Downtown, 28805,* ☎ *828/254–5331 or 800/255–4080,* FAX *828/254–5331. 79 rooms. Pool, business services, meeting room. AE, D, MC, V. CP.*

Outdoor Activities and Sports

GOLF

Colony Lake Lure Golf Resort (⊠ 201 Blvd. of the Mountains, Lake Lure, ☎ 828/625–2888 or 800/260–1040), 25 mi from Asheville, has two 18-hole, par-72 courses known for their beauty. **Etowah Valley Country Club and Golf Lodge** (⊠ U.S. 64, Etowah, ☎ 828/891–7141 or 800/451–8174), about 20 mi from Asheville, has three very different (one par-72, two par-73) 18-hole courses with good package deals. **Grove Park Inn Resort** (⊠ 290 Macon Ave., North Metro, ☎ 828/252–2711 or 800/438–5800) has a beautiful par-71 course.

HORSEBACK RIDING

Trail rides are offered by stables throughout the region between April and November, including **Pisgah View Ranch** (⊠ Rte. 1, Candler, ☎ 828/667–9100), where you can gallop through the wooded mountainside. **Cataloochee Ranch** (⊠ 119 Ranch Rd. [Rte. 1], Maggie Valley, ☎ 828/926–1401 or 800/868–1401) allows riders to explore the property's mile-high vistas on horseback.

LLAMA TREKS

One-day and overnight hikes with llamas carrying your pack through local forests are arranged by **Windsong Llama Treks, Ltd.** (⊠ 120 Ferguson Ridge Rd., Clyde, ☎ 828/627–6111). **Avalon Llama Trek** (⊠ 310 Wilson Cove Rd., Swannanoa, ☎ 828/298–5637) leads trips on the lush trails of the Pisgah National Forest.

SKIING

In addition to having outstanding skiing, **Cataloochee Resort** (⊠ Rte. 1, Maggie Valley, ☎ 828/926–0285 or 800/768–0285) hosts lots of different activities for the whole family. **Fairfield-Sapphire Valley** (⊠ 4000 U.S. 64W, Sapphire Valley, ☎ 828/743–3441 or 800/533–8268) offers basic skiing despite minimal snowfall. **Wolf Laurel** (⊠ Rte. 3, Mars Hill, ☎ 828/689–4111) has night skiing and excellent snowmaking capabilities.

Shopping

Biltmore Village (⊠ Hendersonville Rd., South Metro, ☎ 828/274–5570), on the Biltmore Estate, is a cluster of specialty shops, restaurants, galleries, and hotels in a decidedly early 20th-century-English-hamlet style. You'll find everything from children's books to music, antiques, and wearable art.

Grovewood Gallery at the Homespun Shops (⊠ 111 Grovewood Rd., North Metro, ☎ 828/253–7651, WEB www.grovewood.com), adjacent to the Grove Park Inn and established by Mrs. George Vanderbilt, sells furniture and contemporary and traditionally crafted woven goods made on the premises.

ARTS AND CRAFTS IN THE MOUNTAINS

A CENTURY AGO, AS YOUNG GEORGE VANDERBILT prepared to build a retreat in then-bucolic Asheville, he and an architect traveled the French countryside looking for designs that could be incorporated into the home he was going to model after a 16th-century Loire Valley château. Craftspeople labored long to create the Biltmore Mansion, including its unlikely gargoyles and grotesques.

The message is this: when it comes to arts and crafts in western North Carolina, expect the unexpected. (Note: if a place mentioned here isn't described elsewhere in the chapter, an address or telephone number is given.) There's so much more going on than first meets the eye. And that's the fun of it: the hunt. Sometimes handmade treasures are found out in the open: more than 85 crafts fairs are held annually throughout the rural 21-county region. At the **Balsam Mountain Inn** (✉ off Rte. 23/74, Balsam, ☎ 828/456–9498), just off the Blue Ridge Parkway near Waynesville, the work of a number of artisans is tastefully showcased year-round.

More than 4,000 people here earn part or all of their living from crafts, and many of them can be found "around the bend" and in homes tucked back in forested hollows. They patiently coax form from clay and wood and metal, and they are usually happy to talk about what they do—so explore. Interesting roads that are off the map can lead to workshops. If hours are posted, however, it's best to respect them.

In the beginning it was practical function, not notions of folk art, behind all the quilting, weaving, woodworking, and pottery making. But by the late 19th century missionaries, social workers, and women of means—Frances Goodrich and Edith Vanderbilt among them—began to recognize that the things of day-to-day life contained artistry and thus economic salvation for a beautiful but isolated and impoverished area.

Today utility and aesthetics have melded. From furnaces in the northwest counties of Mitchell and Yancey come gobs of hot liquid shaped by hand into art glass prized by collectors and dealers worldwide. Many glassblowers have perfected their métier at the prestigious Penland School of Crafts, whose courses include printmaking, wood, surface design, metals, drawing, clay, and fibers. The work of students and graduates, much of it contemporary, is on display in area galleries, including Penland's own extensive gallery shop.

In the tiny village of Crossnore, in southern Avery County, a rock cottage houses the **Crossnore School's Weaving Room** (✉ U.S. 221, ☎ 828/733–4660). Favored here are patterns used by the early settlers of the Appalachians; however, in a nod to modernity the ladies spin with easy-care rayon and synthetics as well as with cotton, wool, and linen.

On the Cherokee Reservation, in the shadow of the Smoky Mountains, elders pass on to children the secrets of finger weaving, wood carving, and mask and beaded jewelry making. Their work, intricate and colorful and found in shops such as **Medicine Man Crafts** (✉ U.S. 441, ☎ 828/497–2202) in downtown Cherokee, is ageless, a connective thread to a time that predates the United States by thousands of years.

Side Trips from Asheville

Within 40 mi of Asheville are towns with parks and historic sites. Some are resort destinations in themselves.

BREVARD

40 mi southwest of Asheville on Rte. 280.

Plenty of nearby waterfalls and the **Brevard Music Center** (☎ 828/884–2011, WEB www.brevardmusic.org), which has a seven-week music festival each summer, are draws in this resort town. Nearby Pisgah National Forest has the **Cradle of Forestry in America National Historic Site** (⊠ 1001 Pisgah Hwy., ☎ 828/884–5823, WEB www.cradleofforestry.com).

☾ At **Sliding Rock** in summer you can skid 60 ft on a natural water slide. Wear old jeans and tennis shoes and bring a towel. ⊠ *Pisgah National Forest, north of Brevard, off U.S. 276,* ☎ *828/877–3265.* ☒ *Free.* ☉ *Late May–early Sept., daily 10–5:30.*

CHIMNEY ROCK

25 mi southeast of Asheville on U.S. 64/74A.

This town is deep in the Blue Ridge Mountains. At privately owned **Chimney Rock Park** an elevator travels through a 26-story shaft of rock for a staggering view of Hickory Nut Gorge and the surrounding mountains. Trails, open year-round, lead to 400-ft Hickory Nut Falls, where *The Last of the Mohicans* was filmed. The Old Rock Café can prepare picnics to go. ⊠ *U.S. 64/74A,* ☎ *828/625–9611 or 800/277–9611,* WEB *www.chimneyrockpark.com.* ☒ *$12.* ☉ *Daily 8:30–4:30.*

FLAT ROCK

21 mi southwest of Chimney Rock, 25 mi south of Asheville via I–26.

Flat Rock has been a summer resort since the mid-19th century. The

★ **Carl Sandburg Home National Historic Site** is the spot to which the poet and Lincoln biographer Carl Sandburg moved with his wife, Lillian, in 1945. Guided tours of their house, Connemara, where Sandburg's papers still lie scattered on his desk, are given by the National Park Service. In summer *The World of Carl Sandburg* and *Rootabaga Stories* are presented at the amphitheater. ⊠ *1928 Little River Rd.,* ☎ *828/693–4178,* WEB *www.nps.gov/carl.* ☒ *$3.* ☉ *Daily 9–5.*

The **Flat Rock Playhouse** (⊠ 2661 Greenville Hwy., ☎ 828/693–0731, WEB www.flatrockplayhouse.org) has a high reputation for summer stock theater. The season runs from May to mid-December.

SALUDA

30 mi southeast of Asheville.

At the top of the steepest railroad grade east of the Rockies, this salubrious town along the tracks is strung with antiques and crafts shops in 19th-century brick buildings. The surrounding area has apple orchards, woods, and waterfalls.

WEAVERVILLE

18 mi north of Asheville via U.S. 23/19.

This town's state historic site, the **Zebulon B. Vance Birthplace,** has a reconstructed two-story log cabin and several outbuildings. This is where Vance, governor of North Carolina during the Civil War and later a U.S. senator, grew up. Crafts and chores typical of his period are often demonstrated. Picnic facilities are available. An entrance to the Blue Ridge Parkway is nearby. ⊠ *911 Reems Creek Rd. (Rte. 1103),* ☎ *828/645–6706.* ☒ *Free.* ☉ *Apr.–Oct., Mon.–Sat. 9–5, Sun. 1–5; Nov.–Mar., Tues.–Sat. 10–4, Sun. 1–4.*

Lake Toxaway

40 mi southwest of Asheville.

A century ago a group called the Lake Toxaway Company created a 640-acre lake in the high mountains between Brevard and Cashiers. Nearby, a grand 500-room hotel built with the finest materials, providing the most modern conveniences, and serving European cuisine attracted many of the country's elite. That hotel is long gone, but the scenic area, which some still call "America's Switzerland," has a number of fine resorts and some of the priciest real estate in the North Carolina mountains.

Those who love nature, even if it's just looking at it, will enjoy being in this mountain wilderness. And for those to whom shopping is a sport, a number of upscale stores—many specializing in antiques and regional arts and crafts—can be found.

Lodging

$$$$ ⊡ **Earthshine Mountain Lodge.** You can have as much solitude or adventure as you want at this spacious cedar log cabin with stone fireplaces. The lodge, which sits on 70 acres midway between Brevard and Cashiers on a ridge that adjoins the Pisgah National Forest, offers horseback riding, hiking, fishing, and even an opportunity to gather berries, feed the goats, pan for gems, take guided trail rides, or master some Cherokee skills. In the evening people gather around an open fire to sing songs, square dance, or exchange stories. A minimum stay of two nights is required. ⊠ *Golden Rd., off Silversteen Rd. off U.S. 64, Box 216C, 28747,* ☏ *828/862–4207,* WEB *www.earthshinemtnlodge.com. 10 rooms. Dining room, fishing, hiking, horseback riding, baby-sitting, children's programs, meeting room. D, MC, V. FAP.*

$$$$ ⊡ **Greystone Inn.** In 1915 Savannah resident Lucy Molz built a second home in Lake Toxaway. Today the six-level Swiss-style mansion is an inn listed on the National Register of Historic Places. Guest rooms have antiques or period reproductions, and suites that border the lake of this mountain resort are modern. Rates include breakfast and dinner, afternoon tea and cake, and cocktails. The inn is open weekends only January through March. ⊠ *Greystone La., 28747,* ☏ *828/966–4700; 800/824–5766 outside NC,* FAX *828/862–5689,* WEB *www.greystoneinn.com. 33 rooms. Dining room, in-room VCRs, golf privileges, putting green, 5 tennis courts, pool, lake, massage, spa, dock, waterskiing, fishing, children's programs, business services. AE, MC, V. MAP.*

Hot Springs

30 mi northwest of Asheville via U.S. 23/19 and U.S. 25/70 past Marshall.

This picturesque village is a way station for hikers on the Appalachian Trail. The **Hot Springs Spa**'s mineral springs maintain a natural 100°F temperature year-round and since the turn of the 20th century have provided relief for those suffering various ailments, including rheumatism and pelvic troubles. Massage therapy is also available. ⊠ *315 Bridge St.,* ☏ *828/622–7676 or 800/462–0933,* WEB *www.hotspringsspa-nc. com.* ☞ *$10–$30 per hr, depending on time of day and number of people in tub.* ☉ *Feb.–Nov., daily 9 AM–11 PM; Dec.–Jan., hrs vary, call in advance.*

Dining and Lodging

$ ✕⊡ **Bridge Street Café & Inn.** This renovated storefront, circa 1922, is right on the Appalachian Trail and overlooks Spring Creek. Upstairs are simply decorated rooms and two baths filled with antiques. One bathroom has a claw-foot tub. The café ($–$$$) downstairs has a wood-fired oven and grill from which emerge delicious pizzas. There's also a Sunday brunch. ⊠ *Bridge St., Box 502, 28743,* ☎ *828/622–0002,* FAX *828/622–7282,* WEB *www.main.nc.us/bridgecafe/. 4 rooms without bath. Restaurant. AE, D, MC, V. Closed Nov.–mid-Mar.*

Blue Ridge Parkway

Entrance 2 mi east of Asheville, off I–40.

★ The beautiful **Blue Ridge Parkway** (⊠ Superintendent, Blue Ridge Pkwy., 199 Hemphill Knob Rd., Asheville 28803, ☎ 828/298–0398, WEB www.nps.gov/blri) gently winds through mountains and meadows and crosses mountain streams for more than 469 mi on its way from Cherokee, North Carolina, to Waynesboro, Virginia. This is the most scenic route from Asheville to Boone and Blowing Rock. The parkway is generally open year-round but often closes during inclement weather. Maps and information are available at visitor centers along the highway. Mile markers (MMs) identify points of interest and indicate the distance from the parkway's starting point in Virginia.

The **Folk Art Center** sells authentic mountain crafts made by members of the Southern Highland Craft Guild. ⊠ *Blue Ridge Pkwy., MM 382,* ☎ *828/298–7928.* ☉ *Jan.–Mar., daily 9–5; Apr.–Dec., daily 9–6.*

You can tour an underground mine or dig for gems of your own at ♺ **Emerald Village.** ⊠ *McKinney Mine Rd. at Blue Ridge Pkwy., MM 334, Little Switzerland,* ☎ *828/765–6463 or 877/389–4653,* WEB *www.emeraldvillage.com.* ⊡ *Mine $4, plus cost of gem bucket chosen ($3–$100).* ☉ *June–early Sept., daily 9–6; May and early Sept.–Oct., daily 9–5.*

Linville Caverns are the only caverns in the Carolinas. The caverns go 2,000 ft beneath Humpback Mountain and have a year-round temperature of 51°F. North of Asheville, exit the parkway at mile marker 317.4 and turn left onto U.S. 221. ⊠ *U.S. 221 between Linville and Marion,* ☎ *828/756–4171,* WEB *www.linvillecaverns.com.* ⊡ *$5.* ☉ *June–early Sept., daily 9–6; Apr.–May and early Sept.–Oct., daily 9–5; Nov. and Mar., daily 9–4:30; Dec.–Feb., weekends 9–4:30.*

From the **Linville Falls Visitor Center** (⊠ Rte. 1, Spruce Pine, ☎ 828/765–1045), at mile marker 316.3, a half-mile hike leads to one of North Carolina's most photographed waterfalls. The easy trail winds through evergreens and rhododendrons to overlooks with views of the series of cascades tumbling into Linville Gorge. There are also a campground and a picnic area.

Just off the parkway at mile marker 305, **Grandfather Mountain** soars to 6,000 ft and is famous for its Mile-High Swinging Bridge, a 228-ft-long bridge that sways over a 1,000-ft drop into the Linville Valley. The **Natural History Museum** has exhibits on native minerals, flora and fauna, and pioneer life. The annual **Singing on the Mountain,** in June, is an opportunity to hear old-time gospel music and preaching, and the **Highland Games** in July bring together Scottish clans from all over North America for athletic events and Highland dancing. ⊠ *Blue Ridge Pkwy. and U.S. 221, Linville,* ☎ *828/733–4337 or 800/468–7325,* WEB *www.grandfather.com.* ⊡ *$12.* ☉ *Apr.–mid-Nov., daily 8–dusk; mid-Nov.–Mar., daily 8–5, weather permitting.*

Green spaces along the parkway include **Julian Price Park** (MM 295–MM 298.1), which has hiking, canoeing on a mountain lake, trout fishing, and camping. The **Moses H. Cone Park** (MM 292.7–MM 295) has a turn-of-the-20th-century manor house that's now the **Parkway Craft Center.** The center sells fine work by area craftspeople.

Dining and Lodging

$$$$ ✕⊞ **Eseeola Lodge and Restaurant.** Rebuilt in 1936 after a fire, this lake-
★   side lodge, best described as dressed-up rustic, sits 3,800 ft above sea
level and is one sure way to beat summer's heat. Golf is a passion here,
but the diversions are many. All rooms overlook the manicured grounds
and gardens. Rich chestnut paneling and stonework grace the public areas.
Entrées at the restaurant may include free-range chicken and rainbow
trout; jacket and tie are required at dinner. ⊠ *175 Linville Ave., off U.S.
221, Linville 28646,* ☎ *828/733–4311 or 800/742–6717,* FAX *828/733–
3227,* WEB *www.eseeola.com. 19 rooms, 5 suites, 1 cottage. Restaurant,
18-hole golf course, putting green, 8 tennis courts, pool, exercise room,
boating, fishing, hiking, croquet, bar, children's programs, playground,
business services. MC, V. Closed late Oct.–mid-May. MAP.*

Outdoor Activities and Sports

HIKING

More than 100 trails lead off the Blue Ridge Parkway, from easy strolls
to strenuous hikes. For more information on parkway trails, contact
the Blue Ridge Parkway. Another good source is *Walking the Blue Ridge:
A Guide to the Trails of the Blue Ridge Parkway,* by Leonard Adkins,
available at most parkway visitor center gift shops. The **Bluff Moun-
tain Trail,** at Doughton Park (MM 238.5), is a moderately strenuous
7½-mi trail winding through forests, pastures, and valleys, and along
the mountainside. Moses H. Cone Park's (MM 292.7) **Figure 8 Trail**
is an easy and beautiful trail that the Cone family designed for their
morning walks. The half-mile loop winds through a tunnel of rhodo-
dendrons and a hardwood forest. Those who tackle the half-mile,
strenuous **Waterrock Knob Trail** (MM 451.2), near the south end of
the parkway, will be rewarded with spectacular views from the 6,400-
ft-high Waterrock Knob summit.

ROCK CLIMBING

One of the most challenging climbs in the country is the **Linville Gorge**
(MM 317), often called "the Grand Canyon of North Carolina." Per-
mits are available from the district forest ranger's office in Nebo (☎
828/652–2144) or from the Linville Falls Texaco station on U.S. 221.

SKIING

Moses H. Cone Park (☎ 828/295–7591) is known for its cross-coun-
try skiing trails. On the Blue Ridge Parkway, **Roan Mountain** (☎ 615/
772–3303), open daily during the winter, is famous for its deep pow-
der. Tours and equipment are available from **High Country Ski Shop**
(☎ 828/733–2008), in Pineola on U.S. 221.

Blowing Rock

86 mi northeast of Asheville, 93 mi west of Winston-Salem.

Blowing Rock, a draw for mountain visitors since the 1880s, has re-
tained the flavor of a quiet village. About 1,000 people are permanent
residents, but the population swells each summer. To ensure that the
town would remain rural, the community banded together to prohibit
large hotels and motels. Blowing Rock is the inspiration for the small
town in resident Jan Karon's novels about country life in the fictional
town of Mitford. To get here from the Blue Ridge Parkway, take U.S.
221/321 to just north of the entrance to Moses H. Cone Park.

The **Blowing Rock** looms 4,000 ft over the Johns River Gorge. If you
throw your hat over the sheer precipice, it may come back to you, should

the wind gods be playful. The story goes that a Cherokee man and a Chickasaw maiden fell in love. Torn between his tribe and his love, he jumped from the cliff, but she prayed to the Great Spirit, and he was blown safely back to her. ✉ *Off U.S. 321,* ☎ *828/295–7111,* WEB *www.blowingrock. org.* ✑ *$4.* ☉ *June–Oct., Sun.–Thurs. 8:30–7, Fri.–Sat. 8:30–8; Nov.– Dec. and Mar.–May, daily 9–5; Jan.–Feb., weekends 8–5.*

🅲 The **Tweetsie Railroad** is a popular Wild West theme park built into the side of a mountain and centered on a steam locomotive beset by robbers. A petting zoo, carnival amusements, gem panning, shows, and concessions are also here. Several of the attractions are at the top of the mountain and can be reached by foot or ski lift. ✉ *U.S. 321/221, off Blue Ridge Pkwy., MM 291,* ☎ *828/264–9061 or 800/526–5740,* WEB *www.tweetsie-railroad.com.* ✑ *$23.* ☉ *Early May and mid-Aug.– Oct., Fri.–Sun. 9–6; mid-May–mid-Aug., daily 9–6.*

Lodging

$$$–$$$$ 🏨 **Chetola Resort.** This small gem, named for the Cherokee word meaning "haven of rest," grew out of an early 20th-century stone-and-wood lodge. The original building now houses the resort's restaurant and meeting rooms and is adjacent to the 1988 lodge. Many guest rooms in the lodge have private balconies facing either the mountains, the lake, or both. Condominiums are spread among the hills. The property adjoins Moses H. Cone Park, with hiking trails and riding facilities. ✉ *N. Main St., Box 17, 28605,* ☎ *828/295–5500 or 800/243–8652,* FAX *828/295–5529,* WEB *www.chetola.com. 37 rooms, 5 suites, 62 condominiums. 2 restaurants, minibars, 5 tennis courts, indoor pool, health club, hot tub, massage, boating, fishing, bicycles, racquetball, piano bar, playground, business services, meeting room. AE, D, MC, V.*

$$$–$$$$ 🏨 **Inn at Ragged Gardens.** With a grand stone staircase in the entry hall, colorful gardens, richly toned chestnut paneling, and the chestnut bark siding found on many older homes in the High Country, it's no wonder that this manor-style house in the heart of Blowing Rock gets rave reviews. You'll definitely appreciate the attention to detail: the European and American antiques blended with contemporary art and the all-hours butler's pantry. All rooms have fireplaces, and some have private balconies. It's best for older children. A two-night minimum is required on weekends. ✉ *203 Sunset Dr., 28605,* ☎ *828/295– 9703,* WEB *www.ragged-gardens.com. 6 rooms, 6 suites. Dining room, some hot tubs, meeting room. MC, V. BP.*

$$$ 🏨 **Maple Lodge Bed & Breakfast.** Blowing Rock's oldest continuously operating B&B is just off Main Street. Built in 1946, the inn has a wonderful garden, pine paneling in the foyer and twin parlors, and pine ceilings and woodwork throughout. Some rooms are small, but most can hold a queen-size bed and antique dresser, table, and chair comfortably. The full breakfast, served in an enclosed porch, includes delicious homemade breads and muffins. There's a two-night minimum many weekends. ✉ *152 Sunset Dr., 28605,* ☎ *828/295–3331,* FAX *828/295–9986,* WEB *www.maplelodge.net. 10 rooms, 1 suite. Dining room. AE, D, MC, V. BP.*

$–$$ 🏨 **Alpine Village Inn.** This motel in the heart of Blowing Rock harks back to a simpler time. Rooms are neat and attractive in a homey way. Owners Rudy and Lynn Cutrera have decorated them with antiques, quilts, even flowers on holidays. Room refrigerators are available, and morning coffee is served. ✉ *297 Sunset Dr., 28605,* ☎ *828/295–7206,* WEB *www.alpine-village-inn.com. 15 rooms. AE, D, MC, V.*

Outdoor Activities and Sports

HORSEBACK RIDING

Blowing Rock Stables (✉ U.S. 221, ☎ 828/295–7847) runs trail rides.

SKIING

There's downhill skiing at **Appalachian Ski Mountain** (⊠ 940 Ski Mountain Rd., ☎ 828/295–7828 or 800/322–2373).

Shopping

Bolick Pottery (⊠ Rte. 8 off U.S. 321, Lenoir, ☎ 828/295–3862), 3 mi southeast of Blowing Rock, sells mountain crafts and pottery hand-crafted by Glenn and Lula Bolick, fifth-generation potters.

Boone

8 mi north of Blowing Rock.

Boone, named for frontiersman Daniel Boone, is a city of several thousand residents at the convergence of three major highways—U.S. 321, U.S. 421, and Route 105. You'll find mountain crafts in stores and at crafts fairs here. **Mast General Store,** at the Old Boone Mercantile (⊠ 630 W. King St., ☎ 828/262–0000), is a classic general store.

Horn in the West, a project of the Southern Appalachian Historical Association, is an outdoor drama that traces the story of the lives of Daniel Boone and other pioneers, as well as the Cherokee, during the American Revolution. ⊠ *Amphitheater off U.S. 321,* ☎ *828/264–2120.* ☜ *$12.* ☉ *Performances mid-June–mid-Aug., Tues.–Sun. at 8 PM.*

The **Appalachian Cultural Museum** at Appalachian State University examines the lives of Native Americans and African-Americans in the High Country, showcases the successes of such mountain residents as stock-car racer Junior Johnson and country singers Lula Belle and Scotty Wiseman, and exhibits a vast collection of antique quilts, fiddles, and handcrafted furniture. ⊠ *University Hall Dr., near Greene's Motel, U.S. 321,* ☎ *828/262–3117,* WEB *www.museum.appstate.edu.* ☜ *$4.* ☉ *Tues.–Sat. 10–5, Sun. 1–5.*

OFF THE BEATEN PATH

BLUE RIDGE MOUNTAIN FRESCOES – In the 1970s North Carolina artist Ben Long and his students painted four luminous big-as-life frescoes in two churches about 45 mi northeast of Boone, in Ashe County, past Blue Ridge Parkway mile marker 258.6. *The Last Supper* is in the Glendale Springs Holy Trinity Church; the others, including *Mary, Great with Child,* are in St. Mary's Episcopal Church at Beaver Creek near West Jefferson. Signs from the parkway lead to the churches. ☎ *336/982–3076.* ☜ *Free.* ☉ *Freely accessible. Guide service available by prior arrangement.*

Dining and Lodging

$$ ✕ **Dan'l Boone Inn Restaurant.** Very near Appalachian State University, in a former hospital surrounded by a picket fence and flowers, Dan'l Boone offers old-fashioned food served family style. Warning: the portions of fried chicken, country-style steak, mashed potatoes, scrambled eggs, bacon, and breads (to name a few) are extremely generous. (You can't get breakfast on weekdays.) A gift shop sells food items, among other things. ⊠ *130 Hardin St.,* ☎ *828/264–8657,* WEB *www.danlbooneinn. com. No credit cards. No lunch weekdays, Nov.–late May.*

$$$$ 🏨 **Hound Ears Lodge and Club.** This alpine inn, overlooking Grandfather Mountain and a lush golf course, offers amenities such as a swimming pool secluded in a natural grotto and comfortable, well-kept rooms dressed in Waverly print fabrics. From April through October the room rate for special packages includes breakfast and dinner. The dining area is open only to guests and members; reservations are required, as are a jacket and tie for dinner. ⊠ *328 Shulls Mill Rd., off Rte. 105,*

6 mi from Boone, Box 188, 28605, ☏ *828/963–4321,* FAX *828/963–8030,* WEB *www.houndears.com. 29 rooms. Dining room, 18-hole golf course, 6 tennis courts, pool, fishing, business services, meeting room. AE, MC, V.*

$$$–$$$$ 🏨 **Lovill House Inn.** This restored two-story country farmhouse built in 1875 occupies 11 wooded acres at the western edge of Boone. On the grounds are a picnic area, gardens, and a stream with a waterfall. Some rooms have antique iron bedsteads or sleigh beds, and fireplaces. Every evening the owners host a beer and wine social hour. Kids 12 and up are welcome. ⊠ *404 Old Bristol Rd., 28607,* ☏ *828/264–4204 or 800/849–9466,* WEB *www.lovillhouseinn.com. 6 rooms. Dining room. MC, V. Closed Mar. BP.*

$–$$ 🏨 **Smoketree Lodge.** Views of Grandfather Mountain and an in-house art gallery that shows the work of local artists are the highlights of this mountain inn near the ski slopes. All rooms are fully equipped and have a kitchenette; use of the laundry facilities is free. ⊠ *11914 Rte. 105, Box 3407, 28607,* ☏ *828/963–6505 or 800/422–1880,* FAX *828/963–7815,* WEB *www.smoketreelodge.com. 46 rooms. Room service, indoor pool, exercise room, hot tub, recreation room. AE, D, MC, V.*

Outdoor Activities and Sports

CANOEING AND WHITE-WATER RAFTING
Near Boone and Blowing Rock, the New River, a federally designated Wild and Scenic River (Classes I and II rapids) provides excitement for canoeists and rafters, as do the Watauga River, Wilson Creek, and the Toe River. One outfitter is **Wahoo's Adventures** (☏ 828/262–5774 or 800/444–7238, WEB www.wahoosadventures.com).

GOLF
Western North Carolina has many challenging courses. **Boone Golf Club** (⊠ Fairway Dr., ☏ 828/264–8760) is a good par-71 course for the whole family. **Hound Ears Club** (⊠ Rte. 105, ☏ 828/963–4312) has a par-72 18-hole course with great mountain views. **Linville Golf Club** (⊠ Linville, ☏ 828/733–4363), 17 mi from Boone, has a par-72 Donald Ross course.

Valle Crucis

5 mi south of Boone.

This tiny mountain town has the state's first rural historic district; vintage stores line the downtown streets. Everything from ribbons and overalls to yard art and cookware is sold in the **Mast General Store** (⊠ Rte. 194, ☏ 828/963–6511, WEB www.mastgeneralstore.com). Built in 1882, the store has plank floors worn to a soft sheen and an active old-timey post office. You can take a shopping break by sipping bottled soda pop while sitting in a rocking chair on the store's back porch.

Dining and Lodging

$$$–$$$$ ✕🏨 **Mast Farm Inn.** You can turn back the clock and still enjoy modern amenities at this charming pastoral inn, built in the 1800s and now on the National Register of Historic Places. Rooms are in the farmhouse or in log outbuildings. The restaurant uses locally and organically grown vegetables to enhance its innovative uptown menu. Organic gardening demonstrations are held in the inn's gardens. ⊠ *2543 Broadstone Rd., Box 704, 28691,* ☏ *828/963–5857,* FAX *828/963–6404 or 888/963–5857,* WEB *www.mastfarminn.com. 9 rooms, 6 cottages. Restaurant. MC, V. BP.*

Banner Elk

6 mi southwest of Valle Crucis, 11 mi southwest of Boone.

Banner Elk is a popular ski resort town surrounded by the lofty peaks of Grandfather, Hanging Rock, Beech, and Sugar mountains.

Dining and Lodging

$$$-$$$$ ✕ **Jackalope's View.** The outside is brought indoors at this restaurant, at Archer's Inn, whose plentiful and oversize picture windows upstairs and down look out over the countryside (there's also a dining deck on the lower level). Jackalope classics include Jamaican jerk shrimp over linguine and Wiener schnitzel. The chef also prepares weekly specials, such as duck confit with a raspberry glaze over matchstick vegetables and potatoes. In the summer season there's live music on weekends. ✉ *2489 Beech Mountain Pkwy.,* ☎ *828/898–9004. D, MC, V. Closed Mon.*

$$-$$$ 🏠 **The Inns of Beech Mountain.** As these two Appalachian Mountain resorts—the Beech Alpen Inn and the Top of Beech Inn—are in eastern America's highest town, they overlook the slopes of the Blue Ridge Mountains. The staff is friendly at these country inns, and some rooms have fireplaces and balconies. The restaurant at Beech Alpen is open for dinner only. ✉ *700 Beech Mountain Pkwy., 28604,* ☎ *828/387–2252,* WEB *www.beechalpen.com. 48 rooms. Restaurant. AE, D, MC, V. CP.*

Outdoor Activities and Sports

CANOEING AND WHITE-WATER RAFTING

Edge of the World Outfitters (✉ Rte. 184, ☎ 828/898–9550 or 800/789–3343) offers white-water rafting, rappelling, canoeing, and snowboarding lessons in the Banner Elk area.

HORSEBACK RIDING

Banner Elk Riding Stables (✉ Rte. 184, ☎ 828/898–5424) runs trail rides.

SKIING

At 5,506 ft above sea level, **Ski Beech** (✉ Rte. 184, Beech Mountain, ☎ 828/387–2011 or 800/438–2093) is the highest resort in the eastern United States. One of the larger resorts in the area, **Sugar Mountain** (✉ off Rte. 184, Banner Elk, ☎ 828/898–4521 or 800/784–2768) has an equipment shop and lessons and tubing for the kids. A higher-end resort, **Hawksnest Golf and Ski Resort** (✉ 1800 Skyland Dr., Seven Devils, ☎ 828/963–6561 or 800/822–4295) has full snowmaking capability and challenging slopes. For **ski conditions** call ☎ 800/962–2322.

The Mountains A to Z

To research prices, get advice from other travelers, and book travel arrangements, visit www.fodors.com.

AIR TRAVEL

CARRIERS

➤ AIRLINES AND CONTACTS: **US Airways Express** (☎ 800/428–4322, WEB www.usair.com).

AIRPORTS

Asheville Regional Airport is served by Midway Connections, Atlantic Southeast Airlines, ComAir, and US Airways. US Airways Express serves the Hickory Airport, about 40 mi from Blowing Rock.
➤ AIRPORT INFORMATION: **Asheville Regional Airport** (✉ 708 Airport Rd., Fletcher, ☎ 828/684–2226, WEB www.ashevilleregionalairport.com). **Hickory Airport** (✉ U.S. 321, ☎ 828/323–7408).

BUS TRAVEL

Greyhound/Carolina Trailways serves Asheville.

➤ Bus Information: **Greyhound/Carolina Trailways** (☎ 800/231–2222, WEB www.greyhound.com).

CAR TRAVEL

I–40 runs east and west through Asheville. I–26 runs from Charleston, South Carolina, to Asheville. I–240 forms a perimeter around the city. U.S. 23–19A is a major north and west route. The Blue Ridge Parkway runs northeast from Great Smoky Mountains National Park to Shenandoah National Park in Virginia, passing Cherokee, Asheville, and the High Country. U.S. 221 runs north to the Virginia border through Blowing Rock and Boone and intersects I–40 at Marion. U.S. 321 intersects I–40 at Hickory and heads to Blowing Rock and Boone.

EMERGENCIES

Dial 911 for police and ambulance service everywhere but the Cherokee Reservation, where the police and the EMS can be reached at the numbers listed below.

➤ Doctors and Dentists: **Mission St. Joseph's** (✉ 509 Biltmore Ave., Asheville, ☎ 828/213–1111). **Watauga Medical Center** (✉ 336 Deerfield Rd., Boone, ☎ 828/262–4100).

➤ Emergency Services: **Ambulance, police** (☎ 911). **Cherokee Reservation Police and EMS** (☎ 828/497–4131 for police; 828/497–6402 for EMS).

➤ Hospitals: **Blowing Rock Hospital** (✉ 416 Chestnut Dr., Blowing Rock, ☎ 828/295–3136). **Cannon Memorial Hospital** (✉ 805 Shawneehaw Ave., Banner Elk, ☎ 828/898–5111).

LODGING

CAMPING

You can camp at the five developed, or "frontcountry," campgrounds in the North Carolina part of Great Smoky Mountains National Park; one of these, Smokemont, accepts reservations through the National Park Service Reservation Service. The remaining four campgrounds—Balsam Mountain, Big Creek, Cataloochee, and Deep Creek—are first come, first served only. All frontcountry camping in the park is primitive by design.

➤ Contacts: **Great Smoky Mountains National Park Headquarters** (✉ 107 Park Headquarters Rd., Gatlinburg, TN 37738, ☎ 865/436–1230; 865/436–1231 for inquiries about backcountry camping, WEB www.gsmnp.com). **National Park Service Reservation Service** (☎ 800/365–2267).

OUTDOORS AND SPORTS

CANOEING AND RAFTING

For canoeing and white-water rafting in the Asheville area, the Chattooga, Nolichucky, French Broad, Nantahala, Ocoee, and Green rivers offer Class I–V rapids. One of the largest area outfitters is Nantahala Outdoor Center.

➤ Contacts: **Nantahala Outdoor Center** (✉ 13077 U.S. 19W, Bryson City, ☎ 828/488–2175 or 800/232–7238, WEB ww.noc.com).

GOLF

Western North Carolina offers many challenging golf courses. For a complete listing of public courses in Asheville, Black Mountain, Brevard, Hendersonville, Lake Lure, Old Fort, and Waynesville, contact the Asheville Convention and Visitors Bureau.

HIKING

Anyone into serious hiking can explore the Appalachian Trail, which runs along the crest of the Appalachian Mountains at the North Car-

olina–Tennessee border. It can be picked up at several points, including the Newfound Gap parking area in the Great Smoky Mountains National Park and Grandfather Mountain, where you can get trail maps.
➤ CONTACTS: **Grandfather Mountain** (☎ 828/733–4337). **Great Smoky Mountains National Park** (☎ 615/436–5615).

VISITOR INFORMATION

In Asheville, the Asheville Convention and Visitors Bureau will answer questions and provide maps. The Cherokee Visitors Center provides information on the reservation. North Carolina High Country Host is a complete information center for the High Country counties of Watauga, Ashe, and Avery. Smoky Mountain Host of North Carolina has information about the state's seven westernmost counties.
➤ TOURIST INFORMATION: **Asheville Convention and Visitors Bureau** (✉ 151 Haywood St., Box 1010, 28802, ☎ 828/258–6102 or 800/257–1300, WEB www.ashevillechamber.org). **Cherokee Visitors Center** (✉ U.S. 441 Business, ☎ 828/497–9195 or 800/438–1601, WEB www.cherokee-nc.com). **North Carolina High Country Host** (✉ 1701 Blowing Rock Rd., Boone 28607, ☎ 828/264–1299 or 800/438–7500, WEB www.visitboonenc.com). **Smoky Mountain Host of NC** (✉ 4437 Georgia Rd., Franklin 28734, ☎ 828/369–9606 or 800/432–4678, WEB www.visitsmokies.org).

NORTH CAROLINA A TO Z

To research prices, get advice from other travelers, and book travel arrangements, visit www.fodors.com.

AIR TRAVEL

AIRPORTS

Among the major airports in the state are Charlotte-Douglas International Airport, the Piedmont Triad International Airport, and the Raleigh-Durham International Airport.
➤ AIRPORT INFORMATION: **Charlotte-Douglas International Airport** (✉ 5501 Josh Birmingham Blvd., ☎ 704/359–4013). **Piedmont Triad International Airport** (✉ 6451 Bryan Blvd., Greensboro, ☎ 336/665–5666). **Raleigh-Durham International Airport** (✉ 1600 Terminal Blvd., Morrisville, ☎ 919/840–2123).

BIKE TRAVEL

North Carolina has more than 5,000 mi of mapped and signed bicycle routes, many on scenic country roads. For maps and information contact the Division of Bicycle and Pedestrian Transportation.
➤ BIKE MAPS: **Division of Bicycle and Pedestrian Transportation** (✉ Box 25201, Raleigh 27611, ☎ 919/733–2804).

BOAT AND FERRY TRAVEL

Ferries connect coastal communities. Routes and schedules are printed on the official North Carolina State Transportation Map and are available by phone from the Department of Transportation.

FARES AND SCHEDULES

➤ BOAT AND FERRY INFORMATION: **Department of Transportation** (☎ 800/293–3779).

BUS TRAVEL

Greyhound/Carolina Trailways links the cities of North Carolina with major cities in the southeastern United States and links cities and towns throughout the state.
➤ BUS INFORMATION: **Greyhound/Carolina Trailways** (☎ 800/231–2222, WEB www.greyhound.com).

CAR TRAVEL

I–40 traverses the state from Asheville, in the west, to Wilmington, in the east. I–85 passes through the Triangle, the Triad, and Charlotte as it crosses from northeast to southwest. I–77 passes through the western part of the state from Virginia through Charlotte to South Carolina, and I–95 carries north–south traffic in the eastern part of the state.

➤ CONTACTS: **North Carolina Department of Transportation** (✉ Public Affairs Division, Box 25201, Raleigh 27611, ☎ 919/733–7600; 800/847–4862 outside NC). **Scenic Byways information** (☎ 919/733–2920).

RULES OF THE ROAD

The speed limit on interstates varies; it's generally 65 or 70 mph. Right turns on red are permitted unless otherwise indicated.

EMERGENCIES

In almost all cities and towns dial 911 for police or ambulance in an emergency. Most hospital emergency rooms are open 24 hours a day. Smaller ones are often connected by air evacuation systems to major trauma centers.

➤ EMERGENCY SERVICES: **Ambulance, police** (☎ 911).

OUTDOORS AND SPORTS

FISHING

A mandatory state license can be bought at local bait and tackle shops or over the phone (with a credit card) from the North Carolina Wildlife Commission. The cost for nonresidents is as follows: one day, $10; three days, $15; and a one-year pass $30.

➤ CONTACTS: **North Carolina Wildlife Commission** (☎ 919/715–4091).

TRAIN TRAVEL

Amtrak offers daily service from major cities on the eastern seaboard to the state's main population centers, including Charlotte, Greensboro, Raleigh, Cary, Durham, and Southern Pines; Amtrak also offers daily service between a number of cities and towns within the state.

➤ TRAIN INFORMATION: **Amtrak** (☎ 800/872–7245, WEB www.amtrak.com).

VISITOR INFORMATION

The North Carolina Division of Tourism, Film and Sports Development has information packets and an information line. Operators will answer questions about everything from beaches to snow conditions.

➤ TOURIST INFORMATION: **North Carolina Division of Tourism, Film and Sports Development** (✉ 301 N. Wilmington St., Raleigh 27601, ☎ 919/733–4171 or 800/847–4862, FAX 919/733–8582).

4 SOUTH CAROLINA

South Carolina's scenic Lowcountry shoreline is punctuated by the historic yet vibrant port city of Charleston, known for its elegant homes and fine museums. The recreational resorts of Myrtle Beach and Hilton Head anchor each end of the coast. Columbia, the state capital, is in the fertile interior of the state, which stretches toward the Blue Ridge Mountains. Also to the west are the rolling fields of Thoroughbred Country. Upcountry South Carolina, at the northwestern tip of the state, has incredible mountain scenery and white-water rafting.

Updated by
Mary Sue
Lawrence

F ROM ITS LOWCOUNTRY SHORELINE, with wide sand beaches, spacious bays, and forests of palmettos and moss-draped live oaks, South Carolina extends into an undulating interior region rich with fertile farmlands, then reaches toward the Blue Ridge Mountains, whose foothills are studded with scenic lakes, forests, and wilderness hideaways. What this smallest of Southern states lacks in land area it makes up for in diversity and enthusiasm. People here like to celebrate. Every month of the year there's a local festival that turns on regional pride, feting critters such as jumping frogs, edibles such as peaches and watermelons, or rarefied delicacies such as okra and chitterlings. South Carolina owes much of its growth to the tourism industry, which brings in billions of dollars and millions of people annually.

The historic port city of Charleston, although beautifully preserved, is not a museum city. Many of its treasured double-galleried antebellum homes are authentically furnished house museums, but just as many are homes for Charlestonians and newcomers. Residents air their quilts over piazzas, walk their dogs down cobblestone streets, and tend their famous gardens in much the same way their ancestors did 300 years ago. Locals bravely rebounded from Hurricane Hugo, which hit in 1989, to painstakingly rebuild and renovate, making the city seem as gleaming and fresh as it must have been during the 18th century. Renovation continues to expand to the far reaches of the downtown historic district, extending across the Cooper River Bridge and out of the town of Mount Pleasant into Awendaw and McClellanville. Culturally vibrant, Charleston nurtures theater, dance, music, and visual arts, showcased each spring during the internationally acclaimed Spoleto Festival USA.

Myrtle Beach is the glitzy jewel of the Grand Strand, a 60-mi stretch of wide white-sand beaches and recreational activities, especially golf, a top attraction throughout the state. South from Myrtle Beach to Georgetown, it's almost one continuous community. Georgetown itself is enjoying a healthy tourism trade, offering a small-town respite smack-dab between the urbane sophistication of Charleston and the amusement-park excitement of Myrtle Beach.

To the south, tasteful, low-key Hilton Head—divided into several self-contained resorts—also offers beautiful beaches and wonderful golf and tennis. A toll expressway handles traffic to the resort areas. Sun City, a large, newly developed retirement community, is attracting scores of fiftysomethings to the area.

Nearby is the port city of Beaufort, with lovely streets dotted with preserved 18th-century homes. A stopover popular with New York–to–Florida commuters, it's also the favorite of early retirees in search of small-town life and great deals on real estate; many have converted its historic houses into bed-and-breakfasts.

Columbia, the state capital, is a busy and historic city blessed by three rushing rivers. Besides museums and a good minor-league baseball team, the city has one of the country's top zoos and a riverside botanical garden. The presence of the University of South Carolina, with a student body of 40,000, means that nightlife and cheap and cheerful restaurants are plentiful. Nearby lakes and state parks provide abundant outdoor recreation and first-rate fishing, and the Congaree Swamp National Monument has the oldest and largest trees east of the Mississippi.

Thoroughbred Country, centered on the town of Aiken, is a peaceful area of rolling pastures where top racehorses are trained. In this part of the state, charming, old-fashioned towns such as Abbeville and Cheraw draw more and more interest for their history, abundant outdoor activities, sleepy main streets, and friendly residents.

Upcountry South Carolina, at the northwestern tip, is less visited than the rest of the state but repays time spent here with dramatic mountain scenery, excellent hiking, and challenging white-water rafting. Greenville has seen a dramatic growth spurt in the last few years. Downtown Greenville is changing rapidly; trendy cafés, shops, and boutiques, plus a newfound cultural diversity, are vivifying the city.

Pleasures and Pastimes

Beaches

South Carolina's mild climate makes the surf enjoyable from April through October. The beaches are expanses of white sand—some serene and secluded, others bustling and lined with high-rises. You can choose the high-voltage action at busy Myrtle Beach or the more low-key scene on the resort island of Hilton Head, or just stroll the sands at Huntington Beach State Park.

Dining

South Carolinians love to cook and share good food, from dishes marinated in tradition to the creatively contemporary. Lowcountry specialties include she-crab soup, stuffed oysters, and infinite variations on pecan pie. Seafood—often the fresh catch of the day—is likely to be traditionally prepared on the Grand Strand and gussied up on Hilton Head. Elsewhere in the state, try barbecue and look for various cuisines, from cosmopolitan to country cookery. And don't write off grits until you've tasted them laced with cheese and cream, topped with *tasso* (spiced ham) gravy, or folded into a veal or quail entrée.

CATEGORY	COST*
$$$$	over $25
$$$	$17–$25
$$	$10–$17
$	under $10

*per person for a main course at dinner

Gardens

Gardening devotees can and do build vacations around South Carolina gardens, where camellias, azaleas, other flowering shrubs, and blooming trees abound. Along the coast are some of the nation's most famous, including Middleton Place, with the oldest landscaped garden in America; Cypress Gardens, where cypress trees tower in dark waters with azaleas on the banks; and Brookgreen Gardens, with a superb outdoor sculpture collection set amid giant oaks and colorful flowers. Inland, remarkable gardens planted with roses, irises, or mountain laurel make some small towns a worthwhile side trip. Along the way you can see peach orchards in bloom in spring.

Lodging

From predictable but dependable chains to luxurious resort hotels and quaint B&Bs, accommodations are available for every budget. Reservations are a must, especially on the coast, and prices do vary with the seasons—in fact, winter rates in Charleston and along the coast can be a pleasant surprise.

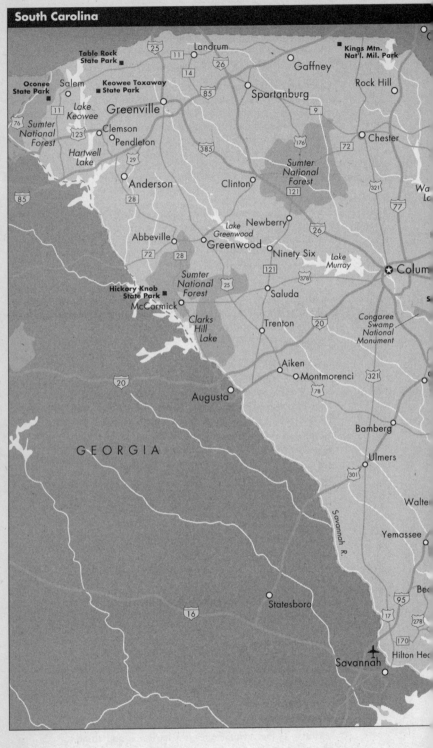

Kings Mtn.
Nat'l. Mil. Park

Table Rock
State Park

Landrum

Gaffney

Rock Hill

Oconee
State Park

Salem

Keowee Toxaway
State Park

Spartanburg

Chester

Sumter
National
Forest

Lake
Keowee

Greenville

Clemson

Pendleton

Hartwell
Lake

Sumter
National
Forest

Wa
La

Anderson

Clinton

Lake
Greenwood

Newberry

Abbeville

Greenwood

Ninety Six

Lake
Murray

Colum

Sumter
National
Forest

Saluda

Hickory Knob
State Park

McCormick

Clarks
Hill
Lake

Trenton

Congaree
Swamp
National
Monument

Aiken

Montmorenci

Augusta

GEORGIA

Bamberg

Ulmers

Walte

Savannah R.

Yemassee

Bec

Statesboro

Savannah

Hilton Hea

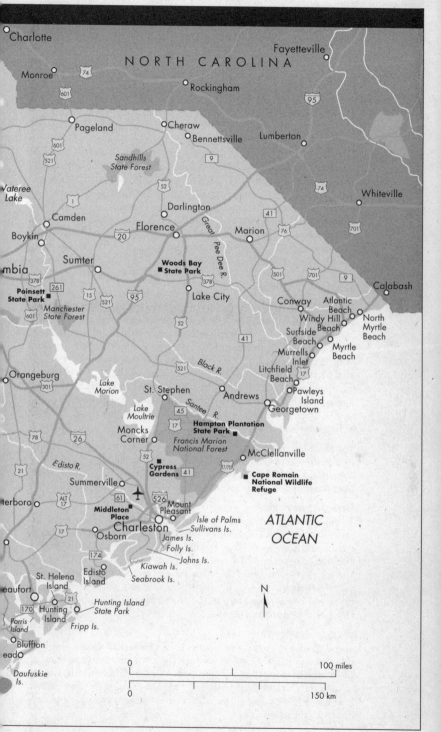

Charlotte

Monroe

NORTH CAROLINA

Fayetteville

74

601

Rockingham

95

Pageland

Cheraw

Bennettsville

Lumberton

601

Sandhills
State Force

9

74

Whiteville

521

Vateree
Lake

52

Darlington

41

76

701

1

Camden

20

Florence

Marion

Boykin

Great

501

701

9

Calabash

Sumter

378

261

Woods Bay
State Park

Pee Dee R.

378

Conway

Atlantic
Beach

Poinsett
State Park

15

521

95

Lake City

Windy Hill
Beach

North
Myrtle
Beach

mbia

Manchester
State Forest

601

52

41

Surfside
Beach

Murrells
Inlet

Myrtle
Beach

Black R.

Litchfield
Beach

17

Orangeburg

301

521

St. Stephen

Andrews

Pawleys
Island

Lake
Marion

Santee

45

Georgetown

Lake
Moultrie

17

Hampton Plantation
State Park

78

26

Moncks
Corner

Francis Marion
National Forest

McClellanville

21

Edisto R.

52

Cypress
Gardens

41

17/70

Cape Romain
National Wildlife
Refuge

Summerville

ALT
17

61

526

Mount
Pleasant

ATLANTIC
OCEAN

terboro

Middleton
Place

Isle of Palms

17

Osborn

Charleston

Sullivans Is.

James Is.

St. Helena
Island

174

Edisto
Island

Folly Is.

Johns Is.

Kiawah Is.

N

eaufort

21

Seabrook Is.

170

Hunting
Island

Hunting Island
State Park

Parris
Island

Fripp Is.

Bluffton

eado

Daufuskie
Is.

0   100 miles

0   150 km

CATEGORY	CHARLESTON, HILTON HEAD, MYRTLE BEACH, AND THE COAST*	OTHER AREAS*
$$$$	over $200	over $150
$$$	$150–$200	$110–$150
$$	$100–$150	$75–$110
$	under $100	under $75

All prices are for a standard double room, excluding 7% tax.

Outdoor Activities

On South Carolina's many rivers and lakes you can indulge in boating, fly- and deep-water fishing, kayaking, sailboarding, sailing, tubing, and, in the Upcountry, white-water rafting. Canoeing is popular on waters near Columbia. Anglers frequently break records with hauls of largemouth bass, stripers, crappie, and catfish caught in Lakes Marion and Moultrie. The first passages of the Palmetto Trail—a hiking, mountain-biking, and horseback-riding trail that will eventually wind 400 mi across the state—are open: the High Hills of Santee Passage, the Lake Moultrie Passage, and the Swamp Fox Passage, in Francis Marion National Forest. Golfing, of course, reigns supreme practically year-round; the state has more than 380 courses.

Exploring South Carolina

South Carolina has three regions—its 200-mi coastline, its interior heart, and its hilly north country. Charleston and points south are the Lowcountry, distinguished by aristocratic elegance and an accent unlike any other in the South. Because Hilton Head Island, in the southern part of the state, has become world renowned as a posh resort, it is treated separately here, along with the coastal towns near it. Natives consider the upper coasts part of what they call the Pee Dee (after the Pee Dee River), but the world knows Myrtle Beach and its environs by their more famous other name—the Grand Strand. It refers to the sandy strip of beaches more than 60 mi long.

The Heartland, including the Midlands core of the state, is an eclectic collection of towns and the capital city, Columbia. It also includes Thoroughbred Country, lush pasture for Triple Crown contenders. The Upcountry, noted for mountain scenery, is in the northwest.

Great Itineraries

To enjoy South Carolina to the fullest, you need a week or more to savor the coast and visit briefly inland. But you can have a memorable experience, however fleeting, by choosing sights that strike your fancy and promising yourself to return another time for more. The Lowcountry and Charleston are priorities; every traveler to South Carolina should visit that historic city—and most want to. With a bit more time you can travel north from there to the Grand Strand or south to Hilton Head or west into the Heartland.

IF YOU HAVE 1 DAY

Spend the day in the historic district in 🔝 **Charleston.** Take a carriage ride through it for a look at some of the city's most elegant homes. Then browse through the shops in the Old City Market area, where most of the carriage tours begin and end. After that, walk south along East Bay Street or any of the side streets on your way to a couple of the area's museums.

IF YOU HAVE 2–3 DAYS

🔝 **Charleston** has so many charms—a rich antebellum and Civil War history, plantations and historic homes, beaches, golf, and superb restaurants—that you could spend a week here. Expand your itinerary on Day 2 by adding more sights within the historic district, by browsing along King Street, and by including the Charleston Museum and other nearby museums. On the afternoon of Day 2 or Day 3, you could visit Mount Pleasant, with access to Fort Sumter National Monument, nice beaches, and Boone Hall Plantation to the north. Or you could head west of the Ashley River to visit Charles Towne Landing State Park and Magnolia Plantation and Gardens.

IF YOU HAVE 5–6 DAYS

On Day 4 take a leisurely exit from Charleston along Route 61 and see **Drayton Hall** and **Middleton Place** as you make your way inland for a quick visit to ☶ **Columbia,** with its State House, historic university campus, and zoo and botanical garden. Another choice is to take U.S. 17 north toward the beaches of the **Grand Strand,** where you can stay in busy ☶ **Myrtle Beach** or the more quiet ☶ **Pawleys Island,** or south toward ☶ **Beaufort** or ☶ **Hilton Head Island.** There are beautiful gardens, stately plantations, and fine museums in both directions.

IF YOU HAVE 10 DAYS

Follow the itineraries above and then extend your time in ☶ **Columbia.** Take a canoe ride on the scenic Saluda River or down the Congaree River, and visit Congaree Swamp National Monument. Take a day trip to historic, horsey **Camden** or **Aiken** to get the flavor of other Heartland towns. On Day 8 head to the Upcountry for magnificent scenery. You can explore ☶ **Greenville,** perhaps driving north to the Cherokee Foothills Scenic Highway or to Kings Mountain National Military Park. You might head west and raft on the Chattooga River and spend your last day in ☶ **Pendleton,** with its historic district and proximity to Clemson and the South Carolina State Botanical Garden.

When to Tour South Carolina

South Carolina is loveliest in spring, when azaleas, dogwood, and other flowering bushes and trees are in bloom, but flowers brighten every season—even winter, when pansies and camellias thrive. Between mid-March and mid-April you can catch tours of private mansions in Charleston, and the city is alive with Spoleto events in May and June. Beaufort holds its Water Festival in mid-July. For price breaks on the coast, consider visiting in the off-season, October through February, but remember that some restaurants and a few attractions close around that time, and the water may be cool.

CHARLESTON

At first glimpse Charleston resembles an 18th-century etching come to life. Its low-profile skyline is punctuated with the spires and steeples of 181 churches, representing 25 denominations—the reason that Charleston, known for religious freedom during its formation, is called the Holy City. Parts of the city appear frozen in time; block after block of old downtown structures have been preserved and restored for residential and commercial use, and some brick and cobblestone streets remain. Charleston has survived three centuries of epidemics, earthquakes, fires, and hurricanes, and it is today one of the South's loveliest and best-preserved cities. It is not a museum, however: throughout the year festivals add excitement and sophistication.

Besides the historic district (which we've divided, for ease of exploration, into two parts: the area north of Broad Street, and the Battery and area south of Broad Street), a visit to the city can easily include nearby towns, plantations and outstanding gardens, and historic sites, whether in Mount Pleasant or the area west of the Ashley River.

North of Broad

To really appreciate Charleston, you must walk its streets. The downtown historic district, roughly bounded by Calhoun Street to the north, the Cooper River to the east, the Battery to the south, and Legare Street to the west, is large, with 2,000 historic homes and buildings on the southeastern tip of the Charleston peninsula. In a fairly compact area you'll find churches, museums, and lovely views at every turn.

The area north of Broad Street has some of the finest historic homes and neighborhoods in the city, including the Mazyck/Wraggborough neighborhood, where you'll find the Aiken-Rhett House. Large tracts of land made this area ideal for urban plantations during the early 1800s. Although there are a number of prerevolutionary buildings here (including the Old Powder Magazine, the oldest public building in Charleston), in general, the farther north you travel on the peninsula, the newer the development. Still, because the peninsula was built-out by the early 1900s, North of Broad is rich with historic buildings from the 19th century and can be lovely—especially since most tourists are busy conquering the waterfront area.

Numbers in the text correspond to numbers in the margin and on the Charleston map.

A Good Walk

Before you begin touring, drop by the **visitor information center** ① on Meeting Street for an overview of the city, a map, and tickets for shuttle services if you want to give your feet a break. Start across the street at the **Charleston Museum** ②, with its large decorative arts collection; then turn right on Ann Street and follow it to Elizabeth Street to the palatial **Aiken-Rhett House** ③. After touring the house, head south down Elizabeth Street and turn right on John Street for the **Joseph Manigault Mansion** ④, another impressive house museum dating to the early 1800s. Continue on John Street to reach the **American Military Museum** ⑤. Return to Meeting Street and walk south toward Calhoun Street, passing the **Old Citadel Building** ⑥, converted into an Embassy Suites. Take a left on Calhoun Street; a half block down on your left is the **Emanuel African Methodist Episcopal Church** ⑦, where slave rebellion leader Denmark Vesey was a member. From here you may want to use the shuttle bus DASH to give your feet a rest, or cross the street to Marion Square Mall for a drink and a break.

Retrace your steps on Calhoun Street (passing the Francis Marion Hotel, in the 1920s the highest building in the Carolinas) and continue two blocks west to St. Phillips Street, where you turn left to end up in the midst of the romantic campus of the **College of Charleston** ⑩, the oldest municipal college in the country. Enter through one of the gated openings on St. Phillips Street for a stroll under the many moss-draped trees. Then head east to King Street, Charleston's main shopping thoroughfare, and turn right; turn left on Hasell Street to see **Kahal Kadosh Beth Elohim Reform Temple** ⑪, a Greek Revival building. Across the street is **St. Mary's Catholic Church** ⑫. Keep walking down Hasell Street and turn right on Meeting Street. Two blocks to the south are **Market Hall** ⑭ and the bustling **Old City Market** ⑮. Now is a good time for a carriage tour, many of which leave from here. Across Meeting Street is the classy **Charleston Place** ⑬, with its graceful hotel and cluster of shops. You can browse from one end to the other, exiting on King Street.

Cross the street and walk a block down Market Street, turning left on quiet Archdale Street to wander through **St. John's Lutheran Church** ⑯ and the peaceful graveyard of the **Unitarian Church** ⑰. Turn left on Queen

Charleston

Street at the bottom of Archdale and walk two blocks to Meeting Street, where you turn left for the **Gibbes Museum of Art** ⑱, with its spectacular stained-glass dome. Across the street is the **Circular Congregational Church** ⑲. Behind it, on Cumberland Street, is the **Old Powder Magazine** ⑳. To the left as you face the building, you'll catch a glimpse of the steeple of **St. Philip's Episcopal Church** ㉑, famous in the city's skyline; it's around the corner on Church Street.

Cross over to picturesque Church Street to the **French Protestant (Huguenot) Church** ㉔ and the **Dock Street Theatre** ㉓, across the street. You might detour east here, down Queen Street and along Vendue Range to **Waterfront Park** ㉒, to relax in a bench swing overlooking beautiful river views, dramatic fountains, and a fishing pier.

TIMING

Set aside from two to four hours for this walk, depending on your pace. Most of the house-museum tours last about 40 minutes, so you might choose the two or three that interest you most. Charleston rickshaws (bicycle-powered two-seaters), which can take you anywhere downtown for $6, can ease the trip back.

Sights to See

❸ **Aiken-Rhett House.** This stately 1819 mansion, with its original wallpaper, paint colors, and some of its furnishings, was the headquarters of Confederate general P. G. T. Beauregard during his 1864 Civil War defense of Charleston. The house, kitchen, slave quarters, and work yard are maintained much as they were when the original occupants lived here, making this one of the most complete examples of African-American urban life of the period. ⊠ *48 Elizabeth St., Upper King,* ☎ *843/ 723–1159,* WEB *www.historiccharleston.org.* ☞ *$7; combination ticket with Nathaniel Russell House $12.* ☉ *Mon.–Sat. 10–5, Sun. 2–5.*

❺ **American Military Museum.** The museum displays hundreds of uniforms and artifacts from all branches of service, beginning with the Revolutionary War. Its collections also include antique toy soldiers, war toys, miniatures, and weaponry. ⊠ *44 John St., Upper King,* ☎ *843/723– 9620.* ☞ *$5.* ☉ *Mon.–Sat. 10–6, Sun. 1–6.*

★ ❷ **Charleston Museum.** Founded in 1773, the country's oldest city museum is in a contemporary complex. The 500,000 items in the collection—in addition to Charleston silver, fashions, toys, snuffboxes, and the like—include objects relating to natural history, archaeology, and ornithology. Its South Carolina decorative arts holdings are extraordinary. The Discover Me Room, designed just for children, has computers and other hands-on exhibits. Two historic homes—the **Joseph Manigault Mansion** and the **Heyward-Washington House**—are owned and managed by the museum. ⊠ *360 Meeting St., Upper King,* ☎ *843/ 722–2996,* WEB *www.charlestonmuseum.com.* ☞ *$8; museum and houses $18; 2 of the 3 sights $12.* ☉ *Mon.–Sat. 9–5, Sun. 1–5.*

⑬ **Charleston Place.** The city's only world-class hotel, this Orient-Express property is flanked by a complex of upscale boutiques and specialty shops. Peek into the lobby or have cocktails or tea in the intimate Lobby Lounge. Entrances for the garage and reception area are on Hasell Street between Meeting and King streets. ⊠ *130 Market St., Market area,* ☎ *843/722–4900.*

⑲ **Circular Congregational Church.** The corners of this unusual Romanesque church were rounded off, they say, so the devil would have no place to hide. Simple but pretty, it has a beamed, vaulted ceiling. ⊠ *150 Meeting St., Market area,* ☎ *843/577–6400.* ☉ *Call for tour schedule.*

⑩ College of Charleston. The lovely, tree-shaded campus of this college, founded in 1770, has a graceful main building, the Randolph House (1828), designed by Philadelphia architect William Strickland. It's a romantic backdrop for the Cistern, often used as a grassy stage for concerts and other activities. Within the college, centered at the corner of George and St. Phillips streets in what was once a school for freed slaves, is the **Avery Research Center for African-American History and Culture,** which traces the heritage of Lowcountry African-Americans. Civil Rights activist Cleveland Seller's personal letters, telegrams, newspaper clippings, and other papers—one of the best series of manuscript collections documenting the Civil Rights movement—is here. ⊠ *Avery Research Center, 125 Bull St., College of Charleston Campus,* ☎ *843/953–7609,* WEB *www.cofc.edu/INSERT TILDEaveryrsc.* ☜ *Free.* ☉ *Mon.–Sat. noon–5, mornings by appointment.*

㉓ Dock Street Theatre. Built on the site of one of the nation's first playhouses, the building combines the reconstructed early Georgian playhouse and the preserved Old Planter's Hotel (circa 1809). The theater, which offers fascinating backstage views, welcomes visitors except when technical work for a show is under way. ⊠ *135 Church St., Market area,* ☎ *843/720–3968.* ☜ *Free tours; call ahead for ticket prices and performance times.* ☉ *Weekdays 10–4.*

❼ Emanuel African Methodist Episcopal Church. Home of the South's oldest A.M.E. congregation, the church had its beginnings in 1818. It was closed in 1822 when authorities learned that Denmark Vesey had used the sanctuary to plan his slave insurrection, but the church reopened in 1865 at the present site. ⊠ *110 Calhoun St., Upper King,* ☎ *843/722–2561.* ☉ *Daily 9–4.*

㉔ French Protestant (Huguenot) Church. This church is the only one in the country still using the original Huguenot liturgy, which can be heard in a special service held each spring. ⊠ *110 Church St., Market area,* ☎ *843/722–4385.* ☉ *Weekdays 10–12:30 and 2–4.*

⑱ Gibbes Museum of Art. The collections of American art include notable 18th- and 19th-century portraits of Carolinians and an outstanding group of more than 400 miniature portraits. Don't miss the miniature rooms—intricately detailed with fabrics and furnishings and nicely displayed in shadowboxes inset in dark-paneled walls—or the Tiffany-style stained-glass dome in the rotunda. ⊠ *135 Meeting St., Market area,* ☎ *843/722–2706,* WEB *www.gibbes.com.* ☜ *$5.* ☉ *Tues.–Sat. 10–5, Sun.–Mon. 1–5.*

NEED A BREAK?

Just across the street from the Gibbes Museum, **Joseph's** (⊠ 129 Meeting St., Market area, ☎ 843/958–8500) serves a great Southern breakfast, lovely lunch, and super Sunday brunch in its courtyard garden.

❹ Joseph Manigault Mansion. A National Historic Landmark and an outstanding example of neoclassical architecture, this home was designed by Charleston architect Gabriel Manigault in 1803 and is noted for its carved-wood mantels and elaborate plasterwork. Some furnishings are British and French, but most are Charleston antiques; some rare tricolor Wedgwood pieces are noteworthy. ⊠ *350 Meeting St., Upper King,* ☎ *843/723–2926,* WEB *www.charlestonmuseum.com.* ☜ *$7; museum and houses $18; 2 of the 3 sights $12.* ☉ *Mon.–Sat. 10–5, Sun. 1–5.*

⑪ Kahal Kadosh Beth Elohim Reform Temple. Considered one of the nation's finest examples of Greek Revival architecture, this temple was built in 1840 to replace an earlier one—the birthplace of American reform Judaism in 1824—that was destroyed by fire. ✉ *86 Hasell St., Market area,* ☎ *843/723–1090,* WEB *www.kkbe.org.* ⊙ *Weekdays 10–noon.*

⓮ Market Hall. Built in 1841 and modeled after the Temple of Nike in Athens, this imposing landmark, now open after a five-year renovation, includes the **Confederate Museum,** where the Daughters of the Confederacy preserve and display flags, uniforms, swords, and other Civil War memorabilia. ✉ *188 Meeting St., Market area,* ☎ *843/723–1541,* ▨ *$5.* ⊙ *Mon–Sat. 10–4, Sun. 1–4.*

❻ Old Citadel Building. Built in 1822 to house state troops and arms, this fortresslike building—now the Embassy Suites Historic Charleston—faces Marion Square. This is where the Carolina Military College—the Citadel—had its start. (The Citadel is now on the Ashley River.) ✉ *Upper King.*

✆ ⓯ Old City Market. A series of low sheds that once housed produce and fish markets, this area is often called the Slave Market, although Charlestonians dispute that slaves ever were sold there. It now has restaurants, shops, gimcracks and gewgaws for children, vegetable-and-fruit vendors, and local "basket ladies" weaving and selling sweet-grass, pine-straw, and palmetto-leaf baskets—a craft passed down through generations from their West African ancestors. ✉ *Market St. between Meeting and E. Bay Sts., Market area.* ⊙ *Daily 9–sunset, hrs may vary.*

⓴ Old Powder Magazine. This structure was built in 1713 and used during the Revolutionary War. It is now a museum with costumes, armor, and other artifacts from 18th-century Charleston, plus a fascinating audiovisual tour. ✉ *79 Cumberland St., Market area,* ☎ *843/805–6730,* WEB *www.historiccharleston.org.* ▨ *Free.* ⊙ *Apr.–Oct., Mon.–Sat. 10–5, Sun. 2–5.*

⓰ St. John's Lutheran Church. This Greek Revival church was built in 1817 for a congregation that was established in 1742. Notice the fine craftsmanship in the delicate wrought-iron gates and fence. Musicians may be interested in the 1823 Thomas Hall organ case. ✉ *5 Clifford St., Market area,* ☎ *843/723–2426,* WEB *www.stjohns-lutheran.org.* ⊙ *Weekdays 9:30–3:30.*

⓬ St. Mary's Catholic Church. Established in 1839, this pretty white-pillared church is the earliest Roman Catholic church in the Carolinas and Georgia. Beautiful stained glass, wall paintings, and an enchanting cemetery tucked between stone walls are highlights. ✉ *89 Hasell St., Market area,* ☎ *843/722–7696.* ⊙ *By appointment.*

㉑ St. Philip's Episcopal Church. The graceful late-Georgian church is the second on its site; the congregation's first building burned down in 1838. You find the burial places of Charlestonians in the graveyard on the church side of the street; "foreigners" (including John C. Calhoun, who was from the faraway location of Abbeville, South Carolina) lie in the graveyard on the other side. ✉ *146 Church St., Market area,* ☎ *843/722–7734.* ⊙ *By appointment.*

㉕ Slave Mart Museum. Here—at a spot where slaves were once bought and sold—exhibits highlight the African-American experience in Charleston, from slavery to emancipation and reconstruction and, finally, to the civil rights movement. ✉ *6 Chalmers St., Market area.* ⊙ *Mon.–Sat. 9–5.*

⓱ Unitarian Church. Completed in 1787, this church was remodeled in the mid-19th century using plans inspired by the Chapel of Henry VII in Westminster Abbey. The Gothic fan-tracery ceiling was added during that renovation. An entrance to the church grounds is on 161½–163 King Street. The secluded and romantically overgrown graveyard invites contemplation. ⊠ *8 Archdale St., Market area,* ☎ *843/723–4617 weekdays 8:30–2:30.* ☉ *Sept.–May, 11 AM service.*

❶ Visitor Information Center. The center gives a fine introduction to the city and sells tickets for shuttle services. Garage parking is $1 per hour; the first hour is free if you purchase a $2 shuttle pass. Take time to see *Forever Charleston,* an insightful 20-minute film. For $32.95 you can also buy a Charleston Heritage Passport, good for admission at Gibbes Museum of Art, Nathaniel Russell House, Edmondston-Alston House, Aiken-Rhett House, Drayton Hall, and Middleton Place. ⊠ *375 Meeting St., Upper King,* ☎ *843/853–8000 or 800/868–8118.* WEB *www.charlestoncvb.com.* ⊠ *Film $2.50.* ☉ *Mar.–Oct., daily 8:30–5:30; Nov.–Feb., daily 8:30–5; shows daily 9–5 on the ½ hr.*

㉒ Waterfront Park. A sprinkle from the park's interactive fountain will refresh you on hot summer days. Here you'll also find swings, a fishing pier, picnic tables, and gardens overlooking Charleston Harbor. It's at the foot of Vendue Range, along the east side of Charleston Harbor. *Market area,* ☎ *843/724–7321.* ⊠ *Free.* ☉ *Daily 6 AM–midnight.*

NEED A BREAK?	With a great view of the harbor and Waterfront Park, the **Rooftop Lounge at Vendue Inn** (⊠ 19 Vendue Range, Market area, ☎ 843/577–7970 or 800/845–7900) serves drinks and appetizers alfresco.

The Battery and South of Broad

Along the Battery, on the point of a narrow peninsula bounded by the Ashley and Cooper rivers, handsome mansions surrounded by gardens face the harbor. Their distinctive look is reminiscent of the West Indies: before coming to the Carolinas in the late 17th century, many early British colonists had first settled on Barbados and other Caribbean isles, where they'd built houses with high ceilings and broad piazzas at each level to catch the sea breezes. In Charleston they adapted these designs. One type—narrow two- to four-story "single houses" built at right angles to the street—emerged partly because buildings were taxed according to the length of their frontage.

Heavily residential, the area south of Broad Street has many beautiful private homes, almost all of which have a plaque with a short written description of the home's history. You might get a peek at tucked-away English-style gardens, too. An open gate in Charleston once signified that all were welcome to venture inside for a closer look at the owner's garden. Open gates are rare today, but keep an eye out, as you never know when you'll get lucky.

Numbers in the text correspond to numbers in the margin and on the Charleston map.

A Good Walk

Start at the top of Broad Street at the **Old Exchange Building/Provost Dungeon** ㉘, which held prisoners during the American Revolution. Two blocks down Broad Street are the Four Corners of Law, including **City Hall** ㉖, with some historical displays and portraits, and **St. Michael's Episcopal Church** ㉗, the city's oldest surviving church. In the famously affluent South of Broad neighborhood are several of the city's lavish house museums. The **Heyward-Washington House** ㉙ is a block south of Broad Street on Church Street. Next to it is picturesque Cabbage Row, the inspiration for Catfish Row in *Porgy and Bess.* The **Nathaniel**

ANTEBELLUM CHARLESTON: THE GOLDEN YEARS

CHARLESTON, CALLED CHARLES TOWNE until the British left in 1783, boomed with the plantation economy in the years before the Civil War. South Carolina's rice, indigo, and cotton crops produced an extraordinary concentration of wealth, enriching a few hundred plantation owners, merchants, and shippers. Rice was the most profitable export in large part because the enormous labor necessary to grow the rice was supplied by slaves. Cotton, too, was a huge moneymaker; by the outbreak of the Civil War, in 1861, cotton accounted for 57% of the nation's exports.

From Charleston's beginnings the planter aristocracy set out to entertain itself in style, seeking a social and cultural lifestyle to match its financial success. By the mid-17th century the city had a thriving musical community. The first playhouse, the original Dock Street Theatre, was open for business. There were dances and concerts; the town attracted some of the most important performers in colonial America. During the 1770s there were more than 23 singing and dancing masters teaching in the city, which also had a reputation for turning out the Colonies' best Shakespearean productions.

The city was known for its talented goldsmiths, silversmiths, gunsmiths, tobacconists, brewers, and cabinetmakers, and was one of the best shopping towns in North America. Immigrants and others seeking religious freedom poured into Charleston. More than 200 private residences were built during this boom. Although Charleston had half the population of New York during the early 1770s, its annual export trade exceeded the tonnage that passed through New York's port.

Until the Civil War Charleston's fortunes continued to grow. The city's native sons played a huge part in the forming of the new national government; four Charlestonians signed the U.S. Constitution. Writers and artists filled the city. Charlestonian Robert Mills, who designed the Washington Monument, also designed many buildings in Charleston. George Washington toured Charleston in 1791, staying in many of the city's now-historic homes.

Charleston thrived as the social and cultural center of planter families. The social season, from late January to March, was defined by balls, dinners, masquerades, concerts, plays, and horse races. The elite and their slaves moved from the plantations to their Charleston residences, embellished with silk curtains, Dutch linens, French china, English silver, and lavish ornamental gardens. They commissioned famous portrait artists and European craftsmen and gave extravagant dinners where guests were served by black slaves. Lowcountry gentlemen joined private clubs and favored foxhunts, races, and gambling. Lowcountry sons traveled to England for their education. By the 1840s construction pervaded the city: City Hall was under renovation, the Battery was being made into a city park, and such buildings as the four-story Charleston Hotel had become part of the emerging cityscape. By 1850 the city's population had grown to nearly 43,000.

When the Union-held Fort Sumter was bombarded on April 11, 1861, signaling the beginning of the Civil War, Charlestonians celebrated. But the merriment, along with the years of splendor and luxury, was soon over; the collapse of slavery ended the plantation system, sending much of the state's economy into depression.

Russell House ㉚ and the **Calhoun Mansion** ㉛ are on Meeting Street, are about two blocks apart on Meeting Street. Around the corner is the **Edmondston-Alston House** ㉜, overlooking Charleston's famous **Battery** ㉞ and Charleston Harbor. A park bench in the shade of **White Point Gardens** ㉝, so named because of the bleached whiteness of oyster shells left here by Native Americans, is a splendid spot for a rest. From here go north along the Cooper River by shuttle, car, or rickshaw to the **South Carolina Aquarium** ⑧. Next door, at the Fort Sumter Visitor Education Center, at Liberty Square, you can catch the ferry for a harbor ride to **Fort Sumter National Monument** ⑨.

TIMING

Plan to spend from two to four hours doing this walk, depending on your pace and which buildings you visit. A trip to the aquarium can add two or so hours, as will a trip to Fort Sumter; you may wish to split the trip into two half-days.

Sights to See

㉞ **The Battery.** This sea wall and promenade has sweeping views of Charleston Harbor. ⊠ *Murray Blvd., South of Broad*

㉛ **Calhoun Mansion.** Opulent by Charleston standards, this is a no-holds-barred example of Victorian taste. Built in 1876, this 24,000-square-ft mansion is full of ornate plasterwork and fine wood moldings and has a 75-ft dome ceiling. ⊠ *16 Meeting St., South of Broad,* ☎ 843/722–8205. ▧ *$15.* ☼ *Feb.–Dec., Wed.–Sun. 10–4.*

㉖ **City Hall.** The intersection of Meeting and Broad streets is known as the Four Corners of Law, representing the laws of nation, state, city, and church. On the northeast corner is the graceful City Hall, dating from 1801. The second-floor council chambers has historical displays and portraits, including John Trumbull's 1791 satirical portrait of George Washington and Samuel F. B. Morse's likeness of James Monroe. ⊠ *80 Broad St., South of Broad,* ☎ 843/577–6970 *or* 843/724–3799. ▧ *Free.* ☼ *Weekdays 10–5.*

OFF THE
BEATEN PATH

COLONIAL LAKE – Joggers, walkers, and folks looking for a tranquil city spot flock to this small man-made lake circled by a wide sidewalk, trees, and benches. In the late 19th century Colonial Common, as it was called at the time, was a popular gathering place for Victorian Charleston. Today it is surrounded by stately Victorian buildings. ⊠ *Ashley and Rutledge Aves. to the east and west, Broad and Beaufain Sts. to the north and south, South of Broad,* ☎ 843/724–7327.

㉜ **Edmondston-Alston House.** With commanding views of Charleston Harbor, this imposing home was built in 1825 in late-federal style and transformed into a Greek Revival structure during the 1840s. It is tastefully furnished with antiques, portraits, Piranesi prints, silver, and fine china. ⊠ *21 E. Battery, South of Broad,* ☎ 843/722–7171, WEB *www.middletonplace.org.* ▧ *$8; combination ticket with Middleton Place $27.* ☼ *Tues.–Sat. 10–4:30, Sun.–Mon. 1:30–4:30.*

★ ☾ ⑨ **Fort Sumter National Monument.** It was here, on a man-made island in Charleston Harbor, that Confederate forces fired the first shot of the Civil War, on April 12, 1861. After a 34-hour bombardment Union forces surrendered and Confederate troops occupied Sumter, which became a symbol of Southern resistance. The Confederacy held the fort, despite almost continual bombardment, for nearly four years, and when it was finally evacuated, it was a heap of rubble. Today National Park Service rangers conduct free guided tours of the restored structure, which includes a free **museum** (☎ 843/883–3123) with historical displays. The fort is accessible only by boat; ferries depart from Patriots Point or the **Fort Sumter Visitor Center at Liberty Square**, next to the South Carolina Aquarium, which contains exhibits on the introduction of the war. ⊠ *340 Concord St., Upper King,* ☎ *843/727–4739 for visitor center; 843/881–7337 or 800/789–3678 for Fort Sumter Tours Inc.,* WEB *www.nps.gov/fosu.* ☐ *Museum free, ferry fare $11.* ☉ *Tours Apr.–early Sept., 9:30, noon, 2:30, and 4; early Sept.–Mar., 9:30, noon, and 2:30.*

㉙ Heyward-Washington House. Built in 1772 by rice king Daniel Heyward, this home was the backdrop for DuBose Heyward's book *Porgy,* which was the basis for the beloved folk opera *Porgy and Bess.* The neighborhood, known as Cabbage Row, is central to Charleston's African-American history. President George Washington stayed in the house during his 1791 visit. It is full of fine period furnishings by such local craftsmen as Thomas Elfe, and its restored 18th-century kitchen is the only one in Charleston open to visitors. ⊠ *87 Church St., South of Broad,* ☎ *843/722–0354,* WEB *www.charlestonmuseum.com.* ☐ *$8; museum and houses $18; 2 of 3 sights $12.* ☉ *Mon.–Sat. 10–5, Sun. 1–5.*

★ ㉚ Nathaniel Russell House. One of the nation's finest examples of Adam-style architecture, the Nathaniel Russell House was built in 1808. The interior is distinguished by its ornate detailing, its lavish period furnishings, and the "flying" circular staircase that spirals three stories with no apparent support. ⊠ *51 Meeting St., South of Broad,* ☎ *843/724–8481,* WEB *www.historiccharleston.org.* ☐ *$7, combination ticket with Aiken-Rhett House $12.* ☉ *Mon.–Sat. 10–5, Sun. 2–5.*

㊀ ㉘ Old Exchange Building/Provost Dungeon. Originally a customs house, this building was used by the British to house prisoners during the Revolutionary War. Today a tableau of lifelike mannequins recalls this era. ⊠ *122 E. Bay St., South of Broad,* ☎ *843/727–2165,* WEB *www.old-exchange.com.* ☐ *$6.* ☉ *Daily 9–5.*

㉗ St. Michael's Episcopal Church. Modeled after London's St. Martin-in-the-Fields and completed in 1761, this is Charleston's oldest surviving church. Its steeple clock and bells were imported from England in 1764. ⊠ *14 St. Michael's Alley, South of Broad,* ☎ *843/723–0603,* WEB *www.stmichaelschurch.net.* ☉ *Weekdays 9–5, Sat. 9–noon.*

NEED A
BREAK?

On your way down Broad Street toward Church Street, duck into the dark-paneled, tin-ceiling **Blind Tiger Pub** (⊠ 38 Broad St., South of Broad, ☎ 843/577–0088) for a drink or beer on the patio out back, or a meal from the Four Corners Cafe next door.

★ ㊀ ❽ South Carolina Aquarium. The 322,000-gallon Great Ocean Tank has the tallest aquarium window in North America. Exhibits display more than 10,000 living organisms, representing more than 500 species. You travel through the five major regions of the Southeast Appalachian Watershed as found in South Carolina: the Blue Ridge Mountains, the Piedmont, the coastal plain, the coast, and the ocean. The little ones can pet stingrays at one touch tank and horseshoe crabs and conchs at another. ⊠ *3250 Concord St., Upper King,* ☎ *843/720–1990 or 800/722–6455,* WEB *www.scaquarium.org.* ☐ *$14.* ☉ *July–Aug., daily 9–7; Mar.–June and Sept.–Oct., daily 9–5; Nov.–Feb., daily 10–5.*

㊀ ㉝ White Point Gardens. Pirates once hung from gallows here; now this park, with a gazebo, Charleston benches, and views of the harbor and Fort Sumter, is the number one marriage site in the city. Children love to climb on the cannon and cannonball replicas. ⊠ *Murray Blvd. and*

E. Battery, South of Broad, ☎ *843/724–7327.* ⊘ *Weekdays 9–5, Sat. 9–noon.*

Mount Pleasant and Vicinity

East of Charleston across the Cooper River Bridge, via U.S. 17N, is the town of Mount Pleasant, named not for a mountain or a hill but for a plantation in England from which some of the area's settlers hailed. In its Old Village neighborhood are antebellum homes and a sleepy, old-time town center that has a drugstore with an old-fashioned soda fountain. Along Shem Creek, where the local fishing fleet brings in the daily catch, are several seafood restaurants. Other attractions in the area are museums, plantations, and, farther north, the Cape Romain National Wildlife Refuge.

A Good Tour

There's enough adventure here to stretch over a number of days, especially if you're a war history buff. On the first day you might drive to **Patriots Point,** veering right from the Cooper River Bridge onto Coleman Boulevard in the direction of Sullivan's Island and the Isle of Palms. Later, continue along Coleman Boulevard and, just after crossing the boat-lined docks and restaurants at Shem Creek, turn right at Whilden Street for a drive through the Old Village. Returning to Coleman Boulevard, you'll pass the Common, a cluster of shops on your left. Stop here for the **Museum on the Common,** featuring the *Hurricane Hugo Revisited* exhibit. Follow the signs to **Fort Moultrie.** Spend the rest of the day relaxing on the beach or bicycling through Sullivan's Island, a residential community of early 20th-century beach houses, or the Isle of Palms, which has a pavilion and more abundant parking.

On another day, drive out U.S. 17N 8 mi to **Boone Hall Plantation** and its famous Avenue of Oaks, stopping at nearby **Charles Pinckney National Historic Site,** with interpretations of African-American life on the plantation. Bring a picnic and rent bikes at **Palmetto Islands County Park,** across Boone Hall Creek from the plantation; you'll need a swimsuit for Splash Island, a mini–water park. Another option is a ferry ride and visit to Bull Island, part of the **Cape Romain National Wildlife Refuge,** one of the nation's most pristine wildlife areas. The Sewee Visitor & Environmental Education Center (on U.S. 17, 35 mi north of Charleston) has information and exhibits on the refuge as well as live birds of prey, red wolves, and trails.

TIMING
You need three days to see all the attractions here; if you have one day or less, choose a few based on your interests.

Sights to See

★ **Boone Hall Plantation.** This plantation is approached along one of the South's most majestic avenues of oaks, which was the model for the grounds of Tara in *Gone With the Wind.* You can tour the first floor of the classic columned mansion, which was built in 1935, incorporating woodwork and flooring from the original house. The primary attraction is the grounds, with formal azalea and camellia gardens, as well as the original slave quarters—the only "slave street" still intact in the Southeast—and the cotton-gin house used in the made-for-television movies *North and South* and *Queen.* ⊠ *1235 Long Point Rd., off U.S. 17N, Mount Pleasant/East Cooper,* ☎ *843/884–4371.* 🖾 *$12.50.* ⊘ *Apr.–early Sept., Mon.–Sat. 8:30–6:30, Sun. 1–5; early Sept.–Mar., Mon.–Sat. 9–5, Sun. 1–4.*

NEED A
BREAK?

Driving north of Mount Pleasant along U.S. 17, you'll see **basket ladies** at roadside stands. If you have the heart to bargain, you *may* be able to purchase the baskets at somewhat lower prices than in Charleston. But remember that you are buying a nearly lost art, and sweet grass is no longer plentiful in the wild.

Cape Romain National Wildlife Refuge. A grouping of barrier islands and salt marshes, this 60,000-acre refuge is one of the most outstanding in the country. At the **Sewee Visitor & Environmental Education Center** you can view exhibits about the refuge and arrange to take a ferry to Bull Island for a day visit. The island is a nearly untouched wilderness; the beach here, strewn with bleached driftwood, is nicknamed Bone Beach. ⊠ *5821 U.S. 17N, Awendaw,* ☎ *843/928–3368.* 🖾 *Free.* ⊙ *Daily 9–5.*

Charles Pinckney National Historic Site. Across the street from Boone Hall, this is the only protected remnant of the country estate of Charles Pinckney, drafter and signer of the Constitution. A self-guided tour explores many fascinating interpretations of African-American life, including the plantation owner–slave relationship. You can also tour an 1820s tidewater cottage. ⊠ *1254 Long Point Rd., off U.S. 17N, Mount Pleasant/East Cooper,* ☎ *843/881–5516,* FAX *843/881–7070,* WEB *www.nps.gov/chpi.* 🖾 *Free.* ⊙ *Daily 9–5.*

☜ **Fort Moultrie.** Here Colonel William Moultrie's South Carolinians repelled a British assault in one of the first Patriot victories of the Revolutionary War. Completed in 1809, this is the third fort on this site at **Sullivan's Island,** which you'll reach on Route 703 off U.S. 17N (8 mi southeast of Charleston). A 20-minute film tells the history of the fort. ⊠ *W. Middle St., Mount Pleasant/East Cooper Sullivan's Island,* ☎ *843/883–3123.* 🖾 *$2.* ⊙ *Daily 9–5.*

☜ **Museum on the Common.** This small museum has an outdoor maritime museum and a Hurricane Hugo exhibit prepared by the South Carolina State Museum; it shows the 1989 storm damage through video and photos. ⊠ *217 Lucas St., Mount Pleasant/East Cooper, Shem Creek Village, Mount Pleasant,* ☎ *843/849–9000.* 🖾 *Free.* ⊙ *Mon.–Sat. 10–4.*

☜ **Palmetto Islands County Park.** You'll find a Big Toy playground, 2-acre pond, paved trails, an observation tower, marsh boardwalks, and a "water island" at this park across Boone Hall Creek from Boone Hall Plantation. Bicycles and paddleboats can be rented in season. ⊠ *Long Point Rd. (½ mi past Boone Hall Plantation), Mount Pleasant/East Cooper,* ☎ *843/884–0832.* 🖾 *$2.* ⊙ *Apr. and Sept.–Oct., daily 9–6; May–Aug., daily 9–7; Nov.–Feb., daily 10–5; Mar., daily 10–6.*

★ ☜ **Patriots Point.** Tours are available on all vessels here at the world's largest naval and maritime museum, now houses the Medal of Honor Society. Berthed here are the aircraft carrier USS *Yorktown,* the World War II submarine USS *Clamagore,* the destroyer USS *Laffey,* the nuclear merchant ship *Savannah,* and the Coast Guard cutter *Ingham,* responsible for sinking a U-boat during World War II. The film *The Fighting Lady* is shown regularly aboard the *Yorktown,* and there is a Vietnam exhibit. ⊠ *Foot of Cooper River Bridge, Mount Pleasant/East Cooper,* ☎ *843/884–2727,* WEB *www.state.sc.us/patpt.* 🖾 *$11.* ⊙ *Early Sept.–Mar., daily 9–6:30; Apr.–early Sept., daily 9–7:30.*

West of the Ashley River

A Good Tour

The sights covered here are each a few miles apart along Ashley River Road, Route 61, which begins a few miles northwest of downtown

Charleston over the Ashley River Bridge. Still, you'll need time to see them all. One day you could spend a few hours exploring **Charles Towne Landing State Park,** veering off Route 61 onto Old Towne Road (Route 171); then finish your day at **Middleton Gardens.** Another day you might tour the majestic simplicity of **Drayton Hall** before continuing on to **Magnolia Plantation and Gardens** and all their splendor.

TIMING

Nature and garden enthusiasts can easily spend a full day at Magnolia Gardens, Middleton Gardens, or Charles Towne Landing State Park, so budget your time accordingly. Spring is a peak time for the gardens, although they are lovely throughout the year.

Sights to See

★ ♻ **Charles Towne Landing State Park.** Commemorating the site of the original 1670 Charleston settlement, this park on Route 171 has a reconstructed village and fortifications, English park gardens with bicycle trails and walkways, and a replica 17th-century vessel moored in the creek. In the animal park native species roam freely—among them alligators, bison, pumas, bears, and wolves. Bicycle and kayak rentals and cassette and tram tours are available. The park has begun a $5 million renovation that includes a comprehensive archaeological dig and a new visitor center–museum. ⊠ *1500 Old Towne Rd., West Ashley,* ☎ *843/852–4200,* WEB *www.southcarolinaparks.com.* ⌧ *$5.* ⊙ *Late May–early Sept., daily 9–6; early Sept.–late May, daily 9–5.*

★ **Drayton Hall.** Considered the nation's finest example of unspoiled Georgian-Palladian architecture, this mansion is the only plantation house on the Ashley River to have survived the Civil War. A National Historic Landmark, built between 1738 and 1742, it is an invaluable lesson in history as well as in architecture. Drayton Hall has been left unfurnished to highlight the original plaster moldings, opulent hand-carved woodwork, and other ornamental details. Connections, an African-American focus presentation offered before the tour, is fascinating. You will learn about the conditions under which slaves were brought from Africa and can view copies of documents recording the buying and selling of local plantation slaves. ⊠ *3380 Ashley River Rd., 13 mi north of Charleston, West Ashley,* ☎ *843/766–0188,* WEB *www.draytonhall.org.* ⌧ *$12.* ⊙ *Guided tours Mar.–Oct., daily 10–4; Nov.–Feb., daily 10–3.*

♻ **Magnolia Plantation and Gardens.** The 50-acre informal garden, begun in 1685, has a huge collection of azaleas and camellias. A tram will take you for an overall tour with three stops. You can canoe through the 125-acre Waterfowl Refuge, explore the 30-acre **Audubon Swamp Garden** along boardwalks and bridges, or walk or bicycle more than 500 acres of wildlife trails. Tours of the manor house, built during Reconstruction, depict plantation life. The grounds also hold a petting zoo and a miniature-horse ranch. ⊠ *3550 Ashley River Rd., just north of Drayton Hall, West Ashley,* ☎ *843/571–1266 or 800/367–3517,* WEB *www.magnoliaplantation.com.* ⌧ *$12; house tour $7 extra; nature tram $6 extra; nature boat tour $5 extra; swamp garden $6; canoe and bike rentals.* ⊙ *Daily 8–5:30.*

★ ♻ **Middleton Place.** The nation's oldest landscaped gardens, dating from 1741, are magnificently ablaze with camellias, magnolias, azaleas, roses, and flowers of all seasons planted in floral *allées* and terraced lawns and around ornamental lakes. Much of the mansion was destroyed during the Civil War, but the south wing has been restored and houses impressive collections of silver, furniture, paintings, and historic documents. In the stable yard craftspeople use authentic tools and equipment to demonstrate spinning, blacksmithing, and other domestic skills from the plantation era. Farm animals, peacocks, and other creatures roam freely. The Middleton Place restaurant serves Lowcountry specialties for lunch daily; a gift shop carries local arts, crafts, and souvenirs. Also on the grounds is a modern Danish-style inn (access to the gardens is included in the room price) with floor-to-ceiling windows dramatizing views of the Ashley River; here you can sign up for kayaking and biking tours. ⊠ *Ashley River Rd. (4 mi north of Magnolia Plantation), West Ashley,* ☎ *843/556–6020 or 800/782–3608,* WEB *www. middletonplace.org.* ⊠ *$15; house tours $8 extra.* ☉ *Daily 9–5; house tours Tues.–Sun. 10–4:30, Mon. 1:30–4:30.*

OFF THE BEATEN PATH

AMERICAN CLASSIC TEA PLANTATION – On a small rural island about 20 mi southwest of Charleston on Route 700 is the country's only commercial tea plantation. Tours run from May through October and cover tea history, harvesting, and production and include a discussion with the plantation's official tea taster. The tour ends with tea and cookies. ⊠ *6617 Maybank Hwy., Wadmalaw Island,* ☎ *800/443–5987.* ⊠ *Free.* ☉ *May–Oct., 1st Sat. each month 10–1:30.*

☺ **ANGEL OAK –** This magnificent live oak has a massive canopy that creates 17,000 square ft of shade. Long a favorite with local children because of its bending branches that slope gently, armlike to the ground, Angel Oak is believed to be more than 1,400 years old. It's about 12 mi southwest of Charleston off Route 700. ⊠ *3688 Angel Oak Rd., Johns Island,* ☎ *843/559–3496.* ⊠ *Free.* ☉ *Daily 9–4:45.*

☺ **CAW CAW INTERPRETIVE CENTER –** Once part of a 1700s rice plantation, this 650-acre cypress swamp park has 8 mi of historical and interpretive trails that include a 1,200-ft marsh boardwalk, informative and well-executed exhibits on rice cultivation, Gullah storytelling, and African-American music and craft demonstrations, and an in-depth documentation of the vital role slaves played in the rice fields. It's about 15 mi west of Charleston on U.S. 17. ⊠ *5200 Savannah Hwy., Ravenel,* ☎ *843/889–8898,* WEB *www.ccprc.com/cawcaw.htm.* ⊠ *$4.* ☉ *Nov.– Feb., Tues.–Sun. 9–5; Mar.–Apr. and Sept.–Oct., Tues.–Sun. 9–6; May– Aug., Tues.–Sun. 8–7.*

Dining

She-crab soup, sautéed shrimp and grits, variations on pecan pie, and other Lowcountry specialties are served all over the Charleston area—as are creative contemporary dishes crafted by local chefs. Outstanding eateries, from seafood houses to elegant French restaurants, make Charleston a favorite for gastronomes. Trendy Mount Pleasant, across the East Cooper Bridge, has a number of good restaurants.

Contemporary

$$$–$$$$ ✕ **Circa 1886.** If you've got an occasion for champagne cocktails and foie gras, celebrate at this formal, conducive-to-conversation dining room in a carriage house behind the Wentworth Mansion. Grilled antelope loin with sweet-potato spoon bread and chocolate Bailey's Irish cream soufflé are the signature dishes. ⊠ *149 Wentworth St., Market area,* ☎ *843/853–7828. AE, D, DC, MC, V. No lunch.*

$$$–$$$$ ✕ **McCrady's.** This elegant restaurant, in a 1778 tavern, has locals rav-
★ ing over its potato gnocchi, tuna tartare, grouper with a creamy leek sauce and truffle oil, herb-marinated rack of lamb with mint drizzle, and bitter-chocolate bread pudding. The dining room is elegant and somewhat formal; the long bar has cozy booths. ⊠ *2 Unity Alley, Market area,* ☎ *843/577–0025. AE, MC, V. No lunch.*

$$$–$$$$ ✕ **Peninsula Grill.** Surrounded by walls covered in olive-green velvet,
★ black-iron chandeliers, and 18th-century-style portraits, diners at this
busy spot in the Planters Inn can feast on such delights as lobster cit-
ron, rabbit loin wrapped in veal bacon with tapenade linguine and mus-
tard vinaigrette, and New Zealand benne-seed-encrusted rack of lamb
with wild mushroom potatoes and coconut-mint pesto. ⊠ *112 N.
Market St., Market area,* ☎ *843/723–0700. AE, D, DC, MC, V. No
lunch. Jackets essential.*

$$$ ✕ **Cypress.** From the owners of Magnolias and Blossom Cafe comes
this sleek restaurant in a renovated 1834 brick-wall building, now very
groovy with rust-color leather booths, a ceiling with circular lights that
change color, and an entire "wine wall" of 4,000 bottles under glass.
Here you'll find not only wonderful vino, but also a fabulous arugula
salad with apples, Gorgonzola and pecans; green tea-smoked duck; and
hickory-grilled fillet with a house-made Boursin cheese and Madeira
sauce. If you've forgotten the jacket, dine upstairs. ⊠ *167 E. Bay St.,
Market area,* ☎ *843/727–0111. AE, D, DC, MC, V. No lunch.*

$$ ✕ **Sermet's Corner.** Colorful, bold artwork by chef Sermet Aslan dec-
orates the walls of this lively eatery. The Mediterranean-influenced menu
has *panini* (grilled Italian sandwiches), seafood, and flavorful pastas.
The poached pear salad and lavender pork are favorites. ⊠ *276 King
St., Market area,* ☎ *843/853–7775. AE, MC, V.*

French

$$$$ ✕ **Robert's of Charleston.** A classically trained singer and chef, Robert
offers a special experience: four rich, generously portioned courses (scal-
lop mousse with lobster sauce, duckling with grilled vegetables, roast
tenderloin with bordelaise sauce, and dessert) with lovely wines, im-
peccable service, and the best of Broadway tunes in a warm, intimate
dining room. ⊠ *182 E. Bay St., Market area,* ☎ *843/577–7565. MC,
V. Closed Sun.–Wed. No lunch.*

$$–$$$ ✕ **39 Rue de Jean Bar Cafe.** In classy, traditionally French style—gleam-
ing wood, white-papered tables, and booths—the trendy set dines late
(until 1 AM, except Sunday) on wonderful mussels, steak frites, scal-
lops St. Jacques, and even sushi. It's noisy and happening, but there's
a quiet back room. ⊠ *39 John St., Upper King,* ☎ *843/722–8881. AE,
D, DC, MC, V. No lunch weekends.*

$–$$ ✕ **Gaulart and Maliclet Café.** This casual, chic eatery serves Continental
dishes—breads and pastries, soups, salads, sandwiches, and specials
such as seafood Normandy and chicken sesame. ⊠ *98 Broad St.,
South of Broad,* ☎ *843/577–9797. AE, D, MC, V. Closed Sun. No dinner Mon.*

Italian

$$$–$$$$ ✕ **Fulton Five.** There are just 15 tables in this romantic restaurant on
a side road off King Street. The chartreuse walls and antique brass ac-
cents provide the perfect environment for savoring northern Italian spe-
cialties, such as risotto, lemon sherbet with Campari, and antipasto
Spoleto (mozzarella and prosciutto wrapped in a romaine lettuce leaf
and drizzled with olive oil and diced tomatoes). ⊠ *5 Fulton St., Mar-
ket area,* ☎ *843/853–5555. AE, DC, MC, V. Closed Sun. and late Aug.–
1st wk Sept. No lunch.*

$$–$$$ ✕ **Il Cortile del Re.** Great wines, hearty soups and pastas, and lovely
cheeses and breads make it feel just like Tuscany here. Tucked off King
Street behind a women's clothing shop, this hard-to-find spot has a cozy
back room and a romantic courtyard with a crumbling brick wall. ⊠
193 King St., Market area, ☎ *843/853–1888. AE, DC, MC, V. Closed
Sun.–Mon. No lunch Thurs.–Sat.*

240

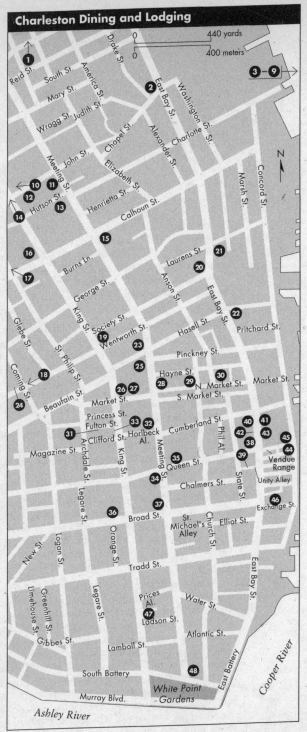

Charleston Dining and Lodging

Lowcountry

$$–$$$$ ✕ **Slightly North of Broad.** This high-ceiling former warehouse with
★ brick-and-stucco walls has several seats looking directly into the exposed kitchen (great for single diners). Chef Frank Lee's inventive dishes include grilled barbecued tuna with fried oysters and sautéed squab with coriander. You can order most items as either a small plate or a main course. The extensive wine list is moderately priced. A sister restaurant, **Slightly Up the Creek** (⊠ 130 Mill St., Mt. Pleasant, ☎ 843/884–5005; no lunch; brunch only on Sun.), at Shem Creek in Mount Pleasant, has waterfront views and more seafood dishes. ⊠ 192 E. Bay St., Market area, ☎ 843/723–3424. Reservations not accepted for lunch. AE, D, DC, MC, V. No lunch weekends.

$$–$$$ ✕ **Carolina's.** This lively, casual bistro, styled in black and white, with terra-cotta tiles and 1920s French posters, has long been a favorite. Fans return for the "appeteasers" such as Crowder pea cakes (made with Crowder peas, spices, egg, and bread crumbs) and fried calamari, plus smoked baby-back ribs and pasta with crawfish and tasso. Dinner entrées are selections from the grill, including pork tenderloin with Jamaican seasoning and salmon with cilantro, ginger, and lime butter. ⊠ 10 Exchange St., South of Broad, ☎ 843/724–3800. Reservations essential. D, MC, V. No lunch.

Lowcountry/Southern

$$$–$$$$ ✕ **Anson.** After an afternoon of strolling through the Old City Market, you can walk up Anson Street to this softly lighted, gilt-trimmed dining room. Framed by about a dozen French windows, Anson's has elegant booths anchored by marble-top tables. New South specialties include shrimp and grits, fried corn-bread oysters, and barbecued grouper. The she-crab soup is some of the best around. ⊠ 12 Anson St., Market area, ☎ 843/577–0551. AE, D, DC, MC, V. No lunch.

$$$–$$$$ ✕ **Charleston Grill.** Its clubby chairs and dark paneling create a com-
★ fortably elegant venue for chef Bob Waggoner's famously fabulous new South cuisine. Dishes include lump crab cake over yellow tomato coulis, venison tenderloin with caramelized mushrooms and truffle potatoes, zucchini blossoms stuffed with lobster mousse, and beef medallions over garlic grits. Many nights there's live jazz. ⊠ 224 King St., Charleston Place Hotel, Market area, ☎ 843/577–4522. AE, D, DC, MC, V.

$$$–$$$$ ✕ **High Cotton.** Feast on spit-roasted and grilled meats and fish in this elegant and airy, brick-walled eatery studded with palm trees. Weeknight specials are great deals; at the popular bar there is live jazz. The chocolate soufflé with blackberry sauce and the praline soufflé are fabulous. ⊠ 199 E. Bay St., Market area, ☎ 843/724–3815. AE, D, DC, MC, V. No lunch weekdays.

$$$–$$$$ ✕ **Magnolias.** Locals love this popular place, in an 1823 warehouse,
★ with a magnolia theme evident in its vivid paintings, etched glass, wrought iron, and candlesticks. The uptown down-South cuisine shines with its specialties: egg roll stuffed with chicken and collard greens with a spicy mustard sauce and sweet pepper purée. Equally innovative appetizers include seared yellow-grits cakes with tasso gravy, yellow corn relish, and sautéed greens. You may also want to try the **Blossom Café** (⊠ 171 E. Bay St., Market area, ☎ 843/722–9200), owned by the same people but with a more Continental menu, including pizzas cooked in a wood-burning oven, pastas, and fish. ⊠ 185 E. Bay St., Market area, ☎ 843/577–7771. Reservations essential. AE, DC, MC, V.

$$–$$$ ✕ **Elliott's on the Square.** Come to this bright and cheerful restaurant if you have a hankering for Southern Sunday-dinner-style entrées for lunch and dinner, including black-eyed pea cakes, fried chicken, barbecued salmon over grits, and butter pound cake. The food may be

down-home, but the service is not. ✉ *387 King St., Francis Marion Hotel, Upper King,* ☎ *843/724–8888. AE, D, DC, MC, V.*

$$–$$$ ✕ **J. Bistro.** Funky steel cutouts liven up the outside and inside walls, and the lighting is whimsical—hanging low over tables lined up against a banquette. A varied list of appetizers and small plates makes this a great place to graze. Choose from such innovations as steamed lobster wontons, grouper with a champagne-crabmeat cream sauce, and pecan-crusted catfish over grits. The lamb chops are superb. It's about 7 to 10 mi from town. ✉ *819 Coleman Blvd., Mount Pleasant/East Cooper,* ☎ *843/971–7778. Reservations essential. AE, MC, V.* ✆ *Closed Mon. No dinner Sun. No lunch.*

$–$$$ ✕ **Hominy Grill.** Locals lunch and brunch at this breezy café-style restaurant. Although a bit off the beaten path (a few blocks east of King Street), it's worth a special trip. The young chef's Southern upbringing is evident in everything from the vegetable plate (collards, squash casserole, black-eyed pea cakes with guacamole, and mushroom hominy) to the pimiento cheese sandwich and the turkey club with homemade french fries. The avocado and *wehani* rice (a clay-colored, aromatic variety of brown rice) salad with grilled vegetables is a refreshing don't-miss in summer. Leave room for the excellent buttermilk pie or bread pudding. ✉ *207 Rutledge Ave., Upper King,* ☎ *843/937–0930. AE, MC, V.* ✆ *No dinner Sun.*

$–$$$ ✕ **Sticky Fingers.** Specializing in ribs six ways (Memphis style wet and dry, Texas style wet and dry, Carolina sweet, and Tennessee whiskey) and barbecue, this family-friendly restaurant has locations downtown and in Mount Pleasant and Summerville. Tuesday night is children's night, with supervised games and cartoons in a playroom. ✉ *235 Meeting St., Market area,* ☎ *843/853–7427 or 800/671–5966;* ✉ *341 Johnnie Dodds Blvd., Mount Pleasant/East Cooper,* ☎ *843/856–9840;* ✉ *1200 N. Main St., Summerville,* ☎ *843/875–7969. AE, DC, MC, V.*

$–$$
★ ✕ **Alice's Fine Foods.** The food Southerners crave is here in its original, beloved form: baked or fried chicken, ribs, fried fish, and other entrées come with a choice of three home-cooked vegetables and side dishes, including green beans, collard greens, red rice, macaroni-and-cheese pie, okra and tomatoes, lima beans, rice and gravy, yams, and squash. The tone here is very casual, and the buffet is cafeteria-style. ✉ *468–470 King St., Upper King,* ☎ *843/853–9366. MC, V.*

$–$$ ✕ **Boulevard Diner.** There are no frills at this simple diner with booths and a counter and booths where the service is friendly and attentive, and the food is quite decent. Among the winners are: the daily variety of homemade veggies, the fried eggplant-and-blue-cheese sandwich, and the Cajun meatloaf and chili. ✉ *409 W. Coleman Blvd., Mount Pleasant/East Cooper,* ☎ *843/216–2611. MC, V.* ✆ *Closed Sun.*

Middle Eastern

$ ✕ **Doe's Pita Plus.** This is a favorite spot, at lunch in particular, among locals working downtown. Among the best-sellers: pitas stuffed with chicken salad, Greek salad, or avocado salad, pita chips, hummus, meat pies, tabbouleh. There's a simple grouping of small tables and chairs, as well as some outdoor seating. ✉ *334 E. Bay St., Market area,* ☎ *843/577–3179. AE. No dinner weekends.*

Seafood

$$–$$$
★ ✕ **Boathouse Restaurant.** Large portions of fresh seafood at reasonable prices make both locations of the Boathouse Restaurant wildly popular. The crab dip, fish specials, and lightly battered fried shrimp and oysters are irresistible. Entrées come with nice helpings of mashed potatoes, grits, collard greens, or blue-cheese coleslaw. The original Isle of Palms location is right on the water. ✉ *101 Palm Blvd., Isle of Palms,*

☎ *843/886–8000;* ✉ *14 Chapel St., Upper King,* ☎ *843/577–7171. Reservations essential. AE, DC, MC, V.*

$$–$$$ ✕ **The Wreck.** Dockside and full of wacky character, this spot serves up such traditional dishes as boiled peanuts, fried shrimp, shrimp pilaf, deviled crab, and oyster platters. They weren't kidding with the name—expect a shabby, candlelighted screened-in porch and small dining area. Nonetheless, it has a kind of seaside-joint charm. ✉ *106 Haddrell St., Mount Pleasant/East Cooper,* ☎ *843/884–0052. Reservations not accepted. No credit cards.*

Lodging

Rates tend to be highest during the spring and fall (except at resort areas, when summer is high season) and during special events, including the Spring Festival of Houses and Spoleto—when reservations are essential.

Hotels and Motels

$$$$ 🏨 **Best Western King Charles Inn.** This inn in the historic district is a cut above the typical chain, with a welcoming lobby and sitting area and spacious rooms furnished with 18th-century period reproductions. ✉ *237 Meeting St., Market area, 29401,* ☎ *843/723–7451 or 800/528–1234,* FAX *843/723–2041,* WEB *www.kingcharlesinn.com. 91 rooms. Restaurant, in-room data ports, pool, free parking. AE, D, DC, MC, V.*

$$$$ 🏨 **Charleston Place.** This Orient-Express property, a graceful low-rise
★ structure in the historic district, is surrounded by upscale boutiques and specialty shops. The lobby has a magnificent handblown Venetian-glass chandelier, an Italian marble floor, and antiques from Sotheby's. Rooms are furnished with period reproductions, linen sheets and robes, and fax machines. Overall, this hotel is simply world class. ✉ *130 Market St., Market area, 29401,* ☎ *843/722–4900 or 800/611–5545,* FAX *843/724–7215,* WEB *www.charlestonplacehotel.com. 400 rooms, 40 suites. 2 restaurants, minibars, 2 tennis courts, indoor pool, hot tub, health club, spa, bar, lobby lounge, concierge, concierge floor, business services, meeting rooms. AE, D, DC, MC, V.*

$$$–$$$$ 🏨 **Embassy Suites Historic Charleston.** The courtyard of the Old Citadel military school where cadets once marched is now a skylighted atrium with stone floors, armchairs, palm trees, and a fountain. The restored brick walls of the breakfast room and some guest rooms in this contemporary hotel contain original gun ports, reminders that the 1822 building was originally a fortification. Teak and mahogany furniture, safari motifs, and sisal carpeting recall the British colonial era. Breakfast and evening refreshments are complimentary. ✉ *341 Meeting St., Upper King, 29403,* ☎ *843/723–6900 or 800/362–2779,* FAX *843/ 723–6938,* WEB *www.embassysuites.com. 153 suites. Restaurant, room service, some in-room hot tubs, outdoor hot tubs, microwaves, refrigerators, pool, gym, lounge, shop, meeting rooms, business services. AE, D, DC, MC, V. BP.*

$$$–$$$$ 🏨 **Hampton Inn–Historic District.** This downtown chain has hardwood
★ floors and a fireplace in the elegant lobby, guest rooms with period reproductions, and a courtyard garden. It's also conveniently near a DASH shuttle stop. ✉ *345 Meeting St., Upper King, 29403,* ☎ *843/ 723–4000 or 800/426–7866,* FAX *843/722–3725,* WEB *www.hamptoninn.com. 166 rooms, 5 suites. Some refrigerators, some microwaves, pool, meeting rooms. AE, D, DC, MC, V. CP.*

$$$–$$$$ 🏨 **HarborView Inn.** Overlooking the harbor and Waterfront Park, this inn is close to most downtown attractions. Calming earth tones and rattan are abundant; high ceilings, four-poster beds, and sea-grass rugs complete the Lowcountry look. Some of the rooms are in a former 19th-century shipping warehouse with exposed brick walls; some have fireplaces and whirlpool tubs. Afternoon wine and cheese as well as evening cookies are included. ⊠ *2 Vendue Range, Market area, 29401,* ☎ *843/853–8439 or 888/853–8439,* FAX *843/853–4034,* WEB *www. charlestownmanagement.com/hvi. 51 rooms, 1 suite. Some in-room hot tubs, in-room data ports, concierge, business services. AE, D, DC, MC, V. CP.*

$$$–$$$$ ⊞ **Mills House Hotel.** Antique furnishings and period furnishings give this luxurious Holiday Inn property plenty of charm. It's a reconstruction of an old hostelry on its original site in the historic district, and although rooms are small and a bit standard, the hotel has a lounge with live entertainment and a nice dining room. ⊠ *115 Meeting St., Market area, 29401,* ☎ *843/577–2400 or 800/874–9600,* FAX *843/722–0623,* WEB *www.millshouse.com. 199 rooms, 16 suites. Pool, restaurant, room service, bar, lounge, concierge, concierge floor, business services, meeting rooms, parking (fee). AE, D, DC, MC, V.*

$$–$$$$ ⊞ **Doubletree Guest Suites Historic Charleston.** Across from the City Market, this hotel has a restored entrance portico from an 1874 bank, a refurbished 1866 firehouse, and three lush gardens. The spacious suites, all decorated with 18th-century reproductions and canopy beds, have wet bars with microwave ovens and refrigerators. ⊠ *181 Church St., Market area, 29401,* ☎ *843/577–2644 or 877/408–8733,* FAX *843/577– 2697,* WEB *www.doubletree.com. 182 suites. Gym, lounge, business services, meeting room. AE, D, DC, MC, V.*

$$$ ⊞ **Meeting Street Inn.** Built in 1874, this salmon-color former tavern in the historic district overlooks a lovely courtyard with fountains and gardens. Spacious rooms have hardwood floors, high ceilings, and reproduction furniture including four-poster rice beds. ⊠ *173 Meeting St., Market area, 29401,* ☎ *843/723–1882 or 800/842–8022,* FAX *843/ 577–0851,* WEB *www.meetingstreetinn.com. 54 rooms. Some refrigerators, outdoor hot tub, bar. AE, D, DC, MC, V. CP.*

$$–$$$ ⊞ **Holiday Inn Charleston/Mount Pleasant.** Just over the Cooper River Bridge, the Holiday Inn is a 10-minute drive from the downtown historic district. Everything has been gracefully done: big banana trees in the lobby, brass lamps, crystal chandeliers, contemporary furniture. ⊠ *250 U.S. 17, Mount Pleasant/East Cooper 29464,* ☎ *843/884–6000 or 800/290–4004,* FAX *843/881–1786,* WEB *www.holidayinn-mtpleasant.com. 158 rooms. Restaurant, some refrigerators and microwaves, pool, gym, sauna, lounge, meeting room. AE, D, DC, MC, V.*

$$–$$$ ⊞ **Westin Francis Marion Hotel.** Built in 1924 as the largest hotel in ★   the Carolinas, the restored Francis Marion is now a Westin property. However, it has retained its big-band and tea-dance glamour with its windowed ballrooms, wrought-iron railings, columns, high ceilings, crown moldings, decorative plasterwork, and views of Marion Square and the harbor. Excellent Southern cuisine can be had at Elliott's on the Square. ⊠ *387 King St., Upper King, 29403,* ☎ *843/722–0600 or 888/625–5144,* FAX *843/723–4633,* WEB *www.westinfm.com. 160 rooms, 66 suites. Restaurant, coffee shop, in-room data ports, gym, lounge, Internet, concierge, business services, meeting rooms, parking (fee). AE, D, DC, MC, V.*

$$ ⊞ **Holiday Inn Historic District.** Although this hotel changed hands and went through a major renovation, it still draws loyal repeat visitors because of its free parking and location—a block from the Gaillard Municipal Auditorium and within walking distance of many must-see spots. Rooms are motel modern. ⊠ *125 Calhoun St., Upper King, 29401,* ☎ *843/805–7900 or 877/805–7900,* FAX *843/805–7700,* WEB *www.charlestonhotel.com. 126 rooms. Restaurant, in-room data ports, pool, bar, concierge, concierge floor, Internet, business services, meeting rooms, parking. AE, D, DC, MC, V.*

$–$$ 🏨 **Hampton Inn Charleston–North.** This upscale Hampton Inn, just off Ashley Phosphate Rd., has a grand marble lobby, a solarium over-looking the pool, crown moldings, and Lowcountry-style furniture. The mostly business clientele rates it tops for service and design. ✉ 7424 *Northside Dr., North Charleston, 29420,* ☎ 843/820–2030 or 877/ 870–2030, 🆆 843/820–2010, 🕸 *www.hamptoninncharleston.com. 102 rooms. In-room data ports, some hot tubs, some kitchens, in-room VCRs, pool, gym, business services, laundry service, meeting room. AE, D, DC, MC, V.*

$ 🏨 **Red Roof Inn.** At the foot of the Cooper River Bridge in Mt. Pleas-ant, about 10 minutes from historic Charleston, this chain motel is clean and well lighted. Some rooms have work areas. ✉ *301 Johnnie Dodds Blvd., Mount Pleasant/East Cooper, 29403,* ☎ 843/884–1411 or 800/ 843–7663, 🆆 843/884–1411, 🕸 *www.redroof.com. 124 rooms. Pool, some refrigerators, some microwaves. AE, D, DC, MC, V.*

Inns and Guest Houses

$$$$ ✕🏨 **Wentworth Mansion.** This spectacular brick mansion, built around 1886 as a private home, is now a luxury inn. Hand-carved marble fire-places, rich woodwork, chandeliers, 14-foot ceilings, and Second Em-pire reproductions create a sense of elegance in the spacious guest rooms. Breakfast buffet, evening wine and cheese, sherry, and turndown ser-vice are included. Rooms have king-size beds and CD players; most have gas fireplaces and some have daybeds. Circa 1886, in the former carriage house, serves inventive food and is the perfect spot for a spe-cial occasion. ✉ *149 Wentworth St., College of Charleston, 29403,* ☎ 843/853–1886 or 888/466–1886, 🆆 843/723–8634, 🕸 *www.went-worthmansion.com. 21 rooms. Restaurant, hot tubs, lounge, free park-ing. AE, D, DC, MC, V. BP.*

$$$$ 🏨 **John Rutledge House Inn.** This 1763 house, built by John Rutledge,
★ one of the framers of the U.S. Constitution, is one of Charleston's most luxurious inns. The ornate ironwork, original woodwork, plaster mold-ings, parquet floors, marble fireplaces, and 14-ft ceilings are impressive. A lovely afternoon tea including wine is served in the ballroom, and a Continental breakfast is served—on the patio, if you prefer sitting out-side. Newspapers are delivered to your room. Some guest rooms have fireplaces. There are also two charming period carriage houses that you can stay in. ✉ *116 Broad St., South of Broad, 29401,* ☎ 843/723–7999 or 800/476–9741, 🆆 843/720–2615, 🕸 *www.charminginns.com. 11 rooms in mansion, 4 in each of 2 carriage houses. Some hot tubs, re-frigerators, business services. AE, D, DC, MC, V. CP.*

$$$$ 🏨 **Planters Inn.** High-ceiling rooms and suites are beautifully ap-pointed with opulent furnishings, including mahogany four-poster beds and marble baths. Twenty-one rooms have a piazza overlooking the garden courtyard. The inn's Peninsula Grill is wonderful. ✉ *112 N. Market St., Market area, 29401,* ☎ 843/722–2345 or 800/845–7082, 🆆 843/577–2125, 🕸 *www.plantersinn.com. 56 rooms, 6 suites. Restaurant, some hot tubs, room service, concierge, business services; no-smoking floors. AE, D, DC, MC, V.*

$$$–$$$$ 🏨 **Ansonborough Inn.** Formerly a stationer's warehouse dating from the early 1900s, this spacious all-suites inn is furnished in period re-productions. It offers hair dryers, irons, a morning newspaper, mes-sage service, wine reception, and rooftop terrace, but it's best known for its friendly staff. ✉ *21 Hasell St., Market area, 29401,* ☎ 843/723–1655 or 800/522–2073, 🆆 843/527–6888, 🕸 *www.ansonborough-inn.com. 37 suites. Bar, meeting room. AE, MC, V. CP.*

$$$–$$$$ 🏨 **Hayne House.** One block from the Battery, in Charleston's presti-gious South of Broad neighborhood, the Hayne house was built in 1755. It has old furnishings but a fresh, light spirit. Rooms have Federal antiques and other heirlooms from the proprietors' families. Two of the guest rooms are in the main house; the other four are in the kitchen house, with its narrow stairway, colonial brickwork, and chimney. ⊠ *30 King St., South of Broad, 29401,* ☎ *843/577–2633,* FAX *843/577–5906,* WEB *www.haynehouse.com. 4 rooms, 2 suites. MC, V. CP.*

$$$–$$$$ 🏠 **Phoebe Pember House.** Built in 1807, the mansion has a separate carriage house, which has two guest rooms upstairs and a living room, dining room, kitchenette, and garden downstairs. Colors and fabrics are cheerful yet refined; artwork is by Charleston artists. The inn is off a busy street, but the piazza is cocooned by a walled garden overlooking Charleston's port. A nearby studio offers yoga classes and workshops. ⊠ *26 Society St., Market area, 29401,* ☎ *843/722–4186,* FAX *843/722–0557,* WEB *www.phoebepemberhouse.com. 6 rooms. Massage, free parking; no smoking. AE, MC, V. CP.*

$$$–$$$$ 🏠 **Two Meeting Street.** As pretty as a wedding cake and just as romantic,
★   this early 20th-century inn on the Battery has two suites with working fireplaces and balconies. In the public spaces there are Tiffany windows, carved English oak paneling, and a chandelier from the former Czechoslovakia. Expect to be treated to afternoon high tea and a Continental breakfast. ⊠ *2 Meeting St., South of Broad, 29401,* ☎ *843/723–7322,* WEB *www.twomeetingstreet.com. 7 rooms, 2 suites. No credit cards. CP.*

$$$ 🏠 **Cannonboro Inn and Ashley Inn.** Two of the most elegant inns in town, these B&B neighbors on the edge of the historic district near the Medical University of South Carolina have luxurious rooms, tastefully decorated in period furnishings. Expect to be treated to a full English breakfast on a piazza overlooking the Charleston gardens. Use of the bicycles and afternoon refreshments are included. ⊠ *Cannonboro: 184 Ashley Ave., Medical University of South Carolina, 29403,* ☎ *843/723–8572,* FAX *843/723–8007,* WEB *www.charleston-sc-inns.com. 6 rooms. Bicycles, business services, free parking. MC, V. BP.* ⊠ *Ashley: 201 Ashley Ave., Medical University of South Carolina, 29403,* ☎ *843/723–1848,* FAX *843/579–9080. 6 rooms, 1 suite. Bicycles, business services, free parking. AE, D, MC, V. BP.*

$$$ 🏠 **Vendue Inn.** This elegant yet friendly inn is close to the harbor and Waterfront Park (though its views are now obstructed by a condo building). Guest rooms have four-poster beds, cozy seating areas, and large bathrooms. A full buffet breakfast, afternoon wine and cheese, and evening milk and cookies are complimentary. The inn's rooftop terrace bar has sweeping harbor views. ⊠ *19 Vendue Range, Market area, 29401,* ☎ *843/577–7970 or 800/845–7900,* WEB *www.vendueinn.com. 31 rooms, 35 suites. Restaurant, in-room data ports, bicycles, bar, business services, meeting room. AE, D, DC, MC, V. BP.*

$$–$$$ 🏠 **1837 Bed and Breakfast and Tea Room.** Although not as fancy as some of the B&Bs in town, this inn has an extremely hospitable staff; you'll get a sense of what it's really like to live in one of Charleston's beloved homes. Restored and operated by two artists-teachers, the home and carriage house have rooms filled with antiques, including romantic canopied beds. The delicious breakfast includes homemade breads and hot entrées such as sausage pie or ham frittatas. ⊠ *126 Wentworth St., Market area, 29401,* ☎ *843/723–7166 or 877/723–1837,* FAX *843/722–7179,* WEB *www.1837bb.com. 8 rooms, 1 suite. AE, D, MC, V. BP.*

$$–$$$ 🏠 **Elliott House Inn.** Listen to the chimes of St. Michael's Episcopal Church as you sip wine in the courtyard of this lovely old inn in the heart of the historic district. You can then retreat to a cozy room with period furniture, including canopied four-posters and Oriental carpets. ⊠ *78 Queen St., Market area, 29401,* ☎ *843/723–1855 or 800/729–*

*1855, FAX 843/722–1567, WEB www.elliotthouseinn.com. 24 rooms.
Hot tub, bicycles. AE, D, MC, V. CP.*

$$–$$$ 🏨 **Guilds Inn.** An easygoing elegance characterizes this place in Mount
Pleasant's historic and scenic Old Village, a residential area with a pharmacy whose soda fountain will take you back in time. The National
Historic Register property has hardwood floors, traditional Lowcountry furnishings, and a mix of antiques and reproductions. Rooms
have whirlpool tubs. Although the self-serve morning pastries are grocery store–bought, the laid-back management is part of the unstuffy
charm of this inn. ⊠ *101 Pitt St., Mount Pleasant/East Cooper, 29464,*
☎ *843/881–0510 or 800/569–4038, FAX 843/884–5020, WEB www.
guildsinn.com. 5 rooms, 1 suite. AE, D, MC, V. CP.*

Resort Islands

On the semitropical islands dotting the South Carolina coast near
Charleston you'll find several sumptuous resorts that offer lots of different packages. Peak season rates (during spring and summer vacations) range from $140 to $300 per day, double occupancy for stays
up to five nights; rates drop for weekly stays and during off-season.

$$$$ 🏨 **Wild Dunes.** This 1,600-acre resort on the Isle of Palms has one- to
six-bedroom villas and homes for rent, plus the plantation-style Boardwalk Inn. Rental locations range from oceanfront to courtside to
marsh side. The inn is just off the beach, in a relaxing boardwalk cluster of villas and shops; guest rooms have balconies and overlook the
ocean. Nearby is a yacht harbor on the Intracoastal Waterway. You
have a long list of recreational options here. ⊠ *Palm Blvd. at 41st Ave.,
Isle of Palms (Box 20575, Charleston 29413),* ☎ *843/886–6000 or
888/845–8926, FAX 843/886–2916, WEB www.wilddunes.com. 430 units,
93 rooms. 2 restaurants, pizzeria, snack bar, ice cream parlor, fans, some
in-room hot tubs, 2 18-hole golf courses, 17 tennis courts, 4 pools, indoor pool, wading pool, health club, boating, fishing, bicycles, volleyball,
lounge, video game room, children's programs (ages 3–12), concierge,
meeting rooms, airport shuttle. AE, D, DC, MC, V.*

$$$–$$$$ 🏨 **Kiawah Island Resort.** Choose from newly renovated inn rooms and
completely equipped one- to five-bedroom villas and private homes in
two luxurious resort villages on 10,000 wooded acres. There are 10
mi of fine broad beaches and plenty of recreational opportunities.
Dining options are many and varied. ⊠ *12 Kiawah Beach Dr., Kiawah
Island 29455,* ☎ *843/768–2121 or 800/654–2924, FAX 843/768–6099,
WEB www.kiawahresort.com. 150 rooms, 430 villas and private homes.
8 restaurants, 5 18-hole golf courses, 28 tennis courts, pro shop, 5 pools,
wading pool, boating, fishing, bicycles, lounges, shops, children's pro-
grams (ages 3–12). AE, D, DC, MC, V.*

$$$–$$$$ 🏨 **Seabrook Island Resort.** About 200 completely equipped one- to six-
bedroom villas, cottages, and beach houses occupy this property (the num-
ber varies according to how many homeowners sign up for the rental
program). The resort is noted for its secluded wooded areas and abun-
dance of wildlife—look for bobcats and white-tailed deer. The Beach Club
and Island House, open to guests, are centers for dining and leisure ac-
tivities. Bohicket Marina Village, the hub of activity around the island,
offers restaurants as well as pizza and sub shops, plus opportunities for
scuba diving, deep-sea- and inshore-fishing charters, and small-boat
rentals. ⊠ *1002 Landfall Way, Seabrook Island 29455,* ☎ *843/768–1000
or 800/845–2475, FAX 843/768–3096, WEB www.seabrookresort.com.
200 units. 3 restaurants, 2 18-hole golf courses, 13 tennis courts, 2
pools, wading pool, boating, parasailing, fishing, bicycles, horseback rid-
ing, children's programs. AE, D, DC, MC, V.*

Nightlife and the Arts

The Arts

CONCERTS

The **Charleston Concert Association** (☎ 843/722–7667) has information on visiting performing arts groups including symphonies, ballets, and operas. The **Charleston Symphony Orchestra** (843/723–7528) presents MasterWorks Series, Downtown Pops, Family Series, and an annual holiday concert at Gaillard Municipal Auditorium (⊠ 77 Calhoun St., Upper King, ☎ 843/577–4500). The orchestra also performs the Sotille Chamber Series at the Sotille Theater (⊠ 44 George St., Market area, ☎ 843/953–6340) and the Light and Lively Pops at Charleston Southern University (⊠ U.S. 78, ☎ 843/953–6340). The College of Charleston has a free **Monday Night Recital Series** (☎ 843/953–8228).

DANCE

Anonymity Dance Company (☎ 843/886–6104), a modern dance troupe, performs throughout the city. The **Charleston Ballet Theatre** (⊠ 477 King St., Upper King, ☎ 843/723–7334) performs everything from classical to contemporary dance at locations around the city. The **Robert Ivey Ballet Company** (☎ 843/556–1343), a semiprofessional company that includes College of Charleston students, gives a fall and spring program of jazz, classical, and modern dance at the Sotille Theater (⊠ 44 George St., Market area, ☎ 843/953–6340).

FESTIVALS

The **Fall Candlelight Tours of Homes and Gardens** (☎ 843/722–4630), sponsored by the Preservation Society of Charleston in September and October, offers an inside look at Charleston's private buildings and gardens.

During the **Festival of Houses and Gardens** (☎ 843/724–8484), held during March and April each year, more than 100 private homes, gardens, and historic churches are open to the public for tours sponsored by the Historic Charleston Foundation. There are also symphony galas in stately drawing rooms, plantation oyster roasts, and candlelight tours.

The **MOJA Arts Festival** (☎ 843/724–7305), which takes place during the last week of September and first week of October, celebrates the rich heritage of the African continent and Caribbean influences on African-American culture. It includes theater, dance, and music performances; art shows; films; lectures; and tours of the historic district.

Piccolo Spoleto Festival (☎ 843/724–7305) is the spirited companion festival of Spoleto Festival USA, showcasing the best in local and regional talent from every artistic discipline. There are about 300 events—from jazz performances to puppet shows—held at 60 sites in 17 days from mid-May through early June, and most performances are free.

The **Southeastern Wildlife Exposition** (☎ 843/723–1748 or 800/221–5273), in mid-February, is one of Charleston's biggest annual events. You'll find art by renowned wildlife artists, live animal demonstrations, and a chili cook-off.

Spoleto Festival USA (☎ 843/722–2764), founded by the composer Gian Carlo Menotti in 1977, has become a world-famous celebration of the arts. For two weeks, from late May to early June, opera, dance, theater, symphonic and chamber music, jazz, and the visual arts are showcased in concert halls, theaters, parks, churches, streets, and gardens throughout the city.

FILM

The **American Theater** (⊠ 446 King St., Upper King, ☎ 843/722–3456), a renovated theater from the 1940s, shows current movies in a table-and-chairs setting with pizza, burgers, finger foods, beer, and wine. Upstairs there's a virtual reality game center. IMAX fans should check out the **IMAX Theater** (⊠ 360 Concord St., Upper King, ☎ 843/725–4629) next to the South Carolina Aquarium.

THEATER

Several groups, including the Footlight Players and Charleston Stage Company, perform at the **Dock Street Theatre** (⊠ 135 Church St., Market area, ☎ 843/723–5648). **Pluff Mud Productions** puts on comedies at the Isle of Palms's Windjammer (⊠ 1000 Ocean Blvd., Mount Pleasant/East Cooper, ☎ 843/886–8596). The Footlight Players regularly perform at the **Footlight Players Theatre** (⊠ 20 Queen St., Market area, ☎ 843/722–4487). Performances by the College of Charleston's theater department and guest theatrical groups are presented during the school year at the **Simons Center for the Arts** (⊠ 54 St. Phillips St., Market area, ☎ 843/953–5604).

Nightlife

DANCING AND MUSIC

Cumberland's (⊠ 26 Cumberland St., Market area, ☎ 843/577–9469) has live blues, rock, reggae, and bluegrass; the place is also known for buffalo wings and cheap beer. There's live music and dancing at the **City Bar** (⊠ 5 Faber St., Market area, ☎ 843/577–7383) each weekend. The **Mills House Hotel** (⊠ 115 Meeting St., Market area, ☎ 843/577–2400), favored by an elegant, mature crowd, has a lively bar. Most evenings **Momma's Blues Palace** (⊠ 46 John St., Upper King, ☎ 843/853–2221) has live music starting at 10 PM. The cavernous **Music Farm** (⊠ 32 Ann St., Upper King, ☎ 843/853–3276), in a renovated train station, showcases live national and local alternative bands. There are dancing and funky '70s music at **Trio Club** (⊠ 139 Calhoun St., Upper King, ☎ 843/965–5333) Wednesday through Saturday. The **Windjammer** (⊠ 1000 Ocean Blvd., Mount Pleasant/East Cooper, ☎ 843/886–8596), on the Isle of Palms, is an oceanfront spot with live rock. Nearby on Sullivan's Island, **Bert's Bar** (⊠ 2209 Middle St., Mount Pleasant/East Cooper, ☎ 843/883–3924), a true beach-bum neighborhood joint, has live music on weekends and a great all-you-can-eat fish fry on Friday night from 6 to 9.

DINNER CRUISES

For an evening of dining and dancing, climb aboard the luxury yacht *Spirit of Carolina* (☎ 843/722–2628). Reservations are essential; there are no cruises Sunday and Monday. Breakfast, brunch, deli, and hot luncheons are prepared on board the *Charlestowne Princess* (☎ 843/722–1112), which also offers its Harborlites Dinner with live entertainment and dancing while cruising the harbor and rivers.

HOTEL AND JAZZ BARS

The **Best Friend Lounge** (⊠ 115 Meeting St., Market area, ☎ 843/577–2400), in the Mills House Hotel, has a guitarist playing light tunes most nights. The elegant **Charleston Grill** (⊠ 224 King St., Market area, ☎ 843/577–4522), in Charleston Place, offers live jazz nightly. In the **Lobby Lounge** (⊠ 130 Market St., Market area, ☎ 843/722–4900), on Charleston Place, afternoon high tea, cocktails, and appetizers are accompanied by piano. At **Mistral Restaurant** (⊠ 99 S. Market St., Market area, ☎ 843/722–5709) there's a regular four-piece jazz band on weekends. **Mitchell's** (⊠ 102 N. Market St., Market area, ☎ 843/722–0732) has nightly acts, from jazz pianists to Latin dance bands.

Charlie's Little Bar (⊠ 141 E. Bay St., Market area, ☎ 843/723–6242), above Saracen Restaurant, is intimate, cozy, and popular with young professionals. **Club Habana** (⊠ 177 Meeting St., Market area, ☎ 843/853–5900) is a chic wood-paneled martini bar (open late) with a cigar shop downstairs. **Southend Brewery** (⊠ 161 E. Bay St., Market area, ☎ 843/853–4677) has a lively bar with beer brewed on the premises; the food is good, especially the soups. You'll find authentic Irish music at **Tommy Condon's Irish Pub & Restaurant** (⊠ 160 Church St., Market area, ☎ 843/577–3818). **Vickery's Bar & Grill** (⊠ 139 Calhoun St., Market area, ☎ 843/723–1558) is a festive nightspot with a spacious outdoor patio and good late-night food. There's another equally popular location in Mount Pleasant (⊠ 1205 Shrimp Boat La., Mount Pleasant/East Cooper, ☎ 843/849–6770).

Outdoor Activities and Sports

Beaches

The Charleston area's mild climate generally is conducive to swimming from April through October. This is definitely not a "swingles" area; all public and private beaches are family oriented, providing a choice of water sports, sunbathing, shelling, fishing, or quiet moonlight strolling. The **Charleston County Parks and Recreation Commission** (☎ 843/762–2172) operates several public beach facilities.

Beachwalker Park, on the west end of Kiawah Island (which is otherwise a private resort), has 300 ft of beach frontage, seasonal lifeguard service, rest rooms, outdoor showers, a picnic area, snack bar, and a 150-car parking lot. ⊠ *Beachwalker Dr., Kiawah Island,* ☎ *843/768–2395.* ⊠ *$5 per car (up to 8 passengers).* ☽ *June–Aug., daily 10–7; May and Sept., daily 10–6; Apr. and Oct., weekends 10–6.*

Folly Beach County Park, 12 mi south of Charleston via U.S. 17 and Route 171 (Folly Road), has 4,000 ft of ocean frontage and 2,000 ft of river frontage. Lifeguards are on duty seasonally. Facilities include dressing areas, outdoor showers, rest rooms, and picnicking areas; beach chair, raft, and umbrella rentals; and parking. ⊠ *1100 W. Ashley Ave., Folly Island,* ☎ *843/588–2426.* ⊠ *$5 per car (up to 8 passengers).* ☽ *May–Aug., daily 9–7; Apr. and Sept.,–Oct., daily 10–6; Nov.–Mar., daily 10–5.*

Isle of Palms County Park is on the Isle of Palms at the foot of the Isle of Palms connector. Lifeguards are on duty seasonally along a 600-ft section of the beach. Facilities include dressing areas, outdoor showers, rest rooms, picnicking areas, beach chair and raft rentals, and a 350-vehicle parking lot. ⊠ *1 14th Ave., Isle of Palms, Mount Pleasant/East Cooper,* ☎ *843/886–3863.* ⊠ *$5 per car (up to 8 passengers).* ☽ *May–Aug., daily 9–7; Apr. and Sept.–Oct., daily 10–6; Nov.–Mar., daily 10–5.*

Participant Sports

The historic district is ideal for bicycling as long as you stay off the main, busy roads; many city parks have biking trails. Palmetto Islands County Park also has trails. Bikes can be rented at the **Bicycle Shoppe** (⊠ 280 Meeting St., Market area, ☎ 843/722–8168; also Kiawah Island, ☎ 843/768–9122). **Island Bike and Surf Shop** (⊠ Kiawah Island, ☎ 843/768–1158) rents bikes, surfboards, and Rollerblades. You'll get a better deal at **Alligator Bike** (⊠ 1823 Paulette Dr., Johns Island, ☎ 843/559–8200), which serves Kiawah and Seabrook islands. **Sea Island Cycle** (⊠ 4053 Rhett Ave., North Charleston, ☎ 843/747–2453) serves all the local islands.

GOLF

One of the most appealing aspects of golfing in the Charleston area is the relaxing pace. With fewer golfers playing the courses than in destinations that are primarily golf oriented, players find choice starting times and an unhurried environment. Nonguests may play on a space-available basis at private island resorts, such as Kiawah Island, Seabrook Island, and Wild Dunes. Top public courses in the area are 18-hole, par-72 courses. For a listing of area golf packages, contact **Charleston Golf Inc.** (☎ 800/774–4444).

The prestigious Pete Dye–designed **Ocean Course at Kiawah Island Resort** (⊠ 1000 Ocean Course Dr., Kiawah Island, ☎ 843/768–7272) is an 18-hole, par-72 course that was the site of the 1991 Ryder Cup. Championship **Kiawah courses,** all 18 holes and par 72, are the Gary Player–designed Marsh Point; Osprey Point, by Tom Fazio; and Turtle Point, a Jack Nicklaus layout (for all three: ⊠ 12 Kiawah Beach Dr.). **Seabrook Island Resort,** a secluded hideaway on Johns Island, offers two more 18-hole, par-72 championship courses: Crooked Oaks, by Robert Trent Jones Sr., and Ocean Winds, designed by William Byrd (for both: ⊠ Seabrook Island Rd., ☎ 843/768–2529). **Wild Dunes Resort,** on the Isle of Palms, has two 18-hole, par-72 Tom Fazio designs: the Links (⊠ 10001 Back Bay Dr., Mount Pleasant/East Cooper, ☎ 843/886–2180) and Harbor Course (⊠ 5881 Palmetto Dr., Mount Pleasant/East Cooper, ☎ 843/886–2301).

Charleston Municipal (⊠ 2110 Maybank Hwy., James Island, ☎ 843/795–6517) is a public, walker-friendly course. **Charleston National Country Club** (⊠ 1360 National Dr., Mount Pleasant/East Cooper, ☎ 843/884–7799) is well maintained and tends to be quiet on weekdays. The **Dunes West Golf Club** (⊠ 3535 Wando Plantation Way, Mount Pleasant/East Cooper, ☎ 843/856–9000) has great marshland views and lots of modulation on the greens. **Links at Stono Ferry** (⊠ 5365 Forest Oaks Dr., Hollywood, ☎ 843/763–1817) is a popular public course with great rates. **Oak Point Golf Course** (⊠ 4255 Bohicket Rd., Johns Island, ☎ 843/768–7431) has water on 16 holes, narrow fairways, and lots of chances to spot wildlife. **Patriots Point** (⊠ 1 Patriots Point Rd., Mount Pleasant/East Cooper, ☎ 843/881–0042) has a partly covered driving range and spectacular harbor views. **Shadowmoss Golf Club** (⊠ 20 Dunvegan Dr., West Ashley, ☎ 843/556–8251) is a well-marked, forgiving course with one of the best finishing holes in the area.

HORSEBACK RIDING

M & M Farms (⊠ Mount Pleasant/East Cooper, ☎ 843/336–4886), in the National Forest Equestrian Center of Francis Marion Forest, offers guided trail tours. **Seabrook Island Equestrian Center** (⊠ Seabrook Island, ☎ 843/768–7541) is open to the public and offers trail rides on the beach and through maritime forests and has pony rides for the kids.

SCUBA DIVING

The **Cooper River Underwater Heritage Diving Trail** is more than 2 mi long and consists of six submerged sites, including ships that date to the Revolutionary War. Contact the **East Coast Dive Connection** (⊠ 206B E. 5th North St., Hwy. 78, Summerville, ☎ 843/821–0001) for lessons, rentals, and information. **Charleston Scuba** (⊠ 335 Savannah Hwy., West Ashley, ☎ 843/763–3483) for maps, rentals, and excursion information.

TENNIS

You can play for free at neighborhood courts, including several across the street from Colonial Lake and at the Isle of Palms Recreation Center on the Isle of Palms. Courts are open to the public at **Kiawah Is-**

land (☎ 843/768–2121). **Shadowmoss Plantation** (☎ 843/556–8251) has public courts available. **Wild Dunes** (☎ 843/886–6000) is a swanky resort with nice courts and a full tennis shop. **Maybank Tennis Center** (✉ 1880 Houghton Dr., James Island, ☎ 843/406–8814) has lights on its six courts. **Charleston Tennis Center** (✉ 19 Farmfield Ave., West Ashley, ☎ 843/724–7402) is a city facility with lots of courts and locker rooms. The Family Circle Cup takes place at the **Town Center Park on Daniel Island** (☎ 843/534–2400), a 32-acre tennis and recreational park with a racquet club and 17 public tennis courts.

Shopping

Shopping Districts

The Market is a complex of specialty shops and restaurants. Vendors sell beaded jewelry, hats, clothing, T-shirts, antique silver, and more in the open-air flea market called **Old City Market** (✉ E. Bay and Market Sts., Market area). You'll find locally made sweet-grass baskets here—and can even watch as they're crafted. **Rainbow Market** (✉ 40 N. Market St., Market area) occupies two interconnected mid-19th-century buildings (don't miss the filled-to-the-hilt **Good Scents** in Rainbow Market, known for its perfume oils and lotions). **Shops at Charleston Place** (✉ 130 Market St., Market area) has Gucci, Caché, Limited Express, and Brookstone. **King Street** has some of Charleston's oldest and finest shops, including **Croghan's Jewel Box** (✉ 308 King St., Market area, ☎ 843/723–3594), **Saks Fifth Avenue** (✉ 211 King St., Market area, ☎ 843/853–9888), and the chichi **Christian Michi** (✉ 220 King St., Market area, ☎ 843/723–0575), which carries elegant women's clothes, makeup, and housewares. From May until September a festive **farmers' market** takes place Saturday mornings at Marion Square.

Antiques

King Street is the center for antiques shopping. **Birlant & Co.** (✉ 191 King St., Market area, ☎ 843/722–3842) presents fine 18th- and 19th-century English antiques, as well as the famous Charleston Battery bench, a small wood-slat bench with cast-iron sides. **Period Antiques** (✉ 194 King St., Market area, ☎ 843/723–2724) has 18th- and 19th-century pieces. **Petterson Antiques** (✉ 201 King St., Market area, ☎ 843/723–5714) offers curious objets d'art, books, furniture, porcelain, and glass. **Livingston & Sons Antiques,** dealers in 18th- and 19th-century English and Continental furniture, clocks, and bric-a-brac, has a large shop west of the Ashley River (✉ 2137 Savannah Hwy., West Ashley, ☎ 843/556–6162) and a smaller one on King Street (✉ 163 King St., Market area, ☎ 843/723–9697).

On James Island, a 10-minute drive from downtown, **Carolopolis Antiques** (✉ 2000 Wappoo Dr., ☎ 843/795–7724) has good bargains on country pieces, many of which are bought by downtown stores. On U.S. 17 in Mount Pleasant, **Hungryneck Mall** (✉ 401 Johnnie Dodds Blvd., Mount Pleaant/East Cooper, ☎ 843/849–1744) has more than 60 dealers hawking sterling silver, oak and mahogany furnishings, linens, and Civil War memorabilia. In Mount Pleasant, **Page's Thieves Market** (✉ 1460 Ben Sawyer Blvd., Mount Pleasant/East Cooper, ☎ 843/884–9672) has furniture, glassware, and "junque."

Art and Crafts Galleries

The **Birds I View Gallery** (✉ 119A Church St., Market area, ☎ 843/723–1276) sells bird paintings and prints by Anne Worsham Richardson. **Charleston Crafts** (✉ 87 Hasell St., Market area, ☎ 843/723–2938) has a fine selection of pottery, quilts, weavings, sculptures, and jewelry fashioned mostly by local artists. The **Pink House Gallery** (✉ 17 Chalmers St., Market area, ☎ 843/723–3608), in the oldest stone house in the city, has prints and paintings of traditional Charleston scenes by local artists. Be sure to go all the way to the third floor to get a look at the small, 17th-century living quarters. Prints of Elizabeth O'Neill Verner's pastels and etchings are on sale at **Elizabeth O'Neill Verner Studio & Gallery** (⊠ 38 Tradd St., South of Broad, ☎ 843/722–4246). The **Marty Whaley Adams Gallery** (⊠ 2 Queen St., Market area, ☎ 843/853–8512) has original vivid watercolors and monotypes, plus prints and posters by this Charleston artist. At **Nina Liu and Friends** (⊠ 24 State St., Market area, ☎ 843/722–2724), you'll find contemporary art objects including handblown glass, pottery, jewelry, and photographs. Famous for his Lowcountry beach scenes, local watercolorist Steven Jordan displays his best at **Steven Jordan Gallery** (⊠ 463 Coleman Blvd., Mount Pleasant/East Cooper, ☎ 843/881–1644).

Books

Atlantic Books (⊠ 191 E. Bay St., Market area, ☎ 843/723–7654; ⊠ 310 King St., Upper King, ☎ 843/723–4751), in two downtown locations, has historic, rare, and out-of-print books. The **Preservation Society of Charleston** (⊠ King and Queen Sts., Market area, ☎ 843/722–4630) carries books and tapes of historic and local interest, sweetgrass baskets, prints, and posters.

Gifts

Charleston's and London's own **Ben Silver** (⊠ 149 King St., Market area, ☎ 843/577–4556), premier purveyor of blazer buttons, has more than 800 designs, including college and British regimental motifs. He also sells British neckties, embroidered polo shirts, and blazers. **Blink** (⊠ 62B Queen St., Market area, ☎ 843/577–5688) has regionally and locally produced paintings, photos, pottery, jewelry, and garden art. **Charleston Collections** (⊠ Straw Market, Kiawah Island Resort, Johns Island, ☎ 843/768–7487; ⊠ 625 Skylark Dr., West Ashley, ☎ 843/556–8911) has Charleston chimes, Rainbow Row prints, Charleston rice spoons and rice steamers, and more. **East Bay Gallery** (⊠ 280 W. Coleman Blvd., Mount Pleasant/East Cooper, ☎ 843/216–8010) has jewelry, chess sets, chimes, and ceramics by local artists. The **Sugar Plantation** (⊠ 48 N. Market St., Market area, ☎ 843/853–3924) has melt-in-your mouth pralines, fudge, Charleston chews, and benne-seed wafers. You can find Charleston foods, including benne-seed wafers, pepper jelly, she-crab soup, and pickled okra, at area **Piggly Wiggly** grocery stores (two locations: ⊠ 1501 U.S. 17N, Mount Pleasant/East Cooper, ☎ 843/881–7921; ⊠ IOP Connector, Mount Pleasant/East Cooper, ☎ 843/881–8939).

Period Reproductions

Historic Charleston Reproductions (⊠ 105 Broad St., South of Broad, ☎ 843/723–8292) has superb replicas of Charleston furniture and accessories, all authorized by the Historic Charleston Foundation. Royalties from sales contribute to restoration projects. At the **Old Charleston Joggling Board Co.** (⊠ 652 King St., Upper King, ☎ 843/723–4331), these Lowcountry oddities (on which people bounce) can be purchased.

Side Trips from Charleston

Gardens, parks, and the charming town of Summerville are good reasons to travel a bit farther afield for day trips.

Moncks Corner

30 mi north of Charleston on U.S. 52.

This town is a gateway to a number of attractions in Santee Cooper Country. Named for the two rivers that form a 171,000-acre basin, the area brims with outdoor pleasures centered on the basin and nearby Lakes Marion and Moultrie.

Cypress Gardens, a swamp garden created from what was once the freshwater reserve of the vast Dean Hall rice plantation, is about 24 mi north of Charleston via U.S. 52, between Goose Creek and Moncks Corner. You can explore the inky waters by boat or walk along paths lined with moss-draped cypress trees, azaleas, camellias, daffodils, wisteria, and dogwood. ⊠ *3030 Cypress Gardens Rd.,* ☎ *843/553–0515.* 🎫 *$7.* ☉ *Daily 9–5.*

Mepkin Abbey, overlooking the Cooper River, is an active Trappist monastery and former plantation home of Henry Laurens and, later, of publisher Henry Luce. You can tour the gardens and abbey, take a look at the egg-farming business, or even stay here on a long retreat— these one- to six-night stays are open to anybody willing to observe the rules of the abbey (including married couples); reservations are required, and donations greatly appreciated. ⊠ *Dr. Evans Rd. (about 8 mi southeast of Moncks Corner via Rte. 402),* ☎ *843/761–8509,* WEB *www.mepkinabbey.org.* 🎫 *Free.* ☉ *Daily 9–4:30.*

On the banks of the Old Santee Canal is the **Old Santee Canal Park.** You can explore on foot or take a canoe. The park includes a 19th-century plantation house; the Berkeley Museum, focusing on cultural and natural history; and an interpretive center. ⊠ *Rembert C. Dennis Blvd.,* ☎ *843/899–5200,* WEB *www.oldsanteecanalpark.org.* 🎫 *$3.* ☉ *Sept.–May, daily 9–5; June–Aug., daily 9–6.*

Francis Marion National Forest consists of 250,000 acres of swamps, vast oaks and pines, and little lakes thought to have been formed by falling meteors. It's a good place for picnicking, camping, boating, and swimming. At the park's **Rembert Dennis Wildlife Center** (⊠ off U.S. 52 in Bonneau, just north of Moncks Corner, ☎ 843/825–3387) deer, wild turkey, and striped bass are reared and studied. ⊠ *U.S. 52 (35 mi north of Charleston),* ☎ *843/336–3248.* 🎫 *Free.* ☉ *Daily 9–5.*

LODGING

$$$–$$$$ 🏨 **Rice Hope Plantation.** A former rice plantation in Moncks Corner overlooking the Cooper River, this inn is on 11 acres of live oaks and gardens designed by landscape architect Loutrell Briggs. The house has six working fireplaces and antiques and reproductions. Guest rooms have four-poster beds, comfortable seating, and private baths; the suite has a porch overlooking the river. ⊠ *206 Rice Hope Dr., 29461,* ☎ *843/761–4832 or 800/569–4038,* FAX *843/884–5020,* WEB *www.ricehope.com.* 4 rooms, 1 suite. Tennis court, boating, fishing, basketball; no smoking. AE, MC, V. CP.

OUTDOOR ACTIVITIES AND SPORTS

Two good fishing spots are **Lakes Marion** and **Moultrie,** both full of bream, striped bass, catfish, and large- and smallmouth bass. For information about fishing, contact **Santee Cooper Counties Promotion Commission** (⊠ Drawer 40, Santee 29142, ☎ 843/854–2131; 800/227–8510 outside SC).

Summerville

25 mi northwest of Charleston via I–26 (Exit 199) to Rte. 165.

Built by wealthy planters, this picturesque town has lots of lovely of Victorian buildings, many of which are listed on the National Register of Historic Places. Colorful gardens of camellias, azaleas, and wisteria abound, and many streets curve around tall pines, as a local ordinance prohibits cutting them down. This is a good place for antiquing. To get oriented, stop by the **Greater Summerville/Dorchester County Chamber of Commerce and Visitor Center** (⌧ 402 N. Main St., Box 670, 29484, ☎ 843/873–2931).

DINING AND LODGING

$$$$ ✕⌆ **Woodlands Inn.** People drive from Charleston for superb meals
★ ($$$$) at this luxury inn, part of the prestigious Relais & Châteaux group. A four-course menu and a five-course menu with wine are available at the restaurant. Delicate sauces and subtle touches are key in entrées— Angus beef with a Barolo wine reduction, potato-encrusted crab cakes, and Asian-spiced lobster. Although the inn, built in 1906 as a winter home, backs up to a suburb, it's a first-rate getaway, with such niceties as fireplaces, whirlpool or claw-foot tubs, and heated towel racks. Rates include a split of champagne at arrival and afternoon tea. ⌧ *125 Parsons Rd., 29483, ☎ 843/875–2600 or 800/774–9999, FAX 843/875– 2603,* WEB *www.woodlandsinn.com. 15 rooms, 4 suites. Restaurant, 2 tennis courts, pool, bicycles, croquet, lounge. AE, D, DC, MC, V.*

Charleston A to Z

To research prices, get advice from other travelers, and book travel arrangements, visit www.fodors.com.

AIRPORTS AND TRANSFERS

Charleston International Airport on I–26, 12 mi west of downtown, is served by Continental, Comair, Delta, Midway Express, United Express, Northwest, TWA, and US Airways.
➤ AIRPORT INFORMATION: **Charleston International Airport** (⌧ 5500 International Blvd., North Charleston, ☎ 843/767–1100).

AIRPORT TRANSFERS

Several shuttle and cab companies service the airport. It costs about $18–$22 to travel downtown by taxi; to Mount Pleasant, $23–$35. Fares are approximately $1.65 per mile. Airport Ground Transportation arranges shuttles, which cost $10 per person to the downtown area. Some hotels provide shuttle service.
➤ TAXIS AND SHUTTLES: **Thurman's Limo** (☎ 843/607–2912). **Absolute Charleston** (☎ 843/817–4044). **Harvie's Taxi Limo Service** (☎ 843/709–4276). **Lee's Limousine** (☎ 843/797–0041). **Airport Ground Transportation** (☎ 843/767–1100).

BOAT AND FERRY TRAVEL

Boaters on the Intracoastal Waterway may dock at Ashley Marina and City Marina, in Charleston Harbor, or at Wild Dunes Yacht Harbor, on the Isle of Palms.

CHARTS is the only full-service water taxi providing transportation to and from Patriots Point naval and maritime museum. It also offers harbor cruises.

FARES AND SCHEDULES

➤ BOAT AND FERRY INFORMATION: **Ashley Marina** (⌧ Lockwood Blvd., Medical University of South Carolina, ☎ 843/722–1996). **CHARTS** (⌧ 196A Concord St., North of Calhoun, ☎ 843/853–4700). **City Marina** (⌧ Lockwood Blvd., Medical University of South Carolina, ☎ 843/723–5098). **Wild Dunes Yacht Harbor** (☎ 843/886–5100).

BUS TRAVEL TO AND FROM CHARLESTON

Greyhound serves Charleston and Moncks Corner.
➤ BUS INFORMATION: **Greyhound** (☎ 800/231–2222).

BUS TRAVEL WITHIN CHARLESTON

Charleston Area Regional Transit Authority (CARTA) runs buses on routes that cover most of Charleston from 5:35 AM until 10 PM, until 1 AM in and to North Charleston. The cost is $1 (free transfers). DASH (Downtown Area Shuttle) trolley-style buses provide fast service in the main downtown areas. A single fare is $1; $3 is the cost of an all-day pass.

FARES AND SCHEDULES

➤ BUS INFORMATION: **CARTA** (☎ 843/724–7420).

CAR TRAVEL

I–26 traverses the state from northwest to southeast and terminates at Charleston. U.S. 17, the coast road, passes through Charleston. I–526, also called the Mark Clark Expressway, runs primarily east–west, connecting the West Ashley area to Mount Pleasant.

EMERGENCIES

The emergency rooms are open all night at Charleston Memorial Hospital, MUSC Hospital, and Roper Hospital all have 24-hour emergency rooms.

➤ EMERGENCY SERVICES: **Ambulance, police** (☎ 911).

➤ HOSPITALS: **Charleston Memorial Hospital** (✉ 326 Calhoun St., Upper King, ☎ 843/577–0600). **MUSC Hospital** (✉ 169 Ashley Ave., Upper King, ☎ 843/792–3826). **Roper Hospital** (✉ 316 Calhoun St., Upper King, ☎ 843/724–2000).

➤ LATE-NIGHT PHARMACIES: **Eckerds** (✉ Calhoun St. and Rutledge Ave., Upper King, ☎ 843/805–6022).

LODGING

APARTMENT AND HOUSE RENTALS

Rates tend to increase and reservations are essential during both the Spring Festival of Houses and Spoleto. For historic home rentals in Charleston, contact Charleston Carriage Houses–Oceanfront Realty. For condo and house rentals on Kiawah Island, Sullivan's Island, and the Isle of Palms—some with private pools and tennis courts—try Great Beach Vacations.

➤ LOCAL AGENTS: **Great Beach Vacations** (✉ 1517 Palm Blvd., Isle of Palms 29451, ☎ 843/886–9704). **Charleston Carriage Houses–Oceanfront Realty** (✉ Box 6151, Hilton Head 29938, ☎ 843/785–8161).

BED-AND-BREAKFASTS

To find rooms in homes, cottages, and carriage houses, try Historic Charleston Bed and Breakfast. Southern Hospitality B&B Reservations handles rooms in homes and carriage houses.

➤ RESERVATION SERVICES: **Historic Charleston Bed and Breakfast** (✉ 60 Broad St., South of Broad, Charleston 29401, ☎ 843/722–6606). **Southern Hospitality B&B Reservations** (✉ 110 Amelia Dr., Lexington 29072, ☎ 843/356–6238 or 800/374–7422).

TAXIS

Fares within the city average $3–$4 per trip. Companies include Safety Cab, Checker Cab, and Yellow Cab.

Charleston Rickshaw Company has two-adult pedicabs that will take you anywhere in the historic district for about $6–$12.

➤ TAXI COMPANIES: **Charleston Rickshaw Company** (✉ 21 George St., Market area, ☎ 843/723–5685). **Safety Cab** (☎ 843/722–4066). **Yellow Cab** (☎ 843/577–6565). **Checker Taxi** (☎ 843/747–9200).

TOURS

BOAT TOURS

Charleston Harbor Tour and Princess Gray Line Harbor Tours ply the harbor. Fort Sumter Tours includes a stop at Fort Sumter and also offers Starlight dinner cruises aboard a luxury yacht.

➤ FEES AND SCHEDULES: **Charleston Harbor Tour** (☎ 843/722–1691). **Fort Sumter Tours** (☎ 843/722–1691, 843/881–7337, or 800/789–3678). **Princess Gray Line Harbor Tours** (☎ 843/722–1112 or 800/344–4483).

BUS TOURS

Adventure Sightseeing and the Colonial Coach and Trolley Company do motor-coach tours of the historic district. Gray Line has tours of the historic district plus seasonal trips to gardens and plantations. Doin' the Charleston, a van tour, combines its narration with audiovisuals and makes a stop at the Battery.

➤ FEES AND SCHEDULES: **Adventure Sightseeing** (☎ 843/762–0088 or 800/722–5394). **Colonial Coach and Trolley Company** (☎ 843/795–3000). **Doin' the Charleston** (☎ 843/763–1233 or 800/647–4487). **Gray Line** (☎ 843/722–4444).

CARRIAGE TOURS

Lowcountry Carriage Co., Old South Carriage Company, and Palmetto Carriage Tours run horse- and mule-drawn carriage tours of the historic district, some conducted by guides in Confederate uniforms, that each last about one hour. We highly recommend carriage tours if you want a great overview of Charleston. They have a set itinerary and cover one of four zones in the historic district; once the carriages have picked up passengers the drivers draw from a lottery to decide which zone each carriage will cover. Go before 5 PM so you'll get to see the residential section.

➤ FEES AND SCHEDULES: **Lowcountry Carriage Co.** (☎ 843/577–0042). **Old South Carriage Company** (☎ 843/723–9712). **Palmetto Carriage Tours** (☎ 843/723–8145).

ECOTOURS

Barrior Island Ecotours, at the Isle of Palms Marina, offers three-hour pontoon-boat tours to a barrier island, sunset tours, crabbing and fishing expeditions, and even a day camp for kids. Coastal Expeditions Kayak Tours offers half-day and full-day naturalist-led kayak tours down historic rivers. You can also rent kayaks. Cap'n Richard's ACE Basin Nature Tour takes you into the ACE (for Ashepoo, Cumbahee, and Edisto rivers) Basin—a managed wilderness that includes 350,000 acres of wetlands—for a river tour as well as a land tour of a private plantation.

➤ FEES AND SCHEDULES: **Barrior Island Ecotours** (☎ 843/886–5000). **Cap'n Richard's ACE Basin Nature Tour** (☎ 843/766–9664). **Coastal Expeditions Kayak Tours** (☎ 843/884–7684).

SPECIAL-INTEREST TOURS

Flying High over Charleston provides aerial tours. Chai Y'All shares stories and sites of Jewish interest. Gullah Tours is expert in local African-American culture. Sweetgrass Tours focuses on African-American influences on Charleston architecture, history, and culture.

➤ FEES AND SCHEDULES: **Chai Y'All** (☎ 843/556–0664). **Flying High over Charleston** (☎ 843/569–6148). **Gullah Tours** (☎ 843/763–7551). **Sweetgrass Tours** (☎ 843/556–0664 for groups).

PRIVATE GUIDES

To hire a private guide, contact Associated Guides of Historic Charleston; Charleston's Finest Historic Tours, which offers tours of the city and plantations; or Janice Kahn, who has been doing individualized guiding for more than 25 years.

➤ CONTACTS: **Associated Guides of Historic Charleston** (☎ 843/724–6419). **Charleston's Finest Historic Tours** (☎ 843/577–3311). **Janice Kahn** (☎ 843/556–0664).

WALKING TOURS

Walking tours are given by Charleston Strolls; Charleston Tea Party Walking Tour, whose walks include tea in a private garden; On the Market Tours; and the Original Charleston Walks. For a spookier view of the city, take the Ghosts of Charleston walking tour. The same guides also celebrate the city in the Story of Charleston walking tour.

➤ FEES AND SCHEDULES: **Charleston Strolls** (☎ 843/766–2080). **Charleston Tea Party Walking Tour** (☎ 843/577–5896 or 843/722–1779). **Ghosts of Charleston** (☎ 843/723–1670 or 800/854–1670). **On the Market Tours** (☎ 843/853–8687). **Original Charleston Walks** (☎ 843/577–3800 or 800/729–3420).

TRAIN TRAVEL

➤ TRAIN INFORMATION: **Amtrak** (✉ 4565 Gaynor Ave., North Charleston, ☎ 843/744–8264 or 800/872–7245).

VISITOR INFORMATION

You can pick up a schedule of events at the visitor center or at area hotels, inns, and restaurants. Also see "Tips for Tourists" each Saturday in the *Post & Courier*. The Charleston Area Convention and Visitors Bureau has information on the city and also on Kiawah Island, Seabrook Island, Mount Pleasant, North Charleston, Edisto Island, Summerville, and the Isle of Palms. The Historic Charleston Foundation and the Preservation Society of Charleston have information on house tours.

➤ TOURIST INFORMATION: **Charleston Area Convention and Visitors Bureau** (✉ Box 975, Charleston 29402, ☎ 843/853–8000 or 800/868–8118, WEB www.charlestoncvb.com). **Historic Charleston Foundation** (✉ Box 1120, Charleston 29402, ☎ 843/723–1623). **Preservation Society of Charleston** (✉ Box 521, Charleston 29402, ☎ 843/722–4630). **Visitor Center** (✉ 375 Meeting St., Upper King).

MYRTLE BEACH AND THE GRAND STRAND

The lively, family-oriented Grand Strand, a booming resort area along the South Carolina coast, is one of the eastern seaboard's megavacation centers. Myrtle Beach alone accounts for about 40% of the state's tourism revenue. The main attraction, of course, is the broad, beckoning beach—60 mi of white sand, stretching from the North Carolina border south to Georgetown, with Myrtle Beach as the hub. All along the Strand you can enjoy shell hunting, fishing, swimming, sunbathing, sailing, surfing, jogging, or just strolling on the beach. Here you'll find more than 100 championship golf courses, designed by Arnold Palmer, Robert Trent Jones, Jack Nicklaus, and Tom and George Fazio, among others; excellent seafood restaurants; giant shopping malls and factory outlets; amusement parks, water slides, and arcades; a dozen shipwrecks for divers to explore; fine fishing; campgrounds, most of which are on the beach; plus antique-car and wax museums, the world's largest outdoor sculpture garden, an antique pipe organ and merry-go-round, and a museum dedicated entirely to rice. The Strand has also emerged as a major center for country music, with an expanding number of theaters.

Myrtle Beach—whose population of 26,000 explodes to about 450,000 in summer—is the center of activity on the Grand Strand. It is here that you'll find the amusement parks and other children's activities that make the area so popular with families, as well as most of the nightlife that keeps parents and teenagers alike happy. On the North Strand are Little River, with a thriving fishing and charter industry, and the several communities that make up North Myrtle Beach. On the South Strand the family retreats of Surfside Beach and Garden City offer more summer homes and condominiums. Farther south are towns as alluring to visit as are the sights along the way: Murrells Inlet, once a pirates' haven and now a scenic fishing village and port; and Pawleys Island, one of the East Coast's oldest resorts, which prides itself on being "arrogantly shabby." Historic Georgetown forms the southern tip.

Myrtle Beach

94 mi northeast of Charleston via U.S. 17, 138 mi east of Columbia via U.S. 76 to U.S. 378 to U.S. 501.

Myrtle Beach, with its high-rises and hyperdevelopment, is a swirl of seaside activity. To capture its flavor, start at the Myrtle Beach Pavilion Amusement Park and wind your way north on Ocean Boulevard. Here's where you'll find an eclectic assortment of gift and novelty shops, a wax museum, and a museum of oddities. Turn east when it suits your fancy and make your way back on the beach amid children building sand castles and kids-at-heart flying kites.

Dozens of colorful streetlight displays around major intersections add yet a few more volts of energy to the already pulsating scene, and at Christmas Myrtle Beach stages one of the largest, most colorful light shows in the South.

Myrtle Beach Pavilion Amusement Park has thrill and children's rides, the Carolinas' largest flume, a wooden roller coaster, video games, a teen nightclub, specialty shops, antique cars, and sidewalk cafés. ⊠ *9th Ave. N and Ocean Blvd., the Strip,* ☎ *843/448–6456,* WEB *www.mb-pavilion.com.* ☎ *Fees for individual attractions; 1-day pass for unlimited access to most rides $22.* ☉ *Mid-Mar.–May and mid-Aug.–Sept., weekdays 6 PM–10 PM, Sat. 1–10, Sun. 1–8; June–mid-Aug., daily 1 PM–midnight, operating hrs can vary, so call ahead.*

Ripley's Haunted Adventure. Convincing vampires and other costumed characters will taunt and entice you to come inside this fun, creepy haunted house. ⊠ *915 N. Ocean Blvd., the Strip,* ☎ *843/448–2261.* ☎ *$10.* ☉ *Late Feb.–May and Sept.–mid-Oct., daily 9 AM–11 PM; June–Aug., daily 9 AM–2 AM.*

Hawaiian Rumble is the crown jewel of Myrtle Beach, the minigolf capital of the world. The course, the site of several championship tournaments, has a smoking mountain that erupts with fire and rumbles at timed intervals. ⊠ *3210 33rd Ave. S, at U.S. 17, North Myrtle Beach,* ☎ *843/458–2585.* ☎ *$8 all day (9–5), $6 per round after 5 PM.* ☉ *Mar.–Dec., daily 9 AM–midnight.*

★ **Alligator Adventure** has exciting interactive reptile shows, including an alligator-feeding demonstration. The boardwalks go through marshes and swamps on the 15-acre property, where you'll see wildlife of the wetlands, including the only known collection of the rare white albino alligator; the gavial, an exotic crocodilian from Asia; giant Galápagos tortoises; and all manner of other reptiles, including boas, pythons, and anacondas. Unusual plants and exotic birds also thrive here. ⊠ *U.S. 17 at Barefoot Landing, North Myrtle Beach,* ☎ *843/361–0789,* FAX *843/361–0742,* WEB *www.alligatoradventure.com.* ☎ *$12.95.* ☉ *Daily 10–9.*

🕭 **Myrtle Beach Grand Prix Family Thrill Park** is auto-mania heaven with Formula 1 race cars, go-carts, bumper boats, mini-go-carts, and bumper boats, plus a kids' park for children ages 3 and up with mini-go-carts, kids' cars, and mini–bumper boats. New is a log flume and music express ride. ✉ *3201 U.S. 17, North Myrtle Beach,* ☎ *843/272–7770;* ✉ *Windy Hill, 3900 U.S. 17S, North End,* ☎ *843/272–7770,* WEB *www.mbgrandprix.com.* 🎟 *$29.95 unlimited rides or individual rides $3–$5 each.* ☉ *Mar.–Oct., daily 3–midnight.*

🕭 At **NASCAR Speedpark** you can drive on seven different NASCAR-replica tracks; the 26-acre facility also has racing memorabilia, an arcade, and miniature golf. ✉ *U.S. 17 Bypass and 21st Ave. N, at Broadway at the Beach, Central Myrtle Beach,* ☎ *843/918–8725,* WEB *www.nascarspeedpark.com.* 🎟 *$21.95 unlimited day pass or $5 each ride.* ☉ *Mar.–Oct., weekdays 5 PM–midnight, weekends noon–midnight; hrs vary, so call to confirm.*

🕭 The **Butterfly Pavilion** has a fully enclosed glass butterfly conservatory where you can walk among 2,000 native North American and tropical butterflies. The Nature Zone Discovery Center has 22 animal exhibits including those featuring exotic frogs, insects, and a working beehive; in the Lorikeet Aviary you're surrounded by and can hand-feed colorful lorikeets. ✉ *1185 Celebrity Circle, at Broadway at the Beach, Central Myrtle Beach,* ☎ *843/839–4444 or 877/280–2751,* WEB *www.butterflypavilion.com.* 🎟 *$12.95.* ☉ *Jan.–early Mar., daily 9–6; early Mar.–late Mar., daily 9–8; Apr.–May, daily 9 AM–10 PM; June–early Sept., daily 9 AM–11 PM; early Sept.–Dec., daily 9–9.*

🕭 The **Ripley's Aquarium** has an underwater tunnel exhibit longer than a football field and exotic marine creatures from poisonous lionfish to moray eels and an octopus. Children can examine horseshoe crabs and eels in touch tanks. ✉ *9th Ave. N and U.S. 17N Bypass, at Broadway at the Beach, Central Myrtle Beach,* ☎ *843/916–0888 or 800/734–8888,* WEB *www.ripleysaquarium.com.* 🎟 *$14.95.* ☉ *Sun.–Thurs. 9–9, Fri.–Sat. 9 AM–10 PM; closing time varies.*

🕭 South of Myrtle Beach about 9 mi, **Wild Water** provides splashy family fun for all ages in 25 water-oriented rides and activities. ✉ *910 U.S. 17S, Surfside Beach,* ☎ *843/238–3787,* WEB *www.wild-water.com.* 🎟 *$20, $13 after 3 PM.* ☉ *Late May–early Sept., daily 10–7.*

🕭 **Myrtle Waves** is a huge water park. ✉ *Hwy. 17 Bypass and 19th Ave. N, South End,* ☎ *843/448–1026 or 800/524–9283,* WEB *www.myrtle-waves.com.* 🎟 *$22 for full day, $13.95 for ½ day.* ☉ *Late May–early Sept., daily 10–6.*

Dining and Lodging

MYRTLE BEACH

$$$–$$$$ ✕ **Collectors Cafe.** A successful restaurant, art gallery, and coffeehouse
★ rolled into one, this unpretentious arty spot has bright, funky paintings and tile work covering its walls and tabletops. You can shop for a painting while enjoying black-bean cakes, grilled tuna, or pan-sautéed scallop cakes. ✉ *7726 N. Kings Hwy., North Myrtle Beach,* ☎ *843/449–9370. AE, D, DC, MC, V. Closed Sun. No lunch.*

$$–$$$ ✕ **Sea Captain's House.** At this picturesque restaurant with a nautical theme, the best seats are in the windowed porch room, which overlooks the ocean. The fireplace in the wood-paneled dining room inside is warmly welcoming on cool off-season evenings. Menu highlights include Lowcountry crab casserole and avocado-seafood salad. The breads and desserts are baked on the premises. ✉ *3000 N. Ocean Blvd., the Strip,* ☎ *843/448–8082. AE, D, MC, V.*

$–$$ ✕ **Villa Katrina's Underground Cantina.** Head downstairs into a fun, tavernlike space for Mexican fare of the elegant variety, including flaming coffees and desserts. Chicken-and-spinach burritos and tacos are a specialty. ⊠ *821 Main St., the Strip,* ☎ *843/946–6216. No credit cards. Closed Sun.*

$–$$ ✕ **Vintage House Café.** Locals dine here on beef tips, smoked chicken ravioli, and homemade bananas Foster cheesecake. The style hints of Granny's house: entrées are served on an assortment of vintage china; old sideboards, pitchers, and lace doilies are among the accents. ⊠ *1210 N. Kings Hwy., the Strip,* ☎ *843/626–3918. AE, D, DC, MC, V. Closed Sun. No dinner Mon.*

$ ✕ **Croissants Bakery & Café.** The lunch crowd loves this spot, which has an on-site bakery. Black-and-white tile floors, café tables, checked tablecloths, and glass pastry cases filled with sweets create an appetizing feel to the place. Try the chicken or broccoli salads, a Reuben sandwich, the pasta specials, a Monte Cristo sandwich, and the peanut butter cheesecake. ⊠ *504A 27th Ave. N, the Strip,* ☎ *843/448–2253. D, MC, V. Closed Sun. No dinner.*

$$ ✕▥ **Sea Island Inn.** In the quiet residential end of Myrtle Beach, this inn has oceanfront rooms with comfortable standard furnishings plus several social areas. Breakfast and dinner are served in the elegant oceanfront dining room. ⊠ *6000 N. Ocean Blvd., North End, 29577,* ☎ *843/449–6406 or 800/548–0767,* ℻ *843/449–4102,* ⊞ *www.seaislandinn.com. 113 rooms, 1 suite, 1 penthouse. Restaurant, 2 pools, Ping-Pong, children's programs. AE, D, MC, V. MAP.*

$$$–$$$$ ▥ **Kingston Plantation.** The Grand Strand's most luxurious property,
★   the 20-story glass-sheathed tower is part of a complex of shops, restaurants, hotels, and one- to three-bedroom condominiums in 145 acres of ocean-side woodlands. An Embassy Suites property, the hotel has guest rooms with bleached-wood furnishings and a whimsical theme; all have kitchenettes. ⊠ *9800 Lake Dr., North End, 29572,* ☎ *843/449–0006 or 800/876–0010,* ℻ *843/497–1110,* ⊞ *www.kingstonplantation.com. 255 suites, 510 villas and condos. 2 restaurants, tennis court, indoor pool, aerobics, health club, sauna, racquetball, lounge. AE, D, DC, MC, V.*

$$$ ▥ **Hampton Inn and Suites Oceanfront.** This property combines the classic reliability of this respected midpriced range with the joys of a beach resort. Rooms have balconies and a cheerful style; all rooms have ocean views, and there's a lazy river—a pool with a moving current—that carries swimmers along its course. ⊠ *1803 S. Ocean Blvd, South End, 29577,* ☎ *843/946–6400 or 877/946–6400,* ℻ *843/236–9415,* ⊞ *www.hamptoninnoceanfront.com. 80 rooms, 36 suites. Microwaves, refrigerators, 2 indoor pools, 2 outdoor pools, gym, hot tub, business services, meeting rooms. AE, D, DC, MC, V. CP.*

$$–$$$ ▥ **Breakers Resort Hotel.** The rooms in this tall oceanfront hotel (within walking distance of the Pavilion) are airy and spacious, with contemporary furnishings. Most have kitchenettes and Murphy beds; the new Paradise Tower (next door to the original tower) has one-, two-, and three-bedroom suites, a lazy river, and a pirate-ship facade that kids can swim in and around. ⊠ *2006 N. Ocean Blvd., Box 485, 29578,* ☎ *843/444–4444 or 800/845–0688,* ℻ *843/626–5001,* ⊞ *www.breakers.com. 204 rooms, 186 suites. 2 restaurants, room service, refrigerators, 2 pools, indoor-outdoor pool, gym, outdoor hot tubs, saunas, lounge, video game room, children's programs, laundry service. AE, D, DC, MC, V.*

$$–$$$ ▥ **Holiday Inn Oceanfront.** This oceanfront inn is right in the heart of the action. The spacious rooms are done in cool sea tones. After beach basking you can prolong the mood in the inn's spacious, plant-bedecked indoor recreation center. ⊠ *415 S. Ocean Blvd., the Strip, 29577,* ☎

843/448–4481 or 800/845–0313, FAX 843/448–0086, WEB www.bassho-tels.com. 306 rooms. 2 restaurants, snack bar, indoor pool, hot tub, sauna, lounge, recreation room. AE, D, DC, MC, V.

$$-$$$ 🏨 **Sheraton Myrtle Beach Resort.** All rooms and suites have a fresh, contemporary look. Oceanfront Lounge, highlighted by tropical colors and rattan furnishings, is a lively evening gathering spot. There are a lazy river (artificial stream) and an arcade nearby. ⌂ *2701 S. Ocean Blvd., South End, 29577,* ☎ *843/448–2518 or 800/992–1055,* FAX *843/449–1879,* WEB *www.sheratonresort.com. 211 rooms, 8 suites. Restaurant, indoor pool, health club. AE, D, DC, MC, V.*

$$ 🏨 **Chesterfield Inn.** A remnant from the past, this oceanfront brick inn, hidden beneath the towers of Myrtle Beach's glitzier hotels, has been in operation for more than a half century. The rooms in the original building are plain and a bit worn, but many people prefer them to those in the newer wing. The highlight here is the family-style meals, served on white tablecloths in the seafront dining room. ⌂ *700 N. Ocean Blvd., the Strip, 29578,* ☎ *843/448–3177,* FAX *843/626–4736,* WEB *www.chester-fieldinnmb.com. 63 rooms. Restaurant, some kitchenettes, pool, shuffleboard. AE, D, DC, MC, V. MAP.*

$$ 🏨 **Landmark Resort Hotel.** This high-rise oceanfront resort hotel has artificial "lazy rivers" indoors and out. Rooms are colorfully decorated in a Caribbean motif. All have balconies and refrigerators; some have kitchenettes. ⌂ *1501 S. Ocean Blvd., South End, 29577,* ☎ *843/448–9441 or 800/845–0658,* FAX *843/448–6701,* WEB *www.landmarkresort.com. 313 rooms, 257 suites. Restaurant, snack bar, 2 pools, 2 indoor pools, wading pool, gym, sauna, hot tubs, pub, video game room, laundry facilities, airport shuttle; no-smoking rooms. AE, D, DC, MC, V.*

$ 🏨 **Days Inn at Waccamaw.** Relax by the pool or in the gazebo after a day of shopping at the nearby Waccamaw Pottery and Factory Shoppes. The theaters of the Fantasy Harbor complex are also close at hand. Rooms here are clean and functional and filled with contemporary furnishings. ⌂ *3650 U.S. 501, Waccamaw Pottery Area, 29577,* ☎ *843/236–1950 or 800/325–2525,* FAX *843/236–9415,* WEB *www.daysinn.com. 157 rooms. Pool, hot tub. AE, D, DC, MC, V.*

$ 🏨 **Driftwood on the Oceanfront.** Under the same ownership for more than 65 years, the Driftwood is popular with families. Some rooms are on the oceanfront, and all are decorated in sea, sky, or earth tones. ⌂ *1600 N. Ocean Blvd., Box 275, 29578,* ☎ *843/448–1544 or 800/942–3456,* FAX *843/448–2917,* WEB *www.driftwoodlodge.com. 90 rooms. Microwaves, refrigerators, 2 pools, gym, shuffleboard, laundry facilities. AE, D, MC, V.*

$ 🏨 **Serendipity Inn.** This cozy Spanish villa-style inn is about 300 yards from the beach. Though the layout is much like a hotel, each guest room is decorated in a different way. There's also a colorful pool area dotted with hanging flowers and a trickling fountain. A breakfast of homemade coffee cake, hardboiled eggs, yogurt, cereal, and fruit is served in the white-wicker Garden Room. ⌂ *407 71st Ave. N, North End, 29572,* ☎ *843/449–5268 or 800/762–3229,* WEB *www.serendipi-tyinn.com. 12 rooms, 1 suite. Refrigerators, some kitchenettes, pool, outdoor hot tub, Ping-Pong, shuffleboard; no room phones. MC, V.*

NORTH MYRTLE BEACH

Dinner cruises are a popular dining option here. The cruise ship **Hurricane** and yachts of the Hurricane pleasure fleet (☎ 843/249–3571) depart from Vereen's Marina (⌂ U.S. 17N and 11th Ave., North Myrtle Beach). The **Barefoot Princess** (☎ 843/272–7743 or 800/685–6601), a replica of a side-wheel riverboat, offers dinner, sunset, and sightseeing cruises along the Intracoastal Waterway from Barefoot Landing (⌂ 4898 U.S. 17S, North Myrtle Beach).

$$–$$$$ ✕ **Greg Norman's Australian Grille.** Overlooking the Intracoastal Waterway, this large restaurant in Barefoot Landing has leather booths, hand-painted walls, an extensive wine list, and a classy bar area. There's an extensive choice of grilled meats, and much of the menu has an Asian flair; try the lobster dumplings, miso-marinated sea bass, or habanero-rubbed tenderloin. ⊠ *4930 U.S. 17S, North Myrtle Beach,* ☎ *843/361–0000. Reservations essential. AE, D, MC, V.*

$$$ 🏨 **Barefoot Resort and Golf.** This golf resort—which when complete (in 2005) will total 500-plus condos—includes one- to- four-bedroom units along fairways as well as in the 118-unit North Tower, which overlooks the Intracoastal Waterway. There are a man-made sandy beach and a waterfront pool. When fully completed, there will be meeting spaces, restaurants, shops, and a water taxi to transport you to Barefoot Landing. ⊠ *Harborpoint Blvd., North Myrtle Beach (mail: 4980 Barefoot Resort Bridge Rd., North Myrtle Beach 29577),* ☎ *866/ 888–6606,* WEB *www.bfresort.com. 118 condos. Pool, 4 18-hole golf courses, spa. AE, D, DC, MC, V.*

Nightlife and the Arts

CLUBS AND LOUNGES

Clubs offer varying fare, including beach music, the Grand Strand's unique '50s-style sound. Some clubs and resorts have sophisticated live entertainment in summer. Some hotels and resorts also have piano bars or lounges with easy-listening music.

South Carolina's only Hard Rock Cafe, Planet Hollywood, and NASCAR Cafe are just a few of the hot spots in **Broadway at the Beach** (⊠ U.S. 17 Bypass between 21st and 29th Aves. N, the Strip, ☎ 843/ 444–3200), which also has shopping. You can dance the shag (the state dance) at **Duck's** (⊠ 229 Main St., North Myrtle Beach, ☎ 843/249– 3858). **Gypsy's** (⊠ 501 8th Ave. N, the Strip, ☎ 843/916–2244) is great for late-night blues music and has a nice wine selection. **Sandals** (⊠ 500 Shore Dr., North Myrtle Beach, ☎ 843/449–6461) is an intimate lounge with live entertainment. The shag is popular at **Studebaker's** (⊠ 2000 N. Kings Hwy., the Strip, ☎ 843/448–9747 or 843/626–3855).

FILM

The **IMAX Discovery Theater** at Broadway at the Beach (⊠ U.S. 17 Bypass between 21st and 29th Aves. N, the Strip, ☎ 843/448–4629) shows educational films on a six-story-high screen.

MUSIC AND LIVE SHOWS

Live acts, and country-and-western shows in particular, are a big draw at the Grand Strand. Music lovers have many family-oriented shows to choose from. The 2,250-seat **Alabama Theater** (⊠ Barefoot Landing, 4750 U.S. 17, North Myrtle Beach, ☎ 843/272–1111) has a regular variety show with a wonderful patriotic closing; the theater also hosts different guest music and comedy artists during the year. **Carolina Opry** (⊠ 82nd Ave. N, North End, ☎ 843/238–8888 or 800/843–6779) is a family-oriented variety show featuring country, light rock, show tunes and gospel music. At **Dolly Parton's Dixie Stampede** (⊠ 8901B U.S. 17 Business, next door to Carolina Opry, North End, ☎ 843/497– 9700 or 800/843–6779), you can dine and enjoy a rousing horse-based show. **Legends in Concert** (⊠ 301 U.S. 17 Business, Surfside Beach, ☎ 843/238–7827 or 800/843–6779) has high-energy shows by impersonators of Little Richard, Elvis, Cher, and the Blues Brothers. The elegant **Palace Theater** (⊠ Broadway at the Beach, U.S. 17 Bypass between 21st and 29th Aves. N, the Strip, ☎ 843/448–0588 or 800/905– 4228) hosts performances by the likes of Aretha Franklin, Kenny Rogers, and the Radio City Rockettes.

The **Fantasy Harbor** complex (✉ Rte. 51, across from Waccamaw Factory Shoppes, Waccamaw Pottery Area) includes several theaters: the 2,000-seat **Crook and Chase Theater** (☎ 843/236–8500 or 800/681–5209), the **Savoy** (☎ 843/236–2200 or 800/681–5209), **Medieval Times Dinner & Tournament** (☎ 843/236–8080 or 800/436–4386), and the 2,000-seat **Forum Theater** (☎ 843/236–8500).

The **House of Blues** (✉ 4640 U.S. 17S, North Myrtle Beach, ☎ 843/272–3000 for tickets), adjacent to Barefoot Landing, showcases big names and up-and-coming talent in blues, rock, jazz, country, and R&B on stages in its Southern-style restaurant and patio as well as in its 2,000-seat concert hall. The gospel brunch is a great deal.

PERFORMING ARTS

Theater productions, concerts, art exhibits, and other cultural events are regularly offered at the **Myrtle Beach Convention Center** (✉ Oak and 21st Ave. N, the Strip, ☎ 843/448–7166).

Outdoor Activities and Sports

BEACHES

All the region's beaches are family oriented, and most are public. The widest expanses are in North Myrtle Beach, where at low tide the sand stretches as far as 650 ft from the dunes to the water. Those who wish to combine their sunning with enjoying nightlife and amusement-park attractions can enjoy it all at Myrtle Beach, the Strand's longtime hub. Vacationers seeking a quieter day in the sun head for the South Strand communities of Surfside Beach and Garden City.

Besides ocean swimming, **Myrtle Beach State Park** has surf fishing, a nature trail, and a pool; there's camping, too, but book in advance. ✉ U.S. 17, 3 mi south of Myrtle Beach, Surfside Beach, ☎ 843/238–5325. ☞ $2 (age 17 and older).

FISHING

The Gulf Stream makes fishing usually good from early spring through December. Anglers can fish from 10 piers and jetties for amberjack, sea trout, and king mackerel. Surfcasters may snare bluefish, whiting, flounder, pompano, and channel bass. In the South Strand, salt marshes, inlets, and tidal creeks yield flounder, blues, croakers, spots, shrimp, clams, oysters, and blue crabs. The annual **Grand Strand Fishing Rodeo** (☎ 843/626–7444 Apr.–Oct.) hosts a fish-of-the-month contest, with prizes for the largest catch of a designated species.

GOLF

Many of the Grand Strand's nearly 100 courses are championship layouts; most are public. **Tee Times Central** (☎ 843/347–4653 or 800/344–5590) books tee times for eight courses, including 18-hole, par-72 **Long Bay** (✉ 350 Foxtail Dr., Longs, ☎ 843/399–2222); 18-hole, par-72 **Myrtle Beach National Golf Club** (✉ 4900 National Dr., Waccamaw Pottery area, ☎ 843/448–2308); and 9-hole, par-36 **Waterway Hills** (✉ U.S. 17N, North Myrtle Beach, ☎ 843/449–6488). A popular course in Myrtle Beach is the 18-hole, par-72 **Arcadian Shores Golf Club** (✉ 701 Hilton Rd., North End, ☎ 843/449–5217). In North Myrtle Beach you'll find the three 18-hole, par-72 courses of the **Legends** (✉ U.S. 501, North Myrtle Beach, ☎ 843/236–9318). The 18-hole, par-72 **Bay Tree Golf Plantation** (✉ Rte. 9, North Myrtle Beach, ☎ 843/249–1487 or 800/845–6191) has varying degrees of difficulty on its silver, gold and green courses. Nine holes of the **Grande Dunes Golf Course** (✉ U.S. 17N, North End 1000 Grande Dunes Blvd., ☎ 888/886–8877) play along the Intracoastal waterway; the course also has elevated vistas. **Heather Glen Golf Links** (✉ U.S. 17N, Little River, ☎ 843/249–9000) is a links-style course with lots of pot-bunkers and pretty water holes. **Robbers Roost Golf Club** (⊠ 1400 U.S. 17N, North Myrtle Beach, ☎ 843/249–1471 or 800/352–2384) has wide fairways and lots of holes with water. Near Surfside Beach is the 18-hole, par-72 **Blackmoor Golf Club** (⊠ Rte. 707, Murrells Inlet, ☎ 843/650–5555), one of the country's top women-friendly courses. In Cherry Grove Beach you'll find the much-touted 18-hole, par-72 **Tidewater** (⊠ 4901 Little River Neck Rd., North Myrtle Beach, ☎ 800/446–5363), one of just two courses in the area that offer ocean views.

SCUBA DIVING

In summer, many warm-water tropical fish travel to the area from the Gulf Stream. Off the coast of Little River, near the North Carolina border, rock and coral ledges teem with coral, sea fans, sponges, reef fish, anemones, urchins, and crabs. Several outlying shipwrecks are flush with schools of spadefish, amberjack, grouper, and barracuda. Instruction and equipment rentals, as well as an indoor dive tank, are available from **New Horizons Dive and Travel,** in the Sports Corner shopping center (⊠ 515 Hwy. 501, Suite A, the Strip, ☎ 843/839–1932).

TENNIS

There are more than 200 courts on the Grand Strand. Facilities include hotel and resort courts, as well as free municipal courts in Myrtle Beach, North Myrtle Beach, and Surfside Beach. **Prestwick Tennis and Swim Club** (☎ 843/828–1000) offers court time, rental equipment, and instruction. **Grande Dunes Tennis** (☎ 843/449–4486) is a full fitness facility with 10 Har-Tru courts, two of which are lighted; the club also offers private and group lessons.

WATER SPORTS

Surfboards, Hobie Cats, Jet Skis, Windsurfers, and sailboats are available for rent at **Downwind Sails** (⊠ Ocean Blvd. at 29th Ave. S, South End, ☎ 843/448–7245). **Myrtle Beach Yacht Club** (⊠ 720 Hwy. 17, Coquina Harbor, Little River, ☎ 843/249–5376) rents water-sports equipment.

Shopping

DISCOUNT OUTLETS

The **Factory Shoppes** (⊠ U.S. 501, Waccamaw Pottery area, ☎ 843/236–6152) is a large outlet center with Gap, Nike, Polo, and Off 5th (a division of Saks Fifth Avenue). In North Myrtle Beach head for the **Myrtle Beach Factory Stores** (⊠ U.S. 501 and Waccamaw Pines Dr., Waccamaw Pottery area, ☎ 843/903–1614) for Brooks Brothers, Donna Karan, Banana Republic, and Eddie Bauer. **Tanger Outlet** (⊠ 10785 Kings Rd., Waccamaw Pottery area, ☎ 843/449–0491) has 75 factory outlet stores, including Polo and Old Navy. At **Waccamaw Pottery and Linen** (⊠ U.S. 501 at the Waterway, Waccamaw Pottery area, ☎ 843/236–1100) more than 3 mi of shelves in several buildings are stocked with china, glassware, brass, pewter, and other items, and about 50 factory outlets sell clothing, furniture, books, jewelry, and more.

MALLS

Barefoot Landing in North Myrtle Beach (⊠ 4898 S. Kings Hwy., North Myrtle Beach, ☎ 843/272–8349), built over marshland and water, has scores of shops and restaurants, plus rides—including a thrill ride called the Accelerator.

Murrells Inlet

15 mi south of Myrtle Beach on U.S. 17.

Murrells Inlet, a fishing village with some popular seafood restaurants, is a perfect place to rent a fishing boat or join an excursion. A notable garden and state park provide other diversions from the beach.

★ **Brookgreen Gardens,** begun in 1931 by railroad magnate–philanthropist Archer Huntington and his wife, Anna (herself a sculptor), displays more than 500 sculptures by such artists as Frederic Remington and Daniel Chester French. The works are set amid beautifully landscaped grounds, with avenues of live oaks, reflecting pools, and more than 2,000 plant species. Also on the site are a wildlife park, an aviary, a cypress swamp, nature trails, and an education center. Summer nights sculptures are illuminated. ⊠ *West of U.S. 17, 3 mi south of Murrells Inlet,* ☎ *843/237–4218 or 800/849–1931,* WEB *www.brookgreen.org.* 🖅 *$12.* ☉ *Oct.–May, daily 9:30–5; June–Sept., Wed.–Fri. 9:30–9:30, Sat.–Tues. 9:30–5.*

Huntington Beach State Park, the 2,500-acre former estate of Archer and Anna Huntington, lies east of U.S. 17, across from the couple's Brookgreen Gardens. The park's focal point is **Atalaya** (circa 1933), their Moorish-style 30-room home, open to visitors in season. In addition to the splendid beach, there are nature trails, fishing, an interpretive center, and an education center with fresh- and saltwater aquariums and a loggerhead sea turtle nesting habitat. There are also picnic areas, a playground, concessions, and a campground. ⊠ *East of U.S. 17, 3 mi south of Murrells Inlet,* ☎ *843/237–4440,* WEB *www.southcarolinaparks.com.* 🖅 *$4.* ☉ *Nov.–mid-Mar., daily 6–6; mid-Mar.–Oct., daily 6 AM–10 PM.*

Nightlife and the Arts

In the fall the **Atalaya Arts Festival** (☎ 843/237–4440), at Huntington Beach State Park, is a big draw.

Drunken Jack's (⊠ U.S. Business 17, ☎ 843/651–2044 or 843/651–3232), overlooking the docks, has been a popular restaurant for 23 years. It has a lounge, waterfront deck, and working crab traps to occupy young diners.

Outdoor Activities and Sports

Capt. Dick's (⊠ U.S. Business 17, ☎ 843/651–3676) runs half- and full-day fishing and sightseeing trips.

Pawleys Island

10 mi south of Murrells Inlet via U.S. 17.

About 4 mi long and ½ mi wide, this island, referred to as "arrogantly shabby" by locals, began as a resort before the Civil War, when wealthy planters and their families summered here. It's mostly made up of weathered old summer cottages nestled in groves of oleander and oak trees. You can watch the famous Pawleys Island hammocks being made and bicycle around admiring the beach houses, many dating to the early 1800s. Golf and tennis are nearby.

Dining and Lodging

$$$–$$$$ ✕ **Frank's.** Seasonal ingredients make this a local favorite. In a former 1930s grocery store with wood floors, framed French posters, and cozy fireside seating, diners indulge in large portions of fish, seafood, beef, and lamb cooked over an oak-burning grill. The roasted asparagus with prosciutto in phyllo and the pork tenderloin with shiitake mushrooms and a Dijon cream sauce are two highlights. Behind Frank's is the casual (but still pricey) Outback at Frank's, specializing in rotisserie chicken, salads, and lighter fare. ⊠ *10434 Ocean Hwy. (U.S. 17),* ☎ *843/237–3030. Reservations essential. D, MC, V. Closed Sun.*

$$-$$$ ✗ **Pawleys Island Tavern.** This little eatery has terrific crab cakes, hickory-smoked barbecue, roasted chicken, and pizza (they deliver). Summer weekend nights tiki torches outside blaze and live music rocks the place. ⊠ *The Island Shops, U.S. 17,* ☎ *843/237–8465. AE, MC, V.*

$ ✗ **Landolphi's.** This Italian pastry shop and deli, fourth generation owned, has excellent coffee, hearty hoagies, pizzas, homemade sorbet, and delicious and authentic pastries, including cannoli and *pasticciotti* (a rich pastry). ⊠ *9305 Ocean Hwy.,* ☎ *843/237–7900. AE, MC, V. Closed Sun. No dinner Mon.–Thurs.*

$$$$ ✗🏨 **Litchfield Plantation.** Period furnishings adorn four spacious suites of this impeccably restored 1750 rice-plantation manor house–turned–country inn. Use of a beach-house club a short drive away is part of the package, as is a full breakfast at the elegant Carriage House Club ($$–$$$); guests also have golf privileges at eight nearby courses. The resort is approximately 2 mi south of Brookgreen Gardens on U.S. 17 (turn right at the Litchfield Country Club entrance and follow the signs). ⊠ *River Rd., Box 290, 29585,* ☎ *843/237–9121 or 800/869–1410,* FAX *843/237–8558,* WEB *www.litchfieldplantation.com. 38 rooms, 4 suites, 10 2- and 3-bedroom cottages. Restaurant, 2 tennis courts, pool, library, concierge. AE, D, DC, MC, V. BP.*

$$$–$$$$ 🏨 **Sea View Inn.** A "barefoot paradise," Sea View is a no-frills beachside boardinghouse with long porches. Rooms, with views of the ocean or marsh, have half baths; showers are down the hall and outside. Three meals, served family style—with grits, gumbo, crab salad, pecan pie, and oyster pie—make this an unbeatable deal. There is a 2-night minimum during May and September and a 1-wk minimum from June through August. ⊠ *Myrtle Ave., 29585,* ☎ *843/237–4253,* FAX *843/237–7909,* WEB *www.seaviewinn.net. 20 rooms. Dining room. No credit cards. Closed Nov.–Mar. FAP.*

$$–$$$ 🏨 **Litchfield Beach and Golf Resort.** Rentals from one-bedroom condos to four-bedroom villas are available at this 4,500-acre resort, which runs along both sides of U.S. 17. The almost 2-mi stretch of oceanfront accommodations ranges from condos to the 160-room Litchfield Inn, which has standard motel rooms; other units overlook fairways or lakes and are within a 10-minute walk to the beach. The 120-unit Bridgewater, with its oceanfront pool, lazy river (an artificial, moving, river-shaped pool that carries swimmers along its course) and clubhouse, is popular with families. Most suites are decorated in pastel tones and light woods. ⊠ *U.S. 17, 2 mi north of Pawleys Island (Drawer 320, 29585),* ☎ *843/237–3000 or 800/845–1897,* FAX *843/237–4282,* WEB *www.litchfieldbeach.com. 140 rooms, 216 suites, 200 condominiums, cottages, and villas. 2 restaurants, 9 18-hole golf courses, 26 tennis courts, 2 indoor pools, 18 pools, health club, bicycles, children's programs. AE, D, DC, MC, V.*

$ 🏨 **The Inn at Pawleys.** You'll find that excellent golf packages are available at this well-maintained inn (however, the 18-hole course next door is not affiliated with the hotel). Outfitted with motel-modern furnishings, the rooms are spacious, bright, and airy. ⊠ *U.S. 17S, Box 2217, 29585,* ☎ *843/237–4261 or 800/272–6232,* FAX *843/237–9703,* WEB *www.ramada.com. 100 rooms. Café, pool, lounge. AE, D, DC, MC, V.*

Outdoor Activities and Sports

GOLF

The **Litchfield Beach and Golf Resort** (⊠ U.S. 17S, Litchfield Beach, ☎ 843/237–3000 or 800/845–1897) is a popular 18-hole course. **Pawleys Plantation Golf & Country Club** (⊠ U.S. 17S, Pawleys Island, ☎ 843/237–8497 or 800/367–9959) is a Jack Nicklaus–signature course; several holes play along saltwater marshes. **Tee Times Central** (☎ 843/347–4653 or 800/344–5590) books tee times—though you can also call courses directly to book time. **Litchfield Country Club** (⊠ U.S. 17S, Pawleys Island, ☎ 843/237–3411) is a mature, old-style course with tight fairways and moss-laden oaks. The newly renovated **River Club** (⊠ U.S. 17S, Pawleys Island, ☎ 843/626–9069) has water on 14 of its holes. **Willbrook** (⊠ U.S. 17S, Pawleys Island, ☎ 843/247–4900) is on a former rice plantation and winds past historical markers, a slave cemetery, and a tobacco shack.

TENNIS

You can get court time, rental equipment, and instruction at **Litchfield Country Club** (☎ 843/237–3411).

Shopping

The **Hammock Shops at Pawleys Island** (⊠ 10880 Ocean Hwy., ☎ 843/237–8448) is a complex of two dozen boutiques, gift shops, and restaurants built with old beams, timber, and ballast brick. Outside the Original Hammock Shop, in the Hammock Weavers' Pavilion, craftspeople demonstrate the 19th-century art of weaving the famous cotton-rope Pawleys Island hammocks. Also look for jewelry, toys, antiques, and designer fashions.

Georgetown

13 mi south of Pawleys Island via U.S. 17.

Founded on Winyah Bay in 1729, Georgetown became the center of America's colonial rice empire. A rich plantation culture developed on a scale comparable to Charleston's, and the historic district, which can be walked in a couple of hours, is among the prettiest in the state. Today oceangoing vessels still come to Georgetown's busy port, and the **Harborwalk**, the restored waterfront, hums with activity.

The graceful market and meeting building in the heart of Georgetown, topped by an 1842 clock and tower, has been converted into the **Rice Museum**, with maps, tools, and dioramas. At the museum's Prevost Gallery next door, you can buy glass, local pearls, African dolls, and art. ⊠ *Front and Screven Sts.,* ☎ *843/546–7423.* ☞ *$5; combination ticket for Rice Museum, Harold Kaminski House, and tour of Georgetown $13.50.* ☉ *Mon.–Sat. 9:30–4:30.*

Prince George Winyah Episcopal Church (named after King George II) still serves the parish established in 1721. It was built in 1737 with bricks brought from England. ⊠ *Broad and Highmarket Sts., Georgetown,* ☎ *843/546–4358.* ☞ *Donation suggested.* ☉ *Mar.–Oct., weekdays 11:30–4:30.*

Overlooking the Sampit River from a bluff is the **Harold Kaminski House** (circa 1769). It's especially notable for its collections of regional antiques and furnishings, its Chippendale and Duncan Phyfe furniture, Royal Doulton vases, and silver. ⊠ *1003 Front St.,* ☎ *843/546–7706.* ☞ *$4; combination ticket for Rice Museum, Harold Kaminski House, and tour of Georgetown $13.50.* ☉ *Mon.–Sat. 10–5, Sun. 1–4.*

Hobcaw Barony Visitors Center is at the entrance of Hobcaw Barony, on the vast estate of the late Bernard M. Baruch; Franklin D. Roosevelt and Winston Churchill came here to confer with him. A small interpretive center has exhibits on coastal history and ecology, with special emphasis on the Baruch family. There are aquariums, touch tanks, and video presentations; you can also tour the 17,500-acre wildlife refuge. ⊠ *On U.S. 17, 2 mi north of Georgetown,* ☎ *843/546–4623,* WEB *www.hobcawbarony.com.* ☞ *Visitors center free, tours $15.* ☉ *Weekdays 10–5; reservations necessary.*

Hopsewee Plantation, surrounded by moss-draped live oaks, magnolias, and tree-size camellias, overlooks the North Santee River. The circa-1740 mansion has a fine Georgian staircase and hand-carved Adam lighted-candle moldings. ⊠ *U.S. 17, 12 mi south of Georgetown,* ☎ *843/546–7891 or 800/648–0478,* WEB *www.hopsewee.com.* 🌫 *Mansion $8; grounds $5 per car; parking fees apply toward tour, if taken.* ☉ *Mansion Mar.–Nov., Tues.–Fri. 10–4; Dec.–Feb., by appointment (if you come across a tour group already on the grounds, you can join them). Grounds, including nature trail, daily dawn–dusk.*

Hampton Plantation State Historic Site preserves the home of Archibald Rutledge, poet laureate of South Carolina for 39 years until his death in 1973. The 18th-century plantation house is a fine example of a Lowcountry mansion. The exterior has been restored; cutaway sections in the finely crafted interior show the changes made through the centuries. The grounds are landscaped, and there are picnic areas. ⊠ *Off U.S. 17, at edge of Francis Marion National Forest, 16 mi south of Georgetown,* ☎ *843/546–9361.* 🌫 *Mansion $2, grounds free.* ☉ *Mansion June–Aug., daily 11–4; Sept.–May, Thurs.–Mon. 11–4. Grounds Thurs.–Mon. 9–6.*

Dining and Lodging

$$$–$$$$
★
✕ **Rice Paddy.** Locals flock in for vegetable soup, garden-fresh salads, and sandwiches at lunch, when this Lowcountry restaurant tends to get crowded. Dinner in the Victorian building is more relaxed; options might include broiled seafood, crab cakes, or quail with ham-and-cream grits. ⊠ *732 Front St.,* ☎ *843/546–2021. AE, D, MC, V. Closed Sun.*

$$–$$$
✕ **River Room.** This restaurant on the Sampit River specializes in char-grilled fish, Cajun fried oysters, seafood pastas, and steaks. For lunch you can have shrimp and grits or your choice of sandwiches and salads. The dining room has river views from most tables. It's especially romantic at night, when the oil lamps and brass fixtures cast a warm glow on the dark wood and brick interior of the early 20th-century building. ⊠ *801 Front St.,* ☎ *843/527–4110. Reservations not accepted. AE, MC, V. Closed Sun.*

$$
✕ **Kudzu Bakery.** Indulge in some of the best desserts in town: deep-dish pecan pie and red velvet cake. There's also fresh bread, deli items, and jams and jellies. Sit at the counter if you want a quick bite. ⊠ *714 Front St.,* ☎ *843/546–1847. MC, V. Closed Sun. No dinner.*

$
✕ **Thomas Cafe.** There's great fried chicken, homemade biscuits, and pie here at this dinerlike lunch counter with stools, booths, and café tables, in a 1920s storefront building. ⊠ *714 Front St.,* ☎ *843/546–7776. MC, V. Closed Sun. No dinner.*

$$$$
🏠 **Lodge at Lofton Landing.** To stay here you must rent this entire lodge, a modern facility overlooking the marshland of Cape Romain National Wildlife Refuge. It has a furnished kitchen, a wraparound porch, and a dock for fishing and crabbing, and it sleeps eight. ⊠ *8889 U.S. 17 (about 22 mi south of Georgetown), McClellanville 29458,* ☎ *843/720–7332,* FAX *843/856–8468. 1 lodge with 3 rooms. Boating, fishing. AE, D, DC, MC, V.*

$$
🏠 **Laurel Hill Plantation.** This B&B overlooks the marsh close to the Intracoastal Waterway, near the quaint shrimping village of McClellanville. It's furnished with country antiques and folk art. Here relaxation is key: you can read in the hammock, go fishing or crabbing, take a boat ride, or watch the birds. ⊠ *8913 U.S. 17N (22 mi south of Georgetown), Box 190, McClellanville 29458,* ☎ *843/887–3708 or 888/887–3708. 4 rooms. Fishing. AE, D, DC, MC, V. BP.*

$$
🏠 **Mansfield Plantation.** As you drive up the unpaved road to the 760-acre plantation, past former slave quarters and under a canopy of moss-draped oaks, you'll sense what a plantation must have looked like 200

years ago. You can stay in one of three historic redbrick outbuildings—
the old kitchen, the former schoolhouse, and the 1930s guest house—
that overlook the Black River. Rooms have hardwood pine floors,
reproduction period antiques, four-poster rice beds, and wood-burn-
ing fireplaces. Children and pets are welcome, and you can roam freely
on the plantation grounds. ⊠ *U.S. 701N (Rte. 8, Box 590), 29440,*
☎ *843/546–6961 or 800/355–3223,* FAX *843/546–5235,* WEB *www.bbon-
line.com/sc/mansfield. 8 rooms. In-room VCRs, boating, fishing, bicycles. No credit cards. BP.*

$$ ⊞ **1790 House.** Built in the center of town after the revolution, at the
peak of Georgetown's rice culture, this lovely restored white Georgian
house with a wraparound porch contains 18th- and 19th-century Asian
and European pieces brought by new owners, who've also added
bathrobes, turndown service, and whirlpools. Besides a (very) full break-
fast, you can also expect evening refreshments. Guest rooms downstairs
in the former slave quarters have exposed brick walls. ⊠ *630 Highmarket
St., 29440,* ☎ *843/546–4821 or 800/890–7432,* WEB *www.1790house.com.
4 rooms, 1 suite, 1 cottage. Bicycles. AE, D, MC, V. BP.*

Outdoor Activities and Sports

CANOEING AND KAYAKING

Black River Expeditions (⊠ 21 Garden Ave., U.S. 701, ☎ 843/546–
4840) offers naturalist-guided canoe and kayak day and evening (in-
cluding moonlight) tours of the tidelands of Georgetown. They also
do rentals and sales.

BOATING

The **tall ships *Jolly Roger & Carolina Rover*** (⊠ 735 Front St., ☎ 843/
546–8822 or 800/705–9063) are docked at the Harborwalk at the foot
of Broad Street. Kids will love the two-hour sailing adventure aboard
the *Jolly Roger* along the Intracoastal Waterway, with Captain Kidd
in period dress telling pirate tales. Three-hour ecotours on the *Carolina
Rover* include a visit to a historic lighthouse.

GOLF

The city of Georgetown's premier course is the nearby 18-hole, par-
73 **Wedgefield Plantation** (⊠ 129 Club House La., off U.S. 701, ☎
843/448–2124 or 843/546–8587). The 18-hole, par-70 **Winyah Bay
Golf Club** (☎ 877/527–7765) is a popular option.

TARGET SHOOTING

At the **Back Woods Quail Club** (⊠ Rte. 51 at Rte. 41, ☎ 843/546–1466),
there are target shooting, gun rentals, a skeet shooting center, and quail
hunting.

Myrtle Beach and the Grand Strand A to Z

*To research prices, get advice from other travelers, and book travel ar-
rangements, visit www.fodors.com.*

AIRPORTS

The Myrtle Beach International Airport is served by Air Canada, Air-
Tran, Continental, COMAIR, Delta's regional carrier Atlantic South-
east, Spirit, Vanguard, and US Airways.
➤ AIRPORT INFORMATION: **Myrtle Beach International Airport** (⊠ 1100
Jetport Rd., ☎ 843/448–1580).

BOAT AND FERRY TRAVEL

Boaters traveling the Intracoastal Waterway may dock at Hague Ma-
rina, Harbor Gate, and Marlin Quay.

➤ Boat and Ferry Information: **Hague Marina** (✉ Myrtle Beach, ☎ 843/293–2141). **Harbor Gate** (✉ North Myrtle Beach, ☎ 843/249–8888). **Marlin Quay** (✉ Murrells Inlet, ☎ 843/651–4444).

BUS TRAVEL

Greyhound Bus Lines serves Myrtle Beach, Georgetown, and McClellanville.

➤ Bus Information: **Greyhound Bus Lines** (☎ 800/231–2222).

CAR TRAVEL

Midway between New York and Miami, the Grand Strand isn't connected directly by any interstate highways but is within an hour's drive of I–95, I–20, I–26, and I–40. U.S. 17 is the major north–south coastal route through the Strand.

EMERGENCIES

Both the Grand Strand Regional Medical Center and Georgetown Memorial Hospital have emergency rooms open 24 hours a day. The Grand Strand Regional Medical Center also has the only pharmacy in the area open all night.

➤ Emergency Services: **Ambulance, fire, police** (☎ 911).

➤ Hospitals: **Georgetown Memorial Hospital** (✉ 606 Black River Rd., Georgetown, ☎ 843/527–7000). **Grand Strand Regional Medical Center** (✉ 809 82nd Pkwy., off U.S. 17, Myrtle Beach, ☎ 843/692–1000).

➤ 24-Hour Pharmacies: **Grand Strand Regional Medical Center Pharmacy** (✉ 809 82nd Pkwy., off U.S. 17, Myrtle Beach, ☎ 843/692–1000).

LODGING

With more than 60,000 rooms available along the Grand Strand, it's seldom difficult to find a place to stay, and discounting is rampant. Package deals are offered year-round, the most attractive of them between Labor Day and spring break. You can choose among cottages, villas, condominiums, and hotel-style high-rise units.

APARTMENT AND VILLA RENTALS

For the free directory *Where to Stay and Play,* call the Myrtle Beach Area Convention Bureau. For Pawleys Island and Litchfield Beach, try Pawleys Island Realty.

➤ Local Agents: **Myrtle Beach Area Convention Bureau** (☎ 843/448–1629 or 800/356–3016). **Pawleys Island Realty** (☎ 843/237–4257 or 800/937–7352).

OUTDOOR ACTIVITIES AND SPORTS

GOLF

Spring and fall, when off-season rates are offered, are the busiest times for golf, and there are many packages available in the area; call Golf Holiday. Tee Times Central books tee times at a number of area courses.

➤ Contacts: **Golf Holiday** (☎ 843/448–5942 or 800/845–4653). **Tee Times Central** (☎ 843/347–4653 or 800/344–5590).

TAXIS

Taxi service in Myrtle Beach is provided by Coastal Cab Service.

➤ Taxi Companies: **Coastal Cab Service** (☎ 843/448–4444).

TOURS

Through Georgetown County Chamber of Commerce and Information Center, you can arrange to tour historic areas March through October by tram, by 1840 horse-drawn carriage, or by boat. You can also pick up free driving- and walking-tour maps. Georgetown Tour Company offers tram tours of the historic district, the Ghostbusting Tour, and the afternoon Tea 'n' Tour. It also offers tram tours of the historic district on the hour, departing from the chamber of commerce Monday through Saturday. For an insider's view hire Georgetown native Miss Nell to take you on one of Miss Nell's "Real South" Tours. Palmetto Tour & Travel and Leisure Time Unlimited/Gray Line, both in Myrtle Beach, offer tour packages and guide services.

➤ FEES AND SCHEDULES: **Georgetown County Chamber of Commerce and Information Center** (☎ 843/546–8436 or 800/777–7705). **Georgetown Tour Company** (☎ 843/546–6827). **Leisure Time Unlimited/Gray Line** (☎ 843/448–9483). **Miss Nell's "Real South" Tours** (☎ 843/546–3975). **Palmetto Tour & Travel** (☎ 843/626–2660).

TRAIN TRAVEL

Amtrak service for the Grand Strand is available through a terminal in Florence. Buses connect with Amtrak there for the 65-mi drive to Myrtle Beach.

➤ TRAIN INFORMATION: **Amtrak** (☎ 800/872–7245).

VISITOR INFORMATION

➤ TOURIST INFORMATION: **Georgetown County Chamber of Commerce and Information Center** (✉ 1001 Front St., Box 1776, Georgetown 29442, ☎ 843/546–8436, WEB www.georgetownsc.com). **Myrtle Beach Area Chamber of Commerce and Information Center** (✉ 1200 N. Oak St., Box 2115, Myrtle Beach 29578, ☎ 843/626–7444 or 800/356–3016, WEB www.myrtlebeachlive.com). **Pawleys Island Chamber of Commerce** (✉ U.S. 17, Box 569, Pawleys Island 29585, ☎ 843/237–1921).

HILTON HEAD AND BEYOND

Anchoring the southern tip of South Carolina's coastline is Hilton Head Island, named after English sea captain William Hilton, who claimed the 42 square mi for England in 1663. It was settled by planters in the 1700s and flourished until the Civil War. Thereafter, the economy declined and the island languished until Charles E. Fraser, a visionary South Carolina attorney, began developing the Sea Pines resort in 1956. Other developments followed, and today Hilton Head's casual pace, broad beaches, myriad activities, and genteel good life make it one of the East Coast's most popular vacation getaways.

Beaufort, some 40 mi north of Hilton Head, is a graceful antebellum town with a compact historic district preserving lavish 18th- and 19th-century homes from an era of immense prosperity, based on silky-textured Sea Island cotton. The *beau* in Beaufort is pronounced as in "beautiful," and Beaufort certainly is. Southeast, on the ocean, lies Fripp Island, a self-contained resort with controlled access. And midway between Beaufort and Charleston is Edisto (pronounced *ed*-is-toh) Island, settled in 1690, also once notable for its Sea Island cotton. Some of its elaborate mansions have been restored; others are in disrepair.

Hilton Head Island

108 mi southwest of Charleston via U.S. 17, 164 mi southeast of Columbia via I–26, I–95, and U.S. 278.

Lined by towering pines, palmetto trees, and wind-sculpted live oaks, Hilton Head's 12 mi of beaches are a major attraction, and the semitropical barrier island also has oak and pine woodlands and meandering lagoons. Choice stretches are occupied by various resorts, called "plantations," among them Sea Pines, Shipyard, Palmetto Dunes, and Port Royal. In these areas accommodations range from rental villas and lavish private houses to luxury hotels. The resorts are also private residential communities, although many have public restaurants, marinas, shopping areas, and recreational facilities. All are secured, and cannot be toured unless arrangements are made at the visitor office near the main gate of each plantation. A 5¾-mi Cross Island Parkway toll bridge ($1) makes it easy to bypass traffic and reach the south end of the island, where most of the resort areas and hotels are.

Hilton Head prides itself on its strict regulations that keep "light pollution" to a minimum; but the lack of neon and streetlights also makes it difficult to find your way at night, so be sure to get good directions.

Audubon-Newhall Preserve, in the south of the island, is 50 acres of pristine forest, where you'll find native plant life identified and tagged. There are trails, a self-guided tour, and seasonal plant walks. ⊠ *Palmetto Bay Rd., South End,* ☎ *843/785–5775.* ⊠ *Free.* ⊙ *Daily dawn–dusk.*

Sea Pines Forest Preserve is a 605-acre public wilderness tract on Sea Pines Plantation with walking trails, a well-stocked fishing pond, a waterfowl pond, and a 3,400-year-old Indian shell ring. Both guided and self-guided tours are available. ⊠ *Southwest tip of island, accessible via U.S. 278, South End,* ☎ *843/363–1872.* ⊠ *Sea Pines Plantation $5 per car for nonguests, includes access to preserve.* ⊙ *Daily dawn–dusk; closed during MCI Heritage golf tournament in Apr.*

The **Coastal Discovery Museum** has a permanent collection depicting Native American life and hosts changing exhibits. The museum also sponsors historical and natural history tours of Native American sites, forts, and plantations as well as kayak trips, turtle watches, cruises, birding, and visits to wildlife preserves. ⊠ *100 William Hilton Pkwy., North End,* ☎ *843/689–6767.* ⊠ *Free.* ⊙ *Mon.–Sat. 9–5, Sun. 10–4.*

At the **James M. Waddell Jr. Mariculture Research & Development Center,** 3 mi west of Hilton Head Island, you may tour the 24 ponds and the research building to see how methods of raising seafood commercially are studied. ⊠ *Sawmill Creek Rd. near U.S. 278 at Rte. 46,* ☎ *843/837–3795.* ⊠ *Free.* ⊙ *Tours weekdays at 10 AM and by appointment.*

···········

OFF THE
BEATEN PATH

DAUFUSKIE ISLAND – From Hilton Head you can go by boat to nearby Daufuskie Island, the setting for Pat Conroy's novel *The Water Is Wide,* which was made into the movie *Conrack.* The Daufuskie Island Club & Resort—with an oceanfront inn, cottages, golf courses, tennis, pools, water sports, and several restaurants—is a wonderful getaway (☎ 843/ 341–4820 or 800/648–6778). Amidst increasing development on the island, a few descendants of former slaves live on small farms among remnants of churches, homes, and schools—reminders of antebellum times. Excursions to Daufuskie are run out of Hilton Head by **Adventure Cruises** (⊠ Shelter Cove Marina, Mid-Island, ☎ 843/785–4558), **Calibogue Cruises** (⊠ 164B Palmetto Bay Rd., Mid-Island, ☎ 843/785–8242), and **Vagabond Cruises** (⊠ Harbour Town Marina, South End, ☎ 843/842–4155).

BLUFFTON – Tucked away from the bustle of Hilton Head's resorts, charming Bluffton village has several historic homes and churches, a growing artists' colony, and oak-lined streets dripping with moss. There are several great little shops around here, including **Eggs'n'tricities** (⊠ 71 Calhoun St., Bluffton, ☎ 843/757–3446), with fun and funky gifts, clothes, and even home accessories, and **Red Stripe Gallery** (⊠ 69 Calhoun St., Bluffton, ☎ 843/757–2318), with pottery, ironwork, and outdoor art. You could grab delicious picnic food from **Vino & Vitto** (☎ 843/815–7777) and head to the boat dock at the end of Pritchard

Street or the boat landing at Brighton Beach for great views. From Hilton Head backtrack about 6 mi up U.S. 278, then make a left on Route 46.

Dining

$$$–$$$$ ✕ **Old Fort Pub.** Tucked away on a quiet site overlooking the sweeping marshlands of the Intracoastal Waterway and beside the Civil War ruins of Fort Mitchell, this romantic restaurant specializes in such dishes as grilled scallops, duck confit, crab cakes, and fresh fish. The views are almost panoramic, the wine list extensive, and there's outdoor seating plus a third-floor porch for toasting the sunset. Sunday brunch is also a good bet. ✉ *65 Skull Creek Dr., North End,* ☎ *843/ 681–2386. AE, D, DC, MC, V. No lunch.*

$$–$$$ ✕ **Brick Oven Café.** Velvet drapes, chandeliers, booths, and '40s lounge-style entertainment—on top of good, reasonably priced food served late—make this the trendy place to be. There's a nice wine selection. ✉ *Park Plaza, South End,* ☎ *843/686–2233. Reservations essential. AE, D, DC, MC, V. No lunch.*

$$–$$$ ✕ **Juleps.** In this dimly lit terrace-style restaurant, Southern ingredients—grits, cured ham, fresh fish, and peach preserves—add sparkle to the menu. The mint juleps are incredible; try the magnolia salad with hearts of palm, apples, pecans, and mint vinaigrette; the barbecued duck with cornmeal pancake; or the quail stuffed with andouille and greens. ✉ *14 Greenwood Dr., the Galley of Shops, South End,* ☎ *843/842– 5857. AE, D, MC, V. No lunch.*

$–$$ ✕ **Kenny B's French Quarter Cafe.** Surrounded by Mardi Gras memorabilia, Kenny serves jambalaya, po'boys, muffalettas, and gumbo against a wall mural of Bourbon Street. A local favorite, this café—in a strip mall—is open from morning until 9 PM; at the Sunday buffet brunch you can get chicory coffee, beignets, and Cajun omelettes. ✉ *70 Pope Ave., BiLo Circle, Mid-island,* ☎ *843/785–3315. AE, D, MC, V. Closed Mon.*

$–$$ ✕ **Mi Tierra.** At this friendly Mexican restaurant (easy to miss, in a rather run-down strip mall), freshness is the key to such tasty fare as ceviche fish tacos. Next door, **Baja Tacos**—run by the same people—is a simple taco stand with counter service, café tables, and a condiments bar with fresh, fresh salsas and relishes. ✉ *160 Fairfield Sq., North End,* ☎ *843/342–3409. MC, V.*

$–$$ ✕ **Upper Crust.** Dine on great pizza with creative combinations at this traditional family-friendly eatery with booths and café tables. There's also a bar; sodas come with a long noodle "straw." ✉ *Moss Creek Shopping Center, U.S. 278, Bluffton,* ☎ *843/837–5111. AE, DC, MC, V. No lunch Sun.*

Lodging

Sea Pines, the oldest and best known of Hilton Head's resort developments, or plantations, occupies 4,500 thickly wooded acres with three golf courses, a fine beach, tennis clubs, stables, and shopping plazas. The focus of Sea Pines is **Harbour Town,** built around the charming marina, which has shops, restaurants, some condominiums, and the landmark Hilton Head Lighthouse. Accommodations are in luxurious houses and villas facing the ocean or the golf courses.

The **Crowne Plaza Resort** is the oceanfront centerpiece of **Shipyard Plantation,** which also has villa condominiums, three 9-hole golf courses, a tennis club, and a small beach club. **Palmetto Dunes Resort** has the oceanfront Hilton Head Marriott Beach & Golf Resort, Hilton Resort, and other accommodations, along with the renowned Rod Laver Tennis Center, a good stretch of beach, three golf courses, and several oceanfront rental villa complexes. At **Port Royal Plantation** there's the posh

Westin Resort, which is on the beach and has three golf courses and a tennis club.

Hilton Head Central Reservations (☎ 843/785–9050 or 800/845–7018, FAX 843/686–3255, WEB www.vacationcompany.com) represents almost every hotel, motel, and rental agency on the island. Other options are available through the **Hilton Head Condo Hotline** (☎ 843/785–2939), which handles condo accommodations for all of Hilton Head. **Hilton Head Reservations and Golf Line** (☎ 843/444–4772) books both hotels and tee time. **Island Rentals** (☎ 800/845–6134, WEB www.irhhi.com) offers oceanfront, ocean-oriented, and golf-oriented home, condo and villa rentals, as well as a concierge service.

$$$$ 🖼 **Crowne Plaza Resort.** This oceanfront resort glimmers with brass railings and accents, and shiny wood floors and trim. Decorated in a nautical theme and set in a luxuriant garden, the Crowne Plaza has access to all the amenities of Shipyard Plantation. ⊠ *130 Shipyard Dr., Mid-Island, 29928,* ☎ *843/842–2400 or 800/334–1881,* FAX *843/785–8463,* WEB *www.crowneplazaresort.com. 331 rooms, 9 suites. 2 restaurants, snack bar, room service, 3 18-hole golf courses, indoor pool, 2 pools, hot tub, outdoor hot tub, health club, biking, racquetball, lounge, children's programs (ages 3–12), business services, meeting room. AE, D, DC, MC, V.*

$$$$ 🖼 **Disney's Hilton Head Island Resort.** The villas here have fully fur-
★ nished dining, living, and sleeping areas. The smallest is a studio villa, and the largest has three bedrooms, four baths, and sleeping accommodations for 12; all have marsh or marina views. The villas are decorated in cheerful colors and have porches with rocking chairs and picnic tables—it all gives off the rusticity of Adirondack cabins. The resort offers golf, tennis, and romance packages, beach shuttle service, and a fishing pier. The resort's 13,000-square-ft cabana has a fireplace in the living room, a heated pool, an adult lounge, and a video game room. ⊠ *22 Harbourside La., Mid-Island, 29928,* ☎ *843/341–4100 or 800/ 453–4911,* FAX *843/341–4130,* WEB *www.disney.com/vacation. 102 units. Snack bar, kitchens, fans, some in-room hot tubs, golf privileges, 2 pools, gym, outdoor hot tub, dock, boating, marina, fishing, bicycles, billiards, horseshoes, Ping-Pong, shuffleboard, recreation room, video game room, children's programs, playground, laundry service. AE, MC, V.*

$$$$ 🖼 **Hilton Oceanfront Resort.** There's a Caribbean sensibility to this five-story resort hotel, located mid-island. The grounds are beautifully landscaped, and the spacious rooms, all ocean side, are spacious and decorated with contemporary wood furniture and warm colors. ⊠ *23 Ocean La., Box 6165, 29938,* ☎ *843/842–8000 or 800/845–8001,* FAX *843/842–4988,* WEB *www.hiltonheadhilton.com. 303 rooms, 20 suites. 2 restaurants, kitchenettes, 3 18-hole golf courses, 2 pools, health club, hot tub, sauna, boating, fishing, bicycles, Ping-Pong, volleyball, lounge, children's programs. AE, D, DC, MC, V.*

$$$$ 🖼 **Holiday Inn Oceanfront Resort.** A handsome high-rise motor hotel, this property is on one of the busiest stretches of beach on the island— at the south end, within walking distance of shops and restaurants. The rooms are spacious and furnished in a contemporary style; golf and tennis packages are available. The outdoor Tiki Hut lounge, a poolside bar, is hugely popular. ⊠ *S. Forest Beach Dr., Box 5728, 29938,* ☎ *843/785–5126 or 800/423–9897,* FAX *843/785–6678,* WEB *www.hi-hiltonhead.com. 201 rooms. Restaurant, snack bar, pool, wading pool, bicycles, volleyball, gym, lounge, children's programs (ages 3–12), meeting rooms; no-smoking rooms. AE, D, DC, MC, V.*

$$$$ 🖼 **Main Street Inn.** The outside of this inn looks like an Italianate villa, with gardens, shuttered French doors, and iron railings. Luxury abounds inside, too, in the antique furnishings and the heart-pine floors covered in Turkish and sisal rugs. Guest rooms have velvet and silk brocade linens, feather duvets, and porcelain and brass sinks. The European breakfast includes imported meats, cheeses, quiches, breads, and pastries. ⊠ *2200 Main St., North End, 29926,* ☎ *843/681–3001 or 800/ 471–3001,* FAX *843/681–5541,* WEB *www.mainstreetinn.com. 34 rooms. Pool, hot tub, bar. AE, MC, V. BP.*

$$$–$$$$ ⊞ **Hilton Head Marriott Beach & Golf Resort.** After a complete renovation and flag change, this new property opened in 2002. All guest rooms have private balconies, desk areas, contemporary cherry furniture with sunny yellow and green floral fabrics, and down comforters. ⊠ *One Hotel Circle, South End, 29928,* ☎ *843/686–8400,* FAX *843/ 686–8450,* WEB *www.marriotthiltonhead.com. 452 rooms, 31 suites. Restaurant, café, pizzeria, room service, some kitchens, some minibars, driving range, 3 18-hole golf courses, putting green, 26 tennis courts, outdoor pool, indoor pool, beach, biking, hot tubs, outdoor hot tubs, gym, piano bar, bar, shop, baby-sitting, children's programs (ages 3– 12), concierge, business services, meeting rooms. AE, D, DC, MC, V.*

$$$ ⊞ **Westin Resort, Hilton Head Island.** One of the area's most luxuri-
★ ous properties, the horseshoe-shape Westin sprawls on lushly landscaped oceanfront (and it's on the island's quietest, least inhabited stretch). The hotel guest rooms, most with ocean views, have crown molding and, because of the down pillows, rich colors, and comfortable wicker and contemporary furniture, it manages to seem somewhat residential. All rooms have seating areas and desks. The resort also includes 100 two- and three-bedroom villas, each with a kitchen, VCR, and washer-dryer. ⊠ *2 Grass Lawn Ave., North End, 29928,* ☎ *843/681– 4000 or 800/228–3000,* FAX *843/681–1087,* WEB *www.westin.com. 412 rooms, 29 suites. 3 restaurants, in-room data ports, driving range, 3 18-hole golf courses, 16 tennis courts, pro shop, indoor pool, pool, wading pool, health club, outdoor hot tub, beach, bicycles, Ping-Pong, lounges, children's programs (ages 4–12), concierge, concierge floor, business services, meeting rooms. AE, D, DC, MC, V.*

$$ ⊞ **Hampton Inn.** A short drive from the public beaches, this inn is clean, nicely landscaped, and sheltered from the noise and traffic, making it popular with business and leisure travelers alike. Rooms have one king or two double beds; some double rooms have refrigerators and microwaves; some king rooms have sleeper sofas. A friendly staff keeps customers coming back year after year. ⊠ *1 Dillon Rd., Mid-Island, 29926,* ☎ *843/681–7900,* FAX *843/681–4330,* WEB *www.hampton-inn.com. 124 rooms. Some microwaves, some refrigerators, pool. AE, D, DC, MC, V.*

$ ⊞ **Best Western Inn.** Just a five-minute walk from the beach, this is a front-runner in the budget category; rooms are smallish but clean, with standard furnishings. ⊠ *40 Waterside Dr., South End, 29928,* ☎ *843/ 842–8888,* FAX *843/842–5948,* WEB *www.bestwestern.com. 91 rooms. Pool. AE, D, DC, MC, V.*

$ ⊞ **Red Roof Inn.** This two-story inn is popular with families. Clean and functional rooms are just a short drive from the public beaches. ⊠ *5 Regency Pkwy., Mid-Island, 29928,* ☎ *843/686–6808 or 800/843–7663,* FAX *843/842–3352,* WEB *www.redroof.com. 111 rooms. In-room data ports, refrigerators, pool. AE, D, DC, MC, V.*

Nightlife and the Arts

THE ARTS

The **Self Family Arts Center** (⊠ Shelter Cove La., Mid-Island, ☎ 843/ 686–3945) has details on Hilton Head arts events; it includes an art gallery, a theater, and a theater program for youth. In warm weather free **outdoor concerts** are held at Harbour Town and Shelter Cove. Concerts, plays, films, art shows, sporting events, food fairs, and mini-tournaments make up Hilton Head's **SpringFest** (☎ 843/686–4944 or 800/424–3387), which runs for the month of March. The Winter Carnival and Winefest are held each year.

NIGHTLIFE

Bars, like everything else in Hilton Head, are often in strip malls. Try the **Blue Nite** (⊠ 4 Target Rd., South End, ☎ 843/842–6683) for live music. **Hilton Head Brewing Co.** (⊠ Hilton Head Plaza, South End, ☎ 843/785–2739) has late-night disco every Wednesday. The **Lodge** (⊠ Hilton Head Plaza, South End, ☎ 843/842–8966) has pool tables and roaring fires in the stone fireplaces. **Moneypenny's** (⊠ Palmetto Bay Rd., Village Exchange, South End, ☎ 843/785–7878) is a cozy spot with acoustic music. **Monkey Business** (⊠ Park Plaza, South End, ☎ 843/686–3545) is a dance club popular with young professionals. During the summer Monday and Tuesday are teen nights. **Salty Dog Cafe** (⊠ South Beach Marina, Sea Pines, South End, ☎ 843/671–2233) has a great dockside happy hour, ice cream shop for kids, and live music.

The **Pelican Poolside** (☎ 843/681–4000), an oceanfront lounge at the Westin Resort, offers informal entertainment every night but Sunday. **Regatta** (⊠ 23 Ocean La., Mid-Island, ☎ 843/842–8000), a sophisticated oceanfront nightspot in the Hilton Resort, has live beach and jazz music nightly. **Tiki Hut** (⊠ S. Forest Beach Dr., South End, ☎ 843/785–5126), a locally popular beachside bar at the Holiday Inn Oceanfront Resort, has live music during the high season.

Outdoor Activities and Sports

BEACHES

Although the resort beaches are reserved for guests and residents, there are four public entrances to Hilton Head's 12 mi of ocean beach. Two of the main parking and changing areas are at Coligny Circle, near the Holiday Inn, and on Folly Field Road off U.S. 278. Signs along U.S. 278 point the way to Bradley and Singleton beaches, where parking space is limited.

BIKING

There are pathways in several areas of Hilton Head (many in the resorts), and pedaling is popular along the firmly packed beach. Bicycles can be rented at most hotels and resorts. You can also rent bicycles from the **Hilton Head Bicycle Company** (⊠ 11B Archer Rd., South End, ☎ 843/686–6888). **South Beach Cycles** (⊠ Sea Pines Plantation, South End, ☎ 843/671–2453) rents bikes, helmets, tandems, and adult tricycles. **Outside Hilton Head** (⊠ South Beach Marina, South End, ☎ 843/671–2643 or 800/686–6996; ⊠ Shelter Cove Plaza, Mid-Island, ☎ 843/686–6996 or 800/686–6996) rents bikes and Rollerblades.

CANOEING AND KAYAKING

Outside Hilton Head (⊠ South Beach Marina, South End, ☎ 843/671–2643 or 800/686–6996; ⊠ Shelter Cove Plaza, Mid-Island, ☎ 843/686–6996 or 800/686–6996) is an ecologically sensitive company that rents canoes and kayaks; it also has nature tours.

FISHING

On Hilton Head you can pick oysters, dig for clams, or cast for shrimp; supplies are available at the **Shelter Cove Marina**, at Palmetto Dunes (☎ 843/842–7001). Local marinas offer inshore and deep-sea fishing charters. Each year a billfishing tournament and two king mackerel tournaments attract anglers.

GOLF

Many of Hilton Head's nearly 30 championship courses are open to the public. The **Island West Golf Course** (⊠ U.S. 278, 8 mi before bridge to Hilton Head, ☎ 843/689–6660) is an 18-hole course. **Old South Golf Links** (⊠ U.S. 278, Bluffton, ☎ 843/785–5353) has scenic holes with marshland and intracoastal waterway views. **Palmetto Dunes** (⊠ Ocean La., Mid-Island, ☎ 843/785–1138) includes two 18-hole courses, including an Arthur Hills course with an old lighthouse (and lots of alligator sightings). **Port Royal** (⊠ Grass Lawn Ave., North End, ☎ 843/689–5600) has three 18-hole courses, all on Bermuda grass. **Ocean Course at Sea Pines** (⊠ 100 North Sea Pines Dr., South End, ☎ 843/842–8484) is a championship course with narrow fairways and water on all but four holes. **Harbour Town Golf Links at Sea Pines** (⊠ 11 Lighthouse La., South End, ☎ 843/671–2448 or 800/955–8337) hosts the MCI Heritage Classic every spring.

HORSEBACK RIDING

Many trails wind through woods and nature preserves. **Lawton Stables** (⊠ Sea Pines Plantation, South End, ☎ 843/671–2586) also offers pony rides and lessons. At **Sea Horse Farms** (⊠ 34 Mitchellville Rd., North End, ☎ 843/681–7746) you can ride on the beach on ponies or horses. **Old South** (⊠ Fording Island Rd., Bluffton, ☎ 843/842–7433) offers riding. Rates are generally per person by the hour. **Rose Hill Plantation** (⊠ 1 Equestrian Way, Bluffton, ☎ 843/757–3082) welcomes experienced riders only.

SUMMER CAMP

On Hilton Head Island all major hotels offer summer youth activities; some have full-scale youth programs. The **Island Recreation Center** runs a summer camp that visiting youngsters can join. ⊠ *Hilton Head Island Recreation Association, Wilborn Rd., Box 22593, North End, Hilton Head Island 29925,* ☎ *843/681–7273.* ☉ *Camp mid-June–late Aug., weekdays.*

TENNIS

There are more than 300 courts on Hilton Head. **Port Royal** (⊠ 15 Wimbledon Ct., North End, ☎ 843/686–8803) has 16 courts, including two grass. **Sea Pines Racquet Club** (⊠ 32 Greenwood Dr., South End, ☎ 843/842–8484) has 23 courts, instructional programs and a pro shop. **Shipyard** (⊠ Shipyard Dr. next to Crowne Plaza Resort, Mid-Island, ☎ 843/686–8804) has clay courts and hard courts, a few of which are lighted. **Palmetto Dunes** (⊠ 6 Trent Jones La., Mid-Island, ☎ 843/785–1151) welcomes guests. **Van der Meer Tennis Center** (⊠ 19 deAllyon Rd., Shipyard Plantation, Mid-Island, ☎ 843/785–8388) is highly rated and is recognized for tennis instruction; 4 of its 28 courts are covered.

Shopping

MALLS AND OUTLETS

Hilton Head Factory Stores 1 & 2 (⊠ U.S. 278 at island gateway, Bluffton, ☎ 843/837–4339 or 888/746–7333) has more than 80 clothing and housewares outlets, including J. Crew, Gap, Brooks Brothers, Harry & David, and Coach. The **Mall at Shelter Cove** (⊠ U.S. 278, ½ mi north of Palmetto Dunes Resort, Mid-Island, ☎ 843/686–3090) has 55 shops and four restaurants. **Shoppes on the Parkway** (⊠ U.S. 278, 1 mi south of Palmetto Dunes Resort, Mid-Island, ☎ 843/686–6233) comprises 30 outlets, including Dansk, Gorham, and Van Heusen.

ART GALLERIES

The **Red Piano Art Gallery** (⊠ 220 Cordillo Pkwy., Mid-Island, ☎ 843/785–2318) showcases 19th- and 20th-century works by regional and national contemporary artists.

BOOKS

Authors Bookstore (⊠ The Village at Wexford, Mid-Island) carries a good selection of books on local history and culture.

JEWELRY

The **Bird's Nest** (⊠ Coligny Plaza, South End, ☎ 843/785–3737) sells locally made shell and sand-dollar jewelry, plus island-theme charms. The **Goldsmith Shop** (⊠ 3 Lagoon Rd., Mid-Island, ☎ 843/785–2538) carries classic jewelry and island charms.

NATURE

The **Audubon Nature Store** (⊠ The Village at Wexford, Mid-Island, ☎ 843/785–4311) has items with a nature theme. The **Hammock Store** (⊠ The Plaza at Shelter Cove Mid-Island, ☎ 843/686–6996 or 800/686–6996) sells Pawleys Island hammocks, swings, and other items that have an emphasis on nature and gardening.

Beaufort

38 mi north of Hilton Head via U.S. 278 and Rte. 170, 70 mi southwest of Charleston via U.S. 17 and U.S. 21.

Charming homes and churches from Beaufort's prosperous antebellum days as a cotton center grace this historic town on Port Royal Island. Although it is unusual for the private homes in the historic district of Old Point to be open to visitors, some may be included in the annual Fall House Tour, in mid-October, and the Spring Tour of Homes and Gardens, in April or May. The **Greater Beaufort Chamber of Commerce** (☎ 843/524–3163) can provide more information about house-tour schedules. The Gullah Festival, which takes place Memorial Day weekend, celebrates Lowcountry and West African culture.

The **John Mark Verdier House Museum,** built about 1790 in the federal style, has been restored and furnished as it would have been between 1790 and the visit of Lafayette in 1825. It was the headquarters for Union forces during the Civil War. ⊠ *801 Bay St., Historic Downtown,* ☎ *843/524–6334.* ⚏ *$4.* ⊙ *Mon.–Sat. 10–4:30.*

Built in 1795 and remodeled in 1852, the Gothic-style arsenal that was the home of the Beaufort Volunteer Artillery now houses the **Beaufort Museum,** with prehistoric relics, native pottery, and Revolutionary War and Civil War exhibits. ⊠ *713 Craven St., Historic Downtown,* ☎ *843/525–7077.* ⚏ *$2.* ⊙ *Mon.–Tues. and Thurs.–Sat. 10–5.*

St. Helena's Episcopal Church (1724) was turned into a hospital during the Civil War, and gravestones were brought inside to serve as operating tables. ⊠ *501 Church St., Historic Downtown,* ☎ *843/522–1712.* ⊙ *Mon.–Sat. 10–4.*

Henry C. Chambers Waterfront Park, off Bay Street in historic Beaufort, is a great place to survey the scene. Barbra Streisand filmed *Prince of Tides* here. Its seven landscaped acres along the Beaufort River, part of the Intracoastal Waterway, include a seawall promenade, a crafts market, gardens, and a marina. Some events of the popular mid-July Beaufort Water Festival, as well as a seasonal farmers' market, take place here.

At **Parris Island,** 10 mi south of Beaufort via Route 802, you can observe U.S. Marine Corps recruit training and either take a guided tour or drive through the base on your own. There's a replica of the Iwo Jima flag-raising monument on the base.

The **Parris Island Museum** exhibits uniforms, photographs, and weapons chronicling military history since 1562, when the French Huguenots

THE WORLD OF GULLAH

IN THE LOWCOUNTRY, Gullah refers to several things: language, people, and a culture. Gullah (the word itself is believed to be a version of Angola), an English-based dialect rooted in African languages, is the unique language of the African-Americans of the Sea Islands of South Carolina and Georgia. More than 300 years old, this rhythmic language has survived, in part, because of the geographic isolation of the people who speak it; most locally born African-Americans of the area can understand, if not speak, Gullah.

Descended from thousands of slaves who were imported by planters in the Carolinas during the 18th century, the Gullah people have maintained not only their dialect but also their heritage. Much of Gullah culture traces back to the African rice-coast culture and survives today in the art forms and skills, including sweet-grass basket making, of Sea Islanders. During the colonial period, when rice was king, Africans from the West African rice kingdoms drew high premiums as slaves. Those with basket-making skills were extremely valuable because baskets were needed for agricultural and household use. Still made by hand, sweet-grass baskets are intricate coils of a marsh grass called sweet grass. Highly prized by residents and visitors alike, the baskets are named for the sweet, haylike aroma of the sweet grass. Other Gullah art forms can be seen in hand-carved bateaus and gourds and in hand-tied nets used to catch shrimp in local creeks and rivers.

Nowhere is Gullah culture more evident than in the foods of the region. Rice appears at nearly every meal—Africans taught planters how to grow rice and how to cook and serve it as well. Like many African dishes, Lowcountry dishes use okra, peanuts, benne (the African word for sesame seeds), field peas, and hot peppers. Gullah food reflects the bounty of the islands: shrimp, crabs, oysters, fish, and such vegetables as greens, tomatoes, and corn. Watermelons, indigenous to West Africa, are grown all over the Lowcountry.

Many dishes are prepared in one pot, similar to the stew-pot cooking of West Africa. Frogmore stew calls for cooking shrimp, potatoes, sausage, and corn together in one large pot. Hoppin' John—a one-pot mixture of rice and field peas traditionally served on New Year's Day—is similar to rice and pigeon peas, a mainstay in West Africa.

The practices of plantation owners unknowingly helped the Gullah culture survive: from praise houses—one-room houses of worship where Christianity was introduced to keep slaves from running away—came plantation melodies. These songs live on in performances by groups including the Hallelujah Singers, Sea Island Singers, Mt. Zion Spiritual Singers, and Ron and Natalie Daise, all of whom perform regularly in Charleston and Beaufort.

The Penn Center, on St. Helena Island near Beaufort, is the unofficial Gullah headquarters, preserving the culture and developing opportunities for Gullahs. Until 1927 or so St. Helena felt little influence from the outside world. Blacks retained the land, their language, and their unique culture. Many still go shrimping with hand-tied nets, harvest oysters, and grow their own vegetables. Nearby on Daufuskie Island, as well as on Edisto, Wadmalaw and Johns islands near Charleston, Gullah communities can still be found, although development continues to encroach. A number of companies can help visitors you this world.

A famous Gullah proverb says: *If oonuh ent kno weh oonuh dah gwine, oonuh should kno weh oonuh come f'um.* Translation: If you don't know where you're going, you should know where you come from.

built a fort on St. Helena. ☎ 843/525–2951. 📧 *Free.* ⊙ *Fri.–Wed. 10–4:30, Thurs. 10–7.*

St. Helena Island, 9 mi southeast of Beaufort via U.S. 21, is the site of the **Penn Center Historic District** and **York W. Bailey Museum.** Penn Center, established in the middle of the Civil War as the South's first school for freed slaves, today provides community services and has cottages for rent. The **York W. Bailey Museum** (formerly a clinic) has displays reflecting the heritage of Sea Island blacks. These islands are where Gullah, a musical language that combines English and African languages, developed. ✉ *Land's End Rd., St. Helena Island,* ☎ *843/838–2432.* 📧 *Donation suggested.* ⊙ *Tues.–Fri. 11–4 and by appointment.*

OFF THE BEATEN PATH

HUNTING ISLAND STATE PARK – This secluded domain of beach, nature trails, and varied fishing has about 3 mi of public beaches—some of it dramatically yet beautifully eroding. The 1,120-ft fishing pier is among the longest on the East Coast. You can climb the 181 steps of the 140-ft **Hunting Island Lighthouse** (built in 1859 and abandoned in 1933) for sweeping views. The park is 18 mi southeast of Beaufort via U.S. 21; write for cabin and camping reservations. ✉ *1775 Sea Island Pkwy., St. Helena 29920,* ☎ *843/838–2011.* 📧 *$2 per person Mar.–Oct., free rest of year; 50¢ to climb lighthouse.* ⊙ *Lighthouse daily 10–5. Gates close at sunset.*

Dining and Lodging

$$$–$$$$ ✗ **Bistro 205.** This well-lit spot, with a comfortable counter bar and indoor courtyard motif, is popular with the lunch crowd. Try the rack of lamb, beef fillet with Brie quesadilla, coriander-encrusted pork, or macadamia-dusted mahimahi. ✉ *205 West St., Historic Downtown,* ☎ *843/524–4994. AE, D, MC, V. No lunch Sun. and Mon.*

$$–$$$ ✗ **11th Street Dockside.** The succulent fried oysters, shrimp, and fish here are some of the best around. Other seafood specialties are the steamed seafood pot and, by request only, Frogmore stew (with shrimp, potatoes, sausage, and corn). It's all served in a classic wharf-side environment—you can eat in a screened porch (if you prefer), and you'll get water views from nearly every table. ✉ *11th St. W, Port Royal,* ☎ *843/524–7433. AE, D, DC, MC, V. No lunch.*

$$–$$$ ✗ **Emily's.** Long, narrow, and wood-paneled, Emily's is a lively restaurant and tapas bar that serves until 11 PM. The crowds linger over tapas including chicken spring rolls, lamb chops, and crab wontons. This is definitely *not* a no-smoking haven. ✉ *906 Port Republic St., Historic Downtown,* ☎ *843/522–1866. AE, MC, V. Closed Sun. No lunch.*

$–$$ ✗ **Shrimp Shack.** On the way to Hunting Island, stop here, as locals have for 20 years—for shrimp burgers, sweet-potato fries, and sweet tea. On weekends dinner is served only until 7 PM. ✉ *1929 Sea Island Pkwy., St. Helena,* ☎ *843/838–2962. AE, D, DC, MC, V. Closed Sun. No dinner Mon.–Thurs.*

$$–$$$ ✗🏠 **Beaufort Inn and Restaurant.** This peach-color 1897 Victorian inn, with its many gables and porches, has a superb restaurant ($$$–$$$$) with two mahogany-paneled dining rooms, porch dining, and a wine bar. Among the classy seafood dishes are crispy flounder with yucca chips and sashimi tuna in peanut sauce. Guest rooms are decorated with period reproductions, tasteful fabrics, and comfortable chairs. All have pine floors; several have fireplaces and four-poster beds. ✉ *809 Port Republic St., Historic Downtown, 29902,* ☎ *843/521–9000,* 📠 *843/521–9500,* 🌐 *www.beaufortinn.com. 15 rooms. Restaurant. AE, D, MC, V. BP.*

$$$–$$$$ 🏠 **Rhett House Inn.** This storybook inn (circa 1820) in the heart of the
★ historic district is filled with art and antiques and abounds in little lux-

uries—down pillows and duvets, cotton linens, a CD player in each room, and fresh flowers. Breakfast, afternoon tea, evening hors d'oeuvres, and dessert are included in the rate. Visiting celebrities have included Barbra Streisand, Jeff Bridges, and Dennis Quaid. The remodeled house across the street has eight rooms, each of which has a gas fireplace, a whirlpool bath, a private entrance, and a porch. ⊠ *1009 Craven St., Historic Downtown, 29902,* ☎ *843/524–9030,* FAX *843/524–1310,* WEB *www.rhetthouseinn.com. 16 rooms, 1 suite. Bicycles. AE, MC, V. BP.*

$$$ 🏨 **Cuthbert House Inn.** Overlooking the bay, this pillared 1790 home has original federal fireplaces and crown and rope molding. The owners have filled it with 18th- and 19th-century heirlooms; rooms are elegant yet comfortable, with Oriental rugs on pine floors, commanding beds, quilts, and books. ⊠ *1203 Bay St., Historic Downtown, 29902,* ☎ *843/521–1315 or 800/327–9275,* FAX *843/521–1314,* WEB *www.cuthberthouseinn.com. 7 rooms, 1 suite. Bicycles. AE, D, MC, V. BP.*

$$–$$$ 🏨 **Craven Street Inn.** This double-piazza 1870 inn is decorated in clean, Pottery Barn–style, with olive and neutral tones, hand-crafted cabinets, wreaths, and baskets. Spacious guest rooms in the main house have pine floors, high ceilings, and fireplaces; those in the 1920s garden house are small but cozy and comfortable. Breakfast might be stuffed French toast or a ham-and-cheese omelet with homemade crumpets. ⊠ *1103 Craven St., Historic Downtown, 29902,* ☎ *843/522–1668 or 888/522–0250,* FAX *843/522–9975,* WEB *www.craven-streetinn.com. 7 rooms, 2 suites. AE, D, MC, V. BP.*

$$–$$$ 🏨 **Fripp Island Resort.** This highly exclusive resort encompasses the entire island; access is limited to guests only. Two- and three-bedroom villas and homes are contemporary in style. The island is 19 mi south of Beaufort via U.S. 21, just beyond Hunting Island State Park. There's a pavilion with shops, restaurants, and a marina. During peak season a 4-night minimum is required; off-peak there is a 2-night minimum. ⊠ *1 Tarpon Blvd., Fripp Island 29920,* ☎ *843/838–3535 or 800/845–4100,* FAX *843/838–9079,* WEB *www.frippislandresort.com. 240 units. 5 restaurants, 2 18-hole golf courses, 10 tennis courts, 4 pools, boating, bicycles, children's programs. AE, D, DC, MC, V.*

$$ 🏨 **Best Western Sea Island Inn.** At this well-maintained but standard inn in the downtown historic district, rooms are basic. The inn is centrally located, however, and within walking distance of shops, restaurants, and the waterfront area. ⊠ *1015 Bay St., Box 532, Historic Downtown, 29902,* ☎ *843/522–2090 or 800/528–1234,* FAX *843/521–4858,* WEB *www.sea-island-inn.com. 43 rooms. Refrigerators, pool, gym. AE, D, DC, MC, V. CP.*

$ 🏨 **Howard Johnson.** This clean and cheerfully staffed hotel sits on the edge of the marsh a few miles from the historic district. Rooms are spacious and have desks; many have views of the river and marsh. ⊠ *3651 Trask Pkwy. (U.S. 21), Outskirts, 29902,* ☎ *843/524–6020 or 800/528–1234,* FAX *843/521–4858. 63 rooms. Microwaves, refrigerators, pool. AE, D, DC, MC, V. CP.*

Nightlife and the Arts

Plum's (⊠ 904½ Bay St., Historic Downtown, ☎ 843/525–1946) is good for a late drink and has live bands during the weekend.

Outdoor Activities and Sports

BIKING

Beaufort is great for bicycling. Rentals are available from **Lowcountry Bicycles** (⊠ 904 Port Republic St., Historic Downtown, ☎ 843/524–9585).

Most golf courses are about a 10- to 20-minute drive from Beaufort. Try the 27 holes designed by Tom Fazio at **Callawassie Island Club** (⊠ Rte. 170, Callawassie Island, ☎ 800/221–8431). The 18-hole **Cat Island Golf Club** (⊠ 8 Waveland Ave., Port Royal, ☎ 843/524–0300) is challenging and beautiful. **Dataw Island** has two 18-hole, par-72 courses (⊠ Dataw Club Rd., 6 mi east of Beaufort off U.S. 21, Dataw Island, ☎ 843/838–8250).

Shopping

ART GALLERIES

On canvas and sculpture as well as on bits of tin roofing, rugs, frames, and furniture, the colorful, whimsical designs of Suzanne and Eric Longo decorate their **Longo Gallery** (⊠ 407 Carteret St., Historic Downtown; 103 Charles St., Historic Downtown; ☎ 843/522–8933 for both). The **Rhett Gallery** (⊠ 901 Bay St., Historic Downtown, ☎ 843/524–3339) sells Lowcountry art by members of the Rhett family and antique maps and prints, including Audubons. On nearby St. Helena Island, the **Red Piano Too Art Gallery** (⊠ 853 Sea Island Pkwy., St. Helena Island, ☎ 843/838–2241), in a huge old wooden building, is filled with quirky Southern and folk art, beads, and pottery.

GIFTS

Browse for gifts—handcrafted jewelry, candles, purses, hats, perfume, wall clocks—at **Out of Hand** (⊠ 915 Greene, Historic Downtown, ☎ 843/522–8525). Art supplies and classes are also offered. **Juxtaposition** (⊠ 720 Bay St., Historic Downtown; ☎ 843/521–1415) has beaded bags, copper-roof birdhouses, beautiful cards, potpourri and more. Just outside Beaufort, in the charming little town of Walterboro, the **SC Artisans Center** (⊠ 334 Wichmann St., Walterboro, ☎ 843/549–0011) carries the works of more than 200 South Carolina artists, with pottery, glass, folk art, furniture, quilts and metalwork for sale. Most Saturdays there are craft demonstrations.

JEWELRY

The **Craftseller** (⊠ 818 Bay St., Historic Downtown, ☎ 843/525–6104) displays jewelry and other items by Southern craftspeople.

En Route The ruins of **Sheldon Church,** built in 1753, make an interesting stop if you're driving from Beaufort to Edisto Island. The church was burned in 1779 and again in 1865. Only the brick walls and columns remain beside the old cemetery. The place is lovely—it's dripping with moss—and has become a favorite spot for people to get married. Get here from Beaufort on U.S. 21; it's about 1 mi west of Gardens Corner.

Edisto Island

62 mi northeast of Beaufort via U.S. 17 and Rte. 174, 44 mi southwest of Charleston via U.S. 17 and Rte. 174.

On this rural island, magnificent stands of age-old oaks festooned with Spanish moss border quiet streams and side roads; wild turkeys may still be spotted on open grasslands and amid palmetto palms. Many of the island's inhabitants are descendants of former slaves. **Edisto Beach State Park** has 3 mi of beach with excellent shelling, housekeeping cabins by the marsh, and campsites by the ocean (although severe erosion is limiting availability). Luxury resort development has begun to encroach around the edges of the park. For camping reservations call ☎ 843/869–2156 or 843/869–3396.

Dining and Lodging

$$$ ✕ **Old Post Office.** Try the fussed-over pork chop or the blue-crab-and-
★ asparagus pie, served with the house salad, vegetables, and fresh-
baked bread. The house specialty at this restaurant on Store Creek is
shrimp and grits and, well, *anything* with grits, rumored to be the best
around these parts. ⊠ *1442 Rte. 174,* ☎ *843/869–2339. MC, V.
Closed Sun. Closed Mon. Oct.–May. No lunch.*

$$ 🏨 **Fairfield Ocean Ridge Resort.** Although not on the beach, most accommodations are a short walk away from it, and combine resort ameni-
ties with a get-away-from-it-all environment. Well-furnished one- to
five-bedroom villas and homes tastefully decorated in contemporary
style are available. A trolley transports you to the resort's beach shelter. ⊠ *1 King Cotton Rd., Box 27, 29438,* ☎ *843/869–2561 or 800/
845–8500,* FAX *843/869–2384,* WEB *www.efairfield.com. 100 units.
Restaurant, 18-hole golf course, miniature golf, 4 tennis courts, pool,
wading pool, beach, boating, fishing, hiking, lounge. AE, D, MC, V.*

Hilton Head and Beyond A to Z

*To research prices, get advice from other travelers, and book travel ar-
rangements, visit www.fodors.com.*

AIRPORTS

Hilton Head Island Airport is served by US Airways Express and Midway. Most travelers use the Savannah International Airport, about an
hour from Hilton Head, which is served by AirTran, ComAir, Continental Express, Delta, and US Airways.

➤ AIRPORT INFORMATION: **Hilton Head Island Airport** (☎ 843/681–
6386). **Savannah International Airport** (⊠ 400 Airways Ave., ☎ 912/
964–0514).

BOAT AND FERRY TRAVEL

Hilton Head is accessible via the Intracoastal Waterway, with docking available at Harbour Town Marina, Schilling Boathouse, and Shelter Cove Marina.

➤ BOAT AND FERRY INFORMATION: **Harbour Town Marina** (☎ 843/671–
2704). **Schilling Boathouse** (☎ 843/681–2628). **Shelter Cove Marina**
(☎ 843/842–7001).

CAR TRAVEL

Hilton Head Island is 40 mi east of I–95 (Exit 28 off I–95S, Exit 5 off
I–95N). If you're heading to the south end of the island, your best bet
to save time and avoid traffic is to take the Toll Expressway ($1 each
way). Beaufort is 25 mi east of I–95, on U.S. 21.

EMERGENCIES

Emergency medical service is available at the Hilton Head Medical Center and Clinics. CVS is open until 9 PM.

➤ EMERGENCY SERVICES: **Ambulance, fire, police** (☎ 911).

➤ HOSPITALS: **Hilton Head Medical Center and Clinics** (⊠ Hospital
Center Blvd., ☎ 843/681–6122).

➤ LATE-NIGHT PHARMACIES: **CVS** (⊠ 95 Matthews Dr., Hilton Head,
☎ 843/681–8363).

TAXIS

Lowcountry Taxi and Limousine Service and Yellow Cab provide service in Hilton Head. Other options include At Your Service and Lowcountry Adventures. In Beaufort Point Tours and Yellow Cab provide
service.

➤ TAXI COMPANIES: **At Your Service** (☎ 843/837–3783). **Greyline
Lowcountry Adventures** (☎ 843/681–8212). **Lowcountry Taxi and**

Limousine Service (☎ 843/681–8294). **Point Tours** (☎ 843/522–3576). **Yellow Cab** (☎ 843/686–6666 in Hilton Head; 843/522–1121 in Beaufort).

TOURS

Hilton Head's Adventure Cruises offers dinner, sightseeing, and murder-mystery cruises. Several companies, including Harbour Town Charters in Hilton Head, run dolphin sightseeing and environmental trips. Lowcountry Adventures offers tours of Hilton Head, Beaufort, and Charleston.

Carolina Buggy Tours will show you Beaufort's historic district. Carriage Tours of Beaufort has tours of the historic district by horse-drawn carriage. Gullah 'n' Geechie Mahn Tours provides tours of Beaufort and sea islands such as St. Helena, which focus on the traditions of African-American culture. Costumed guides sing and act out history during walking tours by the Spirit of Old Beaufort tour group. Call the Greater Beaufort Chamber of Commerce to find out about self-guided walking or driving tours of Beaufort.

➤ FEES AND SCHEDULES: **Adventure Cruises** (☎ 843/785–4558). **Carolina Buggy Tours** (☎ 843/525–1300). **Carriage Tours of Beaufort** (☎ 843/221–1651). **Greater Beaufort Chamber of Commerce** (☎ 843/524–3163). **Gullah 'n' Geechie Mahn Tours** (☎ 843/838–7516). **Harbour Town Charters** (☎ 843/363–2628). **Lowcountry Adventures** (☎ 843/681–8212). **Spirit of Old Beaufort** (☎ 843/525–0459).

VISITOR INFORMATION

For information on Edisto, call the Edisto Island Chamber of Commerce. The Greater Beaufort Chamber of Commerce has information about Beaufort and the surrounding area. Two Hilton Head welcome centers, run by a private real-estate firm, are on U.S. 278 next to the bridge to Hilton Head and at 6 Lagoon Road, at the island's south end. The centers provide visitor information and also attempt to entice you into purchasing real estate. In Hilton Head your best bet is to stop by the Welcome Center and Museum of Hilton Head.

➤ TOURIST INFORMATION: **Edisto Island Chamber of Commerce** (✉ 430 Rte. 174, Box 206, Edisto Island 29438, ☎ 843/869–3867 or 888/333–2781, WEB www.edistochamber.com). **Greater Beaufort Chamber of Commerce** (✉ 1006 Bay St., Box 910, Beaufort 29901, ☎ 843/524–3163, WEB www.beaufortsc.org). **Welcome Center and Museum of Hilton Head** (✉ 100 William Hilton Pkwy., 29938, ☎ 800/523–3373, WEB www.hiltonheadisland.org).

COLUMBIA AND THE HEARTLAND
Camden, Cheraw, Sumter, Aiken, Greenwood

South Carolina's Heartland, between the coastal Lowcountry and the mountains, is a varied region of swamps and flowing rivers, fertile farmland, and vast forests of pines and hardwoods. Lakes Murray, Marion, and Moultrie have wonderful fishing, and the many state parks are popular for hiking, swimming, and camping. At the center of the region is the state capital, Columbia, an engaging contemporary city superimposed on cherished historic remnants. It has restored mansions, several museums, a university, lots of restaurants, a lively arts scene, and a fine zoo and botanical garden.

In Aiken, the center of South Carolina's Thoroughbred Country, such champions as Sea Hero and Pleasant Colony were trained. The beautiful landscape is studded with the fine mansions of wealthy Northerners such as the Vanderbilts and Whitneys. Throughout the region, such towns as Ninety Six, Sumter, and Camden preserve and interpret the past, with historic re-creations, exhibits, and restorations. Several public gardens provide islands of color during most of the year.

Columbia

112 mi northwest of Charleston via I–26, 101 mi southeast of Greenville via I–395 to I–26.

In 1786 South Carolina's capital was moved from Charleston to Columbia, in the center of the state along the banks of the Congaree River. One of the nation's first planned cities, Columbia has streets that are among the widest in America—because it was then thought that stagnant air in narrow streets fostered the spread of malaria. The city soon grew into a center of political, commercial, cultural, and social activity, but in early 1865 General William Tecumseh Sherman invaded South Carolina and incinerated two-thirds of Columbia. A few homes and public buildings were spared—as was the First Baptist Church, where secession was declared, because a janitor directed Sherman's troops to a Methodist church when asked directions. Today the city is a sprawling blend of modern office blocks, suburban neighborhoods, and the occasional antebellum home. Here, too, is the expansive main campus of the University of South Carolina, including the historic and scenic Horseshoe.

The **Columbia Museum of Art** contains art from the Kress Foundation Collection of Renaissance and baroque treasures, sculpture, decorative arts, including art glass, and European and American paintings, including a Monet and a Botticelli; there are also changing exhibitions. Kids love this place, especially when they get to see mummies; if you have children with you, the guides will often tailor the tour to them. ✉ *Main and Hampton Sts., Main St. Area,* ☎ *803/799–2810.* ⊙ *$4.* ☉ *Tues. and Thurs.–Sat. 10–5, Wed. 10–9, Sun. 1–5.*

Stop by the **Museum Shop** of the Historic Columbia Foundation in the Robert Mills House (✉ 1616 Blanding St., Main St. Area, ☎ 803/252–1770), in the historic district, to get a map and buy tickets to tour four Columbia houses: the Hampton-Preston Mansion, the Robert Mills House, the Mann-Simons Cottage, and the Woodrow Wilson Boyhood Home. ⊙ *Each house $4.* ☉ *All houses Tues.–Sat. 10:15–3:15, Sun. 1:15–4:15.*

The **Hampton-Preston Mansion** (✉ 1615 Blanding St., Main St. Area, ☎ 803/252–1770), dating from 1818, is filled with lavish furnishings collected by three generations of two influential families.

The classic, columned 1823 **Robert Mills House** (✉ 1616 Blanding St., Main St. Area, ☎ 803/252–1770) was named for its architect, who later designed the Washington Monument. It has opulent Regency furniture, marble mantels, and spacious grounds.

The **Mann-Simons Cottage** (✉ 1403 Richland St., Main St. Area, ☎ 803/252–1770) was the home of Celia Mann, one of only 200 free African-Americans in Columbia in the mid-1800s.

The **Woodrow Wilson Boyhood Home** (✉ 1705 Hampton St., Main St. Area, ☎ 803/252–1770) displays the gaslights, arched doorways, and ornate furnishings of the Victorian period.

The **Fort Jackson Museum,** on the grounds of a U.S. army training center, displays heavy equipment from the two world wars and has exhibits on the history of the fort from 1917 to the present. ✉ *Bldg. 4442, Jackson Blvd.,* ☎ *803/751–7419.* ✉ *Free.* ☉ *Tues.–Fri. 10–4, Sat. 1–4.*

Ⓒ Exhibits at the **South Carolina State Museum,** in a refurbished textile mill, interpret the state's natural history, archaeology, historical development, and technological and artistic accomplishments. One exhibit portrays noted black astronauts (dedicated to South Carolina native Dr. Ronald McNair, who died on the *Challenger*); one focuses on the Confederate submarine the *Hunley;* and another focuses on the cotton industry and slavery. An iron gate made for the museum by Phillip Simmons, the "dean of Charleston blacksmiths," is on display, as is the surfboard that biochemist Kary Mullis was riding when he heard he'd won the Nobel Prize. In the Stringer Discovery Center, an interactive display, children can check out microorganisms under a microscope and climb trees to observe the animals that live in the branches. ✉ *301 Gervais St., Vista,* ☎ *803/898–4921.* ✉ *$4.* ☉ *Mon.–Sat. 10–5, Sun. 1–5.*

South Carolina's capitol, the **State House,** started in 1855 and completed in 1950, is made of native blue granite in the Italian Renaissance style. Six bronze stars on the western wall mark direct hits by Sherman's cannons. The interior is richly appointed with brass, marble, mahogany, and artwork. ✉ *Main and Gervais Sts., Main St. Area,* ☎ *803/734–9818.* ✉ *Free.* ☉ *Weekdays 9–5, Sat. 10–5, 1st Sun. of month 1–5.*

Ⓒ Make sure it's dark out when you drive by **Tunnelvision,** an optical illusion painted on the wall of the Federal Land Bank Building by local artist Blue Sky. Next to it is Sky's bigger-than-life silver "busted" **Fire Hydrant,** a working fountain. ✉ *Taylor and Marion Sts., Main St. Area.*

A highlight of the sprawling **University of South Carolina** is its original campus—the scenic, tree-lined **Horseshoe**—dating to 1801. Researchers explore the special collections on state history and genealogy at the **South Caroliniana Library** (✉ *Sumter St., USC Campus,* ☎ *803/ 777–3131*), established in 1840. Here, too, is the **McKissick Museum** (✉ *Sumter St., USC Campus,* ☎ *803/777–7251*), with geology and gemstone exhibits and a fine display of silver.

Ⓒ **Riverfront Park and Historic Columbia Canal,** where the Broad and Saluda rivers form the Congaree River, was created around the city's original waterworks and hydroelectric plant. Interpretive markers describe the area's plant and animal life and tell the history of the buildings. ✉ *312 Laurel St., Vista,* ☎ *803/733–8613.* ✉ *Free.* ☉ *Daily dawn–dusk.*

★ Ⓒ **Riverbanks Zoological Park and Botanical Garden** contains more than 2,000 animals and birds, some endangered, in natural habitats. Walk along pathways and through landscaped gardens to see sea lions, polar bears, Siberian tigers, and black rhinos. Koalas are the latest addition. The South American primate collection has won international acclaim, and the park is noted for its success in breeding endangered and fragile species. The Aquarium/Reptile Complex has South Carolina, desert, tropical, and marine specimens. At the Bird Pavilion you can view birds and wildlife under a safarilike tent. You can ride the carousel and also take a tram over the Saluda River to the 70-acre botanical gardens on the west bank. (A new entrance in West Columbia, off Highway 378, takes you directly to the botanical gardens.) A forested section with walking trails travels past historic ruins and spectacular views of the river. ✉ *I–126 and U.S. 76 at Greystone Riverbanks exit, West Columbia,* ☎ *803/779–8717,* ⓦⒺⒷ *www.riverbanks.org.* ✉ *$76.25.* ☉ *Apr.–Oct., weekdays 9–4, weekends 9–5; Nov.–Mar., daily 9–4.*

Dining and Lodging

$$$ ✕ **Motor Supply Co. Bistro.** This elegant but casual bistro-style eatery has wooden tables, dim lighting, and an outdoor patio (with heat lamps in cold months). You can choose from such entrées as seared grouper with tomato basil relish, pork chops with Gorgonzola sauce, or spinach and walnut stuffed mushrooms over pasta. On Sunday there's a bountiful brunch. ✉ *920 Gervais St., Vista,* ☎ *803/256–6687. AE, DC, MC, V. Closed Mon.*

$$–$$$ ✕ **California Dreaming.** This airy, greenery-bedecked space is the renovated old Union train station. The only drawback is an echo that's noticeable when it's crowded. Specialties include prime rib, barbecued baby-back ribs, Mexican dishes, and homemade pasta. ✉ *401 S. Main St., USC Campus,* ☎ *803/254–6767. AE, MC, V.*

$$–$$$ ✕ **Mangia! Mangia!** Earth tones, hammered copper, and mosaic tiles
★   transform an early 20th-century building into an elegant place to dine. Window-side tables have a view of the Columbia skyline across the Congaree River; there's a lively outdoor patio, too, with heaters for chilly nights. Try the mussels steamed in a garlicky wine sauce, followed by wild-mushroom pizza baked in the wood-burning oven. The Tuscan-influenced menu also includes lamb shank roasted in red wine with herbs. The entire restaurant, except for the bar, is no-smoking. ✉ *100 State St., West Columbia,* ☎ *803/791–3443. AE, D, DC, MC, V. Closed Sun.*

$$ ✕ **Blue Marlin.** With polished wood, lines of booths, and an oceanic mural over the bar, this restaurant speaks of bygone years—fitting for an eatery that was once a train station. Seafood and pasta dishes include talapia with shrimp and crabmeat sauce, lobster ravioli, and a basic lobster or fish filet–all mains are served with steaming collard greens and grits. Fruit cobblers come topped with liqueur-laced whipped cream. It's great for late lunches or early dinners because it opens at 11 and stops serving around 10 PM. ✉ *1200 Lincoln St., Vista,* ☎ *803/799–3838. Reservations not accepted. AE, D, DC, MC, V.*

$–$$ ✕ **Maurice Gourmet Barbecue–Piggie Park.** One of the South's best-known barbecue chefs, Maurice Bessinger has a fervent national following for his mustard-sauce-based, pit-cooked ham barbecue. Fans also love the chicken, ribs, hash over rice, and thick-battered onion rings. ✉ *1600 Charleston Hwy., Cayce,* ☎ *803/796–0220;* ✉ *800 Elmwood Ave., Main St. Area,* ☎ *803/256–4377;* ✉ *1141 Lake Murray Blvd., Irmo,* ☎ *803/732–5555. Reservations not accepted. AE, D, MC, V.*

$ ✕ **The Gourmet Shop.** This French-style café, styled in black and white, with mirrors and French art prints, has long been serving wonderful coffee, sandwiches, and salads, including a super chicken salad, potato salad, and tomato, feta, and basil salad. Next door, the shop sells food to go (great for picnics), wine, and fancy food items. ✉ *724 Saluda Ave., Five Points,* ☎ *803/799–9463. AE, MC, V. No dinner Sun.*

$$$–$$$$ ▥ **Embassy Suites Hotel Columbia–Greystone.** In the spacious seven-story atrium lobby with skylights, fountains, pool, and live plants, you can enjoy full breakfasts and evening cocktails. All rooms are suites with sleeper sofas. The staff, which caters mainly to a business clientele, works hard to please. ✉ *200 Stoneridge Dr., St. Andrews, 29210,* ☎ *803/252–8700 or 800/362–2779,* ℻ *803/256–8749,* ⓦⓔⓑ *www.embassysuites.com. 214 suites. Restaurant, microwaves, refrigerators, indoor pool, hot tub, gym, lounge, recreation room, business services, meeting rooms. AE, D, DC, MC, V. BP.*

$$–$$$$ ▥ **Adam's Mark.** This upscale downtown hotel is near state offices and the University of South Carolina. It has leather armchairs, suspended lights, and brass accents in public areas. Guest rooms are contemporary, with armoires and desks. ✉ *1200 Hampton St., Five Points, 29201,* ☎ *803/771–7000 or 800/444–2326,* ℻ *803/254–8307,* ⓦⓔⓑ

www.adamsmark.com. 296 rooms, 4 suites. Restaurant, indoor pool, health club, hot tub, lounge, sports bar, business services. AE, D, DC, MC, V.

$$–$$$$ ⊞ **Hampton Inn Downtown Historic District.** This classy chain is conveniently located within walking distance of restaurants and nightlife in the Vista. The hotel's staff offers attentive service, and rooms have comfortable, though standard, furnishings, including desks and blonde-color wood furniture. ⊠ *822 Gervais St., Vista 29201,* ☎ *803/231– 2000,* FAX *803/231–2868,* WEB *www.hamptoninncolumbia.com. 102 rooms. Some microwaves and refrigerators, some hot tubs. AE, D, DC, MC, V. BP.*

$$$ ⊞ **Claussen's Inn.** It's a small hotel in a converted bakery warehouse in the attractive Five Points area, and near lively nightlife and specialty shops. The open, airy lobby has a Mexican-tile floor; the rooms are arranged around the lobby. The eight loft suites have downstairs sitting rooms, period reproductions, spiral staircases, and four-poster beds. Some of the rooms have modern metallic furniture; generally rooms have floral or print fabrics and desk areas. ⊠ *2003 Greene St., Five Points, 29205,* ☎ *803/765–0440 or 800/622–3382,* FAX *803/799–7924. 21 rooms, 8 suites. Hot tub, meeting room. AE, D, MC, V. CP.*

$ ⊞ **La Quinta Motor Inn.** At this three-story inn on a quiet street near the zoo, the rooms are spacious and well lighted, with very large working areas. ⊠ *1335 Garner La., St. Andrews, 29210,* ☎ *803/798–9590 or 800/531–5900,* FAX *803/731–5574,* WEB *www.laquinta.com. 120 rooms. Pool. AE, D, DC, MC, V.*

$ ⊞ **Riverside Inn.** Close to the University of South Carolina's Williams-Brice Stadium, this inn has comfortable rooms and a cheerful staff. Locally owned, the Riverside is a favorite with state senators and legislators who stay here during legislative sessions. Rooms were upgraded in 2002 to include new carpet, mattresses, and bedspreads. The Continental breakfast includes breads, fruit, yogurt, grits, and oatmeal. ⊠ *111 Knox Abbott Dr., West Columbia, 29033,* ☎ *803/939–4688,* FAX *803/926– 5547,* WEB *www.riversideinn.com. 64 rooms. Putting green, pool. AE, D, DC, MC, V. CP.*

Nightlife and the Arts

THE ARTS

The **Columbia Music Festival Association** (☎ 803/771–6303) will provide information by phone about events of the Choral Society, the opera, Opera Guild, Dance Theatre, Brass Band, Caroliers, and Cabaret Company. The **Koger Center for the Arts** (⊠ Assembly St., USC Campus, ☎ 803/777–7500) presents national and international theater, ballet, and musical groups, as well as individual performers. Call the **South Carolina Philharmonic** (☎ 803/254–7445) for information about scheduled concerts of the Philharmonic, chamber orchestra, and youth orchestra.

The **Town Theatre** (⊠ 1012 Sumter St., USC Campus, ☎ 803/799–2510), founded in 1919, stages six plays a year from September to late May, plus a special summer show. The **Workshop Theatre of South Carolina** (⊠ 1136 Bull St., USC Campus, ☎ 803/799–4876) produces a number of plays.

NIGHTLIFE

In the hopping Vista neighborhood, the **Art Bar** (⊠ 1211 Park St., Vista, ☎ 803/254–4792) is funky, with splash-painted walls, lighted lunch boxes, and dancing to world music. At **Billy G's** (⊠ 828 Gervais Rd., Vista, ☎ 803/806–8870) you'll find live bands. **Willy's Restaurant & Grill** (⊠ 1200B Lincoln St., Vista, ☎ 803/799–3111), in a former train station waiting room, has live music and an outdoor patio. In Five Points, **Goatfeathers** (⊠ 2017 Devine St., Five Points, ☎ 803/256–3325 or

803/256–8133) is a bohemian spot that's popular with university and law-school students, and it also appeals to late-night coffee and dessert seekers.

Outdoor Activities and Sports

BASEBALL

The **Capital City Bombers** (☎ 803/256–4110), a Class-A affiliate of the New York Mets, play from mid-April through August at **Capital City Stadium** (⊠ 301 S. Assembly St., USC Campus) downtown.

CANOEING AND KAYAKING

Self-guided canoe trails traverse an alluvial floodplain bordered by high bluffs at the 22,200-acre, **Congaree Swamp National Monument** (⊠ 20 mi southeast of Columbia, off Rte. 48, Old Bluff Rd., Hopkins, ☎ 803/776–4396). The beautifully eerie water and trees here, including many old-growth bottomland hardwoods (the oldest and largest trees east of the Mississippi River) are full of wildlife. The Saluda River near Columbia offers challenging Class III and Class IV rapids for kayaking and canoeing. Guided river and swamp canoeing excursions can be arranged, as can canoe rentals, from **Adventure Carolina** (⊠ 1107 State St., Cayce, ☎ 803/796–4505), which is just outside Columbia. You can rent canoes or take a guide river or swamp expedition through the **River Runner Outdoor Center** (⊠ 905 Gervais St., Vista Columbia, ☎ 803/771–0353). Canoe and kayak rentals are available at **Saluda Shoals Park** (⊠ 5605 Bush River Rd., Irmo, ☎ 803/772–1228).

GOLF

Sedgewood (⊠ Sumter Hwy., Hopkins, ☎ 803/776–2177), with 18 holes at par 72, is among the many fine area courses. Call the booking company **Golf Vacations of Columbia** (☎ 888/501–0954) for tee times.

HIKING

Congaree Swamp National Monument (⊠ 20 mi southeast of Columbia, off Rte. 48, Old Bluff Rd., Hopkins, ☎ 803/776–4396) has 22 mi of trails for hikers and nature lovers and a ¼-mi boardwalk for people with disabilities. Guided nature walks leave Saturday at 1:30.

Shopping

ANTIQUES AND FLEA MARKETS

Many of Columbia's antiques outlets, boutique shops, and restaurants are in the ever-growing **Congaree Vista** around Huger and Gervais streets, between the state house and the river. A number of intriguing shops and cafés are in **Five Points,** around Blossom at Harden streets. There are antiques shops across the river on Meeting and State streets in **West Columbia.** The **Old Mill Antique Mall** (⊠ 310 State St., West Columbia, ☎ 803/796–4229) has items from many dealers, including furniture, glassware, jewelry, and books.

FARMERS' MARKET

The **State Farmers' Market** (⊠ Bluff Rd., USC Campus, ☎ 803/737–4664) is one of the 10 largest in the country. Fresh vegetables, along with flowers, plants, seafood, and more, are sold weekdays 6 AM–9 PM and Sunday 1–6.

Camden

32 mi northeast of Columbia via I–20.

Charming Camden, a town with a horsey history and grand Southern colonial homes, has never paved its fanciest roads for the sake of the hooves of the horses that regularly trot over them. The Carolina Cup and Colonial Cup are run here; in addition to the horse races, you'll see champagne tailgate parties with elegant crystal and china.

Camden is South Carolina's oldest inland town, dating from 1732. British general Lord Cornwallis established a garrison here during the Revolutionary War and burned most of Camden before evacuating it. A center of textile trade from the late 19th century through the 1940s, Camden attracted Northerners escaping the cold winters; DuPont is one of Camden's major employers. Because General Sherman spared the town during the Civil War, most of its antebellum homes still stand.

The **Bonds Conway House** was built by the first black man in Camden to buy his freedom. The circa-1812 home has the fine details of a skilled craftsman, including wonderful woodwork and heart-pine floors. ⊠ *811 Fair St.,* ☎ *803/425–1123.* 🖭 *Free.* ☉ *Thurs. 1–5 or by appointment.*

☙ The **Historic Camden Revolutionary War Site** re-creates and interprets historical structures of 18th- and early 19th-century Camden, with an emphasis on the British occupation of 1780. Several structures dot the site, including the 1789 **Craven House** and the **Blacksmith Shed.** The **Kershaw House,** a reconstruction of the circa-1770 home of Camden's founder, Joseph Kershaw, also served as Cornwallis's headquarters; it's furnished with period pieces. A nature trail, fortifications, powder magazine, picnic area, and crafts shop are also here. ⊠ *U.S. 521, 1½ mi north of I-20,* ☎ *803/432–9841,* 🕸 *www.historic-camden.org.* 🖭 *$5; admission to grounds and trail free.* ☉ *Tues.–Sat. 10–5, Sun. 1–5; call for guided tours.*

OFF THE BEATEN PATH

HISTORIC BOYKIN – This 19th-century agricultural community, on the National Register of Historic Places, was once centered around the now restored and working grist mill. You can visit the mill; buy freshly ground grits or cornmeal from the Boykin Mill General Store, which has floor-to-ceiling shelves; step inside a restored 1740 slave house (Broom Place) and see brooms being handmade on late-19th-century equipment; and visit the 1820s Swift Creek Baptist Church. The Mill Pond Restaurant occupies two historic buildings. ⊠ *Rtes. 261 and 28 (10 mi south of Camden via U.S. 521),* ☎ *803/424–4731.* 🖭 *Free.* ☉ *Broom Place weekdays 10–5; Sat. 10:30–2; general store Mon.–Sat. 7–6; church and mill open by appointment.*

Dining and Lodging

$$$–$$$$ ★ ✕ **Mill Pond Restaurant.** In a pair of historic buildings overlooking a sprawling millpond, this restaurant, about a 10-minute drive south of Camden in Boykin, specializes in Mediterranean-influenced dishes. You can dine alfresco, close enough to see pond wildlife, on the spicy, perfectly fried Cajun oysters, bacon-wrapped scallops, or crab cakes with shrimp tartar sauce. The more casual side of the restaurant has a vintage saloon-style bar. ⊠ *84 Boykin Mill Rd., Boykin,* ☎ *803/425–8825. MC, V. Closed Sun.–Mon. No lunch.*

$$ ✕ **The Pearl.** Chances are Ms. Pearl has put out her sign and is serving her famous collards, pork chops, catfish, fried chicken, and banana pudding, but you'll have to call or drop by to be sure. A meat-and-two (lunch) or -three (dinner) comes with salad and beverage. Each room has a theme: for example, the Pearl Room has framed pearl necklaces on the wall. ⊠ *707 DeKalb St.,* ☎ *803/713–8009. AE, MC, V.*

$–$$ ✕ **Lucy's Food & Spirits.** You can sit at the immense wooden bar or at café tables in this high-ceilinged, brick-walled turn-of-the-20th-century building. Veal, pork, quail, and lamb are specialties; don't miss the sweet-potato chips, the pear and endive salad, or, for lunch, the curried-chicken salad. ✉ *1034 Broad St.,* ☎ *803/432–9096. AE, D, MC, V. Closed Mon.–Sun. No lunch Tues.*

$$ ✕🅷 **Greenleaf Inn of Camden.** You won't find a nicer or better-value
★ lodging in the region. This property, in Camden's historic district, consists of the main inn, with four rooms on the second floor above the inn's restaurant; a nearby house, circa 1805, with seven rooms; and a 1930s bungalow, which is good for families. The grander rooms in the inn are spacious and have classic Victorian furniture; rooms in the other house are smaller but more private. All baths are modern. High ceilings, elaborately tiled fireplaces, and patio dining set the tone for an elegant yet casual meal in the restaurant ($–$$$; no lunch). Try the wonderful eggplant Parmesan, crispy whole flounder, or seafood lasagna. ✉ *1308 Broad St., 29020,* ☎ *803/425–1806 or 800/437–5874,* FAX *803/425–5853,* WEB *www.greenleafinncamden.com.* 10 *rooms, 2 suites, 1 bungalow. Restaurant. AE, D, MC, V. BP.*

$$–$$$ 🅷 **A Camden Bed & Breakfast.** This federal-style 1920s home in Camden's historic district has wood-burning fireplaces in every room, both in the main house and in one of the cottages, and antiques and Persian rugs. The three-bedroom suite in the main house is perfect for families and contains a VCR, computer with Internet access, microwave, and refrigerator. Breakfast might include a Canadian ham casserole or French toast. ✉ *127 Union St., 29020,* ☎ *803/432–2366,* WEB *www.camdenscbandb.com. 1 suite, 2 cottages. AE, MC, V. BP.*

$–$$ 🅷 **Holiday Inn.** This well-maintained two-story chain property has cheerfully decorated rooms; refrigerators and microwaves are available on request. The hotel is 3 mi west of downtown Camden. The restaurant serves commendable home-style fare—the Sunday buffet is a favorite among locals. ✉ *U.S. 1/601S, Box 96, Lugoff 29078,* ☎ *803/438–9441 or 800/465–4329,* FAX *803/438–9441,* WEB *www.basshotels.com. 117 rooms. Restaurant, pool, lounge. AE, D, DC, MC, V.*

$ 🅷 **Colony Inn.** A short drive from the historic district, this well-maintained hotel is popular with business travelers. Because of the friendly staff, clean rooms, and the great location, the inn is always busy. ✉ *2020 W. DeKalb St. (U.S. 1), 29020,* ☎ *803/432–5508 or 800/356–9801,* FAX *803/432–0920. 71 rooms. Restaurant, pool. AE, DC, MC, V.*

Nightlife and the Arts

The **Paddock Restaurant & Pub** (✉ 514 Rutledge St., ☎ 803/432–3222) has music and dancing weekends. The prolific **Fine Arts Center of Kershaw County** (✉ 810 Lyttleton St., ☎ 803/425–7676) sponsors many events, including a blues festival, music and theater performances, and art shows.

Shopping

Real European butter is key to the divine cheese sticks at the **Mulberry Market Bake Shop** (✉ 536 E. DeKalb St., ☎ 803/424–8401); also sample almond Danishes, lemon bars, and macaroons. It's a delightful culinary asset in a small town.

Camden is known for its antiques shopping, with several shops and multidealer malls along Broad Street, including the **Camden Antique Mall** (✉ 830 Broad St., ☎ 803/432–0818), with furniture, sterling, glassware, and reproduction pieces in some 30 stalls. The **Granary** (✉ 830 Broad St., ☎ 803/432–8811) specializes in English and American items and has whimsical garden furniture.

Nearby, **Charles Dixon Antiques & Auction Co.** (✉ 818 Broad St., ☎ 803/432–3676) has distinctive architectural pieces. At **Springdale Antiques** (✉ 951 Broad St., ☎ 803/432–0312), the proprietor always provides great history on his items.

Outdoor Activities and Sports

EQUESTRIAN EVENTS

Camden puts on two steeplechase events at the **Springdale Race Course** (⊠ 200 Knights Hill Rd., ☎ 803/432–6513): the Carolina Cup, in late March or early April; and the Colonial Cup, in November. You're likely to see Thoroughbreds working out most mornings October through April; also on site, the **National Steeplechase Museum** (☎ 803/432–6513, WEB www.carolina-cup.org; ☞ free; ☉ Sept.–Apr., daily 10–5; May–Aug., by appointment) shows off National Steeplechase artifacts and horse memorabilia.

Polo matches are held annually in May at **Camden Polo Field** (⊠ Polo La., ☎ 803/425–7676).

GOLF

White Pines Golf Club (⊠ 615 Mary La., ☎ 803/432–7442) is an 18-hole, par-72 course.

Cheraw

55 mi northeast of Camden via U.S. 1.

The small and historic town of Cheraw, named for the Native American tribe that once thrived in this region, is worth visiting to see its well-preserved 213-acre historic district, anchored by the town green, which dates to the original 1768 village plan. The district encompasses more than 50 antebellum public buildings and homes, including Victorian, classical revival, Federal, upcountry farmhouse, and colonial styles, plus some mill buildings. The **Greater Cheraw Chamber of Commerce** (⊠ 221 Market St., ☎ 843/537–8425 or 888/537–0014) distributes brochures that delineate self-guided-tours.

Notable buildings on the **town green** include the Cheraw Town Hall, built in 1858, which has massive columns and now contains city offices. Brokers once bought and sold cotton in **Market Hall,** which dates to 1837.

The small brick **Lyceum,** which dates to 1820, has served as a chancery court and as headquarters for both Confederate and Union quartermasters. Now a small museum with Indian artifacts and local historical relics, it includes engaging artifacts on the late jazz musician Dizzy Gillespie, who hailed from Cheraw. ⊠ *220 Market St., ☎ 843/537–8425. ☞ Free. ☉ Obtain key from chamber of commerce, weekdays 9–5, or call for appointment.*

The **Old St. David's Episcopal Church** dates to the early 1770s and was the last Anglican church built in South Carolina under King George III. Inside you can view simple box pews and gaze out the windows toward graceful magnolias; outside in the graveyard, soldiers from every American war have been buried. Both the Americans and the British used Old St. David's as quarters during the revolution; both the Confederate and the Union armies used it as a hospital during the Civil War. The acoustics are splendid. ⊠ *91 Church St., ☎ 843/537–8425. ☞ Free. ☉ Obtain key from chamber of commerce, weekdays 9–5, or call for appointment.*

Dining and Lodging

$ ✕ **Country Kitchen.** This no-frills lunch place—a short drive from the historic district—serves all-you-can-eat home-cooked fried chicken, macaroni and cheese, squash, corn bread, peach pie, vegetable soup, and other delights. Every Friday there's fried fish. ⊠ *908 Chesterfield Hwy. (Rte. 9), ☎ 843/537–3662. AE, MC, V. Closed Sat. No dinner.*

$ ✕ **El-Sherif's House of Pizza.** Expect great pizza, fair prices, and tasty chicken salad at this casual spot in the former soda fountain of an early 20th-century hotel, right behind Town Hall. ⊠ *217 2nd St.,* ☎ *843/ 921–0066. AE, MC, V. Closed Sun.*

$ ▣ **501 Kershaw and Spears Guest House.** Accommodations at this inn consist of four rooms in the Spears Guest House (a 1940s cottage with an enchanting front porch) and one in the owner's 1845 federal-style home across the street. Although on the small side, rooms have antique and reproduction furnishings. You have access to a fully equipped kitchen and a gas grill. Breakfast is self-serve: the refrigerator is stocked with juice and packaged foods. ⊠ *501 Kershaw St., 29520,* ☎ *843/537– 7733 or 888/424–3729,* FAX *843/537–0302,* WEB *www.bbonline.com/sc/ kershaw. 5 rooms. AE, D, DC, MC, V. CP.*

$ ▣ **314 Market Street B&B.** In the historic district, this 1904 home has spacious guest rooms, four porches (upstairs and down), huge mahogany pocket doors, and inviting period fireplaces. The inn is known for its delicious (and filling) breakfasts. ⊠ *314 Market St., 29520,* ☎ *843/ 537–5797. 3 rooms. AE, MC, V. BP.*

Shopping

A few miles west at the **Chesterfield Outlet** (⊠ Rte. 9, Chesterfield, ☎ 843/623–7474), you'll find knit polo shirts embroidered with the state palmetto tree logo, made of local cotton grown and spun here in Chesterfield County.

Outdoor Activities and Sports

Cheraw State Park, about 4 mi south of Cheraw off U.S. 52, contains a terrific golf course. Also within the park's 6,000 acres are the Turkey Oak Trail and the scenic Boardwalk Trail, the latter jutting into the lake for awesome views (pack lunch and a swimsuit because this trail leads to a lovely picnic area and a small beach with lifeguards). There are a cypress swamp that's ideal for canoeing (canoes and paddleboat rentals are available) and great fishing. Overnighters can consider eight log cabins built by the Civilian Conservation Corps in the 1930s that are fully furnished, quaint, and comfortable. ⊠ *100 State Park Rd.,* ☎ *843/537–2215 or 800/868–9630.* ▣ *Free.* ⊙ *Daily 7–7.*

Golf

The championship Tom Jackson–designed 18-hole course at **Cheraw State Park** (⊠ 100 State Park Rd., ☎ 843/537–2215 or 800/868–9630) has been rated by *Golf Digest* as one of the best buys in the nation (ask about the $50 per person deal that includes overnight cabin accommodations, greens fees, and a cart). The course takes in beautiful pine forest and lake views. Right by the state park, **Cheraw Country Club** (⊠ 1601 Cash Rd., ☎ 843/537–3412) has a short but heavily bunkered 18-hole course that's nice for beginners because it's unintimidating and unhurried.

Sumter

70 mi south of Cheraw via U.S. 52 to U.S. 15, 30 mi southeast of Camden on U.S. 521, 44 mi east of Columbia on U.S. 378/76.

Sumter—named for the Revolutionary War hero and statesman General Thomas Sumter—was settled about 1740 as the center of a cultivated plantation district. Today it houses varied industries, lumbering, agricultural marketing, and nearby Shaw Air Force Base.

The **Sumter County Museum** (headquarters of the Sumter County Historical Society), in a lovely 1845 Victorian Gothic house, exhibits fine period furnishings, Oriental carpets, vintage carriages, dolls, and various memorabilia. Behind the museum is an 1800s re-created "old South" village with live reenactments. ⊠ *122 N. Washington St.,* ☏ *803/775–0908.* 🎟 *Free.* ☉ *Tues.–Sat. 10–5, Sun. 2–5.*

The **Sumter Opera House,** built in 1892, has a clock tower and a stunning art deco interior, including detailed plasterwork and an intricate, hand-painted stage area. Theater, film, and music performances are held here. ⊠ *21 N. Main St.,* ☏ *803/436–2581.* 🎟 *Free.* ☉ *Tours by appointment weekdays 8:30–5.*

Swan Lake Iris Gardens is like Eden when its thousands of irises are in bloom. All eight known species of swans—including the *coscoroba,* whooper, trumpeter, and black Australian varieties—paddle leisurely about the 45-acre lake. The 150-acre park also includes walking trails, picnic areas, tennis courts, a playground, and concessions. ⊠ *W. Liberty St.,* ☏ *803/775–1231.* 🎟 *Free.* ☉ *Daily 8–sunset.*

Lodging

$$ 🏨 **Magnolia House.** In Sumter's historic district, this four-column Greek Revival structure is a pleasing alternative to the region's generic chain properties. Antiques, many of which are French, furnish the rooms; there are also stained-glass windows, inlaid oak floors, and five fireplaces. ⊠ *230 Church St., 29150,* ☏ *803/775–6694 or 888/666–0296,* 🕸 *www.bbonline.com/sc/magnolia. 3 rooms, 1 suite. AE, D, MC, V. BP.*

$–$$ 🏨 **Holiday Inn.** This well-maintained motor inn is 4 mi west of town, near Shaw Air Force Base. Simple, clean rooms are as you would expect from this chain. ⊠ *2390 Broad St. Ext., 29150,* ☏ *803/469–9001 or 800/465–4329,* 📠 *803/469–7001,* 🕸 *www.basshotels.com. 124 rooms. Café, pool, gym. AE, D, DC, MC, V.*

Outdoor Activities and Sports

About 20 mi east of Sumter, a mysterious canoe trail leads into a remote swampy depression at **Woods Bay State Park** (⊠ east on U.S. 378, then north on U.S. 301, ☏ 803/659–4445), where rentals are available for $3 per hour or $10 for a full day. About 20 mi southwest of Sumter, **Poinsett State Park** (⊠ west on U.S. 378, then south on Route 261, ☏ 803/494–8177) is part of the state-wide Palmetto Trail and offers great hiking.

GOLF

Inveterate duffers appreciate the affordable, unhurried golfing at several nearby 18-hole courses, including **Lakewood Links** (⊠ 3600 Greenview Pkwy., ☏ 803/481–5700). You can walk the par 71 course at **Pocalla Springs** (⊠ 1700 U.S. 15S, ☏ 803/481–8322). **Crystal Lakes Golf Course** (⊠ 1305 Clara Louise Kellogg Dr., ☏ 803/775–1902) offers nine holes.

Aiken

100 mi southwest of Sumter via U.S. 378/76 to I–20 to U.S. 1, 56 mi southwest of Columbia via I–20 to U.S. 1.

Aiken, in Thoroughbred Country, first earned its fame in the 1890s, when wealthy Northerners wintering here built stately mansions and entertained one another with lavish parties, horse shows, and hunts. Many of the mansions—some with up to 60 rooms—remain as a testament to this era of opulence. The town is still a center for all kinds of outdoor activity, including the equestrian events of the Triple Crown, as well as tennis and golf.

The area's horse farms have produced many national champions, which are commemorated at the **Aiken Thoroughbred Hall of Fame** with exhibitions of horse-related decorations, paintings, and sculptures, plus racing silks and trophies. The Hall of Fame is on the grounds of the 14-acre **Hopeland Gardens**, with winding paths, quiet terraces, and reflecting pools. There's a Touch and Scent Trail with Braille plaques. Open-air free concerts and plays are presented on Monday evening May through August. ⊠ *Dupree Pl. and Whiskey Rd.*, ☏ *803/642–7630.* ⊡ *Free.* ☉ *Museum Oct.–May, Tues.–Sun. 2–5; grounds daily dawn–dusk.*

The **Aiken County Historical Museum**, in one wing of an 1860 estate, is devoted to early regional culture. It has Native American artifacts, firearms, an authentically furnished 1808 log cabin, a schoolhouse, and a miniature circus display. ⊠ *433 Newberry St. SW*, ☏ *803/642–2015.* ⊡ *Donations suggested.* ☉ *Tues.–Fri. 9:30–4:30, weekends 2–5.*

Aiken surrounds the serene and wild **Hitchcock Woods** (⊠ enter from junction of Clark Rd. and Whitney Dr., Berrie Rd., and Dibble Rd.), 2,000 acres of Southern forest with hiking trails and bridal paths. Listed on the National Register of Historic Places and three times the size of New York's Central Park, it's the largest urban forest in the country.

The renovated 1951 **Monetta Drive-In** (⊠ US 1, Monetta, ☏ 803/685–7949) plays past and present favorites every weekend and some weekdays.

Stop for a wine tasting at **Montmorenci Vineyards** (⊠ U.S. 78, 2½ mi east of Aiken, ☏ 803/649–4870, ☉ Wed.–Sat. 10–6). Montmorenci wines are made from French-American hybrid grapes, many typical of the Southeast, and include rosés, blushes, whites, and reds.

Dining and Lodging

$$–$$$ ✕ **Malia's.** Locals love this busy lunch and dinner spot, with dim lighting and dark fabrics that convey a cool, classy style. You can sample creative international cuisine, including lamb soup with curry, veal with shiitake mushrooms and brandy demiglace, or the baked ham, Brie, and Portobello mushroom sandwich. ⊠ *120 Laurens St.*, ☏ *803/643–3086. D, MC, V. No lunch weekends, No dinner Sun.–Tues.*

$$ ✕ **Linda's Bistro.** In an open and clean bistro-style environment, chef Linda Rooney elevates traditional favorites, turning out mushroom-Gruyère tarts, risotto with roasted mushrooms and Asiago, steak *frites*, and rum–coconut cream bread pudding. Main courses come with a salad, a vegetable, and potatoes. ⊠ *210 The Alley*, ☏ *803/648–4853. AE, D, DC, MC, V. Closed Sun.–Mon. No lunch.*

$ ✕ **Track Kitchen.** The who's who of Aiken's horsey set can be found here most mornings, feasting on the heavy and hearty cooking of Carol and Pockets Curtis. The small dining room is unpretentious, with walls of mint-green cinder block and simple Formica counters. ⊠ *420 Mead Ave.*, ☏ *803/641–9628. No credit cards. No dinner.*

$$$$ ⊡ **The Willcox.** Winston Churchill, Franklin D. Roosevelt, and the Astors have slept at this elegant inn, built in the grand style in the late 19th century and now newly renovated. The lobby is graced with massive stone fireplaces, rosewood woodwork, heart-pine floors, Oriental rugs, and antiques. Most rooms are well-proportioned suites with high four-poster beds, soaking tubs, and fireplaces. Some of the special details include bedside lavender linen spray and CD players. ⊠ *100 Colleton Ave., 29801*, ☏ *803/648–1898 or 877/648–2200,* FAX *803/643–0971,* WEB *www.thewillcox.com. 7 rooms, 15 suites. Dining room, room service, gym, spa, lobby lounge. AE, D, DC, MC, V. CP.*

$ ⊡ **Briar Patch.** You can learn plenty about both the Old and New South ★ from the knowledgeable innkeepers of this terrific B&B, which was formerly tack rooms in Aiken's stable district. You get two choices—either the frilly room with French provincial furniture or the less dramatic one with pine antiques and a weather vane. ⊠ *544 Magnolia*

La. SE, 29801, ☎ *803/649–2010,* WEB *www.bbonline.com/sc/briar. 2 rooms. Tennis court. No credit cards. CP.*

Outdoor Activities and Sports

EQUESTRIAN EVENTS

In Aiken **polo matches** are played at Whitney Field (☎ 803/648–7874) on Sunday afternoon September through November and March through July. Three weekends in late March and early April are set aside for the famed **Triple Crown** (☎ 803/641–1111)—Thoroughbred trials of promising yearlings, a steeplechase, and harness races by young horses making their debut.

GOLF

Aiken Golf Club (✉ 555 Highland Park Ave., ☎ 803/649–6029) is one of the many fine 18-hole, par-70 courses in the area. The **River Golf Club** (✉ 307 Riverside Blvd., North Augusta, ☎ 803/202–0110), just outside Aiken, is adjacent to the Savannah River.

Greenwood

60 mi northwest of Aiken via Rte. 19 to U.S. 25, 75 mi west of Columbia via U.S. 378 to U.S. 178.

Founded by Irish settlers in 1802, Greenwood received its name from the site's gently rolling landscape and dense forests. Andrew Johnson, the 17th U.S. president, operated a tailor shop at Courthouse Square before migrating to East Tennessee. Anglers, swimmers, and boaters head for nearby Lake Greenwood's 200-mi shore. Two sections of Sumter National Forest are nearby.

The **museum** has more than 7,000 items in eclectic displays: Native American artifacts, natural history and geology exhibits, and a replicated village street, including a one-room school and a general store. ✉ *106 Main St.,* ☎ *864/229–7093.* 🎫 *$2.* ◷ *Wed.–Sun. 10–5.*

The **Gardens of Park Seed Co.,** one of the nation's largest seed supply houses, maintains colorful experimental gardens and greenhouses 6 mi north on U.S. 178 at Hodges. The flower beds are especially vivid June 15 through July, and seeds and bulbs are for sale in the company store. The **South Carolina Festival of Flowers**—with a performing-artists contest, a beauty pageant, private house and garden tours, and live entertainment—is held at Park's headquarters annually at the end of June. ✉ *On Rte. 254, 7 mi north of town,* ☎ *864/941–4213 or 800/845–3369.* 🎫 *Free.* ◷ *Gardens daily dawn–dusk; store Mon.–Sat. 9–5.*

Lodging

$$ 🏨 **Inn on the Square.** This inn, renovated in 2001, was fashioned out of a warehouse in the heart of town. New carpet, drapes, and linens brighten spacious guest rooms furnished with reproduction 18th-century antiques, four-poster beds, and writing desks. Also note thoughtful touches such as turndown service and complimentary morning newspapers. ✉ *104 Court St., 29648,* ☎ *864/223–4488 or 800/231–9109,* FAX *864/223–7067,* WEB *www.innonthesquare.com. 48 rooms. Restaurant, pool, lounge. AE, D, DC, MC, V.*

Ninety Six

10 mi east of Greenwood on Rte. 248.

The town of Ninety Six, on an old Native American trade route, is so named for being 96 mi from the Cherokee village of Keowee in the Blue Ridge Mountains—the distance a young Cherokee maiden, Cateechee, is supposed to have ridden to warn her English lover of a threatened Native American massacre. The **Ninety Six National Historic Site** commemorates two Revolutionary War battles. The visitor center's museum has descriptive displays, and there are remnants of the old village, a reconstructed French and Indian War stockade, and revolutionary-era fortifications. ⊠ *Rte. 248,* ☎ *864/543–4068,* WEB *www.nps.gov/nisi.* ⊡ *Free.* ⊙ *Daily 8–5.*

Abbeville

14 mi west of Greenwood on Rte. 72.

★ **Abbeville** may well be one of inland South Carolina's most satisfying although lesser-known small towns. An appealing historic district includes the old business district, early churches, and residential areas. What was called the "Southern cause" by supporters of the Confederacy was born and died here, where the first organized secession meeting was held and where, on May 2, 1865, Confederate president Jefferson Davis officially disbanded the defeated armies of the South in the last meeting of his war council. The Confederate council met at the 1830 **Burt-Stark House.** ⊠ *306 N. Main St.,* ☎ *864/459–4297 or 864/459–2181.* ⊡ *$3.* ⊙ *Sept.–May, Fri.–Sat. 1–5 or by appointment; June–Aug., Tues.–Sat. 1–5 or by appointment.*

An 1850s jail houses the **Abbeville County Museum,** which contains area memorabilia. It's adjacent to the 1837 log-cabin home of Marie Cromer Siegler, founder of the 4-H clubs, and to an educational garden. ⊠ *Poplar and Cherry Sts.,* ☎ *864/459–4600.* ⊡ *Free.* ⊙ *Wed. and Sun. 3–5 or by appointment.*

The **Abbeville Opera House** (⊠ *Town Sq.,* ☎ *864/459–2157*) faces the historic town square. Built in 1908, it has been renovated to reflect the grandeur of the days when lavish road shows and stellar entertainers were center stage here. Current productions range from contemporary light comedies to local renderings of Broadway musicals. Call about tours.

OFF THE BEATEN PATH

HICKORY KNOB STATE RESORT PARK – This park on the shore of Strom Thurmond Lake, about 20 mi south of Abbeville, has everything for a complete vacation: fishing, waterskiing, sailing, motorboating, a swimming pool, a tackle shop, nature trails, an 18-hole championship golf course, a pro shop, tennis courts, and a skeet/archery range. A 1770s log cabin, a 78-room motel ($), nine duplex lakeside cottages, campgrounds, and a restaurant round out Hickory Knob's offerings. You're also near a stretch of the **Savannah River Scenic Highway,** which follows the Savannah River along the Georgia border, winding 100 mi and past three lakes. ⊠ *Rte. 1, Box 199B (off Rte. 33, just north of U.S. 378), McCormick 29835,* ☎ *864/391–2450 or 800/491–1764.* ⊡ *Free; fees for some activities.* ⊙ *Office daily 7 AM–11 PM.*

Dining and Lodging

$–$$ ★ ✕ **Village Grille.** Locals come to this high-ceiling room with pomegranate-color walls and antique mirrors for the herb rotisserie chicken. Other choices are the ribs, homemade pastas, and cordial-laced desserts. The feeling here is trendy yet easygoing; the staff bend over backward to please. ⊠ *114 Trinity St.,* ☎ *864/459–2500. AE, D, MC, V. Closed Sun.–Mon.*

$ ✕ **Yoder's Dutch Kitchen.** You'll find authentic Pennsylvania Dutch home cooking in this unassuming redbrick building. There are a lunch buffet and evening smorgasbord with fried chicken, stuffed cabbage, Dutch meat loaf, breaded veal Parmesan, and plenty of vegetables. Shoofly pie, Dutch bread, and apple butter can be purchased to go. ⊠

Rte. 72 (east of downtown), ☎ *864/459–5556. No credit cards. Closed Sun.–Tues. No dinner Wed.*

$$ ⊞ **Belmont Inn.** Built in the early 1900s, this restored Spanish-style structure is a popular overnight stop with opera house visitors. Guest rooms are spacious, with high ceilings and pine floors. Theater-and-dining package plans are available. ⊠ *104 E. Pickens St., 29620,* ☎ *864/459–9625 or 877/459–8118,* WEB *www.belmontinn.net. 25 rooms. Restaurant, lounge, business services, meeting rooms. AE, D, DC, MC, V. CP.*

Nightlife and the Arts

The **Abbeville Opera House** (⊠ Town Sq., ☎ 864/459–2157) stages high-caliber productions in an early 20th-century setting.

Shopping

Abbeville's **Town Square** is lined with attractive gift and specialty shops in restored historic buildings dating from the late 1800s.

Columbia and the Heartland A to Z

To research prices, get advice from other travelers, and book travel arrangements, visit www.fodors.com.

AIRPORTS

Columbia Metropolitan Airport, 10 mi west of downtown, is served by ASA/Delta, ComAir, Continental, Delta, United Express, and US Airways/Express.

➤ AIRPORT INFORMATION: **Columbia Metropolitan Airport** (⊠ 3000 Aviation Way, ☎ 803/822–5000).

BUS TRAVEL

The Columbia Trolley runs a midday route weekdays 11:20–2:30 along Main Street and around the Congaree Vista; fare is 25¢; there's also evening service Sunday–Thursday 5:30–11, which also covers Five Points and Devine Street.

Greyhound serves Aiken, Camden, Columbia, Greenwood, and Sumter.
➤ BUS INFORMATION: **Columbia Trolley** (☎ 803/748–3019). **Greyhound** (☎ 800/231–2222).

CAR TRAVEL

I–77 leads into Columbia from the north, I–26 runs through north–south, and I–20 east–west.

EMERGENCIES

Emergency room services are available at Richland Memorial Hospital. Kroger Sav-on has a pharmacy open 24 hours; other regional locations are open until 9.
➤ EMERGENCY SERVICES: **Ambulance, fire, police** (☎ 911).
➤ HOSPITALS: **Richland Memorial Hospital** (⊠ 5 Richland Medical Park, Columbia, ☎ 803/434–7000).
➤ 24-HOUR PHARMACIES: **Kroger Sav-On** (⊠ 7467 Woodrow St., Irmo, ☎ 803/732–0426).

OUTDOORS AND SPORTS

FISHING

For fishing, Lakes Marion and Moultrie attract anglers after bream, crappie, catfish, and several kinds of bass. Supplies, camps, guides, rentals, and accommodations abound. For information contact Santee Cooper Counties Promotion Commission & Visitors Center.
➤ CONTACTS: **Santee Cooper Counties Promotion Commission & Visitors Center** (⊠ 9302 Old Hwy. 6, Drawer 40, Santee 29142, ☎ 803/854–2131; 800/227–8510 outside SC, WEB www.santeecoopercountry.org).

HIKING

For information on hiking trails in the Francis Marion National Forest and the Sumter National Forest, contact the National Forest Service.

➤ CONTACTS: **National Forest Service** (✉ 4931 Broad River Rd., Columbia 29210-4021, ☎ 803/561–4000).

LAKES

The 41-mi-long Lake Murray, just 15 mi west of Columbia via I–26 (Irmo exit), has swimming, boating, picnicking, and superb fishing. There are many marinas and campgrounds in the area. For information contact the Capital City/Lake Murray Country Visitors Center.

➤ CONTACTS: **Capital City/Lake Murray Country Visitors Center** (✉ 2184 N. Lake Dr., Irmo 29063, ☎ 803/781–5940 or 866/785–3935, WEB www.scjewel.com).

TAXIS

Companies providing service in Columbia include AAATaxi and Airport Shuttle Service, Blue Ribbon, and Checker-Yellow. Gamecock Cab Co. offers citywide service as well as service to other cities statewide. It's about $15–$17 from the airport to downtown Columbia.

➤ TAXI COMPANIES: **AAATaxi and Airport Shuttle Service** (☎ 803/796–3626). **Blue Ribbon** (☎ 803/754–8163). **Checker-Yellow** (☎ 803/799–3311). **Gamecock Cab Co.** (☎ 803/796–7700).

TOURS

The Aiken Chamber of Commerce runs a 90-minute tour of the historic district ($6) and will customize tours to suit individual interests. In Sumter the charismatic former mayor "Bubba" McElveen gives walking, bus, and auto tours of the area. In Camden, Camden Carriage Company takes you on a tour on a horse-drawn carriage through Camden's loveliest neighborhood and down unpaved roads. Customized excursions of Camden are available from Greenleaf Tours. Richland County Historic Preservation Commission runs guided tours of Columbia and rents out historic properties.

➤ FEES AND SCHEDULES: **"Bubba" McElveen** (☎ 803/775–2851). **Camden Carriage Company** (☎ 803/425–5737). **Greenleaf Tours** (contact Louise Burns, ☎ 803/432–1515). **Richland County Historic Preservation Commission** (☎ 803/252–1770).

TRAIN TRAVEL

Amtrak makes stops at Camden, Columbia, Denmark, Florence, and Kingstree in the Heartland.

➤ TRAIN INFORMATION: **Amtrak** (☎ 800/872–7245).

VISITOR INFORMATION

➤ TOURIST INFORMATION: **Columbia Metropolitan Convention and Visitors Bureau** (✉ Box 15, 29202; visitor center: ✉ 1012 Gervais St., ☎ 803/254–0479 or 800/264–4884, WEB www.columbiasc.net). **Capital City/Lake Murray Country Visitors Center** (✉ 2184 N. Lake Dr., Irmo 29063, ☎ 803/781–5940 or 866/785–3935, WEB www. scjewel.com). **Greater Abbeville Chamber of Commerce** (✉ 104 Pickens St., Abbeville 29620, ☎ 864/459–4600, WEB www.emeraldis.com/ abbeville). **Greater Aiken Chamber of Commerce** (✉ 121 Richland Ave. E, Box 892, Aiken 29802, ☎ 803/641–1111, WEB www.chamber.aiken. net). **Greater Cheraw Chamber of Commerce** (✉ 221 Market St., 29520, ☎ 843/537–8425 or 888/537–0014, WEB www.cheraw.com). **Kershaw County Chamber of Commerce** (✉ 724 S. Broad St., Box 605, Camden 29020, ☎ 803/432–2525 or 800/968–4037, WEB www. camden-sc.org). **Ninety Six Chamber of Commerce** (✉ 112 N. Cambridge St., Box 8, 29666, ☎ 864/543–2900). **Greater Sumter Convention & Visitors Bureau** (⊠ 32 E. Calhoun St., Sumter 29150, ☎ 803/436–2640 or 800/688–4748, WEB www.sumter.sc.us).

THE UPCOUNTRY

The Upcountry, in the northwest corner of the state, has long been a favorite for family vacations because of its temperate climate and natural beauty. The abundant lakes and waterfalls and several state parks (including Caesar's Head, Keowee-Toxaway, Oconee, Table Rock, and the Chattooga National Wild and Scenic River) provide all manner of recreational activities. Beautiful anytime, the 130-mi Cherokee Foothills Scenic Highway (Route 11), which goes through the Blue Ridge Mountains, is especially delightful in spring (when the peach trees are in bloom) and autumn.

Greenville is growing fast and attracting lots of industry, much of it textile-related, in keeping with the area's history. Clemson, home of Clemson University and the "Orange Wave," is pretty much a university town. Pendleton, just a few miles away, has one of the nation's largest historic districts. With its village green, surrounded by shops and restaurants, it's a lovely step back in time. The comfortable communities of Spartanburg and Anderson are beginning to rejuvenate their downtown areas.

Greenville

100 mi northwest of Columbia via I–26 and I–385.

Known for its textile and other manufacturing plants, Greenville has many tree-lined streets and a revitalized turn-of-the-20th-century downtown. It also claims a number of attractions, including a zoo, and nearby state parks, such as Caesar's Head and Table Rock. Here you'll also find Bob Jones University, which has a gallery of religious art and antiquities.

The renowned international collection of religious art at **Bob Jones University Art Gallery and Museum** includes works by Botticelli, Rembrandt, Rubens, and Titian. ⊠ *Bob Jones University, 1700 Wade Hampton Blvd.,* ☎ *864/242–5100.* ☑ *$5, free Sun.* ☉ *Tues.–Sun. 2–5.*

Housed in an innovative modern building, the **Greenville County Museum of Art** displays American works dating from the colonial era. Exhibited are works by Paul Jenkins, Jamie Wyeth, Jasper Johns, and noted Southern artists. ⊠ *420 College St.,* ☎ *864/271–7570.* ☑ *Free.* ☉ *Tues.–Sat. 10–5, Sun. 1–5.*

Dining and Lodging

$$–$$$ ✕ **Augusta Grill.** At this local favorite the menu changes daily depending on what's in season and on the whims of the chef. Seafood and beef with French-influenced sauces are typical; there's a martini bar, too. The crab cake special on Wednesday night packs the restaurant. Lunch service is brisk. ⊠ *1818 Augusta St.,* ☎ *864/242–0316. AE, D, MC, V. Closed Sun. No lunch Sat.*

$$–$$$ ✕ **Johann's.** In a high-ceilinged, spacious structure inside the West End Market (a former mill building), Johann's makes appealing use of the building's industrial history, with exposed brick walls and large windows upstairs. Sample crepes, salmon steak, honey-glazed duck, sea bass, and pastas. Sunday brunch is a big to-do. ⊠ *1 Augusta St.,* ☎ *864/235–2774. MC, V. Closed Mon. No lunch Sat.*

$–$$ ✕ **Stax's Omega Diner.** This contemporary diner with booths and a half-circle counter with stools serves everything from bacon and eggs and burgers to souvlaki, Greek-style chicken, and shrimp and grits. It's all good, and it's open almost around-the-clock. ⊠ *72 Orchard Park Dr.,* ☎ *864/297–6639. AE, DC, MC, V.*

$ ✕ **Two Chefs Delicatessen.** You can mix and match from this often-packed deli's selection of delicious homemade sandwiches and salads. Try the roasted potato salad, Asian chicken salad, dried cranberry–and–grilled chicken salad or pepper-crusted turkey on rosemary sourdough. There are a lot of tempting desserts, too, including apple brandy cake, flourless chocolate cake, and fruit tarts. There's a second location, **Two Chefs To Go** (⊠ *29 Pelham Rd.,* ☎ *864/284–9970*), on the east side. ⊠ *104 S. Main St., Suite 105,* ☎ *864/370–9336. MC, V. Closed Sun. No dinner Sat.*

$$$$ ✕▥ **La Bastide.** About 19 mi northwest (30 minutes) of Greenville in the sloping Piedmont hills, this French provincial–style inn with surrounding vineyard re-creates the French countryside experience. Rooms have European linens, French antiques and reproductions, elaborate chandeliers, wrought iron, gas fireplaces, and hillside views. Guests have access to golf and a nearby country club. Prix-fixe French country meals and fine wine are served at the restaurant ($$$–$$$$). ⊠ *10 Road of Vines, Travelers Rest 29690,* ☎ *864/836–8463 or 877/836–8463,* ℻ *864/836–4820,* ⊞ *www.cliffscommunities.com. 12 rooms, 2 suites. Restaurant, croquet. AE, D, DC, MC, V. BP.*

$$$ ✕▥ **Phoenix–Greenville's Inn.** Plantation shutters, gardens, and four-poster beds create the residential feel of a Southern inn; the service is excellent. Ask for a room overlooking the courtyard pool area. Palms Restaurant ($$–$$$$), one of Greenville's best, serves sophisticated dishes—grilled peach salad with strawberry-basil vinaigrette, and grouper with risotto cake and shrimp vermouth sauce. ⊠ *246 N. Pleasantburg Dr., 29607,* ☎ *800/257–3529,* ☎ ℻ *864/233–4651,* ⊞ *www.phoenixgreenvillesinn.com. 181 rooms, 3 suites. Restaurant, pool, lounge, piano bar, pub, business services, meeting room, airport shuttle. AE, D, DC, MC, V. BP.*

$$$–$$$$ ▥ **Hyatt Regency Hotel.** This upscale chain offering's best asset is its central location in the midst of the revitalized downtown of shops and restaurants. Make sure you ask for a room overlooking the atrium, which are far lovelier than those without views. ⊠ *220 N. Main St., 29601,* ☎ *864/235–1234 or 800/633–7313,* ℻ *864/232–7584,* ⊞ *www.hyatt. com. 330 rooms. Restaurant, pool, health club, lounge, airport shuttle. AE, D, DC, MC, V.*

$$–$$$ ▥ **Westin Poinsett Hotel.** After sitting dormant for many years, this historic 12-story hotel, dating to 1925, opened to an enthusiastic and supportive community. The large guest rooms have down comforters, marble baths, and high ceilings. All public spaces are back in their original opulence, including ornate plaster details and mosaic tile work. ⊠ *120 S. Main St., 29601,* ☎ *864/421–9700,* ℻ *864/421–9719. 181 rooms, 9 suites. Restaurant, coffee shop, health club, lounge, concierge. AE, D, DC, MC, V.*

Nightlife and the Arts

The **Peace Center for the Arts** (⊠ 101 W. Broad St., ☎ 864/467–3030), which sits along the Reedy River, presents star performers, touring Broadway shows, dance companies, chamber music, and local groups.

Outdoor Activities and Sports

GOLF

South Carolinians sometimes prefer Upcountry courses to those on the coast, as they're less crowded and enjoy a slightly cooler climate. The area's rolling hills provide challenging courses. **Links O'Tryon** (⊠ 11250 New Cut Rd., Campobello, ☎ 864/468–4995) is an Upcountry 18-hole course. **Rock at Jocassee** (⊠ 171 Sliding Rock Rd., Pickens, ☎ 864/878–2030) is a mountain course with many water hazards; its signature hole has a waterfall view.

Spartanburg

31 mi east of Greenville via I–85.

Spartanburg once produced the state's largest peach crop. Lovely country drives in the area meander through peach orchards, which delight with fragrant, papery blossoms each spring and juicy treats at roadside stands each summer. Although it's still part of the state's largest peach-producing area, today the town is better known as an international business center. So many foreign corporations have plants here that some local attractions provide brochures in German, French, and Spanish. In Spartanburg county 20 German (including a BMW plant), Swiss, and Austrian companies are visible from I–85. The town's early 20th-century downtown is slowly being revitalized with trendy shops and cafés. The NFL's Carolina Panthers train here each summer; their practice sessions at Wofford College (☎ 704/358–7000) are free and open to the public.

The **BMW Zentrum** plant, the company's only one in North America, exhibits BMW engineering in the auto, motorcycle, and aviation industries. On display is the Z3 James Bond drove in the film *Golden Eye*, classics dating to the 1910s, and BMWs painted by artists including Warhol and Lichtenstein. The Virtual Factory Tour, about the making of the BMW Z3 roadster, takes you down the factory line. ⊠ *Rte. 101S, Exit 60 off I–85 (18 mi west of Spartanburg), Greer,* ☎ *864/989–5297 or 888/868–7269.* ☜ *Free; plant tours $5.* ☉ *Tues.–Sat. 9:30–5:30; plant tours by appointment.*

More than 10,000 plants make **Hatcher Gardens** a refuge for birds and wildlife. It also has walking trails and ponds. ⊠ *Reidville Rd.,* ☎ *864/574–7724.* ☜ *Free.* ☉ *Daily dawn–dusk.*

Dining and Lodging

$$–$$$ ✕ **Abby's Grill.** A classy eatery downtown, Abby's has a lounge and live piano most evenings. High ceilings make the dining room open and airy. The menu changes nightly to include such items as smoked salmon *bruschetta,* panfried flounder, grilled salmon with lemon-caper sauce, and roasted pork loin with red-wine mushroom sauce. ⊠ *149 W. Main St.,* ☎ *864/583–4660. AE, DC, MC, V. Closed Sun.*

$ ✕ **Beacon Drive-In.** This Spartanburg institution—and some of its staff—have been around for 50 years. They'll serve you curbside, but the action is inside at the counter. Locals come for the Beacon burgers (hamburgers with all the fixin's), onion rings, hot dogs, fried fish sandwiches, and sundaes. ⊠ *255 Reidville Rd.,* ☎ *864/585–9387. AE, DC, MC, V. Closed Sun.*

$$ ▥ **Brookwood Inn.** You'll find comfort and simple style here, as well as clean rooms and a welcoming staff. It's at I–26 and I–85, on the west side of town. ⊠ *4930 College Dr., 29301,* ☎ *864/576–6080 or 800/426–7866,* ℻ *864/587–8901,* ⦿ *www.hamptoninn.com. 112 rooms. Pool, business services, meeting room. AE, D, DC, MC, V. CP.*

$$ ▥ **Inn at Merridun.** This antebellum 1855 home in Union, about 27 mi south of Spartanburg, has country style and cozy floral rooms. Rates include full breakfast and evening dessert. Afternoon tea, picnic lunches, and dinners are available. ⊠ *100 Merridun Pl., off U.S. 176, Union 29379,* ☎ *864/427–7052 or 888/892–6020,* ℻ *864/429–0373,* ⦿ *www.merridun.com. 5 rooms. Dining room. AE, D, MC, V. BP.*

$$ ⊞ **Red Horse Inn.** You'll travel through pretty countryside to get to this inn, near several state parks and the North Carolina border. Victorian-style cottages with porches and hand-painted murals are scattered on the inn's 190 acres, about 25 mi north of Greenville and near the charming Upcountry village of Landrum. Each cottage has a sitting area, fireplace, and board games; some have lofts and whirlpools. In each cottage's small kitchen you'll find a nice basket of breakfast items. ⊠ *4930 College Dr., Landrum 29301,* ☎ *864/895–4968,* FAX *864/587–8901,* WEB *www.bedandbreakfast.com. 9 cottages. AE, D, DC, MC, V. BP.*

Shopping
The more than 90 outlets at the **Prime Outlets of Gaffney** include the Gap, Nike, Levi's, and Donna Karan. The playground will keep older kids busy while you shop. ⊠ *I–85, Exit 90, Gaffney,* ☎ *864/902–9900 for information center.*

Pendleton

30 mi southwest of Greenville via U.S. 123.

Charming Pendleton, a few miles from Clemson University, has a historic district and interesting architecture. The Farmers Hall, built in 1826, was originally built to be a courthouse. The Square, a district of restaurants and shops, faces the Village Green.

☁ The **South Carolina State Botanical Garden,** on the Clemson University campus in nearby Clemson, holds more than 2,000 varieties of plants on more than 270 acres, including wildflower, fern, and bog gardens, as well as nature trails. The **Fran Hanson Discovery Center** has information on regional history and cultural heritage, and a hands-on learning station on natural history, a microscope with a big-screen monitor, and a talking animated raccoon. ⊠ *102 Garden Trail,* ☎ *864/656–3405,* WEB *www.clemson.edu/scbg.* ⊡ *Free.* ☉ *Daily dawn–dusk.*

Dining and Lodging
$$ ✕⊞ **Liberty Hall Inn.** There's great food and lodging at this country inn in the heart of town. Built in the 1840s, the inn caters to business travelers and vacationers. New owners now live on-site and have freshened up the house and rooms, which are furnished with antiques and family heirlooms. Breakfast is a choice of yogurt parfait or French toast. The restaurant, Café Leisure ($$–$$$), displays intensely colorful art on red walls and serves dishes ranging from grilled Cornish hen with Madeira mushroom sauce to panfried sea bass with cucumber-dill sauce. ⊠ *621 S. Mechanic St., 29670,* ☎ *800/643–7944,* ☎ FAX *864/646–7500,* WEB *www.bbonline.com/sc/liberty. 7 rooms. Restaurant. AE, D, MC, V. BP.*

Kings Mountain National Military and State Park

70 mi northeast of Greenville via I–85.

A Revolutionary War battle considered an important turning point was fought here on October 7, 1780. Colonial Tories commanded by British major Patrick Ferguson were soundly defeated by ragtag patriot forces from the southern Appalachians. Visitor center exhibits, dioramas, and an orientation film describe the action. A paved self-guided trail leads through the battlefield. ⊠ *20 mi northeast of Gaffney, SC, off I–85 (exit 2) via a marked side road in NC,* ☎ *864/936–7921,* WEB *www.south-*

carolinaparks.com. ✉ *Free.* ☉ *Early Sept.–late May, daily 9–5; late May–early Sept., daily 9–6.*

The 6,000-acre **Kings Mountain State Park** (☎ 864/222–3209), adjacent to the national military park, has camping, swimming, fishing, boating, and nature and hiking trails.

Upcountry A to Z

To research prices, get advice from other travelers, and book travel arrangements, visit www.fodors.com.

AIRPORTS

Greenville-Spartanburg Airport, off I–85 between the two cities, is served by US Airways, Delta ComAir, United Express, Northwest, American Eagle, and Continental.

➤ AIRPORT INFORMATION: **Greenville-Spartanburg Airport** (✉ 2000 G.S.P. Dr., ☎ 864/867–7426).

BUS TRAVEL

Greyhound serves Greenville and Spartanburg.

➤ BUS INFORMATION: **Greyhound** (☎ 800/231–2222).

CAR TRAVEL

I–85 provides access to Greenville, Spartanburg, Pendleton, and Anderson. I–26 runs from Charleston through Columbia to the Upcountry, connecting with I–385 into Greenville.

EMERGENCIES

➤ EMERGENCY SERVICES: **Ambulance, police** (☎ 911).

OUTDOORS AND SPORTS

CANOEING AND RAFTING

The Chattooga National Wild and Scenic River, on the border of South Carolina and Georgia, is excellent for guided rafting, canoeing, and kayaking trips. Contact Nantahala Outdoor Center, Southeastern Expeditions, or Wildwater Ltd.

➤ CONTACTS: **Nantahala Outdoor Center** (☎ 864/647–9014 or 800/232–7238). **Southeastern Expeditions** (☎ 800/868–7238). **Wildwater Ltd.** (☎ 864/647–9587 or 800/451–9972).

STATE PARKS

Devils Fork State Park, on Lake Jocassee, has luxurious villas and facilities.

➤ CONTACTS: **Devils Fork State Park** (✉ 161 Holcombe Circle, Salem 29676, ☎ 864/944–2639).

TRAIN TRAVEL

Amtrak stops in Greenville and Spartanburg.

➤ TRAIN INFORMATION: **Amtrak** (☎ 800/872–7245).

VISITOR INFORMATION

➤ TOURIST INFORMATION: **Discover Upcountry Carolina Association** (✉ Box 3116, Greenville 29602, ☎ 864/233–2690 or 800/849–4766, WEB www.the upcountry.com). **Greater Greenville Convention and Visitors Bureau** (✉ 206 S. Main St., Box 10527, 29603, ☎ 864/421–0000 or 800/351–7180, WEB www.greatergreenville.com). **Spartanburg Convention and Visitors Bureau** (✉ 298 Magnolia St., 29306, ☎ 864/594–5050 or 800/374–8326, WEB www.spartanburgsc.org).

SOUTH CAROLINA A TO Z

To research prices, get advice from other travelers, and book travel arrangements, visit www.fodors.com.

AIR TRAVEL

CARRIERS

South Carolina is served by Air Canada, AirTran, American Eagle, ASA, ComAir, Continental, Delta, Midway, Northwest, Spirit, United Express, US Airways, and Vanguard.

AIRPORTS

Major airports are Charleston International Airport; Columbia Metropolitan Airport; Greenville-Spartanburg Airport; Hilton Head Island Airport, served by US Airways Express; Myrtle Beach International Airport; and Savannah International Airport, about an hour's drive from Hilton Head.

➤ AIRPORT INFORMATION: **Charleston International Airport** (✉ 5500 International Blvd., ☎ 843/767–1100). **Columbia Metropolitan Airport** (✉ 3000 Aviation Way, ☎ 803/822–5000). **Greenville-Spartanburg Airport** (✉ 2000 G.S.P. Dr., ☎ 864/867–7426). **Hilton Head Island Airport** (☎ 843/681–6386). **Myrtle Beach International Airport** (✉ 1100 Jetport Rd., ☎ 843/448–1589). **Savannah International Airport** (✉ 400 Airways Ave., ☎ 912/964–0514).

BUS TRAVEL

Greyhound serves many towns and cities throughout South Carolina and links several cities and towns throughout South Carolina.

➤ BUS INFORMATION: **Greyhound** (☎ 800/231–2222).

CAR TRAVEL

Many interstates lead into South Carolina from its neighbors Georgia and North Carolina. From western North Carolina I–26 runs southeast through Greenville, Columbia, and Charleston; from central North Carolina I–77 leads south into Columbia and I–85 leads southwest into Greenville; and from eastern North Carolina I–95 leads southwest through Florence, intersecting with I–20 and I–26. From Atlanta, Georgia, I–85 runs northeast into Greenville, and I–20 leads east via Augusta into Columbia; from southern Georgia I–95 leads northeast into the state. U.S. 17, a north–south coastal route, runs along the coastal edge of the entire state.

RULES OF THE ROAD

The speed limit on interstates can run as high as 70 mph but is lower in congested areas. You can turn right at a red light unless otherwise noted by street signs. If it's raining and you have your windshield wipers on, you must have your headlights on, too.

EMERGENCIES

➤ CONTACTS: **Ambulance, fire, police** (☎ 911).

LODGING

BED-AND-BREAKFASTS

Contact the South Carolina Bed and Breakfast Association for a current state directory of member B&Bs. For a complete list of B&Bs contact the South Carolina Division of Tourism and ask for the pamphlet *Bed & Breakfasts of South Carolina.*

➤ RESERVATION SERVICES: **South Carolina Bed and Breakfast Association** (✉ Box 1275, Sumter 29150-1275, ☎ 888/599–1234, WEB www.southcarolinabedandbreakfast.com).

TOURS

Lowcountry Adventures offers tours of Hilton Head, Beaufort, and Charleston. For information about other specific tours contact the South Carolina Division of Tourism.

➤ FEES AND SCHEDULES: **Lowcountry Adventures** (☎ 843/681–8212).

TRAIN TRAVEL

Amtrak stops in Charleston, Camden, Columbia, Denmark, Florence, Greenville, Kingstree, and Yemassee (near Beaufort). Amtrak provides service to these cities along an East Coast route that runs from Boston to Miami.

➤ TRAIN INFORMATION: **Amtrak** (☎ 800/872–7245).

TRANSPORTATION AROUND SOUTH CAROLINA

A car is easily the best way to get around South Carolina; however, if you're spending most of your time in Charleston, you can get by fairly easily either on foot or using public transportation. In virtually every other city you need a car to get to and from attractions, accommodations, and restaurants.

VISITOR INFORMATION

➤ TOURIST INFORMATION: **South Carolina Department of Parks, Recreation, and Tourism** (✉ 1205 Pendleton St., Suite 106, Columbia 29201, ☎ 803/734–0122 or 800/872–3505, WEB www.travelsc.com). **Tourist welcome centers** ✉ U.S. 17, near Little River; I–95, near Dillon, Santee and Lake Marion, and Hardeeville; I–77, near Fort Mill; I–85, near Blacksburg and Fair Play; I–26, near Landrum; I–20, at North Augusta; and U.S. 301, near Allendale.

INDEX

Icons and Symbols

★ Our special recommendations

✕ Restaurant

🏠 Lodging establishment

✕🏠 Lodging establishment whose restaurant warrants a special trip

🐣 Good for kids (rubber duck)

☞ Sends you to another section of the guide for more information

✉ Address

☎ Telephone number

🕐 Opening and closing times

💰 Admission prices

Numbers in white and black circles ③ ❸ that appear on the maps, in the margins, and within the tours correspond to one another.

NOTES

NOTES

NOTES

NOTES

Fodor's Key to the Guides

America's guidebook leader publishes guides for every kind of traveler. Check out our many series and find your perfect match.

Fodor's Gold Guides
America's favorite travel-guide series offers the most detailed insider reviews of hotels, restaurants, and attractions in all price ranges, plus great background information, smart tips, and useful maps.

Fodor's Road Guide USA
Big guides for a big country—the most comprehensive guides to America's roads, packed with places to stay, eat, and play across the U.S.A. Just right for road warriors, family vacationers, and cross-country trekkers.

COMPASS AMERICAN GUIDES
Stunning guides from top local writers and photographers, with gorgeous photos, literary excerpts, and colorful anecdotes. A must-have for culture mavens, history buffs, and new residents.

Fodor's CITYPACKS
Concise city coverage with a foldout map. The right choice for urban travelers who want everything under one cover.

Fodor's EXPLORING GUIDES
Hundreds of color photos bring your destination to life. Lively stories lend insight into the culture, history, and people.

Fodor's POCKET GUIDES
For travelers who need only the essentials. The best of Fodor's in pocket-size packages for just $9.95.

Fodor's To Go
Credit-card–size, magnetized color microguides that fit in the palm of your hand—perfect for "stealth" travelers or as gifts.

Fodor's FLASHMAPS
Every resident's map guide. 60 easy-to-follow maps of public transit, parks, museums, zip codes, and more.

Fodor's CITYGUIDES
Sourcebooks for living in the city: Thousands of in-the-know listings for restaurants, shops, sports, nightlife, and other city resources.

Fodor's AROUND THE CITY WITH KIDS
68 great ideas for family days, recommended by resident parents. Perfect for exploring in your own backyard or on the road.

Fodor's ESCAPES
Fill your trip with once-in-a-lifetime experiences, from ballooning in Chianti to overnighting in the Moroccan desert. These full-color dream books point the way.

Fodor's FYI
Get tips from the pros on planning the perfect trip. Learn how to pack, fly hassle-free, plan a honeymoon or cruise, stay healthy on the road, and travel with your baby.

Fodor's Languages for Travelers
Practice the local language before hitting the road. Available in phrase books, cassette sets, and CD sets.

Karen Brown's Guides
Engaging guides to the most charming inns and B&Bs in the U.S.A. and Europe, with easy-to-follow inn-to-inn itineraries.

Baedeker's Guides
Comprehensive guides, trusted since 1829, packed with A–Z reviews and star ratings.

At bookstores everywhere.   www.fodors.com/books